A History of EDUCATION
in American Culture

A History of

in

EDUCATION
American Culture

R. FREEMAN BUTTS

LAWRENCE A. CREMIN

Teachers College, Columbia University

HENRY HOLT AND COMPANY · New York

PREFACE

THIS BOOK is addressed to all who are interested in the improvement of education in the United States. In recent years more and more people have become vitally concerned about the future of American education. Individual parents and citizens and organized groups of all kinds are taking a renewed interest in the conduct of schools and colleges. Inevitably, differences of attitude and opinion have arisen; sometimes these differences have led to vigorous controversy charged with emotional overtones. In a word, education has become a paramount matter of public interest that ranges in scope from the private discussions between parent and teacher in a local school to the widely publicized debates in the legislative halls and public forums of the state and nation.

In this setting of public interest in education it is vitally important that judgments be based upon the best evidence available and the most intelligent processes of thought and discussion. In education, as in all matters of important public policy, the hope of the democratic way of life rests upon reasoned intelligence, sober regard for the truth, and free and open discussion of the merits of opposing points of view. Emotional appeals to prejudice, reliance upon half-truths or invalid generalizations, or simple lack of knowledge are dangerous bases upon which to form public or private judgments.

This book is designed to provide a sound historical foundation upon which to base judgments about American education. It is addressed not only to prospective teachers but also to the members of the educational profession and to the American public, who share the responsibility for the conduct of educational institutions in the United States. It assumes that all present practices and all proposals for the future rest upon some interpretation of the past. Educational policies and decisions look both forward and backward. Whenever judgments are made, they rest upon some assumption or presupposition about the past as well as upon some hope or preference about the future. A careful study of history is therefore an indispensable element in evaluating the present and in making plans for the future. The study of history will not solve our present problems nor will it dictate the roads to the future, but intelligent decisions cannot be reached without it. We believe, therefore, that the study of the history of education is one of the ways in which the profession

v

and the public together should prepare themselves for making better judgments about American education.

We hope this book will be especially useful in the professional preparation of teachers and administrators. It is designed specifically for use in courses in the history of education in teachers colleges, liberal arts colleges, and universities. It is also designed for study in connection with other professional courses that deal with the principles of education, philosophy of education, educational psychology, administration, and curriculum and teaching. It is our hope that it will be useful for the college student who is entering upon his professional preparation and needs an orientation to the whole scope of the educational enterprise. It is also our hope that it will be of service to the advanced student who may need an opportunity to achieve integration and synthesis after his study of the specialized aspects of his professional task. It is, finally, our hope that the profession at large and the general public will find opportunity herein to enlarge their understanding of the great achievements already made and the problems and difficulties that still face American education.

The history of education is one of the oldest and most persistent elements in the professional preparation of teachers and administrators. In its earlier forms it had two dominant characteristics. It was concerned primarily with presenting factual information about the development of schools, their organization, administration, curriculum, and methods, but it gave relatively little attention to the role of education in the surrounding society and culture. Furthermore, it was often taught in a systematic chronological way that failed to relate the past to the present and gave little help in bringing historical interpretations to bear upon the making of valid decisions about the present problems that face education.

We have sought to preserve the merit of these earlier forms while avoiding their shortcomings. We have attempted to include basic factual information about the actual development of school practices, and we have maintained a basically chronological organization which remains one of the distinctive values of the historical approach. We have, however, tried to remedy the failures by attempting to take account of the newer outlooks that have come to characterize more recent writing and teaching in the fields of history and the history of education.

One of these characteristics is the cultural approach to the study of history and of education. Recent developments in the social sciences have stressed the importance of the concept of culture. The distinctive way of life of a society, developed in the traditions of the past and living on in the institutions, ideas, beliefs, and customs of the people, is summed up in the term culture. If educators and citizens alike are to understand and be able to deal with the problems of education, they need to understand the culture in which education operates and to which it contributes. Our cultural traditions are not things dead and gone; they live on in us and act as guides to our thought and action.

If we are to know ourselves, our problems, and our society, we need to know our culture. If educators are genuinely to face the problems of the role of education in culture, they need to study the role of education as an institution among other social institutions in society, and they need to study the underlying ideas, values, beliefs, and attitudes that motivate human behavior in and out of school. Thus, if the educational profession is to analyze carefully the present problems that face education, professional workers need to know how and why people act as they do. People act as they do, at least in part, as a result of the inherited values and ideals that live on in them as traditions.

The history of education, therefore, should be designed to help educators understand what their present problems are, how the problems have arisen, what the advantages and dangers of the past have been, what forces from the past are still at work in the present, and what we have to reckon with as we move into the future. The teaching and writing of history must be selective. Since we cannot bring to bear all recorded history upon present-day problems, we should bring to bear upon the present that experience of the past which is pertinent and relevant to the resolution of present problems. Thus, the history of education should no longer be confined to the factual recital of school data of the past but should see education in vital relationship to the culture of its times. It should no longer be a simple chronological recital of happenings from year to year or century to century, but it should take off from present problems and issues and return to the present as an aid in deciding what should be done in the future.

In this view the historical approach to educational foundations becomes a reassessing of our cultural and educational traditions. It should help educators make judgments concerning what of our past culture is good for the future and thus needs to be strengthened, and what is destructive of democratic ends and thus needs to be changed. All of this can and must be done with no abatement or relaxing of the rigorous requirements of historical scholarship. Much has been achieved in the university disciplines of history and the social sciences. The history of education should put some of the resources of these disciplines at the disposal of the professional educator.

Since the chronological approach in historical foundations remains one of the distinctive values of the historical method, we have tried to combine it with the cultural approach. There is great value in gaining perspective on our own present times by seeing how education has been related to its culture in past eras. We have tried to show how education was viewed in colonial culture and in nineteenth-century culture and how its methods and content have been shaped by prescientific and earlier philosophical and religious orientations. This attempt is essential to an understanding of the way these inherited outlooks and practices continue to operate at the present time. Such an understanding of the past is indispensable to a sound analysis of the conflicting points of view that exist at the present time. Present judgment of present practice cannot escape making judgments of those past practices which so largely continue to operate in the present.

A second characteristic of recent scholarship in history and in education is increased attention to the persistent problems that face education in our culture. The "problems approach" is a significant development in teaching and learning at all levels of the educative process. We have tried to incorporate much of this problems approach along with the cultural-chronological approach. In this way we have hoped to make the book useful in courses dealing with the social and philosophical foundations of education where attention is centered upon certain critical problems or conflict areas as related to education in our culture. These courses often include such topics as the struggles over the meaning of our democratic traditions, ideals, and practices; economic theories and institutions; political outlooks and various conceptions of the state; the impact of science and technology; church-state controversies; intergroup relations; conflicting theories of human nature, intelligence, and learning; moral and religious experience; esthetic and vocational experience, and the like. Much perspective on these current problems can be gained by acquiring an historical orientation to each problem along with its social and philosophical bearings.

In order to preserve the values of the factual and chronological treatment of history and also to incorporate the values of the cultural and problems approach to the study of education, the book is organized in the following way:

Four rather well-accepted and familiar chronological periods in American history are presented in the four parts of the book. Part I deals with the colonial period; Part II with the period from the Revolutionary War to the Civil War; Part III with the period from the Civil War to World War I; and Part IV with the period from World War I to the middle of the twentieth century. Within each part education is treated as a phase of the distinctive cultural developments of the particular chronological period under consideration. An effort is made not only to describe the major cultural developments and trends that affected education but also to identify the persistent problems that appeared in each period.

The first chapter in each part (Chapters 1, 5, 9, and 13) deals principally with the political, economic, social, and religious institutions that most vitally influenced education. We have not tried to present a digest or summary of all of American history in each period, but we have tried to select those phases of our history which are indispensable for an understanding of the role played by education in each period. There is value in gaining perspective on the present by seeing what happened to education in times that are removed from our own—times which created traditions, outlooks, and practices that still affect our own thinking and methods. The emphasis in these chapters is upon the social institutions, the social forces, and the social trends that shaped education. These are the social foundations of education viewed historically.

The second chapter in each part (Chapters 2, 6, 10, and 14) deals with the intellectual, philosophical, psychological, religious, and scientific outlooks that influenced education in the period under consideration. Conceptions of man's relation to nature, human growth and development, methods of thinking and intelligence, and the developing bodies of organized knowledge all played their part in shaping educational goals, content, and methods. As philosophical, religious, and scientific orientations changed or came into conflict with one another, they produced conflicting views of the desirable role of education in their times. Many such views continue to affect us in modified forms. These are the philosophical, psychological, and intellectual foundations of education viewed historically.

The third chapter in each part (Chapters 3, 7, 11, and 15) treats the educational points of view that marked each period. Some of these points of view represent the more or less settled agreements and consensus among educators and the majority groups in the public, but others represent proposals for change that rested upon dissatisfaction with existing educational patterns. Here are thus described the conflicting demands made upon schools by those who held differing educational outlooks with respect to the persistent problems of education. These are the controversial questions upon which the public was making up its mind with respect to the social role of education, educational control and support, the educational program, and the role of the educational profession.

Finally, the fourth chapter in each Part (Chapters 4, 8, 12, and 16) describes the actual practices in education that came to prevail as a result of the interplay of social forces, intellectual orientations, and educational points of view. As new conditions and new outlooks press for change, they are often reflected in educational innovations, experiments, and new trends. Some of these educational changes took place more rapidly than others, leaving a residue of many unresolved problems for ensuing periods. These chapters will describe what actually happened in practice, the dominant patterns of administration, control, and support, of curriculum and methods, the unresolved issues of policy, and the meaning for the present.

Throughout all of the chapters we have been at pains to stress factual and scholarly information based upon the best available primary and secondary sources. In addition to the resources of general history, we have tried to use the results of recent scholarship in social history, intellectual history, philosophy, psychology, and other social sciences. Footnoting has been kept to a minimum except in the four chapters that deal with various educational outlooks and conflicting proposals for education (Chapters 3, 7, 11, and 15). In these chapters there is considerable quotation and frequent reference to primary source material. Therefore footnotes have been more liberally used as a guide to the serious reader who may wish to probe more deeply into the historical roots of persistent educational issues.

At the end of each chapter a few suggestions for further reading are listed. The more readily available publications have been selected in order to enable the reader to widen or deepen his understanding of those phases of history that cannot be enlarged upon in a general volume of this kind. Also at the end of each chapter several issues are defined to elicit discussion and further study. These depart from the usual "Questions for Discussion" which are so often purely factual in nature and so often stress relatively unimportant historical details. These issues have been designed to bring to the surface the kind of historical assumption or generalization that is commonly used as an argument to support present-day points of view. They are deliberately intended to stimulate critical re-examination of prevailing attitudes and to promote further inquiry into the historical materials in a way that will increase historical understanding and bring the history to bear upon present problems and issues. They are also designed to be useful as guides for public study and discussion whereever groups of citizens and educators are attempting to face seriously and to solve thoughtfully the critical problems of education.

Our hope is thus that this book will be useful in preserving the long-established values of the history of education as well as promoting the revitalization of the history of education as an essential and prominent part of the preparation of professional educators. The authors have had several years experience in teaching courses in the history of education at Teachers College, Columbia University. They have also had the opportunity of working in courses in the foundational problems of education in close cooperation with their colleagues in the Department of Social and Philosophical Foundations at Teachers College. They have profited much from the leadership exerted in recent years by the History of Education Section of the National Society of College Teachers of Education. This organization has promoted renewed interest in the history of education by publication of the *History of Education Journal* and by undertaking a nation-wide study of the role of the history of education in the preparation of the educational profession.

If there is merit in this book, much of it is undoubtedly a result of these several influences, but its shortcomings will easily be identified exclusively as the authors' own. Particular thanks should be extended to Miss Priscilla Aiken for her special services in helping to prepare the manuscript for the publisher.

New York, N. Y.   R. F. B.
December 1952   L. A. C.

CONTENTS

441
151

PART 1

COLONIAL FOUNDATIONS
OF AMERICAN EDUCATION
(1600-1779)

OLD WORLD CULTURE
IN A NEW SETTING

TO MANY Americans the term "colonial period" calls to mind a hodge-podge vision of Captain John Smith being saved by Pocahontas, of Pilgrims landing on Plymouth Rock and catching turkeys for Thanksgiving, of Peter Stuyvesant stomping angrily about New Amsterdam, of Indian wars and scalpings along the Mohawk Valley, of the tea party in Boston harbor, of Paul Revere riding through the night, of Washington at Valley Forge, and of the surrender of Cornwallis at Yorktown. The "colonial period" in this view is a romantic and picturesque subject appropriate primarily for story, fable, and song. To many other Americans the "colonial period" is associated mainly with the first chapter of tedious textbooks in American history and a long series of now vaguely remembered dates, names, and events: Queen Anne's War, King George's War, the French and Indian War, the Quebec Act, the Sugar Act, the Stamp Act, the Tea Act, and the Declaration of Independence.

Let it be said at once that the intention here is neither to try to glamorize our remote past nor to repeat the usual formulas of chronological history. It is important, however, for anyone who would face realistically the problems of American education to look again at the roots of our American traditions. They are important for understanding and dealing with the present. And the roots of some of our most controversial and urgent problems of the present are firmly imbedded in the colonial period. We cannot deal exhaustively with all or even a large part of the colonial history that would be considered important by general historians. What we can do is to select those basic patterns which help to explain the education of the past and which help to throw light upon the present. When we combine these interests and attempt to select those educational problems that were of greatest importance to the colonists in their own day and that remain of most importance to our day, we have a promising principle by which to select and organize our re-examination of American culture and education.

Of all the present problems that have their roots in the colonial period, three stand out as most essential for study. First, American educators are arguing about the proper role of education in relation to the state; in the colonial period the distinctive American patterns of political and state authority were being hammered out. Secondly, the problem of the proper role of religion and education is being vigorously debated; in the colonial period the seeds of our present controversies were being planted. Thirdly, the merits of equality of educational opportunity as a present goal for American education are being hotly disputed; in the colonial period the basic patterns of economic, class, and sectional distinctions were being laid. This chapter, then, will attempt to highlight these three problems as they appeared in the colonial period, and a study of them may help to deal with their present versions.

This effort may require looking again at some more or less familiar historical material, but we believe that even old material looks new when looked at with the purpose of facing the important tasks of today. We hope that many readers will look at our history again with renewed interest, spurred by the desire to untangle present confusions. We believe that many will find here new material they have not seen before in histories whose concern has not been focused upon education. Our aim is to combine the values of historical scholarship with an emphasis upon the persistent problems of education. No one can face the deeper issues of American education without a concern for understanding the basic theory and practice of political authority in American life. To this problem we turn first.

POLITICAL AUTHORITY MOVES TOWARD REPRESENTATIVE GOVERNMENT

The foundations of American culture and education took their character in the colonial period largely from North European sources and particularly from the British Isles. This fact does not discount the contributions of other European peoples; it simply means that English institutions and ideas became, after a long struggle, the dominant pattern of life and thought along the eastern seaboard of America from Maine to Georgia. During the sixteenth, seventeenth, and eighteenth centuries the Western Hemisphere was the scene of military and commercial rivalries of the great European empires. By 1600, after 100 years of conquest, Spain held most of South America and laid claim to much of North America. Spain's supremacy, however, was soon challenged in the seventeenth century by England and France, who began a long duel for control of the eastern half of North America. England emerged as victor in the Treaty of Paris in 1763.

Thus, by the end of the eighteenth century Spain had been confined to the territory west of the Mississippi River and to Florida; France had been largely pushed off the continent; and French Canada had become politically tied to Britain even though not entirely British in culture or loyalty. As a result, the colonial history of the United States, from founding to independence, was to be dominated by the relationship of England to its several American colonies. The thirteen colonies inherited and made significant adaptations in the institutions and ideas carried from Britain to American shores. A thorough understanding of American colonial history would require an understanding of British political, economic, and religious history, but only a very few generalizations can be made as a background for developments in the colonies.

Politically, the seventeenth and eighteenth centuries in England were marked by a continuing struggle for power between the royal authority of the crown and the authority of Parliament. Becoming increasingly representative of the middle class and commercial interests of the nation, Parliament grew restive under the Stuart kings, James I and Charles I. Civil War finally broke out in 1642 and led to the execution of Charles I in 1649 and the establishment of the Puritan Commonwealth. After some ten years of Puritan rule with Oliver Cromwell as Lord Protector for part of the time, the Stuarts came back with a vengeance in 1660, only to be cast out again by Parliament in favor of William and Mary in 1688. So it went, with the executive functions of government gradually moving into the hands of the Parliamentary cabinet until George III's willful desire to run his own foreign affairs helped to precipitate the American War of Independence. The real point is that the political struggles between Parliament and crown played a large part in the changing attitude of Englishmen toward the colonies and gave scope to the interplay of forces and interests in England which had their counterparts in the colonies. Whenever possible the colonists tried to take advantage of these struggles for their own benefit.

Of great and enduring importance was the gradual growth of institutional forms of government that tended to reduce arbitrary royal power and tended to achieve a tradition of representative forms of government and civil liberties for Englishmen. Once transferred to American soil this tradition of liberty was developed by Americans and turned back against Parliament as well as the crown in the Revolutionary period. It was permanently important for the history of America that its political foundations reflected these representative forms of government based upon a growing tradition of liberty rather than upon the feudal or military aristocracy that marked so many of the nations of the Old World in the seventeenth century. Whatever else may be said about colonial culture, this fact was of superlative importance for the development of education and made it possible for a new conception of the role of education in society to be developed when the time was ripe.

A glance at Table 1 on page 7 will show that there were two major periods in the founding of the principal English colonies. The first took place in about thirty years of the reigns of James I and Charles I, the second in about twenty years in the reign of Charles II after the Stuart Restoration in 1660. Political authority was exerted in three typical ways among the colonies of the first period, all of which had significance for the pattern of relationship with England and the development of representative government in America. Virginia and Massachusetts were founded under the authority of charters granted by the crown to commercial stock companies; Maryland was founded as a proprietary grant of land to and individual; and Connecticut and Rhode Island were founded as disaffection arose in Massachusetts and groups of settlers in the new "plantations" drew up constitutional agreements under which they exercised almost independent political authority.

England as well as other nations promoted foreign trade around the world in the sixteenth and seventeenth centuries by the organization of joint-stock corporations. This invention of mercantile capitalism made it possible for many individuals to combine their resources, sell stock to a large number of persons, receive the monopoly of trade in certain sections of the world, choose directors to manage affairs, and pay dividends from the profits to the stockholders. The London Company was thus organized to develop trade in Virginia, which at first vaguely included most of the English claims in America. The company in London sent out a small colonizing group to establish the Jamestown settlement in 1606. Government was in the hands of a resident governor and council under directions from the company in London, which operated under a grant of powers in a charter from the king. After many difficulties and hardships the company ordered the governor to establish a local representative assembly with power to make laws subject to the approval of the company in London. In 1619 the first representative assembly in America was chosen by vote of the freeholders, and a new pattern of government was initiated. Because of misfortune in Virginia and controversy in the company in England, the London Company was dissolved, and Virginia became a royal province in 1624. The governor and council were thereupon appointed directly by the king rather than by the stock company, but the representative assembly was retained along with courts of justice and a fair measure of English common law. The Virginia Assembly proceeded to establish the Church of England, organize a parish system, and pass laws that affected education throughout the colonial period. The important thing is that direct legislative authority gradually passed into the hands of representatives of the colonists themselves.

Similarly, Massachusetts received its political authority as a stock company by royal charter from the king in 1629. However, a significant difference arose. Control of the stock company was captured by a group of Puritans who de-

Table 1—Political Chronology in the Colonial Period

English Rulers	Founding of American Colonies *
Elizabeth (Tudor) 1558–1603	Exploration of Drake, Gilbert, and Raleigh
James I (Stuart) 1603–1625	Virginia (1607) Plymouth (1620)
Charles I (Stuart) 1625–1649 (Civil War 1642–1649)	Massachusetts (1629) Maryland (1632) New Netherland (1638) Rhode Island (1638 and 1644) Connecticut (1639)
Commonwealth (Puritan) 1649–1660	
Charles II (Stuart) 1660–1685	Carolinas (1663) New Jersey (1664) New York (1664) New Hampshire (1679) Pennsylvania (1681) (and Delaware)
James II (Stuart) 1685–1688 William and Mary (Orange) 1688–1702 Anne (Stuart) 1702–1714 George I (Hanover) 1714–1727 George II (Hanover) 1727–1760	Georgia (1732)
George III (Hanover) 1760–1820	Continental Congress (1774) State Constitutions (1776 and 1777) Articles of Confederation (1777; ratified 1781) Constitutional Convention (1787) U. S. Constitution in effect (1789)

* Some dates refer to legal charters granted by the crown; others refer to local compacts or agreements in the colonies themselves. They do not necessarily refer to time of first settlement.

cided to try to escape the persecutions imposed upon them by the Stuarts and the leaders of the Church of England. They, therefore, picked up and moved bodily to Massachusetts, stockholders, directors, charter, and all. With the corporation itself located in Massachusetts the members of the company felt much less dependent upon England.

In effect, the directors of the company became the governor, council, and magistrates of a civil government, and the stockholders became not only owners of the corporation but free citizens in a political commonwealth. The voters who made up the General Court of stockholders soon found that it was too difficult for them all to gather together from the several towns they had established; so a representative assembly of deputies was soon devised in which the deputies were elected by the freemen (stockholders who had become voting citizens). The governor, deputy-governor, and his assistants, elected regularly from among the men of more substantial property, comprised a kind of upper legislative chamber, and the basic pattern of political organization in America was forecast. Even when the original Massachusetts charter was abrogated and a new one making Massachusetts a royal province was established in 1691, the power and authority of the General Court were strong enough to carry on a running battle with the royal governors appointed by the king for nearly a century.

This precedent in which a commercial charter became virtually a political constitution was of enormous significance. The idea of a written contract as the basis of political authority found its way eventually into the American system of state and federal constitutions. It found expression more immediately in the colonies that were offshoots of Massachusetts. When the followers of Anne Hutchinson went to lower Rhode Island, they drew up a compact to govern themselves in 1638; Thomas Hooker and his Puritan followers in upper Connecticut adopted a constitution in 1639; and the Puritan settlers under John Davenport and Theodore Eaton adopted a covenant for the "plantation" of New Haven in 1638. These were all in effect mutual contracts establishing a body politic with virtually sovereign powers. Upper Connecticut and New Haven were joined together as the colony of Connecticut in a royal charter of 1662 from Charles II under which Connecticut governed herself until her first state constitution of 1818. Roger Williams had obtained a separate royal charter for the Providence settlement in 1644 and was instrumental in obtaining another charter in 1663 which incorporated both parts of Rhode Island and which remained the organic law of Rhode Island until the first state constitution was adopted in 1842. Connecticut and Rhode Island were never brought to heel by the crown to become royal provinces as was done in several other cases. For example, New Hampshire was colonized by several independent companies directly from England, while other towns were settled from Massachusetts and looked to her for law making. From 1641 to 1679 Massachusetts laws had force in New Hampshire, but the crown made New Hampshire into a royal province in 1679, and a separate legislature was authorized in 1680. After a period of uncertainty New Hampshire was again created a royal province in 1691 with a royal governor and a local assembly.

The third type of political organization used by the English king in this first period of settlement was the proprietary grant of land to an individual

Catholic

who was given rights to political authority as well as landed property. This was the case with Maryland when the king granted a large share of Virginia to the first Lord Baltimore (Sir George Calvert). Calvert died before he could take advantage of the grant but his son, the second Lord Baltimore, Cecil Calvert, became Lord Proprietor of Maryland by charter in 1632. By this time the pattern of rule included the appointment of a governor by the Lord Proprietor and the election of a representative assembly by the freemen of the colony. The Catholic leanings of the Lord Proprietor and his successors and the conflict between a Catholic minority and a Protestant majority led to many complications in Maryland. The colony was made a royal province for two decades but was returned to the proprietors again prior to the Revolution. Through all these changes, representative government continued to play a large role.

When the second wave of colonization began in the 1660's, the pattern of commercial stock companies dropped out of the picture and the pattern of proprietary grants became the rule. Thus, in 1663 eight land and trade promoters received proprietary rights to all the land south of Virginia and north of Florida to be known as Carolina and to be ruled on the ground by a governor and elected assembly. Much of the political and economic power centered in Charleston, and somewhat later a separate assembly was authorized for the northern and distant regions which came to be North Carolina. The government shifted back to the crown in 1729. North Carolina and South Carolina were separated. Both became royal provinces, but their assemblies continued to function and to grow in power.

Dutch

New York and New Jersey became proprietary colonies in 1664 when Charles II gave the conquered Dutch colony of New Netherland to his brother, the Duke of York (later James II). New York had originally been settled by the Dutch under authority of the States General of the Netherlands by grant of power to the Dutch West India Company in 1621. The company established trading posts at Albany in 1624 and on Manhattan Island in 1626. It drew up a series of articles for colonization which, when approved by the States General in 1640, set the governmental policy for New Netherland. Government was vested in a governor and council appointed by the company. No representative assembly was instituted until one was called by the English governor under the Duke of York in 1683. With a mixed population and large political control exerted in the assembly by the Dutch elements because of their vast property holdings along the Hudson, the assembly fought long and hard against the governor, especially over matters of taxation and religion. The Duke of York granted the territory of New Jersey to two of his friends in 1664, who, as proprietors, split up the territory and then sold out to other groups of proprietors. A representative assembly appeared by 1683 in the Jerseys and continued to function even after the charters of both Jerseys were annulled, and they were joined with New York when the whole territory became a royal province in 1702 under a single royal governor.

The Duke of York's grant was further whittled down when William Penn obtained a large part of his lands in consideration of a debt owed by the duke to Penn's father. Penn received a proprietary charter from the king in 1681 and proceeded to draw up his liberal *Frame of Government* of 1682, which was incorporated in the Great Law of the first legislative assembly that met in the same year. Penn lost his charter in 1693, and Pennsylvania was joined as a royal province to New York. But the proprietary charter was restored in 1694, and Penn's Charter of Privileges of 1700 continued to govern Pennsylvania until its constitution of 1776. The lower counties of Delaware had been settled by a Swedish trading company, were absorbed by New Netherland and New York, and then went along with Pennsylvania until they were granted their own assembly in 1702. Penn's Charter of Privileges continued to apply to Delaware, and the governor of Pennsylvania was also the governor of Delaware, until *its* constitution of 1776. Economic, political, and religious liberty of a generous sort rapidly attracted many people of varied backgrounds to Pennsylvania and made it quickly one of the largest and most prosperous of the colonies.

The last of the original colonies to be established was Georgia, founded as a proprietary grant in 1732 by a group of humanitarians and philanthropists whose major concern was to provide a haven for the oppressed and the unfortunate. An assembly was organized in 1751, but the conditions were so untoward for the proprietors that the colony was turned back to the crown and became a royal province in 1752, but, as in all other cases, it retained its representative assembly.

Thus, the American colonies in the eighteenth century became somewhat more consolidated under English political control, and the main outlines of a colonial imperial policy emerged. After 1752 nine of the colonies were royal provinces with royal governors appointed by the king and ostensibly under the rule of the instructions given by the king to his governors. Nevertheless, every colony had its representative assembly which was free to make laws but whose validity was theoretically subject to the king's privy council and to Parliament. Court decisions were also subject to review by the privy council. Two colonies remained proprietary (Maryland and Pennsylvania) with governors appointed by the proprietors, subject to approval by the crown and obliged to deal with the colonial assemblies. Two colonies were allowed to keep their corporate charters (Rhode Island and Connecticut) with their governors elected by the colonists but their assemblies' laws theoretically subject to royal and parliamentary approval.

Thus, all colonies maintained their representative assemblies which increasingly tried to expand their legislative powers and even to take on executive functions. They thereupon came to political blows with the royal and proprietary governors and with the crown and Parliament. All governors (except in Virginia) were paid by the colonial legislatures and thus were handicapped in their dealings with the assemblies. England's colonial policy began more and more to irk the colonists. Beginning with the Acts of Trade and Navigation (1660-1672), the freedom of the colonies to trade with other countries was limited, and colonial imports and exports were restricted to English ships, English ports, and English trading companies. So long as the colonists could get away with avoiding these laws (as they did in large part for nearly a hundred years), little real conflict developed; but when England began to tighten up its imperial and colonial policy after 1760, it ran head on into bitter resistance from a group of colonies that had tasted commercial prosperity and a large measure of political independence. A political and military showdown was quickly precipitated.

With a vast new empire to rule after the victory over France in 1763, England began to try to raise revenue from the colonists to help defray the military and political expenses of ruling an empire. Prior to this time the duties were largely to protect trade and profits of English merchants, but now the colonists were required to contribute financially to a larger share of military defense of the empire and of colonial administration. This meant more centralized control from England and less control by the colonial legislatures. By the Royal Proclamation of 1763 the crown took over the lands west of the Alleghanies, wiped out the claims of the several colonies, and prohibited purchase of the western land or settlement on it. The Sugar Act of 1764 increased duties on sugar and added many other items to the list. The Stamp Act of 1765 levied an indirect tax upon all kinds of legal documents, commercial bills, newspapers, pamphlets, licenses, and other papers. This brought such an outcry and violent resistance that it was repealed in 1768, but it helped to bring to a head the constitutional issue of representation.

The Americans argued that they could not be taxed by a body in which they were not represented; the Parliament said they were "virtually" represented by class and interest rather than by locality. Then the Townshend Acts of 1767 increased duties on a number of items, established new courts and a customs office in Boston, and aroused more violence, this time in the Boston Massacre of 1770. All the Townshend duties were repealed except that on tea, which was kept as a symbol of parliamentary authority. When in 1773 the East India Company was given a monopoly on the importing of all tea into the colonies, the merchants joined with the radicals who were preaching independence and resistance. The Boston Tea Party of December 1773 stung Parliament to retaliation by means of a whole series of "intolerable acts" closing the port of Boston, forbidding town governments, requiring trial of certain offenders in England rather than in Massachusetts, and removing from the colonists the right to elect the governor's council. Meanwhile, the Quebec Act of 1774 restored civil rights and religious liberty to the French Catholics and added the Northwest Territory above the Ohio River to Quebec. This further alarmed and antagonized the colonists who smelled a plot to capture the West for Catholicism.

The coercive acts aimed at Massachusetts prompted the calling of the first Continental Congress in September 1774 which proceeded to take retaliatory measures of its own and to state the case that Parliament had no jurisdiction over the colonies except in matters of commerce and imperial affairs. The theory of federalism was enunciated whereby the colonies admitted loyalty to the crown's wars and treaties but maintained that they should be free to govern themselves in all other matters. But George III was in no mood to be conciliatory. The fighting began at Lexington and Concord and the Second Continental Congress assembled in May 1775 and took over direction of the war. The king declared the colonies in rebellion, and Parliament stopped all trade with the colonies. Backed by a public opinion that had been pushed to favor independence by Thomas Paine's *Common Sense,* the Congress asked the colonies in May 1776 to constitute themselves as independent governments and adopted the Declaration of Independence on July 4.

In response to the call of the Continental Congress and to their own sense of necessity, the several colonies moved promptly to transform themselves from dependent colonies to independent commonwealths. They built upon the past and went beyond it. In framing their written constitutions [1] they drew upon the precedent of contract and charter that had marked their colonial status, but they changed the basis of political authority from royal or proprietary sovereignty to the sovereignty of the people. They solidified the developing theory of the separation of powers by placing legislative powers in the hands of representative assemblies, executive powers in the hands of governors, and judiciary or interpretative powers in the hands of independent courts.

They drew upon the natural rights philosophy of the Declaration of Independence to incorporate declarations of rights or bills of rights into the organic law of their constitutions. Notable among these was the Declaration of Rights of the Virginia Constitution. Here were summaries of the great tradition of civil liberties which have marked Western and American political theory since that time: sovereignty in the hands of the people, free elections,

---

[1] State constitutions were framed and adopted as follows:

New Hampshire (1) Jan. 1776	Vermont July 1777
South Carolina (1) March 1776	(not admitted to Union until 1791)
Virginia June 1776	South Carolina (2) March 1776
New Jersey July 1776	Massachusetts June 1780
Delaware Aug. 1776	(Provisional government from 1774 to 1780)
Pennsylvania Sept. 1776	New Hampshire (2) June 1784
Maryland Nov. 1776	Connecticut and Rhode Island
North Carolina Dec. 1776	continued to operate under their colonial charters until 1818 and 1842 respectively

fair and speedy trials by one's peers, the right of *habeas corpus,* reasonable bail and punishment, freedom of religious conscience, freedom of the press, assembly, and petition, protection against general search and seizure of personal property and domicile, protection against imprisonment without warrant and *ex post facto* laws, prohibition of military law in time of peace, and superiority of the civil authority over military authority.

All in all, the new state constitutions were something new in the world and marked a milestone in human liberty. Seen at this distance, however, some of them revealed weaknesses that were later to be remedied. Some gave too little power to the executive branch of government; others put too much check upon the legislative branch in order to prevent the popular will from touching vested interests; all retained property qualifications or poll taxes for the suffrage (except Vermont) and higher property qualifications for office holding; and many retained religious qualifications or religious oaths for office holding. Many constitutions discriminated against the western frontier and debtor sections of the states by giving them proportionately less representation in the legislature than the eastern and creditor regions. Some were more democratic than others and represented a victory for democratic forces, as in Pennsylvania, North Carolina, and Georgia; others gave notable advantages to the conservatives, as in Virginia, South Carolina, Maryland, Massachusetts, and New York.

This, then, in barest outline was the political framework that developed in the colonial period. It was extremely important for education and provided the basic foundations for state control of education. Education throughout the colonial period was a function of political sovereignty. Even where education was conducted by private or religious agencies, it was a grant of power by the political authority whether king, proprietor, or colonial legislature. When the colonies became independent states, they assumed similar prerogatives in law, no matter how much or how little freedom was given to private or religious groups to conduct education. Without this fundamental tradition of political and state authority the states of the nineteenth century would have found it extremely difficult to extend public control over education or to establish the public systems of education which became so important a feature of American life.

Two other cultural patterns of the colonial period were of prime importance for education. One was the inherited alliance between church and state, which meant that the political authority could properly legislate on religious matters and on religious education. The significant changes and developments that took place in this pattern during the colonial period led to the separation of church and state in the Revolutionary and early national periods. The other was the pattern of economic–class-sectional relationships which created serious problems and conflicts within the colonies and vitally influenced the kind of schooling and opportunity for education that developed in colonial times. Of all the problems that could be treated, these two deserve the closest attention of educators; and of these two, the more prominent problem throughout colonial times was the religious.

ESTABLISHMENT OF RELIGION MOVES TOWARD SEPARATION OF CHURCH AND STATE [2]

Among the many knotty problems that face American education today, one of the oldest and most difficult is the problem of the relation of religion and education. The American people and American educators have long debated whether religious instruction should be given in the public schools and whether public funds should be allocated to religious schools. Questions such as these stir the emotions and elicit hot arguments on both sides.(Inevitably the decision on these educational matters rests upon the more fundamental issues concerning the proper relation between church and state. If church and state are considered to be allies in any proper sense, then religion and education should go hand in hand in public as well as in private schools. If church and state are considered to be separate in function and structure, then state schools should not promote religious instruction and state funds should not be used to promote religious education.)

Of all the legacies that we have inherited from the colonial period in American history, the most important to understand clearly is an awareness of the patterns of church-state relations as they were brought from Europe to these shores and modified under the peculiar conditions of American life. Colonial history is replete with interesting developments, but the most fascinating and the least understood by American educators is this question: What *was* the authentic tradition of religion and education in colonial times and what does it mean for us today?

Establishment of a Single Church in the Seventeenth Century

The dominant pattern of relationship between church and state as developed in Europe in the sixteenth and seventeenth centuries was one of close alliance between the state and a single established church. The majority outlooks of the major religious groups in Europe rested upon a belief that the welfare of society required that certain religious doctrines be promoted and supported by the civil authority of the state. Despite genuine differences of religious doctrine, the most powerful churches, Protestant and Roman Catholic alike, believed that their own church should be the preferred church and should be protected and aided by the state in return for the propagation of

---

[2] This section is based upon and partially drawn from R. Freeman Butts, *The American Tradition in Religion and Education* (Boston, Beacon Press, 1950). Permission granted by Beacon Press to select from Chapters II and III.

the true faith and morality. The religious wars of the Reformation broke the universal power of the Catholic Church in Europe, but they reaffirmed the principle that religion is a proper concern of the state and that cooperation between church and state was a desirable political arrangement. Thus the idea of a single established church was current in the countries of Europe at the time of American colonization, and the colonists brought their establishments of religion with them in various forms. In the sixteenth and seventeenth centuries the various Protestant groups waged their battles to break the hold of the Roman Catholic Church in Europe by relying upon the rising national states for financial, military, and moral support. The major religious settlements were thus basically political settlements.

In those national states where the Roman Church was overthrown, the various Protestant churches were established by law in place of the Catholic Church. In some German states and in Scandanavia Lutheranism was established; in the Netherlands, the Reformed Church; in England, the Church of England; in Geneva, Calvinism; in Scotland, Presbyterianism. In all these cases it was assumed that religion was a concern of the whole community and hence should be supported by the state.

Thus the Dutch brought their established Reformed Church to New Netherland; the English Anglicans brought their established Church of England to Virginia and the Carolinas; the Swedes brought their established Lutheranism to the Delaware region; and the English Puritans brought their established Congregationalism and Presbyterianism to New England. Now, what was the essence of "an establishment of religion" as conceived by these colonists? It always had two parts: establishment meant (1) that the state gave financial support to the church, and (2) that the state enforced by law the public worship and doctrines of the established church with punishment and penalties for offenders. To illustrate just how the established churches operated in law and in practice, the two most powerful and most firmly entrenched establishments will be described, namely the Anglican in the South and the Puritan in New England.

The Anglican establishment in the South. The Church of England became the established church in England as a result of a long series of conflicts with Rome. The changes in the relationship between church and state were embodied in the legal enactments of Parliament under Henry VIII, Edward VI, and Elizabeth, whereby the English crown displaced the Pope as the supreme head of the English church. The Act of Uniformity of Parliament required the Book of Common Prayer to be the only legal form of public worship and fixed penalties for clergymen who did not follow the orders set down therein. Opposition to the articles of faith or to the methods of public worship constituted a breach of civil law and could be punished by the civil authorities. The state required attendance at church, prohibited public worship by dissenters, prohibited dissenters from holding public office, and punished offenders in any of these respects. All persons were forced to pay taxes for the support of the parish church, no matter what their own religious beliefs might be.

This system of establishment was carried in substance to Virginia, where the commercial company in charge was authorized by the royal charter of 1607 to give financial support to ministers, require church attendance of all settlers, and levy penalties upon any who spoke blasphemy or heresy. Virginia thus followed in essence the pattern from the homeland. Under the rule of the commercial company harsh laws were ordained in 1611 by the governor, Sir Thomas Dale, against religious dissenters. For example, the death penalty was laid upon anyone who spoke impiously of the Trinity or for repeated blasphemy. Whippings were decreed for those who showed disrespect for a minister, for not attending church, and for breaking the Sabbath. These laws were aimed at Romanists, Puritans, and other dissenters. Laws were soon passed against Quakers—levying fines upon shipmasters who brought Quakers to the colony, upon any who gave them aid, and upon any magistrate who did not enforce the laws against them in addition to fines, imprisonment, and banishment for Quakers themselves. Later on, Baptists, Presbyterians, Lutherans, Mennonites, and Moravians all felt the lash of discrimination from the civil government operating in favor of the established church.

Financial support for ministers of the Church of England also appeared as early as 1618 under the rule of the commercial company. When a colonial assembly was established in 1619 and when Virginia became a royal province in 1624, the legislature proceeded to enact a whole series of laws for the support of the church. Taxes were levied for the support of clergymen, church buildings were built with the aid of taxes and public lands, glebe lands were allocated to ministers for their support, and workmen were assigned at public expense to till the lands for the clergymen. The state not only supported the ministers but laid down rules to control the conduct of the ministers in and out of church. Ministers should not drink to excess, nor riot, nor be idle or waste time at cards or dice, and they must conduct services in conformity with the orders of the Church of England, preach regularly on Sundays, and administer the sacraments. Penalties were to be exacted from reluctant or recalcitrant ministers.

In addition to the ultimate legal establishment of the Church of England by grant of power from the English crown and enactment by the Virginia assembly, the structure and administration of local government reinforced the close alliance of church and state throughout the colonial period in Virginia. This took the form of the parish system.

The parish was originally the local form of church government, paralleling the county as the local form of civil government, but it came to serve as an agency of civil as well as ecclesiastical administration. The parish boundaries were sometimes larger than those of the county, sometimes smaller, and often coincided. The parish was governed by a board of vestry, appointed at first by the county court, then later chosen by parishioners, and finally becoming self-perpetuating. The vestry's main duties were to choose the parish minister, levy the parish tax for support of the minister, administer the church lands, property, and buildings, administer poor relief and care for the aged, investigate moral and religious offenses and present offenders to the county court for trial and punishment. After 1661–1662 the vestry also was given power over the care and apprenticeship of orphans and illegitimate and poor children. This function gradually led to wider educational activities on the part of the vestry and the parish, especially during the eighteenth century in Virginia (see pp. 105–107 and 116–118).

In brief, establishment meant that the Church of England not only received legal privileges of public worship and faith which were accorded to no other belief, but also the compulsive and legal force of the state was used to enforce these privileges and to support the clergy and property of the established church by aid of lands and taxes. To give effect to these principles, the legislature passed many laws "respecting an establishment of religion" as well as "prohibiting the free exercise thereof." Somewhat similar forms of Anglican establishment were enacted in the Carolinas and eventually in Maryland and Georgia. This form of single establishment was one kind of "cooperation" between church and state which the American people sought to prevent when they began the long struggle toward separation of church and state in the late eighteenth century.

The Puritan establishment in New England. The English Puritans followed in general John Calvin's doctrines in their efforts to reform the Church of England and also to counteract the "radical" Protestant sects who wanted free exercise of religion and separation of church and state. Despite Calvin's great hostility to the Roman Catholic Church, his position was somewhat similar to that of the Catholic Church regarding the relation of church and state. He insisted that it was the obligation of the state to enforce the church's pronouncements on religion. On this basis the Puritans in England could not accept the Anglican doctrine that the civil ruler in the person of the crown was the supreme authority in religious affairs. They were not by any means arguing for separation of church and state. They simply wanted to be sure that the state enforced the orthodox religion as defined by the Puritan church.

Thus, when the Puritans came to New England, one of their primary concerns was to establish their own religious orthodoxy as the law of the land in Massachusetts, Connecticut, and New Hampshire. In many ways they showed their intent that the state should support the Congregational Church in accordance with Calvin's outlook. The principle of "cooperation" between church and state was fully in operation in the full meaning of the

Puritan Congregational establishment. The close alliance of church and state in Massachusetts was early revealed by the two qualifications for free citizenship that were instituted, namely, a free man was one who owned a certain amount of property and who was a member of an authorized church. A law of 1631 required church membership as a qualification for voting:

> . . . to the end the body of the commons may be preserved of honest and good men, it was likewise ordered and agreed that for time to come no man shall be admitted to the freedom of this body politic, but such as are members of some of the churches within the limits of the same.[3]

Thus it was assumed that good citizenship required adherence to the true religion as expressed in membership in the approved churches. Hence, Anglicans, Baptists, Quakers, and Catholics could not be given the freedom of citizenship because their religious beliefs made them a threat to the civil welfare.

Two other approaches to maintaining a single establishment of religion were soon evident. One was the providing of tax support for the established church. The other was the legal outlawing of unorthodox religious views and organizations. A law of 1638 provided that all persons, irrespective of religious belief, were compelled to support by taxation the established church:

> . . . every inhabitant in any town is liable to contribute to all charges, both in church and commonwealth, whereof he doth or may receive benefit; and withal it is also ordered, that every such inhabitant who shall not voluntarily contribute, proportionately to his ability, with other freemen of the same town, to all common charges, as well for upholding the ordinances in the churches as otherwise, shall be compelled thereto by assessment and distress to be levied by the constable, or other officer of the town, as in other cases.[4]

From that time forward a whole series of laws during the seventeenth century reinforced the principle that all persons must not only attend church on Sundays (with fines and imprisonment as penalties) but also must pay taxes for the support of the established ministers.

The converse of using the coercive power of the state to require financial support for the established church was to use the force of law to punish any who dissented from the established religion. As early as 1644 a law was passed decreeing banishment for Baptists, three years later the same for Jesuits, and in 1658-1659 not only banishment but death for Quakers who persisted in their activities. Numerous laws defined heresy with respect to immortality of the soul, the resurrection, sin, redemption, repentance, and the meaning of the Bible. Fines, whippings, banishment, and even death were

[3] *Records of the Governor and Company of Massachusetts Bay in New England,* Nathaniel B. Shurtleff, ed. (Boston, William White, 1853), Vol. I, p. 87. [Spelling modernized.]

[4] *Ibid.,* Vol. I, p. 240. "Distress" and "distrain" meant the legal seizure of property or goods and the sale of such goods to obtain payment for a debt owed by the owner, in this case assessment for support of the ministers. [Spelling modernized.]

devised for various degrees of refusal to accept the orthodoxies so defined in law by the General Court. Even contemptuous conduct toward the minister led to fines and punishments by law. A law of 1659 has an oddly curious sound to modern ears when the Puritans outlawed the observance of Christmas as a punishable offense because it reeked of a popish holiday. As the seventeenth century moved to its close, however, the most stringent of these laws against dissenters in Massachusetts were reduced by the growth of dissenting groups and by the interference of the home government in England.

The establishment of religion in Connecticut paralleled in many respects that of Massachusetts. Actual church membership was not required for citizenship, but heretics, blasphemers, idolators, infidels, and Quakers were to be punished by law, and all taxpayers were compelled to support the established Congregational Church.

The compulsory support of ministers was elaborated in a law of 1644 which required every man to indicate what he could pay for the minister; if he refused to pay voluntarily, he was to be assessed by the magistrates and the assessment to be collected by force of law.[5] A comprehensive statement of the alliance of church and state was developed in the Cambridge Platform of 1648 which was drawn up by a church synod and given the force of law by enactment of the General Courts of Massachusetts and Connecticut. Here, the maintenance of the church by taxation upon all was further legalized, and civil magistrates were given authority to define and punish heresy, blasphemy and idolatry, profaners of the Sabbath, and disturbers of public worship. A whole series of laws gave effect to these principles as illustrated in the "True Blue Laws of Connecticut" of 1672, which defined the capital laws for which death was the penalty. Quakers were especially singled out for punishment in laws of 1656, 1657, and 1658, but the penalties were largely in terms of fines rather than punishment or death.

New Hampshire followed the main outlines of establishment as set up in Massachusetts and Connecticut. The laws of Massachusetts governed New Hampshire from 1641 to 1679, and then after a period of uncertainty New Hampshire was finally separated in the charter of 1691. Laws of New Hampshire in 1692, 1702, and 1714 reaffirmed religious assessment upon all taxpayers for support of the minister who was to be elected by the freeholders of the town and paid by the constable who was authorized to collect the tax funds.

Summary of meaning of single establishment of religion. In the seventeenth century colonial Americans living in Massachusetts, Connecticut, New Hampshire, Virginia, Maryland, and the Carolinas knew well what a single established church meant. It meant two things:

1. The state gave positive support to religion by levying taxes and using public funds and public property for the benefit of the established church.

---

[5] J. Hammond Trumbull (ed.), *The Public Records of the Colony of Connecticut,* (Hartford, Brown & Parsons, 1850), Vol. I, pp. 111–112.

2. The state enforced by law the exclusive rights of the preferred church to conduct public worship and compelled all persons to attend these church services no matter what their own religious beliefs. Conversely, the state used its coercive power to deny equal rights of worship to the unorthodox and in some cases even denied civil rights of suffrage and office holding in the state to the religiously unorthodox. Not only were dissenters often denied political rights, but they also were subject to civil trial and punishment by the state for heresy, blasphemy, and idolatry, for holding private religious opinions or engaging in public worship contrary to law, and in some cases even for criticizing the established ministers.

The Struggle for Free Exercise of Religion up to the Revolution

From the foregoing descriptions it is clear that one of the dominant traditions in early colonial America was the acceptance of the principle that church and state were legitimate partners in the propagation and maintenance of an established religion. It should be noted immediately, however, that a second and equally authentic tradition was present in America from almost the beginning. This was the tradition of separation of church and state which began as a minority viewpoint in the early seventeenth century but which became a majority point of view toward the end of the eighteenth century. As the tradition of separation won its way in principle, the practice of establishment began to crumble on many fronts until a high degree of separation was eventually won.

Perhaps the most effective early American statement of the principle of separation of church and state was made by Roger Williams in the course of his bitter conflict with the Massachusetts authorities under the leadership of the Puritan clergyman John Cotton. Williams believed that conflict between various religions could end only when there was essential separation between church and state, when the legal connections between civil and religious authorities were cut away. Civil authorities have their secular sphere and religious authorities have their religious sphere; neither should try to control the affairs of the other. All religious beliefs should not only be allowed freedom to exist, but also the state must not infringe the *equal* rights of any religious belief—Christian or non-Christian. He even held that freedom of nonbelief should be allowed by the state. He believed that only in these ways may the true welfare of the state as well as of all religions be achieved. Williams' famous tract entitled *Bloudy Tenent of Persecution* elaborated these ideas in 1644.

Needless to say, such "radical" views as these expressed by Roger Williams in 1644 did not immediately change the picture of the dominant outlook toward establishment, but they did take root increasingly and ever more firmly among larger numbers of people, especially among the noncomformist and dissenting groups that came to America in increasing numbers in the seventeenth and eighteenth centuries. Although the roots of establishment seemed firmly grounded in the soil of the seventeenth century, new seeds were soon planted that began rapidly to sprout and blossom into sturdy plants of religious freedom. An added factor in the growth of freedom was the rapid increase of a wide variety of religious groups which soon began to attack the entrenched establishments where they existed and which effectively prevented the spread of establishment to ground where it had not originally been.

In general, there were three types of attitudes toward religious establishments among the thirteen colonies. There was, first, the group of colonies where strong establishments existed for relatively long periods of time. These, as we have seen, included Massachusetts, Connecticut, and New Hampshire, where the Congregational Church was most commonly recognized as the established church, and Virginia, South Carolina, and North Carolina, where the Church of England was established.

There was a second group in which the status of establishment was uncertain or changed as the complexion of the religious population changed. These were New York, New Jersey, Maryland, and Georgia.

There was, finally, a third group of colonies in which little or no establishment of religion existed and in which a large measure of religious freedom was present from their beginnings and in general was maintained throughout the colonial period. These were Rhode Island, Pennsylvania, and Delaware.

In the founding of Providence Plantation, Roger Williams put into practice what he had preached. In the royal charter granted to Rhode Island in 1663 no one was to be asked to account for his religious beliefs so long as he did not disturb the civil peace. The British crown apparently felt that it would be good policy to encourage a colony that seemed likely to be advantageous for the empire. If religious freedom contributed to prosperity, then religious freedom was to be encouraged. In general, Rhode Island was able to maintain its liberal record, although later, citizenship was limited to Protestant Christians, but this rule was not rigorously enforced, and some Jews and Catholics became citizens. There was no penal legislation against Quakers, Jews, or Catholics, and one of the strongest Jewish congregations grew up in Newport in the eighteenth century. Rhode Island steadfastly refused to tax its citizens for the support of religion and in 1716 passed a law stating that "what maintenance or salary may be thought needful or necessary by any churches, congregations, or societies . . . for the support of their, or either of their minister or ministers may be raised by a free contribution, and no other ways." [6]

[6] *Records of the Colony of Rhode Island and Providence Plantations, in New England,* John Russell Bartlett, ed. (Providence, Knowles, Anthony, 1859), Vol. IV, p. 206.

To William Penn the ideal of toleration and commercial interest were strong motives for founding Pennsylvania. Freedom of conscience and of worship was included in Penn's *Frame of Government* and was further re-enforced in the Great Law of 1682. The state was not to compel individuals to attend any public worship they did not wish to attend nor penalize them for their beliefs. Society was to be founded upon Christian principles but without enforced conformity or uniformity. Freedom of conscience thus came to mean freedom from obligation to support anyone else's religion by taxation. The growth and prosperity of Pennsylvania stimulated other colonies to try more religious freedom. When Delaware was separated from Pennsylvania in 1702, Delaware continued the policy of permitting a wide range of religious freedom with no establishment of religion.

Emergence of Multiple Establishment of Religion

By the time of the Revolution all colonies were trying in greater or lesser degree the experiment of allowing more freedom of religious worship. This process gained headway in the eighteenth century but met most opposition in those colonies where established churches claimed special prerogatives on the basis of laws passed in the seventeenth century. The established churches were reluctant to relinquish their privileges but gradually gave in to growing dissenter groups. Two stages were apparent in the eighteenth century. The first was granting the privilege of freedom of worship to dissenting groups but maintaining tax support for the established church. When the dissenters proved not to be satisfied with this arrangement and continued to fight to be relieved of the burden of paying taxes for a religion in which they did not believe, the standing orders tried another compromise which has been little understood in American history.

At this point several colonies tried the experiment of expanding the privileges of the establishment by allowing *more than one church* to use the taxing machinery of the state for the support *for their own ministers* and religious worship. This meant that legislatures were persuaded to open up the taxing power of the state to the dissenting groups one by one; gradually more and more churches were admitted into the establishment and given the legal right of taxation for their own public worship. Thus, the term "establishment of religion" came to be applied not just to one preferred church, but to *all* churches that had legal and financial connections with the state. The term used here to refer to this development is "multiple establishment of religion." It was the only form of establishment left in any American state at the time the United States Constitution was put into effect in 1789. Multiple establishment became the policy for varying lengths of time in New York, Massachusetts, Connecticut, New Hampshire, Maryland, and South Carolina. It was attempted but not achieved in Virginia.

Under the Dutch commercial company which founded New Netherland the Dutch Reformed Church was established, but a distinction was made between public worship on one hand and private religious beliefs and private worship on the other. Even though public worship was confined to the Dutch Reformed Church, considerable toleration was given to freedom of private conscience. This developed partly from indifference on the part of the governing company and partly from the desire to maintain a prosperous colony that would attract settlers. As a result, a heterogeneous religious population soon appeared, including Calvinists, Lutherans, Mennonites, Quakers, Catholics, and Jews.

When the English took over New Netherland and made it into New York, the principle of toleration was continued. The inclinations of the Duke of York toward Catholicism led to a modification of the harsh measures against Catholics, and toleration for public worship was given to all Protestant groups who could produce an ordained minister. This principle of free exercise of religion, as set down in the *Duke's Laws* of 1664, is interesting because no mention is made of the Church of England by name. The usual provisions for churches to be built and ministers to be supported by a public tax upon all inhabitants are included, but the Church of England was not singled out for special privilege. Each township was required to support a minister, but the minister was to be elected by the majority vote of the inhabitants of the town.

Thus, no specific church was to be established for the whole colony, but simply Christian Protestant religion in general was to be established. Each town must have some kind of church and support, but its denomination was to be left to the locality. Here is an early case where establishment did *not* mean preference of one religious group over all others; the preacher merely had to produce a certificate of ordination from some Protestant bishop or minister. The early English governors followed this practice of multiple establishment by recognizing that the Dutch Reformed Church be maintained as the established church and the Dutch minister be paid by public funds in certain towns.

After the Duke of York became king, he then specifically instructed the royal governors to single out the Church of England for preference as the established church in New York and for public support of Anglican ministers. This set off a long period of conflict with the New York Assembly which consistently refused to pass such laws. Upon the insistence of the royal governor, the New York Assembly finally passed a compromise law in 1693 which carefully refrained from giving preference to the Church of England. The act simply provided that in six towns of the four southern counties of New York there should be "established a good, sufficient, Protestant Minister" to be supported by a public tax. This act did not mention the Church of England, it applied only to New York City, Richmond, Westchester, and Queens, it made no mention of the denomination of the ministers to be chosen, and it did not apply to the whole province.[7] .

From then on the battle raged between the royal governors and the Anglican clergymen on one side, who maintained that the Church of England was established, and the legislature and the dissenters on the other side who insisted that it was not. In 1695 the Assembly specifically resolved that a town in the four counties specified could select a dissenting Protestant minister and pay him from public tax funds. Controversy ensued in many disputes and court cases. One of the most notable cases was decided in 1731 when a court ruled that the town of Jamaica in Queens could select and support a Presbyterian minister rather than a Church of England minister as the established minister of the town. Here was the principle of "cooperation," between the state and a variety of churches. This policy of multiple establishment was maintained in New York until the time of the Revolution when it was abrogated in the New York Constitution of 1777.

The trend toward multiple establishment was even more clearly evident in Massachusetts, Connecticut, and New Hampshire. In Massachusetts the single establishment of the Congregational Church received a body blow when William and Mary issued a new charter in 1691, making Massachusetts a royal province, granting toleration to all Protestants, and removing membership in the Congregational Church as a prerequisite for the suffrage. Thus, the groundwork was laid for the growth of other religious groups which were to challenge the dominance of the single establishment. These were principally Anglicans, Baptists, and Quakers. The Congregationalist majority in the General Court, however, circumvented the edict of toleration by promptly passing a law in 1692 which compelled each *town* to support and maintain "an able, orthodox and learned minister" by means of a religious tax upon all inhabitants. Although the Congregational Church was thus not singled out by name for preference in tax support, the Congregationalists had a sufficient majority in the towns to make sure that the voters would for a long time choose a Congregationalist minister to be the established minister. From then on it was a battle between the Congregationalist majority, who tried to use the civil machinery of the state to protect their privileges, and the dissenters, who, on their part, tried to gain privileges or exemptions for themselves.

The first groups to be successful in this effort were Church of England members who were given the privilege in a law of 1727 to have their religious taxes paid to their own ministers for their support. Here was recognition of the principle of multiple establishment. There was no longer a single establishment when the civil taxing authorities were used to aid the Anglicans

[7] For a general summary of the development in New York, see Sanford H. Cobb, *The Rise of Religious Liberty in America* (New York, Macmillan, 1902), pp. 303 ff.

to support their churches along with the Congregational churches. Then, in the following years the Quakers and Baptists were granted exemption by law from paying taxes for the Congregational town churches if they could obtain certificates showing that they were regular attending members of the own services. All others were required to pay taxes for the support of the town churches.

The dissenters kept up a constant running fight against the principle of establishment, during and after the Revolutionary period, but they lost their fight in the Massachusetts Constitution of 1780 which gave the legislature authority to compel the towns to levy a general tax to support "public Protestant teachers of piety, religion, and morality" to be chosen by the "several towns, parishes, precincts, and other bodies politic, or religious societies." The constitution of 1780 and the laws soon passed under it were a step backward for the Quakers and Baptists who now were not exempt from religious taxes, but had to pay the taxes and then obtain a certificate which entitled *their own* ministers or religious teachers to obtain their share of the taxes from the taxing authorities.

Article III of the Massachusetts Constitution of 1780 contains the following provision:

> And all moneys paid by the subject to the support of public worship, and of the public teachers aforesaid, shall, if he require it, be uniformly applied to *the support of the public teacher or teachers of his own religious sect or denomination,* provided there be any on whose instructions he attends; otherwise it may be paid towards the support of the teacher or teachers of the parish or precinct in which the said moneys are raised.[8]

Here was a thoroughgoing multiple establishment in which everyone still paid a general tax for religion, but the way had been opened for all Protestant groups to participate equally in the privileges of the establishment. Any Protestant group could claim its share of religious taxes. A court decided that even so radical a dissenter as a Universalist minister in Gloucester was entitled to recover the taxes that his parishioners had paid to the town treasury. The town form of multiple establishment was the constitutional policy of Massachusetts in 1789 when the First Amendment was framed and continued to be until an amendment to the Massachusetts Constitution was adopted in 1833. New Hampshire followed in main respects the Massachusetts town form of multiple establishment from its law of 1714, down to and including its constitution of 1784.

The story of multiple establishment in Connecticut was similar. Connecticut named the Congregational Church as the establishment when the General Court approved the Saybrook Platform in 1708 and then moved to the town

[8] F. N. Thorpe, *The Federal and State Constitutions, Colonial Charters and Other Organic Laws* . . . (Washington, D.C., Government Printing Office, 1909), pp. 1889–1890. [Italics added.]

form of multiple establishment by a law of 1717 which provided for the election of the town minister by a majority of the voters and empowered the town to levy taxes for his support. Connecticut also passed a law in 1727 giving Church of England members the right to use their taxes for the support of their own ministers and even to levy further taxes if the original taxes were not deemed sufficient.[9] Quakers and Baptists were also given exemption from paying taxes for the town establishments.

In 1784 in its first code of laws as a state Connecticut authorized each town to form one or more ecclesiastical societies as the majority of inhabitants so voted in order to levy taxes for the support of public ministers. It also authorized dissenters to form their own societies which were to be on an equal footing with the same privileges of supporting their ministers by taxation as those of the majority churches. *Everyone had to support some kind of religious worship, but he could choose which kind.* This was the general form of multiple establishment which obtained in Connecticut from 1784 until the dissenting groups became strong enough to oust the Congregationalists from political power and adopt the Connecticut Constitution of 1818 which finally wiped out the town form of multiple establishment and made religious support a purely voluntary matter. The state could no longer use its civil machinery to support or promote one or more forms of religion.

In the South the efforts to arrive at multiple establishment achieved greater success in Maryland and South Carolina. The first Lord Baltimore hoped that Maryland would become a refuge for Roman Catholics, but he was in an anomalous position as a Catholic holding a patent from Charles I as head of the Church of England and wishing to attract Protestants as settlers for the sake of the prosperity of his colony. Thus when the first Maryland assembly adopted an "Act for Church Liberties" in 1637, it included the rather equivocal statement that the "Holy Church within this province shall have and enjoy all her Rights, liberties, and Franchises wholly and without blemish." [10] Scholars dispute whether "Holy Church" meant the Roman Catholic Church or the Church of England. In any case, the population was divided sharply between Protestants and Catholics. A kind of truce was signed when the Protestants and Catholics in the legislature agreed with the lord proprietor to enact the famous Toleration Act of 1649, granting freedom to the various sects of Trinitarian Christians of Protestant and Catholic persuasion. This was an attempt to make possible a peaceful truce among the many warring factors that had come to Maryland.

The political balance, however, soon swung sharply to the Protestants, who revoked the Toleration Act and persecuted Catholics, only to be reprimanded by Cromwell, whereupon the Toleration Act was reinstated. When

[9] For details of the Connecticut establishment, see M. Louise Green, *The Development of Religious Liberty in Connecticut* (Boston, Houghton Mifflin, 1905).
[10] *Maryland Acts of Assembly,* Vol. I, p. 96.

the proprietorship was ended in 1692 and Maryland became a royal province, the Church of England was established with all the details of the parish system and taxation upon all for the Anglican clergymen. From then on a three-cornered struggle ensued between Anglicans, nonconformist Protestants, and Catholics. By the time of the Revolution the Church of England was able to hold off complete separation of church and state only by making it possible for Protestants and Catholics alike to use their religious taxes for support of their own churches. Maryland tried to reach a compromise whereby free exercise of religion would be achieved while at the same time provision was made for multiple establishment and protection for the property of the Church of England.

A close reading of the Maryland Constitution of 1776 will reveal how the attempt was made to serve all of these varying interests at the same time. First, respects were paid to free exercise of religion; then, secondly, multiple establishment was made legal; and, finally, the property of the Church of England was safeguarded.

That, as it is the duty of every man to worship God in such manner as he thinks most acceptable to him; all persons, professing the Christian religion, are equally entitled to protection in their religious liberty; wherefore no person ought by any law to be molested in his person or estate on account of his religious persuasion or profession, or for his religious practice; unless, under colour of religion, any man shall disturb the good order, peace or safety of the State, or shall infringe the laws of morality, or injure others, in their natural, civil, or religious rights; *nor ought any person to be compelled to frequent or maintain, or contribute, unless on contract, to maintain any particular place of worship, or any particular ministry; yet the Legislature may, in their discretion, lay a general and equal tax, for the support of the Christian religion; leaving to each individual the power of appointing the payment over of the money, collected from him, to the support of any particular place of worship or minister*, or for the benefit of the poor of his own denomination, or the poor in general of any particular county: but the churches, chapels, glebes, and all other property now belonging to the church of England, ought to remain to the church of England forever.[11]

A careful reading of these provisions will show that the meaning of establishment had definitely moved away from support of a single preferred church to support for any Christian sect so designated by the taxpayer. All Christian churches were on an equal footing in the eyes of the law. This was multiple establishment. The people of Maryland recognized it as multiple establishment when they ratified a constitutional amendment in 1810 specifically outlawing this provision in the following words:

Art. XIII. That it shall not be lawful for the general assembly of this State to lay an equal and general tax, or any other tax, on the people of this State, for the support of *any religion*.[12]

[11] Thorpe, *op. cit.*, p. 1689. [Italics added.]
[12] *Ibid.*, p. 1705. [Italics added.]

Similar, but much more elaborate, provisions for multiple establishment were included in the South Carolina Constitution of 1778. These provisions illustrate so clearly the common and widespread understanding that establishment of religion meant multiple establishment that they deserve to be studied carefully.

That all persons and religious societies who acknowledge that there is one God, and a future state of rewards and punishments, and that God is publicly to be worshipped, shall be freely tolerated. *The Christian Protestant religion shall be deemed, and is hereby constituted and declared to be, the established religion of this State. That all denominations of Christian Protestants in this State, demeaning themselves peaceably and faithfully, shall enjoy equal religious and civil privileges.* . . . And that whenever fifteen or more male persons, not under twenty-one years of age, professing the Christian Protestant religion, and agreeing to unite themselves in a society for the purposes of religious worship, they shall, (on complying with the terms hereinafter mentioned,) be, and be constituted a church, and be *esteemed and regarded in law as of the established religion of the State,* and on a petition to the legislature shall be *entitled* to be incorporated and *to enjoy equal privileges.* That every society of Christians so formed shall give themselves a name or denomination by which they shall be called and known in law, and all that associate with them for the purposes of worship shall be esteemed as belonging to the society so called. But that previous to *the establishment and incorporation of the respective societies of every denomination* as aforesaid, and in order to entitle them thereto, each society so petitioning shall have agreed to and subscribed in a book the following five articles, without which no agreement or union of men upon *pretence of religion* shall entitle them to be incorporated and *esteemed as a church of the established religion of this state:*

> 1st. That there is one eternal God, and a future state of rewards and punishments.
> 2d. That God is publicly to be worshipped.
> 3d. That the Christian religion is the true religion.
> 4th. That the holy scriptures of the Old and New Testaments are of divine inspiration, and are the rule of faith and practice.
> 5th. That it is lawful and the duty of every man being thereunto called by those that govern, to bear witness to the truth.[13]

It is true, of course, that the South Carolina Constitution still discriminated against Roman Catholics and non-Christians, but it is clear that "establishment of religion" no longer meant simply a privilege for a single religious sect or denomination in preference to all others. All Protestant Christian sects were to be treated equally and impartially by the state. This was a great broadening of the meaning of establishment from the days when the Church of England was actually a single establishment and civil disabilities were laid upon Puritans, Presbyterians, Baptists, Quakers, and all other dissenting Protestant sects as well as upon Roman Catholics and non-Christians. Virtually

[13] *Ibid.,* pp. 3255–3256. [Italics added.]

all religious groups then in South Carolina could thus participate equally in the multiple establishment. This was "cooperation" between the state and all legitimate churches.

In summary, then, as revealed in the new constitutions that were adopted by the states in 1776 and 1777 at the beginning of the Revolution, the status of religious freedom was as follows: Freedom of religious conscience was largely won in all states but some of them retained in their early constitutions religious qualifications or religious oaths for office holding. Among the latter were Delaware, Pennsylvania, New Jersey, North Carolina, South Carolina, and Maryland. Many of these restrictions were deleted from later constitutions.

With respect to compulsory support of religion by state taxes or public funds, the organic laws of a majority of the new states prohibited such support. In this sense, both single and multiple establishment of religion was effectively prohibited in eight states (by charter in Rhode Island, and by constitutions in Pennsylvania, Delaware, New York, New Jersey, North Carolina, Georgia, and Virginia [14]). In the remaining five states compulsory taxation for religion was permitted or required in their organic laws (by charter and codified laws in Connecticut and by constitutions in Massachusetts, New Hampshire, Maryland, and South Carolina). In all of the five states where establishment of religion was still permitted it was a multiple form of establishment. None of them required a single establishment of religion or preference for one church over all others. When church was separated from state, the state retained its legal rights to control education and to authorize private and religious education under a grant of power from the state by charter and legislative enactment. This is of paramount importance in the history of American education.

It is no accident that by and large it was the more liberal constitutions that provided for separation of church and state, whereas the more conservative state constitutions continued to permit an establishment of religion. This indicated that the struggle for religious liberty was not only allied with the struggle for political democracy but was also involved in the struggle for social democracy. This then raises the problem of conflict between economic interests, class differences, and sectional antagonisms which acted at once as threat to and as seed bed for a growing democracy.

CONFLICT OF ECONOMIC, CLASS, AND SECTIONAL INTERESTS

Americans have long been proud of their tradition of equality as well as their tradition of liberty and popular government. The American dream has been shaped by our belief that "all men are created equal" or at least that all men

---

[14] It took a ten-year legislative battle to apply the constitution of Virginia into agreement with this principle (see pp. 153–155).

should be treated as though they have an equal opportunity to make of themselves what they will. This ideal has been the motivating force behind much of the humanitarian and reform movement which led eventually to the abolition of slavery, universal suffrage, and universal free education. Much of the ideal has found realization in the actual conditions of American life, but it is also true that the realities of American culture have often delayed and even denied the ideal in practice. American educators who deal with all the children of all the people must be aware of the conditions that have fostered the ideal as well as the conditions that have stood in the way of its realization. These conditions have taken the form principally of economic, class, and sectional differences, some of which were inherited from Europe in the colonial period and some of which developed indigenously on the American continent.

Class distinctions were deeply imbedded in the feudal arrangements of medieval and Reformation Europe. Based largely upon the ownership of landed property, the class system of Europe in the sixteenth century consisted of three principal groups. At the top were the landed nobility and higher clergy; in the middle were the merchants, smaller landowners, freehold farmers, lower clergy, scholarly and professional people, tradesmen, free artisans, craftsmen, and skilled workers; at the bottom of the heap and representing the largest numbers were the peasants, serfs, slaves, tenants, servants, and unskilled or menial laborers most of whom were not considered free men (see Table 2, p. 32). In most European countries the class lines were rather rigidly drawn, and movement from one class to the other was very difficult.

One of the great and good fortunes of the American colonies was the fact that they were settled by Northern European countries which were among the first to begin to break the pattern of feudal institutions and to give greater scope and freedom to the growth of the middle classes. As noted earlier, the colonization of America was in large part a phenomenon of an expanding middle class that had joined forces with the royal authority to win colonies and expand trade for their mutual benefit. The merchants within the middle class were the leaders in this movement in England. Their hope of finding raw materials to bring to England for manufacture and for sale at home or abroad was the dynamic motive behind the rise of merchant capitalism. The encouragement of foreign trade was similarly useful to the crown in the pursuit of competition for markets and imperial wars on the continent of Europe and throughout the world.

In the seventeenth and eighteenth centuries this form of merchant capitalism was known as mercantilism. According to this doctrine, the profits from international trade should go to the merchants in England, and the tariffs or duties on import and export of goods should go to swell the treasuries of the king's central government. To obtain the raw materials quickly, it was desirable for people to be sent to the colonies to clear the land, raise the crops, and produce the raw materials. Land was the principal resource the crown had; it was abundant in America and could be granted freely without too many questions asked concerning the religious or class affiliations of those who were willing to brave the rigors of the New World. This was fortunate for the colonists because the land provided opportunity for a better life for those who were free at home; it provided the means of acquiring economic freedom for those who were oppressed or underprivileged at home; and it gave opportunity for religious freedom for those who were persecuted at home. The early land policies in the colonies of the seventeenth centuries were thus a great boon for potential erasure of the rigid class lines of feudal Europe.

On the other hand, many of the American colonists soon turned to trade rather than to agriculture, and they then ran up against the intention of the English merchants, Parliament, and the crown to control colonial trade for England's benefit, not for the colonists'. The English merchants were not so willing to give the same freedom and privileges to colonial merchants that they had won for themselves from the crown. This brought the economic interests of the merchants in the colonies into conflict with those of the merchants in England and contributed, as we have seen, to the causes of the Revolution. The colonial merchants came to look upon royal or proprietary governors, tax collectors, and English company agents as "foreign" oppressors of their political as well as their economic rights.

Further complications arose in the colonies by the establishment of class distinctions in the colonies themselves. Some of these were the result of carrying to America the class system of England, and some were the result of indigenous distinctions (see Table 2, p. 32). While it is true that the feudal privileges of landed property for nobility and church were not established in America, and few nobles actually came, it is, nevertheless, true that the rest of the class system was transferred in large measure. Colonial life in the seventeenth century revealed very definite class lines even though the highest classes of the feudal system were lopped off the top and the great preponderance of peasants and serfs was lopped off the bottom. In colonial towns the highest class consisted of royal officials, magistrates, merchants, and established clergy; below them were the substantial shopkeepers and tradesmen and master craftsmen; still lower were the skilled artisans and mechanics, clerks, sailors, and fishermen; and at the bottom were the unfree indentured servants, unskilled labor, and drifters or vagabonds. In the rural regions the highest class was made up of the landed gentry (planters in the South and patroons in New York), magistrates, and established clergy; below them were the substantial but lesser planters and farmers; still lower were the small freehold farmers or yeomen and tenants, and at the bottom were the unfree indentured servants and Negro slaves.

These class lines were just as definite in colonial seventeenth-century cul-

Table 2—Transfer of Class Distinctions from Europe to America

Feudal European Classes	American Colonial Classes

Upper Classes of Privilege
Landed nobility
Higher clergy

Upper Classes of Free Men

In Towns	In Rural Regions	
Merchants		⎡planters
Magistrates	Landed gentry	⎨ country gentlemen
and		⎣patroons
officials	Magistrates	
Established	Established clergy	
clergy		

Middle Classes of Free Men
Merchants
Landed gentry
Lower clergy
Scholars and professionals
Artisans, skilled craftsmen
Small traders
Freehold farmers (yeomen)

Middle Classes of Free Men

In Towns	In Rural Regions
Substantial	Substantial farmers
shopkeepers	Dissenting clergy
Master craftsmen	
Lawyers and	
college teachers	

Lower Classes of Free Men

In Towns	In Rural Regions
Mechanics,	Small freehold farmers
artisans	Renters and tenants
Clerks in	
business	
Fishermen and	
sailors	
Teachers	

Lower Classes of Servitude
Tenants and servants
Peasants and serfs
Slaves

Servile Classes of Unfree Men

In Towns	In Rural Regions
Indentured	Indentured white
white	servants and
servants	workers
Negro servants	Negro slaves

ture as in England. The difference was twofold: (1) The numbers in the middle categories of free men in town and country in America were far larger in proportion to the classes above and below than in Europe. In other words, most of the people in America either came from or were able to move into what had been called the "middle classes" in Europe. Few of the "upper classes" of Europe came to America and relatively few who remained in the condition of permanent servitude were transported to America with the exception of African slaves. (2) There was much more chance in America for those in the lower classes (except slaves) to rise into the classes above. The possibility of this social mobility upward gave great reality to the American dream of equality. The rapid expansion of population in the eighteenth century gave further impetus to social mobility. Whereas the total population of the colonies was about 360,000 in 1713, it had grown to 1,600,000 in 1760; to 2,200,000 by 1770; and to 3,900,000 by 1790. This amounted to more than a tenfold increase in population in the course of some seventy-five years.

The fact of class lines, however, found expression in the limitation of the suffrage to those who owned a certain defined amount of landed property or personal wealth and served to give the wealthier groups greater control over the colonial legislatures. Increased property qualifications for office holding meant that the actual reigns of government were conducted by a relatively few from the upper classes. The educational systems set up in the several colonies served, by and large, to perpetuate these class divisions with notable exceptions to be discussed in Chapter 4.

The land policies and the eagerness of certain of the proprietors to attract settlers led to a great influx of immigrants in the later seventeenth and middle eighteenth centuries who represented a wide variety of national, ethnic, and religious backgrounds as well as of economic and social class. This was a great boon as it gave them a chance to improve their economic positions, and it launched one of the most significant adventures in all human history—the task of developing a common society out of a variety of cultures without destroying the values of the contributing cultures. This adventure had its grave difficulties, however, and posed enormous problems for education. National and religious differences were added to economic and class distinctions, further complicating the achievement of a genuinely democratic society. Antagonisms, suspicions, and hatreds often flared into violent controversies.

Finally, a clash of sectional interests appeared on the scene to make difficulties for the struggling young colonies. The political and economic control of the colonies was substantially in the hands of the landed gentry or planters or merchants by the end of the eighteenth century, and they were mostly located in the towns or plantations nearest to the eastern seacoast of the several colonies. As indentured servants were freed, as renters gained enough money to buy cheap land, and as newcomers to the colonies found the seaboard lands taken up, they moved into the outskirts, into the "back country" or the "up-country" away from the settled regions near the shore. These back-country settlements or western counties soon developed different interests from those to the east. They found that they were at the mercy of land speculators from the towns or plantations; they had to borrow money to buy their land and equipment. They found that their small holdings did not entitle them to vote or hold office and that their regions were not given proportionate representation in the legislatures even when they outnumbered the eastern towns or counties. And they found that they had to pay taxes to support the established church even though they were dominantly dis-senters and often in a majority.

In all of these ways the "frontier" sections began to come to blows with the eastern sections. They developed more democratic and radical notions of taxation, easy credit, easy currency, and popular government which came into conflict and sometimes erupted in violence and pitched battles with the more conservative forces of the East. These differences carried into the struggles attendant upon forming the state constitutions and into the fram-ing of the United States Constitution and on into the nineteenth century. Sec-tionalism within the states was soon to be further complicated by a develop-ing sectional interest that divided the North from the South. Even before the Revolution certain distinctive patterns appeared in the colonies which began to have their effect upon schools and education.

New England Colonies

The most distinctive economic factor in seventeenth-century New England was the land policy that was appropriate to a fairly well-knit and compact town form of community life. The original settlers were organized into small social groups before they came to America. They were neighbors and families and congregations who moved to the New World in groups. Quite naturally a group would ask for and receive a common grant of land from the General Court. Certain parts of the land grant would be allocated for common purposes upon which to build a meeting house that would serve as church, town hall, and sometimes as school. The central common land then became the "green" or simply the "common" around which would cluster the shops and houses of most of the inhabitants. Part of the outlying woods or meadows would also be allocated for the common use of the inhabitants. The rest of the land was then assigned to individuals as their private prop-erty upon which to build houses and to farm and work as they could.

This meant that people lived close together, going out from the center of town to work their land and returning to their homes near the village green at night. The outlying land along with the central village green com-prised the "town." The church meeting thus became the principal intel-lectual, religious, and social center of life, and the town meeting became the principal agency for conducting and controlling the political and economic affairs of the town. Indeed, town meetings not only chose their selectmen and town clerk but also were authorized to choose many town officials to exert strict control over economic affairs. Modern New Englanders, proud of their rugged individualism, might be surprised to be subjected to the scrutiny of official "fence viewers," "leather sealers," "tything-men," "haywards" (to impound stray cattle), "chimney-viewers," "gaugers" (to measure the contents of casks), "packers" (to inspect goods packed for export), "sealers of weights and measures," and "key-keepers." [15] As new settlers came to New England or as the older towns became more crowded, new groups would gather and move on toward the west to form new towns on the same pattern. No wonder, then, that most decisions were common decisions of church and town.

In all New England colonies a property qualification was necessary for voting in the town meeting. With land fairly easily available for much of the colonial period, most men could become freeholders and thus voters. Therefore, a considerable amount of actual and potential democracy was present in the New England towns. Despite the widespread land-owning policy, however, class lines were marked and followed in general the class distinctions indicated in Table 2. Among the freeholders the highest rank was given to magistrates and other officials, the larger property owners, and the established or "settled" ministers. Below them were the smaller farmers and free artisans and tradesmen (coopers, tanners, blacksmiths, shoemakers, wheelwrights, and all the others necessary to produce the necessities of town life). At the bottom of the scale were servants, unskilled laborers, and a few slaves. Indentured servants were those who could not afford to pay for their passage from England and thus signed a contract or indenture whereby the servant would agree to work for a period of years for the person who paid his passage. After the expiration of the term and depending on good behavior, the indentured servant was free to acquire land for himself, perhaps by joining another group and moving on west to obtain some land and a freehold. This fluidity of land ownership formed the basis of a fairly widespread ownership of land and prevented the type of exclusive aristocracy based on land ownership that characterized most of Europe.

Nevertheless, considerable privilege went to the "gentlemen" of the upper classes in the form of office holding, of title of address, of dress, and of preference in town meeting and in church meeting. And in the course of the eighteenth century class differences began to come into sharp conflict, largely as a result of two factors. The influx of new immigrants who needed land led the older inhabitants to try to take advantage of the newcomers. The colonial assemblies began to allow the unsettled land to be bought up in fairly large tracts by land speculators who would then sell it to those who

[15] *Acts and Laws of the State of Connecticut in America* (New London, Timothy Green, 1784), pp. 247-249.

had no land. This meant that it became harder and harder to acquire free land and that the newcomers or free servants would have to borrow money to buy their land or simply "squat" on someone else's land. The back-country farmers thus often became debtors or renters, irritated by the economic control of absentee landlords and the creditors of the eastern section of the colonies. Interestingly enough they also became less interested in paying taxes for the town schools that were required by the colonial assemblies. (See district system, pp. 103–104).

A second factor of strife was the rapid increase in trade and commerce that marked the period after 1713. A profitable trade to Europe and the West Indies grew up in which New England timber and wood products, furs, fish, grain, livestock, and shipbuilding materials were eagerly sought. As a result, the quickest way to wealth in eastern New England was via commerce and business. This shift is summed up nicely in the following words, "In 1660 New England traded for a living; in 1760 New England lived for trade." [16] The merchant class thus began to overshadow the landed gentry as the arbiters of political and economic affairs in the eastern towns and helped to stimulate the need for a lawyer class that also joined the upper ranks. These facts gave added impetus to a new and more cultivated style of life and of social accomplishments and to a new kind of practical education (see pp. 124–126) that further distinguished the eastern towns from the rural and agricultural back country.

Within the towns this emphasis on trade and commerce created a growing class of "mechanics," clerks, fishermen, and sailors who had no property in land and precious little of personal wealth or money. They became resentful of the fact that they had no vote, little or no representation in the assemblies, and suffered discriminations in the laws and the courts and in punishments. They began to feel toward the merchant owners in the towns and cities as the debtors and the renters of the rural regions felt toward the landed gentry and officials. Both groups resented the tax for the established churches and eventually formed the backbone of the revivalistic movements and the agitation against the established churches. An increasing secularization of life stemming from the commercial revolution also tended to weaken the hold of established churches. These groups saw little need for the classical education of the town grammar schools. The lower classes in the backwoods felt that the rudiments of elementary education were enough education for their purposes and began to agitate for control of their own elementary schools. On the other hand, the lower classes in the towns of the seaboard began to take advantage of a new type of secondary education more suitable to their commercial and trade interests (see p. 124). Nevertheless, education was much more a class phenomenon even in colonial New England than is

---

[16] S. E. Morison and H. S. Commager, *The Growth of the American Republic* (New York, Oxford University Press, 1950), Vol. I, p. 181.

usually realized. Despite these class and sectional differences in education, the pattern of town life, a fairly democratic land policy, and a strong religious motivation in early Puritan days led to a pattern of school control and support that provided the New England colonies with the most widespread network of schools and more opportunity for education than was present elsewhere in the thirteen colonies.

Middle Colonies

The pattern of class distinctions, the rise of commercial interests, and sectional conflicts in the middle colonies paralleled in large measure those of New England. Major differences arose in the matters of land policy, characteristics of the immigration, and religious freedom.

Under Dutch rule in New York trade and commerce set the pattern for the lower counties around the mouth of the Hudson River, but along the upper Hudson vast tracts of land were granted to "patroons" in return for bringing fifty families or more to act as tenants on the lands. These owners, or patroons, were given what almost amounted to feudal rights of political, economic, and judicial control over their estates. This meant that from Poughkeepsie to Albany the gap between patroons and tenants was almost that between nobility and peasant in Europe. The economic, political, and religious rights of this landed aristocracy were retained when the English took over in 1664. The pattern of religious toleration initiated under the Dutch West India Company attracted a religiously heterogeneous population to southern New York, and the proprietary system applied to New Jersey after 1664 also meant that a variety of religious and national stocks came into New Jersey.

In eighteenth-century New York the class distinctions survived and were further implemented by the rapid immigration. At the top of the scale in New York were the landed aristocrats of the upper Hudson region and the wealthy merchants of lower New York; below these were the smaller farmers of the regions back away from the Hudson River and in the Mohawk Valley and the city shopkeepers and master craftsmen in New York City and Albany; still lower were the tenants on the landed estates and the artisans, mechanics, fishermen, and sailors in the cities; and at the bottom the indentured servants and slave servants. New Jersey did not have the same problem of semifeudal estates as in New York, but there was much difficulty over the haphazard system of granting land with consequent legal and political battles over land titles and rights.

In Pennsylvania the religious and nationality heterogeneity was even more marked than in New York and New Jersey, and in some respects the class and sectional rivalries were more marked too. Dutch, Swedes, and Finns had already settled along the Delaware River before Penn gained his proprietary grant. When he announced a policy of religious liberty and easy land (50 acres free; 200 acres on a tenant basis at a penny of rent per acre; and grants of 5,000 acres for £100), people flocked to Pennsylvania. By 1770 only Virginia and Massachusetts were still larger in population (Pennsylvania had passed Massachusetts by 1790), and in many respects Philadelphia challenged Boston and New York as the leading city in the colonies.

The Quakers dominated the political and economic life of southeastern Pennsylvania; thus when the new immigration swelled the population after 1713, the newcomers swept on to the western sections of Pennsylvania. The newcomers were principally Germans and Scots-Irish. The Germans, representing a variety of religious outlooks (Lutherans, Pietists, Mennonites, Moravians, and Dunkards) settled in and through the rich mountain and valley regions of central Pennsylvania. The Scots-Irish, who came principally from the northern colonies of Ireland and who settled in the western sections of Pennsylvania, were largely Presbyterian in outlook. Many of the German and Scots-Irish immigrants were from the lower classes of European society, but through the acquisition of cheap land and habits of industry and thrift they became substantial farmers and pioneers of the western sections, swelling the ranks of those who resisted the Quaker political and economic control of the Pennsylvania legislature. For a long time they held to their own religious and cultural patterns of education based upon a frontier rather than an urban and commercial conception of education. Public and state control of education in the colonial period was thus less advanced in the Middle Colonies than in New England because of the diversity in religion, nationality, and culture.

Southern Colonies

During the seventeenth century the class distinctions in the South were not too much different from those in the North, and the land policy was at first conducive to widespread ownership. But by the end of the seventeenth century the economic conditions of the South were such that the gap between upper and lower classes began to widen rather than to lessen.

At the beginning settlers came to Virginia in groups under the sponsorship of some wealthy person and were granted fairly large tracts of lands known as "hundreds." Each person who could pay his own way received fifty acres of free land as a head-right and another fifty acres for each person he could bring over. Indentured servants could become tenants when their contracts ended and could hope to acquire their own land further west. Most of the early settlers were small farmers back in England. As tobacco became a profitable staple, the tendency was for the larger planters to try to acquire still larger holdings.

The large plantation thus gradually began to be the pattern of the low lying Tidewater region near the coast and along the rivers, and the importation of Negro slaves became more profitable to the planters than indentured white servants. In the later eighteenth century cotton reinforced the plantation system, promoted slavery, and prevented the development of a compact town life except in a few centers along the mouths of the rivers. The small free-hold farmers were gradually squeezed out and became tenants or moved further west to pick up land in the Piedmont region and Shenandoah Valley where their numbers were swelled by the Scots-Irish, English, and Germans who came down the valleys from the North. These back-country people formed a strong resistance to the domination of the Tidewater landed aristocracy, which had reinforced its pattern by laws of primogeniture and entail, establishment of religion, and representation in the legislature favoring the eastern regions. This resentment of the poor farmers broke out into violence as early as Bacon's Rebellion of 1675 and continued to grow in various ways until the time of the Revolutionary reforms when Virginia became an independent state.

In Maryland and the Carolinas the proprietary system of land granting led to a heterogeneous population both with respect to religion and nationality. Differences appeared, however, with respect to class distinctions. With the development of plantation systems in Maryland and South Carolina the pattern more nearly approached that of Virginia. In South Carolina where the staple crops were rice and indigo, slavery became very profitable, and a unique arrangement was worked out whereby the planters clustered for their social life around Charleston.

North Carolina presented marked contrasts. Slavery was not so profitable, the plantation system never displaced the small farms so fully, and city life did not play a large part in the social life of the people who were poorer, more rebellious, and more democratic in religion, economics, and politics. This meant that the conflict between the up-country farmers and the Tidewater gentry was bound to be even more acute than where the lower classes were relatively weaker. Sectional violence broke out between the Regulator associations of western North Carolina and forces led by the royal governor in the east in 1770. When North Carolina became a state, the western counties had much more to say in the state constitution than they did in South Carolina, whose constitution was therefore much more conservative. Slavery had a firm hold in South Carolina; slaves well outnumbered whites by the time of the Revolution.

In Georgia the liberal and humanitarian motives of the proprietors led them to establish a relatively easy land policy of fifty acres free for poor colonists and to exert efforts to prohibit slavery and the rum trade and to build friendly relations with the Indians. Despite these good intentions the land was so poor that fifty acres could not produce a satisfactory living. So, gradually the grants of land became larger, the plantation system was expanded, and slavery was permitted. Georgia thus moved toward the class system and economic basis of Virginia and South Carolina, but by the time of the Revolution it was still the poorest and feeblest of the thirteen colonies.

This chapter has described some of the most important institutional patterns that were inherited from England and from Europe in colonial times. From the beginning American education reflected these political, religious, economic, class, and sectional arrangements. The details of the interaction between these aspects of colonial culture and education will be described in Chapters 3 and 4.

ISSUES FOR STUDY AND DISCUSSION

1. Criticize the following proposition: "From the beginning of the American colonial period, education has been a function of political sovereignty and the right to conduct schools has been a grant of power from the state." In what respects is this true and in what respects false?

2. Some people today argue that private schools are better than public schools and that education therefore should not be a monopoly of the state. Is there any historical sense in which educational authority is properly a monopoly of the state?

3. Some people today argue that the authentic American tradition is one of co-operation between church and state. Others say it is one of separation between church and state. Which do you think is more justifiable and what difference would it make for education?

4. Criticize this proposition: "Where religious and national diversity was strongest in the American colonies, there public education was the weakest." Do you think that public education helps to promote unity among diversity?

5. To what extent was equality of opportunity a goal of American life in the colonial period? Did education contribute to this ideal or hinder it?

SUGGESTIONS FOR FURTHER READING

Adams, James Truslow, *The Founding of New England*, Boston, Atlantic Monthly, 1921.
———, *Provincial Society, 1690–1763*, New York, Macmillan, 1928.
Beard, Charles A. and Beard, Mary R., *The Rise of American Civilization*, New York, Macmillan, 1936.
Butts, R. Freeman, *The American Tradition in Religion and Education*, Boston, Beacon, 1950.
Greene, Evarts B., *Religion and the State*, New York, New York University Press, 1941.
———, *The Revolutionary Generation, 1763–1790*, New York, Macmillan, 1943.
Hacker, Louis M., *The Triumph of American Capitalism*, New York, Simon & Shuster, 1940.

Hansen, Marcus L., *The Immigrant in American History*, Cambridge, Harvard University Press, 1940.

Herskovits, Melville J., *The Myth of the Negro Past*, New York, Harper, 1941.

Jernegan, Marcus W., *Laboring and Dependent Classes in Colonial America, 1607–1783*, Chicago, University of Chicago Press, 1931.

Morris, Richard B., *Government and Labor in Early America*, New York, Columbia University Press, 1946.

Nettels, Curtis P., *The Roots of American Civilization*, New York, Crofts, 1938.

Stokes, Anson Phelps, *Church and State in the United States*, Vol. I, New York, Harper, 1950.

Sweet, William W., *Religion in Colonial America*, New York, Scribner, 1942.

Wertenbaker, Thomas Jefferson, *The First Americans, 1607–1690*, New York, Macmillan, 1927.

——, *The Founding of American Civilization; the Middle Colonies*, New York, Scribner, 1938.

——, *The Old South, the Founding of American Civilization*, New York, Scribner, 1942.

Wittke, Carl, *We Who Built America*, New York, Prentice-Hall, 1939.

BIBLIOGRAPHICAL NOTE

The reader is referred to the following books that may be useful to him throughout this study of the history of education in the United States. They include recent textbooks in the history of European and American education for those who wish to relate developments in America to those in Europe. They also include books on historical method and bibliographical suggestions for those interested in specific topics or in research in the history of education. These books are not listed again at the end of succeeding chapters.

American Educational Research Association, *Review of Educational Research*, "History of Education and Comparative Education," Vol. 6, October 1936.

——, "History of Education and Comparative Education," Vol. 9, October 1939.

——, "Historical and Philosophical Foundations of Education," Chapter 1 in the "Social Framework of Education," Vol. 22, February 1952.

Brickman, William W., *Guide to Research in Educational History*, New York, New York University Bookstore, 1949.

Brubacher, John S., *A History of the Problems of Education*, New York, McGraw-Hill, 1947.

Butts, R. Freeman, *A Cultural History of Education*, New York, McGraw-Hill, 1947.

Cubberley, Ellwood P., *Public Education in the United States*, Boston, Houghton Mifflin, 1934.

——, *Readings in Public Education in the United States*, Boston, Houghton Mifflin, 1934.

Eby, Frederick, *The Development of Modern Education*, 2d ed., New York, Prentice-Hall, 1952.

Edwards, Newton, and Richey, Herman G., *The School in the American Social Order*, Boston, Houghton Mifflin, 1947.

Good, Harry G., *A History of Western Education*, New York, Macmillan, 1947.

Gottschalk, Louis, *Understanding History, A Primer of Historical Method*, New York, Knopf, 1950.

Knight, Edgar W., *Education in the United States*, 3d rev. ed., Boston, Ginn, 1951 (c1922).

———, and Hall, Clifton L., *Readings in American Educational History*, New York, Appleton-Century-Crofts, 1951.

McCormick, Patrick J., and Cassidy, Frank P., *History of Education*, rev. ed., Washington, D. C., Catholic Education Press, 1946.

Monroe, Paul (ed.), *A Cyclopedia of Education*, New York, Macmillan, 1911–1919, 5 vols.

Mulhern, James, *A History of Education*, New York, Ronald, 1946.

Noble, Stuart G., *A History of American Education*, New York, Farrar and Rinehart, 1938.

2

THE COLONIAL MIND

THE SHAPE of education in any time and place is largely a function of the interaction of the institutionalized forms of behaving solidified or leavened by the dominant beliefs and ideas of the people who control the educative process. Chapter 1 described some of the most important cultural patterns and institutions that provided the setting in which education operated. These gave character to the organization and framework of education which, as will be shown in Chapter 4, was a mixture of political, religious, and social-class factors. Before the heart of the aims, curriculum, and methods of education can be understood adequately, however, the texture and context of the prevailing ideas, beliefs, and motivations of the colonial period must be briefly sketched. This chapter seeks to identify some of the most important currents of thought that molded the ideas about education that will be described in Chapter 3.

In the course of more than 150 years the colonial mind of America which formed the intellectual setting for educational theory became increasingly complex and representative of the crosscurrents of thought that swept over Western Europe. At the beginning of the colonial period the prevailing orthodoxies in America were based upon theological conceptions and reinforced by religious sanctions. By the end of the colonial period, however, new sanctions had appeared and were receiving some acceptance as a basis for approved right thinking. This change from religious to nonreligious or secular sanctions for thought and action is usually summed up by historians in the term Enlightenment. Especially during the eighteenth century proposals for change in the older ways of thinking and acting carried appeals to *human* reason rather than divine law, to *natural* rights rather than supernatural rights, to *scientific* method rather than to established truths, to *social* agreements and *individual* freedom rather than authoritarian control, and to *humanitarian* and *democratic* faith rather than aristocratic privilege. The results of this shift in emphasis in intellectual sanctions were felt in theology and religion, in philosophy, and in political, economic, and social theory. They were likewise seen in the emergence of new forms of educational theory and proposals for educational change that eventually led to changes in educational practice.

THE CHALLENGE TO THEOLOGICAL AND RELIGIOUS ORTHODOXIES

At the beginning of the colonial period traditional Christian theism held almost universal sway among colonists of an intellectual turn of mind. Differences there were, to be sure, but these were almost entirely within the Christian fold itself and had to do with conflicts over the nature of God, man's role in salvation, and the authority of the clergy or the state in matters religious. By the end of the colonial period rationalism and liberalism and scepticism had grown markedly. They had resulted in various forms of religious liberalism and even gave strength and sanction to outlooks that embraced a full-fledged theory of the universe and of man without reliance upon theology or religion at all. Such views were not widely or openly stated in the early seventeenth century in America, but they had gained considerable notoriety by the end of the eighteenth century. In the course of this shift in intellectual concerns it became possible for the goals and conduct of education to be discussed without exclusive reliance upon religious motivations and sanctions. The religious element remained strong and even dominant, but the trend was building up with such strength and impetus that the religious sanctions for education become somewhat overshadowed by the secular in the course of the nineteenth century.

Traditional Christian Theism

Except for relatively few Roman Catholics, the dominant theological outlook of seventeenth-century America was traditional Christian theism as interpreted by European Protestantism. The fundamental tenet centered upon belief in God, whose essence was described, in the words of the Westminister Catechism, as "a Spirit, Infinite, Eternal and Unchangeable, in his Being, Wisdom, Power, Holiness, Justice, Goodness and Truth." There is only one God, but there are three persons in the God Head—the Father, the Son, and the Holy Ghost. God created the universe and all living beings and nonliving things out of nothing in the space of six days. God's powers did not cease with creation but continued to operate through miracles in the natural world whenever necessary for God to achieve his purposes.

God created man in his own image, and man's purpose on earth was to glorify God and enjoy him forever. Man was made of flesh, but he was distinguished from other living beings by God's action in endowing him with an immortal spirit or soul. Man was also originally endowed with an intellect, a moral conscience, and a free will as a means of choosing the good and avoiding evil. But because of the temptation and sin of Adam and Eve, man fell from his original state of happiness and fell from God's grace, thus passing on to all future men the fruits of the original sin. No man could thereafter arise out of sin and misery and achieve the good life on this earth or enduring happiness in heaven without God's help and grace. As a gift to man and as a means by which man could escape the pains of hell in the next life, God sent to earth his son Jesus Christ in the form of man. Christ brought word to man of God's will for man's salvation and offered himself as a sacrifice to satisfy divine justice so that man might overcome the effects of original sin, avoid eternal damnation, and achieve salvation. To instruct man in what he should believe and in the ways he must trod if he were to be saved, God revealed his word in the divinely inspired writings of the Bible and laid down the moral law for man to follow in the Ten Commandments.

Any satisfactory summary of the Christian epic and the Christian conception of God and man was as difficult to make then as it is now because of the variety of interpretations that arose among the several Protestant sects in the Reformation period of the sixteenth and seventeenth centuries. Perhaps the best that can be done is to cite a few of the orthodoxies that competed for men's loyalties in the American colonies of the seventeenth and eighteenth centuries. Outstanding among the early orthodoxies was that of John Calvin, which was promoted by English Puritans, Scottish Presbyterians, Dutch Reformed, German Reformed, and French Huguenots. Inspired by John Calvin's *Institutes of the Christian Religion,* the Synod of Dort in 1619 drew up a systematic interpretation of salvation which gave a primary role to God and a very much smaller role to man. This took the form of an emphasis upon predestination, a doctrine which remained a characteristic of orthodox Calvinism throughout most of the colonial period. Inherent in this view were the following beliefs: (1) God selects those individuals who are to be saved, and man's will has no part in deciding whether or not he will be saved (unconditional predestination); (2) Christ's sacrifice is limited to the elect, namely, those chosen by God to be saved (limited atonement); (3) because of original sin man is incapable of repentance or salvation through his own efforts (total depravity and human inability); (4) the elect cannot resist being saved by the operation of God's will and grace no matter what they do (irresistibility of grace); and (5) when a person has been elected to be a saint and thus saved, he cannot again fall from grace but will certainly be saved (perseverance of saints).

Something of this emphasis upon original sin and predestination, whereby eternal salvation was marked out for the elect and eternal punishment was meted out to the sinners, remained in the thought of orthdox Calvinism throughout the colonial period. It can be seen in the theological writings of such Puritan divines as John Cotton, Increase Mather, Cotton Mather, and Jonathan Edwards. This basic view of human nature found its way into the poetry of Michael Wigglesworth, into educational theory, into the catechisms for children, and into the school books of the time, notably the *New England Primer*.

Reactions Against Orthodox Calvinism

The rigorous doctrines of Calvinism gave great moral strength to Puritan leaders who were convinced of the righteousness of their views and thus could persuade their followers that, being elected for salvation, they had the full force and power of God's will at their hand. There were, however, stubborn believers that man's role in salvation could not be so small as the Puritan Calvinists insisted. These rebellious groups exercised their Protestant rights to call to witness the Bible to justify *their* outlooks in defiance of the orthodoxy established in New England and wherever the Calvinists took root. By and large this protest took two forms. One type emphasized man's faith and piety as an aid to salvation, and the other form argued that man's reason and good works could play an important part in man's salvation. They agreed that man's own efforts should be and were rewarded by a just and loving God, but they disagreed among themselves concerning the specifics of their beliefs.

Prominent among those who elevated the role of faith and piety in salvation were the Baptists, Quakers, the German Pietists of Lutheran Europe, and other individualistic Protestant sects. They argued in effect that if the elect were predestined to salvation through no merit or effort of their own, there would be no reason why the elect should continue to be morally good or to study the Bible or even to adhere to belief in God or Christ. They therefore insisted that the heart of the religious experience was in the direct and personal relationship between the individual and God which must be sealed by a vital faith and emotional piety. The adherence to religious forms or rituals or even the adherence to customary moral and civic virtues could not be a sign of religious rectitude without religious fervor. Man has free will to believe or not to believe, and God will forgive all those who do repent and believe in Christ. Therefore, faith alone is the prime necessity for salvation, and this faith is a matter of intimate and immediate union of the individual with God. It is this direct union that assures salvation rather than predestination or even the doing of good works or living up to the obligations of the moral and civil law. It was this latter de-emphasis on the importance of living up to established moral and civil law that led them to be dubbed "antinomians" (*anti* == against and *nomos* == the law) by their opponents.

The Baptists were an outgrowth of several small sects that grew up in southern Germany, Switzerland, and the Low Countries in the sixteenth and seventeenth centuries. Their radical rejection of infant baptism, and their insistence that baptism should come only upon confession of faith among adults gave them the name Anabaptists (*ana* = again or anew). The Anabaptists felt that they must separate themselves from impure religious domination as well as from civil authorities that would dictate religious conformity. They thus arrived early at the conception of separation of church and state and insisted that religion arose from the heart rather than in observance of ecclesiastical or civil forms or professions of creed and doctrine. Their views and followers spread to England and then to America where Anne Hutchinson and Roger Williams came into conflict with the Puritan orthodoxy because of their "antinomian" views.

Stemming from the work of George Fox in seventeenth-century England, the Quakers emphasized the "inner light" received directly from God as the signpost of spiritual guidance rather than observance of outward forms. This led them to reject the creeds, the ritual, the oaths, the preaching of an authoritative clergy, and even to do away with the whole ecclesiastical arrangement of regular churches and a permanent or continuing clergy. Their religious enthusiasm and deviation from the established forms thus brought them into disfavor with all orthodoxies, resulted in the laws passed against them, and made them the objects of persecution and witch hunts. By the eighteenth century, however, they were beginning to gain status and recognition in many colonies and contributed the writings of such men as William Penn and John Woolman to the intellectual, humanitarian, and social as well as the religious literature of colonial America.

Similarly, the Pietistic movement of German Lutheranism contributed a resurgence of feeling and emotion to the religious outlooks of many offshoots of the Lutheran faith along with the Moravians, the Mennonites, the Dunkards, the Amish, and other "plain sects." They all reinforced the growing reliance upon faith and piety as the road to salvation.

The second major type of reaction against orthodox Calvinism took the form of an elevation of man's efforts to aid in his salvation by his attention to living a good life and to the exercise of his reason. This emphasis on good works stemmed from a position known as Arminianism and flowed into the Methodism of John and Charles Wesley. The followers of Jacobus Arminius, a Dutch cleric, were defeated at the Synod of Dort in 1619 and their views rejected. Arminianism argued in opposition to Calvinism that (1) human effort and will could play a part in salvation (conditional predestination or election); (2) Christ had atoned for the sins of all men if they believed in him, not just for a few (universal redemption); (3) man may be regenerated and renewed by the exercise of faith granted to man as a gift of God through the Holy Spirit; (4) by the exercise of free will man may persist in sin and resist divine grace (resistibility of grace); and (5) man, if he is not careful, may fall from a state of grace. Thus, the Arminians and later the Methodists argued that if salvation depended upon God's election and predestination, the elect would have no obligation to continue in the path of righteousness and the unchosen would have no motive for struggling to be good. They insisted that man's efforts did make a difference, and the grace that God offered to man would be efficacious only if man exerted moral effort to be good. Human will and effort were necessary, and the better the life a man lived here and now the better were his chances for salvation.

As a result of the growth of a concern for faith and piety and the concern for doing good works and living a strictly moral life, the middle of the eighteenth century in America was marked by a great outpouring of religious fervor that has been called "The Great Awakening." Nearly all sects were affected by the appeals made by a growing number of ministers who turned to evangelical preaching among the masses of people. Among these were Theodore Frelinghuysen (Dutch Reformed), William Tennent (Presbyterian), Heinrich Muhlenberg (Lutheran), Francis Asbury (Methodist), Jonathan Edwards (Congregational), and George Whitefield (Anglican). The religious zeal that was generated attracted thousands into the churches to listen and be converted and become members. It increased the feelings of altruism, charity, and philanthropy either through an awakened sympathy for the downtrodden or a realizing fear of what happened to sinners and the unrepentant. It increased the desires of thousands to make something of themselves and to atone for their sins, and a ready channel by which men could show evidence of their desire for good works was the contribution of money and energy to the founding of schools and colleges.

Orthodox Calvinism as reflected in the Congregational and Presbyterian churches was torn apart by the religious revivals of the middle decades of the eighteenth century. Those who tried to hold on to an unrelieved predestination and election (the "Old Lights") found themselves beset by attacks from several sides. Some of the Congregational ministers began to preach the spirit of repentance and salvation by conversion (the "New Lights"). Congregations were split asunder, and the members followed the ministers of their choice.

Other Congregational ministers began to give greater and greater stress to the role of human reason in solving religious problems and to the doctrine that scriptural truth should be in conformity with the test of rational truth. They began to desert the authoritarianism of the older orthodoxy and to turn away from the emotional hysteria of the "fire and brimstone" preaching of the New Lights. They began instead to find the principles of human rationality expressed in God's nature and in God's creations. Reason and revelation must go hand in hand. So spoke John Wise, Jonathan Mayhew, Simon Howard, Thomas Emlyn, and Charles Chauncy. God's goodness, mercy, benevolence, and wisdom began to overshadow the traditional Calvinist stress on God's anger and vindictiveness toward man as expressed by Cotton Mather and Jonathan Edwards.

This rationalism in religion even led some of the Congregational theologians to approach a liberalism that laid the groundwork for the development of Unitarianism and Universalism. They trod close to heresy in their questioning of the Trinitarian conception of God and their denial of the divinity of Christ, of the personal existence of the Devil, of total depravity and original sin, and of the eternity of punishment in Hell. In these views they hearkened back to the Socinian doctrines of Laelius Socinius and Faustus Socinius, two Italian theologians of the sixteenth century. Socinianism had asserted that Christ was human rather than divine, that human sin was not passed on by Adam but was simply an imitation of Adam's sin, that salvation was to be achieved not by the literal atonement of Christ but by man's imitation of Christ's virtuous life, and that the Bible was to be interpreted by human reason and in accordance with rational understanding. In their hands theology came down to earth, and Christianity became a way of life rather than an adherence to dogma revealed to man by an authoritative clergy or authoritative Scriptures that could not be questioned. The role of man in the epic of salvation was achieving an ever greater place within the fold of the churches. Anglicanism reflected this trend in the outlooks of William Smith, provost at the College of Philadelphia, and of Samuel Johnson, president of King's College.

Outside the churches the currents of thought centering on man's reason took the form of deism, a rationalistic view developed by philosophers and scientists in France and England in the seventeenth and eighteenth centuries. Deism was an attempt to build a world view that would embrace the new conceptions in science that had emerged after Sir Isaac Newton's publication of his *Mathematical Principles of Natural Philosophy* in 1687. Newton's view of the universe as a great machine in which all parts fit perfectly together according to discoverable natural laws left little room for the divine intervention and miracles of a personal God. Deism was an attempt to explain natural laws without explaining them away or simply reconciling them with orthodox Christianity. Thus, the deists thought of God, not as the personal being of Christian theism who looked out for each individual person, but as a great spirit or first cause or prime mover who set the machine of the universe in motion but who did not interfere with it once it had begun to run according to exact definable natural law. In this way natural laws were to be discovered by scientific methods and by human reason without reliance upon the revelation of the Scriptures or the theology of the drama of human salvation, original sin, atonement of Christ, sacraments, faith, and good works.

Discussion of deistic writings and views began to appear in American periodicals, books, and discussion groups and began to attract a small but a growing group of intellectuals who included among their numbers in varying degrees of sympathy such outstanding persons as William Livingston, John Adams, Benjamin Franklin, and Thomas Jefferson. Where religious liberalism left off and deism began was a difficult matter to determine, but certain it is that rationalism and a faith in the intelligence and reason of man were on the upswing during the eighteenth century in intellectual circles and among college students. Faith in human reason was especially prominent in proposals for a new education that would embrace the findings of science and philosophy along with religion as the sanctions for intellectual achievement.

THE RISE OF SECULAR THOUGHT

While religion held the center of the intellectual stage throughout most of the colonial period in America, a new voice was being heard in Europe which was little more than an echo in America in the seventeenth century but which grew rapidly in volume and authority by the end of the colonial period. This was the voice of modern science. Beginning with the scientific investigations of the fifteenth and sixteenth centuries, the cumulative effect of scientific evidence and scientific method rose to a crescendo in the seventeenth and eighteenth centuries until it could no longer be ignored. The growing respect for the voice of science was one of the most profound intellectual revolutions that came out of the Reformation and the Enlightenment periods, and its effect was to be felt in all ranges of philosophy and social theory.

New World Views

The traditional religious view of the universe had put the earth at the center of the universe and had asserted that all of nature had been created by God for divine purposes. The most important of all the heavenly bodies was the earth as the habitat of man; the sun and stars revolved about the earth (geocentric view). However, as a notable company of astronomers, scientists, and mathematicians pursued their investigations in the sixteenth and seventeenth centuries, the picture of an immense solar system with the sun at the center (heliocentric view) around which the earth and other planets revolved began to emerge. Copernicus, Kepler, Galileo, Brahe, Bruno, and Huygens contributed to this view, which began to have serious implications far beyond the realm of physical science, for if the scientists were right, the orthodox religious view of creation would have to be reinterpreted or modified. The divine law as revealed in the Scriptures was challenged by the conception of natural law as revealed by human reason working through the scientific method. The battle of authorities and of sanctions for belief was about to be joined.

The churches in Europe were at first hostile to science and able to win temporary victories in the sixteenth and early seventeenth centuries. Copernicus did not publish his views; Bruno was burned at the stake when he did publish his; Galileo was forced to recant his; and Kepler was ostracized. But by the end of the seventeenth century the scientific view became somewhat safer. Following Newton's epoch-making work in 1687, the victory for natural law was in the making, and rival philosophic conceptions of the origin and nature of the physical universe were being freely expounded in the eighteenth century. The "law" of gravitation and the "law" of cause and effect became models of the kinds of natural laws that were then promulgated as the basis for new beliefs concerning human nature, human reason, and social affairs.

Philosophy and religion were then faced with the problem of what to do with the new scientific findings and scientific theories. In general three kinds of responses were made. Some religious leaders felt that they had to reassert the claims of the spiritual world over against the claims of the material or natural world as described by science. They could do this by denying the reality of the physical world and insisting that the only true reality was spiritual or mental. This was done by such philosophers as Bishop George Berkeley of the Church of England in his outlook known as idealism. Berkeley asserted that the essence of existence is spiritual and that physical things exist only in the mind of God and have no independent existence or reality of their own. Similarly, the essence of man is his spirit, consisting of soul and mind which perceive things as appearing to exist in time and space. However, this appearance of continuity and substance in physical objects is created because God continues to "think" of them beyond the life span of individual men. In this way the existence and importance of God were reasserted, and the presumption of an independent physical world was discounted. Philosophic idealism gave a new lease on life to theology and a religious orientation by putting science into its proper subordinate place.

A second philosophic response to the new science was to try to give equal recognition to spiritual affairs and to the physical world. This effort to reconcile theology and science was notably worked out by Réne Descartes in his philosophy of dualism. Descartes asserted that all existence is of two kinds or substances, mind and matter, which are independent of each other. Mind is a spiritual substance whose essence is the source of thinking not bound by the physical or natural laws but free to follow its own nature and make choices. Matter is a material substance whose essence is expressed in the "real" objects of space and time which obey the fixed laws of nature and operate as a great natural machine. Mind and matter are entirely separated from each other and operate according to their respective laws and do not interact with each other. Descartes tried to make his peace with theology by asserting that both mind and matter were created by God, but he granted independence to the real world of physical nature by removing it from further interference from God once it was created. This kind of reconciliation between theology and science made it possible for deism to become increasingly popular in the eighteenth century as a haven for intellectuals who did not wish to break away entirely from religious sanctions but who did see merit in the scientific approach.

A third philosophic position, known as materialism, rejected the idealistic defense of religion and also rejected dualism as a half-hearted compromise. Materialists boldly asserted that the only reality was the material universe which was a machine operating according to mechanical laws: they left no place for spirit or mental substance or God. They asserted that all existence could be explained simply by the laws of matter in motion, and thus all explanations were material explanations. Stemming from the philosophies of Thomas Hobbes in England and Pierre Gassendi in France in the seventeenth century, the philosophy of materialism gained new support in the eighteenth century from such philosophers as Julian de La Mettrie, Baron Holbach, and Claude Helvetius. They were the philosophic extremists who brought down upon their heads the wrath of the orthodox religionists. American intellectual leaders in the eighteenth century were by and large content to explore the possibilities of dualism and deism without going the whole way with materialism and atheism. The dominant intellectual patterns in colonial America continued to embrace some form of theological or religious outlook as represented in idealism or dualism rather than in materialism.

New Conceptions of Human Nature

The traditional concept of man as born in original sin continued to dominate American thought throughout most of the colonial period. Religious orthodoxy posited human nature as made up of a spiritual and immortal soul breathed into man by God and a material body which links him to nature and thus provides a continuing source of temptation and evil. The Calvinist thus felt that man must constantly be on his guard against the temptations of the body and must cultivate and discipline the resources of the soul and the mind in order to help man exert control over his weaknesses. Since a constant guard must be kept, education must therefore aid in this task by combining at least equal shares of "learnin' and lickin'" on the lower levels of education. On the higher levels of education the mind became the most important element in the development of a truly educated man. For, after all, had not Bishop Berkeley said that the essence of man was his spirit or perceiving mind and that the body was simply an appearance or perception of the mind?

Again, however, as in the case of the world views, dissatisfaction began to arise with the view that human nature was conceived in original sin. Men like William Harvey in their studies of anatomy, physiology, and medicine had begun to show that the human body operated according to discoverable and definable natural laws. Descartes' dualism when applied to man insisted that human nature, like the universe, was composed of two independent, separate, and coequal substances—mind and body. In this view the mind can think and can operate according to the laws of logic and mathematics, but the body is a machine and operates according to scientific and mechanical laws. This elevated the body to a subject worthy of study along with the mind. Then along came John Locke with his background in medicine and philosophy to urge the scientific study of human nature. He argued that human nature was not wholly preformed at birth but was formed at least partly out of the action of the surrounding environment upon the pliable raw material of the physical organism. He gave at least equal importance to the development of a sound body along with a sound mind. Each had their laws of sane growth and development.

In this view the body could no longer be looked upon as carrying the taint of original sin nor could human nature be conceived as totally depraved because of the sin of man's ancestors thousands of years before. Weakness and evil were a function of individual effort and surrounding environment which, if controlled carefully enough, could result in any number of possible characteristics. Human nature, being formless and neutral with respect to goodness or evil, had great possibilities. The ground was being laid thereby for the doctrines of innate human goodness and perfectibility that received their most influential formulation by Jean Jacques Rousseau and the French humanitarians.

Rousseau bitterly attacked the orthodox view of human nature as innately sinful, and he swung to the opposite extreme to argue that human nature, if left to itself, was essentially and inherently good. It is the impact of environment and of social institutions upon man that makes him evil, not his own nature. If human nature is allowed to take its course, all will be well. This philosophy of the dignity of the "natural man" or of "naturalism" began to attract more and more attention among intellectuals and led some religionists to adapt their theological and educational theories accordingly, but it also led such men as Jonathan Edwards to reject bitterly the belief that "natural man" could stand on his own feet without divine help. Indeed, if "natural men" persist in their ways they will call down divine wrath upon them and be subject to eternal punishment.

American intellectuals began to respond favorably to the views of Locke and the naturalists and to think of ways that education could be revised accordingly. Few Americans, however, openly propounded the extreme materialistic views of human nature that had begun to find expression among European philosophers. Men like Hobbes, Gassendi, Toland, La Mettrie, Helvetius, Holbach, and Hartley were arguing that human nature is entirely materialistic. The body, being a machine, may be studied according to mechanical laws, but since mind cannot be studied this way, then the "mind" is just a word for the body in motion, and it has no existence apart from the body. In either case the effect was to deny either the importance of the soul or to deny its existence altogether. Few reputable American intellectuals

wished to go to these extremes and incur the charge of atheism, but by the
end of the colonial period the way was open for human reason to explore the
nature of human nature more freely than at any prior time. A secular basis
for the study of man was gradually winning its way, but as yet no full-bodied
conception of human nature was being formulated in America on a secular
underpinning.

New Conceptions of Method

In the long run the most telling intellectual revolution of the seventeenth and
eighteenth centuries was probably not in the specific world views or conceptions of human nature that appeared; it was probably the formulation and
application of a new method of thinking, a new method of arriving at truth
and acquiring knowledge, a new method of human learning and intelligence.
This was the scientific method, which gradually came to attract the imaginations of men and which produced such revolutionary changes in the actual
conditions of life that its power became most persuasive.

The traditional method of thinking that had dominated Western thought
for some four centuries had its roots in the deductive methods of Aristotle
which were adopted by Scholasticism and given theological sanction by St.
Thomas Aquinas. In his famous work on logic known as the *Organon*
(*Method*) Aristotle had set forth a rigorous system of thought centering upon
the formal syllogism. Syllogistic method started with an accepted or authoritative generalization (major premise) under which a specific statement is
classified (minor premise) and from which a logical conclusion can be drawn.
For example:

> Whatever is bad for society ought not to be practiced (major premise)
> Lying is bad for society (minor premise)
> Therefore, lying ought not to be practiced (conclusion)

This was the dominant intellectual method of Western Europe for several
hundred years. In the hands of Scholasticism major premises were derived
from religious or traditional authorities, specific arguments were classified
under the accepted generalizations, authorities were compared and distinctions were made, and systematic and consistent conclusions were achieved
that reconciled seemingly divergent views. Those views that could not come
consistently within the formulas that had been logically deduced from the
accepted authorities were rejected.

Dissatisfaction arose with this closed and authoritative approach to the
phenomena of the natural world. One of the most popular of the dissidents
was Francis Bacon in the seventeenth century. He began to attack the Aristotelian and Scholastic methods on the grounds that they simply perpetuated
superstition and outworn traditions in philosophy, theology, and physical
knowledge. He charged that the deductive method was simply a playing with

words and a refinement of language with little or no regard to actuality and present experience. Greatly impressed with the possibilities of science and of scientific method, Bacon wrote his *Novum Organum* (*New Method*) in which he set forth the claims of the inductive method of science. The essentials of the new method were: (1) careful observation of nature, (2) collection of facts upon the basis of direct observation, and (3) arrival at general propositions on the basis of observable relations among individual cases or facts. Instead of starting with the authoritative generalization of some writer of the past, the scientist should start with individual specific things and arrive at his generalizations at the end of the process of thought rather than beginning with uncriticized authorities. Truth and knowledge thus arise out of observation and experience rather than from manipulation of accepted or given ideas. Here was a bold affirmation that human reason could, by using a controlled method of investigation, arrive at sound knowledge unaided by revelation or accepted authorities. This opening wedge in traditional methods of thought was made wider and wider as great strides in knowledge of the natural world were made by the scientists of the eighteenth century.

A most important result was the gradual building up of a theory of the way people acquired ideas and knowledge of the external world, in short, a philosophy of learning. The traditional view had been that man was born with a faculty of reason as a part of his spiritual equipment, that his rational faculty simply needed to be developed and formed by the proper discipline and methods of study, and that the best studies for this purpose were the classical languages, mathematics, and philosophy. True ideas were either implanted at birth in the child (innate ideas) and simply awaited the training of the reason, or ideas existed apart from man in an independent realm and simply awaited to be grasped by the mind when it had been trained to "see" or to reach out and grasp the true ideas. These were the elements of the main stream of philosophy known as rationalism.

In contrast to rationalism the inductive and scientific method led other thinkers to say that man is not endowed with innate ideas but rather that he learns about the external world through sense experience, through his senses of smell, taste, sight, touch, and hearing. Knowledge is acquired through experiences coming to the individual through his senses. Learning through experience came to be known as empiricism and rested upon the assumption that observation of phenomena was the surest guide to accurate knowledge.

John Locke was a great popularizer of the empirical approach to learning by his insistence that at birth the human mind was not preformed and ready to function but that the individual simply possessed a blank but sensitive tablet (*tabula rasa*) that was ready to receive impressions or perceptions from the external world through his senses. Ideas were thus not already present in the individual and waiting to find expression, but ideas arise from the perceptions that the individual receives from outside himself, from his physical environment, and from other people. In a similar way individuals acquired a sense of values, morality, and religion through the empirical process of experience, but while Locke stressed sense experience, he also reserved a place for internal mental activity through the process of reflection whereby the individual gives form to his perceptions and builds up complex ideas from the simple perceptions received through his senses.

Some thinkers went to a more extreme position and even rejected Locke's faculty of reflection. Such men as Hume, Hartley, and Condillac began to say that the *only* source of ideas was the sensations received through the five senses. By the process of association the repetition of one sensation will call up other sensations, and thus more complex ideas arise simply by association and combination of simple sensations. Their view came to be called sensationalism, but it was often considered to be atheistic because it left no room for the mind or the soul as traditionally conceived.

Again, it was not the extremist views of the sensationalists that gained adherents in colonial America but rather the views of Locke and other empiricists who applied their doctrines to education. Even before Locke, some European educators had begun to apply empirical outlooks to the learning process of children. Bacon himself urged that learning would be best if teachers rejected traditional methods of verbal and linguistic emphasis upon books and instead would start with the observation of nature and then cultivate the habits of induction and scientific method. The Moravian bishop, Comenius, urged that the child should start from simple, known, everyday observation of things and move on to the more complex and unknown. He urged the use of pictures and actual objects as a means of developing the sense experience of children.

This view came to be known as sense realism and was firmly based upon the empirical assumptions that learning is best when the child's senses are cultivated. Similar propositions were being made in the seventeenth century by Wolfgang Ratke in Germany and by a number of educational reformers in England, including Richard Mulcaster, Edmund Coote, John Brinsley, John Dury, Charles Hoole, and Sir William Petty. For young children greater emphasis was put upon manipulation of objects, singing, drawing, and physical activity as a means of developing sense experience. For older youth it was argued that the study of nature and of science and practical activities leading to a life of action and usefulness would be better than exclusive emphasis upon books or upon the classical languages.

In the eighteenth century such German educators as Johann Hecker and Johann Basedow gave further expression to the use of realism in education by setting up schools (*Realschulen*) that would capitalize upon the use of actual objects and models and excursions to observe life at firsthand. Toward the end of the eighteenth century Rousseau became the greatest popularizer of all when he urged that the natural impulses of the child should be set free by removing the restrictions and disciplines of the traditional books and linguistic subject matters in favor of learning through play, games, actual objects, manual activities, and direct acquaintance with nature through the observation and study of the sciences. The ideas of sense realism began to germinate in America in the eighteenth century, new schools arose, and new proposals for education were made to reform education along the lines of the empirical emphasis upon sense realism. Appropriately enough, the most notable of these proposals came from the pen of Benjamin Franklin.

The Power of Knowledge

In the more than 150 years of the colonial period in America the respect for the usefulness of knowledge followed two general patterns. The first was a gradual shift of interest away from knowledge that was based upon religious and supernatural sanctions toward knowledge that originated in secular and human investigations. The second was a shift away from knowledge that served principally as a sign of ornamental and gentlemanly accomplishment toward the kind of knowledge that would contribute to practical usefulness and the utilitarian business of living.

Humanistic interest in the classical languages and literature had been the badge of an educated person in Western Europe since the time of the Renaissance. Upper-class planters, gentry, and officials in America tried to keep this tradition alive by cultivating alike the arts of the classical scholar and the status of a gentleman. The Latin grammar schools and the colonial colleges kept alive this alliance between classical scholarship and social status. The movement to expand the intellectual interests of the early colonists beyond the classics, however, was not to be denied as the eighteenth century ran its course. Expansion of interest appeared in three ways, all of which reflected growing secular concerns. These were the growth of the vernacular literatures, the growth of the physical sciences, and the growth of the social sciences.

Whereas Latin had been the language of literature and scholarship for centuries in Europe, the seventeenth and eighteenth centuries saw the rise of a great literature in the modern languages. One need only mention the English writings of such men as Bacon, Hobbes, Locke, Shakespeare, Johnson, Bunyan, Milton, Dryden, Pope, Swift, Addison, Steele, Defoe, and Fielding; or the French writings of Descartes, Corneille, Racine, Molière, La Fontaine, Voltaire, Rousseau, Diderot, Montesquieu, and Condorcet; or the German of Goethe, Leibnitz, and Kant. Despite the mixtures of tongues that had come to America the English language became the common language of the colonies by the time of the Revolution, and French had become the international language of diplomacy and society. No wonder that forward-looking Americans began to clamor for more attention to the modern languages in the schools and colleges of America.

Even more spectacular were the achievements in science, some of which have already been mentioned with respect to new philosophies and new methods, but most impressive were the practical accomplishments made possible by the application of science to the development of new tools and machines. The technical arts and technology were producing a new world. Accurate measurements were made possible by the microscope, the telescope, the barometer, the thermometer, and the clock. The mariner's compass and other navigational instruments had made world-wide trade and communication possible. The refinements of gunpowder and military weapons had made centralized political authority more possible. The study of the effects of heat, light, electricity, and mechanics led to the development of machines and processes that improved mining, farming, stock raising, the manufacture of goods, and the methods of communication and transportation. A new technological era was ushered in with the appearance of James Watt's steam engine in the same year the Declaration of Independence was signed.

With characteristic American zeal for the new and the changing, American intellectuals began to press forward in the areas of science and to apply scientific techniques to surveying, navigation, agriculture, mining, and medicine. Outstanding for their work in such practical applications of science as well as pushing back the frontiers of scientific investigation were such men as Thomas Brattle, Charles Morton, Isaac Greenwood, and John Winthrop at Harvard, William Small at the College of William and Mary, William Smith and Benjamin Rush at the College of Philadelphia; and outside the colleges many amateur and professional scientists added their contributions, most notable of whom were Cadwallader Colden and, of course, Benjamin Franklin. The interests of these men ranged over the areas of natural philosophy (physics, astronomy, mechanics, mathematics, and chemistry) and natural history (botany, zoology, and geology), and as they did so, they began to aid in the process of removing traditional superstitions concerning witches, demons, ghosts and spirits as the causes of disease, evil, and fell events.

The respect for "natural" knowledge thus worked two ways. It worked as a leaven to remove unfounded beliefs in a fearsome and unseen world beyond the control of normal men, and it prompted men to claim for knowledge the power to improve the conditions of life and to control nature for the welfare of man. The belief spread that if man could just know more he would be prepared to improve himself as well as to improve business, his country, and society in general. This growing respect for secular knowledge thus fitted into the new conceptions of political, economic, and social welfare that began to capture the imaginations of Americans as they moved from colonial status to independence. Demands for a more utilitarian education accompanied these changes in respect for practical knowledge.

GROWING LIBERALISM IN SOCIAL THEORY

American social theory underwent a most significant change in its fundamental assumptions during the colonial period. At the beginning of the seventeenth century it was assumed that the social order was of divine inspiration and rested upon supernatural authorities. Governments and social classes were believed to be ordained by God and their purpose was to carry God's laws into effect on this earth. It was further assumed that only a few leaders could rightfully carry out God's injunctions and that the majority of people were simply ordained to carry out the decrees of God which had been embodied in the laws of the state by God's elect. This view supported monarchical or aristocratic views of society and the state.

Gradually, however, the belief grew that men had certain natural rights, whether accruing from God's gift or simply from natural sources, that could not be abrogated by society. In either case more and more people began to believe that men themselves, indeed the majority of men or all men, should have some share in formulating the civil policies by which they were to be governed. This outlook took the form of a belief in natural rights, in a more democratic form of government, and in a humanitarian social philosophy. Again, the emergence of these views represented a growing belief in the secular assumptions underlying organized society and resulted in demands for a greater role for ordinary men in the conduct of their own affairs.

Political Theory

The shift in political theory can be highlighted in the views of a few outstanding American spokesmen. In the seventeenth century the dominant views of Puritan political theory can be illustrated by John Winthrop, John Cotton, and Nathaniel Ward. They grounded their political beliefs in the doctrine of original sin. If man had maintained his original estate of happiness, governments among men would have been unnecessary, but with the fall from grace the evil nature of man made necessary the compulsive power of the state to keep men from robbing, harming, and murdering each other. Obviously, in this view, the authority of civil governments could not be allowed to fall into the hands of evil or unregenerate men, or else society itself would be swept to destruction. Thus, governments were ordained by God to prevent such calamities and to aid in achieving man's last end—salvation. Consequently, the magistrates must rule on earth for God, and the people must be given only that liberty which will lead them to justice, truth, and goodness as defined by the magistrates.

The early Puritans rejected the monarchical theory of the divine right of kings as formulated by the Stuart kings of England, but maintained the divine right of elected magistrates. They applied the covenant or compact theory to civil government as they applied it to theology. To be sure, government is brought into being by the act of men and rests on a compact between the people for the assurance of good government, but the compact was not a free compact of naturally free men but was simply a gift of God by which men obeyed God's commands to set up a government on earth. Once the compact has been made according to God's will, then only those who were "saints" or religiously regenerate (members of approved churches) could share in the election of rulers, and the rulers must consider God's will as revealed in the Scriptures as their authority rather than the will of the people among whom the majority were unregenerate or sinners. Thus, we find Winthrop saying that people are not equal and that the people should have only that liberty which is good for them; Cotton asserting that democracy was not ordained by God as a fit government either for church or commonwealth; and Ward asserting that religious liberty could not be permitted by a stable government, for it would be tantamount to permitting error and sin to be propagated. All agreed that government must thus be dictatorial and authoritarian with respect to the beliefs and practices of the inhabitants.

Objections to this view of the state were being expressed in the seventeenth century by such men as Roger Williams, who argued for separation of church and state and insisted that civil government should rest upon the consent of the people who should be allowed liberty of conscience. But it was not until the eighteenth century that such views began to enlist widespread popular support. Samuel Willard represented a kind of transition to this more liberal view in his arguments that the magistrate rules by the authority of men as well as from God and thus must be responsible to men as well as to God. Much more important, though, was the position of Reverend John Wise who elaborated the view that government rests upon the natural rights of man. To be sure, government stems from God's will, but it is brought into being by man's natural reason and turns for its authority not to the Scriptures but to the basic ingredients of man's nature which has a threefold character: internal liberty of mind and reason, external liberty of person, and equality. Similarly, Wise rejected monarchy and aristocracy because they do not rest upon man's natural rights and accepted democracy as the best form of government because it does exactly protect and promote the essential elements in human nature.

It was but a step then to the full-fledged philosophy of natural rights as expressed in the later eighteenth century by such men as James Otis, John Adams, Samuel Adams, Benjamin Franklin, Tom Paine, and, above all, Thomas Jefferson. Life, liberty, equality, property, and the pursuit of happiness were grounded in the basic nature and rights of man with little or no reliance upon supernatural sanctions. The shift from Winthrop and Cotton to Franklin and Jefferson can be seen most vividly by comparing the early Puritan statements with the Declaration of Independence and the bills of rights of the Virginia and Pennsylvania constitutions. Whereas references were made to God in the eighteenth-century statements, the meaning was much more evidently related to a deistic or naturalistic God rather than the personalized theistic God of the Puritans, and the main burden of argument rested upon the natural laws of human rights and the inherent dignity and worth of men because they are men. This shift to natural rights as the basis of government drew upon the thought of Montesquieu, Harrington, Sidney, and John Locke and was reflected within Puritan thought itself in the eighteenth-century writings of such ministers as John Barnard and Jonathan Mayhew. Belief in human rights and human action were winning out over belief in supernatural rights as the basis of human and civil government. The secular revolution in American government was sealed with the adoption of the United States Constitution, ordained and established by the compact of "We, the people of the United States."

Economic Theory

As pointed out in Chapter 1 the great economic change in the world of the seventeenth and eighteenth century was the shift from an agrarian feudalism to a commercial capitalism. The basic theory underlying this shift was associated with the rise to power of the middle classes and the assertion of middle-class belief in the ownership of property, the profit motive, and the moral virtues attached thereto. Feudalism had been based upon a theoretical compact between the aristocratic owner of property and the landless serf who owed him service. The capitalistic view had asserted the rights of all to acquire property and enjoy the fruits of his labor whether in land or trade and commerce. The theory of mercantilist capitalism had asserted the right of the civil ruler to control the ownership of property and the conduct of business, but in the eighteenth century the restrictions by English and French kings had led spokesmen for the middle classes to argue for greater freedom for the propertied classes against government. When such spokesmen as Locke and Adam Smith in England and Quesnay and Turgot in France began to insist that the propertied classes should be let alone by the government, the philosophy of laissez-faire capitalism was born and rapidly gained adherents in Europe and America. Conveniently, the theory of natural law that was being applied to philosophy and politics was found to be appropriate also to economics. Natural laws of economics were found in the essentially profit-seeking motives of human nature, the natural laws of the free market, competition, and supply and demand as natural regulators for the production, distribution, and prices of goods. These "laws" appealed to the business classes who were restive under government control.

The popularity of these views led to the desire to incorporate protection for property interests and freedom for property owners in the basic laws of the state. Of even more importance here is the popularity of the moral virtues associated with success in economic enterprises. Easily the most outstanding in this respect in eighteenth-century America was Benjamin Franklin, the apostle of middle-class morality. His "Advice to a Young Tradesman" and his "Poor Richard Almanacs" glorified the models upon which personal success was to be built. Honesty, frugality, hard work, thrift, and perseverance would assuredly pay dividends to the earnest and careful worker. The abundance of free land and the economic opportunities in trade and commerce made this philosophy an appealing one to Americans of high and low station alike. No wonder that education to serve these ends was earnestly desired, but it would need to be an education that would be practical, utilitarian, and useful for getting ahead and making money. Without neglecting other values, this was just the kind of education that Franklin urged and worked to provide in his academy at Philadelphia. Here was another powerful secular trend in eighteenth-century American education.

An Emergent Humanitarianism

In the eighteenth century the beginnings of social reform were clearly evident, much of it stemming from an awakening of social conscience and desire to improve the lot of the unfortunate and underprivileged. This had two principal sources: a benevolent religious impulse and a secular humanitarianism. The religious benevolence grew from the more sympathetic forms of evangelical Christianity which began to look upon the unfortunate not as visitations of the wrath of God but as the result of wretched human environment. With a belief in the essential worth of all individuals in the sight of God and the possibility of salvation open to all, some religious groups turned to charitable aid for the downtrodden. Notable among these were the Quakers under the leadership of William Penn and John Woolman, the Anglicans in their philanthropic societies, and the Wesleyan movement for religious philanthropy. Campaigns for more humane treatment of offenders and criminals, reform of the penal codes, prison reform, almshouses for the poor and aged, abolition of slavery, temperance, emancipation of women, and charitable education all had their advocates before the Revolutionary War. Much of religious thought and sentiment, however, continued to be callous to economic and social misfortune, looking upon it as a sign of human weakness, and even justifying the distinctions between rich and poor as essential for social stability and the welfare of society.

A more secular approach to humanitarian services stemmed from the doctrines of inherent goodness and perfectibility of human nature. This view looked upon poverty and misfortune as the result of environmental conditions, not of personal inadequacy or weakness, and began to urge similar social reforms as a means of improving society, not for the glory of God but for the sake of man and human progress. Gaining strength from the writings of Lord Shaftesbury, Alexander Pope, and the French Encyclopedists, men like Franklin, Paine, and Jefferson in America took up the cause of the common man and shifted the locus of improvement from the concept of individual charity to the need for organized effort, even through governmental sponsorship of measures to promote the general welfare by the state. Eventually, humanitarianism became a powerful movement for social reform and included public education as one of the most potent weapons in the battle against poverty, ignorance, disease, and inequality.

ISSUES FOR STUDY AND DISCUSSION

1. Before you read Chapters 3 and 4, try to predict what differences in educational outlook might follow from the more liberal religious views in contrast to the orthodox Calvinist view. Do you find such differences still present today?

2. Similarly, what differences in educational outlook or practice would you expect to flow from the scientific outlook of the eighteenth-century Enlightenment in contrast to the religious views? Do you find any such conflict today?

3. Do you find any parallel between the more liberal religious outlooks of the colonial period and the more liberal political and economic views? Between religious orthodoxy and conservative social points of view? What do you find to be the essence of eighteenth-century liberalism? Is it the same today?

4. What surprises you most or what impresses you as most significant about the developments described in Chapters 1 and 2 in comparison with the impressions you have had about the colonial period and its influence upon the present? From your other reading how would you criticize the interpretations given so far in this book?

SUGGESTIONS FOR FURTHER READING

Adams, James Truslow, *The Founding of New England,* Boston, Atlantic Monthly, 1921.
————, *Provincial Society, 1690–1763,* New York, Macmillan, 1928.
Blau, Joseph L. (ed.), *American Philosophic Addresses, 1700–1900,* New York, Columbia University Press, 1946.
————, *Men and Movements in American Philosophy,* New York, Prentice-Hall, 1952.
Curti, Merle, *The Growth of American Thought,* 2nd ed., New York, Harper, 1951.
Dorfman, Joseph, *The Economic Mind in American Civilization, 1806–1865,* Vol. I, New York, Viking, 1946.
Greene, Evarts B., *The Revolutionary Generation, 1763–1790,* New York, Macmillan, 1943.
Hacker, Louis M. (ed.), *The Shaping of the American Tradition,* New York, Columbia University Press, 1947.
Miller, Perry, *The New England Mind,* New York, Macmillan, 1939.

Miller, Perry, and Johnson, Thomas H., *The Puritans*, New York, American Book, 1938.

Morais, Herbert W., *Deism in 18th Century America*, New York, Columbia University Press, 1934.

Nettels, Curtis P., *The Roots of American Civilization*, New York, Crofts, 1938.

Parrington, Vernon Louis, *Main Currents in American Thought*, Vol. I, *The Colonial Mind, 1620–1800*, New York, Harcourt, 1927.

Perry, Ralph Barton, *Puritanism and Democracy*, New York, Vanguard, 1944.

Schneider, Herbert W., *A History of American Philosophy*, New York, Columbia University Press, 1945.

———, *The Puritan Mind*, New York, Holt, 1930.

Smith, Bernard, *The Democratic Spirit: A Collection of American Writings from the Earliest Times to the Present Day*, New York, Knopf, 1941.

Thorp, Willard, Curti, Merle, and Baker, Carlos (eds.), *American Issues: The Social Record*, Vol. I, *The Literary Record*, Vol. II, Philadelphia, Lippincott, 1941.

Wertenbaker, Thomas Jefferson, *The First Americans, 1607–1690*, New York, Macmillan, 1927.

———, *The Founding of American Civilization; the Middle Colonies*, New York, Scribner, 1938.

———, *The Old South, the Founding of American Civilization*, New York, Scribner, 1942.

Wish, Harvey, *Society and Thought in Early America*, New York, Longmans, 1950.

3

CROSSCURRENTS IN EDUCATIONAL THOUGHT

THE PROFOUND changes in the institutional life of colonial America described in Chapter 1 and the ferment in the intellectual life described in Chapter 2 led men to begin to think harder and harder about education. The actual conditions under which men lived and the changes they worked and fought for prompted them to look more critically at the kind of education they saw about them and to visualize an education that would be more appropriate to the times. New outlooks on life and man and nature caused some to bring their ideas to bear upon educational goals, content, and practice. Traditional intellectual outlooks were reflected in a reassertion of traditional conceptions of education, whereas those who saw value in the new religious, philosophic, and scientific attitudes began to argue for a newer conception of education.

At the beginning of the colonial period educational thought was dominated by theological, philosophical, political, and social orthodoxies; by the end of the colonial period more and more voices were being heard proposing an education that would be more liberal, more secular, more scientific, more utilitarian, more humanitarian, and more democratic. An authoritarian conception of child nature and the educative process began to be softened by a less severe attitude toward discipline and more careful attention to the child as a person to be valued for himself. The dominantly religious content and goal for education began to give way to greater emphasis upon the desirability of secular and scientific studies. The exclusively classical and humanistic quality of secondary and higher education began to be widened to include practical and utilitarian goals and opportunities. The aristocratic and private character of education began to be challenged by proposals for a more democratic kind of education to be achieved by public control and support of schools and colleges.

These generalizations should not be taken to mean that educational institutions and practices were revolutionized during the colonial period. By and large movement was slow, and new ideas had difficulty in gaining acceptance. In general, the earlier patterns of education continued to dominate education until after the American Revolution, but the new ideas *were* abroad in the land and many of them forecast the shape of things to come in the nineteenth century. They served to awaken the consciousness of need for change, or they served to plant the seeds of discontent with the old. Some of the ideas caught on sufficiently to enlist support for new kinds of schools or new content or methods in old schools. Most of the new educational ideas had to wait until the changed conditions of life added their thrust to arguments and proposals for change. Genuine change requires some kind of alliance between ideas and the brute conditions of life. The history of education must record the history of ideas as instruments of educational change as well as the social conditions that serve to accelerate or thwart educational change.

CALVINIST VIEWS OF THE CHILD AND EDUCATIONAL METHOD

The most persistent and lasting concept of the child to be found in the colonial period was an outgrowth of the Puritan outlook that permeated much of the religious thinking of Americans for 150 years. It stemmed directly from the religious orthodoxy of Calvinism with its emphasis upon God's power and wrath, original sin, reverence and fear of God, obedience to His commandments, and obedience to the authority of parents and elders. An authoritarian education was seen as the only possible way to implement beliefs that the child's nature was inherently evil. Since the child was prone to sin, the best way to keep him under control was to instill in him a fear of breaking God's laws and a fear of the awful and dreadful consequences of sin. Fear, discipline, and obedience were the by-words of this conception of child nature. These formed the staples of educational method throughout the colonial period for those who fully accepted this view of religious orthodoxy. Notable illustrations can be drawn from outstanding spokesmen whose lives and influence span most of the seventeenth and eighteenth century. Their views became firmly embedded in the traditional authoritarian attitudes toward the child in the family, the church, and the school. So strong is the tradition that it still survives in much of contemporary life even where the original religious motivations are not so extreme nor so real as once they were.

One of the most influential of the early Puritan spokesmen was the famous Boston minister, John Cotton, who wrote a short catechism designed especially for children. It was called *Spiritual Milk for American Babes Drawn out of the Breasts of Both Testaments for their Souls Nourishment*. Published perhaps as early as 1641 but certainly by 1646, this catechism was read and learned by many generations of children not only as a separate piece but also as a part of the *New England Primer*.[1] In this catechism the child learned that he was conceived in sin and born in iniquity, that his corrupt nature bent him to sin and transgression of God's commandments, and that the wages of sin were death and damnation. In interpreting the Ten Commandments to the child, Cotton emphasized that "Honor thy father and thy mother" meant reverence, obedience, and recompense for all his superiors in family, school, church, and state, obviously referring to parents, teachers, ministers, and magistrates. Salvation might come for the child only through the sacrifice of Christ, the word of God contained in the Bible, adherence to the law of God, faith in the gospel, prayer, repentance, obedience to the church, and observance of the seals of the covenant in baptism and the Last Supper.

Cotton not only believed in education as a means of inculcating proper obedience and behavior of children, he favored the use of law as a final resort for undisciplined children. One of his proposals in his elaborate code of laws which he drew up for the consideration of the Massachusetts General Court in 1641 read as follows:

> Rebellious children, whether they continue in riott or drunkenesse, after due correction from their parents, or whether they curse or smite their parents, to be put to death.[2]

Connecticut followed Cotton's lead and included even more elaborate provisions to the same effect and quoted the same Biblical authority for the death penalty in its code of colonial laws of 1672.[3]

Not only through catechisms, school books, and laws but also through poetry, sermons, and published advice to parents and ministers was the authoritarian Calvinist outlook on children kept alive in the literature of the colonial period.

A widely read poetic description of sinners facing the last judgment was writen by Michael Wigglesworth, minister and Harvard teacher, entitled *The Day of Doom*.[4] From the time it was published in 1662, it is estimated that one copy was sold for every twenty persons in New England and one for every forty-five persons in all the colonies. A large section of the long poem was devoted to a pitiful picture of unhappy children faced with the prospect of eternal damnation. Although extreme in its doctrines, this view probably represented the general outlook of most Calvinists and of many other religious

---

[1] Paul L. Ford, ed., *The New England Primer* (New York, Dodd, Mead, 1899).

[2] *The Hutchinson Papers*, publications of the Prince Society (Albany, 1865), Vol. II, p. 198.

[3] A. B. Hart, *American History Told by Contemporaries* (New York, Macmillan, 1919), Vol. I, pp. 488–490.

[4] Michael Wigglesworth, *The Day of Doom*, edited by Kenneth B. Murdock (New York, Spiral Press, 1929).

sects through much of the colonial period. When brought to the bar of judgment, the children who died in infancy pleaded that they had had no chance to sin and thus should not be punished. They begged for mercy, but the stern judge argued that their natures were depraved as a result of the original sin of Adam and that therefore they had sinned fully as much as had Adam. If Adam had not sinned, the children would have happily received the blessings and benefits that would have flowed to them, so the chi'dren must accept a share in the punishment along with all other men beca' se Adam had not lived up to his promise. And besides, the children would ʲrobably have done no better than Adam if they had been in his place, so they must suffer the consequences. Furthermore, the judge reminded them that God alone could choose those to be saved, but since the children had not had as much opportunity to sin as adults had, they could not expect eternal happiness, but still they might hope for the "easiest room in Hell."

Countless sermons by Puritan ministers reiterated this general theme, but perhaps the best and most complete statement of this position, especially as it applied to the family duties of parents to children and the duties of children to their parents, is contained in a tract published in 1699 by Cotton Mather entitled *A Family Well-Ordered*.[5] This little book, now quite rare, paints a vivid picture of the authoritarian family based upon orthodox Calvinist religious principles. It came at the end of the seventeenth century when many New Englanders were growing restless under the Puritanical theocracy, and Mather carried John Cotton's stern warnings to the extreme in sermons, tracts, books, and a catechism of his own.

A Family Well-Ordered is divided into two parts, one addressed to parents and one addressed to children. In the first section Mather alternately threatened, warned, and pleaded with parents to care for the piety and salvation of their children. He elaborated in dire detail how children were born in sin and were creatures of Hell, Death, and Wrath and therefore had corrupt natures. He insisted that parents have their children baptized, that parents constantly "charge their children vehemently" and command them to obey, that prayer was essential, and that parents must be good examples to their children.

Of most importance and interest to educators were the sections on instruction and authority. Instruction should consist of reading, writing, ciphering, and preparation for an honorable calling, but above all instruction should lead to salvation by means of Bible reading, the catechism, public worship, and continuing religious teaching at home by the parents. In the section on authority Mather argued that if parents wanted their children to fear God, the home must be ruled with absolute authority, children must be kept in subjection, and the parents' word must be law. To be sure, the authority must

---

[5] Cotton Mather, *A Family Well-Ordered* (Boston, Green & Allen, 1699). Available on microfilm in the Special Collection of the Library of Columbia University.

be tempered with kindness, meekness, and loving tenderness so that children will love as well as fear their parents. But children must be held in rein and parents must keep vigilant watch over their activities and their friends, rebuking and restraining them when necessary, even to liberal use of the rod but never whipping in anger.

The second part of the well-ordered family described with even more vehemence the duties of the child to his parents. Vivid and awful consequences will be visited upon the undutiful child. The vengeful curse of God will lead him into ever worse sins, will make all of his plans and efforts go wrong, will result in untimely and especially horrible deaths of hanging, suicide, and being eaten by vultures, and will result after death in eternal punishment in the utter darkness of Hell. The motivation of fear of wrong doing runs throughout the major part of the tract. The dutiful child, on the other hand, will receive singular blessings, favor on his enterprises, and prosperity and happiness. The keys to being dutiful were reverence, obedience, and recompense to one's parents. And these duties were to be paid not only to one's natural parents but also to his political parents (magistrates), ecclesiastical parents (ministers), and scholastical parents (teachers).

Mather thus visualized fear, obedience, discipline, and absolute authority as the essential ingredients of the teaching methods in schools as well as in the home, church, and the state. A long passage was addressed to servants enjoining them to pay the same respects and observe the same duties to their masters that children should pay to their parents, or they too would suffer the same curse of God and the same terrible consequences. "Good order" in the family would produce a well-ordered society, but poor discipline would result in chaotic society. That Cotton Mather's injunctions were not simply the ravings of a morbid and petulant minister is attested by the whole content and spirit of the New England Primer which was the most widely read school book in America for 100 years. The best estimate is made that some 3,000,000 copies were sold from 1700 to 1850.

The traditional Calvinist view of human nature and its motivations carried on well into the eighteenth century. The writings and sermons of the great apologist for original sin and for emotional awakening to religion attest to the continuing vitality of Puritanism in the hands of Jonathan Edwards despite the fact that his efforts were being eclipsed by other interests and other outlooks by the end of the colonial period. In his *Thoughts Concerning the Present Revival of Religion in New-England,* published in 1741, Edwards made an exhaustive defense of the Great Awakening that was sweeping New England.[6] Edwards reviewed in detail the ways that multitudes of people had been emotionally affected by an awakened feeling of sin and "vileness" and the new feeling of peace and contentment that comes from

[6] Jonathan Edwards, *Thoughts Concerning the Present Revival of Religion in New-England,* abridged by John Wesley (London, W. Strahan, 1745).

a sweet love of Christ. He commented especially upon a similar effect among little children. He defended the methods used by himself and other preachers to play upon the emotions of people and the use of fear and terror as a means of awakening them out of their natural and sinful state. Sinners *ought* to be terrified, including children.

He eloquently defended the practice of "frighting poor children with Talk of Hell and Damnation" and any who complained of the practice betrayed weakness and doubts about the corrupt nature of man and child alike. If parents are too tender and loving with their children, they will live to regret their folly in exposing children to "eternal Burnings." Edwards asserted confidently that he believed in dealing plainly with children and never had known any ill consequences from such severe practices.

He had earlier reported (1736) in a detailed letter to a colleague in Boston the story of Phebe Bartlet who had been greatly affected by his own preaching. This case study of a child in religious terror and anguish is a remarkable picture of emotional and mental tension; it is contained in Edwards' *Faithful Narrative of the Surprising Work of God*.[7] At the age of four years Phebe began to retire to her room for secret prayer five or six times a day and to engage in fits of crying and writhing. She showed an overwhelming interest in adult conversations on religious matters, talked constantly of her own feelings of sin and terror of damnation, and talked with parents, adults, the minister, and other children about sin, death, and salvation. She recited her complete catechism several times a day to herself and to others. She could not wait for Sunday to come and would count the days and hours until the next opportunity to attend church to hear Edwards preach. The taking of some plums from a neighbor's tree with other children brought on great remorse and a sense of guilt because of the sinful act. Edwards spoke proudly of Phebe as a prime example of a desirable and all consuming religious involvement among children and as evidence of the effectiveness of his style of preaching and justification of his emphasis on sin and fear as a proper educational method.

For further elaboration of the dominant view of human nature and its effect upon children the reader is referred to two interesting and well-documented studies of this aspect of colonial life, Fleming's *Children and Puritanism* and Kiefer's *American Children Through Their Books*.[8] These books document with much detail the emotional excesses, the feelings of guilt and fear that were instilled in children by the great emphasis upon sin, obedience, and authoritarianism in dealing with children. Evidence is mar-

[7] Carl Van Doren, ed., *Benjamin Franklin and Jonathan Edwards* (New York, Scribner's 1920), pp. 332–338.

[8] Sandford Fleming, *Children and Puritanism; The Place of Children in the Life and Thought of the New England Churches, 1620–1847* (New Haven, Yale University Press, 1933); and Monica Kiefer, *American Children Through Their Books, 1700–1835* (Philadelphia, University of Pennsylvania Press, 1948).

shalled in the latter study to show that such approaches and effects were not confined to New England Calvinists but were common among nearly all the religious sects and in all parts of the country during much of the colonial period.

LIBERALIZING VIEW OF THE CHILD AND EDUCATIONAL METHOD

Despite the prevailing attitudes toward child nature that led to the treatment of the child as a sinful though miniature version of an adult person, there were signs that a change in outlook was in the making in the educational thought of the eighteenth century. It seems clear from most descriptions of colonial schools that discipline was harsh and punishment was severe in actual practice, but here and there a voice was raised expressing the belief that children should be treated more gently and tenderly as befits the peculiar characteristics of childhood. More and more persons began to sound the theme that children have some rights of their own, at least the right to be treated as an immature being whose interests and capacities should be enlisted in the educative enterprise. Gradually it came to be felt that the child should not be expected to live up to the rigorous exactions of an adult standard of religious and moral authority.

By and large, such views came from those who held religious outlooks that departed from the harsh Calvinist doctrines of predestination and original sin and came to look upon salvation as possible of achievement through human faith and human effort along with the grace and foregiveness of God. Such views came not only from the liberalizing religious views of Quakers, Anglicans, and minority religious sects, but also from those who began to emphasize the moral values that stemmed from deistic and secular outlooks concerning human nature and morality. Those who held the more liberal religious outlooks were no less concerned for the religious motivations and inculcation of religious principles among children, but they believed that more genuine religious behavior could be achieved by methods that emphasized love rather than fear, tenderness and gentleness rather than harsh discipline, sympathy and understanding for childish weaknesses rather than vindictive authority and punishment, and learning through positive motivations of interest in a wider range of activities rather than through rote memorization of verbal symbols. These methods were supported by arguments that the child should be accepted on his own grounds as a child and that children vary in their individual aptitudes and interests. Thus the groundwork was being laid in the eighteenth century for the geater emancipation and freeing of the child from complete adult domination that marked the developments of educational theory in the nineteenth and twentieth centuries. To be sure, such voices were as yet largely crying in the wilderness of authoritarianism.

The principal strain of Quaker thought on education throughout the eighteenth century seemed to stress these arguments concerning the reform of education. In his *Reflections and Maxims* William Penn wrote a remarkably modern sounding statement on educational methods in which he urged the study of nature through sense experience rather than simply the memorizing of words and the rules of grammar and rhetoric.[9] Children's "natural genius to *mechanical* and *physical,* or *natural* knowledge" is neglected, whereas things are to be preferred to language. The order of nature should be followed in teaching children as the best revelation of God's power and wisdom.

Later in the century the noted and liberal Quaker writer, John Woolman, carried forward the basic doctrines of the Friends as applied to political, economic, and educational affairs. In his short treatise on schools Woolman urged patient attention to children, sympathetic regard to their innocent and tender natures, careful attention to the varying spirit, inclinations, and conduct of each individual child in order to arouse their love and admiration for their teachers and in order to lead them to become genuinely children of God.[10] Similarly, the famous Quaker teacher, Anthony Benezet, urged that stern discipline in school be replaced with kindliness and appeals to the child's sense of the important and the just as the heart of an education "founded upon Christian and reasonable principles." Method should be based upon a religious plan that is delightful and interesting to children rather than a "painful labor." [11] The whole spirit of Penn, Woolman, and Benezet is a far cry from the fear-ridden bombast of Cotton Mather and Jonathan Edwards. It is no wonder that the thought of these Quaker leaders led them to be concerned too for the education of Indians, Negroes, and women on a level of equality with the usually more privileged status of whites and males of the times.

The outlook of Anglicans toward children in the eighteenth century also seemed to reflect a more reasonable attitude toward child nature. The instructions of the Society for the Propagation of the Gospel in Foreign Parts to its schoolmasters in 1706 contained injunctions that the teachers should use "all kind and gentle Methods in the Government of their Scholars, that they may be loved as well as feared by them" and that when punishment was necessary, the child should understand that it was given out of kindness and reason rather than simply out of vindictiveness to maintain the teacher's authority and to command obedience.[12] Part of the purpose of the society was also to

---

[9] *The Select Works of William Penn,* 3rd ed. (London, Phillips, 1782), Vol. V, pp. 120–122.

[10] John Woolman, *A Journal* (Philadelphia, Association of Friends for the Diffusion of Religious and Useful Knowledge, 1860), pp. 329–332.

[11] James P. Wickersham, *History of Education in Pennsylvania* (Lancaster, Pa., 1886), pp. 216–217.

[12] Quoted in E. W. Knight, and C. L. Hall, *Readings in American Educational History* (New York, Appleton-Century-Crofts, 1951).

carry religious instruction to Indians and Negroes in the South as well as in the North.

The generally more humane tone of the Anglican theology as applied to children is illustrated by the catechism for children written in several editions in the middle of the eighteenth century by Samuel Johnson, the first president of King's College, who gave up Calvinism in favor of Anglicanism. Johnson's catechism when compared with John Cotton's or Cotton Mather's shows much less emphasis on sin and fear of God and much more emphasis upon the wisdom, justice, goodness, kindness, and mercy of God.[13] The more gentle outlook in religion is carried over to educational method by Johnson in his plan for education contained in his important work entitled the *Elements of Philosophy* first published in 1752.[14] Following the idealistic philosophy of Bishop George Berkeley, Johnson pointed out the social origins of the moral sense of right and wrong and urged that the development of the intellect should be assisted by knowledge and experience that is pleasing, useful, and appropriate to the children themselves. Children should be treated with candor, patience, decency, honor, and integrity and should be led gradually and tenderly from concern with the family into the activities of neighborhood, community, and state.

A liberalizing outlook toward child nature and educational method also began to appear among some of the smaller Protestant sects, such as the Moravians, Dunkards, and Mennonites. The most elaborate treatise in this respect was drawn up by the Mennonite teacher in Pennsylvania, Christopher Dock, who made much of his methods of gentleness and the motivation of love as an educational goal and instrument.[15] He believed it was far better to bring children to do things from a love of doing rather than to force them by threat of physical punishment. The stubborn child must, of course, be sharply punished by the rod but only as a last resort after other methods of group censure have failed rather than to be beaten soundly and often as part of a common or standard operating procedure. He realized that different children need different treatment and that the shy and slow-learning pupils could be definitely harmed by harsh words and much whipping. Gentleness, loving care, and admonition to follow the ways of God were the foundations of his method for both parents and teachers who should not remain aloof from children nor insist on distance as Cotton Mather did, but rather should humble themselves to the level of children in order to attain "a community with the children."

The rigid sectarianism of the seventeenth and eighteenth centuries began to be softened, too, in Dock's outlook. In his school he had children of various

---

[13] Samuel Johnson, *A Short Catechism for Young Children* (New York, Holt, 1765).

[14] Samuel Johnson, *Elementa Philosophica* (Philadelphia, Franklin & Hall, 1752), Chap. VI.

[15] Martin G. Brumbaugh, *The Life and Works of Christopher Dock* (Philadelphia, Lippincott, 1908).

denominations and thus reserved the teaching of the catechism to the parents. In school he concentrated on general religious injunctions, prayers, reading the Bible, and the singing of hymns and psalms. Nonsectarian religious instruction was often the outcome of the less severe and more humane attitudes toward the child and the necessity of teaching children of different sects some of the common principles of religion and morality.

In fact, definite efforts to establish schools through interdenominational cooperation appeared as early as the middle of the eighteenth century. Appropriately enough, the occasion and the need were most apparent in Pennsylvania with its wide variety of sectarian groups.[16] Michael Schlatter, minister of the German Reformed Church, publicized through Europe the need of educational facilities among the Pennsylvania Germans and found a willing ear among members of the Society for the Propagation of the Gospel. William Smith, later provost of the University of Pennsylvania, proposed a plan whereby the Anglican society as well as Englishmen of nonconformist beliefs should join together to found English schools in Pennsylvania for the Germans. A Society for Propagating Christian Knowledge among the Germans in America was formed in London in 1754. When schools were set up in Pennsylvania, it was provided that the trustees for each school should consist of Calvinists, Lutheran Germans, and Englishmen of any Protestant profession whatever.

To be sure, the Pennsylvania Germans were suspicious that political motives were at work to Anglicize the Germans both religiously and politically, and doubtless that motive was present. But, nevertheless, it is important that religious diversity was seen as making necessary a common form of instruction based upon "the English language and the common principles of the Christian religion and morality" wherein children of both English and German ancestry could be educated together in a common school. Sectarian suspicion eventually prevented the continuation of such schools beyond 1763, but it was an interesting experiment forecasting the conditions and arguments that eventually led to the establishment of a common school system under public rather than private auspices in the nineteenth century. Appeal to a state that had become neutral religiously could achieve in the nineteenth century what voluntary interdenominational cooperation could not achieve in the eighteenth century. The softening of the doctrinal rivalry among sectarian outlooks on human nature was part of the necessary condition of such an achievement along with the institutional separation of church and state.

Most important, too, in the development of a more humane attitude toward children and educational method was the emergence of nonreligious and secular concerns among an increasingly large proportion of the population. This could not be called an antireligious movement, but rather a growing

16 Wickersham, *op. cit.,* pp. 66–69, 151, 172, 236, *et passim.*

interest in and respect for activities of a political, economic, and scientific kind which did not deny the religious motivations but recognized them as one among many motivations that impelled men to the good and the true and the useful in life. The secular concerns of preparation for citizenship, for government, for business, for labor, for the professions, for the intellectual life, and for leisure pursuits all served to lay claim to the energies of men. These were not antireligious in character so much as they were nonreligious in character. They signalized the advent of a cultural and social situation in which the religious motivations were to be no longer all consuming and exclusive. The development of this utilitarian outlook to be discussed in the next section carried with it an outlook that passed over the beliefs of predestination, original sin, depraved human nature, and authoritarian methods of inculcating fear and obedience and turned rather to a wider range of child interests. These embraced sense experience, physical, mental, and emotional activities, and preparation for a wider range of legitimate and useful adult vocations and activites in an increasingly secular culture.

THE CLASSICAL VERSUS THE PRACTICAL VIEW OF EDUCATION

Although the intellectual leaders of the colonies made much in their writings of the religious aspect of life and to this extent they were children of the Protestant Reformation of the sixteenth and seventeenth centuries in Europe, they were just as truly proponents of the classical Humanism of the Renaissance of the fourteenth, fifteenth, and sixteenth centuries. When the colonists came to America in the seventeenth century the study of the classical languages and literature of Greek, Latin, and Hebrew had become the staples of secondary and higher education. Devotion to the study of the classics for upper-class boys was part and parcel of Protestant and Catholic alike in Western Europe. The religious controversies of the sixteenth century had made it necessary for Protestants who would battle toe to toe with learned Catholic philosophers and theologians to become just as well grounded in the sacred and classical languages.

Agreement on the importance of classical learning among the colonial intellectuals was so widespread that relatively little dissent can be found in the literature of much of the colonial period, especially among Calvinist and Anglican writers. The Protestant sects were divided on doctrinal and theological grounds, and thus they thundered against each other over matters of original sin, free will, the authority and literal interpretation of the Bible, the inner light, the role of emotion and faith in salvation, persecution for cause of conscience, and the separation of church and state. But they were all more or less agreed upon the importance of the study of the classics for those who would become leaders in church or state. Most of the earliest Puritan ✓

and Anglican leaders had been grounded in the classics in the grammar schools or universities of England, and they moved promptly to establish similar Latin grammar schools in America.

The polemic literature in seventeenth-century America is relatively silent on the question of the value of the classics. To be sure, John Winthrop as governor of Massachusetts was apprehensive that the Puritan clergy made too much of the classical authors rather than sticking to the Bible, but he was quickly reassured by the ministers themselves that humanistic learning was as necessary for development of human reason as revelation and grace were necessary for faith and salvation. John Cotton, Nathaniel Ward, Thomas Shepard, Increase Mather, Cotton Mather, and a host of learned Puritan ministers consistently paid their tributes to classical learning. No less enthusiastic were the Anglican, Presbyterian, Catholic, and Lutheran proponents of classical learning as the staple of training for leadership. Indeed, Cotton Mather's funeral sermon and eulogy on the life and contributions of Ezekiel Cheever, famed New England schoolmaster, is usually taken as a high point in the admiration for the value of the classics in the early eighteenth century.[17] Mather looked upon the learned languages as the keys to understanding of human life without which man would remain dumb, ignorant, uncouth, wild, and foolish.

In the course of the eighteenth century another and increasingly formidable claimant to the intellectual allegiances of men began to challenge the dominant claims of the religious and classical foundations of a liberal education. This was the ideal of practical utility with its roots in economic motives, political ideals, and scientific interest in the wonders of nature and human invention. The demand for attention to these intellectual interests was relatively mild and scattered during the eighteenth century and thus did not meet the religious and classical in mortal combat but rather was often accepted as rounding out a full blown philosophy of education. It was not until the nineteenth century that the utilitarian and scientific challenge achieved the proportions of a head-on conflict with the humanistic and classical tradition. At that time the controversy became shrill and bitter, enlisted vigorous support on both sides, and caused cleavages in the body educational that have not been healed to this day.

In the eighteenth century, indeed, some of the religious sects themselves were the most hospitable to the new secular concerns of society and argued that vocational preparation should be combined with the religious. In 1682 William Penn desired that his children should be taught "the useful parts of mathematics, as building houses or ships, measuring, surveying, dialling, navigation; but agriculture is especially in my eyes; let my children be hus-

---

[17] Cotton Mather, *Corderius Americanus. An Essay upon the Good Education of Children* (Boston, 1708). Quoted in Perry Miller and Thomas H. Johnson, *The Puritans* (New York, American Book, 1938).

bandmen and housewives; it is industrious, healthy, honest, and of good example." [18] The Puritans of New England, the Anglicans of the South, and the Dutch in New York all moved early by custom and by law to provide for preparation in a trade through apprenticeship of children, especially children of the poorer and underprivileged classes (see Chapter 4).

A most interesting proposal for vocational training of a highly practical kind was made in 1685 by a canny Quaker, Thomas Budd.[19] He argued that not only should boys and girls learn the most useful arts and sciences, such as reading and writing English, Latin, arithmetic, and bookkeeping but also that the boys should learn a useful trade (woodworking, clockmaking, weaving, or shoemaking) and the girls should be instructed in spinning, knitting, needle work, and straw work. Apparently Budd was impressed by the possibilities in the establishment of public spinning schools whereby children could earn money for their parents and for the school by making linen cloth that could undersell English cloth in the colonies and still earn double the profit that English manufacturers obtained. If children were required by law to attend such schools and the profits were turned over to the schools, there would be enough income to enable poor children and Indian children to be maintained free of charge in the school and thus be educated along with children of the rich.

The noted Anglican minister, Thomas Bray, who was so effective in promoting the work of the Society for the Propagation of the Gospel in Maryland, Virginia, and in other colonies wrote *An Essay Towards Promoting All Necessary and Useful Knowledge* in which he outlined an entire course of reading that would be useful to clergymen, physicians, lawyers, and merchants. He included the study of history, humanities, natural history, gardening, agriculture, mathematics, physics, and law as well as theology.[20]

The most elaborate plan for a utilitarian education in the colonial period was set forth, appropriately enough, by Benjamin Franklin, the apostle of practicality.[21] In 1749 he published his *Proposals Relating to the Education of Youth in Pensilvania.* Franklin's plan for a new type of school to be known as an academy was distinctly secular in tone and content. Apparently he realized that opposition would come from religious and classical sources; so he bulwarked his arguments with elaborate references to such European authorities as John Milton, John Locke, Charles Rollin of the University of Paris, and Francis Hutcheson (University of Glasgow). His proposals thus provide a clear channel by which the newer philosophies of sense realism and empiricism flowed into American educational thought to give support to the

[18] Samuel M. Janney, *The Life of William Penn,* 6th rev. ed. (Philadelphia, 1882), pp. 198–203.
[19] Thomas Budd, *Good Order Established in Pennsylvania and New Jersey,* edited by Frederick J. Shepard (Cleveland, Burrows, 1902).
[20] See Bernard C. Steiner, *Rev. Thomas Bray* (Baltimore, Maryland Historical Society, Fund Publication No. 37, 1901), pp. 53–70.
[21] Thomas Woody, *Educational Views of Benjamin Franklin* (New York, McGraw-Hill, 1931).

desires for vocational training and practical preparation for a life of usefulness in society, government, occupation, and professional service. He even hoped the trustees would "look on the students as in some sort their children, treat them with familiarity and affection, and when they have behaved well, and gone through their studies, and are to enter the world, zealously unite, and make all the interest that can be made to establish them, whether in business, offices, marriages, or any other thing for their advantage, preferably to all other persons whatsoever even of equal merit." This faint reference to the good offices of a vocational placement bureau is a far cry from the attitude toward the "children of wrath and sin" envisioned by Cotton Mather and Jonathan Edwards.

Franklin also envisioned a pleasant and attractive school life for the students in his hope that the school would have a garden, orchard, meadow, and fields and be well stocked with books, maps, globes, scientific apparatus, and machines. Attention to physical education was also recommended for its pleasure in running, leaping, wrestling, and swimming as well as an aid to healthy bodies.

The practical and vocational motive runs throughout Franklin's suggestions for a curriculum which are summarized in the following paragraphs. Study of the English language was a prime purpose; reading to be learned through the English classics; pronouncing, by means of declarations, speeches, and orations; writing of letters and stories; and grammar, rhetoric, and logic. Long footnotes citing Locke and Hutcheson argued that expertness in the use of the English language is one of the most useful accomplishments a person can acquire.

Elementary art work in drawing and perspective were early mentioned by Franklin as an aid to creative expression. He quoted Locke on the usefulness to gentlemen of drawing as a means of communication and expression of ideas, and added that it was no less useful to a mechanic who can improve the design of his work in carpentry, ship building, engraving, painting, cabinet making, carving, and gardening and thus impress his employer.

Mathematics in the form of arithmetic, geometry, astronomy, and especially accounting was another important item of the proposed curriculum. The most space and attention were given by Franklin to what we would call the social studies. These were to include history through translations of the Greek and Roman historians, modern history especially of Britain and the colonies, chronology of the principal epochs in human history, geography with large attention to maps, social history of customs, political history and political science, and the history of religions and morality.

Franklin paid his respects to the learned languages and insisted that the classics be taught in the school for all who want or need them but argued that they should not be required of everyone. Prospective professional occupation should be the determinant: Latin and Greek should be taught to those preparing for the ministry; Latin, Greek, and French to those preparing for medicine; and French, German, and Spanish to prospective merchants.

Natural science came in for a large share of attention as a necessary accomplishment for merchants and mechanics in order that they might know more about their commodities and materials; for physicians to help them understand drugs and aid in preserving health; for ministers as an aid in strengthening their proofs of Divine Providence; and an improvement of the conversation and instruction of all.

Practical experiences in agriculture should accompany the reading in natural history; experience in gardening and planting, and excursions to the best farms would heighten learning and enjoyment.

The history of technology and actual experiences with machines would contribute to a knowledge of the applications of science to the arts of commerce, inventions, manufactures, machines of war, and to the improvement of civilization.

Throughout all the curriculum should be a concern for good breeding, manners, and morals which should result in a desire to serve others by means of true virtue and good conduct. The aim of knowledge and learning is not to acquire information for its own sake but as a means of improving conduct. In this emphasis upon the moral quality in education Franklin agreed with the religionists and classicists, but he differed in that he found the standards of conduct in human nature and human society rather than in appeal to sectarian religious sanctions.

Franklin's real hope was to enlarge and make respectable an education for civil and occupational life that would not need to rest upon religious instruction nor upon the classics. He hoped his academy would have an English school that would be on a level of equality and even more valuable than its classical school. Franklin summed up this view in the conclusion of his *Idea of the English School* written in 1751 as a further plea for support of the English department of the academy:

Thus instructed, youth will come out of this school fitted for learning any business, calling or profession, except such wherein languages are required; and though unacquainted with any ancient or foreign tongue, they will be masters of their own, which is of more immediate and general use; and withal will have attained many other valuable accomplishments; the time usually spent in acquiring those languages, often without success, being here employed in laying such a foundation of knowledge and ability as, properly improved, may qualify them to pass through and execute the several offices of civil life, with advantage and reputation to themselves and country.[22]

Franklin's ideas received an immediate and widespread response from people representing a curious variety of backgrounds. He received support from the middle-class merchants of Philadelphia who saw in his plans a useful

[22] *Ibid.*, pp. 129–130.

education for their sons that would aid them in business and who therefore put money into the venture. He received an enthusiastic reply from Samuel Johnson, the noted Anglican philosopher and intellectual who was later to become president of King's College. Though somewhat surprised that a "tradesman" could devise such an excellent plan, Johnson heartily approved the *Idea of the English School* and could find no basic criticism of it or suggestions for improvement. William Smith, who himself wrote extensively on educational matters and later became provost of the College of Philadelphia, urged the establishment of a mechanics' school to teach tradesmen useful subjects exactly along the lines of Franklin's academy.[23] And Cadwallader Colden, Tory member of the governor's council in New York for fifty-five years and ranked with Franklin as an outstanding scientist and man of learning, wrote Franklin a letter giving hearty approval to the whole design of Franklin's *Proposals*. Colden was especially pleased at the emphasis upon agriculture and the sciences to be taught, urging the techniques of an agricultural experiment station, praising the instruction in English, and suggesting dancing as a means of forming the manners and carriage appropriate to young gentlemen of high station.[24]

Despite this response from middle-class merchants, Anglican scholars, and aristocratic public officials, Franklin's appeal to the doctrine of usefulness was doomed to failure for the moment. He laid the blame upon the heavy hand of the traditional power and prestige of the "Latinists" in the academy. He wrote a long complaint in 1789 describing the various ways that his beloved English school had been starved and neglected in favor of the Latin school at the academy.[25] He discussed at length how the masters and trustees had not lived up to the intentions of the founders and of the charter, and how they had cut the English master's salary and increased his duties while paying twice as much to the Latin master to do half as much work and teach half as many boys. Thus, good Latin teachers were secured, and poor English teachers could not hold their own against the skillful Latinists who pled for more tutors and higher salaries and even plotted to do away with the English school entirely. Disappointed parents withdrew their children from the school and sent them to private teachers.

For these reasons Franklin then demanded that the English school be separated entirely from the Latin school, the stock divided up, and the corporation dissolved. He was ready to call a failure the first experiment in developing an education that would combine the values of the classical hu-

---

[23] William Smith, *Discourses on Public Occasions in America* (London, 1762), Appendix II, No. 1; also see Thomas H. Montgomery, *History of the University of Pennsylvania* (Philadelphia, Jacobs, 1900), p. 187.

[24] "Letters and Papers of Cadwallader Colden," in *Collections of the New York Historical Society*, Vol. 53, pp. 156–158.

[25] See Woody, *op. cit.*, pp. 192–228.

manism and modern science and utility. This was an illustration in the first twenty or thirty years of the life of this institution of the prevailing outlook in favor of a classical education. But the issue was soon to be joined on wider grounds, and the classicists were gradually to lose ground throughout the nineteenth century but never to admit defeat. Franklin had lived 100 years too soon, but his ideas were abroad, and they were not to be permanently defeated. The impetus given to the academy movement and eventually to the public high school movement was one of the basic revolutions in the conception of a proper secondary education for all American youth.

CONSERVATIVE VERSUS LIBERAL VIEWS OF HIGHER EDUCATION

The trend of thought concerning the nature and purposes of colleges in the colonial period reflected a similar threefold controversy among the religious, the classical, and the practical interests. In general, the religious and the classical were strong allies and dominated the field in the first part of the period, but signs soon appeared that the practical and scientific concerns would rise to the challenge in the latter part of the period. The motives in establishing the first three colonial colleges, Harvard in 1636, William and Mary in 1693, and Yale in 1701, were definitely religious. Indeed, they were religious motives of a distinctly sectarian flavor, and they continued to dominate four of the six colleges that were founded in the middle of the eighteenth century. But two of the colleges founded in this latter period showed signs of the growing practical and scientific interest. Several examples will show how this shift in interest began to gain recognition alongside the older classical and religious outlooks.

Yale represented the continuing strength of the religious and classical tradition undimmed. In its very origin one of the principal motives of the founders was to counteract the growing signs that Harvard was developing a more liberal religious outlook and was beginning to soften the rigorous Calvinist doctrines. The training of "learned, pious, and orthodox" ministers through the classical arts and sciences was one of the primary purposes of the founding of the College and this goal was reasserted by act of the Connecticut General Court in 1735. Yale's belligerent and able president, Thomas Clap, stated this outlook in 1754 as clearly as it could be stated:

> Colleges, are *Religious Societies,* of a Superior Nature to all others. For whereas *Parishes,* are Societies, for training up the *common People;* Colleges, are *Societies of Ministers,* for training up Persons for the Work of the *Ministry.* . . . Some indeed, have supposed, that, the only Design of Colleges, was to teach the Arts, and Sciences. . . . But, it is probable, that there is not a College, to be found upon Earth, upon such a Constitution . . .[26]

[26] Thomas Clap, *The Religious Constitution of Colleges, Especially of Yale-College in New-Haven* (New London, Conn., T. Green, 1754), p. 4 and 12.

Clap was somewhat more vigorous than accurate in his claims, for great reform movements in science and philosophy were sweeping the universities of Aberdeen and Edinburgh in Scotland and of Halle and Göttingen in Germany prior to the time he wrote.

Jonathan Edwards took much the same position as Clap in his even more vigorous way which must have favorably impressed Princeton, for he was offered its presidency. Edwards hammered away at the colleges for not paying enough attention to religion; he thereby helped to disprove Clap's claims by inference. Edwards claimed that since the main design of colleges should be to train for the ministry, they, therefore, should resolutely become "Nurseries of Piety" and "Schools of the Prophets" to prepare persons to be "Ambassadors of Jesus Christ." [27]

The public discussions, however, that went on in connection with the founding of King's College (later Columbia) and the College at Philadelphia revealed a startling contrast to the temper and content of the statements by Clap and Edwards, both staunch Calvinists in their own ways. One cannot read the statements by Samuel Johnson, president of King's College in New York, and of William Smith, provost of the College of Philadelphia, without sensing immediately the change in tone and the interests to be served. Perhaps it was their more generous Anglican outlook; perhaps it was their concern for the business and commercial interests of two thriving trading communities; perhaps it was their greater interest in the Enlightenment and consequent concern for intellectual studies of a scientific nature; perhaps it was their contact with Benjamin Franklin and his practical proposals for a new type academy. Likely it was some combination of all.

No one could doubt Samuel Johnson's earnest and pious religious outlook, but it was far more generous than that of Edwards and Clap. In his advertisement in a New York newspaper describing his plan for King's College, Johnson made clear his conviction that the boys in his college should be trained up in religion, but he emphasized that there was no intention to impose on the students the tenets of any particular sect, but only to teach them the great principles of a common Christianity upon which all denominations are generally agreed.[28] He then went on to describe the plan of instruction which was to include the classical languages, grammar, rhetoric, logic, mathematics, surveying, navigation, geography, history, husbandry, commerce, government, and the several natural sciences of physics, mineralogy, biology, astronomy, and of "everything useful for the comfort, the convenience and elegance of life, in the chief manufactures relating to any of these things." No mention was made of the intent to train ministers for a particular sect, nor to serve the functions of a divinity school.

[27] Jonathan Edwards, *Thoughts Concerning the Present Revival of Religion in New-England*, pp. 112–114.

[28] *New York Gazette, or Weekly Post Boy*, June 3, 1754.

Now, to be sure, Johnson's ambitious plans for a wide and many-sided curriculum did not pan out as he proclaimed them, for it was not long before King's College was definitely Anglican in flavor, many of its students did become ministers, and the practical studies found little place in the actual curriculum in comparison to the attention given to the classics and traditional liberal arts. But, again, as in the case of Franklin, the idea was hard to down and Columbia eventually had to meet the competition of the technical and scientific offerings of other institutions.

The plan of William Smith for the College at Philadelphia was quite similar to the plans of Johnson and Franklin.[29] Utilizing his acquaintance with the scientific strides being made at his alma mater, the University of Aberdeen, Smith wrote several educational plans, one proposing a college in New York City, another proposing special schools appropriate to preparation for the learned professions and for the mechanical trades, and one proposing a broad scheme of liberal education that was eventually adopted by the trustees of the Philadelphia College. In the latter plan, as in Johnson's, there was no mention of training for the ministry, only the most general statements concerning religion, and no course of study in religion or divinity. The curriculum as planned rivaled in scope the proposals of Franklin and were definitely aimed at a higher level of attainment as befitted a college curriculum rather than that of an academy. Not only were the classical studies to be pursued, but also the several branches of logic, mathematics, ethics, history, law and government, trade and commerce, and the whole range of the natural sciences as then known. Enlightenment science and philosophy had found a congenial home.

In these plans the strongholds of sectarian religion and classical study were being attacked, but in actual practice they were to be by no means overwhelmed. Reinforcements were rushed to the scene, the enemy was staved off, and each side girded for the longer and more bitter battles of the nineteenth century.

One other example of the effort to change the character of the colonial college must suffice to illustrate the clash of forces at work. This can be shown clearly in the history of the College of William and Mary. The early intention and motives of the Virginia Assembly in proposing a college to be established was couched in these terms in 1661:

> Whereas the want of able and faithful ministers of this countrey deprives us of those great blessings and mercies that always attend upon the service of God; which want, by reason of our great distance from our native country, cannot in probability be always supplied from thence: Bee it enacted, that for the advance of learning, education of youth, supply of the ministry, and promotion of piety, there be land taken up or purchased for a colledge and free school: . . .[30]

[29] Montgomery, *op. cit.,* pp. 187, 234–241.
[30] Hening, W. W., *Statutes at Large . . . of Virginia* (Richmond, 1809), Vol. II, p. 56.

When the charter was granted in 1693, similar expressions were made concerning the purpose to train ministers, teach youth piety, letters, and manners, and bring Christianity to the Indians. To this end four schools consisting of six professors were established: (1) a school of sacred theology with one professor of Hebrew and the Scriptures and one professor of divinity according to the doctrine of the Church of England; (2) a school of philosophy with one professor teaching rhetoric, logic and ethics and another teaching physics, metaphysics, and mathematics; (3) a school with one professor to teach Greek and Latin; and (4) a school with one professor to teach Indian boys the three R's and religion. This remained the general design of the college until the Revolution.

The change in spirit wrought by the eighteenth-century Enlightenment is strikingly illustrated in the proposals that Thomas Jefferson made for reconstructing the traditional curriculum of William and Mary in 1779.[31] His proposals were not accepted, but they show the more secular and more practical as well as less classical emphasis he would have made if he had been successful. Jefferson discussed the religious intent of the original founders by simply summing up their efforts as "a scheme for cultivating and disseminating useful knowledge in this country, which had been proposed by some of its liberal minded inhabitants." He proposed that the original six professorships be reconstituted into eight professorships as follows:

1. Ethics (moral philosophy, law of nature, law of nations) and fine arts (sculpture, painting, gardening, music, architecture, poetry, oratory, criticism)
2. Law (municipal law—common law, equity, merchant law, maritime law, ecclesiastical law; economics—politics, commerce)
3. History (civil, ecclesiastical)
4. Mathematics (pure—arithmetic, geometry; mixed—mechanics, optics, acoustics, astronomy)
5. Medicine and anatomy
6. Natural philosophy (chemistry, statics, hydrostatics, pneumatics, agriculture) and natural history (animals—zoology; vegetables—botany; minerals—mineralogy)
7. Ancient languages (oriental—Hebrew, Chaldee, Syriac; northern—Gothic, Anglo-Saxon, Old Icelandic)
8. Modern languages (French, Italian, German)

Notice that the following secularizing transformations were proposed: The theological professor of Hebrew and Scriptures was to become a pro-

[31] Roy J. Honeywell, *The Educational Work of Thomas Jefferson* (Cambridge, Harvard University Press, 1931). See also Julian P. Boyd, ed., *The Papers of Thomas Jefferson* (Princeton, Princeton University Press, 1950), Vol. 2, pp. 535–543.

fessor of ancient languages of Northern Europe as well as of the Middle East; Biblical explication was omitted and the origin of modern European languages was emphasized.

The theological professor of divinity and apologetics was to become a professor of civil and ecclesiastical history; thus the character of teaching was changed from inculcation and defense of a specific religious position to the objective study of religious as well as political institutions. The professor of Latin and Greek was to become a professor of the modern languages.

The two professorships in philosophy were to become three professorships with greatly expanded work in modern politics and economics, in the several pure and applied sciences, and in fine and practical arts. The obvious intent was to discard the Aristotelian and scholastic philosophy of the medieval world and to modernize the teaching with strong infusions of Enlightenment political, economic, and scientific and technological thought.

Two entirely new professorships in law and in medicine were to be added.

Here was Jefferson's ideal of a higher education as an instrument of preparation for leadership in public service, in the professions, in science and technology, and in the arts in place of preparation for the ministry, classical scholarship, and the inculcation of the tenets of an established religion. The unkindest cut of all was his suggestion that in place of the religious school for Indians the faculty should appoint "a missionary, of approved veracity, to the several tribes of Indians, whose business shall be to investigate their laws, customs, religions, traditions, and more particularly their languages, constructing grammars thereof, as well as may be, and copious vocabularies, and, on oath, to communicate, from time to time, to the said president and professors, the materials he collects, to be by them laid up and preserved in their library." This proposal would have had the effect of transforming the teacher of the Indians into a missionary-anthropologist.

Presumably this and the other proposals were too much for the Anglican board of control, for they were rejected. Jefferson lived 100 years too soon, but by the end of the nineteenth century what he proposed here was actually taking place in essence in dozens of colleges and universities throughout the United States.

PUBLIC VERSUS PRIVATE CONTROL OF EDUCATION

The foregoing proposals by Jefferson for the reform of higher education in Virginia were a part of a larger plan for a comprehensive scheme of state education from lowest to highest levels under public control. To give meaning to the term "public control" and to indicate why those were fighting words and why Jefferson's scheme for a state system of education was defeated in his day, it is necessary to look at the different meanings given to the term "public school" or "public education" during the colonial period.

To point up the contrast, a "private school" in the colonies referred to a school run for the profit of the teacher as a business venture. The private teacher was free to accept or reject pupils as he saw fit; he could manage his school according to his own ideas apart from public supervision; and he was paid fees according to contractual arrangements as agreed upon between parents and the teacher. In the seventeenth century these schools were largely of an elementary variety designed to teach the mere rudiments of the three R's, but they also sometimes included private tutors who contracted to teach the classics; in the eighteenth century the term also applied to private venture "English" schools designed to teach a wide variety of useful and practical as well as ornamental skills (see p. 113 and pp. 124–126 in Chapter 4).

The term "public school," however, was used in two basically different ways in the American colonies. In general, a "public school" in the colonial period in New England meant a school set up by government authority, whether the colonial legislature or town government, but usually under the direct supervision of town governments through the town meeting and selectmen. This meant that the school came under open inspection and direction by some governmentally appointed official and the teacher was hired and authorized to teach by governmental authority or license. It meant that the school was open to the public and that parents had the right to send their children to the public school; indeed they were often expected to do so. But the school was usually not free of expense to the parents. Parents were expected to pay fees to support the school which often also received some financial support from governmental sources whether by land grant, lottery, tolls, license fees, assessments, or taxes. The school was thus not run for profit but received aid from gifts and endowments; or in some cases public-spirited citizens and parents would voluntarily agree to contribute certain amounts to the support of the school over a specified period of time.

In the South, however, the "public school" followed more closely the English meaning of the term as it had developed over a period of several centuries. The "public school" was typically established under the authority of a governmental agency, whether royal governor or legislature, but its management was delegated by charter or legislative act to a body of men or corporation which was given the power to supervise and direct the conduct of the school. The principal distinction was therefore this: In the South and soon in the middle colonies the government delegated the power to administer the "public school" to a corporate group of persons with the right to collect funds, own property, hire teachers, build buildings, and determine the curriculum and teaching methods; whereas in New England the government entrusted such powers to government officials as such.

The common features of "public schools" throughout the colonies included the following: parents had the right to send their children to a public school; its policies, purposes, standards, and curriculum were determined not by the teacher but by a governing board who exercised some kind of supervision and approval; the school was not run for profit or the private gain of the teacher; the teacher was not a self-employed enterpriser but an employee of the governing board or trustees; the parents paid a larger or smaller share of the financial operation of the school, but government often contributed financial aid; and the curriculum consisted principally of Latin grammar and other liberal arts rather than the rudiments of the three R's in the vernacular.

In common usage in the seventeenth century a "free school" usually meant the same thing as a "public school" with the added stipulation that poor children whose parents could not afford to pay were instructed free of charge. A "free school" in the seventeenth century was not free for all who attended but simply meant that poor children would be taught free. The terms "public school" and "free school" nearly always had the common meaning that they referred to a Latin grammar school rather than a vernacular school for the three R's.

In the course of the eighteenth century certain distinctive changes occurred in the meaning of these terms. A "free school" began to be applied more commonly to schools offering the rudiments of the three R's and giving instruction free to poor children. They changed their character from Latin grammar schools that admitted some poor children on a gratis basis to elementary schools of the three R's designed to give gratis or charity education to children who could not afford it. The stimulus to this change came from the work of organized religious agencies such as the Society for the Propagation of the Gospel and the work of the several denominations in their efforts to promote religious instruction as well as literacy among the common people.

A "free school" thus changed its character. It became less and less a classical grammar school for the upper classes with some free places for poor children. It became more and more an elementary, vernacular, religious, and charity school for the underprivileged, supported by private, voluntary donations, subscriptions, and endowment rather than by government funds. This was substantially the character of elementary education at the end of the eighteenth century when the movement for "free public schools" got under way in the first half of the nineteenth century. It was then realized that if elementary vernacular education was to become genuinely free for all and not just for the poor that the free school would have to become a "common school" under "public," i.e., government control, rather than under private, charitable, or religious control.

In the course of the eighteenth century a significant change likewise began to appear in the meaning of "public school." One of the best examples of this trend was in Pennsylvania where at first William Penn intended that the state government should promote public schools.[32] His *Frame of Government* written in 1682 and approved the same year by the first Assembly of Pennsyl-

[32] Wickersham, *op. cit.*, pp. 33 ff.

vania stated that "the Governor and Provincial Council shall erect and order all public schools. . . ." Penn wrote his *Frame of Government* in England where he had attended the "free grammar school" at Chigwell in Essex County, and he therefore knew at first hand the meaning of an English "public school" and evidently intended to bring the promotion of such schools under the control of his new government in Pennsylvania. If he had been able to pursue his original intentions, Pennsylvania might have followed the New England pattern of government control and supervision of "public schools."

The Quaker intention to follow this lead is further indicated by Thomas Budd's proposals of 1685 in which he urged that public schools be provided in all towns and cities with teachers chosen by the governor and General Assembly. He even went so far as to recommend that parents be required by law to send their children to the public schools for at least seven years, or longer if they desired. But the idea of government control of public schools was not to win out in Pennsylvania for more than 150 years, and the idea of compulsory attendance was even longer in taking hold.

It very soon developed that government control of public schools could not be achieved in a colony where mixed religious beliefs soon developed into hostile sectarian rivalries. Apparently fearing that the Quakers who were in control of the assembly would provide public schools to propagate the Quaker faith, opposition arose to the control by the state of public schools. As early as 1689 Penn ordered the president of the council to set up a "public grammar school," to which Penn issued a formal charter in 1696, but he granted control and supervision of the school to the Monthly Meeting of Quakers rather than to public officials. Then in 1701 a new charter gave all power not to the Monthly Meeting but to a private board of overseers consisting of fifteen Quakers. Now whether this method of delegating control over schools to a private corporation was Penn's original intention or whether he was persuaded to take these steps by the Pennsylvania Quakers or by the opposition to government control on the part of antagonistic sects is a moot question.

Penn's actions might well have been caused by opposition from the other religious sects because the Charter of Privileges granted by Penn in 1701 as the new organic law of the colony contained no provision on education at all, whereupon acts of Assembly in 1712 and 1713 provided that all religious denominations of Protestants would be permitted lawfully to buy land for the erection and support of schools. Thus, by the time that Benjamin Franklin came to propose his "public school" he followed the then current practice of obtaining a charter from the state which granted the privilege of establishing a school to a corporation made up of a board of trustees for the management, conduct, and supervision of the school. This is the pattern that today would be called a private school, but it is noteworthy that Franklin thought of it as a "public school." He did not follow Budd's conception of state control and, probably, in light of the policy that had developed in Pennsylvania of delegating authority to corporations to conduct education he could not have done so.

The middle of the eighteenth century was the high point of private conduct of schools, a pattern stimulated by the rivalry of the religious sects growing out of the Great Awakening. Even New England was faltering in its loyalty to governmental control of "public schools" as the Congregational groups were split asunder by the revivals and Jonathan Edwards was pleading with wealthy men to pour some of their wealth into "establishing and supporting Schools in poor Towns and Villages" in order to help bring up children in common learnings and vital piety. In New York William Livingston in 1753 proposed that the legislature enact a law for establishing two grammar schools in every county to be under the control of a board of guardians who were to be elected by the people and whose job was to hire teachers and pay their salaries out of taxes laid upon the inhabitants.[33] This proposal if it had been accepted would have changed the meaning of "public school" in New York to include government support and control. Livingston's efforts in behalf of state control of secondary schools were only incidental to his basic fight to achieve state control over the projected college in New York City, which became King's College and later Columbia College. But Livingston made little headway with either of these proposals, just as other efforts to increase the range of state or governmental control over education failed in the colonial period.

The battleground over public control prior to the end of the Revolution was principally the colonial colleges. All nine of them were founded largely on the model of the English "public schools" in that they were managed by corporate bodies of trustees or overseers which were charged by the legislatures or the crown with the conduct of the institutions but which received considerable amounts of financial aid from governmental sources. But from the middle of the eighteenth century onward the growing democratic forces in several colonies began to re-examine the principle whereby the governments had delegated so much authority to close corporations to operate as they pleased and free from governmental inspection, supervision, or approval. The idea began to emerge as a part of the Enlightenment philosophy that a republican or democratic government was the only proper agency to represent the whole public in the conduct of an institution that professed to serve the public. This outlook led to several attempts to transform the private, self-perpetuating close corporations of the colleges into genuinely public corporations appointed by the civil authority and responsive to it.

One of the most interesting and illuminating of the conflicts of ideas about the control of education was the controversy over the founding of King's College in New York City. This controversy was not only interesting because the proposals and ideas came into head-on collision, but because it revealed

[33] *The Independent Reflector,* Number L, Thursday, November 8, 1753.

the complicated political, economic, and religious forces that were actually striving in the colony to affect educational policy and practice.[34] The forces lined up something like this: On one side were the Anglican religious forces in favor of an established church; the Tory political forces loyal to the crown and supporting the royal governor and majority of the council (such as James De Lancey and Cadwallader Colden); and the large landed aristocracy and merchant class, who desired conservative economic policies favorable to private property (represented by the De Lancey family). On the other side were the dissenter religious groups, principally the Presbyterians, Baptists, Dutch Reformed, French Huguenots, and German Lutherans, who believed in separation of church and state, at least when it came to opposing the power of Trinity Church and the Anglicans; the republican and democratic political forces, who favored larger authority for the colonial legislature as over against the Crown's royal agents; and large elements of the middle and lower economic classes, whose concerns were cheap land, easy credit, and freedom from the mercantilist restraints of England and the large landlords of the Hudson River Valley.

Therefore, when the proposal was made and acts were passed in the assembly between 1746 and 1751 for the establishment of a college in New York to be founded and supported initially by a public lottery, these forces began to line up and jump into the battle. The act of 1751 vested the public funds in a board of ten trustees, consisting of seven Anglicans, two Dutch Reformists, and one Presbyterian, who were to formulate the plans for incorporating the college and getting it under way. The Presbyterian member of the board was William Livingston, scion of the prominent and wealthy Livingston family which was fighting the De Lanceys for political power. Then the fight began in earnest.

The Anglican members of the board wanted the college to be granted a charter from the crown and to be incorporated as a close corporation according to the common pattern of English control of education. Livingston argued instead that the legislature was the proper authority to control the college and should set up a public corporation to govern the college inasmuch as public funds were involved. Livingston and two of his lawyer associates, John Marin Scott and William Smith, Jr., carried on a most vigorous public campaign in the columns of the weekly paper called the *Independent Reflector,* which they edited.[35] Here Livingston argued that a college chartered by the crown would become a private corporation unresponsive to public needs or requirements and would be used to further the sectarian, political, and economic ambitions of the Church of England and the aristocratic classes. It would

---

[34] See, for example, Dorothy R. Dillon, *The New York Triumvirate* (New York, Columbia University Press), 1949.

[35] See the six issues numbered XVII to XXII of the *Independent Reflector* for March 22, 29, April 5, 12, 19, and 26, 1753.

become a "party college" promoting partisan aims but using public funds to achieve its ends.

He and his friends argued vigorously and repeatedly that the college should be a state institution, established as a public corporation by act of the legislature, whose board of control would be appointed by the legislature, and whose acts would be subject to legislative review and approval. He demanded that no particular religious profession be established in the college and that all members of denominations be equally entitled to hold any office or attend as a student. He argued for regular religious services and compulsory attendance by students twice a day, but he wanted the services to be nonsectarian services agreed upon in common by all Protestant sects; he wanted no professor of divinity or theology. Degrees were to be granted only in the secular fields of the arts, sciences, and civil law, and that while "free Conversation upon polemical and controverted Points in Divinity, be not discountenanced," nevertheless "all public Disputations upon the various Tenets of different Professions of Protestants, be absolutely forbidden."

This was a thoroughgoing attempt to define the role of a college that would serve all the people of a community divided along religious lines. Livingston saw that such a public college could not be in the hands of or under the control of one religious group if it were to serve the genuinely public purpose of preparing *all* youth for citizenship. The only agency that could safely be entrusted to guide the destinies of such a public institution was the agency that represented all the people in common, i.e., the civil authority whose principal agency was the legislature.

Public opinion was raised to fever heat by the pamphleteering that went on, political maneuvering was rampant on both sides, and charges and counter-charges were leveled back and forth. The Anglican party finally won out, and a charter was granted to the college by the crown, but only after certain compromises and concessions were made. The result and the political aspect of the result are clearly revealed in a letter written by the rector of Trinity Church, leader of the Anglican forces, to the prospective president of the new college, Samuel Johnson, whose step-son had been active in the campaign against Livingston. Referring to the protest that Livingston had made in the New York legislature against the granting of a charter by the royal governor in the name of the crown, the Reverend Henry Barclay thus summed up the close call and then the victory that the Anglican party achieved:

> They had a majority of fourteen to eight, but three of our friends were absent, and it was with much difficulty that they were prevented from censuring the conduct of the Trustees and returning thanks to Livingston. We were all afraid that this would have retarded the Sealing of the Charter, and some well-wishers to the thing would have consented to the retarding of it, had not the Governor [James De Lancey] appeared resolute and come to town on Saturday and fixed the Seal to it; and to do him justice, he has given us a good majority of Churchmen

[Anglicans], no less than eleven of the Vestry [of Trinity Parish] being of the number. There are but eight of the Dutch Church, most of them good men and true, and two Dissenters.[36]

The deal by which the Anglicans won the promise of support by the Dutch Reformed group in the legislature to vote for further financial aid to the new college is described by the rector as follows:

I went from Mr. Chambers' to Mr. Watts' . . . , and met two Dutch members coming out of his house, who, as he told me, came to make proposals for an accommodation, and all they desired was a Dutch Professor of Divinity, which, if granted, they would all join us, and give the money. This I doubt not will be done unless the Governor should oppose it, who is much incensed at the Dutch for petitioning the Assembly on that head, but I make no doubt but he may be pacified.[37]

In a postscript Barclay listed the line-up of the original board of trustees and indicated that the college's affairs were safely in the hands of the Anglican contingency:

I have not time to give you a list of the Governors, nor indeed can I recollect them all. The whole number is forty-one: seventeen *ex officio* and twenty-four private gentlemen, in which number there are at present but eight of the Dutch Church, the French, Lutheran, Presbyterian Ministers, and Will. Livingston,—so that we have a majority of twenty-nine to twelve, and in these twelve are included Mr. Richards, John Cruger, Leonard Lispenard, and the Treasurer, all our good friends.[38]

At about the same time and continuing into the next decade a somewhat similar move was made in Connecticut to exert greater legislative control over Yale College. In 1754 the legislature stopped giving public funds to the college, and subsequently several efforts were made to set up visitorial powers over the college corporation whereby the legislature could inspect and approve the actions of the corporation. President Thomas Clap, however, was able to stave off this effort to exert public control over the college by arguing that the college had really been founded by a group of private individuals and that the legislature had merely acquiesced in the establishment of an essentially private and close corporation.

In Pennsylvania the efforts to establish public control over the College of Philadelphia were more successful but only for a short time. In 1779 the charter was revoked by a legislature dominated by Presbyterians, and the University of Pennsylvania was established under public control, but this

---

[36] E. Edwards Beardsley, *Life and Correspondence of Samuel Johnson* (New York, Hurd & Houghton, 1874), p. 196; also contained in Herbert and Carol Schneider, *Samuel Johnson* (New York, Columbia University Press, 1929), Vol. IV, pp. 24–25.

[37] *Ibid.*, pp. 196–197. On May 7, 1755, at the first meeting of the board of trustees of the college after the formal presentation of the charter, the board voted to recommend the establishment of a professor of divinity to teach according to the doctrine, discipline, and worship of the National Synod of Dort (Dutch Reformed).

[38] *Ibid.*, p. 197.

arrangement lasted only ten years at which time a realignment of the political forces in the state resulted in the re-establishment of the original corporation long dominated by the Anglicans. After two years, during which the two institutions existed side by side, the two were merged and control given to a private corporation.

The final instance to be mentioned here of the growth of the idea of public education under public control is seen in Jefferson's attempts to revise the laws of the state of Virginia in 1779. He saw more keenly than anyone up to his time that public schools aiming to serve the whole public must be under governmental direction and free from religious or sectarian or private control. He saw, too, more fully than anyone up to his time that such an education under public control must extend from the lowest to the highest levels and include a comprehensive system of elementary schools and secondary schools capped by a state university. Others had been concerned to achieve direct governmental control of one or more levels of schools, but Jefferson saw the need for a complete system of public education. These proposals were a part of his general concern to revise the whole code of laws in Virginia in order to bring them into line with the needs of an independent and republican state and a democratic form of society and thus do away with the political, economic, and social injustices of a colonial society based upon aristocratic privilege and class distinctions.

Jefferson's proposal for a system of public elementary and secondary schools was contained in his *Bill for the More General Diffusion of Knowledge* introduced in the Virginia Assembly in 1779.[39] He based his argument for public schools upon the grounds that a free society devoted to achieving the natural rights of its citizens can be maintained and tyranny prevented only if the people in general are well educated. Wise laws will be made and well administered only if the capable persons have equal opportunity to achieve a liberal education without regard to wealth or social status. Therefore, all children should have a chance at education at public expense.

Jefferson proposed that the citizens of each county in the state elect three aldermen to have general charge of schools in the county and arrange to divide the county into hundreds (or wards) in each of which an elementary school should be established and maintained at county expense. The aldermen were to appoint an overseer (or superintendent) over every ten of the district schools; his duties were to appoint the teachers, visit and supervise the teaching, examine the pupils, and carry out the instructions of the College of William and Mary. The teachers' salaries and board and lodging were to be paid by public funds levied upon the inhabitants of the wards, and all free children were to be entitled to free tuition for at least three years and as much longer at private expense as their parents wished. The curriculum was to consist of reading, writing, arithmetic, and the history of

[39] Honeywell, *op. cit.,* pp. 199–205. See also Boyd, *op. cit.,* pp. 526–535.

Greece, Rome, England, and America. Notable in this connection was the secular character of the curriculum wherein Jefferson proposed that history be substituted for religious instruction and reading of the Bible.

Jefferson also provided for a system of grammar or secondary schools. The state was to be divided into regional districts consisting of several counties each, and in each regional district a grammar school was to be established. The schools were to be under the supervision of a public board of visitors who were to appoint the teachers, visit the schools, examine the students, and provide for the acquisition of land and the building of the schools at public expense. The maintenance of the schools was to be paid for by private tuition, but also the best students from the elementary schools were to be selected and sent to the grammar schools at public expense. These "public foundationers" should be examined each year and only the best continued on at public expense, and finally the best student in each grammar school was to be chosen to attend the College of William and Mary for a full college course at full public expense.

The curriculum of the grammar schools was to consist of Latin, Greek, English, geography, and higher arithmetic—a typical college preparatory program but again omitting religious instruction. Whereas this was not a proposal for entirely free secondary education, it was a far cry from the attitude of Governor William Berkeley 100 years earlier who exclaimed that he thanked God there were no free schools in Virginia to be the seed beds of disobedience and heresy against the constituted state and church.

To complete his proposals for a public system of education Jefferson introduced an accompanying bill in the legislature in 1779 to amend the charter of the College of William and Mary and to bring it under direct civil direction.[40] Arguing that the college had not fulfilled the expectations of the public for nearly 100 years and that it would become more useful for the public service under a changed form of government, Jefferson proposed that the board of visitors be reduced in number and that they be appointed by vote of the legislature. This was quite similar to Livingston's proposals for King's College. Furthermore, the board so constituted should no longer be constrained by the laws of England or the regulations of the Church of England. The college was to be supported by a duty on the export of tobacco. All this would have had the effect of transforming the college from a private corporation into a public corporation and would have made the sectarian private college into a secular state university.

Jefferson was making a genuine effort to reform education along the lines of the liberal thought of the Enlightenment with its growing respect for human reason, science, humanitarianism, and republicanism (as described in Chapter 2), but he found standing athwart his efforts not only the orthodoxies of the colonial period but also the rigidities of such cultural patterns

[40] Honeywell, *op. cit.*, pp. 205–210.

as established religion and class distinctions (as described in Chapter 1). Until these patterns were changed to provide for separation of church and state and more equal opportunity in political, economic, and social participation, Jefferson found it difficult to make much headway in the reform of education. Gains were being made in some ways and in some places by the time of the Revolutionary period, but the state of Virginia was not yet ready to venture upon the road to genuinely public education at either the lower or higher levels. The hold of the established church had not yet been broken, and the sectarian rivalries were still so great that they could not agree upon the essentials of a common school or a state university. Thus Virginia allowed other states to blaze the way toward the kind of public education under government control which eventually became the most commonly accepted solution for a population of heterogeneous backgrounds and which proved to be one of the most distinctive contributions of American culture to the world.

ISSUES FOR STUDY AND DISCUSSION

1. Many critics of modern education are disturbed about the "soft pedagogy" of today. Do you think they would prefer the viewpoint of Cotton Mather and Jonathan Edwards? Does it help any to realize that the origins of "soft pedagogy" are at least 250 years old?

2. Similarly, many critics of modern education are opposed to the utilitarian and practical nature of recent secondary and higher education. What difference does it make to know that these movements are also at least 200 years old?

3. The development of private education reached its high point in the middle of the eighteenth century. Look again at the reasons for this movement, and try to judge in what respects they are similar to or different from the conditions today.

4. What do you think were the most important obstacles to the achievement of public control of higher education in the eighteenth century? How would you estimate the strength and weaknesses of our inherited traditions in this respect?

5. Some people today argue that private and religious schools are more American than public schools. Is this a sound argument? On the other hand, some argue that a dual system of schools based upon religious or class lines will promote divisions among our people. Does your study of the colonial period lead you to agree or disagree with this proposition?

SUGGESTIONS FOR FURTHER READING

Arrowood, Charles F., *Thomas Jefferson and Education in a Republic,* New York, McGraw-Hill, 1930.
Brumbaugh, Martin G., *The Life and Works of Christopher Dock,* Philadelphia, Lippincott, 1908.
Butts, R. Freeman, *The College Charts Its Course,* New York, McGraw-Hill, 1939.
Curti, Merle, *The Social Ideas of American Educators,* New York, Scribner, 1935.

Fleming, Sandford, *Children and Puritanism,* New Haven, Yale University Press, 1933.

Honeywell, Roy J., *The Educational Work of Thomas Jefferson,* Cambridge, Harvard University Press, 1931.

Kiefer, Monica, *American Children Through Their Books, 1700–1835,* Philadelphia, University of Pennsylvania Press, 1948.

Knight, Edgar W., *A Documentary History of Education in the South before 1860,* Chapel Hill, University of North Carolina Press, 1949–1952, Vols. 1–3.

Morison, Samuel Eliot, *The Founding of Harvard College,* Cambridge, Harvard University Press, 1935.

———, *Harvard College in the Seventeenth Century,* Cambridge, Harvard University Press, 1936, 2 vols.

———, *The Puritan Pronaos,* New York, New York University Press, 1936.

Reisner, Edward H., *The Evolution of the Common School,* New York, Macmillan, 1930.

Ulich, Robert, *History of Educational Thought,* New York, American Book, 1945.

Walsh, James J., *Education of the Founding Fathers; Scholasticism in the Colonial Colleges,* New York, Fordham University Press, 1935.

Wigglesworth, Michael, *The Day of Doom,* New York, Spiral, 1929.

Woody, Thomas, *Educational Views of Benjamin Franklin,* New York, McGraw-Hill, 1931.

———, *A History of Women's Education in the United States,* New York, Science Press, 1929, 2 vols.

PREVAILING PATTERNS
OF EDUCATION

THIS CHAPTER will attempt to describe the dominant forms of education that appeared in the colonial period as a result of the major cultural patterns, the main streams of thought, and the educational outlooks described in the first three chapters. What actually happened in the educational world reflected the interweaving of these social trends and intellectual conflicts. Particular attention will be given to the types of control and support of educational institutions, the dominants in curriculum content and method, and the nature of the teaching profession.

A few generalizations at the outset may help to guide the reader through the various problems to be discussed. In Chapter 1 three major cultural patterns were described. These were: (1) the movement toward representative forms of political control; (2) the gradual weakening of established religions in the face of a growing diversity and freedom of religion; and (3) the emergence of a strong middle class, a capitalistic economic system, and sectional rivalries. All of these developments had profound influence not only upon colonial education but also upon the more recent patterns of American education.

The transfer of political authority to the American colonies by means of delegation of power from the English crown to stock companies, to individual proprietors, to royal governors, or to colonial legislatures included the power to initiate and control education. This meant that the civil government had exerted authority over education from the beginning, whether such authority was exercised by stock company officials, by the proprietors or their agents, or by the royal governor and his council. When the colonial legislatures grew in power either by delegation of right from the crown or by their own insistence, they, too, gradually came to claim responsibility for education and to exert their authority over schools and colleges. This is a most significant principle, for when the colonies became free and independent states, they carried over this authority and responsibility for education into their new status. The right of democratic states to conduct public schools and to permit private schools to operate rests upon the authority, the consent, and the participation of the people of the community as expressed and carried out through the agencies of the civil government.

Schools in the colonial period were not only widely authorized by the civil government, but they were also dominantly religious in purpose and content. This was principally the result of the widespread maintenance of established religions. When the church and the state were allies, it was natural for the state to authorize and indeed require that education be appropriately religious. Thus, in all those colonies where specific churches were established, the publicly approved education would also be concerned to perpetuate the publicly approved religion. When, however, dissident and nonconformist religious groups grew in numbers and strength, they began to agitate for public approval of *their* right to conduct their own religious schools. Great effort and persistent struggles were often required to win this right against the opposition of the established churches and the ruling political groups. This movement led (1) to the demand for private forms of education in addition to or in place of the colonial forms of public education, (2) to a gradual weakening of the public education controlled by the civil government, and (3) to a decline in state systems of education devoted to the religious principles of a single church.

The eighteenth century thus saw the emergence of new forms of educational control, principally to allow for religious diversity. Private corporations were organized to which the state delegated the power to conduct educational institutions. This pattern was borrowed from the practices of merchant capitalism whereby private corporations sought the right to conduct business by charter from the civil authorities. Boards of trustees or boards of governors were set up with the right to hold property and to manage the affairs of a school or college without further supervision from the state authorities. This political and economic invention was resorted to in the effort to grant freedom to religious groups and to private groups of like-minded individuals to conduct education as they saw fit. It was a logical and necessary development in a day when it was commonly agreed that education must be religious and that a state religion should no longer be imposed upon all persons in violation of their own religious beliefs.

In a society where religious freedom is allowed but where education must be religious, a common public school system for all children is well nigh impossible. In the eighteenth century prior to the Revolution the people cherished religious freedom and a diversity of religious education more than they cherished a common school system. To maintain religious freedom and at the same time achieve a common school system the people would have to decide to exclude religion from the common school and to nourish religion in their homes and churches. The American people finally decided to take this route in the nineteenth century, but they we·e not yet ready to do it in the colonial period. The only other alternative is to allow each religious group to control its own schools and to share in public funds. This alternative was also tried in the colonial period and in the nineteenth century, but it was soon realized that the common values of a democratic society could not be achieved by such divisive practices. And so this alternative was likewise abandoned. But in the colonial period diversity of religion and of nationality, which often went together, seemed more important than political or social community. Thus the state patterns of education established in the colonial period began to decline until community values were elevated again in the nineteenth century in the effort to establish a new nation devoted to freedom, equality, and democracy.

Another cultural pattern that stood in the way of democratic ideals in the colonial period was the social class system inherited from Europe. This meant that one kind of education was considered appropriate for the upper classes and another type for the lower class. A dual system of education was almost universally present in the American colonies. Latin grammar schools and colleges were designed for the use of the upper classes, whereas elementary schools and the apprenticeship system were designed for the lower classes. In the course of the eighteenth century some cracks were made in the wall separating the two types of schools, but by and large the dual system was maintained throughout the colonial period.

The principal changes appeared as a rising merchant and trading class began to press for an education more appropriate to their interests. Private instruction in the more useful and utilitarian subjects began to be given in the commercial centers and then appeared in the new type secondary school that came to be known as the academy which held its popularity for over 100 years into the nineteenth century. The expansion of the capitalist movement thus had a democratizing influence in the eighteenth century, but it also helped to heighten the sectional rivalries that grew up between the "backwoods" farmers and the seacoast merchants. This led to battles over town control of schools, weakened further the centralized civil authority over education, and resulted in the emergence of the district system of control.

The backwoods people saw little use in the upper-class Latin schools designed for preparation for college and resisted the taxes required for their support. They wanted simply the rudiments of the three R's as sufficient for their simple needs and occupations. The backwoodsmen were also likely to be religious dissenters and newly arrived "foreigners" from non-English countries of Europe. Desiring to maintain their own religious and national cultures, they sought to conduct their own schools and resisted the effort to Anglicize or Americanize them. State schools under civil authority thus had another obstacle to overcome in the movement toward a common culture.

Until the secular ideas of the Enlightenment could overcome national and religious isolation, the idea of a public school under the control and support of the civil authority could not win its way. Here the development of modern science, rationalism, natural rights, and democratic and humanitarian ideas (as described in Chapters 2 and 3) ultimately became supporters of the public school idea, but not very successfully until the nineteenth century. The colonial period thus established patterns of education that held promise for the kind of educational solutions that were to come but also set loose conflicting forces that have caused serious problems for American society and education that still remain with us.

DOMINANT TYPES OF CONTROL AND SUPPORT OF EDUCATION

Most of the colonies founded in the seventeenth century soon gave evidence that government was looked to as high authority in educational affairs. The records of colonial legislatures, town meetings, parish meetings, and county courts are full of references to educational matters. In the eighteenth century, however, the civil authority began to delegate the management of schools and colleges to private corporations and to permit private individuals to conduct schools. The state did not retreat from its position of authority, but it did retreat in some cases from direct administration and supervision of schools and turned these functions of direct management over to private directors. A few illustrations of these dominant forms of educational control must suffice.

Government Control of Schools and Colleges

New England. In general the New England colonies legislated earlier and oftener on a wider range of educational matters than any other group of colonies. In this process Massachusetts usually took the lead, followed closely by Connecticut and somewhat later by New Hampshire. Rhode Island with its passion for freedom from state control proved the exception and gave relatively little colony-wide attention to education. Stemming from the Puritan zeal for religious conformity, from the group efforts at town making, and from the desire to build a new society upon collective principles, the towns and legislatures of Massachusetts and Connecticut began to legislate on educational matters soon after the colonies were established.

The first steps to establish schools were taken by several Massachusetts towns, and since the town meeting was the principle political agency at work in these early days, it was only natural that the town meeting turned its attention to schools as well as to other political, economic, religious, and social matters. In Massachusetts Boston began the process in 1635 and soon after was followed by the towns of Charlestown, Ipswich, Salem, Dorchester, Newbury, and Cambridge. In Connecticut New Haven and Hartford were among the first towns to establish schools. This early concern for education resulted in the establishment of town schools for the teaching of Latin grammar. This was the means by which boys of that period could proceed to higher education and could gain a liberal education appropriate for leadership in church and state. The motives were mixed. The Puritans were representatives of the Renaissance belief in classical humanism as the best road to a liberal education, the Reformation belief in religion as the staple of any kind of education, and the English class system that looked upon a classical education as the road to upper-class preferment. Thus, the early concern for a Latin school in the New England towns arose because the towns contained a relatively high proportion of persons who had known this type of education in England.

The initiative in founding schools in New England was usually taken by the town governments representing all the free citizens entitled to vote. The town authorities either began by appointing a schoolmaster to open a school or by giving town authority to a schoolmaster who had already opened a school as a private venture. Often the town would grant a parcel of public land for the building and support of a school as well as lending aid to a process of subscriptions voluntarily undertaken by the citizens. Most of the towns accepted as a matter of course that the schools thus set up should be under the supervision of the town authorities, whether selectmen, magistrates, or ministers, all of whom were public officials. The schools were thus "public schools" in the sense that they existed by authority of the town government; all parents had the right to send their children to them; the town contributed public lands and sometimes funds to their support; and the town officials inspected and supervised the conduct of the schools. But they were *not* "public" in the sense that they were totally supported by public funds and thus free of charge to everyone. Certain poor children could occasionally go to the schools free of charge, but commonly the parents who could afford to do so paid fees or tuition for their children's education, and by and large arrangements were made for the education of poor children in other ways than sending them to a Latin school.

Apparently not satisfied with the local initiative of towns in the matter of education and especially concerned about the rudiments of education among the lower classes, the Massachusetts General Court stepped into the picture to see that all children received an education of some kind. In 1641 Massachusetts adopted its first code of laws called *The Body of Liberties,* embodying a summary of English common law and liberties as deemed by the Puritans appropriate to their new commonwealth. It consisted of ninety-five articles dealing with the whole range of freedoms of life, person, property, family, and court proceedings, none of which liberties could be taken away without express law of the General Court or due process of law in the courts. Four of the sections had to do with the "Liberties of Children" concerning the inheritance of property, the rights of children to complain to the authorities about parents who treated them with "unnatural severitie," and the right of orphans to be disposed of only under the supervision of some court of law.[1]

The very next year the Massachusetts General Court undertook a further limitation on the rights of parents by passing its famous act of 1642 requiring parents and masters to see to the education of the children under their control and levying fines upon all adults who failed to do so. This was the first exercise of colonial civil authority requiring compulsory education of children. Parents were no longer to be free to neglect the education of their children. Basing its action upon the English Poor Law of 1601 that gave authority to parishes to see to the apprenticeship of children, the Massachusetts General Court not only required apprenticeship for poor children but also went further to require literacy in reading, orthodoxy in religion, and knowledge of the capital laws as the basic essentials of education necessary for all children in order that they might become good citizens of the state and of the established church. The town selectmen were given the authority to see that the requirements of the law were lived up to and to hail negligent parents or masters into court for punishment by fine.

No schools were established by the law of 1642, but its intent was to lay the obligation for education upon the adults responsible for the care of children. It reflected the political desire that children be educated properly for the sake of the commonwealth to be able to understand its laws; it showed the economic intent to see that children learn a trade that would be profitable to themselves and to society and to prevent the appearance of an unskilled pauper class; and it revealed the religious motive that children be brought up in orthodox religious principles. The ability to read English was considered to be basic to the achievement of these goals. The revision of this law in 1648 stated the case even more explicitly and was undoubtedly the version that was copied in the Connecticut laws of 1650, and in later laws of the New Haven Colony, Plymouth, and New Hampshire when the latter became independent of Massachusetts.

The next step undertaken by the colonial governments of New England was again initiated by the Massachusetts General Court when it passed its famous act of 1647 requiring the towns to establish schools. Apparently feeling that its requirements upon parents to educate their children could not legitimately be enforced unless schools were available for the children to attend, the General Court in the law of 1647 required every town of fifty or more families to appoint a teacher to give instruction in reading and writing,

---

[1] See F. C. Gray, "Remarks on the Early Laws of Massachusetts Bay," in *Collections of the Massachusetts Historical Society* (Boston, Little, Brown, 1848), 3d Series, Vol. VIII, p. 230.

such teacher to be paid by the parents of children who go to him or by the use of tax funds if the town meeting should so decide on that method. In addition, every town of 100 families was also required to appoint a schoolmaster to give instruction in Latin grammar in order to prepare boys for college. The establishment of Latin grammar schools was no longer to be left to local initiative but was to be required of the towns by the authority of the state government, and penalties by means of fines were to be levied upon negligent towns. The other New England colonies, except Rhode Island, soon followed suit, and they all passed a number of subsequent laws increasing the amount of the fines in order to prod reluctant towns into action.

Here was the principle that government had authority to control schools, and it was well enunciated in the New England colonies early in their histories. It was a principle of great importance, for it set a precedent in American life establishing the authority of the state to promote education as a public and civil matter. To be sure, in the colonial period the schools thus established were expected to inculcate the principles of the established religion, but when the separation of church and state was achieved in the late eighteenth and early nineteenth centuries in New England, the right of the state to conduct its own schools and to grant the privileges of education to private agencies rested upon these legal precedents.

The New England pattern consisted of four principles: the state could require children to be educated; the state could require towns to establish schools; the civil government could supervise and control schools by direct management in the hands of public officials; and public funds could be used for the support of public schools. As the eighteenth century progressed, the colonial legislatures showed a slackening of effort to require compulsory education and gave greater freedom to private groups to educate children in schools of their own preference.

Another development of great significance took place in the eighteenth century when the colonial legislatures began to give to the towns the right to divide themselves up into small local districts for the direct conduct and administration of schools. Thus a process of decentralization in control of education was begun. The General Court continued to assert its authority over education, but just as it had delegated the power to conduct schools to the towns in the seventeenth century, now it began to give this power to the local districts in the eighteenth century. This represented a response to the frontier conditions of life, the expansion of population into the backwoods areas and the outlying regions of the towns, and a conflict between the rural, agricultural sections and the urban, commercial sections of the towns. Because of the difficulties of travel, the parents of children in the outlying regions began to object to continuing their support of the school in the central town. It was difficult for the children to reach the town school, and furthermore the farm parents began to see little use in a Latin education for their children. When they saw any need for schooling at all, they thought in terms of the rudiments of the three R's. They, therefore, began to agitate for greater control of their own local district schools.

In response to the agitation of people from these local areas many of the New England towns began to arrange for the town teacher to travel from one part of the town to another and to teach the children in the outlying districts for a limited period each year. The teacher continued to be a town teacher, hired and supported by the selectmen under authority of the town meeting. This was the so-called "moving school." But because the "moving teacher" could spend so little time in each district and because the people of the district had no particular control over the teacher, a new arrangement was sometimes made, called the "divided school." Under this scheme the town authorities kept control over the schools, but they assigned a teacher to conduct a school in each of the districts of the town. But this was still not satisfactory, and by the end of the eighteenth century the legislatures were delegating to the local districts themselves full power to conduct and control schools. Thus arose the "district system" of school control, the ultimate in decentralization of educational administration. Districts were now authorized to establish and maintain a school, to build the school house, appoint the teacher, determine the curriculum and the length of the school year, and provide whatever funds they thought necessary or possible.

As the frontier swept further westward in the late eighteenth and early nineteenth centuries, the district system of administration of schools went along and eventually covered most of America. In a day when population was sparse, when travel was difficult, when the obligations of state governments were small, and when educational aspirations were low, the district system served a useful function. But when all of these conditions began to change in the nineteenth century, the weaknesses of the district system and its inability to provide equal educational opportunity became increasingly apparent. It was then that far-seeing educators began to try to overcome the weaknesses of decentralized control of schools and to reassert the authority of the state governments in educational control and support. But loyalty to the district system proved tenacious in both the nineteenth and twentieth centuries and often served to block educational progress and adaptation to new educational and social needs.

Southern colonies. The principle of state control of education in the South was not nearly so extensively practiced as it was in New England, but it was present from the beginning in several ways. The reasons for this difference are complicated, but some of them are apparent. One of the usual reasons assigned is that the Puritans of New England were more interested in promulgating their Calvinist religious doctrines than was the Church of England in the South. This may have been true in some respects, but perhaps even more important was the difference in attitude toward the educational role of the church in relation to the state. In England the episcopal system of church control had put almost complete authority for the conduct of church affairs into the hands of the bishops subject only to the final authority of the crown and Parliament. In 1603 the Canons of the Church of England had placed authority for the conduct of public and private schools in the hands of the bishop, who had the right to approve all teachers in his diocese. Thus, the Church of England had been given the right to control and supervise schools in England, and this pattern was transferred to the southern colonies where the civil authorities accordingly paid less attention to educational matters than in New England.

In contrast, religious affairs in New England were put into the hands of the local congregations because Congregationalism had revolted against episcopal control of religious affairs by bishops. Thus, when New Englanders came to the problem of establishing a uniform and widespread *system* of schools covering the whole colony, they had no alternative but to turn to the only agency that dealt with colony-wide matters, namely the General Court. Their Congregationalism not only prevented them from relying upon bishops, but they also resisted control by synods or higher church bodies that might exert authoritative direction over individual congregations. As a result, education was transferred from ecclesiastical agencies to the civil government which was represented by the General Court for the colony as a whole and by the town meetings for local affairs. Both of these agencies legislated on religious matters as well as on political, economic, and educational affairs, but they were instruments of civil government, not ecclesiastical.

The theory in the South, however, was that education in general was a matter for the Archbishop of Canterbury or the Bishop of London to decide. What the civil government did do, however, was to exercise authority over apprenticeship and the education of poor children, orphans, and illegitimate children. It thus did not presume to limit the rights of *all* parents but only to exert control over indigent parents and over children who had no parents. In these cases the state stepped in to exercise the functions of parents and to stand in their place.

Following the English pattern of poor laws and apprenticeship systems, the colonial legislatures of the South delegated the power of enforcement not to the town governments as in New England but to the parish authorities made up of the vestry and church wardens and sometimes to the county courts if the parish officials did not carry out their functions. The principal function of the vestry was to see that orphans and poor children were properly apprenticed and taught a trade. The apprenticeship indenture or contract was a matter of public record, and the courts were given jurisdiction to see that the terms of the contract were faithfully carried out.

Beginning in 1642, the colonial assembly of Virginia passed an apprenticeship act asserting its authority to see that guardians and masters undertook their responsibilities and giving power to the justices of the peace in each county to supervise the problem. Here, as in the case of New England, the state undertook to limit the rights of parents to do as they pleased with their children. Virginia was especially active in this field during the colonial period, enacting some seventeen laws concerning orphans and some eighteen laws concerning the apprenticeship of poor children up to the time of the Revolution. Of these, ten laws included reference to reading and writing as a part of the responsibility of the masters of apprenticed children.

The parishes in Virginia also undertook other educational functions but on a rather haphazard and unsystematic basis.[2] Occasionally, the parish minister taught a school for the children of his parish, charging fees for the parents who could pay and sometimes teaching poor children for nothing. Only rarely did a parish build a school building or pay tuition for parish poor children in a private school. Somewhat more common was the practice of asking parish and county officials to act as trustees or guardians for endowments to be administered in establishing and conducting endowed private schools. But here again only nine or ten such schools were established in Virginia in the whole colonial period and only seven of the ninety parishes had such schools. Poor children were given free instruction in these schools, and at least some of them admitted girls. The assembly also made several efforts to encourage parishes to set up workhouses for dependent children as a means of aiding the flax industry and of caring for the children, but the parishes seemed little interested.

Aside from the Virginia legislation concerning apprenticeship, which was followed by the other southern colonies, the most noteworthy action of the civil authorities in education in the South prior to the Revolution was in Maryland. In an act of 1694, amended in 1696, the legislature provided for the establishment of a quasi-public corporation consisting of high government and church officials whose duty it was to secure funds and formulate policy for the governing of schools, one in each county of the colony. The schools were to be Latin grammar schools, supported partially by public funds, and free in the English sense of the word, that is, free for poor children. The rules governing them were to conform with the laws of England, Maryland, and the Church of England. Here was a plan for a state system of schools somewhat like that of New England but even going further in centralized control. The corporation had a vague resemblance to the idea of a state board of education which appeared in many states in the nineteenth century. The Maryland board of trustees established King William's School in Annapolis (later St. John's College), but could get no further in providing schools for other counties. An act of 1723 went still further in envisioning a system of free schools, one for each county, to be supervised by a county board

[2] See Guy F. Wells, *Parish Education in Colonial Virginia* (New York, Teachers College, Columbia University, 1923), Chap. III.

of visitors and to be supported by public land and public salary for the school-master. Several such schools were established, but the going was difficult and the counties seemed more reluctant than the New England towns in lending their continuing support in a colony of divided religious loyalties.

South Carolina made several attempts to establish by legislative enactment free Latin schools, but little came of it. One act in 1710 set up a corporation like that of Maryland; in 1712 public funds were added to the corporation's funds; and in 1722 an act authorized the county courts to establish Latin schools and to levy taxes for their support, but the economic and social conditions or the motivation to respond to this legislative leadership were apparently too weak to result in much activity. The growing heterogeneity of the religious population, the sparsity of population, the tradition of private and parental initiative in providing education for upper-class children, and the class differences that divided the people, all seemed to conspire to weaken public promotion of education in the South until after the Revolutionary War. But weak and faltering as it was, the governmental authorities did establish some aspects of responsibility for educational activity.

Middle colonies. In New York and Pennsylvania an interesting development took place that illustrated a kind of transition that occurred somewhat less dramatically and less rapidly in the other colonies. During the early years of colonization in the seventeenth century when the Dutch dominated New York and the Quakers dominated Pennsylvania, serious efforts were made to promote education by public authority, but when the colonies soon became heterogeneous in religion and nationality, the efforts to control education by the civil authorities began to give way to private control. Under Dutch rule, for example, the Dutch West India Company, exercising its political powers, moved to establish schools in the several towns somewhat along the lines of the New England colonies. Indeed the Dutch Reformed Church was linked through its Calvinism to the Puritan outlook on education. But when the English took over New Netherland in 1664 and transformed it into the royal province of New York, the state could no longer enforce a common religion through public schools. The Dutch schools became church schools rather than town schools, and the other religious groups moved to establish their own schools.

The state maintained a form of control inasmuch as the royal governor asserted the right to license teachers. The Assembly also tried on a few occasions to establish schools. For example, an act was passed in 1702 to establish a Latin school in New York City with the schoolmaster's salary to be paid by tax funds in the same way in which ministers were supported. Another such effort was made by an act of 1732, but in general the religious and national diversity of the population militated against such efforts. Jealous political and religious forces were afraid that public funds might go to the aid of some sectarian interests in discrimination against others. The colony therefore settled for a large measure of private control of education until after the Revolution.

Similarly in Pennsylvania, as we have seen in Chapter 3, William Penn set out upon a policy of public and state responsibility for education. His first frames of government and the early acts of the legislature asserted this principle, but soon after the turn of the eighteenth century the religious and national rivalries forced a retreat from public responsibility and prompted a granting of rights to religious and private groups to conduct education for their own purposes. Interestingly enough, however, when Pennsylvania came to draw up its state constitution in 1776, it was the first state to assert state responsibility for education and did so in these words:

> A school or schools shall be established in every county by the legislature, for the convenient instruction of youth, with such salaries to the masters, paid by the public, as may enable them to instruct youth at low prices; and all useful learning shall be duly encouraged and promoted in one or more universities.

This was a victory for the democratic forces in the state, and, strikingly, the other two states which drew up notably liberal constitutions also embodied similar provisions for public schools despite their rather feeble efforts in this direction as colonies. North Carolina's Constitution of 1776 contained a provision almost identical with that of Pennsylvania, and Georgia's Constitution of 1777 simply said "Schools shall be erected in each county, and supported at the general expense of the State, as the Legislature shall hereafter point out."

New England lagged somewhat behind in the assertion of state responsibility for education during the Revolutionary period. Massachusetts did not adopt a constitution until 1780, at which time it inserted a somewhat equivocal provision enjoining the legislature to "cherish the interests of literature and the sciences, and all seminaries of them; especially the university at Cambridge, public schools, and grammar-schools in the towns. . . ." New Hampshire followed suit in its constituion of 1784. Connecticut and Rhode Island did not adopt constitutions until the nineteenth century. The rest of the original thirteen states moved by law and by constitution in the nineteenth century to assert public responsibility for school systems. By the time that Ohio was admitted to the Union in 1803 the principle of state responsibility for education was thereafter firmly incorporated in the constitutions of the new states.

Growth of Private Control and Support of Education

In addition to the stimulus and support for education given by various governmental agencies as illustrated in the foregoing section, considerable impetus to the establishment of schools came from nongovernmental sources. Private effort by individuals and by groups of like-minded people appeared very early on the scene and came to be the dominant method of promoting education by the middle of the eighteenth century in many of the colonies. The principal means employed included endowment of schools by individuals, establishment of denominational schools by churches and religious societies, private-venture instruction by individual teachers, and founding of private corporations for the continuing management of private academies.

The lines of distinction between private and public management of schools were often blurred. When church and state were close allies, there is no easy way to distinguish between what today would be termed public in contrast to private support and control. Individuals gave private bequests to town schools or to public authorities for the use of public schools; and public funds or other aid were often given by towns or legislatures to private agencies and religious schools. The state continued to assert its authority over education and continued direct mangement of public schools where they existed, but also delegated to individuals the right to teach by means of license or granted to corporate enterprises the privilege of carrying on education by means of legal charters. When the state began to assign direct management of schools to individuals and to self-perpetuating boards of trustees, private control of education could more easily be distinguished from public control.

The pattern of private control was largely a result of the growing diversity of religious organization. This meant that the state could no longer require religious conformity in public schools but could maintain a measure of state authority by giving each religious group the right to conduct schools of its own. It was also a phase of the growing laissez-faire pattern of capitalism of the eighteenth century. Under the earlier form of capitalism known as mercantilism the state closely regulated business and trade, but under laissez-faire capitalism, business was given much more freedom to operate without state regulation. So when the state began to grant to private corporations the right and freedom to conduct continuing businesses and enterprises of various kinds, education came to be one of the activities which individuals and corporations could conduct with a minimum of direction from the state. Private initiative in education was stimulated by this means. Flexibility in religious outlook might not have otherwise been possible at a time when public schools so often represented a single dominant or established religious outlook rather than the whole community. The establishment of private schools also gave an educational opportunity to the rising middle classes whose desires for practical studies were not being met by the traditional classical and religious schools of town and country.

Endowed schools. An important method of making funds available for educational purposes was by endowment through gifts or bequests. The first endowed school seems to have been contemplated by Benjamin Syms, a Virginia planter, in his will of 1634–1635 in which he provided that 200 acres of his land and eight milch cows should be used for the establishment and maintenance of a free school in Elizabeth City County. In 1642–1643 the Virginia Assembly confirmed this grant by legislative act, and the school probably opened soon after. The county justices of the peace and the minister and churchwardens of the parish were designated in Syms' will as the trustees for the management of the funds. Similarly, Thomas Eaton provided in his will of 1659 for a free school with an endowment of 500 acres of land, two Negro servants, twelve cows, two bulls, and twenty hogs, as well as household effects. He again entrusted this endowment to the county and parish officials. In each case the purpose was apparently to provide an education free of charge to the poor children of the county and parishes.

All together, some ten or eleven such endowed schools were created in Virginia prior to the Revolution along with several free schools not entrusted to the control of public officials. Only seven of the ninety parishes in Virginia had such schools, and apparently little if any parish funds were ever put into the schools. They could thus be thought of as private schools because the public officials did not manage or supervise them nor were public funds used to support them. But they had difficult times: attendance was small, funds were inadequate, and the trustees apparently paid little attention to them.[3]

Consequently, in the middle of the eighteenth century, the Virginia Assembly passed several acts of incorporation authorizing the trustees of some of the schools to form themselves into corporations for the better management of the schools. This was done for the Syms school in 1753, for the Eaton school in 1759, and for the Peasley school in Gloucester County in 1756. The authority of incorporation made it possible for the trustees to use the land, lease it, or otherwise manage the school in ways that they were not sure they had the right to do until that time. There was evidence, too, that some of the masters in these schools had begun to think of themselves as virtually autonomous; therefore, the corporate trustees were given the power by the state to appoint, supervise, and approve the actions of the teachers. Furthermore, in some cases the children of well-to-do families seemed to be crowding out the poor children for whom the schools were principally founded, and the legislature felt that an incorporated board of trustees could be held more responsible for carrying out the original intentions of the donors. Some girls as well as boys seemed to have been admitted to these endowed schools.

In the eighteenth century South Carolina also moved in the direction of granting the right to private donors to conduct schools after little had come of the state's efforts to set up county schools. Free schools were established by individual endowment and by the Winyaw Indigo Society, a group of planters who were interested in philanthropic as well as sociable activities. In Georgia the Bethesda Orphan House was established through the efforts of the Reverend George Whitefield as a free school for orphan children.

In New England the practice of endowing schools was perhaps less common than in the South but nevertheless proved to be an important supple-

[3] Wells, *op. cit.*, Chap. III.

ment to town support. One of the earliest endowments was that of Edward Hopkins, for long a governor of Connecticut. At his death in 1657 Hopkins bequeathed his property in New England to four trustees, of whom the most important was probably the Reverend John Davenport of New Haven. The funds were divided among grammar schools in New Haven, Hartford, and Hadley, and Harvard College. In the eighteenth century the movement away from town control of schools was signalized when Lieutenant Governor William Dummer of Massachusetts gave his house and land at his death in 1761 as an endowment for the establishment of a grammar school which later became the Dummer Academy by incorporation in 1782.

In Connecticut Governor Jonathan Trumbull established a school at Lebanon in 1743 which was incorporated in 1774 as the Union School of New London. Somewhat earlier Joshua Moor had endowed a school with property and house which became the Moor's Indian Charity School taught by the Reverend Eleazor Wheelock who later moved to New Hampshire and was instrumental in carrying on the charity school and eventually building Dartmouth College.

Thus, it is notable that both in the South and in New England, endowments for schools in the seventeenth century were likely to be turned over to public authorities or public officials for management, whereas from the middle of the eighteenth century onward, they were likely to be delegated to a private board of trustees for management under authority of a charter granted by an act of incorporation of the legislatures.

Denominational schools. As the colonial period progressed, the most active promotion of schools was undertaken by religious groups. This took the form of schools established by an individual congregation or minister, by neighboring churches as a cooperative undertaking, or by religious societies organized on a wider basis. The most characteristic educational pattern of the middle colonies was the development in the eighteenth century of denominational schools sponsored by a local church or by denominational effort.

In Pennsylvania, after the first efforts at state promotion of schools, the several denominations promoted their own schools. The Quakers established schools in Philadelphia and eastern Pennsylvania; such sectarian groups as Lutherans, German Reformed, Moravians, and Mennonites established their elementary schools in the middle counties of Pennsylvania; the Scots-Irish Presbyterians were especially enterprising in setting up schools in the western counties; and the Puritans who settled in the Wyoming Valley in northeastern Pennsylvania brought their New England type of schools with them. As noted earlier, the Pennsylvania legislature passed acts in the early eighteenth century making it possible for the various religious groups to own property for educational purposes. This was particularly helpful to the foreign-language sects who could then feel free to develop their schools unmolested by the state. Prominent among these were Nazareth Hall, established by the Moravians in 1759, the Moravian school of Christopher Dock, and the Lutheran schools promoted by Heinrich Muhlenberg.

Similarly in New York and New Jersey the denominations were active in establishing their sectarian schools, especially the Presbyterians, Quakers, Anglicans, Dutch Reformed, Congregationalists, and Baptists. Notable among these was the "log college" conducted by William Tennent as a training school for Presbyterian ministers at Neshaminy, New Jersey. Other Presbyterian ministers conducted schools at Newark and Elizabethtown, and a Baptist school was established at Hopewell in 1756. Two Jesuit priests conducted a Latin school for Catholic children in New York until the advent of William and Mary as sovereigns of England in 1688 when Catholics were no longer tolerated as fully as they had been under Charles II and James II.

In the South the dissenting religious groups gradually won the right to establish their own schools. Quick to promote the idea were the Presbyterians, Quakers, Baptists, and the German sects who settled in the western counties of Virginia and North Carolina. Catholic schools were conducted in Maryland during the middle decades of the seventeenth century. Ministers of the established Church of England sometimes conducted classical schools; even though these were private ventures, they carried weight because of the privileged position of ministers as public officials maintained by public taxes. The most widespread organized effort to conduct schools in the South and in the middle colonies was undertaken by the Society for the Propagation of the Gospel in Foreign Parts organized in 1701, especially through the instigation of the Reverend Thomas Bray. Designed to promote the establishment and maintenance of Church of England ministers and hopeful of establishing an Anglican episcopacy in America, the society was very active in founding schools and supporting teachers in elementary charity schools for poor children in most of the American colonies.

On a smaller scale other group efforts were made by the denominations to promote schools. Pennsylvania seemed to be an appropriate center for such efforts. In 1743 three presbyteries of the Presbyterian Church joined together to establish a school and received aid and support from the Synod of Philadelphia. Anglicans organized the short-lived Society for the Propagation of Christian Knowledge Among the Germans in Pennsylvania and established perhaps a dozen schools, but it met the opposition of the smaller German sects and was labeled a political effort to destroy their religion and national culture. More successful were the so-called "neighborhood schools" in Pennsylvania which were established by the concentrated effort of several religious groups which would cooperate to establish a community school in neighborhoods where the population of any one sect was too small to permit each one to maintain its own separate denominational school. Somewhat the same form of private group effort but without the religious diversity was evident in the so-called "old-field" schools in the South where people would construct a school for the neighborhood on one of the old fields that were lying fallow after a series of crops had exhausted their fertility.

Private-venture schools. Alongside the public schools under government control and the permanent private schools established by endowment or religious organizations, the independent enterprising teacher tried to make his living by selling his instructional wares for a fee. Sometimes this type of instruction was given in the teacher's home or in rented rooms; sometimes the teacher would go to the homes of his customers to give the instruction. Perhaps the nearest modern counterpart of this type of teacher is the private music teacher who gives instrumental or vocal lessons to children either at his own home or in a music school or who goes to the home of his pupils.

In this category came the women who conducted "dame schools" in their homes for instruction in the three R's to small children for a fee; the tutors who went to live on the estates of the southern planters or the Dutch patroons in New York, or in the homes of wealthy merchants of Boston, Philadelphia, New York, or Charleston; the minister who taught Latin to some of the boys of his congregation or parish as a means of preparing them for college and thus supplementing his own income; the trained Latin scholar who made a lifetime occupation out of his scholarship; and the private teachers whose repertoire extended to a very wide range of subjects in the seacoast towns of the early eighteenth century.

These latter teachers are best described in the detailed accounts of Seybolt.[4] They ran their schools much as they pleased and were seldom subject to surveillance, supervision, or approval by public officials or private boards of trustees. What they taught did not have to be approved by the colleges or by standardizing agencies. The only check on their teaching or the subjects offered was whether or not their students and parents were satisfied and continued to come for instruction and to recommend the wares to others. But the American people apparently preferred permanence in their schools and some sort of oversight of what was taught to their children. From the middle of the eighteenth century onward, they increasingly turned to control and support of schools through public bodies or private boards of trustees.

Incorporated schools and colleges. In the latter part of the colonial period the corporate school, controlled by a self-perpetuating board of governors or board of trustees, gradually appeared as the typical form of educational control, especially for secondary schools and colleges. This movement was stimulated by the middle class and capitalistic concern for corporate continuity as a means of caring for endowments, bequests of property, and money as well as by the desire of religious societies to maintain permanent schools and

[4] Robert F. Seybolt, *Source Studies in American Colonial Education: The Private School* (Urbana, University of Illinois, 1925) and *The Private Schools of Colonial Boston* (Cambridge, Harvard University Press, 1935).

to be free of government regulation. The patterns of control worked out in the colleges, especially at Yale College, helped also to promote this type of educational management. Several examples of such schools have already been mentioned and little further need be said here. The William Penn Charter School, incorporated in 1697, set the pattern in Pennsylvania, to be followed a half century later by the incorporation of the nonsectarian academy at Philadelphia through the efforts of Benjamin Franklin. The Syms and Eaton schools were given corporate charter in the 1750's in Virginia, Newark Academy was chartered in Delaware in 1769, and the Washington Academy in Hackensack, New Jersey, in the same year. With the chartering of the Phillips Academy in Andover, Massachusetts, in 1778 a new era in secondary education was launched, and the success of the private academy under corporate control was signalized. Religion, capitalist enterprise, class status, and utilitarian motives joined forces to produce an important and influential type of educational control for the new republic about to be founded.

The colleges had led the way in this development of private corporate control and support of schools. When Harvard was founded in 1636 by the Massachusetts General Court, the corporation consisted of the president and resident teachers to whom were entrusted the internal management of the college under the direct supervision of the General Court. Then a board of overseers was set up to act as a supervisory and approval-granting body. Gradually the corporation came to comprise nonresident trustees rather than the teaching staff. Thus, full legal control was taken out of the hands of the faculty and put into the hands of a nonresident board. Harvard remained for long under the jurisdiction of the General Court, and the College of William and Mary in Virginia followed in general the Harvard plan, but with the founding of Yale in 1701 a new pattern was instituted.

A single close corporation, consisting of a self-perpetuating board of trustees, became the governing body and full legal authority at Yale. In the middle of the eighteenth century President Clap won his fight (as earlier described) to keep the college free of visitorial powers from the state. The board did not include faculty members. When the other colonial colleges were founded in the middle of the eighteenth century under the stimulus of the Great Awakening, they followed the Yale pattern with some variations. Brown included some faculty representatives on the board of control; King's had a variety of religious representatives; most had civil officials as ex officio members, but all moved further and further away from direct governmental control or supervision despite the efforts of Livingston, Jefferson, and others to reassert legislative and state control. By and large, the control of schools was greatly influenced by these developments in the colleges.

Interestingly enough, the religious motive worked in various ways. The newer and dissenting religious groups saw the private corporation as a means of freeing themselves from the domination of the established religions, but the established religions had their troubles too. In Connecticut, for example, President Clap agreed that religious orthodoxy could best be maintained at Yale by preserving Yale as a private corporation and not subject to state control, whereas some of the "Old Light" Congregationalists were upholding state authority as the best means of preserving religious orthodoxy by arguing that no group could establish a school without legislative permission. Religious motives thus led to different proposed solutions. Connecticut later on even tried to distribute its public funds to a wide variety of religious groups, but that proved to be an unpopular and unsuccessful solution. It was not until public education came to be recognized as a secular enterprise that it was possible to solve the problem of a common school with due regard to freedom of religious conscience. Meanwhile, private control of schools was the principal eighteenth-century answer to the problem of religious diversity, and public schools genuinely designed for all had to wait upon the arrival of the nineteenth century.

DOMINANT PATTERNS OF INSTRUCTION

During much of the colonial period educational opportunity was available in two different types of institutions, roughly divided according to class lines. Apprenticeship and elementary schools for learning the reading and writing of English were largely designed for the lower classes, whereas secondary schools of the Latin grammar type and the colleges were designed for the upper classes. Instruction in religion was common to both types of education. This form of a dual system of education was widely apparent in the seventeenth century, but it started to break down somewhat in the eighteenth century as the ranks of the middle classes began to swell and as they began to seek a newer type of education that would be more utilitarian and practical for business and trade purposes but would not be tagged with the stigma of lower-class education.

As the eighteenth century progressed, a new type of intermediate education began to appear to meet these demands. This movement took the form first of private "English" schools and then later the academy. These were at first a more democratic type of school that bridged the gap between upper and lower classes. The content of education as reflected in the curriculum of school and college and in the current textbooks of the day began to reflect this readjustment of educational pattern. The way was being prepared for the appearance, in the nineteenth century, of the single-track or ladder system of education, which began with elementary schools and was followed by secondary schools and high schools that led on to college and higher education. When this happened, a distinctive form of American educational system began to make its contribution as one of the most important social inventions of American culture.

Apprenticeship

Apprenticeship was an informal method of teaching sealed by a formal agreement or contract between the master craftsman and the young apprentice. As a practice and a method of education it stemmed back at least to the guild system of medieval times and was a standard method of education in seventeenth-century England and Europe. The colonists of all nationalities were familiar with it and early applied it to their new society. It represented a combination of economic, class, humanitarian, and religious motives. Economically it was a method of teaching a trade to children of the lower classes so that they could become contributing and productive members of society and thus not contribute to the growth of poverty or a vagabond class that would be a threat to the more stable elements in society. It helped to maintain a steady flow of skilled workers into the economic arrangements of a growing commercial and urban society.

Apprenticeship was also a way of providing relief for the poor and avoiding public responsibility for poor relief on a direct basis. In place of poor relief or charity to help poor families to maintain themselves in a precarious economic situation, apprenticeship was a means of caring for poor children or orphans who would render useful service in return for their "keep." Undoubtedly, also, there was an increasing humanitarian and religious drive to provide better care for the sake of the children themselves.

Generally speaking, a child or young person was assigned to a master workman to serve as a helper and later as an assistant as he became more skilled in the trade, whether it be as weaver, tanner, tailor, shoemaker, blacksmith, cooper, wheelwright, carpenter, stonemason, miller, baker, butcher, fisherman, farmer, shopkeeper, merchant, or any other. The apprentice was bound to serve the master for a stated period of time, usually from three to eight or ten years. Sometimes the term ran until the age of twenty-one for boys and the age of eighteen or until married for girls. The apprentice agreed to work hard, learn the trade, keep the secrets, lead a sober and moral life, and obey all directions or commands. Some agreements even specified that the apprentice must not get married, drink, gamble, or in any way harm his master or his goods.

In return for this service, the master agreed to teach the apprentice the art and skill of the trade, provide food, lodging, and clothing as one would for his own child, and grant a sum of money and an outfit of clothing at the end of the period of service. Sometimes these arrangements were spelled out in great detail, but sometimes they were simply assumed as customary. Increasingly in the colonial period the stipulation was made that the apprentice should be taught some rudimentary elements of learning. Most commonly, this was simply reading, but also often included writing and the elements of religion or simply the catechism. In the eighteenth century the added requirement was sometimes made that the master should send the apprentice to school for as much as three years. Some of the earliest contracts made in New England in the 1630's did not contain reference to literary education, but the Massachusetts law of 1642 sought to correct this omission and required masters as well as parents to see that the children under their care were taught to read, know the capital laws, and learn the principles of religion. A regulation of Petsworth Parish in Virginia in 1724 provided that all orphan children who were bound out by the parish and who could not read by the age of 13 should be set free from their masters or taken from them and assigned to another. Girls as well as boys were commonly apprenticed and were to be taught the art of spinning, knitting, or sewing, and sometimes reading, writing, and religion.

Arrangements such as these were formalized by a contract known as an indenture, which was a legal document drawn up between the parties and filed in the town, county, or parish records. Public officials, whether town selectmen, county judges, or parish vestrymen, were usually charged with seeing that the indentures were carried out legally and properly. Orphans were by law to be assigned as apprentices by the selectmen or county judges in New England and by the parish officials or county court in Virginia. A special orphans' court was held in Virginia to handle such cases, to examine masters and apprentices to see if the terms of the indenture were being carried out, and to adjudicate claims of violation. Free parents who could not care for their children because of poverty or who wished the child to learn a trade could voluntarily enter into such contracts before the court. Occasionally, such parents would have to sue in court to require the master to do as he had agreed. For example, parents in York County, Virginia, in 1690, complained that the master had made the apprentice "work in the ground" as a farmer rather than teaching the boy to be a tailor as he had agreed to do and had failed to teach him to read and write.

Here then was one principal means by which education was conducted during the colonial period, especially for orphans and poor children. Most of what we know about the content of such teaching is contained in the indentures kept on file in county, town, and parish records.[5] What we do not know, of course, is how faithfully or well the educational provisions in apprenticeship were carried out. It is entirely likely that they were often honored more in the written indentures than in the actual practice. Masters, themselves, were often poorly equipped to teach their apprentices, and schools were often not easily available in the South or the middle colonies. Furthermore, Wells' study of apprenticeship in the parishes of Virginia shows that the total num-

---

[5] See, for example, M. W. Jenegan, *Laboring and Dependent Classes in Colonial America, 1607-1783* (Chicago, University of Chicago Press, 1931); Lyon G. Tyler, "Education in Colonial Virginia" in *William & Mary College Quarterly Magazine* (April 1897), pp. 219-233; and Wells, *op. cit.*, Chap. V.

ber of orphan and poor children cared for by apprenticeship was only a very small proportion of such children. Many parishes had no record of apprentice indentures in a period of fifty years; others cared for but one or two a year on the average.

Despite these possible inadequacies the practice was common enough to indicate that some attention was being paid to the educational needs of lower-class children in colonial America. Much more successful, probably, was the use of the apprenticeship idea in the advanced training for the professions of law, medicine, teaching, and the ministry. Here young adults who had already acquired considerable educational training would learn the elements of the profession under the direct guidance and help of a practicing lawyer, doctor, teacher, or minister. This was the accepted method of professional preparation until provisions for such training were made available in the colleges in the late eighteenth and nineteenth centuries.

Elementary Education

Elementary education in the colonial period was a relatively simple matter. At the most it included instruction in reading and writing of the vernacular tongue, arithmetic, and the rudiments of religious faith along with some attempt at the shaping of "manners and morals" along the lines of the common virtues. At the least it meant instruction in recognizing the ABC's and some elementary skill at simple reading. In point of time spent at it, the range was from a few weeks to not more than a year or two or three. For those who were intended to go on to a secondary education, the elements of elementary instruction were expected to be achieved by the age of seven or eight; for those who were not expected to go further in school, ability to read was probably hoped for by the age of twelve or so.

There were several ways that children could pick up the common branches of an elementary education. They might learn from one or the other of their parents if the parents themselves could teach their children. Apprentices might learn from their masters. Poor children might be able to attend a school conducted by the town, or by the minister of the church, or in an endowed free school, or in a school run by a religious society. Children of more privileged parents might learn reading, writing, and arithmetic from a tutor brought to the house, or they might attend a private "dame school" or an "old field school," or the Latin grammar schoolmaster might be diverted from his main task to teach the boys their "letters" as a preliminary to their study of Latin.

In New England in the seventeenth century there is some evidence that the European practice of separate schools for reading and writing was in vogue for a time. The reading school was the more elementary of the two, concentrating upon the learning of the ABC's and perhaps some religious instruction. Reading and religion were combined in the hornbook, which was simply a piece of paper or parchment on which were written the alphabet, some simple syllables, a benediction, and the Lord's Prayer. For the sake of durability the paper was attached to a board and covered with transparent horn. The child learned his letters through religious materials.

The "dame school" was a rather fancy name given to the practice wherein a woman, often a widow with children, would take some neighbor's children into her house a few days a week to teach them reading while she carried on her housework. Clearly, only an exceptional woman would have been able to teach the children very much under these circumstances. Boys and girls often attended together; the girls perhaps learning some sewing and cooking as well as their letters.

The writing school was presumably somewhat more advanced in nature and typically concentrated on writing and arithmetic, but probably gave attention to reading also for those who had not advanced very far. It was not long, however, until the reading and writing schools were combined into one elementary school to teach all three subjects. These became the staples of the elementary curriculum in all colonies in the eighteenth century, whether town schools in New England, denominational schools in the middle colonies, or the charity schools of the South. As long as they could, the various nationalities held to their own vernacular languages. Thus, the Dutch Reformed schools were taught in Dutch, the German sects taught in German, the Huguenots in French, the Swedish Lutherans in Swedish, and so on. Gradually, however, as English culture began to predominate in the eighteenth century, elementary education turned more and more commonly to the English language.

As the elementary schools became more formalized in the eighteenth century and as schools became more available, the quantity and quality of teaching began to improve over the very rudimentary and informal methods of the seventeenth century. In general, we must piece together the character of the elementary instruction from a study of the books that were used and the instructions given to teachers concerning their goals and their methods. By far the most widely used textbook in the eighteenth century was the *New England Primer* designed for the Puritans. There were several other primers designed for Anglicans and other Protestant denominations. The *New England Primer,* as well as the others, was based upon the small books published in England designed as first books by which the layman could learn the grounds of his religious faith.

Typically, the *Primer* began with several pages devoted to the alphabet in capital and small letters, lists of two-letter syllables beginning ab, ac, ad, . . . then eb, ec, ed, . . . and so on for each vowel and on through the alphabet. These were followed by lists of words of one syllable, two syllables, and up to five syllables. Almost all the words were of a moral and religious character. Then came the well known woodcuts illustrating each letter in the alphabet by means of two- or three-line rhymed verses. Several pages consisted of reading matter devoted to moral lessons for children, the Lord's Prayer, the Apostles' Creed, the Ten Commandments, the names of the Books of the Bible, and the shorter Westminster Catechism. Many editions of the *Primer* also contained a sorrowful story about John Rogers' martyrdom at the hands of Queen Mary as well as John Cotton's catechism called *Spiritual Milk for New England Babes*. Children were apparently expected to read the material over and over until completely memorized. In the more ambitious schools the children could then progress to reading the Psalter and the Bible.

The dominantly religious character of this instruction goes without saying. The Puritan attitude toward children, considered desirable for teachers to adopt, is revealed in the discussion of John Cotton and Cotton Mather in Chapter 3 (pp. 66–71). The instructions to a Dutch teacher in 1661 emphasized that the children should arrive at school promptly at 8 A.M. and again at 1 P.M., that good discipline must be kept, and that the children should learn their prayers, the Ten Commandments, baptism, Lord's Prayer, and the catechism. In a contract with a Dutch schoolmaster in New Amsterdam in 1682, it was agreed that school should be held from 8 to 11 A.M., from 1 to 4 P.M., and in the evening for nine months a year from September to June. School should always begin with prayer and close with prayer or a psalm; and the teacher was to instruct the children in the catechism on every Wednesday and Saturday to prepare them for public catechising before the church congregation.

One of the most elaborate and thoughtful statements of an ideal elementary education according to the view of the Church of England is contained in the instructions given to their schoolmasters in 1706 by the Society for the Propagation of the Gospel in Foreign Parts. The goal of education was to teach children to believe and live as Christians. In order to achieve this goal, the children must be taught to read English so that they could read the Bible and other religious books, must learn the catechism by heart after being carefully taught its meaning, must learn the prayers appropriate to school and home, and must be taught how to worship in church and take part in the services. The teacher should also teach the children how to write and how to do arithmetic as a preparation for a useful employment. Special attention was to be given to the manners of the children in order that they be "modest, gentle, well-behaved, just and affable, and courteous to all their Companions; respectful to their Superiors," especially to the ministers. They must also be taught to love truth and honesty and to avoid lying and evil speaking. Discipline should be by kind and gentle methods, and punishment given with understanding rather than brutality. Teachers should also be ready to teach Indian and Negro children as well as white children. Whether or not the schoolmasters of the Society for the Propagation of the Gospel could live up to these instructions is a matter of question, but they reveal what these schools would have been like under ideal circumstances.

One of the best descriptions of the way an elementary school was actually conducted is given in some detail by Christopher Dock in his book *Schulordnung* which describes his school in Pennsylvania in the eighteenth century. The boys sat on benches separate from the girls. They were taught to read and write from the Bible, learned the Lord's Prayer and the Ten Commandments, and opened school with a psalm or hymn and prayers. The children then memorized and recited from the Bible. Any who could not recite properly after three attempts were called "Lazy" by the other children and their names written on a slate until they had made good. Then they might be called "Diligent," and their names erased. The smallest children began with spelling and were put in the spelling class. Spelling and pronunciation of words were practiced in groups so that the slow learner could profit from the oral work of the others. When the beginners had learned to spell and to read, they were advanced to the Testament class where they worked further on reading the Bible, newspapers, letters, and on arithmetic. Each group in reading, writing, or in arithmetic worked separately. Dock apparently tried hard to use group praise or blame as motives for good behavior or as punishment for bad behavior rather than simply relying upon his superior authority and the whip. If he did utilize these methods, he was probably far in advance of his age when the common means of "keeping discipline" was the ever present ferule and an eager willingness to use it often and with vigor.

Secondary Education

The American colonists, no matter from what country they came in the seventeenth century, knew what a secondary education was. It was an education in the classical languages of Latin and Greek. Since the time of the Humanistic revival of the Renaissance in the fifteenth and sixteenth centuries, a person who would be called truly educated must have studied the ancient languages as a basis for higher study in the universities and as a basis for leadership in church and state. It was a class education designed for the upper classes and for a few poor boys who might be given a free education in the English "public schools" or Latin grammar schools. The Protestant Reformation of the sixteenth and seventeenth centuries with its concern for religious orthodoxy had adopted the classical heritage of the Latin schools and given it a religious motivation. To be a "learned minister" meant that the minister must know Latin, Greek, and perhaps Hebrew as a means of studying the original languages in which the Scriptures and religious literature had been written.

Thus, in seventeenth-century America the original type of secondary education was a Latin schooling modeled after the classical schools of Europe, and especially of England. In the course of the eighteenth century a new type of secondary education began to appear in America and to challenge the Latin grammar schools for leadership. This took the form of an "English" education devoted to a much broader type of curriculum devoted to mathematics, science, and the modern languages. Its aim was more practical and commercial. It found a ready clientele among the growing middle classes in America and found an outlet in two new types of schools, the private "English" schools and the academies.

Latin grammar schools. Since the bodies of knowledge necessary for a life of scholarship and intellectual leadership in the church and other professions were still largely dominated by the classical languages in the seventeenth century, it was necessary to learn these languages in school as a preparation for leadership in such activities. Although the modern languages were beginning to be used in more and more realms of intellectual life, the courses of study in colleges and universities were still based upon Latin books. A boy who would go to college must learn his Latin in a preparatory school. The Latin grammar school was principally a college preparatory institution. The college entrance requirements of the colonial colleges give a fairly good idea of what the Latin grammar schools were supposed to do.

In 1642 Harvard required its freshman students to be able to understand and read at sight some Latin author of the difficulty of Cicero, be able to speak Latin in prose and poetry, and be able to decline Greek nouns and conjugate Greek verbs. A hundred years later the Harvard requirements had not changed substantially; ability to read Vergil in Latin and ability to read a Greek text such as the New Testament or Isocrates were the only additions. The entrance requirements of other colleges were similar; Yale and Princeton had added arithmetic by the middle of the eighteenth century, but the universal requirement was ability to read Latin.

No wonder, then, that the Latin grammar schools concentrated on the study of Latin and to a lesser extent the study of Greek. We have few actual courses of study to indicate the precise nature of the grammar school curriculum, but the picture is simply a variation on the same theme. At the Boston Latin School at the beginning of the eighteenth century the course was seven years in length, the boys beginning at the age of seven or eight years. During the first three years the boys learned by heart a beginning Latin book, often called an "accidence." They read and parsed Latin sentences in such Latin readers as Cato's *Distichs* (dating from the fourth century A.D.), the *Colloquies* of Corderius (a sixteenth-century Humanist), and Aesop's *Fables*. In the fourth year they read Erasmus, Aesop, Ovid, and studied Latin grammar (probably one by Ezekiel Cheever, the famous colonial schoolmaster, or one by William Lily, sixteenth-century English scholar). In the fifth year they continued Erasmus and Ovid and took up Cicero's *Letters* along with practice in composition and verse-making in Latin. The sixth year was devoted to Cicero's *De Officiis,* Vergil's *Aeneid,* Ovid's *Metamorphoses,* Thomas Godwyn's history of Rome, and the beginning of Greek and rhetoric. In the final year the program ranged over a wide list of Latin and Greek authors including Cicero's *Orations,* Vergil, Horace, Juvenal, Homer, Isocrates, Hesiod, and the New Testament. Some students could probably begin Hebrew as well. Considerable attention was given to writing Latin dialogues, verses, and compositions and translating Greek sentences into Latin.

This was a stiff and formidable program of studies, probably matched by only a few other Latin schools in the colonies, but it represents what was meant by a grammar school. If the teaching was good, the boys could learn a lot about Latin culture and ideas. If it was pedestrian, as it was likely to be in many hands, the boys would plod along year after year with technical ability to read Latin but little real grasp or understanding. School hours were typically long, beginning at eight or seven or even six o'clock in the morning and lasting until eleven; after two hours out for lunch, school began again at one and lasted until four or five in the afternoon. Apparently school continued all through the summer and winter and often six days a week. In a large school the boys were divided into classes or forms and progressed a form a year. The word "form" originally meant a long bench without a back on it. The boys of a specific class sat on the same bench and thus the word form came to be applied to a class or a grade in school. In the upper grades of a Latin school the boys would often sit at rows of desks because they needed to be able to write on a flat surface. In some cases the boys in a Latin school would attend a writing school during the late morning or afternoon hours in order to learn how to write, but sometimes the Latin masters also had to teach writing and even English reading. They often objected to this practice as beyond their call of duty or beneath their calling. Sometimes a writing or reading teacher or "usher" would be attached to a Latin school to render this service.

The curriculum of the Boston Latin school showed little evidence of an emphasis on religion, but in the days of Ezekiel Cheever much reading was given from the Bible, and probably other masters also emphasized the religious texts as well as instruction in the catechism, especially on Saturdays. Discipline was likely to be severe with heavy emphasis on corporal punishment, or as was often stated "without respect to person." The boys sat long hours on hard benches with little attention to comfort, relaxation, or play. Little wonder that strict discipline was necessary to keep the kind of order that seemed necessary to the master.

Regulations spoke often of the punishments that should be meted out to fit the offenses of lying, cursing, swearing, quarreling, fighting, and playing cards or dice. Physical education, or music, or art, or science, or mathematics, or any subject that might appeal to the interests of seven- to fifteen-year olds had no place in the curriculum, and methods of active involvement beyond memorizing seldom seemed to occur to the teachers. There was little thought of child study, human psychology, or methods of teaching. When academic scholars of today urge that all a teacher needs to know is his subject matter and that he does not need to know anything about "education," it is well to remember that the teachers of the Latin grammar school certainly knew their subject matter and they certainly knew little about education. They also began to disappear two centuries ago in the face of more useful types of schools based upon newer conceptions of educational method.

Private "English" schools. During the first half of the eighteenth century the increasing tempo of practical and intellectual interests began to lead to demands for new kinds of education. Trade and commerce with foreign countries could be improved if the personnel needed in building and sailing ships were properly trained. Competence in marine engineering and navigation required the study of an increasing number of technical subjects. The amount and quality of goods for sale abroad could be expanded if effort and skill were directed toward opening up the vast land areas of the American continent. Surveying new lands and building roads and bridges required new technical skills, many of which were based upon mathematics. The business and promotional side of an expanding commercial enterprise required skills in bookkeeping, accounting, letter writing, and foreign languages. The colonial wars fought up and down the reaches of America and on the high seas brought demands for personnel trained in military engineering and the arts and sciences of war. And the wider contact with the cultures of other peoples led to a concern for the history, geography, and literature of the European world. As city life made it possible for a greater sophistication to develop among the upper classes, a new demand for music, dancing, and the arts of "polite society" began to appear.

Since the Latin grammar schools were circumscribed in their content and aim by the humanistic tradition of classical scholarship and by the college entrance requirements, new types of schools appeared under private auspices to fill these new needs. A general name that may be used to apply to these private schools of the first half of the eighteenth century is "English grammar schools" or simply "English schools" to distinguish them from the Latin schools. The English schools, responding to the growing commercial interests of the middle classes, were designed to give a practical and vocational education that would prepare young people for the new occupations that were attracting more and more persons. Teachers in these schools were not bound by college entrance requirements although some of them taught the classics. They taught what the young people wanted; they charged fees for specific courses; they held classes early in the morning or in the late afternoon or evening to serve young people who had jobs during the day; and they held classes at regular daytime hours for everyone else. The clientele of such schools was thus much broader than that of the Latin schools which were designed primarily for college-bound boys. Girls as well as boys were often welcomed in the English schools, sometimes in separate classes, sometimes in classes with the boys.

The advertisements that appeared widely in the newspapers of such cities as Boston, New Haven, New York, Philadelphia, Baltimore, and Charleston revealed the range and extent of subjects offered. They were almost entirely of a secular nature and gave little or no emphasis to religious instruction. Commercial subjects seemed to be a popular new field, including commercial arithmetic, accounting, bookkeeping, penmanship, letter writing, and even a rare instance of shorthand. Perhaps even more popular, at least in the advertisements, were the various branches of mathematics, arithmetic, algebra, geometry, trignometry, and astronomy along with the applied mathematics useful for civil and military engineering, namely, surveying, gauging, dialing, navigation, fortifications, and gunnery. Some of the teaching of mathematics in the English schools was as good if not better than that in the colleges of the day, and often the practical applications of the teaching were emphasized. One teacher guaranteed that his students would be so well prepared in navigation that they could sail as mates on their first voyage.

The modern languages were often taught either as aids to dealing with foreign merchants in their own languages as in the case of Portuguese, Spanish, and Italian or as an accomplishment of polite society as in the case of French. Geography and history were often advertised, and much attention was given to the arts of music (singing, violin, flute, spinnet), dancing, fencing, and the handcraft arts of drawing, painting, embroidery, quilting, and fine needlework. Occasionally, a teacher who was a college graduate would advertise studies in the liberal arts appropriate to the colleges, for example, Latin, Greek, Hebrew, ethics, rhetoric, logic, metaphysics, and natural philosophy.

In the long run one of the most important developments of all, was the emergence of English grammar as a subject of instruction in these private schools. Until English became an almost universal study in elementary and secondary schools, there could be no guarantee that America would become and remain a unilingual nation rather than a multilingual one. The first English grammar text to be used in America was Thomas Dilworth's *A New Guide to the English Tongue,* printed in London in 1740 and in Philadelphia by Benjamin Franklin in 1747. This consisted principally of word lists for spelling, easy reading exercises, and the rules of grammar.

President Samuel Johnson wrote in 1765 *The First Easy Rudiments of Grammar applied to the English Tongue.* He described himself on the title page as "one who is extremely desirous to promote good Literature in America, and especially a right English Education." Johnson believed that his grammar contained the first principles of grammar common to *all* languages and thus would be useful as a basis for later study of the learned languages. It was interesting that the study of English had to be justified on the grounds that it would be useful in learning the classical languages. After English had won its way in the curriculum, the argument was turned around, and the classics were justified as an aid to the improvement of English. Johnson felt that all the preparation needed for the use of his book was that the boys be taught to read by a good spelling book. His book consisted principally of definitions of the parts of speech and the rules for the use of words and sentences. A unique feature of this elementary grammar was an appendix that contained Johnson's synopsis of all the elements of a good education designed to show the relation between grammar and the other studies the student would later encounter. This was an idea that might well have been emulated more often as a means of orienting students and teachers alike to the entire curriculum of a school or college education.

The academies. In the latter half of the eighteenth century the private English schools gradually gave way to the academies which were usually founded on a basis more permanent than the private-venture English schools. In a sense the curriculum of the academy was an effort to combine the values and content of the Latin schools and the English schools into one institution. Typically, the early academies had Latin departments and English departments. For a reminder of one of the most elaborate of these arrangements it might be well at this point to look again at Franklin's proposals for an academy as described in Chapter 3 (see pp. 77–81). An excellent example of this process is shown in an advertisement for the Newark Academy in New Jersey in 1775. One department was to teach the classical languages and mathematics; another department called an "English School" was to teach reading, writing, arithmetic, bookkeeping, and English grammar. Girls were invited to attend the English School. Children could board at the Academy, and all were expected to attend the church services of their choice.

Not only were the classical elements of the Latin school incorporated into the academies, but the religious element was also retained along with the more utilitarian and practical studies of the English schools. The Great Awakening of the middle decades of the eighteenth century reasserted the religious concern of the agencies that sponsored and controlled the academies, but the sense realism of the Dissenters' academies of England and the Pietistic schools of Europe were also used to appeal to the merchant and middle classes of America. Thus, both the Latin grammar schools and the private English schools passed away, but their influence lived on in the academies which became the dominant secondary school in America. When, however, the academies became more concerned with the classical training than with a practical "English" education, the academies in turn gave way to the public high school in the nineteenth century.

The academies used English as the basic language rather than Latin, and they were typically boarding schools rather than day schools. Academies for girls were also founded and often became the basis for later foundations of colleges for women in the nineteenth century. It was a great experiment to try to combine the values of a classical and practical education in the same institution. Often the classical function won out, and the academies began to be college preparatory institutions rather than institutions for direct preparation for life.

When the academies took on this character, the public high school filled the need for a terminal type of education. But the academies brought into the secondary school curriculum some attention to English grammar, composition, literature and rhetoric, mathematics, the social studies, the modern languages, the sciences, and the arts and music, none of which were being developed by the Latin schools. The academies showed the way to a broadening of the secondary school curriculum and thereby helped to force the colleges to widen their own requirements. The academies served to illustrate that secondary education would be obliged to change itself to meet changing social needs rather than to wait for the colleges to loosen their requirements from the top down.

Higher Education

When the colonists set up colleges in America they naturally followed the inherited patterns of higher education that they had known in their home lands. Harvard in 1636 and William and Mary in 1693 were patterned after the English and Scottish universities. The prevailing influence was that of Oxford and Cambridge. Harvard's first curriculum as drawn up in organized form in 1642 shows the effect of four streams of influence that had been developing for some four centuries in the universities of Europe.

1. The seven liberal arts of the cathedral schools of the Middle Ages consisted of grammar, rhetoric, logic, arithmetic, geometry, astronomy, and music. All of these except music were present in Harvard's curriculum. These were the studies considered to be the complete curriculum necessary for an educated man during the early medieval period. The books used in these fields were all written in Latin, the language of the intellectual classes of Europe in the Middle Ages.

2. In the later Middle Ages the rediscovery of the philosophy of Aristotle and the translation of his works from Greek into Latin were incidents in the development of the faculty of philosophy and the origin of the universities in the thirteenth century. In Harvard's curriculum the presence of ethics, politics, and physics represented Aristotelian philosophy; metaphysics was also present in the study of theological questions and in the topics for disputation. All of these studies were also carried on in books written in Latin.

3. The Humanist ideal of the Renaissance of the fourteenth to sixteenth centuries required that a liberally educated man not only know Latin, but it must

be the Latin of classical Rome as portrayed best of all by Cicero and Vergil, and to this should be added a knowledge of Greek and perhaps Hebrew and other Eastern tongues. All of these subjects were present in the Harvard curriculum.

4. Finally, the Reformation ideal insisted that a liberal education should be devoted to the development of the religious doctrines of an orthodox faith. With the development of the several Protestant denominations this meant that orthodoxy depended upon sectarian religion. The presence of divinity in the curriculum and the entire atmosphere of Harvard as a Puritan institution represented this ideal of higher education in the seventeenth century.

Here, then, was the dominant conception of a liberal education. Three of the four ingredients could be said to be secular and one religious, although probably not in equal proportions. But it showed the necessity for a student to have a knowledge of Latin as a means of reading and understanding the books in the several studies. The religious emphasis was strong, to be sure, but it was not an exclusive interest. This type of education was considered necessary for the preparation of a learned ministry, but it was also considered essential for anyone who would be prepared for a life of scholarship or leadership in the church and state or for anyone who would consider himself to be a well-rounded and cultivated gentleman. The aristocratic ideal was strong, and the college was looked upon as an institution for the preparation of members of the ruling and upper classes in whatever field of endeavor the individual might choose.

It was primarily an education through language and books. The interests of the students were not to be considered in drawing up the curriculum. Education was conceived to be a fixed and known quantity which should be completely prescribed for all students with no choice or selection to be permitted. College education was designed exclusively for boys, and the boys normally began college work at the age of fourteen or fifteen. The three-year course soon was expanded to four years leading to the Bachelor of Arts degree. Language and mathematics were the staple "arts" which the boys must master. The entering students were grouped in a class, and all the members of the class studied the same books or subjects at the same time under the instruction of a tutor who carried one class in all subjects throughout the four years. Besides reading and learning the required books, the boys would engage in disputation on topics of a wide range and would develop their arguments, questions, and answers according to formal rules of logic and rhetoric. Oratory and declamation also played their part in the curriculum. A little botany on summer Saturday afternoons and a little ancient history on winter Saturday afternoons rounded out the program of studies.

The six-day week with long church services on Sunday left no room for physical exercise or recreation except as adolescent spirits broke out in riots, fights, brawls, and gambling, all of which brought down severe fines or public whippings. The methods of teaching were almost entirely devoted to reading of books by the instructor, the reading back by students, recitation on the content learned, and writing of digests and outlines of the arguments of the books. Student participation of an active sort was largely confined to formal disputations and declamations.

Late in the seventeenth century and increasingly in the eighteenth century there were signs that the Medieval and Renaissance content of education was gradually being changed to conform with the new intellectual currents of thought that were developing in the Enlightenment (see Chapter 2). Aristotelian logic and geometry began to give way to books on logic based on the work of the French scholars Descartes and Ramus; the geocentric astronomy of Ptolemy and Aristotle began to be revised according to the heliocentric theories of Copernicus, Galileo, Kepler, Gassendi, and Newton. The college had a telescope by 1672, and one of the tutors, Thomas Brattle, made observations of the Great Comet of 1680 which contributed usefully to Newton's works. By 1687 Charles Morton wrote a *Compendium Physicae* based largely upon Newtonian physics.

Considerable leadership in the field of natural philosophy and mathematics was exerted by Harvard professors in the eighteenth century. A professorship in these fields was founded by Thomas Hollis in 1728, and the incumbents of this chair made notable contributions. Isaac Greenwood wrote books on the practical applications of arithmetic, meteorology, and astronomy, and John Winthrop was probably, next to Franklin, the most noted scientific investigator in the colonies. By the middle of the century, not only was Enlightenment science having a hearing, but new philosophical and psychological ideas were being propounded in the use of such books as Fordyce's *Moral Philosophy* and John Locke's *Essay concerning Human Understanding*.

This expansion of the college curriculum and increased attention to the intellectual and scientific trends of the Enlightenment led to a significant change in the methods of teaching in 1767. In that year a single tutor was no longer expected to teach all subjects to the members of a class, but specialization in teaching was arranged whereby one tutor would teach one subject and another tutor was to teach another subject. For example, one tutor was to teach Latin; another tutor to teach Greek; a third to teach logic, metaphysics, and ethics; a fourth to teach natural philosophy, geography, astronomy, and mathematics; and a fifth to teach elocution, English composition, rhetoric, and literature. This was not only a significant move toward specialization in teaching but also recognized the importance of the English language and literature as a study worthy of college instruction. In 1769 a further radical departure was achieved when students were permitted to study French if they gained their parents' permission. Apparently the college was not prepared to take sole responsibility for what the students might come across in the way of danger to their morals were they to read French authors without approval.

The content of the courses of study at the other colonial colleges was not significantly different from that of Harvard. It may be that Yale's curriculum was more heavily weighted on the religious side. Yale had held closer to the orthodox Calvinism, whereas Harvard had begun to move more rapidly toward deism and Unitarianism under such presidents as John Leverett and Edward Holyoke and such professors of divinity as Edward Wigglesworth. Even so, Yale, too, began to change the content of its teachings along the lines of Enlightenment philosophy and science. Newton's *Principia* and *Optics* were present at Yale as early as 1715 and were used by Samuel Johnson when he was a tutor there. Bishop Berkeley gave many books to Yale, and other persons, including Franklin, contributed "philosophical apparatus" like that at Harvard, including globes, microscopes, and mechanical instruments. By the time of the Revolution Locke's *Essay* and books on mathematics and English grammar were in use at Yale. Similarly, at William and Mary the mathematical and scientific interest probably kept pace under the guidance of such professors as Hugh Jones and William Small, Scottish scientist, who taught Jefferson.

The other colonial colleges founded in the middle of the eighteenth century followed in general the patterns set by the first three. Princeton (1746), King's (1754), Brown (1764), Rutgers (1766), and Dartmouth (1769) probably had a larger share of sectarian religious concern present in their foundings than did the College at Philadelphia (1755).

King's College made a good deal of the practical and utilitarian concept of higher education in its initial promotional plans, but little came of it except by way of mathematical and philosophical studies. President Johnson himself described the character of the curriculum at King's College in the middle of the eighteenth century. Johnson taught the freshmen Latin, Greek, Hebrew, ethics, rhetoric, and logic and as much Christian morality as he could. In the sophomore year the boys read Cicero's *De Oratore,* and *De Officiis* and Caesar's *Commentaries* in Latin and Aesop's *Fables,* Xenophon's *Cyropaedia,* and Homer in Greek. In the second and third years the boys studied arithmetic, geometry, trigonometry; in the third and fourth they studied natural philosophy, geography, and astronomy. At the end of the fourth year Johnson taught them his own principles of logic and ethics. As can be seen from this description, the King's College curriculum did not depart much from that of the other colonial colleges despite its early advertisements.

The College of Philadelphia did somewhat better if William Smith's plan of a liberal education was actually put into operation. Smith's plan called for the usual classical and rhetorical studies to be taught in the afternoons, but the distinctive emphasis was to be upon three "schools of philosophy" whose classes were to be taught in the mornings. One school was called "instrumental philosophy" and referred to the practical applications of mathematics. The second, called "moral philosophy," included ethics, history, law and government, trade and commerce; and the third, "natural philosophy," included the several branches of physics and other physical sciences. This plan more nearly approached the extensive proposals of Franklin and Jefferson, as described in Chapter 3, than that of any of the other colonial colleges. The colleges were gradually becoming secularized in content and atmosphere as proposed by Enlightenment writers, but at the Revolution the dominant temper continued to be classical and religious.

TEACHERS AND THE PROFESSION

Supervision and Control of Teachers

Throughout the colonial period much attention was paid and effort expended to see that teachers lived up to the expectations of those who controlled education. The appointing officers were given the right to inquire into the qualification of teachers and to see that they did not deviate from community standards whether religious, political, or moral. In New England teachers were approved by town meetings, selectmen, school committees, and ministers; in the middle colonies they were issued certificates by royal governors, royal proprietors, and religious groups; in the South they were certified by governors, parish officials, and religious agencies. Where the Church of England was established, teachers often had to be certified by the Bishop of London; under Dutch rule in New York the certifying agency was the governor by authority of the Classis of Amsterdam or the Dutch West India Company.

The three most common requirements of teachers were that they be religiously orthodox, loyal to the civil government, and morally acceptable. For example, a law of Massachusetts in 1654 required the overseers of Harvard and the selectmen of the towns to see that no teachers were appointed who were "unsound in the faith or scandalous in their lives." Henry Dunster had been dismissed by the General Count the year before because he had adopted views on infant baptism contrary to the reigning Calvinist doctrines. When he opposed infant baptism, he apparently became "unsound in the faith" and therefore a dangerous person to be the head of the college and in charge of the lives of Puritan boys. Similar attention to religious orthodoxy of teachers was paid by the Dutch officials in New York and by the Church of England authorities and the civil authorities in the colonies of the South.

Some gains were made for academic freedom at Harvard in the eighteenth century when the board of overseers overlooked the theological position of John Winthrop upon his appointment in 1738 as Hollis Professor of Mathematics and Natural Philosophy. Similarly, President Clap at Yale argued a few years later that religious orthodoxy would be better served if the faculty and the college supervised themselves rather than submit to the supervision of the legislature. But by and large the legislatures were concerned to keep within their hands the authority to assure themselves of the political loyalty of the teachers.

While the colonies were subject to the crown and Parliament of England, teachers along with other public officials were required to be loyal to England and take oaths of allegiance to the crown. When the Revolution broke out, many of the legislatures quickly moved to pass laws requiring teachers to sign oaths of allegiance to the newly established states. Such laws were passed by Massachusetts in 1776, New Jersey in 1777, and Pennsylvania in 1778. These were aimed at weeding out of the ranks of teachers those who remained loyal to Britain and to retain only those who were loyal to the republican principles of the Revolution. Teachers were thus forced by law to subscribe to the principles of the American Revolution, an interesting forecast of later attempts by state legislatures to require teachers to take oaths of loyalty to constituted governments.

As might be expected, some teachers of the colonial period were prominent for their attitudes for and against the Revolution. John Lovell, master of the Boston Latin School in the eighteenth century, was a Conservative and Tory who left Boston at the onset of the Revolution, and Jonathan Boucher, a Church of England loyalist, who had taught in Virginia and Maryland, went back to England in 1775. On the other hand, notable patriots among teachers were Phillip Vickers Fithian, who was a tutor on a Virginia plantation, Joseph Warren, master of the grammar school at Roxbury, Massachusetts, and Nathan Hale, who taught school in New London, Connecticut. The Quaker meeting in Philadelphia protested in 1779 against the law of Pennsylvania requiring oaths of teachers, and on the basis of religious conscience were able to achieve the revocation of a fine levied upon a Quaker schoolmaster who had refused to sign the oath of allegiance on grounds of conscientious objection to war and to oaths.

The third ground upon which teachers could be dismissed throughout the colonial period related to morality and character. Whereas the grounds of religious orthodoxy began to be softened by the end of the colonial period and the grounds of political loyalty began to harden with the onset of the Revolution, the opposition to immoral behavior by teachers remained a constant source of surveillance over the lives and personal actions of teachers.

Preparation and Qualifications of Teachers

The preparation of teachers for their jobs was a very uncertain and uneven element in colonial education. Some teachers were very well prepared both in temperament and training for the life of a professional educator; these would be found most often in the better known grammar schools and in the colleges. Men like Ezekiel Cheever, Elijah Corlett, William Tennent, John

Lovell, and Francis Pastorius gained rather widespread reputation as school-masters of note. College professors and presidents often achieved considerable reputation for their scholarly and intellectual attainments. Prominent among these were Isaac Greenwood and John Winthrop at Harvard, Thomas Clap at Yale, Hugh Jones and William Small at William and Mary, William Smith at Philadelphia, and Samuel Johnson at King's.

Often, however, teachers and schoolmasters were not guided by any particular professional or long-term motivation. Teaching, then as now, was often looked upon as a waiting station until something better came along or as a part-time job to supplement an otherwise inadequate income. Young prospective clergymen would teach school for a time while waiting for a call to a pastorate, or established clergymen whose main task was their pastorate would teach children or boys for fees to help keep the wolf from the door. Then there were always the adventurers and misfits who had tried other enterprises unsuccessfully and then turned as a last resort to teaching in order to keep body and soul together until a more remunerative business or scheme could be devised. Indentured servants sometimes could use teaching as a means of building up enough of an estate to buy their freedom.

Whereas much was made by the public of the religious, political, and moral worthiness of their teachers, the public seldom had very high expectations concerning the professional training of teachers. The usual thought was that the teacher should know enough about his subject matter to be able to pass his knowledge on to his pupils. Many contracts with elementary teachers simply say that the teacher should know how to read and write or to reckon as qualification for teaching these subjects. For grammar school teachers a knowledge of Latin and Greek as usually obtained in college was deemed sufficient.

Somewhat more elaborate were the qualifications required of teachers for the Society for the Propagation of the Gospel in Foreign Parts as issued in 1711. In this case the teacher had to have certificates signed by reputable persons including the minister of the parish attesting to his age, marital status, temper, prudence, learning, "sober and pious conversation," zeal for the Christian religion, loyalty to the government, conformity to the doctrine and discipline of the Church of England, and ability to teach reading, writing, and the catechism of the Church of England. This set a rather high standard for the times for elementary school teachers.

For most of the colonial period the training of teachers was given little thought or attention by colleges or schools. Grammar school teachers usually had to have college training, but the colleges apparently did not recognize teaching in the schools as an occupation or profession worthy of special training or instruction beyond that of the regular course of study for a liberal arts education. Apprenticeship was sometimes used as a method of preparation for teaching along with tailoring, carpentry, and other trades. From

the middle of the eighteenth century onward the idea grew that one purpose of the academies might be to provide teachers of the English subjects
for the elementary schools. This was one of the arguments used in the
proposals for Franklin's academy in Philadelphia and later became a characteristic part of the academy movement, for which purpose state governments would often contribute public funds to the support of the private
academies.

Status and Salaries of Teachers

In general the status and salaries of teachers in the colonial period set the
pattern that persists to the present day, whereby the highest salaries and
highest social positions were accorded to college teachers, the next best to
secondary school teachers, and the lowest to elementary school teachers.
This represented the upper-class character of secondary and higher education
as over against the lower class character of elementary schools. In general, the
status of teachers was probably best in New England compared to that of
the other colonies as a group. Grammar school masters and their wives were
often assigned fairly high places of honor in the town churches. The salary
of a grammar school teacher in New England probably ranged from 20
to 60 pounds a year, which might mean a salary of anywhere from $50 to
$100 a year in addition to board. This would put the higher paid teachers in
the middle-class status and the more poorly paid teachers in lower-class
status comparable to artisans and tradesmen (see Table 2, p. 32).

Salaries were often irregular in payment and often were paid in produce
or livestock as well as in cash. All sorts of arrangements were made involving
the furnishing of board, houses, lands, exemption from taxation, and the
right to charge fees and tuitions as means of supplementing cash payments.
Even the most notable of teachers had difficulty in making ends meet. President Dunster of Harvard was required to collect his own assessments from
reluctant taxpayers. Elijah Corlett petitioned the General Court of Massachusetts in 1659 for a grant of land because he could not live on his salary,
and the legislature granted the request. Ezekiel Cheever, after fifty years of
teaching, had to make a special petition to the royal governor of Massachusetts
to enable him to maintain his family by asking that the sums of money owed
to him should actually be paid. In some cases the public, then as now, was
reluctant to believe that teachers needed more than a pittance in order to
be able to perform their duties as persons and citizens as well as teachers.

The necessity for the teacher to adapt himself to the pleasure of the people
he served is clearly brought out in the journal and letters of Philip Vickers
Fithian who was born in New Jersey and went to be a tutor to the children
of a wealthy Virginia planter. He reported that it was advisable to attend
church regularly on Sundays, stay close in the retirement of his rooms, pursue
the scholarly life, read his books, and stay totally away from women. In

many quarters of the land the patrons of education often felt that teaching was a fairly undemanding task, and they therefore would add to the duties of the teacher such custodial duties as cleaning out the church, ringing the bell, providing a baptismal basin, running errands, serving as messenger, and digging graves, as well as assisting the pastor in reading the Scriptures and leading the singing at church services, keeping records, issuing invitations, writing letters, visiting the sick, and generally making himself useful. Here is the background of the more modern expectations that teachers will contribute their services to community agencies by teaching Sunday school and otherwise "helping out" where needed. Colonial teachers often had to supplement their meager incomes from teaching by farming, shepherding, keeping taverns, or engaging in skilled labor. This will be no news to many present-day teachers who also work afternoons and evenings in countless ways to augment their still generally inadequate salaries.

In the colonial period teachers seldom thought of themselves as a group having common professional interests and problems. They had no professional organizations and no standards for preparation. When teachers began to organize themselves for mutual discussion and attainment of adequate salaries and working conditions, and when professional training at the college or university level came to be expected for entrance upon the job and for improvement in service, teaching gradually became a profession. Beginnings along these lines were made in the nineteenth century, but the problem still remains a difficult and important one in the twentieth century.

ISSUES FOR STUDY AND DISCUSSION

1. Criticize the following proposition: "In colonial times the paramount authority for education was vested in the civil government, but developing conditions led to increased delegation of power by the state to local units and to private agencies." What were the conditions that led to such delegation of power? Are these conditions still present in the same degree today? Is large freedom for private and religious education as developed in the eighteenth century a good thing for today?

2. What might have happened in America if the dual system of schools of colonial times based upon religion or social class had been maintained to the present time? Is a single-track system of public schools more appropriate to modern American life?

3. Decentralized patterns of educational control appeared in the colonial period. Are the colonial conditions that produced the district school system still operating today or do you think that greater centralization is necessary or desirable?

4. Expansion and change in the educational program of schools and colleges began as early as the eighteenth century. Do you think such trends were on the whole a good thing for American education and for American life? What was lost, and what was gained?

5. What do you think were the most desirable aspects of the role and status of the teaching profession in colonial times? What were its greatest weaknesses? How

would you compare these strengths and weaknesses with those of the profession today?

SUGGESTIONS FOR FURTHER READING

Beale, Howard K., *A History of Freedom of Teaching in American Schools*, New York, Scribner, 1941.

Bell, Sadie, *The Church, the State, and Education in Virginia*, New York, Science Press, 1930.

Brown, Elmer E., *The Making of Our Middle Schools*, New York, Longmans, 1903.

Burns, James A., *The Growth and Development of the Catholic School System in the United States*, New York, Benziger, 1912.

Butler, Vera M., *Education as Revealed by New England Newspapers Prior to 1850*, Philadelphia, Majestic Press, 1935.

Butts, R. Freeman, *The College Charts Its Course*, New York, McGraw-Hill, 1939.

Elsbree, Willard S., *The American Teacher*, New York, American Book, 1939.

Ford, Paul L. (ed.), *The New England Primer*, New York, Dodd, 1899.

Gould, Elizabeth P., *Ezekiel Cheever, Schoolmaster*, Boston, Palmer, 1904.

Heartman, Charles F., *The New England Primer, Issued Prior to 1830*, New York, Bowker, 1934.

Holmes, Pauline, *A Tercentenary History of the Boston Public Latin School, 1635–1935*, Cambridge, Harvard University Press, 1935.

Jackson, George L., *The Development of School Support in Colonial Massachusetts*, New York, Teachers College, Columbia University, 1909.

Jernegan, Marcus W., *Laboring and Dependent Classes in Colonial America, 1607–1783*, Chicago, University of Chicago Press, 1931.

Johnson, Clifton, *Old-Time Schools and Schoolbooks*, New York, Macmillan, 1904.

Kemp, William Webb, *The Support of Schools in Colonial New York by the Society for the Propagation of the Gospel in Foreign Parts*, New York, Teachers College, Columbia University, 1913.

Kilpatrick, William H., *The Dutch Schools of New Netherland and Colonial New York*, Bulletin 12, Washington, D. C., U. S. Bureau of Education, 1912.

Knight, Edgar W., *A Documentary History of Education in the South before 1860*, Chapel Hill, University of North Carolina Press, 1949–1952, Vols. 1–3.

McGucken, William J., *The Jesuits and Education*, Milwaukee, Bruce, 1932.

Meriwether, Colyer, *Our Colonial Curriculum, 1607–1776*, Washington, D. C., Capital Publishing, 1907.

Morison, Samuel Eliot, *The Founding of Harvard College*, Cambridge, Harvard University Press, 1935.

———, *Harvard College in the Seventeenth Century*, Cambridge, Harvard University Press, 1936, 2 vols.

Parsons, Elsie Clews, *Educational Legislation and Administration of Colonial Governments*, New York, Macmillan, 1899.

Seybolt, Robert F., *Apprenticeship and Apprenticeship Education in Colonial New England and New York*, New York, Teachers College, Columbia University, 1916.

———, *The Evening School in Colonial America*, Urbana, University of Illinois Press, 1925.

———, *The Private Schools of Colonial Boston,* Cambridge, Harvard University Press, 1935.

———, *The Public Schools of Colonial Boston, 1635–1775,* Cambridge, Harvard University Press, 1935.

———, *Source Studies in American Colonial Education: The Private School,* Urbana, University of Illinois Press, 1925.

Small, Walter H., *Early New England Schools,* Boston, Ginn, 1914.

Suzzalo, Henry, *The Rise of Local School Supervision in Massachusetts,* New York, Teachers College, Columbia University, 1906.

Tewksbury, Donald G., *The Founding of American Colleges and Universities before the Civil War,* New York, Teachers College, Columbia University, 1932.

Tuer, Andrew, *History of the Horn-book,* New York, Scribner, 1897.

Updegraff, Harlan, *The Origin of the Moving School in Massachusetts,* New York, Teachers College, Columbia University, 1908.

Wells, Guy F., *Parish Education in Colonial Virginia,* New York, Teachers College, Columbia University, 1923.

Woody, Thomas, *Early Quaker Education in Pennsylvania,* New York, Teachers College, Columbia University, 1920.

———, *A History of Women's Education in the United States,* New York, Science Press, 1929, 2 vols.

PART 2

THE DEVELOPMENT OF A DISTINCTIVE AMERICAN EDUCATION
(1779-1865)

5

THE GROWTH OF THE AMERICAN REPUBLIC

THE DISTINCTIVE way of life which we today recognize as "American" did not come into existence with the signing of a declaration or the ratification of a constituion. While such instruments doubtless exerted their profound influence, this way of life was far more a product of geographical, political, economic, social, and intellectual forces which had been maturing for at least a century. Many of them have already been discussed in Part I in connection with the great liberalizing movements of the colonial period. Yet it was largely in the years between 1779 and 1865 that American society really took on a character which set it apart from its European antecedents.

These years saw the gradual extension of the suffrage in the direction of universality, the general democratizing of political processes, the beginnings of industrialism which gave rise to a highly education-conscious labor movement, and the growth of a vigorous, assertive nationalism. Life on the rich, virgin land of the new republic fostered a hardy, independent people whose political and social relations exemplified to an amazing degree the principles of liberty and equality enunciated by the founding fathers. Needless to say, such a people soon demanded sweeping changes in educational institutions which had traditionally catered to a comparatively small segment of society. In response to their demands emerged a school system as different from its predecessors as was the society which it sought to serve.

THE FRONTIER AND THE SELF-SUSTAINING FARM FAMILY

The decades following the founding of the republic were years of expansion. In the older states settlers.quickly moved from the more populated seaboard areas to the back-country wilderness where they carved farms out of the backwoods. By 1860 twenty new states had joined the original thirteen; and the entrance of California and Oregon into the Union had brought the boundaries of the United States to the Pacific. Although the center of population remained in the East, its movement westward was soon begun by the rapid increase of these western populations.

Life in these newly settled regions was unique in character. Remote from the social comforts of the towns and cities and free of constraining European customs and class labels, the self-dependent farm family lived close to the land on which it subsisted. In place of the closely knit European village, where families lived together and only scattered daily to till the surrounding soil, Americans developed the neighborhood community, in which families actually lived out on the land they worked. Communication remained a luxury. Roads were poor at best—valleys of mud in the spring and dusty paths in the summer. It has been estimated, for instance, that in rural New England of the early nineteenth century, only one fourth to one fifth of the population had access to existing market and trade facilities. The remainder was almost completely isolated from commercial relations.

Such conditions of isolation developed in the farm family a versatility which has since become legend. Of necessity, practically everything required to maintain life—food, clothing, shelter, and even many farm utensils—was manufactured on the homestead proper. Young and old alike participated together in the struggle for existence. The family became the fundamental economic unit of the agrarian community. For many weeks of the year it was also a self-sufficient social unit.

Given these conditions of isolated self-sufficiency, there was little to be gained from advantages of wealth or noble birth. Men rapidly became the equals of their fellows as each sought a living by his own efforts. Equality became not only a deeply held value, but at times, almost a fetish. The slightest indication of "aristocracy"—a polished mannerism, perhaps, or a well-turned phrase—was potentially punishable by social ostracism. The individualism of the independent family unit became the keynote of this agricultural society. To be sure, one finds numerous examples of communal activity. The cooperative raising of a new dwelling or neighborhood school or church is a familiar incident in the rural life of the period. Yet these were *voluntary* activities in which individuals participated of their own free will. The proverbial neighborliness of the frontier was the neighborliness of independent yeomen. Fundamentally, this was a society of free and equal families.

It was virtually inevitable that such conditions would profoundly influence American life as a whole. First, there was the strong effect of these democratic values of independence and equality on life in the older Eastern regions. In the bitter struggles over the suffrage in the seaboard states between 1775 and

1850, the small frontier farmers almost unanimously aligned themselves with those forces favoring extension. When the new states entered the Union, almost all joined with constitutional provisions for universal manhood suffrage. In educational conflicts, too, the free western farmers were often on the side of eastern middle-class reformers. Although continued settlement of frontier communities in many cases brought conservative leaders to replace earlier liberals, this democratic effect of the west on America as a whole cannot be underestimated.

A second tremendous influence of the frontier was exerted through the strong drawing power of vast areas of cheap, fertile land on the growing populations of the East. The sons of a New England farmer, after several years of labor and frugal living, could leave the exhausted land of their fathers and strike out with their savings for a homestead in the western territories. German and Scandinavian immigrant farmers could push west to the rich land of Ohio, Illinois, Wisconsin, Minnesota, and the Dakotas rather than settle in the industrial towns of the East. It is true that not everyone could go west. Money, skill, ingenuity, and courage were necessary to meet the rigorous demands of farming on the frontier. But even in light of the selective character of westward migration, thousands who might well have glutted the eastern labor market were drawn off and given an opportunity to start life anew. In this way the frontier provided what Frederick Jackson Turner has called a population "safety valve" for the East.

Politically, economically, and socially, frontier agricultural life exerted a considerable influence on the total picture of American democracy. It injected the tenets of freedom, equality, and individualism not only into the newly settled areas, but well back into the older, more populated regions. In effect, it cast the shadow of its virile character over the whole of the nation.

THE DEMOCRATIZING OF POLITICS

At the outbreak of the Revolution the traditional English notion that only the rich and wellborn should participate in government still prevailed throughout the colonies. The most common qualifications for voting were ownership of property and payment of public taxes, the theory being that society was a giant corporation and those who owned the most "stock" should have the most to say about policy making (see Chapter 1). No one, perhaps, expressed this colonial ideal more clearly than Alexander Hamilton, when he argued in 1787:

> All communities divide themselves into the few and the many. The first are the rich and well born, the other the mass of the people. . . . The people are turbulent and changing; they seldom judge or determine right. Give, therefore, to the first class a distinct, permanent share in the government. They will check

the unsteadiness of the second; and as they cannot receive any advantage by a change, they therefore will maintain good government.[1]

Accordingly, it has been estimated that only one white male in seven was eligible to vote at the time of the ratification of the Constitution in 1789.

Three important influences of the late eighteenth century, however, served increasingly to challenge this conception. First, and perhaps foremost, no policy which excluded most citizens from the suffrage could long remain compatible with the Revolutionary doctrines of equality and "natural rights." When these doctrines were reinforced by the surge of democratic ideas from the frontier areas (and later from the working groups of the towns and cities), they provided powerful arguments for extending voting privileges to all. Finally, the competition of new political parties for votes was also a powerful incentive for universal suffrage.

It was not long before state constitutional conventions began to act on grass roots demands for an extended franchise. Vermont and Kentucky entered the Union in 1791 and 1792, respectively, with neither taxpaying nor property qualifications for voting. By 1821 Connecticut, Delaware, Massachusetts, and New York had liberalized their suffrage provisions regarding property; while Georgia, New Hampshire and South Carolina had removed such requirements completely. At mid-century twelve of the original thirteen states had abolished the property requirement (North Carolina retained one until 1856), while seven had completely done away with taxpaying qualifications (Connecticut, Georgia, Maryland, New Hampshire, New Jersey, New York, South Carolina). After 1817 every new state which entered did so with constitutional provision for universal manhood suffrage.[2] The gradual but important shift in political power which ensued is well reflected in the election of 1828, when Andrew Jackson and the Democratic Party, backed principally by small farmers and urban workers, were elected to head the national government.

Closely paralleling this extension of the suffrage was the movement to liberalize actual political procedures themselves. The founding fathers, for instance, had provided that the President be chosen by electors picked by the legislatures of the various states. It was a means by which they hoped to keep the Presidency out of the hands of the people at large. Gradually, however, the people began to demand this power for themselves, and by 1832 South Carolina was the only state in which the legislature continued to choose presidential electors. Similarly, party organization was changed to allow for greater popular voice in policy making. Whereas formerly candidates for high office had been selected by small party caucuses of national and local legislators,

[1] Jonathan Elliot, ed., *The Debates in the Several State Conventions, on the Adoption of the Federal Constitution, as Recommended by the General Convention at Philadelphia, in 1787* (Philadelphia, Lippincott, 1888), Vol. 1, pp. 421–422.

[2] Kirk H. Porter, *A History of Suffrage in the United States* (Chicago, University of Chicago Press, 1918).

they now began to be chosen by popular conventions which more adequately represented rank and file elements.

Finally, one notes during the first three decades of the nineteenth century, a gradual change in the notion of eligibility for public office. Whereas formerly even the staunchest republicans had doubted the capacity of the "common man" to carry on the actual business of government, the 1830's saw the growth of the conception that any citizen could effectively manage positions of public trust and responsibility. On the frontier the reaction against "aristocratic" officials went so far that often the well-educated candidate for elective office was at a decided disadvantage. Hall, for instance, reports the campaign of an unschooled candidate for the Indiana legislature in 1828 who actually argued that his educational shortcomings might well hinder his chances of doing his constituency too much good but it would also keep him from doing them too much harm.[3] In any case, the shift was a real one. When coupled with the introduction of the "spoils system" in 1828, it significantly changed the character of American government and politics.

Needless to say, these new trends were clearly manifested in the general political developments of the period. With the exception of Whig victories in 1840 and 1848 the Jeffersonian Republicans and their successors, the Democratic Party, won every national election until Lincoln became President in 1860. In the early part of the century the Democratic-Republicans found most of their support among the independent farming groups of the South and West. During and after the 1820's they were joined by increasing numbers of newly enfranchised artisans and workingmen from the eastern cities. The coalition thus formed stood for states' rights, popular suffrage, low tariffs, opposition to "special privileges," and, as they phrased it, the rights of the "common man." On the other hand, their opponents—first the Federalists and later the Whigs—generally proposed high tariffs for the protection of business and industrial interests and appealed more directly to conservative and well-to-do groups. With the heightening of interest in the slavery question during and after the later 1830's, the alignment of forces changed, and in 1860 the newly formed Republican Party (successors to the Whigs) won the Presidency on a platform of opposition to slavery, free land, and a high tariff—a platform designed to appeal both to western farmers and eastern businessmen.

AGRARIAN SOCIAL DEMOCRACY

When the first volume of Alexis de Tocqueville's memorable treatise, *Democracy in America,* was published in 1835, it began with the following observation:

[3] Baynard Rush Hall, *The New Purchase or, Seven and a Half Years in the Far West* (James Albert Woodburn, ed. (Princeton, Princeton University Press, 1918), p. 176.

Among the novel objects that attracted my attention during my stay in the United States, nothing struck me more forcibly than the general equality of condition among the people. I readily discovered the prodigious influence that this primary fact exercises on the whole course of society; it gives a peculiar direction to public opinion and a peculiar tenor to the laws; it imparts new maxims to the governing authorities and peculiar habits to the governed.[4]

To be sure, this was the statement of one French visitor highly favorable to the Americans and their institutions. Yet even its unbounded optimism could not dull its essential accuracy.

Fifty years before, established clergies and politically privileged classes in the several states had been seeking desperately to maintain the foothold they had established in the colonial period. Debtor's prisons were crowded with their unfortunate hordes, and in New York men not far removed from serfdom tilled the vast estates of the Van Rensselaer family. The Constitution, while proclaiming the sovereignty of "we the people," had been originally designed to allow a small, well-educated group to do the ruling. Now, in slightly over one generation, the unbounded resources and unlimited opportunity of a new continent had wrought their effect. Men had achieved a greater degree of equality and security than they had enjoyed, perhaps, at any time in human history.

Although social classes persisted in America, the gulf between them became less and less wide. Francis Grund, a German visitor, observed that the "laboring classes in America are really less removed from the wealthy merchants and professional men than they are in any part of Europe; and the term 'mob,' with which the lower classes in England are honored, does not apply to any portion of the American community."[5] What gulf there was between social classes was fairly easily traversed, and social mobility was everywhere in evidence. The laws of inheritance and entail had been so modified as to leave little chance for a landed aristocracy, after the fashion of Europe, to take root. One European observer, on surveying the social scene in 1839, was led to predict that it would be fully half a century, perhaps, before a select circle of society could be collected together in any one city or region.[6]

What upper-class groups there were in America (the families who had begun to build great trading, manufacturing, or land fortunes) were careful not to stand aloof from the people. Rich and poor alike worked at some trade or profession. Tocqueville noted that he found "no class in America in which

[4] Alexis de Tocqueville, *Democracy in America,* Phillips Bradley, ed. (New York, Knopf, 1946), Vol. I, p. 3.

[5] Francis J. Grund, *The Americans, in their Moral, Social and Political Relations* (Boston, Marsh, Capen and Lyon, 1837), p. 38.

[6] Frederick Marryat, *A Diary in America* (London, Longman, Orme, Brown, Green, and Longmans, 1839), Vol. I, Pt. I, p. 24.

the taste for intellectual pleasures is transmitted with hereditary fortune and leisure and by which the labors of the intellect are held in honor." [7] Sir Charles Lyell, who visited New England in 1846, fancied himself "in a country where all, whether rich or poor, were laboring from morning till night, without ever indulging in a holiday." [8] Even the young sons of southern plantation owners, often under no necessity to work for a living, generally felt obliged to take up some profession. Generally, all Americans followed some trade, calling, or employment.

In the realm of dress, too, class distinctions became less and less obvious during these years. Knee breeches, donned pantaloons, and lace, which had been popular with gentlemen of the Revolutionary era, had all but disappeared by 1830. Good clothing, while it still maintained ornaments and frills, tended to become ever more simple. So also with manners, where the formal graces gradually gave way to simple courtesies. Moreover, while the dropping of upper-class labels tended to narrow social distances, the gaps were closed even further by the never ending efforts of ambitious social climbers to imitate the customs of the wellborn.

Generally, the European contempt for the more humble occupations tended to disappear from the American scene. Nor was the idea of working for remuneration looked down upon. Callings were more or less skilled, and more or less profitable; but none was held either in reverence or disdain. Every honest vocation, and even some dishonest ones, was honorable. In keeping with the spirit of equality, the humbler classes of society exhorted a pride which literally fascinated European observers. Such habits as tipping were not at all common, and personal service was extremely difficult to maintain. "The spirit of the institutions of the States," wrote one French observer, "is so opposed to servitude, that it is chiefly from the emigrants that the Americans obtain their supply of domestics." [9] Even these were rapidly infected by the new spirit, and the diaries of visiting aristocrats were filled with complaints over the inefficiency of American servants. One writer even went so far as to urge Europeans contemplating the journey to America to leave their domestics at home, lest they be ruined by American notions of equality.[10]

On the whole, the lot of the early nineteenth-century American was a good one and a secure one, and a spirit of optimism and progress pervaded his every thought and behavior. Within a context of vertical social movement and equal opportunity, class lines remained largely fluid, and a kind of equalizing, middling tendency colored social, economic, and intellectual life. In effect social democracy had to a great extent been achieved.

[7] de Tocqueville, *op. cit.,* Vol. I, p. 52.
[8] Charles Lyell, *A Second Visit to the United States of North America* (New York, Harper, 1849), Vol. II, p. 91.
[9] Marryat, *op. cit.,* Vol. I, Pt. II, p. 144.
[10] Lyell, *op. cit.,* Vol. II, p. 167.

THE BEGINNINGS OF INDUSTRIAL CAPITALISM

Revolutionary America was predominantly agricultural. It is probable that nine out of ten breadwinners during the late eighteenth century were engaged in some form of farming during the greater part of the year. The existence of vast tracts of cheap, fertile land led rather naturally to such a pattern, and it is not unlikely that the economic security engendered by such conditions contributed powerfully to demands for political and social democracy. But if this agrarianism set the theme, the period also heard the rumblings of a new industrialism. Fertilized by British and American invention, nurtured by the funds of an ever expanding capitalism of trade, this industrialism developed into a force destined to change the American way of life.

One important factor in the early stages of this development was the influx of technological ideas from England. British inventors of the eighteenth century were well along the road to machine production of textiles. A long series of inventions, starting with the flying shuttle in 1733 and moving through Hargreaves' spinning jenny (1764), Arkwright's water frame (1769), and Crompton's spinning mule (1779).found their way to America despite stringent English efforts to keep them at home. As early as 1775 a spinning jenny appeared in Philadelphia, and another with further mechanical improvements made its appearance in the mill of Samuel Slater at Pawtucket, Rhode Island, in 1790. With the great rise in the cotton supply provided by Whitney's cotton gin in 1793, America had all the elements for an unprecedented expansion of textile production. Similar mechanization also came slowly in distilling, canning, tobacco manufacture, lumbering, and shipbuilding.

Paralleling these mechanical developments came rapid exploitation of power. Water power was readily available in the myriad streams of New England, and dams and water wheels soon began to dot the New England countryside. As early as 1801 steam power, based on the principles of Watt in England, made its appearance in connection with American iron-working machinery. Although the ready availability of water power in the New England states won it ascendancy at first, by 1850 steam had far surpassed water as a source of industrial power.

Equally stimulating to the development of industrialism was the expansion of communication and transportation facilities. Within less than a decade after the initial run of Fulton's "Claremont" up the Hudson River in 1807, the steamboat was an established conveyance on the Mississippi River. Congress aided this development during the decade following 1824 by making regular appropriations for the general improvement of these waterways. Undoubtedly, the steamboat was a prime factor in stimulating trade and production in the years following 1820.

Because of the hardship and high cost of overland transportation between the larger waterways, a logical next step was the building of the great canals. The Erie Canal, completed in 1825, and the Pennsylvania Canal, completed in 1834, provided important trade links between the West and the eastern manufacturing centers. So much public enthusiasm developed over canal building that the floating of unscrupulous loans to finance them became one of the prime causes of the depression of 1837.

A third, and perhaps the most important, step in the development of communications was the building of the railroads, coming rapidly on the heels of the canal boom. They provided the final links between the manufacturing and trade centers of the nation. Although the major task of constructing the great railroad networks was not begun in earnest until 1850, by that year there were already 9,000 miles of track in use. These short lines provided the first wide experiments with the railroad and served to link those important areas of the East which lacked water communication.

Finally, the invention of the telegraph by Samuel F. B. Morse in 1844 provided the link of verbal communication across the country. Government appropriations made possible the construction of the first line from Baltimore to Washington; and in less than a decade there were approximately fifty different telegraph companies in the several states. The telegraph, the rapidly developing federal postal service, and new techniques of printing and publishing interacted with the demands of political and commercial interests to usher in an era of unprecedented expansion in the interchange of news and ideas.

The total effect of this development in communications was to enhance greatly America's vigorous capitalism of trade. It was the profit from this merchant capitalism (a capitalism of businessmen who made their profits through trade and commercial activity) which eventually contributed in large part to the rise of later industrial capitalism (a capitalism of businessmen who made their profits through manufacture and production). With both, the spirit of economic individualism remained dominant, and it was expected that free competition and the natural laws of supply and demand would remain unfettered by government restrictions. "Every man is the maker of his own fortune" was the adage which governed the times.

Intimately bound up with the growth of industrialism was the beginning of the great movement to the cities. Although the early censuses considered as urban only communities having populations of 8,000 or more, it is possible to glean from their statistics the general trend toward urbanization. Thus, while the census of 1790 reported six such communities, embracing 3.3 percent of the population, the census of 1830 reported twenty-six, embracing 6.7 percent, and that of 1860 reported one hundred and forty-one, embracing 16.1 percent of the population. Life in these communities quickly became very different from the life of the rural neighborhood. The subsistence farm rapidly became a thing of the past for most families. With their livelihood now fully tied to factory employment, they soon lost the economic independence of the freehold farmer and descended into conditions of economic insecurity and even poverty. Although many maintained the spirit of independent artisans and petty producers, others quickly became simple factory laborers. The first real slums of America came into existence, and all the problems and low standards of crowded urban living made their appearance. Such conditions were only aggravated by the tremendous influx of immigrants who flowed into the cities between 1830 and 1860.

Thus, although industrialism did not by any means set the dominant note of American culture during these years, its influences had begun deeply to affect the lives of many Americans. The disturbances which even these infant beginnings wrought on the agrarian culture presaged the sweeping changes of an age yet to come.

THE GROWTH OF LABOR ORGANIZATIONS

One profoundly important outgrowth of this early industrialism was the development of an education-conscious labor movement. The banding together of workingmen for their mutual interest began in America in the last years of the eighteenth century with the organization of the Federal Society of Journeymen Cordwainers in Philadelphia in 1794. Collective action by such groups began when this society conducted its first strike in 1799 to resist wage cuts on the part of the masters. During the next decades, even though the courts declared strikes to be conspiratorial actions in restraint of trade, such associations multiplied and flourished. To be sure, they experienced their ups and downs in the face of varying economic conditions. By the time of Jackson, however, artisans in every craft had organized in the larger towns, and by 1836 there were some fifty-three unions in Philadelphia, fifty-two in New York, twenty-three in Baltimore, and sixteen in Boston. It seemed virtually inevitable during the period of political unrest characterizing Jackson's administrations that these workingmen's organizations should develop political arms. Accordingly, a workingmen's party appeared in Philadelphia in 1828, one in New York in 1829, and a whole flurry in New England during this same period.

The program of these organizations and their affiliated political parties was broad, progressive, and comprehensive. Furthermore, it was far more a program of *social* protest and reform than it was one of economic protest and reform. Rather than higher wages and shorter hours, it was "equal, universal education" which topped labor's list of demands during this period. Along with this came cries for "abolition of imprisonment for debt," "abolition of all 'licensed monopolies,'" "revision of the military system," and "equal taxation on property." At conventions and meetings resolutions of every kind bearing on these items were debated and adopted, and even though labor organizations suffered terrific loses in membership and funds during such upheavals as the panic of 1837, their effect cannot be underestimated.

It was principally through the intellectuals, writers, and reformers associated with the labor movement that the great wealth of "labor literature" emerged. According to this literature, a great struggle was under way between the great body of people—workers, small producers, and small farmers —on the one hand and a small minority of capitalists and financiers on the other. Whereas the former were woefully unorganized, the latter had extended their "well-ordered tentacles" over the state, the economic system, the press, and education. They saw in the financial systems of an expanding capitalism forces which were rapidly destroying the broad base of social democracy in America. "Thus far," wrote Stephen Simpson, early leader of the Philadelphia Working Men's Party, ". . . we perceive our constitution of *equal rights* to be the merest untenanted skeleton of liberty that the imagination of man can conceive; which, by its *operation,* creates aristocracy, privileges, extortion, monoply, and overgrown fortunes, and which, by its *letter,* declares that equality of rights shall be guaranteed to all and the pursuit of happiness to be a common boon secured to industry by the equity of her principles and the simplicity of her laws." [11]

How were the small farmers, planters, mechanics, and laborers to meet the challenge? Basically, according to the intellectuals, the answer lay in organization for protest, education, and political action. It was inevitable, in this cause, that they would run up against the intense individualism of the age, and they were forced to wage a constant battle against it. Thus, William Leggett, fiery radical editor of the *New York Evening Post* wrote:

> But let us ask what and where is the danger of a combination of the labouring classes, in vindication of their political principles, or in defence of their menaced rights? Have they not the right to act in concert, when their opponents act in concert? Nay, is it not their bounden duty to combine against the only enemy they have to fear as yet in this free country, monopoly and a great paper system that grinds them to the dust? [12]

It was through their newly won franchise that the "people" would triumph over the upper classes. "Teach the lawgivers a salutary lesson at the polls . . . ," preached Theophilus Fisk, a New-England Universalist minister; "vote for no man who is not pledged to maintain your cause at all risks and at every hazard. If you are united, your strength is well nigh omnipotent." [13]

While this "labor literature" was not entirely accepted by a still highly individualistic artisan group, it did make a strong impression on them. Though

[11] Stephen Simpson, "The Working Man's Manual: A New Theory of Political Economy, on the Principle of Production the Source of Wealth," quoted in Joseph Blau, ed., *Social Theories of Jacksonian Democracy* (New York, Hafner, 1947), pp. 141–142.

[12] *New York Evening Post* (Nov. 4, 1834), p. 2, col. 4.

[13] *New York Evening Post* (Aug. 6, 1835), p. 2, col. 2.

a spirited social equality dominated the scene, the long hours, low pay, and sporadic employment of the new industrialism were already to be seen in the mill towns and cities. And though the working groups continued to enjoy a good deal of independence and a reasonable standard of living, they became both frightened of industrial desolation elsewhere and determined to resist miserable social conditions at home.

MOVEMENT TOWARD SEPARATION OF CHURCH AND STATE [14]

The principle of separation of church and state was one of the achievements necessary for the creation of the new society that was in process of formation with the opening of the Revolutionary period. So long as men believed that morality rested upon specific religious beliefs, the state could not tolerate dissenters, for dissenting religious belief would imply immoral conduct inimical to the common welfare of civil society. When men began to grant that a person could be morally good and thus could be a good citizen even though he did not accept the dominant religious doctrines, the idea of establishment was threatened and separation was indicated.

More and more people came to believe that freedom of religion requires the assumption that there are different religious roads to the good life and that genuine religious freedom requires that the state guarantee equal rights of conscience to all religious claimants with no distinctions. They argued that a thorough acceptance of the equal rights of conscience requires that morality cannot be confined to those expressing some recognized religious or church doctrine.

The next step was to grant that in a democratic society the nonbeliever as well as the believer must be accorded the right to be considered capable of good moral conduct and of good citizenship. The test of good citizenship is morality, not religious belief. Thus, when the colonists decided to renounce their connection with Britain and become Americans, they also decided that their differing religious beliefs could not be allowed to stand in the way of the common ties of good citizenship. They therefore moved to separate the state from all churches as well as from any one church so that all Americans could become equally good citizens in the eyes of the civil law and of the state. The recognition that, so far as the state is concerned, good citizenship rests upon good conduct and not upon religious belief was the secular revolution that accompanied the political revolution. This recognition took the institutional form of separation of church and state.

The struggle for separation of church and state was a part of the larger Revolutionary struggle for separation from England; the Church of England was closely identified with the crown in the minds of Americans. Thus,

[14] R. Freeman Butts, *The American Tradition in Religion and Education* (Boston, Beacon Press, 1950), Chap. 4.

religious liberty and civil liberty were often closely associated. Just prior to the Revolution the Anglican groups tried to establish an American bishop to be in charge of all Anglican churches in America rather than to maintain the Anglican Church as subordinate to the Bishop of London. This move intensified the fears of dissenters that they would lose even what liberties they had gained. Also the Quebec Act of 1774 which gave privileges of tax support to the Roman Catholic Church in Canada intensified fears of Protestants in America that the English government was not to be trusted to preserve religious freedom.

On the home front the separation of church and state was a part of the larger revolutionary struggle to replace an aristocratic social, political, and economic system with a more democratic and "republican" system. Thus, in general, the "liberal" groups politically were in favor of separation, and the "conservative" groups politically were defenders of establishment. Insofar as the English political labels applied to America, Whigs were for separation and Tories were for establishment. When party lines were drawn during the early years of the new nation, Federalists tended to favor establishment and Democratic-Republicans tended to favor separation. These are broad generalizations subject to qualification, but, taking the country as a whole, the religious establishments were viewed along with other political, economic, and social privileges of the old order as objects for change in the effort to create a more equalitarian and democratic society along the lines of the natural rights doctrines of the Declaration of Independence. In its broader setting, then, the struggle for separation of church and state was an integral part of the Revolutionary struggle "for home rule" and the struggle to see "who would rule at home."

As described in Chapter 1, eight of the thirteen colonies had gone on record in their organic laws in favor of separation of church and state, but five still held on to a form of multiple establishment in which the state aided more than one religious group. During the course of the early national period these five states all moved to separation, by constitutional provision in South Carolina in 1790, in Maryland in 1810, in Connecticut in 1818, and in Massachusetts in 1833 and by statute in New Hampshire in 1819.

The most significant turning point arose in the critical period before the adoption of the United States Constitution in 1789 and is revealed most clearly in the struggle that took place in Virginia. Virginia's constitution of 1776 guaranteed religious freedom, but it soon became apparent that the state was divided concerning whether this meant that the state could or could not aid by public funds the several religious groups in the state.

After the Revolutionary War was over, the struggle was revived. The conservatives submitted a new religious bill reviving the principle of general assessment for religious support. In 1784 Patrick Henry vigorously supported multiple establishment as embodied in the Bill Establishing a Provision for

Teachers of the Christian Religion. The purpose of the assessment bill of 1784 was in Patrick Henry's words clearly to require all persons ". . . to pay a moderate tax or contribution annually for the support of the Christian religion, or of some Christian church, denomination or communion of Christians, or for some form of Christian worship."

The bill proposed a levy on all persons to be collected by the sheriff, who was to make up and post publicly a list of all taxpayers along with the religious society to which each taxpayer wished his taxes to go "for the inspection of all concerned." The sheriff then was to pay the minister or teacher so designated his share of the tax funds. If any taxpayer did not indicate a choice among the churches, his money was to be given to "seminaries of learning" within the respective counties. All money was to be used for paying clergymen or religious teachers or providing places of divine worship, except that Quakers and Mennonites could use it for any purpose they desired.

Thus, the base of the establishment was to be still broader than that of the bill of 1779, which had set up definite and elaborate stipulations defining a church eligible to receive funds and which had effectively limited such churches to the major Protestant denominations. Now, however, the assessment bill of 1784 did not lay down such restrictions and apparently included all Christians, the small radical sects as well as Catholics, but no non-Christians as yet. Indeed, the Assembly almost took the final step of multiple establishment to include all religious groups equally and impartially. In the debates on the assessment bill on December 22 and 23, 1784, the Assembly in committee of the whole voted by a small majority to substitute the word "religious" for "Christian." This would have levied an assessment "for the support of religious teachers," but in report to the house the conservatives were able to reverse the decision and reinsert "Christian," thus ruling out the non-Christian religious groups. But for this close decision the assessment bill would have arrived at the principle that the state should support all religions equally and impartially.

James Madison saw the implications of the assessment and rallied the democratic forces to oppose it. In order to carry his case to the people, Madison wrote his famous *Memorial and Remonstrance Against Religious Assessments,* which was widely distributed during the summer of 1785. The *Remonstrance* is Madison's most complete statement of what he understood the conservatives to mean by "an establishment of religion." It is unequivocally clear that he identified the assessment proposal to aid all religious groups equally, as "an establishment of religion," as did the proponents of the bill, no less in 1785 than in 1779. It reveals clearly that he opposed any kind of connection between church and state, that he opposed multiple support for all churches as vigorously as he opposed the establishment of a single church.

With the *Remonstrance* as the common underlying principle for action the people of Virginia during the summer and fall of 1785 flooded the legislature with petitions and memorials opposing assessment. The response was so overwhelming that the assessment bill was never brought to a vote. It also had such effect in the elections to the new session of the legislature that Madison and the liberals were in so great a majority that they had no trouble in bringing up Jefferson's Bill for Religious Freedom of 1779 and passing it by the overwhelming majority of seventy-four to twenty in January 1786. This then became the historic Virginia Statute of Religious Freedom. On the eve of the Constitutional Convention the separation of church and state had been completed in Virginia.

Although the struggle for separation of church and state was perhaps more spectacular and thoroughgoing in Virginia than elsewhere, the trend was evident between 1776 and 1791 that disestablishment was definitely the will of a large majority of states by the time the First Amendment was framed and adopted. By 1791 it is clear that virtual separation had already been achieved in the constitutions of nine of the original thirteen states. Despite differences of wording in these nine constitutions, several show unmistakable similarity in wording and all show a basic similarity in purpose and meaning; namely, the protection of free exercise of worship, prohibition of preference to any one or several religious groups, and prohibition of support for any religious worship or instruction.

What made the Virginia contest so important in other respects was that the chief proponent for separation of church and state, James Madison, was the architect of the First Amendment of the Constitution which was adopted by Congress in 1789 and ratified by the states in 1791. The details of the formulation of the First Amendment cannot be discussed here, but the mark of Madison was apparent throughout the initial proposals, the debates, and the final statement which became the historical American formulation of the principle of separation of church and state:

> Congress shall make no law respecting an establishment of religion, or prohibiting the free exercise thereof. . . .

Jefferson and Madison both gave great loyalty to the First Amendment in word and deed in their roles as statesmen and presidents of the United States.

As new states were admitted to the Union throughout the nineteenth century, their constitutions reflected the principle of separation largely as defined in the First Amendment. Despite differences in wording the common characteristics of the religious provisions show the intent to protect freedom and equality of religious conscience by assuring free exercise of religion to all orderly religious groups and by prohibiting public taxation for the support of religious groups. Thomas M. Cooley, eminent authority on constitutional law, summarizes those things that are not lawful under any of the American constitutions: no law may be passed respecting an establishment of religion, compulsory support, by taxation or otherwise, of religious instruction, compulsory attendance upon religious worship, or restraints upon the expression of religious belief.

The states added to the Union in the early nineteenth century reflected these principles in various ways in their constitutions. The Illinois Constitution of 1818 contains provisions that are typical of the provisions in many other state constitutions of that period:

> That all men have a natural and indefeasible right to worship Almighty God according to the dictates of their own consciences; that no man can of right be compelled to attend, erect, or support any place of worship, or to maintain any ministry against his consent; that no human authority can, in any case whatever, control or interfere with the rights of conscience; and that no preference shall ever be given by law to any religious establishments or modes of worship.

These words show the intent to prevent the use of public funds for any religious group, an intent directly in line with the meaning of the "establishment of religion" clause of the First Amendment. The final clause indicates clearly by the use of plurals in the words "religious establishments or modes of worship" that multiple cooperation between the state and a large number of churches is just as much prohibited as is cooperation between the state and a single church.

A careful inspection of all state constitutions will show that every original state constitution outside of the Eastern seaboard (except possibly Louisiana and Mississippi) contains a similar prohibition against compulsory support of any place of worship or maintenance of any ministry of religion. In most cases the actual wording is repeated or parallels the form contained in the constitutions of Pennsylvania, New Jersey, and North Carolina (all framed in 1776) and in the Virginia Statute for Religious Freedom of 1786. The intention in all these provisions is clearly to prohibit "an establishment of religion." The state constitutions as well as the First Amendment were all intended to prohibit multiple establishment as well as single establishment. They are all part of the same historical process.

Several state constitutions in addition to those of Illinois in 1818 and Wisconsin in 1848 use the words in the plural, "religious establishments or modes of worship." The Michigan Constitution of 1837 spells out the prohibition by adding the words "No money shall be drawn from the treasury for the benefit of religious societies, or theological or religious seminaries." The constitutions of Iowa, Utah, South Carolina, and Louisiana use the exact words of the First Amendment. Space will not permit further examples from the state constitutions, but the main lines of the historic principle of separation of church and state are as clear with respect to prohibition of support of religion (meaning no single or multiple establishment) as they are with respect to the free exercise of religion. From 1876 onward all new states added to the Union were required by Congress to include in their basic laws an irrevocable ordi-

nance guaranteeing religious freedom in line with the principles of the First
Amendment.

THE DEVELOPMENT OF NATIONALISM

The delegates to the Continental Congresses were men of conflicting allegiances and divided patriotic sentiments. Many considered themselves loyal
subjects of the British king; others saw their primary loyalties resting with
their respective colonies; still others considered themselves first and foremost
citizens of a somewhat amorphous new nation. Jefferson in his *Notes On
Virginia* conceived of that colony, rather than the "United Colonies" of his
Declaration, as his native land. During his years as President, he often used
the phrase "my country" to apply both to the United States and to Virginia,
and as late as 1809 in a letter to the Virginia Assembly, he declared his native
state endeared to him "by every tie which can attach the human heart." [15]
John Adams, throughout the Revolution and afterwards, made similar references both to the United States and to Massachusetts. This confusion of loyalties was characteristic of most Americans of this period, for the shift of primary allegiance to the new government was a slow and gradual process. As
a matter of fact, it took a major war (1812) and fully a half century of national
life before the new nation could really boast a loyal and devoted citizenry of
its own.

One early indication of growing patriotic sentiment during these years was
the development of American loyalty symbols. Loyalty remains a somewhat
nebulous feeling unless it can attach itself to certain concrete symbols—
symbols which can serve as rallying points for patriotic emotions. Thus, the
development of the flag, the patriotic song and cartoon, and the national
holiday and hero served quickly to crystallize the common attachments which
Americans were building. Beginning with the Bunker Hill Monument near
Boston, a series of monuments commemorating the great battles, heroes, and
events of the Revolution were erected. In 1833 the Washington National
Monument Society was founded specifically to organize and rally American
patriotic sentiment over the country, and by 1850 the myth and symbol of
Washington, together with other towering figures of the colonial period, had
taken its place as the ideal of democratic man and hero. They were to be, as
Ralph Gabriel has pointed out, the newly canonized saints of the young
national faith.

The flag, changing often during the early years of national life, became
among the most concrete of these rallying points, and although the practice
did not become general until the Civil War, authenticated reports of flags

[15] Jefferson to General Assembly of Virginia, Feb. 16, 1809; *The Writings of Thomas Jefferson*,
H. A. Washington, ed. (Washington, United States Congress, 1854), Vol. VIII, p. 148.

flying over schoolhouses date from as early as the War of 1812. Graphic symbols such as Brother Jonathan and Uncle Sam appeared widely in popular songs, sketches, and cartoons. The Fourth of July, in its opportunities for patriotic speeches and raucous celebration, lent itself neatly to the cultivation and expression of nationalist sentiment. In general, there seems little doubt that these more popular symbols of the new spirit helped tremendously to engender patriotic feeling in the great body of the people.

Another evidence of growing nationalism was the appearance of a profound interest in the nation's past. During the decades between 1830 and 1850 at least thirty-five historical societies were organized and began the prodigious tasks of gathering the great historical documents of the republic. The necessity of a new history of the United States, written from a patriotic point of view, was fulfilled by George Bancroft in his first comprehensive *History of the United States of America*. Numerous lesser historical works for school and popular consumption also appeared on the scene.

If reverence for the past was an integral aspect of the new patriotism, it was matched equally by reverence for the future. Francis Grund, a German visitor of the 1830's, observed that the Americans *"love* their country, not, indeed, *as it is,* but *as it will be."* [16] American society was looking forward; progress was inevitable. Bound up with the doctrine of progress and evangelical Christianity was the *mission* that Americans took on to improve democracy not only at home but also all over the world. Central in this missionary conception was the "higher moral law" provided by Christianity, and if given sects had been disestablished, this was for the American far removed from the question of founding republican government on Christian principles. Essentially, the argument ran that Christianity alone could maintain liberty, that the maintenance of liberty was the basis of the national welfare, and thus, that Christianity supported the national welfare. As such, the Bible rapidly became identified as a patriotic symbol of the first order. Through it, the missionary zeal of Christianity easily lent part of its emotional force to the new patriotism; and it quickly became the duty of the nineteenth-century American to carry liberty, democracy, and Christian principles to the world. "He has been educated," observed Frederick Marryat, a French visitor to America, "to despise all other countries, and to look upon his own as the first in the world; he has been taught that all other nations are slaves to despots, and that the American citizen only is free. . . ." [17] It was to these other nations that America would bring freedom.

When this growing nationalism encountered the tremendous waves of immigration from Northern Europe between 1830 and 1860, it yielded a phenomenon formerly alien to the American scene—nativism. Previously, America had beckoned to the weak and downtrodden of the world, offering to all

16 Grund, *op. cit.,* p. 151.
17 Marryat, *op. cit.,* Vol. II, Pt. II, p. 82.

comers the opportunity to carve out a life for themselves and their families. Now, for the first time in earnest, the potential loyalty of the immigrant began to be called into question. Much of this hostility must be seen in such economic terms as labor's resentment of the immigrant's willingness to accept an inferior standard of living. Further understanding must be sought in the feeling that the newcomers, stemming as they did from monarchical traditions, could not possibly participate in a republican community. "The foreigner, who attempts to drive the chariot of American freedom," inveighed a speaker before the *Order of United Americans,* "is but another Phaeton rashly and fatally seeking to guide the fiery coursers of the Sun. . . ." [18] Doubtless, many who shared his sympathies earnestly feared the inundation of the young republic by a flow of immigration far in excess of the number it could healthfully absorb. Others probably welcomed the opportunity to further their own deeply felt bigotry.

The brunt of this resentment was directed toward the Roman Catholic. With regard to numbers, the Catholics in 1830 constituted but a small percentage of the population. It was not until the great European famines of the 1840's that huge immigrations swelled their numbers. In light of deep Protestant suspicion of Catholicism and its clergy, they were logical scapegoats of nativism. Terrorism against Catholic churches, convents, and individuals appeared in many places as the nativist movement gained force. Secret societies such as the Sons of the Sires, the Supreme Order of the Star Spangled Banner, and the Order of United Americans were organized to further nationalist and nativist sentiment. The movement finally culminated in the formation of a Native American Party in the 1850's—a party which essentially amalgamated all the forces of nativism. It was a short-lived effort, however, and by 1860, the political influence of the nativists had declined to insignificance in the face of sectional conflict.

While it is true that the nativist movement represented a kind of fanatical fringe of nationalism, one cannot ignore the unifying element of nationalism in an age of growing sectionalism. It was a force which knitted elements of the most diverse sort—of different population stocks, different cultural backgrounds, and different regional and ideological affiliations—into a mesh of common loyalty and belief that rapidly became the new American nationality.

It is also clear that this sense of nationality both strengthened and was strengthened by the expansion of federal power during the ante-bellum period. Under Jefferson's presidency, in spite of a firm commitment to a weak central government, Louisiana was purchased in 1803, and an embargo on English goods was imposed in 1807. Both vitally affected American industry and agriculture. Monroe raised tariffs, annexed Florida, and formulated the Monroe Doctrine protecting the Western Hemisphere from European im-

[18] Alfred B. Ely, *American Liberty, Its Sources—Its Dangers, and the Means of Its Preservation* (New York, 1850), p. 27.

perialism. Jackson helped to prevent the secession of South Carolina; while under Polk and Pierce, American territory and foreign intercourse was expanded considerably. Needless to say, with the successful prosecution of the Civil War and the maintenance of the Union, federal power and prestige grew immeasurably. As a matter of fact, a strong federal government had by 1865 become a foundational plank in the Republican platform.

THE SOUTH BECOMES A SECTION APART

When Virginia, the Carolinas, and Georgia ratified the Constitution and first entered the Union, there seemed little question about their eventual integration into the new nation. Virginia gave the United States four of its first five presidents; early statesmen from the other southern states are far too numerous to mention. Southern thinking influenced the course of early American politics, and southern practice entered into much of early federal legislation. Yet, slave labor, distinctive agricultural products, and a pattern of decentralized settlement had from its earliest decades created particular political, economic, and social problems for the South. Rather than diminishing during the late eighteenth and early nineteenth centuries, these peculiar problems only intensified. For instance, although men like Jefferson were firmly convinced that the South would eliminate slavery of its own free will, the continuing decline of land productivity, the slackening of the slave trade, and the invention of the cotton gin in 1793 made such a course economically unsound. Such intensification was only heightened by developments on the national scene after 1820, when Virginia's political preeminence gave way to the power of the mercantile-industrial North and the agricultural West. It was not long before peculiar problems began to breed a sense of uniqueness—before the South began to feel itself a section apart. This feeling only increased as new states joined the Union. Sectionalism rapidly changed into a kind of regional nationalism, a nationalism which expressed a sectional political-economic conflict that was ultimately destined to become the Civil War.

Perhaps the principal point of difference between the South and the other regions lay in its economic system. The plantation represented not only a geographical unit for the production of cotton and tobacco but, in a fashion, a whole way of life. Howard Odum has pictured it as a miniature society revolving around a family unit—a society which often maintained schools, local government, religious instruction and worship, agriculture and industry, and entertainment and recreation. As such, it literally set the tempo of southern life. Furthermore, it inevitably determined the pattern of social class relationships.

The owners of these plantations, basing their view of society largely on a conception of the English gentleman class, set out to build what Vernon Parrington has so aptly called "a Greek democracy." It was to be a humane and cultivated society, "set free from the narrow exactions of economics to engage in the higher work of civilization." [19] The concept easily rationalized a pyramidal kind of class structure, with a small, select group of gentleman landholders at the narrow top and the great mass of slaves at the broad base. In between was an almost caste-like array of classes—smaller planters, independent yeomen farmers, and "poor whites"—an arrangement based largely on extent, location, and type of landholding.

It is interesting to note the lack of any vigorous commercial class in this pyramidal scheme. In general, the tendency was for each planter to deal directly with the English and Dutch traders and shippers. The decentralized economy of largely independent plantation communities was not at all conducive to the development of mercantile towns. By 1860 there were only six southern communities with populations in excess of 20,000—Charleston, Richmond, Mobile, Memphis, Savannah, and New Orleans. These cities were inhabited principally by the kind of independent artisan characteristic of earlier European society. Bankers, lawyers, doctors, and other professional men were not found in large numbers, for these men usually pursued their professions only in addition to their duties as lords of their own plantations. If there was no ample evidence of an expanding merchant capitalism, there was considerably less illustrating any impact of industrialism. Manufactures like clothing and implements were largely produced on the plantations proper or by the artisans of the towns. Other needed materials were almost always supplied directly from outside sources.

Nurtured by the ideals of the British gentry and undisturbed by commercial and industrial expansion, the South gradually became a static society, ideologically and intellectually. The humanitarian influences which had dominated the Virginia scene during the days of Jefferson and Madison were now retreating in the face of a vigorous desire to perpetuate the economics of the plantation system. When the effects of diminishing returns, high slave prices, and exhausted lands became increasingly apparent during the 1840's, they only strengthened the determination to preserve the status quo. The capitalist ways of northern industry and commerce were repudiated as utterly plebeian; the strengthening of the national government to aid this capitalism, as authoritarian. The southern response centered in reaction, in a return to decentralized agrarian ways—to local economics and politics.

In the face of such political and economic realities, the forces of dynamic democracy made little headway. With no industrial enterprise developing there was hardly any of the labor unrest of the North. Receiving fewer and fewer of the new immigrants, the South experienced little of the influence of European socialism. What new ideas did manage to find their way into its thinking were quickly stamped out. The society as a whole was little recep-

[19] Vernon Louis Parrington, *Main Currents in American Thought* (New York, Harcourt, Brace, 1927), Vol. 2, p. 99.

tive to change; it bred few leaders to carry the torch of reform. The spirited equality of Jefferson's freehold farmer changed to the benevolent oligarchy of a planter aristocracy. The new system denied democracy in favor of a monarchical brand of republicanism, and it challenged the ways and power of the vigorous northern middle class. It retreated into its reactionary agrarianism until the jolt of the Civil War brought to a head the impending disaster of economic collapse and left only ruin on which to build a new society.

ISSUES FOR STUDY AND DISCUSSION

1. In what ways would the cultural differences between the North and the South during the antebellum period lead you to expect significant educational differences in the two sections?

2. Many Americans have traditionally believed that most of their distinctively democratic institutions date from the founding of the republic. How would you criticize this position?

3. How did the labor unions of 1830 compare in purpose, program, and character with present-day labor unions? Have labor's major goals, particularly with respect to education, changed since that time?

4. Would the growth of a powerful spirit of equality during the early nineteenth century lead you to expect significant changes in the organization of schools as developed by colonial Americans?

SUGGESTIONS FOR FURTHER READING

Beard, Charles A., and Beard, Mary R., *The Rise of American Civilization*, New York, Macmillan, 1936.

Billington, Ray A., *Westward Expansion*, New York, Macmillan, 1949.

Blau, Joseph L. (ed.), *Social Theories of Jacksonian Democracy*, New York, Hafner, 1947.

Butts, R. Freeman, *The American Tradition in Religion and Education*, Boston, Beacon, 1950.

Cole, Arthur Charles, *The Irrepressible Conflict, 1850–1865*, New York, Macmillan, 1934.

Commons, John R., and Associates, *History of Labour in the United States*, New York, Macmillan, 1918–1935, Vol. 1–2.

Dodd, William E., *The Cotton Kingdom: A Chronicle of the Old South*, New Haven, Yale University Press, 1919.

Dorfman, Joseph, *The Economic Mind in American Civilization, 1606–1865*, New York, Viking, 1946, 2 vols.

Fish, Carl Russell, *The Rise of the Common Man, 1830–1850*, New York, Macmillan, 1927.

Hacker, Louis M., *The Triumph of American Capitalism*, New York, Simon & Schuster, 1940.

Krout, John A., and Fox, Dixon Ryan, *The Completion of Independence, 1790–1830*, New York, Macmillan, 1944.

Phillips, Ulrich Bonnell, *Life and Labor in the Old South*, Boston, Little, 1929.

Randall, James G., *The Civil War and Reconstruction*, Boston, Heath, 1937.

Schlesinger, Arthur M., Jr., *The Age of Jackson*, Boston, Little, 1945.

Stokes, Anson Phelps, *Church and State in the United States*, New York, Harper, 1950, Vols. 1–2.

Sydnor, Charles S., *The Development of Southern Sectionalism, 1819–1848*, Baton Rouge, Louisiana State University Press, 1948.

Tocqueville, Alexis de, *Democracy in America*, Phillips Bradley (ed.), New York, Knopf, 1945, 2 vols.

Turner, Frederick Jackson, *The Frontier in American History*, New York, Holt, 1920.

———, *The United States, 1830–1850*, New York, Holt, 1935.

Tyler, Alice Felt, *Freedom's Ferment*, Minneapolis, University of Minnesota Press, 1944.

6

INTELLECTUAL OUTLOOKS
IN THE NEW NATION

AS AMERICANS struggled with their political, economic, and social problems in the formative years of the new republic so they struggled with new ideas in the realms of thought and knowledge. The new nation continued to be swept by European currents of thought and strove to accommodate itself to the patterns of thinking being developed abroad, but in the process the intellectual leaders of the new continent began to think as Americans rather than simply as displaced Europeans in a colonial setting. Many of the same intellectual conflicts that appeared in colonial times continued to disturb the new nation and to rumble through the educational scene. Traditional religious outlooks were maintained and even gained many adherents, but secular ideas continued to make advances among a growing minority of intellectuals.

The problems faced by the molders of the American mind could be stated in a wide variety of ways, but three types pressed to the forefront, the solution of which affected most directly the kind of education deemed appropriate for the new nation. There was, first, the continuing conflict between supernaturalism and naturalism with respect to the nature and destiny of man. The goals of education in any age are related to the underlying conceptions of human nature and the conceptions of man's relation to the seen and unseen world in which he lives and dies. The second set of problems had to do with the beliefs concerning what kind of knowledge is of the most worth, how it should be organized, and what uses should be made of organized knowledge. The content and methods of education are persistently related to the status and kind of knowledge that is valued in any society. The third set of problems had to do with the conflict of ideas between democratic and aristocratic concepts of the individual and his relation to the society in which he lives and finds his fulfillment. The opportunity and kind of education provided in a society is persistently related to social goals and ideals. This chapter will try to describe briefly some of the basic ideas that were being expressed concerning these three sets of problems as they were formulated and propounded in the first eighty or ninety years of the new nation.

CONFLICTING CONCEPTIONS OF MAN AND NATURE

For a time during the first two or three decades following the revolutionary period it looked as though the secular ideas of the Enlightenment might become a dominant intellectual pattern of American thought. Deism and free thought made considerable gains among intellectuals who tried to make of science the religion appropriate to the common people of a democracy. With the onset of the nineteenth century, however, religious conservatism began to reassert itself, and much more traditional supernatural ideas pushed again to the fore on a wave of religious revivalism and evangelism. But the naturalistic and scientific ideas would not be completely downed, and much of deism was incorporated into a new synthesis of liberal and somewhat nonsectarian religion. Unitarianism and transcendentalism represented these newer religious outlooks which captured a large proportion of the intellectual leaders of the first half of the nineteenth century.

This formulation of religious outlooks that embraced spiritual values and yet softened the rigidities of sectarian doctrines was a most important development for education. So long as each religious sect held firmly and uncompromisingly to a set of specific religious doctrines in opposition to all other sects, the tendency would be to insist upon religious schools that taught those tenets and only those tenets. When, however, religion could be looked upon as a belief in God and in common moral and spiritual values, it became possible for different religious sects to cooperate more fully with other sects in the establishment and managing of schools. It is entirely possible that if some kind of nonsectarian outlook in religion had not appeared, the rise of the public school open to all religious groups alike would not have been possible. Similarly, the dominant conception of human nature centering upon the new faculty psychology gave a chance for educational method to look upon human nature as a combination of spiritual, mental, and physical facilities, freed somewhat from the rigid demands of a Calvinist conception of predestination and original sin. The way was thus paved for the new doctrines of sense realism in educational method which could emphasize learning through physical activity and sense impressions without destroying the importance of spiritual and mental development deemed necessary for the development of moral habits and good character.

Liberalism in Religious Thought

The first blush of success over the victories of the Revolutionary War was taken as a repudiation of British religious and intellectual thought as well as political and economic dominance over America. It was only natural then that French ideas of the Enlightenment should be hailed as appropriate to America, especially in view of the felt kinship between the American and French Revolutions. Thus, while the French Revolution went from victory to victory through Europe, the secular outlooks of deism and rationalism became more popular in America. They had quite a vogue in American colleges for some twenty or thirty years. But with the imperialism of Napoleon and his eventual defeat the tide turned away from the secular thought of France and began to turn to German and British romanticism and transcendentalism as a means of reasserting the claims of spirituality over naturalism. The growth of a more lasting and indigenous American secular philosophy was thus delayed until the rise of the tide of evolution and science in the later nineteenth century which in turn led to the formulation of the philosophy of pragmatism and experimental naturalism.

Deism.   In the view of its supporters deism was a religion based upon a conception of God and man's spiritual nature, but it was also based upon human reason as the source of knowledge of God, nature, and man. In the view of its opponents deism was looked upon as atheistic "infidelity" because it did not rely upon the traditional conception of a personal theistic God and denied traditional Christian reliance upon revelation, miracles, and salvation through sacraments or faith. In his *Reason the Only Oracle of Man,* published in 1784, Ethan Allen argued that God's existence could be justified by human reason alone and did not need to rely upon revelation in the Christian Bible. Furthermore, nature was self-sufficient once it had been created by God, and the workings of natural laws did not need nor could they be interfered with by divine miracles. Allen tried to make deism into a religion of law appropriate to a republic rather than a religion of authoritarian fiat appropriate to a monarchy.

Thomas Paine's *Age of Reason* appeared in 1794 in which he attacked much more bitterly the traditional supernatural outlooks of Christianity and argued vehemently for a natural religion based upon scientific laws of nature. Evidence for the existence and power of God could be achieved through human reason and not by the exhortations or bombast of clergymen or the regulations of ecclesiastical hierarchies. Paine's tract was followed by Elihu Palmer's *Principles of Nature* in 1801, a much more sober philosophical analysis of God as a supreme deity or first cause lying behind the phenomena of nature. He departed from his Baptist ministerial outlook as Paine had left his Quakerism. Palmer was a leader in organizing "deistical" clubs and societies throughout the East and in editing journals to spread the deistic "gospel." Central to Palmer's thoughts were such principles as these: nature reveals the existence of one supreme deity; man possesses by nature certain intellectual and moral faculties including reason that are sufficient for good conduct and happiness on this earth; and the religion of nature grows out of the moral relations of intelligent human beings and is connected with the progressive achievement of welfare for mankind if science and education are properly promoted and separation of church and state is maintained.[1]

Unitarianism. Somewhat less radical than deism but incorporating much of Enlightenment thought, Unitarianism began a process of liberal trans-formation of Christian thought which became very influential in New England. It helped to fight the battle for nonsectarian public schools against the forces of narrow sectarianism. It retained its allegiances to Christianity, holding on to revelation and to miracles in contrast to deism, but it emphasized human reason and the goodness and perfectibility of human nature. It broke with the traditional Trinitarian conception of God and looked upon Jesus as a great human ethical teacher rather than a component part of the divine Godhead revealed in the person of God, Christ, and the Holy Ghost. It dropped the stern predestination and original sin of Calvinism in favor of an increasingly individual and personal religious experience. Incorporating a deep respect for the human personality, Unitarianism moved away from an angry, jealous, vindictive, and autocratic God to a warm, beneficent, loving God; from a world of elect and damned to a world where each individual could achieve his own salvation by following the Scriptures and his own individual freedom of conscience. It combined the optimistic faith and the forward-looking social ideals of the Enlightenment with a liberal creed of Christianity dedicated to the improvement of society. Thus, it helped to stimulate the social reform movements of the early nineteenth century of which the public school awakening was a part.

One of the most obvious outgrowths of these intellectual currents was the wave of reform movements which swept the nation in the second quarter of the nineteenth century. The older theology had described life in this world as preparation for life in the next. Now there was increasing emphasis on life in the here and present. Drawing on the ideas of human dignity and the doctrine of progress, and on the knowledge provided by science, reform movements to alleviate every sort of social ill sprang up. Universal peace, prison conditions, capital punishment, temperance, slavery, and, of course, education were all topics for discussion and problems for social action. Groups were organized in every part of the nation to combat this or that social evil. The reform movements attracted widespread interest as Americans embarked on their mission to attain perfectibility in the sphere of human institutions.

Unitarianism gained adherents in the late eighteenth century, especially from upper-class Congregationalists, Presbyterians, and Anglicans. The Epis-

[1] See G. Adolph Koch, *Republican Religion; the American Revolution and the Cult of Reason* (New York, Henry Holt, 1933), p. 79.

copal King's Chapel in Boston under James Freeman adopted Unitarianism in 1783–1784, and when Henry Ware was appointed Hollis Professor of Divinity at Harvard in 1805, Unitarianism gained a firm hold at Harvard. Above all, the chief prophet of Unitarianism was William Ellery Channing, who adapted his zeal for evangelical piety inherited from Puritanism to the new demands of the natural and rational religion of the Enlightenment as well as to the moral enthusiasm for social reform stemming from republicanism and humanitarianism. Thus, salvation in a religious sense became linked more than ever with the moral and human effort to achieve a society and world in harmony with man's own natural inclinations toward goodness and perfectibility. Horace Bushnell in Hartford, Connecticut, stressed still further the doctrine of free will rather than divine election as the means to salvation and argued that all Christian groups had hold of some aspects of religious truth. These trends in Unitarian thought which helped to push Christian beliefs toward a nonsectarian Christianity blurred the lines of sectarian dogma and paved the way for an educational emphasis upon the "common elements of Christianity" which stressed moral virtue rather than adherence to specific theological or dogmatic creeds.

Transcendentalism.   Despite its stimulus to liberal religious thought and social humanitarianism, Unitarianism began to lose its nonsectarian character as the first half of the nineteenth century moved into the fourth and fifth decades. It began to feel the pressures of sectarianism and began to take on the characteristics of a sect by developing a more firmly fixed creed and orthodoxy. Thus Unitarianism began to lose its intellectual leadership and its hold on the liberal movement in American thought. It eventually was overshadowed by a new intellectual movement known as transcendentalism which pushed the nonsectarian aspect of American religion even further. Transcendentalism drew inspiration from such German philosophical idealists as Kant, Schelling, Fichte, and Schleirmacher and from such British romanticists as Coleridge. It was a reaction against the intellectualism, rationalism, and naturalism of the eighteenth-century Enlightenment. In place of the Enlightenment emphasis upon human reason, scientific method, and the discoverable laws of nature, transcendentalists found the mainsprings of human motivation and action in human nature but in a human nature whose essence was spiritual and in tune with the divine spirit. The human spirit was thought to transcend the material and lower aspects of physical nature.

The transcendentalists were not much interested in nature as an object of study to be described painstakingly by the scientific method, but they *were* interested in nature as an evidence of God's provision of a habitat congenial to man's soul and in human nature as a revelation of the spiritual affinity of man with God. Their idealism put them on the side of supernaturalists as opposed to materialistic naturalists, for they emphasized man's spirit in contrast to his body. But their conception of God as an oversoul or divine immanence ranged them against the traditional theologies of their day. In this emphasis upon God as a universal spirit they were akin to the deistic and Unitarian philosophies as befitted nonsectarian spiritualists, and in their rejection of the revelation, creeds, and authority of the Bible they were close to a liberal formulation of religious thought. They gave German idealism an American turn by rejecting the absolutistic and nationalistic trappings of German idealism and by emphasizing the individualistic character of man's spiritual nature, especially his self-reliance and self-cultivation. They glorified man's individuality, asserting that his instincts and moral conscience are essentially good and perfectible; if given freedom from the constraints of convention and authoritarian institutions, man would be able to achieve self-fulfillment and social progress.

Transcendentalism thus saw evil in materialism, industrialism, commercialism, profit seeking, and exploitation of man by man. It stimulated further the note of social protest, reform, and humanitarianism that had been set afoot by the Enlightenment, but the way to reform was not through material improvement as visioned by the Enlightenment rationalists but rather through spiritual freedom and self-realization. Escape from city life "back to nature" would be an aid to this process, but the real clue to progress was the free cultivation of man's spiritual nature—intellectual, moral, and religious. Transcendentalists believed in the power of man's reason, to be sure, but it must be aided by a spiritual motivation whether in the form of a religious piety or a secular moral consciousness that would transcend everyday experience. Knowledge and goodness cannot be achieved by sense experience but must be based upon a spiritual intuition of reality above and beyond the realm of material experience. Reality is not known by the methods of science as claimed by the Enlightenment rationalists but only by an intuitive relationship between man's spirit and the divine spirit of God.

Only a few specific instances of transcendentalism can be mentioned here. Theodore Parker posited an infinite God whose spirit infused all men, but he rejected the traditional Christian reliance on the Bible as revelation and on the sacraments as roads to salvation. It is the appearance of God's divinity in man's soul that must guide experience and conduct. All human beings have a common element derived from the immanence of God's spirit within them; thus there is only one true religion, based not on a church or a creed or revealed word but on the true piety and moral conscience of all individuals. Religious piety is an innate element in man's nature, and since this is a universal fact of human nature, there must exist a divine being to satisfy the love of God that exists in man. Parker often spoke of the "religious faculty" as an instinct or innate quality of human nature along with the intellectual and moral faculties. Cultivation of this religious faculty is the road to spiritual salvation and enables man to go beyond or transcend the kind of life that would be open to him if he were confined to merely rational guides to human conduct. Natural science, therefore, has grave limitations both as a source of knowledge and as a guide to conduct. Parker followed Kant in asserting that conceptions of God, morality, and immortality are instinctive intuitions of human nature and are not to be achieved by logical or rational demonstrations. Knowledge is of less importance than a life of spiritual attunement and moral consciousness. He thus tried to base religion upon man's innate nature and to free religion from theological orthodoxies as well as from materialism and empiricism. Religion was "natural" not because it coincided with scientific laws of nature but because it flowed naturally from man's spirit.

Reverend James Marsh of the University of Vermont also tried to distinguish religion from rational and scientific intelligence as well as from the orthodoxies of revelation. Man has a faculty of "spiritual reflection" which acts as man's guide to spiritual achievement and moral conduct. Caleb Sprague Henry of New York University argued that human reason has its sources spontaneously deep in man's consciousness; independently of human effort, the truth is perceived and received instantaneously before it is elaborated into logical or scientific laws. Holding such doctrines as these the transcendentalists had little to do with laboratory science or experimental research. The road to reality was not through science but through the cultivation of the spiritual self. Preeminent of all transcendentalists in preaching this view was Ralph Waldo Emerson, who emphasized imagination and poetical inspiration rather than scientific knowledge as the road to the good life. Impatient with organized institutions and organized knowledge, Emerson constantly urged individuals to develop their own potentialities through intuition, insight, and poetic vision rather than simply by acquiring scientific or factual knowledge.

In these ways the transcendentalists prepared the minds of Americans for accepting a nonsectarian view of religious and spiritual values. Americans were not ready for a fully secular philosophy based upon science and naturalism, but they did respond to a generalized religious outlook of love, beneficence, and moral virtue that was divorced from specific sectarian creeds but not divorced from Christian idealism in general. Aside from this rather diffuse effect upon American thought, transcendentalists had little direct or immediate effect upon American education compared to that of their arch enemies, natural science and evangelical religion. The transcendentalists lost the field to science, on one hand, because they had little concern with organized knowledge of a scientific or useful kind, and they lost to evangelical religion, on the other hand, because they were impatient with organized efforts to institutionalize their ideas. Organized knowledge was the special forte of scientists who could so evidently portray the usefulness of their knowledge, and the institutionalizing of religious effort was characteristic of the evangelical sects of Protestantism.

Transcendentalists did have their teachers and educators, such as Bronson

Alcott, whose Temple School in Boston tried to develop self-expression among children in line with the idealistic and transcendental emphasis upon spiritual cultivation. But Alcott made relatively little impact on education in general and left the field to the professional educators who were ready to systematize and organize knowledge for teaching purposes. Nevertheless, transcendentalism was important in generating a kind of tolerant religious belief which eventually came to appeal to many Americans, namely, that there are many religious roads to salvation, to morality, and to the good life. Religious bigotry and persecution could have less doctrinal validity when people began to respond to such pleas for unity as those of Henry James the Elder (father of William James and Henry James) in his Fourth of July oration in 1861 at the beginning of the Civil War:

> In short, Revelation ascribes to the whole human race the unity of a man before God, having but one body and one spirit, one Lord, one faith, and one baptism, one God and Father of all, who is above all and through all and in all: this man being evidently social, as implying such a unity of all the members with each individual member and of each with all as will finally obliterate the iniquities of caste upon earth, or do away with all that arbitrary and enforced inequality among men which is the pregnant source of our existing vice and crime.[2]

When people of one religious faith could have a wholesome respect and generous feeling of common fellowship with people of other religious faiths, they could cooperate genuinely in supporting a common school. When doctrinal differences began to seem less important then the fundamental likeness in basic beliefs and in religious values, a nonsectarian school was a possibility. But when doctrinal differences assumed major proportions despite certain elements in common, separate school systems for separate sectarian religious instruction were deemed essential.

Reassertion of Sectarianism in Religious Thought

Despite the attraction of liberal religious ideas for many intellectual and clerical leaders of the new nation, the masses of people were much more vitally and directly touched by religious enthusiasm of more orthodox varieties. The opening decades of the nineteenth century witnessed a widespread revival movement that spread the length and breadth of the land and rivaled the Great Awakening of the mid-eighteenth century to the extent that it has even been called the "Protestant Counter-Reformation." Evangelical Protestantism was a kind of adaptation of Puritanism to frontier life; the highly emotional character of earlier preaching like that of Jonathan Edwards retained its dramatic appeal for the lonely farm family; and the multiplication of sects which began in the eighteenth century continued with increasing vigor. Making wide use of untrained, lay preachers, these sects were a characteristic

---

[2] Henry James, *The Social Significance of Our Institutions* (Boston, Ticknor and Fields, 1861), pp. 44–45.

expression of frontier democracy. Their emphasis, as it had been earlier, remained with the individual conversion experience, providing a distinctive individual link of each person with his God. Combining this experience with communal association, their camp meetings and revivals provided a religious outlet which was uniquely democratic both in form and content.

Protestant evangelism. Reacting alike against the "atheism" and "infidelity" of deism and rationalism and the generous interpretations of Unitarianism and transcendentalism, evangelical Protestantism reasserted the traditional supernatural faiths of orthodox theism. God was looked upon as a personal spirit guiding the destinies of each individual person as directly in the present as He had, according to the Bible, created the world in six days. Some Protestant sects put emphasis upon regeneration of man's spiritual life through piety, faith, and the Scriptures. Other sects stressed "good works" and the moral law. God's moral law was described in the Bible and was to be obeyed by man; the moral law was not a human invention or creation, but rather it set the standards by which man was able to judge right and wrong and himself to be judged if he erred. Moral standards were thus viewed as eternal, absolute, and unchanging, in virtue of which they were also dependable and thus could offer security to the doubting or the unaware. Evangelical Protestantism thus resulted in an intense revivalism and in the splitting up into many denominationalisms, some looking to individual effort for salvation, others to communal effort, and some to the imminent coming of the millennium.

Thousands were swept into the crusading churches and sects, and new organizations were founded to speed the work. The American Tract Society was organized to reestablish orthodoxy. The American Bible Society was organized in 1816 to promote the reading of the Bible by families and to spread its use as a school book. Sunday school societies were established and missionary societies sprang up among the major denominations to promote religion among the people in the West as well as abroad. The Board of Home Missions was founded in 1816 and the Society for the Promotion of Collegiate and Theological Education at the West in 1843.

In addition to the great strides made by the evangelism of such widely popular denominations as the Baptists and Methodists, several new sects broke away from the older denominations in order to follow a variety of leads to religious individualism and self-expression. Appealing especially to the underprivileged little people of the rural regions and holding out the hope of greater equality in economic and social life as well as religious faith, such groups as the Shakers, Perfectionists, Millerites, and Mormons gained numerous adherents. Some groups tried to remedy the excessive sectarianism by appealing to the Bible as a common basis of unity; among these were groups known as the Disciples of Christ and a group known simply as

Christians. The net effect was to add many new Protestant sects to the number already seeking adherents.

Calvinism. Many of the new sects grew as a reaction against the orthodox Calvinism of colonial times which had revealed within itself the split that was taking place between the "Old Light" emphasis on predestination and the "New Light" interest in revivalism following Jonathan Edwards. Such followers of Edwards as Joseph Bellamy and Samuel Hopkins retained their hold upon the branches of Congregationalism that had not moved into Unitarianism, but their justification of a vindictive and jealous God soon led liberals to drop from the fold. Nathanael Whitaker, Nathanael Emmons, Stephen West, Jedidiah Morse, Timothy Dwight, president of Yale, and a host of others carried on the attack against the liberal thought of the Enlightenment and helped to stem the tide of scepticism and reestablish Calvinist orthodoxy of a somewhat softened variety. Nathaniel Walker, working in Yale's Divinity School, and other orthodox Calvinists who founded Andover Theological Seminary in 1808 used these educational means of counteracting the liberalism and Unitarianism that had captured Harvard's Divinity School a few years earlier.

All in all, religious orthodoxy became once again a potent fare in higher education. College professors had to be on the alert concerning their religious beliefs lest they offend the patrons or supporters of the denominational colleges which had mushroomed over the educational landscape. Princeton also moved to the fore as a center from which conservative religious thought went across the land. John Witherspoon, his son-in-law, Samuel Stanhope Smith, and President James McCosh became leaders of a "commonsense" philosophy that gave philosophical underpinnings to a revived Presbyterianism. Borrowing from the Scottish school of common sense realism, they gave considerable attention to reconciling the scientific method with orthodox supernaturalism, theism, and immortality of the soul. They stimulated an interest in metaphysics and in philosophy among the new evangelical colleges and gave a philosophical foundation for orthodox Protestant religion which it had not had since Jonathan Edwards. They helped to regain something of the intellectual leadership which had been lost to Unitarians and transcendentalists of a more liberal outlook.

Roman Catholicism. Not only was sectarianism fed by the crosscurrents of liberal and Protestant thought in the early nineteenth century, but the intellectual scene also became even more complicated by the appearance of a new claimant upon the beliefs of Americans. The Roman Catholic Church, oldest of all, was not new to America, but now it entered the arena to do direct combat with the majority Protestant outlook. It could begin to assert itself more vigorously because of its rapid growth in numbers and power acquired mainly from the great influx of German and Irish immigrants in the 1830's, 1840's, and 1850's. When the Protestants were quarreling among themselves, splitting off in all directions, arguing dozens of interpretations of the Bible, and intensifying their sectarianism, the Catholic Church began to make a bold bid for the merits of an authoritative doctrine that would give security among the rash of sectarian creeds.

Leadership in the Catholic Church in America had been largely imported or labeled as foreign, but now native Americans began to seek intellectual refuge in the Church. Outstanding among these were Orestes Brownson and Isaac Hecker. Brownson moved from Congregationalism to Presbyterianism, to Universalism, to Unitarianism, and finally to Catholicism. In the columns of his *Democratic Review* he argued that American democracy would be safe only in the hands of the Catholic Church. He leveled his guns at Protestant liberalism as well as at Protestant orthodoxy, insisting that Protestantism could not be the basis of democracy. Some Protestants believe in a depraved human nature, and why should a democratic government be entrusted to depraved souls? Other Protestants believe in the essential goodness of human nature, but how can we trust democracy to a human nature that has produced so much evil in the world? The only sure way for democracy to be safe is in the hands of a people who are guided in their religious and moral standards by a Church that is the infallible custodian of God's eternal truth, the Roman Catholic Church.

> We say, then, if democracy commits the government to the people to be taken care of, religion is to take care that they take proper care of the government, rightly direct and wisely administer it.
>
> But what religion? It must be a religion which is above the people and controls them, or it will not answer the purpose. If it depends on the people, if the people are to take care of it, to say what it shall be, what it shall teach, what it shall command, what worship or discipline it shall insist on being observed, we are back in our old difficulty. The people take care of religion; but who or what is to take care of the people? We repeat, then, what religion? It cannot be Protestantism, in all or any of its forms; for Protestantism assumes as its point of departure that Almighty God has indeed given us a religion, but *has given it to us not to take care of us, but to be taken care of by us.* . . .
>
> The Roman Catholic religion, then, is necessary to sustain popular liberty, because popular liberty can be sustained only by a religion free from popular control, above the people, speaking from above and able to command them,—and such a religion is the Roman Catholic. It acknowledges no master but God, and depends only on the divine will in respect to what it shall teach, what it shall ordain, what it shall insist upon as truth, piety, moral and social virtue. It was made not by the people, but for them; is administered not by the people, but for them; is accountable not to the people, but to God.[3]

Similarly, Father Hecker was brought up a Protestant and for a while em-

[3] Orestes A. Brownson, *Essay and Reviews, Chiefly on Theology, Politics, and Socialism* (New York, Sadlier, 1862), pp. 372–373; 381.

braced transcendentalism at Brook Farm and Fruitlands, but he became a Catholic, organized the Paulist order to convert Americans, and edited the first Catholic daily paper in America called *The Catholic World*. Father Hecker carried forward the offensive against Protestantism in terms similar to those of Brownson insisting that Protestantism based on Calvin or Luther could not be a safe framework for democracy but rather that democracy could be safe only in the hands of a people who found authoritative guidance in the Catholic Church.

Naturally enough, the more effective the Catholic offensive became, the more violent became the Protestant opposition. Anti-Catholic organizations were formed against Catholics as Catholics and as foreigners. The patriotic feelings of nationalism were joined with religious antagonism in such secret societies as the Sons of the Sires, United Sons of America, and the Supreme Order of the Star Spangled Banner. Openly condemning Catholicism were such editors as William G. Brownlow, formerly a Methodist preacher in Tennessee, who saw in Catholicism a threat to all that was fine and decent in American life. Anti-Catholicism also broke out into a political movement when the Native American Party (also called Know-Nothing) was formed in the 1850's to defeat Catholic candidates and interests at the polls. On occasion hostility broke out into actual violence, stonings, and burning of church buildings.

Intellectually, the orthodox Protestant and Roman Catholic positions had much in common in their supernatural beliefs, in their conceptions of God as a spirit and of man as made up of immortal soul and physical body, in their view of man's destiny in the next world and the necessity of salvation, and in their moral commitments based upon the Hebraic law and the teachings of Christ. This common Christian heritage, however, was seldom heard over the recriminations that exploded from both sides over the heads of the other. Catholicism became associated with "foreignism," "un-Americanism," and "popery." Underlying many of the differences in sacraments, ritual, beliefs in miracles, saints, and relics, different versions of the Bible, the use of the Latin language, and much else was the claim of the Catholic Church to be the only true church of Christ and therefore entitled to authoritative interpretation of God's word. Nothing aroused Protestants more than to be told that the individual or "the people" were to have no voice in religious or ecclesiastical affairs but they were only to learn and to obey. Protestants could quarrel and fight and split among themselves, but when faced with the voice of authority, they tended to draw together to confront what they thought to be the common enemy. This facet of American religious thought and action accounts for much of America's distinctive approach to public education. The splintering of education along religious lines which had developed in the eighteenth century began to halt in the face of Catholic power in the early nineteenth century, and many Protestant groups began to cooperate in their efforts to establish a common nonsectarian public school and to oppose the diversion of public funds to a separate Catholic school system.

Faculty Psychology Wins the Day

Conceptions of the mind, intelligence, and learning paralleled in general the trend of thought concerning man, nature, and the universe just described. Just as there were some attempts in the late decades of the eighteenth century and early decades of the nineteenth century to construct a world view that was based upon the findings of science instead of the supernatural guidance of man's affairs, so there were some attempts to describe human nature and mental activity in scientific terms. But just as there was a return to supernaturalism in religious thought in the middle decades of the nineteenth century, so was there a reassertion of supernaturalism and retreat from naturalism in conceptions of the mind.

From the 1780's to the 1820's a few Americans began to describe human nature and mental phenomena without reliance upon supernatural causes. Perhaps the most outstanding of these was Dr. Benjamin Rush, whose medical concerns led him to see that the physical states of the brain and nervous system had a close relationship to the functioning of the mental ability to remember, to judge, and to think. Defects or damage or malfunctioning of the brain could result in insanity and poor moral judgment. Rush's treatise entitled *An Inquiry into the Physical Causes upon the Moral Faculty* in 1786 elaborated his view that the physical condition of the body could affect the mental and intellectual functions of the human being. Just as natural causes could explain much of the functioning of the universe so natural causes could explain much of human behavior without reliance upon supernatural direction.

One of Rush's students, Joseph Buchanan, published a *Philosophy of Human Nature* in which he drew upon the sensationalism of Hume and Hartley and the associationism of Thomas Brown and Erasmus Darwin. The mind was not looked upon as a separate spiritual faculty but appears as a result of the total functioning of the human organism. The natural "excitability" or susceptibility of the organism to receiving sensations from the external world leads to the association of feelings and sentiments with actions. As feelings are the sources of action and as they become connected with conduct, mental processes appear. Education and habit formation thus became important agencies in developing intellectual capabilities and capacity. Here was a preview of the associationist psychology which foreshadowed the development of scientific and experimental psychology in the latter part of the nineteenth century.

There were also a few voices raised in the blush of the late eighteenth-century Enlightenment to argue that differences in sex and race were caused not by innate spiritual or mental capacities but by the effects of different environments. The arguments of such European writers as Locke, Hartley, Condorcet, Montesquieu, Rousseau, Godwin, and Mary Wollstonecraft were bought to witness in the 1780's and 1790's. Benjamin Rush, Charles Brockden Brown, and others argued that the unfavorable conditions of women's life, their subordination and lack of education caused the belief that women were not equal to men in intellectual ability rather than any innate inferiority. Similarly, Samuel Stanhope Smith at Princeton and Benjamin Smith Barton in Philadelphia argued that racial differences in mental ability and social habits were caused by environmental conditions of climate, customs, and culture. Thus, any assumed inferiority of Negroes or Indians in mental or moral or social functioning was not the result of any essential or inherited biological or spiritual inferiority. Again, however, the acceptance of such environmental ideas had to wait, as did the scientific conceptions of mind, until the spread of the doctrine of evolution and the development of scientific anthropology, sociology, and psychology in the later nineteenth and early twentieth centuries. Conservative social, economic, and political outlooks favorable to subordination of women, Negroes, and Indians won out over liberal ideas, just as conservative religious and intellectual outlooks on the mind won out over naturalistic conceptions. In this process the Scottish common-sense philosophy and German and British transcendental philosophy helped to transfer attention from the body to the faculties of the soul and the self.

The doctrines of a faculty psychology became the most popular theory of mind and learning largely because they were congenial to religious orthodoxy and served to combat materialism, naturalism, and environmentalism. Faculty psychology was based upon the authority of the consciousness or an awareness of the inner workings of the spiritual faculties of man. The evidence of what one feels inwardly became the prime evidence for the way the mind works. Appeal was made to introspection as the method of analysis rather than to an empirical method of observation of behavior. The mind was conceived to be a spiritual affair separate and distinct from the physical body and having a pattern of functioning all its own, unique to man and common to all men in contrast to the animals. The religionists, of course, argued that the mind, being spiritual, was a special creation of God and His gift to man. The mind was considered a part of the soul.

There were a great many different ways of describing the faculties of the mind, but most commonly the mind was considered to consist of three separate sets of faculties or independent powers and capacities to which various names were given:

1. The understanding, reason, or intellect—those faculties which enable man to think and reason, make judgments, analyze, remember, imagine, reflect, and apprehend meanings.

2. The feelings, desires, sensibilities, affections, appetites, emotions, passions, susceptibilities, taste, the "heart"—those faculties by which man is impressed, feels pain or pleasure, suffers and enjoys, loves and hates.

3. The will or volition—those faculties which enable man to act.

Some proponents of the three-faculty conception of the mind arrived at their views because of their desire to make sure that the will was recognized as a separate and independent faculty. They felt that Jonathan Edwards in his reliance upon Locke had described the mind in too simple terms and had linked the will and the feelings so closely together that he had come out with the will a slave to the feelings, and therefore man had no free will. In their effort to make way for free will in religious terms they insisted that the will be considered a separate faculty. Others were interested in the separation of the feelings from the will, for they thought that the heart of religious faith was in the faculty of religious feelings or affections. Still others with little religious interest were attracted to the three-faculty psychology and sought to reestablish Locke within the new framework; so Locke's emphasis on reflection was taken to be the heart of the intellectual faculty, and from this time on Locke was used to support the disciplinary theories of education on a secular as well as a religious basis.

Whatever the motivations, the faculty psychology began to receive important attention following the publication of works by Reverend Asa Burton in Vermont in 1824. In the 1830's and 1840's orthodox religionists, liberal religionists, and transcendentalists took up the faculty psychology until it became the dominant academic psychology of the day. President Jeremiah Day of Yale, President Asa Mahan of Oberlin, Professor Albert Taylor Bledsoe, Professor Henry P. Tappan of New York University, Professor Thomas C. Upham of Bowdoin, President Francis Wayland of Brown, President Noah Porter of Yale, and President James McCosh of Princeton were a few of the outstanding academicians who embraced and promoted the faculty psychology and gave it great power in the educational world through most of the nineteenth century.

Faculty psychology was especially important as providing the basic justification for mental discipline as the supreme method in college education and for giving first place to the classics, mathematics, and philosophy as the essential content of a liberal education. It was used as a bulwark against admitting new and useful studies to the college curriculum. Of all the educational statements of the time the one that most clearly illustrates the operation of the faculty psychology as the basis for mental discipline and the prescribed curriculum of intellectual studies was the Yale faculty report of 1828 which stated in the words of President Jeremiah Day:

> The two great points to be gained in intellectual culture, are the *discipline* and the *furniture* of the mind; expanding its powers, and storing it with knowledge.

The former of these is, perhaps, the more important of the two. A commanding object, therefore, in a collegiate course, should be, to call into daily and vigorous exercise the faculties of the student. Those branches of study should be prescribed, and those modes of instruction adopted, which are best calculated to teach the art of fixing the attention, directing the train of thought, analyzing a subject proposed for investigation; following, with accurate discrimination, the course of argument; balancing nicely the evidence presented to the judgment; awakening, elevating, and controlling the imagination; arranging, with skill, the treasures which memory gathers; rousing and guiding the powers of genius. . . .

The great object of a collegiate education, preparatory to the study of a profession, is to give that expansion and balance of the mental powers, those liberal and comprehensive views, and those fine proportions of character, which are not to be found in him whose ideas are always confined to one particular channel.[4]

What the proponents of the faculty psychology did, however, was to concentrate so exclusively on the intellectual faculties that they almost forgot the faculties of feeling and the will. They became so absorbed in training the intellectual faculties that they began to assume and then to claim that rigorous training of the mind would be transferred to the other faculties and would develop sound moral character and the proper motivations to conduct and action. They became so concerned with scholarly knowledge and mental discipline that they neglected and even argued against preparation for living in a real world as a proper goal for education. It took the political, economic, and social pressures of the next fifty years and a new kind of behavioral psychology and experimental philosophy before the faculty psychology was removed from its central role in defining the goals and content of American education.

THE GROWTH OF ORGANIZED KNOWLEDGE

Significant developments occurred in the early nineteenth century that changed the character of organized knowledge and thus began a fundamental revolution in the character of higher education and eventually of secondary education. One of the most notable of these changes was what happened to the academic discipline known as "philosophy." Another important development was the alignment of attitudes toward the role of knowledge in education and the role of an intellectual class in society. Some thought of knowledge as a means of self-cultivation for an intellectual elite; others saw knowledge as a potent fare for practical usefulness, for the improvement of society in general, and for the welfare of the common people in particular. Aristocratic gentility was confronted with social responsibility as ideals of education; and

---

[4] "Original Papers in relation to a Course of Liberal Education" *American Journal of Science and Arts*, Vol. 15 (January 1829), pp. 300–301 and 308–309. For a full discussion of the whole report, see R. Freeman Butts, *The College Charts Its Course* (New York, McGraw-Hill, 1939), pp. 118–225.

the conflict of these ideals reverberated through academic halls and public forums.

Philosophy

From the medieval days of a revival of interest in Aristotelian thought, philosophy had been thought of alternately as the "queen of the sciences" or as the "handmaiden of theology." The eighteenth-century Enlightenment had made great strides in freeing philosophy from its apron strings that held it tied to the supernatural interests of theology and religion. The "philosophers" of Enlightenment thought had turned the attention of philosophy to nature and to science as the key to the unlocking of the mysteries of the natural world. Thus, a large part of philosophy came to be known as "natural philosophy," which meant a speculative and scientific investigation of natural laws in realms that would today be classified largely under physics, chemistry, astronomy, and geology.

From about 1750 to 1820 the dominant attention to philosophy in American colleges had been divided between "natural philosophy" and "moral philosophy." Natural philosophy was devoted to the physical sciences, and moral philosophy was the term applied to the whole range of political, economic, legal, and social institutions of man, or what we today would call generally the social sciences. These divisions of philosophical interest could clearly be seen in the interests of Franklin's American Philosophical Society, in the proposals by Jefferson for reform of the curriculum of the College of William and Mary in 1779, and in the writings on philosophy by Samuel Johnson in the 1750's and 1760's. Natural philosophy received a great boost from the growth of interest in science promoted by such leaders in the Revolutionary period as David Rittenhouse, astronomer and mathematician, Joseph Priestley, chemist, Benjamin Rush, physician, and Thomas Cooper, chemist and president of the University of South Carolina. Natural philosophy was on its way to being thoroughly secularized and concerned with developing comprehensive and encyclopedic theories and natural laws concerning the operation of the universe, physical phenomena, and human nature.

The interest in scientific observation and scientific method did not cease; in fact, it was enormously accelerated in the first half of the nineteenth century, but philosophy lost its touch with science. Under the influence of the faculty psychology, philosophy dropped its interest in natural philosophy and turned to "mental philosophy." It turned its attention from investigation of nature to introspection of the human mind. Philosophy forsook the outward world for the delights of the inner spirit. In the 1820's, 1830's, and 1840's under the impetus given to faculty psychology by the Scottish philosophy and by transcendental idealism, the main divisions of philosophy became mental philosophy and moral philosophy. Mental philosophy referred primarily to the faculty of reason or intellect, and moral philosophy turned to the faculties of feeling and will. Mental or intellectual philosophy was devoted to exploring the intricacies of consciousness, perception, memory, judgment, and imagination through logic and metaphysics; and moral philosophy dropped its concern with political economy, history, and law and turned to the role of the will and of feelings in moral conduct and action. For three decades prior to the Civil War many textbooks on mental and moral philosophy were written by such college professors and presidents as Francis Wayland of Brown, Mark Hopkins of Williams, Frederick Beasley of the College of Philadelphia, Thomas C. Upham of Bowdoin, Asa Mahan, Francis Bowen of Harvard, Laurens P. Hickok of Union College, Joseph Haven, Henry N. Day, and Noah Porter of Yale. Supernaturalism had achieved a firm grip in philosophy, from which it did not extricate itself until the pragmatic revolution of the late nineteenth and early twentieth centuries. At the same time "natural philosophy" was taken over by the sciences.

Natural Sciences

Meanwhile, however, the interest in the natural world continued and speeded up as new and fascinating strides were made in the physical sciences ("natural philosophy") and in the biological sciences ("natural history"). Great masses of information were accumulated and classified in an ever widening and growing field. Under the impetus of such expansion of knowledge, the fields of science gradually became more specialized. A professor of "natural philosophy" like Benjamin Silliman of Yale could take the whole range of natural knowledge for his field at the opening of the nineteenth century, but by the 1850's a scientist would have to be a chemist, a physicist, a geologist, a botanist, or a zoologist, if he were to keep up with his specialization.

By the beginning of the nineteenth century, the natural sciences had already firmly taken root on the American scene. The American Academy of Arts and Sciences had been founded in 1780 to promote interest and knowledge in natural history, medicine, mathematics, astronomy, meteorology, geography, the arts, agriculture, manufacture, commerce, and indeed the whole gamut of literary, intellectual, and useful knowledge. Yet, much of what writing and research was in evidence had been the work of men whose interest in science was largely avocational. Thus, Benjamin Franklin's outstanding experiments with electricity were carried on between 1746 and 1752 only in addition to his principal work as statesman, author, and editor. The research for Thomas Jefferson's *Notes on the State of Virginia* (1785), representing probably the earliest scientific survey of a region published in the United States, was also undertaken while Jefferson engaged in the work of state. So it was with most of the sciences. Country planters, ministers, businessmen, and physicians were the men who produced America's initial contributions in botany, geology, astronomy, and physics. To be sure, there was a great deal of dependence upon European scholarship. Furthermore, there was little specialization, the prevailing belief holding that not enough was known in any one field to warrant concentration.

If this amateur interest saw continuing growth during the early decades of the nineteenth century, it was increasingly complemented by the development of professional scholarship in the field. A number of historians have marked the launching of Benjamin Silliman's *American Journal of Science and Arts* in 1818 as the beginning of professional science in America. In any case, the half century following that date witnessed any number of significant developments in that direction. Much of the work, to be sure, simply represented compiling, fact-gathering, describing, and classifying. These were the years of the first precise and extensive coast and geodetic surveys, the years of J. J. Audubon's remarkable work in ornithology and Louis J. R. Agassiz's pioneering research in geology and zoology. The state governments sponsored state surveys and the federal government sponsored wide varying explorations by land and sea. In 1846 Congress chartered the Smithsonian Institution, with physicist Joseph Henry as its head. Through his wise and efficient administration the Institution became a primary agency for disseminating scientific information rather than the limited museum and oddity collection which many of the founding congressmen had envisioned. The rapidly developing industrial system vigorously stimulated investigations with possible practical consequences; and the steady rise in the number of patents documented the skill of American inventors.

Professional associations expanded, and new ones were formed, notably the American Medical Association in 1847. A milestone, perhaps, was the founding of the American Association for the Advancement of Science in 1848. Scientific subjects received increasing attention not only in secondary schools and colleges, but also in popular lectures and forums. The American Society for the Diffusion of Useful Knowledge (1836), the establishment of mercantile and mechanics libraries, the Lowell Institute lectures, and the lyceum movement were all greatly stimulated and nourished by the growing interest in natural science. Generally, if the age failed to produce any outstanding men of science, the groundwork was being laid for future creative thought.

A persistent question arose, of course, concerning the relation of all the scientific knowledge to the supernatural concerns of the religionists in maintaining the authority of the Biblical story of the origin of the world and its creatures. Enlightenment naturalists like Thomas Cooper had seen no point in trying to reunite science and religion, and some religionists opposed the whole idea of scientific investigation by damning it as contributing to infidelity. But many, if not most, writers both scientific and religious tried to show that there was no essential conflict. Prominent among the scientists who took this position were Benjamin Silliman, Louis Agassiz, James Dwight Dana, and Asa Gray. Ministers like Horace Bushnell argued that science simply confirmed the truths of religion. The head-on conflict between science and religion was largely postponed until the battles over evolution in the later nineteenth century.

The Social Sciences

Asserting their independence of moral philosophy, history and political economy were the most active disciplines in the field of the social sciences in the early national period. The nationalistic impulses of the Revolutionary War turned the attention of historians to the history of the American states and to biographies of national leaders. Many of them believed that history should promote attitudes of patriotism and republicanism among citizens and school children. Prominent among these were Theodore Parker and George Bancroft. In the middle decades other phases of the development of the New World were explored by William H. Prescott who chronicled the role of the Spanish, and Francis Parkman did the same for the French. In political economy some authors, like John McVickar of Columbia, followed Adam Smith and portrayed the glories of economic individualism, laissez-faire capitalism, free trade, and the open market of competition as appropriate to the new nation. Others, like Mathew Carey, Henry Carey, and Frederick List protested against Malthusian doctrines of natural law in which disease, war, and famines were looked upon as natural remedies for overpopulation and urged the use of the state as an agency for economic planning through protective tariffs and a managed currency in order to achieve a better society that would serve the welfare of all.

The Humanities

The humanist tradition with its continuing interest in the classical language and literature retained a strong hold on academic loyalties. The humanists eagerly embraced the new faculty psychology as a philosophical justification for a large place in the college curriculum for the classics as unique instruments for mental discipline. The most serious battle the classical humanists had to fight in the early nineteenth century was against the modern languages and literature. Retaining their interest in European culture the classical humanists looked with disdain upon the rising upstarts in English, French, and German. French received a great stimulus in the Enlightenment phase of the Revolutionary sympathy for France, and German received greater attention in the new regard for German idealism among the scholars who were attracted to the German universities. At Harvard George Ticknor, Edward Everett, George Bancroft, Joseph Green Cogswell, Charles Follen, and Charles Beck all joined a clamor to have the modern languages given an equal recognition in the curriculum along with the classics, but they made only a little headway. Meanwhile a new interest in English as the language of America was promoted by the pioneering work of Noah Webster. The classical humanists grudgingly gave way to the modern languages only when they came to see them as allies in holding the fort of "cultural" and humanistic studies against the onslaught of the sciences, technology, and other useful subjects.

The lines of battle were being formed that were to last for a hundred years to the present. The "genteel tradition" held its ground with arguments in favor of mental discipline; knowledge was valuable for its own sake and for the cultivation of the mental and moral faculties. The ideal of aristocratic gentility required quiet and scholarly pursuit of language, history, art, and music as the marks of an educated gentleman. The idealist and transcendental philosophies and the romantic literature of the early nineteenth century glorified this ideal as portrayed by William Wadsworth Longfellow, James Russell Lowell, Oliver Wendell Holmes, and Ralph Waldo Emerson.

In opposition to the refinements of "culture" appropriate to an intellectual elite were heard voices saying that knowledge should be useful in promoting nationalism, utilitarianism, and democracy. Knowledge should be pursued in order to achieve nationalistic American loyalties and patriotism. It should be pursued as a preparation for a life of work in a business and commercial society as a means of improving the arts of manufacturing, commerce, agriculture, and mechanics. This aim would be useful to the individual as a means of getting ahead and to society as a means of improving the production of goods and services. Knowledge should also be widely disseminated among the people in order to enable them to perform their duties in a republican and democratic society where welfare depends upon the knowledge and enlightenment of the people at large. An aristocratic intellectual elite might have been appropriate to the Old World but not to the New. Knowledge should be pursued for the purposes of improving the lot of the common man. Such arguments as these helped to expand the study of the sciences and technologies in many higher institutions and in some secondary schools. The scientific and technical studies were admitted grudgingly, however, and were often assigned positions of inferiority in comparison with the older humanities. They were not to win their way to a position of equality or superiority until the industrialization and democratization of America had made far greater strides in the later nineteenth century.

THE GROUND SWELL OF DEMOCRATIC THOUGHT

The conflict of ideas about the proper role of knowledge just mentioned reflected broader currents of thought that were sweeping the country. Details need not be mentioned here because the broad pattern has been described in connection with the discussion of political, economic, and religious trends in Chapter 5. All that can be done here is to bring some of the basic ideas into perspective that will relate them to the ideas and practices of education. The recurring theme that runs through American social thought of the early period is the gradual advance of democratic ideals against the rugged defenses of aristocracy. The doctrinal winds of naturalism and supernaturalism could alternately require tacking to windward or running free, but the people seemed to find the tide of democracy running ever more strongly in their direction. Public education in the form of common schools for all the people was one of the craft that took advantage of the strongly running tide of democracy.

The eighteenth-century Enlightenment found expression in America in the ideas of progress and humanitarianism as expressed by Tom Paine, Philip Frenau, Joel Barlow and a dozen others. The ideas of equality and democracy were immortally expressed by Jefferson in the Declaration of Independence. The theory of consent of the governed shifted from the federal theology and the covenant of the religious congregation to the secular basis of the compact of the people in the federal and state constitutions. From the 1820's onward the new creed of democracy was the dignity and worth of the "common man."

The heart of the impact of the European Enlightenment on America lay in the notion of progress which gradually began to pervade American democratic thought in the late eighteenth century. The protection of the oceans, the distance from powerful neighbors, huge tracts of fertile land, and the development of an independent yeomanry had since colonial times nurtured republican and equalitarian ideas. The keynote of society, by the end of the eighteenth century, was the ideal of a free individual, possessed of natural rights guaranteed him by the Constitution, participating in the shaping of his own political destiny, and subject in the quest for fortune only to the unrestrained operation of natural laws. Now, in the early nineteenth century, the European Enlightenment richly fertilized the roots of this democratic ideology.

The new doctrine, growing out of the rationalism of John Locke, the utilitarianism of Jeremy Bentham, and the humanitarianism of the French *philosophes,* optimistically proclaimed the dawn of a new era for mankind. Through his reason—through rational treatment of his problems—man could achieve greater happiness and prosperity than he had ever known. Science and political democracy were to be the great tools for the fulfillment of these aspirations. With it, man's perfectibility was indefinite; its limitation, as the French philosopher Condorcet had written, was the duration of the globe upon which nature had placed man. Differences between men were minimized. In the struggle for perfection the accent was on man and mankind. This was the faith of dynamic democracy.

Out of this faith emerged a new conception of the comman man. As the ideals of the Enlightenment joined the ideals of the frontier, the farmers, the mechanics, and the laborers—the men whom President Jackson called "the bone and sinew of the country"—came to symbolize America. Gradually, the literature of the "laborites" and of the Democratic Party began to speak of "the people" in romantic tones suggesting an ideal society. "The exact measure of the progress of civilization," wrote Democrat George Bancroft, "is the degree in which the intelligence of the common mind has prevailed over wealth and brute force; in other words, the measure of the progress of civilization is the progress of the people." America, as the French traveler Michel Chevalier observed, was rapidly becoming "essentially and radically a democracy, not in name merely, but in deed."

This democratic ideology during these years was also closely associated with the Protestant Christian ethic. "The Americans," wrote Alexis de Tocqueville, "combine the notions of Christianity and of liberty so intimately in their minds that it is impossible to make them conceive the one without the other. . . ." Thus, if the Americans had seen fit to disestablish their religion, it was certainly not for lack of interest in religion. Sunday laws were still in effect and observed in most places. Church attendance remained in fashion, ministers continued as important public figures, and religion retained a greater financial support voluntarily than it ever had before under compulsion. Even the new scientists generally accepted Christianity; and most saw their findings completely in accord with the earlier teachings of the Bible.

Richard Hildreth, the historian, in his *Theory of Morals* in 1844 argued that the progress of morality depends upon the progress of knowledge and upon the sentiment of benevolence whereby man is motivated to good acts. Here is a continuation of the secularization of morals that had been so much a part of Franklin's effort to instill habits of virtue but without religious sanctions. Knowledge and education are so important because they enable man to make better judgments concerning the proper course of conduct to be pursued. The people can think for themselves as well as govern for themselves provided they are relieved from pain and suffering and degradation through the reform of social institutions. Simply preaching to people or enjoining them to be good or cultivating their moral faculties will not achieve true morality; only the development of man's intelligence and the reform of his institutions will accomplish this end. A moral society cannot be attained by the dictation or leadership of a few but only by the general enlightenment of all the people, and they are capable of such enlightenment. Similiar outlooks were expressed by Jacksonian Democrats in the 1830's and 1840's, peculiarly well expressed by Walt Whitman in his prose as newspaper editor and in his poetry as singer of the democratic faith in the common man.

In reply spokesmen for the propertied and privileged classes kept up a running barrage against the spokesmen for democracy. Alexander Hamilton, the Hartford Wits, Fisher Ames, and the Federalists in general attacked Jeffersonian republicans as revolutionaries intent on destroying property, decency, and morality. Chief Justice John Marshall upheld the inviolability of contracts and private property even when they contravened the public welfare. The apparent reality of innate inequalities among classes and races was used to hammer away at the ideal of equalitarianism. Superpatriots and conservative intellectuals and religionists jeered at reform movements as the wild-eyed schemes of crackpots. Democracy was dubbed visionary by Melville, Cooper, and Francis Lieber. The feminists were subjected to scorn and ridicule for trying to take women out of the home and raise them to a level of equality with their innately superior men. Southern aristocrats turned from apologizing for Negro slavery as a necessary evil to eulogizing slavery as a desirable value for both the owners and the slaves themselves. But despite all the arguments that could be brought to bear against them, the common people felt confidently optimistic about their own powers and abilities, and they moved to alter their institutions to prove it. Education was one of the most important institutions before the Civil War to feel the effects of the movement of democratic thought.

ISSUES FOR STUDY AND DISCUSSION

1. From your study so far do you think it is fair to say that the development of a nonsectarian religious outlook was important in the development of a nonsectarian public school system?

2. As the faculty psychology is described in this chapter, do you find that it is still an important concept in American education? What is your guess as to its main influence on educational method and content?

3. What do you think were the most important advances in knowledge made in the early nineteenth century? Which do you think had the most influence upon education at that time, and which have had the most persistent influence upon modern education?

4. Criticize the following proposition: "Public education received more support in the early nineteenth century from those who held democratic social outlooks than from those who held aristocratic points of view." Do you think a similar proposition would apply today in lesser or greater degree than it did then?

SUGGESTIONS FOR FURTHER READING

Blau, Joseph L. (ed.), *American Philosophic Addresses, 1700–1900,* New York, Columbia University Press, 1946.
———, *Men and Movements in American Philosophy,* New York, Prentice-Hall, 1952.
Brooks, Van Wyck, *The Flowering of New England, 1815–1865,* New York, Dutton, 1938.
Butts, R. Freeman, *The College Charts Its Course,* New York, McGraw-Hill, 1939.
Curti, Merle, *The Growth of American Thought,* 2d ed., New York, Harper, 1951.
Dorfman, Joseph, *The Economic Mind in American Civilization, 1606–1865,* Vol. II, New York, Viking, 1946.

Fish, Carl R., *The Rise of the Common Man, 1830–1850*, New York, Macmillan, 1927.

Gabriel, Ralph H., *The Course of American Democratic Thought*, New York, Ronald, 1940.

Hacker, Louis M., *The Shaping of the American Tradition*, New York, Columbia University Press, 1947.

Krout, John A., and Fox, Dixon Ryan, *The Completion of Independence, 1790–1830*, New York, Macmillan, 1944.

Miller, Perry, *The Transcendentalists*, Cambridge, Mass., Harvard University Press, 1950.

Parrington, Vernon L., *Main Currents in American Thought*, Vol. II, *The Romantic Revolution in America, 1800–1860*, New York, Harcourt, 1927–1930.

Perry, Ralph Barton, *Puritanism and Democracy*, New York, Vanguard, 1944.

Schlesinger, Arthur M., Jr., *The Age of Jackson*, Boston, Little, 1945.

Schneider, Herbert W., *A History of American Philosophy*, New York, Columbia University Press, 1946.

Smith, Bernard, *The Democratic Spirit: A Collection of American Writings from the Earliest Times to the Present Day*, New York, Knopf, 1941.

Stokes, Anson Phelps, *Church and State in the United States*, New York, Harper, 1950, Vols. I and II.

Thorp, Willard, Curti, Merle, and Baker, Carlos, *American Issues: The Social Record*, Vol. I, *The Literary Record*, Vol. II, Philadelphia, Lippincott, 1941.

Tocqueville, Alexis de, *Democracy in America*, Phillips Bradley (ed.), New York, Knopf, 1945.

Turner, Frederick Jackson, *The Frontier in American History*, New York, Holt, 1920.

Tyler, Alice, *Freedom's Ferment*, Minneapolis, University of Minnesota Press, 1944.

Wish, Harvey, *Society and Thought in Early America*, New York, Longmans, 1950.

7

CONFLICTING CONCEPTIONS
OF EDUCATION

THOMAS JEFFERSON'S *Bill for the More General Diffusion of Knowledge* stands as a landmark in the history of educational thought (see pp. 93–94). Holding that the most effective safeguard against political tyranny is "to illuminate, as far as practicable, the minds of the people at large," Jefferson proposed a system of free public schools which would (1) give every child in the commonwealth a basic elementary education, and (2) give the brightest children the chance to continue on through secondary school and the university. With this system Jefferson hoped not only to provide for the general enlightenment of the citizenry, but also "to avail the state of those talents which nature has sown as liberally among the poor as the rich, but which perish without use, if not sought for and cultivated." Taken with its provisions for public support and control, the bill actually anticipated much of the course of educational reform during the first half century of the republic.

Jefferson's bill, however, did not pass the Virginia legislature in 1779; nor did Virginia adopt anything like it at any time before the Civil War. These latter facts offer another clue to the educational thought of this period. Americans were by no means of a single mind. Many opposing conceptions vied for acceptance, and the conflicts concerning them were often bitter and prolonged. Such issues as universal education versus education for the few, tax support versus private support, state control versus local or church control, election versus prescription, and dozens of others were in the forefront of public discussion throughout the first half of the nineteenth century, and many were by no means solved even after 1850. Yet there can be no denying that out of this clash of ideas emerged a new system of educational thought and practice. By and large, ideals of the common school, the high school, the state university, and normal school were all products of the period. They provided a distinctive American educational ideal which has endured to the present time.

EARLY DEMANDS FOR EQUAL EDUCATIONAL OPPORTUNITY

Universal Elementary Education

Universal education and political enlightenment. The necessity of general literacy and enlightenment in a republican society was vigorously advanced both in France and America during the late eighteenth and early nineteenth centuries. Soon after the French Revolution leaders such as Mirabeau and Tallyrand proposed sweeping educational reforms to the newly organized Constituent Assembly. Both urged the political necessity of universal primary instruction throughout France. In 1792 the philosopher Condorcet presented to the National Assembly his *Report on the General Organization of Public Instruction* in which he argued that only through universal education could citizens be taught effectively to enjoy their rights and fulfill their responsibilities.

In the United States, although the ideal appeared only sporadically at first, it soon entered into the thinking of many prominent persons. As early as 1786 Benjamin Rush, prominent Philadelphia physician and man of affairs, proposed a plan for universal national education in the values and obligations of republican citizenship. Similar ideas were advanced by James Sullivan, a New England jurist, in 1788; by Robert Coram, a Delaware author in 1791; and by Nathaniel Chipman, federal judge of the district of Vermont, in 1793. When the American Philosophical Society in 1796 offered a prize for an educational plan best designed to meet the needs of the infant republic, the two winning essays also embodied this notion of universal instruction. Notwithstanding the fact that none of these plans was put into practice, they had begun to make real the very important relationship between self-government and public enlightenment.[1]

While it is difficult to estimate the circulation of the plans themselves, it is clear that the ideas they embodied received increasing voice following the turn of the century. The writings of every one of the early Presidents, for example, revealed a deep interest in universal education as a bulwark of republican institutions. Washington mentioned it in his farewell address; Adams had been a schoolmaster in his early years; Jefferson was a lifelong supporter of education and actually fathered the University of Virginia; and

---

[1] See Allen Oscar Hansen, *Liberalism and American Education in the Eighteenth Century* (New York, Macmillan, 1926). See also Lawrence A. Cremin, *The American Common School* (New York, Teachers College, Columbia University, 1951), for more extensive discussion of these demands.

Madison wrote in 1822 "A popular Government, without popular information, or the means of acquiring it, is but a Prologue to a Farce or a Tragedy; or, perhaps both. Knowledge will forever govern ignorance: And a people who mean to be their own Governors, must arm themselves with the power which knowledge gives." [2]

As the movement to extend the suffrage and liberalize politics progressed during the 1820's and 1830's, these demands received ever wider enunciation. Moreover, the problem itself became more and more complex. An intelligent electorate was now far from the only need. With the growth of the idea that any citizen could hold any public office, or serve on juries, or in the militia, the dangers of ignorance only multiplied. Furthermore, as political power gradually began to slip from their hands, many upper-class people came to realize that popular education was actually to their own advantage. If the people were going to rule, they ought at least to rule well. More than ever, the education of all was clearly the interest of all.

Universal education and nationalism. Closely related to the above argument, and present in almost all of the early plans and proposals, was the influence of nationalism on education. Whereas much of the guiding purpose of colonial education had been preparation for religious orthodoxy, increasing emphasis was now placed on citizenship in and loyalty to a national state. The movement was by no means confined to the New World; it was in evidence in most of the major nations of Western Europe. Essentially, nationalism demanded an education that would best enable citizens to help the nation realize its political, social, and military aspirations.

Quite appropriately, then, most of these early proposals for "republican education" embodied a conception of education for patriotism. Benjamin Rush, for example, urged that schools carefully nurture in children a "SUPREME REGARD TO THEIR COUNTRY"; Coram, Sullivan, and Chipman were equally vehement in their demand for universal inculcation of American and republican values. All saw in education a prime means of cutting the cultural umbilical cord which tied America to the Old World and of building a vigorous new loyalty to American institutions.

As the forces of nationalism grew stronger in the early decades of the nineteenth century, so did the demands that the school exercise this patriotic duty. When the great immigrations of the 1840's and 1850's came, and stimulated the development of nativism, the argument was substantially reinforced. Leaders began to fear the presence of large bodies of foreigners whose habits of thought and living were incompatible with the American way of life. They felt that such persons could well challenge the very virility of the republic; and gradually, they began to call for some means of inculcating in

[2] Madison to W. T. Barry, Aug. 4, 1822, Gaillard Hunt (ed.), *The Writings of James Madison Comprising his Public Papers and his Private Correspondence, including numerous Letters and Documents now for the First Time Printed.* (New York, Putnam, 1910) Vol. IX, p. 103.

them the basic concepts and practices of republicanism. An *Americanizing* function of the school was clearly indicated. "Shall these adopted citizens," asked Benjamin Labaree, President of Middlebury College in Vermont,[3] "become a part of the body politic, and firm supporters of liberal institutions, or will they prove to our republic what the Goths and Huns were to the Roman Empire?" The answer for Labaree rested in large measure with the wisdom and fidelity of the teacher. The schoolmaster was to be a master builder, and by degrees mold "these unprepared and uncongenial elements" into "intelligent, enterprising and liberal-minded supporters of free institutions."

Universal education and equality of opportunity.   Coming principally from the labor groups in the cities, a third proposal involved the relationship of universal education to equality and equality of opportunity. Generally, two aspects were involved in this educational concern of the workingman. First, viewing the effects of merchant and industrial capitalism on America's relatively fluid class system, he was concerned with the hardening of class lines and the growth of class cleavage. Universal education, he felt, could do much to offset this. Second, in a society paying allegiance to economic individualism, the workingman was particularly concerned with maintaining equality of opportunity. He felt that his son, armed with the preparation for individual success regarded as a direct result of education, could rise to the top of the socio-economic ladder despite humble beginnings. If, on the other hand, the half mysterious power bestowed by education was denied to the lower classes, republican equality would quickly vanish from American society.

Examples of this concern with universal, "republican" education can be found throughout the early labor literature. It was central in an extensive report on Pennsylvania's school system published by a joint committee of Philadelphia workingmen in 1829. Nowhere, however, was it better expressed than in the writings of Robert Dale Owen, early leader of the New York workingmen's movement. Owen, with the failure of his communal experiment at New Harmony, Indiana, had become more and more convinced that reform of the educational system was the only solid foundation on which a more extensive reform program could rest. In the New York Workingmen's Party he saw the opportunity to put his ideas into effect. Insisting that the new party could do well to concentrate on a few basic reforms rather than a widespread, inarticulate program, Owen urged that a system of universal education be placed at the head of its platform. In April of 1830 he set his views before the public in a series of six essays on *Public Education*.[4]

---

[3] Benjamin Labaree, "The Education Demanded by the Peculiar Character of Our Civil Institutions," *Lectures Delivered Before the American Institute of Instruction, at Montpelier, Vt., August, 1849; Including the Journal of Proceedings and a List of the Officers* (Boston, Ticknor, Reed, and Fields, 1850), pp. 27–58.

[4] *The Working Man's Advocate* (New York), Vol. I, No. 25 (Apr. 17, 1830) and Vol. I, No. 26 (Apr. 24, 1830).

Opening with the question *"What sort of Education is befitting a Republic?"*, Owen replied: "No system of education which embraces any thing less than the whole people. . . ." Furthermore, republican education would have to be not only *open* to all, but *equal* to all. It was here that Owen incorporated the most revolutionary aspects of his proposals. On surveying the common day schools of New England, he found that true republican education could not possibly exist. ". . . if the children from these state schools are to go every evening, the one to his wealthy parent's soft carpetted drawing room, and the other to its poor father's or widowed mother's comfortless cabin, will they return the next day as friends and equals? He knows little of human nature who thinks they will." In view of this, the only education which Owen saw as genuinely equal was "one which provides for children at all times; receiving them at the earliest age their parents chose to entrust them to the national care, feeding, clothing, and educating them, until the age of majority." In a system which provided all children with a common totality of experience over a period of years, the republic should bestow an education befitting its citizenry.

As would be fairly obvious in a society where the family was as strong an institution as it was in America of 1830, such proposals stirred up a storm of controversy. Furthermore, the average American workingman of 1830 (bourgeois artisan-producer that he was) really did not want anything quite so radical for his children. Rather, in the spirit of economic individualism, he would have preferred bestowing upon them the trappings of the classical education common among the upper classes. Yet, even though Owen's proposals became a political football which split the New York labor movement wide open, they elicited a surprising degree of genuine interest. They were copied by sixteen newspapers in their entirety and were cited with approval by many others. Some of the rural periodicals are even reported to have given them kindly notices. In sensitizing the workingman and the population at large to the need for universal education, they fortified the arguments from other sources. Even more important, perhaps, was the way in which their conception of equal republican education—in a somewhat modified form— entered into the thinking of educators and statesmen.

Other demands for universal elementary education. A number of other demands which figured prominently in the arguments for universal elementary education bear brief mention at this point. One commonly heard was that widespread schooling would raise the productivity of the people, and thereby increase national prosperity. This contention was widely used to convince taxpaying businessmen that it was to their own economic advantage to support universal education. Two other arguments stemmed principally from the urban life of the period. One urged that universal education would diminish crime; the other, that universal education would prevent poverty. Both were often used to bolster requests for appropriations to support expanding city school systems. Finally, there were the arguments which held basic education to be the *natural right* of every individual and further conceived it to be public duty to furnish such education to all children. At a time when the philosophy of natural rights was so widely accepted as a basic tenet of republican political thought, to establish education as a natural right associated with freedom of speech, conscience, assembly, or the press, or with natural economic laws, was to add great strength to its cause.

The educators conceive an ideal common school. What was the essential element common to all of these demands? Basically, it was this: that the public school would have to undertake certain important social tasks which could no longer be haphazardly entrusted to the family, the church, or even simple participation in the life of the community. In effect, the school would now be entrusted with a responsibility involving the very perpetuation and progress of the republic. Clearly, this was far different from the comparatively secondary role which formal education had played in the life of colonial America.

Gradually, educators in all parts of the Union began to conceive of a new kind of school—a school which would embrace the whole population. It was to be a common school; not common in the European sense of a school for the common people, but common in a new sense of common to all the people. "The Common School," declared Bishop George W. Doane to the legislature of New Jersey, "is *common,* not as inferior, not as the school for poor men's children, but as the light and air are common." [5] Through periodicals, memorials, pamphlets, and petitions, educational reformers pressed this idea of a free school, open and available to rich and poor alike. Not only was it to be free, so that no one would be excluded for inability to pay tuition, but also it was to be of high quality, the equivalent of any institution which could be privately established. Obviously, if this free education were not of such quality, it would soon be tainted with the stigma of "pauper education" and renounced by the proud and independent citizenry of a free republic.

It is important to note, however, that this notion of "availability" was a very positive concept in the eyes of these educators. Accepting the assumption that association will inevitably engender mutual respect and friendship among children, these men hoped that the common school would not only be *open* to all but also *used* by all. The children of all nationalities, religions, creeds, and economic levels would then have an opportunity to mix together in the common schoolroom. ". . . *let the common school be made fit to educate all, and let all send to it,"* urged Orville Taylor in the New York *Common School Assistant.* "This alone will secure an education for everyone, and this is republican. More than all—*this is duty." *[6] Two years later, in 1839, a speaker before the Middlesex County Association for the Improve-

[5] *American Journal of Education,* Vol. 15 (1865), pp. 8–9.
[6] *Common School Assistant,* Vol. 2 (1837), p. 1.

ment of Common Schools expressed all the optimism of this early faith when
he declared: "I want to see the children of the rich and the poor sit down
side by side on equal terms, as members of one family—a great brotherhood
—deeming no one distinguished above the rest but the best scholar and the
best boy—giving free and natural play to their affections, at a time of life
when lasting friendships are often formed, and worldliness and pride, and envy
have not yet alienated heart from heart." [7] It was urged that given such an association in childhood, the different groups in the community would forever
have common memories, faith, and respect on which to build amicable relationships.

Implicit in the notion of a school embracing the whole people was an idea
of the private school as a competing factor inevitably detracting from the
ideal. Not only did the private school draw the children of the upper classes
from the common school, but also their interest and financial backing. "The
spirit of private, select schools," wrote Orville Taylor in 1837, "is a spirit
directly opposed to the FREE, EQUAL spirit of our Institutions." [8] It could
only, he continued, weaken and bring into disrepute the public school. But
how, in a free economy, could this competition be quelled? Certainly, forceful suppression was in direct opposition to an individualist-capitalist system.
Rather, the answer lay in making the common schools of such high quality
that even those who could afford them would not use the private schools.

Opposition to universal education.   Pressure for universal education, while
widespread, was by no means without exception. As a matter of fact in many
areas, especially rural ones, it was weak or nil. Some citizens undoubtedly
viewed mass education as "agrarianism" or "socialism" calculated to disturb
the traditional class arrangements of society. Others argued that all education
demanded leisure—a fact which made universal education an impossible goal
for all but the upper classes. For still others, "booklarnin" was simply not
important for the great body of the people. ". . . children," wrote a corre-
spondent to the Raleigh (North Carolina) *Register* in 1829, "should pass their
days in the cotton patch, or at the plow, or in the cornfield, instead of being
mewed up in a school house, where they are learning nothing. . . . I hope
you do not conceive it at all necessary, that *everybody* should be able to read,
write, and cipher." [9]

Much of this opposition, however, must be seen as opposition to universal
public education rather than to universal education *per se*. In other words,
many of those opposed readily admitted, for instance, that everyone in a republic ought to be educated, but they steadfastly maintained that only paupers
should attend school at public expense. To educate all in public facilities was

---

[7] *Common School Journal*, Vol. 1 (1839), p. 60.
[8] *Common School Assistant*, Vol. 2 (1837), p. 41.
[9] Charles L. Coon, *The Beginnings of Public Education in North Carolina* (Raleigh, Edwards
& Broughton, 1908), p. 432.

a blatant abrogation of the most fundamental natural rights of private property. Others, also believing in universal education, yet continued to view it as a distinctively religious rather than a public function. As such, they were vehemently opposed to the common school idea. In 1845, for example, the Presbyterian Synod of New Jersey expressed alarm that the "race of religious and infidel youth, such as may be expected to issue from public schools, *deteriorating more and more,* with revolving years will not be fit to sustain our free institutions." [10] Only as churches of every denomination opened schools, to be paid for by prorating tax funds, did the Synod see a way out of the problem. Others, particularly foreign-language groups like the Germans in Ohio or Pennsylvania, deeply feared that public schools would deprive their youngsters of both the language and customs of the older culture, patterns which might well be passed on in private schools.

Equality of Further Educational Opportunity

The demand for academies. Just before the end of the Revolution Samuel Phillips and his brother John drew up a proposed constitution for a school at Andover which would provide the more practical kind of secondary education so emphatically urged by Franklin. According to this document, the Phillips brothers planned to "lay the foundations of a public free SCHOOL or ACADEMY for the purpose of instructing Youth, not only in English and Latin Grammar, Writing, Arithmetic, and those Sciences, wherein they are commonly taught; but more especially to learn them the GREAT END AND REAL BUSINESS OF LIVING." [11] By offering such a course, it was hoped that many more youngsters would be given an opportunity to receive an education in skills and knowledge that would be useful (i.e., more often than not, that would increase their earning capacity in the business world) and practical. The course was to be open to all who could meet the modest tuition charges.

The proposals of the Phillips brothers were among the first of a veritable avalanche of similar plans advanced during the next half century. In effect, all aimed at opening up secondary educational opportunity to increasing numbers of people, especially those of the middle class. With the growing need for persons trained in business and commercial skills, such plans could not help but find fertile soil in which to take root. Of the great wealth of literature which appeared, few essays pointed out the relationships between the academy ideal and the unique conditions of American life quite as ex-

---

[10] J. J. Janeway, *Report to the Synod of New Jersey on the Subject of Parochial Schools* (Philadelphia, n.d.), p. 5.

[11] *The Constitution of the Phillips Academy in Andover* (Andover, Flagg and Gould, 1828), p. 3.

plicitly as an address by the Reverend Edward Hitchcock, President of Amherst College, in 1845.[12]

Hitchcock saw the academical plan of education as peculiarly well adapted to the genius, character, and government of the United States. In allowing youth of both sexes and of every class to pursue an "elevated course of instruction" in whatever branches of science or literature they chose, and for as long as they wished, and in enabling youngsters who aimed at the professions to prepare themselves for colleges, the academy both reflected and contributed to American freedom. The fact that it was privately established and supported was typical of American freedom from government interference. ". . . a free and intelligent people prefer to have the control of so important a business themselves. . . ." The fact that academies represented all shades of religious opinion well reflected the American pattern of disestablishment and religious freedom. The freedom of choice among subjects likewise reflected American economic individualism. Inasmuch as "each man is in a great measure the architect of his own future and character . . . he will not consent to have others tell him what course of study he shall adopt, and how far he shall pursue it." Finally, in a newly developing nation Hitchcock saw the need for schools closely conforming to the everyday wants of society. These, he realized, would of necessity be diverse. "Hence, in a country like ours," he concluded, "where every grade of society exists, from the well established organization of the Atlantic coast, to the log cabin of the back-woodsman, we stand in need of a corresponding grade of literary institutions for the great mass of the people." Thus, he saw the local private academy as an institution able easily to adapt to local situations, a school uniquely designed to meet the special needs of nineteenth-century America.

The demand for free secondary education.   As has been pointed out earlier, the great educational demand of the early nineteenth century was the demand for universal elementary schooling. Yet, many saw along with Jefferson that a republic could not long flourish merely by virtue of a generally enlightened electorate. Wise and skilled social, political, and economic leadership was also indispensable. Only, however, as such leadership represented a "natural aristocracy of virtue and talent" rather than a rigid aristocracy of wealth and birth did these early republicans think the best interests of the new society might be served.

The free, universal common school system was to be the first leg in a program for producing such leadership. Yet, early in the century leaders began to see an element of incongruity in following this free common education with a private academy system, for simply by virtue of its tuition charges the academy excluded many qualified candidates who might otherwise have become effective leaders. Labor groups and educational reformers were quick

[12] Edward Hitchcock, *The American Academic System Defended* (Amherst, Adams, 1845).

to point this out, labeling the academies "class" institutions for the instruction of "the rich." Gradually, in pursuit of the Jeffersonian ideal, educational thinking began to carry the unmistakable signs of concern for equality of further educational opportunity for all. This latter goal was to be achieved by establishing higher public schools, by building additional rungs on an educational ladder capable of carrying a highly competent student from the elementary school, through the secondary school, and ultimately to the university at public expense.

Beginning about 1820, pressures for free secondary education appeared in Boston, New York, Philadelphia, and various other cities in New England, the Midwest, and the South. That the republican ideal of equal educational opportunity was present in most of them is clear. On the other hand, this line of reasoning by no means exhausted the arguments. Another powerful reason, for example, was that academies and high schools would exercise a beneficial influence on common schools. A lecturer before the American Institute of Instruction in 1831 suggested at least three ways in which such an influence might be exerted: (1) by raising educational standards in the community, and by educating people to the necessity of good schools; (2) by removing older students from the common schools, thus allowing more space and attention to younger children; and (3) by providing a steady source of well-trained teachers for the common schools.[13] Still another argument urged that high schools kept youngsters at home under parental influence rather than away at boarding schools which tended to subject youngsters to all sorts of temptations. Others discussed the general well-being which would accrue to the state through the extension of high school education. Finally, a host of arguments paralleled the many advanced in favor of universal common education.

The demand for free higher education. In many respects, the arguments favoring the opportunity for qualified young men (and later women) to attend colleges and universities without cost closely paralleled those at the secondary level. In fact, as one views the various rungs of the educational ladder during this period, there appears a tremendous confusion of terms and patterns. In many states and localities the words "academy," "seminary," and "college" referred to institutions furnishing much the same education but offering, perhaps, somewhat different academic degrees or diplomas. In some localities they were used interchangeably. When some of the western state universities began, their curricula were closely similar, if not inferior, to the classical courses of contemporary New England secondary schools. In light of this, it is not difficult to see how the ideal of an aristocracy of virtue and

---

[13] William C. Fowler, "Influence of Academies and High Schools on Common Schools," *Introductory Discourse and Lectures Delivered Before the American Institute of Instruction* (n.p., n.d.), pp. 183–206.

talent would necessitate equal opportunity in colleges and universities as well as in secondary schools. The notion was not only present in Jefferson's plan for the University of Virginia; it also provided much of the force behind the establishment of most of our great state universities.

One of the most outspoken proponents of this rather revolutionary conception of higher education was Philip Lindsley, President of the University of Nashville. Lindsley, a native of New Jersey and a graduate of Princeton, assumed the presidency of Cumberland College (later the University of Nashville) in 1825. He came to Tennessee at a time when the highly dynamic frontier society was just beginning to show signs of its subsequent evolution into a stratified plantation society after the manner of the Old South. Anxious to retain the ways and spirit of democracy, Lindsley pressed for a system of education which would provide continuing support for republican institutions. His inaugural address at Cumberland is indicative of this effort for the next twenty-five years.[14] Proceeding along much the same logic as his contemporary, Jefferson, Lindsley argued: "A free government, like ours, cannot be maintained except by an enlightened and virtuous people." Like Jefferson, he concluded that this could only be accomplished by combining an intelligent electorate with a wise leadership. Only as higher educational opportunity was provided to the whole people could this latter end be accomplished. Thus, he urged: ". . . raise up colleges among yourselves, and you reduce the charges of a liberal education so considerably that hundreds and thousands can immediately avail themselves of their aid. Not only all the middling classes of citizens, but enterprising youth of the poorest families may contrive to enter the lists of honourable competition with the richest. . . . Such is the peculiar genius and excellence of our republican institutions, that, moral and mental worth is the surest passport to distinction." What better statement in educational terms of Jefferson's ideal aristocracy of virtue and talent?

Lindsley was far from alone in his views. Increasing support came from leaders in the more established universities of the Northeast. One of the most important figures among this latter group was Francis Wayland, President of Brown University from 1827 to 1855. On the lecture platform, in pamphlets, and in textbooks, Wayland was a vigorous critic of traditionalism in higher education. An address delivered in Schenectady in 1854, offers an excellent example of his views on the problems at hand.[15] "Shall we," he inquired, "having educated the whole people up to a certain point, giving to all equal advantages for self-development, then reverse our whole system, and bestow the advantages of higher education only upon the few?" His answer was

---

[14] Le Roy J. Halsey (ed.), *The Works of Philip Lindsley, D.D.* (Philadelphia, Lippincott, 1866), Vol. I, pp. 65–118.

[15] Francis Wayland, *The Education Demanded by the People of the U. States* (Boston, Phillips, Sampson, 1855).

decidedly negative. Only as the benefits of higher education were widely disseminated through the community would the colleges and universities truly serve republican ideals.

Another demand for the extension of higher education grew out of the development of religious denominationalism. In many ways it was even more powerful than republican ideals in securing the enlargement of college opportunity for the people. The movement itself received sharp impetus from the Great Awakening. Denied state support after the separation of church and state had been achieved, the various sects and religious groups were more intent than ever on perpetuating their peculiar doctrinal creeds. One obvious way of doing this was to train spirited, vigorous ministers who would carry on the critical task of proselyting, and it was to the colleges that these groups looked for the accomplishment of this end. "The *Ministry*," declared the Society for the Promotion of Collegiate and Theological Education at the West, "is God's instrumentality for the conversion of the world. Colleges and seminaries are God's means of training up a learned and efficient *Ministry*." [16] Once again, higher education was looked upon as a means of providing community leadership, and especially in the case of the more popular sects, opportunity was to be offered to all who were "called," whether of higher or humble origin.

Brief mention should also be made here of the rather concerted, but unsuccessful, attempts to secure a national university during this period. Proposals for such an institution were particularly strong in the thirty years following the Revolution and then again during the fifteen years immediately before the Civil War. For many, a national university would not only serve the purpose of educational equality, but also would be a prime means of furthering the spirit of American nationalism. Undoubtedly this was in Washington's mind when he recommended the establishment of a national institution where "the youth or young men from different parts of the United States would be assembled together, and would by degrees discover that there was not that cause for those jealousies and prejudices which one part of the Union had imbibed against another part. . . ." [17] Presidents Adams, Madison, Monroe, and John Quincy Adams all advanced similar proposals during their administrations; while the effort of Jefferson to transfer the whole faculty of the College of Geneva, Switzerland, to the United States as the nucleus for a national university were notable and excited widespread interest.

Opposition to equality of further education. As has been indicated, the pressure for free further education was by no means as widespread nor as strong

---

[16] *Sixth Annual Report of the Society for the Promotion of Collegiate and Theological Education at the West* (New York, Trow, 1849), p. 62.

[17] Washington to Hamilton, Sept. 1, 1796. *The Writings of George Washington* (Washington, Government Printing Office, 1940), Vol. 35, p. 199.

as the pressure for universal elementary education. One might then justly expect that the opposition to these proposals would be comparatively weaker, and such was the case. Nevertheless, the beginnings of arguments opposing equality of further education were definitely in evidence, and they clearly presaged the more vehement attacks which were destined to come a half century later when the whole problem came to the fore.

Needless to say, all of the arguments which were advanced in opposition to the common school idea were also used to attack the high school and state university idea. High school and college education, especially of the lower classes, would create large groups of idle, useless malcontents. By turning out boys unwilling to do farm work or manual labor, institutions of higher education would be destroying the productive capacity of large segments of the citizenry. Moreover, they urged, if elementary education demands leisure, higher education most certainly does, and inasmuch as there was no leisure class in America, higher institutions would have little purpose to serve. Charges of "infidelity," "error," "communism," "socialism," "atheism," and a host of others were also leveled against high schools and universities. The objections that high schools inculcated communism and socialism were heard more than once in Pennsylvania during the 1850's; while in the struggle between denominational and public schools on both the secondary and higher level, charges of "atheism" and "godlessness," were hurled with quite the same rancor and often selfishness of purpose as was witnessed on lower levels. In opposing a bill for a state university in 1856, a member of the Texas legislature argued that: "Universities are the ovens to heat up and hatch all manner of vice, immorality and crime." [18]

Another argument which was widely used to attack proposals for high schools and state universities was that while all were taxed to support them, only the few would benefit from their services. An observer in Lancaster, Pennsylvania, urged in 1859 that high schools be abolished altogether because it was "an established fact that ninety-seven per cent of all our children drop out of school either before or very soon after entering our high schools;" and "the other three per cent . . . or those who graduate from our high schools, are the children of parents whose financial condition is such that they can well afford to send their children to a seminary, academy or college. . . ." [19] On the higher level, with even smaller percentages of the population in attendance, these arguments assumed even greater force. Closely related to this view was one which held that free higher schools only diverted much-needed funds from elementary schools; and since the latter were by far more democratic and a more important first step, the establishment of higher education should

---

[18] H. Y. Benedict, *A Source Book Relating to the History of the University of Texas* (Austin, University of Texas, 1917), p. 58.

[19] William Riddle, *One Hundred and Fifty Years of School History in Lancaster, Pennsylvania* (Lancaster, Published by the author, 1905), p. 212.

await their success. The fact that as a rule higher education was more costly per pupil than elementary education served only to intensify this argument in the minds of many.

DEMANDS FOR PUBLICLY SUPPORTED AND PUBLICLY CONTROLLED SCHOOLS

Common Schools

Demands for Public Support. As has been brought out in Part I, education during the colonial period was principally a private undertaking—to be paid for according to the ability and desires of the parent. While it is true that a number of church-supported schools were in evidence before the Revolution, these were organized primarily to serve charity students. Other institutions may have received partial state support, but any who attended these without cost were usually those unable to pay tuition. In effect, education was, as it had been for centuries, a luxury available to those who could afford it or to a very few on a charity basis.

During the early years of the republic, however, the new demands described above began to imply new means of support for common schools. Men who were urging that universal education was necessary for the maintenance of republican institutions could not possibly continue to view the school as a private institution. By doing so, they would automatically be excluding all who could not afford tuition. Furthermore, few of the proud and independent farm families were willing to avail themselves of charity facilities. They were far more ready to sacrifice schooling than they were to sacrifice their pride and send their children to pauper schools. If everyone was to have an education, new means of support would have to be proposed. This, of course, was exactly what happened as the proponents of universal elementary education began to urge public support for common schools.

Fundamentally, the new argument held that if an individual failed to receive an education, it was not he alone who suffered the consequences. Society too would suffer, for in his subsequent limitation in knowledge and the skills of getting knowledge, he would not be helping the electorate to make the best possible decisions. Thomas Jefferson saw this well in the struggle for public support in Virginia: "the tax which will be paid for this purpose [education]," he cautioned, "is not more than the thousandth part of what will be paid to kings, priests, & nobles who will rise up among us if we leave the people in ignorance." [20]

Needless to say, proposals for public support were at the heart of the common school argument during the decades following 1830. In 1835, in a

[20] Jefferson to George Wythe, Aug. 13, 1786, Paul Leicester Ford (ed.), *The Writings of Thomas Jefferson* (New York, Putnam, 1894), Vol. IV, p. 269.

brilliant speech to the Pennsylvania legislature opposing repeal of a year-old common school law, Thaddeus Stevens replied to those who complained about the school tax on the principle that it did not benefit them personally. "The industrious, thrifty, rich farmer," he pointed out, "pays a heavy county tax to support criminal courts, build jails, and pay sheriffs and jail-keepers, and yet probably he has never had and never will have any direct personal use for either." [21] To clinch the argument, he showed how the public supports the public hangman, albeit no one hopes ever to avail himself of his services. Similarly, Bishop George Doane, in an *Address to the People of New Jersey* in 1838, argued that the state pays tax funds to punish the child who is not trained up as he should go. Why, then, should not the state pay funds to "train up the child in the way he should go?" [22]

Horace Mann, a vigorous exponent of public support in Massachusetts, introduced a slightly different but no less important dimension to the argument in his *Tenth Annual Report*.[23] Replying to the contention that a school tax would deprive a man of his private property unjustly, Mann held that complete freedom to dispose of property *ad libitum* could exist only in a nonsocial context. Within a society, he argued, successive generations of men constituted one great commonwealth. Inasmuch as it was the natural right of youth to education, the property of the commonwealth was by natural law pledged to this great task. Successive holders of this property are trustees, "bound to the faithful execution of their trust, by the most sacred obligations." To withhold such funds, then, was a neglect of individual and social responsibility—an "embezzlement and pillage from children," Mann called it.

The change in outlook that these proponents of tax support were attempting to effect was clear and sweeping. Primarily, they were trying to move elementary schooling from a private luxury to a public necessity. Assuming that the common school had certain tasks to perform which were vital to the life of the local community and the republic as a whole, they were urging that provision for this school was a community responsibility. If education was to be universal, it would have to be free; if it was to be free, it would have to be publicly supported. To be sure, everyone would be taxed; but everyone would benefit—if not directly through having his own child educated, then indirectly by virtue of an increased general welfare. In sum, then, the proponents of publicly supported common education were seeking to answer the negative argument of unjust deprivation of private property with the positive argument of community need.

Opposition to public support. Few battles in nineteenth-century America were fought as bitterly as the battle over tax support for common schools. In

[21] *Hazard's Register of Pennsylvania*, Vol. XV, p. 284.
[22] *American Journal of Education*, Vol. XV (1865), pp. 6–7.
[23] *Tenth Annual Report of the Board of Education, Together with the Tenth Annual Report of the Secretary of the Board* (Boston, Dutton and Wentworth, 1847), pp. 111–127.

general, the opposition proceeded on two arguments—related in many ways, yet different in others. The first held that it was simple injustice to deprive one man of his private property, by taxation or otherwise, to educate the son of another. Strongly rooted in the tradition of economic individualism, this argument was central in many of the antidemocratic movements of this age. It held that to extend the suffrage would be tantamount to empowering the many who had no property to use taxation to rob the few who did have property. The generalization was quite applicable to education. To tax for schools was the same as to take away one man's plow and give it to another for use in his fields. Such unjust deprivation was inequality and discrimination. It would discourage thrift and frugality and encourage the poor to lean on the public purse while they "proliferated like rabbits."

The second argument was much more moderate, yet related to the first. Proponents of this position opposed tax-supported common schools just as strongly as the others. Universal education, they argued, was of course vital to the life of a republic. But the public purse should not shoulder the whole task. Public funds, they urged, should only be used to educate those who could not afford to educate themselves. "The time has gone by in this country," wrote a citizen to the *Newburgh Telegraph* in 1846, "for the honest poor man to be ashamed of his condition. . . . To be just is always right, and justice demands that those only who need should fall under the public protection.—But justice frowns upon compelling one man to pay towards the education of the children of his rich neighbors, or to go one step beyond his natural duty to his own offspring and to his country in contributing his share in behalf of the poor." [24] This argument was an infinitely more telling one on the part of the opposition, since it agreed with the end of universal education but proposed different means of attaining it. For those who were urging complete tax support, this alternative way could never provide truly *equal* or *republican* facilities, since those supported by public funds would always be stigmatized as pauper or charity cases. Herein lay the nub of the tax-support controversy.

Demands for public control.   Intimately bound up with proposals and counterproposals on public support was the question of who should control the schools. When education was a private affair conducted largely under the auspices of churches and religious groups, the question of control was a simple one. Control rested largely in the hands of private individuals and ecclesiastical authorities. Now, however, just as demands for public support of schools grew out of new life conditions and educational conceptions, so did demands for public control. Generally, such demands were of two sorts: first, demands based on the assumption that public control should inevitably follow public support; and second, demands based on the assumption that if the public did not control the common school, then sectarian interests

[24] Aug. 6, 1846.

would get hold of it and impose their particular political, economic, or religious doctrines on the students. This would obviously force some to withdraw in order to preserve their rights of conscience, and the schools would no longer be "equal and open to all."

As far as the notion of public control following public support was concerned, it was practically implicit in most of the proposals for using public money. The long tradition of control by town authorities had of course taken root in New England by the time of the Revolution. It has already been pointed out that Jefferson's educational proposals for Virginia made specific mention of "three of the most honest and able men" of each county to be elected aldermen and to be charged with responsibility for establishing and maintaining the common schools.

Although many communities were willing to admit this close relationship of public control to public support, once again the question of means brought controversy. One of the most persistent questions, for example, involved the ultimate repository of public control. Would it be the district, the township, the county, or the state? The federal government, to be sure, was one of constitutionally delegated powers, and inasmuch as education was nowhere mentioned in the Constitution, the Tenth Amendment automatically reserved that area to state control. But this by no means settled the problem, for it left open the whole question of whether the states themselves or local communities should control education. It was this question which wracked the Massachusetts and Connecticut schools between 1830 and 1850, and it was the attempt to assert—or reassert—state control which occupied the major attentions of Horace Mann, James G. Carter, Henry Barnard, and others during this period.

Generally, those who urged state control argued that centralization brought rising standards of education to local communities through the diffusion of new techniques, the appropriation of state funds for education, and the collection and dissemination of school data. Only as the power of the state compelled minimum standards and then helped poorer localities to meet them could equal educational opportunity be provided for all. Those favoring state control also continually emphasized the fact that the state acted principally in an advisory and regulatory capacity, delegating much of its power to localities. Opponents of state control brushed aside these arguments. Education was first and foremost a responsibility of parents and local communities. For the state to exercise its authority in this sphere was to tread directly upon individual rights and democratic local government. It was state control which had built the authoritarian and monarchical school system of Prussia; and clearly, state control would soon "Prussianize" American republican education.

Opposition to public control. Much of the opposition to public control of common schools came indirectly rather than directly. Thus, for example, when strong criticism of Massachusetts educational policy regarding religious instruction was voiced in 1844 and 1846 by Reverend Edward A. Newton and Reverend Matthew Hale Smith, respectively, this criticism was directed against the board of education rather than against the principle of public control. Yet ultimately, this criticism really struck against public control in general since it attacked one of the basic principles on which public control was founded: participation of all religious groups in the community, through representatives, in the making of educational policy. Highly similar were the attacks of Roman Catholic citizens on the nonsectarian public schools of New York. The principle of religious neutrality, they held, was impossible in a curriculum. Rather, the choice was between religious indifference or sectarian instruction. The former was entirely unacceptable to them, as was the latter unless it was in Roman Catholic materials and by Roman Catholic teachers. In effect, they too were urging that public control was impossible, principally because of this religious problem. Even if public schools were tax supported, they should be controlled by the respective denominations, with tax money prorated among them.

While religious groups were among the foremost objectors to public control, they by no means stood alone. In a sense, they merely exemplified the fact that opposition usually came from groups whose private purposes seemed to them irreconcilable with public control. Thus, for example, there was considerable opposition to public control from foreign-language groups in Pennsylvania, Ohio, and other states stemming from the desire of these groups to maintain schools where the language and customs of their birthland might be taught. Closely related was the opposition of certain private schools to public control, supervision, or regulation which they viewed as a threat to their individual liberties. All continued to see educational control as a private domain into which state entrance could be only an unwarranted transgression.

Secondary Education

Demands for public support. It has already been pointed out that the most characteristic demand for secondary education in America between 1776 and 1865 was for the academy—a private institution designed to meet the need for newer commercial and scientific skills demanded by the changing American economy. Furthermore, this period witnessed the first demands for public high schools which would provide this same type of further education for rich and poor at public expense. While in principle the academy was more often than not thought of as privately supported while the high school was usually conceived of as publicly supported, the lines of difference in this respect were neither hard and fast, nor clearly defined. Often, the fact that the state incorporated academies to stimulate education was recognized as sufficient ground for the request of public support. For many the academy as a school enjoying partial public support was simply a transition step to totally supported public education. In any case, the period saw numerous demands for public support of both institutions.

Inasmuch as the Reverend Edward Hitchcock's address on the relation of the American academy to American institutions has already been referred to, it might be well to explore his position on the matter of support. Hitchcock, urging the importance of academies in the life of the republic, was deeply interested in their having enough support to carry forward their work with an independence not subject to the whims of individual students. As a first, and most important, improvement, he argued that such institutions "should be more liberally patronized and endowed by the state governments, or by individuals." Pointing to the liberal public support Massachusetts had bestowed upon normal schools while denying it to academies, Hitchcock saw the danger of a definite lowering of elementary and higher education throughout the state. Contrasting this policy with the far more enthusiastic public support of academies in New York State, he warned that educational leadership would soon pass from Massachusetts to other states unless the financial situation was remedied.[25]

This view of the academies as essentially private institutions which, because of their great usefulness to the state, were entitled to substantial public assistance seemed to prevail in most quarters during this period. As a matter of fact, many who opposed complete governmental support of a common school system were far more willing to endorse this pattern of support, and this latter proposal is observable throughout the union, particularly in the middle, southern, and western states.

In the face of movement toward complete systems of public education, however, it is not difficult to see how many would wish to bring the definite advantages of practical secondary instruction—as embodied in the academy idea—within the reach of all. This undoubtedly was in the minds of the Boston School Committee when they proposed in 1821 the establishment of a publicly supported English classical school and in the minds of other boards of education which advanced similar recommendations soon afterward.

Henry Barnard incorporated much of the flavor of these proposals in the commentary on public high schools in his First Annual Report as secretary of the Connecticut Board of Education.[26] Barnard felt that to serve their purpose—"the common benefit of society"—such schools would have to be accessible to youngsters of all classes, especially the comparatively indigent. To be so, there would have to be enough public support "to make them free to children of the proper age and proficiency, be they rich or poor." If money were raised by tuition rates on the scholars themselves, Barnard felt it would

25 Hitchcock, *The American Academic System Defended, op. cit.,* p. 17.
26 *Connecticut Common School Journal,* Vol. I (1839), p. 172.

make a mockery of the whole idea of equal educational opportunity. Only public higher education would equalize education, and thereby equalize society.

Demands for public control. The movements in various states to establish systems of education running from the primary grades through the university, have already been discussed briefly; and the attempt to exercise at least limited supervisory control over academies and secondary seminaries within these frameworks must be assumed as part of the general demand for such unified systems. Yet the problem of direct control of secondary schools was one which attracted considerable attention after 1830. Most academies—as incorporated institutions—were subject to private control. Even though public money might well be appropriated to an academy, its control remained in the hands of its trustees.

Increasingly, however, one is able to see the demand for publicly controlled high schools to serve the higher educational needs of the people. Most often, the reason advanced was that public control would put such institutions in the hands of the people and thereby make them more responsible to public needs and wants. George Boutwell, former governor of Massachusetts and secretary of the State Board of Education, brought this out clearly and forcefully in a lecture before the American Institute of Instruction, entitled "The Relative Merits of Public High Schools and Endowed Academies." "The distinguishing difference between the advocates of endowed schools and of free schools," he argued, "is this: those who advocate the system of endowed academies go back in their arguments to one foundation, which is, that in education of the higher grades the great mass of the people are not to be trusted. And those who advocate a system of free education in high schools put the matter where we have put the rights of property and liberty, where we put the institutions of law and religion—upon the public judgment." [27]

Based on this, Boutwell, in this and other addresses, outlined a view of public secondary school control. Private academies, to be sure, had a function. They might very appropriately offer professional education of various sorts, for Boutwell did not see this as a public function. An academy or similarly private institution might well serve a community or district where the population was too sparse to support a public secondary school. But, in general, he saw private schools passing away. ". . . they cannot stand by the side of a good system of public education." The real hope of a republic, as far as secondary education was concerned, rested in the public high school, for first and foremost, the public school was responsible to the people it served, and the people who paid for it. ". . . in the public school you get the immediate, direct supervision of the public. Not merely in the election of committees, but in a daily interest and vigilance where results are freely disclosed to the super-

[27] George S. Boutwell, *Thoughts on Educational Topics and Institutions* (Boston, Phillips, Sampson, 1859), pp. 152–153.

intending committee, as every inhabitant feels that his contribution, as a taxpayer, gives him the right to judge the character of the school, and makes it his duty to report its defects to those charged with its management." [28] In this situation, as opposed to the nonparticipation of parents in the control of private academies, Boutwell saw the crux of the republican need for public secondary education.

Opposition to public support and control. Not all persons, however, even all those of liberal temper, were willing to see secondary education as a publicly supported, publicly controlled function. For many, as in the case of the common schools, all education was a luxury to be purchased according to a parent's ability to pay. Of these, many believed that the great mass of the people were unfit for education, especially further education, and, therefore, could not profit from it. Others who gladly joined in the drive for publicly supported common schools felt that secondary education was not in the realm of public necessity. Still others hoped that secondary education would be liberally supported from the public till, but that its private control would generally prevail. It will be remembered, for example, that while President Hitchcock of Amherst College saw a crying need for public support of academies, he thought their private control reflected admirably "freedom from governmental interference with our literary institutions." Only in this way could the academy continue to serve the special needs of local communities.

Another argument for private control which appeared sporadically raised grave doubts about the public's willingness to continue support for higher education on a long-term basis. Lower schools, this position maintained, were well sustained, for most voters in the community had themselves been educated in them, understood their importance, and liberally provided for them. But the studies of the high school were unfamiliar to the great body of the people. A new high school, being an oddity, would perhaps receive enthusiastic support in the beginning; but when, after a time, the tax burden began to be felt, the school election would inevitably bring a committee interested in economy and retrenchment. In a single day the fruit of years of labor would be destroyed.

Higher Education

Demands for public support. While it is true that Thomas Jefferson's *Bill for the More General Diffusion of Knowledge* had envisaged the opportunity of a talented individual to advance from the primary schools through his higher education at state expense, those youths who were selected for free higher education were to receive it at William and Mary College, a private institution. To be sure, one of the two companion bills to the education bill did propose amendments to the college's charter and new means of support

[28] *Ibid.,* pp. 193–194.

which would move the institution well along toward becoming a university, and one with a substantial public endowment. Yet it cannot be said that Jefferson's early plan embodied a completely public system; rather it was a judicious admixture of both public and private facilities. Jefferson's later interests, however, increasingly emphasized the need for both colleges (really academies) and a university substantially subsidized by the state. His correspondence with Peter Carr and Joseph C. Cabell after 1814 seem definitely to urge that since an enlightened populace and skilled leadership were both vital to a republic, the means of educating both was public responsibility. It was out of this conviction, of course, that he fathered the University of Virginia.

This idea of a publicly supported university capping the system of publicly supported common schools demanded by a republic, is observable in many states during the first decades of the nineteenth century. The urgings of President Philip Lindsley of the University of Nashville (Tennessee) with respect to making higher education available to all who were qualified, have already been cited. Lindsley was no less vigorous in his urging that such opportunity be provided by a publicly supported institution. "Great is the mistake . . . ," he argued, "that colleges are designed exclusively for the rich—that none but the rich can be benefited by them—and therefore, that the state ought not to patronize or endow them." [29] Rather, the state should liberally endow such institutions that equal opportunity might be afforded to all. "Such is the peculiar genius and excellence of our republican institutions, that, moral and mental worth is the surest passport to distinction. The humblest individual, by the diligent cultivation of his faculties, may, without the aid of family or fortune, attain the most exalted stations within the reach or gift of freemen." [30] The public college and university were for Lindsley uniquely adapted to perpetuating and realizing these ideals. Needless to say, similar arguments were advanced in support of all of the early state universities.

Demands for public control.   It has already been pointed out that during the late colonial period two patterns of action characterized efforts to secure publicly controlled higher education: the attempt to secure state control of existing facilities and the attempt to establish new state controlled facilities. Strengthened by French influences toward unified systems of state control embracing all levels of instruction, these attempts intensified during and following the Revolutionary War. Jefferson's effort to secure a state university for Virginia represents both patterns. His early proposals of 1779 revolved around changing the board of visitors of William and Mary College from a private body of eighteen men to a public body of five "appointed by joint ballot of both houses of the Assembly. . . ." Failing in this attempt, he con-

[29] *The Works of Philip Lindsley, D.D., op. cit.,* Vol. I, p. 77.
[30] *Ibid.,* pp. 78–79.

ceived in his later proposals a new publicly supported institution controlled by a public board of visitors—the University of Virginia. Certainly both attempts were premised on the proposition that a public board could do a better job of keeping such institutions responsible to the general good. Similar efforts with respect to King's College in New York were likewise predicated, and the Tory sentiments of the college during the Revolution strengthened such convictions. Struggles at the College of Philadelphia, at Yale, and at Harvard invoked much the same arguments. That they were also tied in with internecine religious struggles must also be acknowledged.

The attempts to modify the structures of these colonial colleges to allow greater public control in a sense reached a climax in the efforts of New Hampshire to control Dartmouth College. The state in 1816 declared that "the college of the state may, in the opinion of the legislature, be rendered more extensively useful . . ." and enacted legislation converting the college into Dartmouth University, to be supervised by a board of overseers composed of the governor's appointees in addition to a number of ex-officio civil officers. Inasmuch as this legislation was declared unconstitutional by the United States Supreme Court in February 1819, attempts to secure publicly controlled higher education by taking over existing private facilities were effectively checked.

If the Dartmouth College decision put an end to proposals of this kind, it only stimulated the demand for new public facilities subject to public control. Jefferson's proposals which ultimately secured the University of Virginia— advanced in his *Bill to Establish a System of Public Education* (1817)—called for a university whose visitors were annually to be nominated by the president and directors of the Literary Fund. Inasmuch as the latter were all state civil officers, the lines of public responsibility were clear. Visitors were to have control of buildings, officers, selection of faculty, rules and discipline for students, and general regulations for their subsistence.

Such a discussion of direct agencies of control in specific institutions must not ignore the growing idea, patterned after developments in New York, that a good deal of public responsibility be exercised through state boards of control. Thus, for example, when the sponsors of public control in New York failed directly to incorporate King's College into the public system, they proposed a public University of the State of New York, with its board of regents, which would supervise King's College (a private institution) as one of its responsibilities. In general, proposals for public control both on the secondary and higher levels went in both of these directions: public control of specific, individual institutions and public control of the whole system of public and private schools exercised through an overall administrative authority.

Opposition to public support and control. Opposition to public support and public control for colleges and universities was quite similar to the case of the academies. Many persons felt that higher education (even more so, perhaps, than secondary education) was a private undertaking which the public had no right to support. Higher education was clearly a luxury, used by and therefore to be paid for by those who could afford it. There was, of course, an obvious relationship between this argument and the individualism of the period which assumed it illegal to tax one man for a service to be enjoyed by another. Interestingly enough, this latter argument, which was used by many to oppose common schools, was used in turn by some proponents of common schools to oppose secondary and higher schools.

As for opposition to public control of higher education, the matter was far more complex. The college had traditionally, even more so than the lower schools, been dominated by religious aims and religious authorities, and one finds ample evidence of the resistance of more conservative religious groups to proposals for publicly controlled colleges and universities. "Nearly all our colleges," wrote President F. A. P. Barnard of the University of Mississippi in 1856, "are . . . the creations of the different religious denominations which divide our people. They are regarded as important instrumentalities, through which the peculiarities of doctrine which distinguish their founders are to be maintained, propagated, or defended." [31]

In general, resistance to public control tended to follow a pattern. In instances where the attempt was to introduce direct state control into a chartered institution, the resistance to public control came in terms of private property rights and violation of legitimate contracts represented by chartering. Speaking of the original purpose and charter of Dartmouth, Daniel Webster argued in 1818 before the United States Supreme Court: "Individuals have a right to use their own property for purposes of benevolence, either towards the publick, or towards other individuals. They have a right to exercise this benevolence in such lawful manner as they may choose; and when the government has induced and excited it, *by contracting to give perpetuity to the stipulated manner of exercising it,* to rescind this contract, and seize on the property, is not law, but violence." [32]

In cases where the state sought to establish new institutions, opposition to public control, as in the case of common schools, centered in the charge that political strife would soon dominate these schools. "Colleges and halls," threatened Webster, "will be deserted by all better spirits, and become a theatre for the contention of politicks. Party and faction will be cherished in the places consecrated to piety and learning." [33] Moreover, the ability of colleges, as with academies, to serve different needs and purposes would be

[31] F. A. P. Barnard, "On Improvements Practicable in American Colleges," *American Journal of Education and College Review,* Vol. I (1856), p. 176.

[32] Timothy Farrar, *Report of the Case of the Trustees of Dartmouth College Against William H. Woodward* (Portsmouth, N. H., John W. Foster, 1819), p. 260.

[33] *Ibid.,* p. 283.

vastly impaired by state control. In sum, the case of the conservatives was simply stated as follows: private colleges had traditionally done a creditable job; they had demonstrated an ability of "accommodating themselves easily, without sudden change or violence . . . ," and they had remained free of political strife. Why not, then, continue this pattern?

DEMANDS FOR A FUNCTIONAL CURRICULUM

Intellectual and Moral Demands on the Common School

The demand for broader knowledge. Illiteracy at the time of the Revolution was by no means a social stigma. In the rural farm neighborhoods of America the urgently practical affairs of life claimed most of men's energies. The level of technology was low, and the young could learn the livelihoods of their fathers through apprenticeship, through actually engaging in the tasks they needed to know. With only one white male in seven elegible to vote, the political necessity of education was slight. Generally, the young learned the American way of life from their community—from the family, the church, and the neighborhood.

Within such a life the job of the school was a limited one. To be sure, the great majority of the settlers were Protestants, and the Protestant sects preached that each individual should read and interpret the Bible for himself. Household accounts were kept, and money was exchanged; newspapers were read, and letters written and received. All these depended on skills traditionally associated with formal schooling. On the whole, these skills defined the elementary program.

What, then, was the impact of these sweeping cultural changes on proposals regarding the curriculum? Its keynote, perhaps, was expansion. The task of the new common schools was to be the teaching of the *common branches,* those studies necessary to discharge "the ordinary duties of life." This minimum knowledge still centered largely in reading, writing, and common arithmetic, but one of the most characteristic notes of educational activity between 1820 and 1860 was the demand for broader coverage. Spelling, geography, history, government, constitutional law, and any number of other subjects were demanded as "preparation for citizenship." Furthermore, such areas as natural science, natural history, physical training, and drawing (usually mechanical drafting rather than representative or creative art) were urged as vitally necessary to a "complete" common education—one that would yield a truly "liberal spirit" and "trained character." Generally, such demands for expansion reflected an attempt broadly to educate for citizenship and at the same time to bring the new scientific knowledge to the people. Obviously, they tied closely into the republican ideals and scientific interest which characterized the period.

The demand for more functional knowledge. Closely related to the movement for expansion of the curriculum was the effort to make more useful the knowledge that the school did provide. A pamphlet circulated widely in Pennsylvania,[34] pointed to the shortcomings of "documents of various municipal offices, such as the receipts, orders, reports, accounts, records, etc. of commissioners, guardians, administrators, arbitrators, and magistrates," and then concluded: "Surely we are within bounds when we say that to write a common business letter, promissory note, receipt, bill, or account, legibly and in proper form, is the least that should be required of our common schools in this department." The pamphlet further urged that instruction in arithmetic qualify a pupil "for the ordinary business of a farmer, or mechanic."

One is able to find numerous demands along this line in the professional literature of the time. In speeches, in addresses before educational groups, in pamphlets, and in periodicals, educators began to proclaim the "cash value" of a common school education to employers and employees alike. Education with practical value would be a positive personal asset; in an individualist-capitalist society it would be in great demand. Insofar as it succeeded in improving the quality of the workingman, support would be forthcoming from employers. Thus, to press for a more functional education was to press for support from a "functional-minded" society, and educators seldom forgot the need for such support.

One is also able to find between the years 1820 and 1860 the earliest demands for some kind of vocational education in the common school. Although workingmen generally did not want a special education for their children but rather a general education, such proposals were strong in the early labor reports. The 1829 report of a Philadelphia workingman's committee, for example, recommended the establishment of schools patterned after those of Fellenberg at Hofwyl, Switzerland, where youngsters might be taught agriculture, gardening, and the mechanic arts in addition to standard subjects.[35] A year later, Robert Dale Owen in his six essays on *Public Education* made this very same proposal.[36] In 1831 the *American Annals of Education* cited a speech by Governor Enos Thompson Throop of New York in which he asked that attention be given to agriculture and industry in the common schools.[37] Although the real demand for vocational education did not come until after the Civil War, these early proposals are indicative of this movement to make education more directly useful.

The demand for moral education. To the nineteenth-century American knowledge was power—a power which could be used for good or for evil. Inevitably, therefore, when he thought about education, he thought about

[34] F. A. Packard, *Thoughts on the Condition and Prospects of Popular Education in the United States* (n.p., 1836).
[35] *Working Man's Advocate*, Vol. I, No. 19 (Mar. 6, 1830), p. 1.
[36] *Ibid.*, Vol. I, No. 26 (Apr. 24, 1830), p. 4.
[37] *American Annals of Education*, Vol. I (1831), p. 125.

some moral training—or character training—which would channel the use of the power which education bestowed. Here, however, lay a problem which was destined to beset American public education for generations.

When this same American thought about moral or character training, he thought about religious training. Formerly, this was all good and well. When churches had controlled and sponsored education (each for the young of its own faith), each could educate for character improvement through the peculiar doctrines of its own creed. Now, however, statesmen, educators, and interested citizens were urging a common school, not only open to all but also ideally attended by all the children of the community. What religious doctrines could be taught to such a group? If the tenets of any one faith were introduced, the rights of conscience of children of other faiths would be offended. If the tenets of any one faith were introduced, schools supported by public funds would be teaching a specific religion. This would obviously violate the separation of church and state, by 1833 almost a universally accepted legal injunction in America. What, then, were some suggested solutions to this problem?

Two proposals seem to have gained considerable adherence during this period. The first was that the school educate for character by teaching those principles which were "common to all sects"—the "common elements of Christianity." The central plank in this plan, perhaps, was the introduction of Bible reading without comment into the curriculum. The argument ran that the Bible was given by God while sectarianism was made by man. There could be no danger, therefore, in reading the Word of God without human intervention. "That our Public Schools are not theological seminaries," wrote Horace Mann in his monumental Twelfth Annual Report, "is admitted. . . . But our system earnestly inculcates all Christian morals; it founds its morals on the basis of religion; it welcomes the religion of the Bible; and, in receiving the Bible, it allows it to do what it is allowed to do in no other system,—*to speak for itself.*" [38] Obviously, the argument was grounded in Protestantism, in the notion that the individual is capable of reading and interpreting the Bible for himself. Even with the movement toward separation of church and state, the fact that most Americans in the early nineteenth century were committed to Protestant creeds would easily account for the great popularity of such a notion.

As might be expected, however, members of non-Protestant sects could well think that this proposal of reading the Bible (and by Bible, Mann and his Protestant contemporaries generally referred to the King James, or Protestant, version) without comment was itself a vigorous sectarianism. Thus, for example, Catholic religious authorities in New York City in the 1830's and 1840's waged a vehement campaign against what they called the

[38] *Twelfth Annual Report of the Board of Education, Together With the Twelfth Annual Report of the Secretary of the Board* (Boston, Dutton and Wentworth, 1849), pp. 116–117.

sectarian public schools. "The holy scriptures," wrote the Vicar-General of the Roman Catholic Diocese of New York in 1840, "are read every day, with the restriction, that no specific tenets are to be inculcated—Here, Sir, we find the great demarcating principle between the Catholic church and the Sectaries introduced *silently*. The Catholic church tells her children that they must be taught the religion by AUTHORITY—The Sects say, read the bible, judge for yourselves. The bible is read in the public schools, the children are allowed to judge for themselves. The Protestant principle is therefore acted upon, slily inculcated, and the schools are Sectarian." [39] His argument was widely used by Roman Catholics in some of the major cities as the basis of their demand for public support of parochial schools.

Opposition to this proposal for nonsectarian religious instruction, however, was by no means confined to non-Protestant sects. It was also forthcoming from a number of religious conservatives who remained faithful to the idea that character education could be rooted only in the doctrines of the more orthodox Protestant creeds. Two attacks by Protestant ministers on the Massachusetts Board of Education and its secretary, Horace Mann, in 1844 and 1846 will serve well to illustrate the character of this opposition. [40]

The first of these attacks came from the pen of the Reverend E. A. Newton, a former member of the Board of Education who had resigned some years earlier in protest against the board's policy of selecting nonsectarian books for school libraries. Writing in the columns of the *Christian Witness and Church Advocate,* Newton held that a "book upon politics, morals, or religion, containing no party or sectarian views, will be apt to contain no distinct views of any kind, and will be likely to leave the mind in a state of doubt and *skepticism,* much more to be deplored than any party or sectarian bias." Obviously, he was firmly criticizing the above-mentioned view that a useful, nonsectarian religious education as a basis of character training could be provided in the school. What Newton really desired was a return to the older teaching of religion and morality as one, with the catechism reestablished as a school textbook. It must be mentioned, however, that little support was forthcoming for Newton's attack, either in church or secular newspapers. Even among his fellow Episcopalians, his position did not find extensive favor.

The second, and more vitriolic, of these attacks was launched in 1846 by the Reverend Matthew Hale Smith. In a sermon entitled *The Ark of God on a New Cart* Smith accused the program of nonsectarian religious instruction as "Godless" and "corrupting." With its new policy, he declared, the Board of Education had been instrumental in removing the spiritual basis from the common schools. Only by a return to the teaching of those re-

[39] *New-York Freeman's Journal,* Vol. I, No. 2 (July 11, 1840), p. 12.
[40] For complete discussion see Raymond B. Culver, *Horace Mann and Religion in the Massachusetts Public Schools* (New Haven, Yale University Press, 1929).

ligious doctrines "which nine-tenths of professed Christians of all names believe" could the schools again regain their spiritual foundations. Once again, the essential argument was that education could be made meaningful only by teaching specific religious doctrines—and these attackers all meant orthodox, conservative Protestant religious doctrines.

A second proposal which was often advanced as a possible line of character training was the teaching of moral values outside of their religious context. Thus, such virtues as honesty, sincerity, kindness, etc., could be taught from the experiences of everyday life. By his own example, the proponents of this position urged, the schoolmaster could teach these common virtues in a way that would offend the sensibilities of no one. While both of these proposals were far from irreligious or nonreligious in character, both on the other hand moved considerably along the road to securing a nondenominational morality for the schools.

The demand for patriotic education. If one channeling of the power bestowed by education was to be moral or character education, one might well expect a people with a growing spirit of nationalism to introduce another: namely, education for patriotism. The early nineteenth century saw both in Europe and America the growth and development of conceptions which viewed popular education as a tool of the national state. Most of these systems sought to bestow this "power" of reading, writing, and arithmetic, and most saw the crucial factor in assuring the use of this power for the benefit of the state in patriotic education. Thus, this notion in America must be considered just one phase of a broader movement in the Western world toward education for national, as opposed to purely religious or personal, ends.

Immediately, a problem quite similar to the one encountered in the moral sphere was posed. How could the school teach patriotism without teaching this or that political creed? Once again, the question was one of teaching values while retaining the "common" character of the school—that is, while keeping the school truly available to all. The solution again centered in the attempt to teach those aspects of patriotism common to all parties, and it again involved the teaching of great documents, this time the Constitution, the Declaration of Independence, etc. As Mann put it, the sensible course which "all sensible and judicious men, all patriots, and all genuine republicans, must approve" was "that those articles in the creed of republicanism, which are accepted by all, believed in by all, and which form the common basis of our political faith, shall be taught to all." [41]

One consideration is central here. If the school was to teach only those moral and patriotic principles on which different social factions could agree, then the whole area of the controversial was strictly excluded from the curriculum. This point was made clear in no uncertain terms, for instance, by Mann when he counseled: ". . . when the teacher, in the course

[41] *Twelfth Annual Report of the Board of Education* . . . , p. 89.

of his lessons or lectures on the fundamental law, arrives at a controverted text, he is either to read it without comment or remark; or, at most, he is only to say that the passage is the subject of disputation, and that the schoolroom is neither the tribunal to adjudicate, nor the forum to discuss it." [42] One cannot underestimate the importance of this conception of required neutrality in the development of the American curriculum. In its equating of "noncontroversial" with "democratic" education, it stands in sharp contrast to more recent ideas about the value of discussing controversial issues in public schools.

Opposition to expansion of the common school curriculum. While these pressures for the expansion of the common school curriculum gained great force as a response to the new role that educators were defining for the American school, they were by no means without resistance. Part of this opposition has already been alluded to in connection with the idea of a "common elements" curriculum in the moral and religious sphere. Yet much of it was simply the desire to view the "fundamentals" of the curriculum in much narrower terms and to maintain a more limited view with respect to required subjects. Thus, for instance, many still held that the job of the common school was merely to provide only instruction in reading, writing, and arithmetic. Once these tools were mastered, other subjects would not be difficult to handle. Others, continuing to view formal education as a frill, were perhaps inclined to agree with the position that youngsters could get along perfectly well with instruction simply "in the Bible and figgers." One writer in Horace Mann's *Common School Journal* went so far as to remark that if the "passion" for expanding common school curricula continued, "every county in the state will need an insane hospital. . . ." [43] All apparently agreed that the common school should teach that knowledge which ought to be the common property of all citizens. But they could not agree on what this knowledge was to be. Essentially, then, the argument really hinged on what was or was not necessary for all. Once again, it was an argument that has continued to stand at the heart of American educational controversy.

The beginnings of the conflict concerning method. As has been indicated in Chapter 6, a new conception of the child and his education was rooted in the thought of the Enlightenment. John Locke, Jean Jacques Rousseau, and Johann Pestalozzi had urged in Europe that man is born neither good nor evil; it is his environment which makes him one or the other. Born thus neutral, man, according to the Enlightenment thinkers, was infinitely perfectable. Around this conception of man developed a new philosophy of education in Europe. Enunciated by Rousseau in *Emile,* and further developed and actually put into practice by Pestalozzi in Switzerland, this philosophy viewed education as a gentle, enjoyable process by which the child developed

---

[42] *Twelfth Annual Report of the Board of Education* . . . , p. 89.
[43] *Common School Journal,* Vol. 12 (1850), p. 13.

naturally under the influence of a good, sound, and healthy environment. Moreover, these philosophers dropped the conception of ideas as innate in favor of *sense realism,* which held that the mind is blank at birth and that the individual acquires his ideas through sense experience, through seeing, hearing, smelling, tasting, feeling, and doing. Obviously, in view of this education was considered far more as a matter of rich and varied experiences than as a grappling with books and ideas. Furthermore, one might quite properly expect these ideas to cross the Atlantic as part of the general influence of the European Enlightenment on America.

During the early years of the nineteenth century these ideas began increasingly to appear in American educational thought. As early as 1808, a disciple of Pestalozzi named Joseph Neef, who had come to the United States in 1806, published a treatise on educational method advancing an interpretation of Pestalozzi's ideas. Conceiving of education as the gradual unfolding of human powers, Neef proposed a rich variety of experiences in the elementary school designed to draw out individual potentialities. Counting, reading, spelling—all were to revolve around materials of the child's everyday life. Books would be introduced only after the basic groundwork had thus been laid. Twenty years later, in 1826, William Maclure outlined much the same proposal in his plan for the schools of the New Harmony communal experiment.

One area where a considerable change of opinion might well be expected was in the area of discipline. If the child was no longer to be regarded as an evil, sinful creature who had to be rigidly disciplined, but rather a potentially good creature whose goodness had to develop through education, then the teacher had a drastically new role in the sphere of discipline. Instead of punishment with the ferule, kindness and reason were now to dominate the classroom. Samuel R. Hall, for instance, devoted considerable space in his *Lectures on Schoolkeeping*—one of the earliest popular books on pedagogy —to illustrations of this new kind of discipline, and exhibited considerable enthusiasm and optimism over it.

One of the most famous statements on this new concept of discipline was the *Seventh Annual Report* of Horace Mann as secretary of the Massachusetts Board of Education. It was famous not so much because of the novelty or originality of what it stated as because of the educational controversy it provoked. Summarizing a visit to and survey of the Prussian school system, Mann expressed tremendous enthusiasm for the new instructional methods based on sense realism. Above all Mann noted: "Though I saw hundreds of schools, . . . *I never saw one child undergoing punishment, or arraigned for misconduct. I never saw one child in tears from having been punished, or from fear of being punished.*" [44] In this matter of founding the teacher-

[44] *Seventh Annual Report of the Board of Education; Together with the Seventh Annual Report of the Secretary of the Board* (Boston, Dutton and Wentworth, 1844), p. 133.

student relationship on love rather than on authoritarianism, Mann saw the European schools far ahead of those in New England, and, as will be pointed out below, it was with respect to this criticism of American schools that much of the opposition to his report developed.

Spirited opposition to the newer educational conceptions outlined above developed from the large groups of Americans who continued to cling to traditional notions of childhood and of education. For those who viewed the child and the human being as essentially sinful, the religious and disciplinary role of education remained supreme. For such people there was yet no substitute for the book-centered approach, supplemented by the rod of correction. Any other form of instruction was a perversion of the true meaning of education.

Illustrative of opposition from more conservative religious sources was Matthew Hale Smith's sermon, *The Ark of God on a New Cart*, cited on page 216. Smith premised his remarks on the assumption that: "All men are sinners; the results of a depraved nature are daily developed." Pointing to what he believed to be an apparent and alarming increase of crime and juvenile depravity in Boston, he laid the cause squarely with the schools. "Modern reformers," he cried, "have taken the education of youth under their special care. . . . Throwing themselves across the word of God, they practically oppose its lessons. They deny the propriety of an early religious training; they ridicule, as well as forbid, the use of the rod." [45]

Such opposition, of course, was by no means confined to ministers and theologians; a considerable amount was forthcoming from the educational profession itself. When Horace Mann's *Seventh Annual Report* was published, for example, a group of thirty-one Boston schoolmasters resolved themselves into an "Association of Masters of the Boston Public Schools" and published a pamphlet vigorously criticizing the educational notions set forth by Mann in that document. "In matters of education," stated the masters, "how vain and worthless have been spasmodic efforts and hot-bed theories, in which the projectors have disregarded experience and observation." [46] Mann's notions both on method and on discipline were called sharply into question. Authority, the masters stated, not love, must be the backbone of the teacher-student tie. "We object then," they stated, ". . . to the idea, that the relation of a pupil to his teacher is one 'of affection first, and then duty.' We would rather reverse the terms. . . ." [47] And for the masters, duty meant instilling respect for authority through fear and wise punishment. While the controversy between Mann and the masters dragged on through a number

[45] *The Bible, The Rod, and Religion, in Common Schools* (Boston, Redding & Co., 1847), pp. 10–11.
[46] *Remarks on the Seventh Annual Report of the Hon. Horace Mann* (Boston, Little and Brown, 1844), p. 8.
[47] *Ibid.*, p. 127.

of rejoinders and replies to rejoinders, the issues remained essentially those stated in the early phases of the controversy.

The Demand for an Expanded, More Practical Secondary Curriculum

More practical knowledge. It has been pointed out earlier that one of the central purposes of the Phillips brothers in establishing their academy at Andover was to instruct youth in "the GREAT END AND REAL BUSINESS OF LIVING." This latter aim was undoubtedly the really novel aspect of the new secondary education being urged immediately following the Revolutionary War. In the practical tradition of Franklin, who held that secondary education should provide useful training for business and commerce, a flood of proposals argued that the traditional Latin grammar course was far too impractical and sterile to constitute the further education of those who did not intend to go on to college. As with many proponents of the common school, an increasing number of voices proclaimed the "cash value" of a new, useful training. It would not only improve the individual as a person; it would speed him along the road to success.

Nowhere, perhaps, was the notion of practical secondary education seen more clearly than in the early proposals for the high school. An article first published in 1838, probably under the authorship of Henry Barnard, emphatically urged the establishment of high schools that would serve the purposes of everyday life. For the true ideal of the high school to be realized, the curriculum would have to "prepare every young man, whose parents may desire it, for business, or for college, and give to every young woman a well disciplined mind, high moral aims, refined tastes, gentle and graceful manners, practical views of her own duties, and those resources of health, thought, conversation, and occupation, which bless alike the highest and lowest station in life." [48]

Such opinions were widely held by contemporary educational leaders. Clearly, such proposals were a direct outgrowth of the development of commerce and industry in the early national period (with a concomitant demand for skilled workers), of the vast increase in scientific interest and knowledge, and of the growing belief that schooling should serve a useful purpose in the lives of scholars. Yet this much of a qualification should be introduced. When leaders of antebellum America thought about practical education, they did not usually think of a directly applicable industrial arts, vocational, or commercial education as is given today, but rather their thoughts were more of a learning-from-books-about-more-useful-things. Thus, although the new proposals moved far from the older classical secondary education, they maintained fairly clear continuity and similarity with it. What was being

[48] *The American Journal of Education*, Vol. III (1858), p. 187.

proposed was à *more practical* education rather than a completely practical education per se.

Proposals for a moral basis for secondary education. To educate for the great end and real business of living was to be the central purpose of the Phillips Academy. But it must also be pointed out that Samuel Phillips' proposals further declared the "promotion of true piety and virtue" to be the academy's "*first* and *principal* object." As with common school programs, this object became inextricably tied up with the question of what religion should be taught. As also with the common school, this was a problem which faced every maker of an academy curriculum. The deep ties between church, state, and school which characterized the colonial period had, to be sure, weakened. Yet, one would expect to find signs of these ties still existent in the educational proposals of the early national period. And undoubtedly they were there.

The "promotion of piety and virtue" carries a decidedly different flavor from the earlier distinctively sectarian purposes of academies. It would seem that proposals for the academy curriculum, as with the common school curriculum, began to lean toward a "common elements" conception of religious and ethical instruction. Increasingly, they urged the teaching of those Christian principles common to all sects, leaving inculcation in sectarian doctrine and dogma to the home. While it was the bounden duty of the teacher to provide character education, such education was to be free of sectarian instruction that might offend members of one or more sects.

It must be borne in mind, however, that the academy was a transition phase in the movement from private to public secondary education. There were many kinds of academies proposed—varying all the way from those organized purely for private profit, to those enjoying partial public support, to completely public institutions like the Free Academy. The problem of non-sectarian religious instruction certainly presented itself in publicly supported academies. It was often present in privately supported academies which hoped to cater to as wide an audience as possible. But it must be remembered that some private academies were organized by various sects for the express purpose of training persons in a given body of religious doctrine. In a society where churches and their religious schools had recently been deprived of public support which they had enjoyed for a century and a half, one would expect the development of private institutions to take the place of formerly public institutions. And this was one role of the private academy.

Thus, for example, when the Catholics, the Baptists, the Methodists, the Presbyterians, and the Congregationalists sent ministers to the West, these missionaries were interested in establishing schools as well as churches. The constitution of the Foreign Missionary Society of the Valley of the Mississippi gave as one of its objects to promote "by all suitable means, within the Valley of the Mississippi, the missionary spirit in Theological Seminaries, Colleges,

Academies and the community." [49] Not only in the newer frontier states, but in the older northern and southern states, one finds numerous proposals for private academies which might train not only ministers and leaders but the faithful generally in the doctrines of the various denominations. Many agreed, perhaps, with the Illinois Judge James Hall, when he wrote in 1835: "If religious denominations think proper to educate their children in their own tenets, they have a clear right to do so. . . . In a country, where religious opinions are unshackled, and men may believe and worship as they please, it seems to be unfair, that they should not be allowed every facility for educating their children according to the dictates of their own judgment." [50]

Conservative reaction to the demand for an expanded, more practical education. The heart of conservative reaction to the proposals outlined above seems to have centered in the retention of classical languages and studies as the core of the secondary curriculum. While many conservatives were willing to admit the necessity of some expansion in secondary studies, they saw in the time-honored classical curriculum the most perfect means of "refining the taste," of "enlarging the mind and training its powers," and of "storing the mind with useful science and knowledge." First and foremost, however, the study of Greek and Latin would serve to discipline the young, untrained mind. Once disciplined—once trained in powers of memory, taste, reason, and logic—such a mind would have little trouble mastering facts, skills, and knowledge in apparently more practical realms.

It is interesting to note a close similarity in the arguments opposing curriculum expansion on both the elementary and secondary levels. Both sought to provide the student with *preparation* for getting practical knowledge rather than with the practical knowledge itself. On the common school level, the conservative argued that if the *fundamentals*—reading, writing, spelling, arithmetic, and morals—were taught, the remainder of necessary education would come easily. On the secondary level, the conservative argued that if the *fundamentals*—Latin, Greek, and the classics—were taught, the remainder of necessary education would also come easily. Both sought to prepare the individual with a return to fundamentals; both promised usefulness, albeit by an indirect and circuitous route.

The Demand for Expansion, Practicality, and Increased Flexibility of Higher Education

Broader purposes for higher education. Inasmuch as considerable attention has already been given to Jefferson's conception of a unified system of public education, it might well be profitable to turn in some detail to his views

---

[49] Foreign Missionary Society of the Valley of Mississippi, *Auxiliary to the American Board of Commissioners for Foreign Missions* (Cincinnati, Truman, Smith & Co., 1834), p. 4.

[50] James Hall, *Sketches of History, Life, and Manners, in the West* (Philadelphia, Harrison Hall, 1835), Vol. II, pp. 206–207.

on the purposes of higher education. They are present in many of his papers, especially those of his later years, but one finds them best defined, perhaps, in the report of a committee he chaired in 1818, charged with determining site, program, and policy of the University of Virginia.

Although Jefferson conceived the object of primary education as one of enabling citizens to conduct their affairs, improve their personal capabilities, and know, understand, and recognize their social and political rights and duties, the objects of higher education embraced for him much more of a coordinating and leadership function. He listed these objects as follows:

1. to form the statesmen, legislators, and judges on whom public prosperity and individual happiness so greatly depend;

2. to expound the principles and structure of government, the laws which regulate the intercourse of nations, laws formed municipally for our own government, and a sound spirit of legislation, which, banishing all unnecessary restraint on individual action, shall leave us free to do whatever does not violate the equal rights of another;

3. to harmonize and promote the interests of agriculture, manufactures, and commerce, and by well-informed views of political economy to give a free scope to the public industry;

4. to develop the reasoning faculties of our youth, enlarge their minds, cultivate their morals, and instill in them the precepts of virtue and order;

5. to enlighten them with mathematical and physical sciences, which advance the arts, and administer to the health, the subsistence, and the comforts of human life;

6. and, generally, to form them to habits of reflection and correct action, rendering them examples of virtue to others, and of happiness within themselves.[51]

One quickly recognizes in these purposes the social and intellectual climate of Jefferson's age. The spirit of democratic republicanism is implicit in (1) and (2); the laissez-faire conception of government as well as the natural rights conception of politics is implicit in (2) and (3); economic individualism is also evident in (2) and (3); and the enlightenment faith in science and rationality is evident throughout. What is perhaps most significant about the list is its call for a higher education which would serve definite and specific functions in the everyday life of American society. True, Jefferson's conception of utility meant political and social utility rather than vocational utility, but even this was a proposal going far beyond the traditional notion that literary and linguistic training were the best preparation for public and professional service in every sphere.

If breadth and utility were two important criteria of Jefferson's concep-

---

[51] "Report of the Commissioners Appointed to fix the Site of the University of Virginia, &c.," quoted in Roy J. Honeywell, *The Educational Work of Thomas Jefferson* (Cambridge, Harvard University Press, 1931), pp. 249–250.

tion of a republican university offering, freedom of choice among subject areas was a third. True freedom in education for him involved the maximum development of a student's own individual talents for service to himself and society. While the broadest possible offering of both the traditional linguistic and philosophical studies, together with the newer practical scientific and political studies was one cornerstone of such a program, another definitely involved permitting the student to enter the course of studies most suited to his requirements. In line with this conception he proposed that the University of Virginia embrace eight separate "schools" covering the subject areas of ancient languages, modern languages, mathematics, natural philosophy, natural history, medicine, moral philosophy, and law. Furthermore, a student would be "free to attend the schools of his choice, and no other than he chooses." Obviously, while this notion of choice among schools did not by any means go as far as later proposals to allow free choice among subjects, it was a far cry from the total prescription characterizing virtually every contemporary college and university.

Jefferson's ideal, as proposed for the University of Virginia, began to attract wide attention in other parts of the country. In December 1821 he received a letter from a young professor of languages in Harvard College named George Ticknor. Ticknor, who had toured the principal universities of northern Germany with Edward Everett in 1816, had quickly become imbued with the German conception of scholarship and intellectual freedom. Returning to Harvard as professor of French and Spanish, he showed much disaffection for the traditional, mechanical methods of recitation and lecturing. In his above-mentioned letter he expressed interest in Jefferson's plans for the University of Virginia in the hope of gaining useful ideas for reform at Harvard. Continued correspondence led to a visit by Ticknor to Charlottesville, home of the university, in December 1824. This visit undoubtedly furnished the opportunity of spirited interchange between these two leaders—one of whom had drawn much of his thinking from the French enlightenment and the other of whom had become so enthusiastic over nineteenth-century German culture and education.

Ticknor's ideas on higher education were clearly outlined by him in a pamphlet published in 1825,[52] written on the basis of notes made earlier in 1821 and 1823. Perhaps the central point he set forth was the obsolescence of the "class" system as traditionally practiced at Harvard. Under it, a number of young men entered as a group and took all of their courses together in a prescribed four-year sequence. "The attempt," he argued, "to force together sixty or eighty young men, many of whom have nothing, or almost nothing, in common . . . and to compel them to advance *pari passu* during four of the most active and valuable years of life, giving to the most industrious and

[52] George Ticknor, *Remarks on Changes Lately Proposed or Adopted in Harvard University*, 2d. ed. (Boston, Cummings, Hilliard, 1825).

intelligent no more and no other lessons, than to the most dull and idle, is a thing that is unknown to the practical arrangements for education in other countries. . . ." He criticized the formalism of the lecture method for taking no account of individual differences and the recitation method for superficial emphasis on books rather than ideas. The quality of Harvard scholarship could never in his estimation approach that of the German universities without substantial changes in these approaches.

To remedy these shortcomings, Ticknor recommended the division of course offerings into departments and allowing students to choose suitable courses from among these offerings. "And why," he queried, "should not the student or his friends determine in a greater or less degree, what studies he shall pursue, since more may be offered to him than it is possible he should pursue profitably?" He closed his *Remarks* with the plea that Harvard and other private colleges liberalize and make more functional their curricula. Only in this way, he urged, could they "accommodate themselves more wisely to the spirit and wants the times. . . ." Only in this way could they meet the challenge of the new free state universities. Otherwise, he concluded, "they will only be the first victims of the spirit of improvement."

The proposals of Jefferson and Ticknor, although they aimed at somewhat different ends, yet had much in common. It is true that while the paramount interest of Jefferson was a higher education which would serve American society, that of Ticknor was one which would serve the highest ideals of scholarship. Yet were these ends really so far removed? For a ripe scholarship which served the ends of truth would most certainly serve the ends of a republic. One even seems to sense this follow-through in Ticknor's argument. Both urged that respect for the individual necessitated some freedom of choice among courses of study; both urged subjects with social and political utility. In the last analysis both were attempting to adopt higher education to the changing political climate of their times, the movement toward political democracy.

The conservative reaction in the colleges. Conservative reaction to the kind of ideas advanced by Ticknor and Jefferson was quickly forthcoming. As with secondary education, its theme was that no matter what social, political, or economic changes were taking place in the broader society, the fundamentals of a good higher education would remain the same. If the curriculum attempted to adjust to the transient affairs of society, any education provided therein would be worthless. "Should the time ever come," prophesied the *Western Review* of Cincinnati in 1820, "when Latin and Greek should be banished from our Universities, and the study of Cicero and Demosthenes, of Homer and Virgil should be considered as unnecessary for the formation of a scholar, we should regard mankind as fast sinking into absolute barbarism, and the gloom of mental darkness as likely to increase until it should become universal." [53] When this educational conservatism was coupled with the educational efforts of the older denominations to combat the rationalism and deism of French philosophy, it served as a powerful force opposing expansion and election.

The task of leading this conservative opposition fell to the Yale faculty. The monumental report of 1828, the first part of which was written by President Day, has already been discussed (see Chapter 6). Founded on the prevailing conception of mental discipline, the report held that a liberal education which sought to enlarge intellectual powers, could be attained only through pursuit of a fixed course of disciplinary studies. Other expressions, closely paralleling the Yale report, sought to defend the educational status quo along similar lines. Lyman Beecher, in an address at Miami University (Ohio) in 1836, linked the whole future of the West and of the nation with the maintenance of the traditional curriculum. Presidents Thornwell of the College of South Carolina, Swain of the University of North Carolina, Church of the University of Georgia, and Frelinghuysen of Rutgers, all attacked the reforms at the University of Virginia. Support was also forthcoming from Frederick A. P. Barnard, a former student of Day, then professor at the University of Alabama, and later to be distinguished for his pioneering work as president of Columbia College (1864–1889). Thus, although the protest against traditional higher education was forceful and effective, one cannot underestimate the strength of this conservative argument which sought to maintain the older curriculum, changing slowly at best.

THE TEACHER AND TEACHER TRAINING

Demands for Better Teachers in the Elementary Schools

One might properly expect significant changes in the conception of teaching and the teacher in light of the sweeping new educational proposals discussed heretofore. In a society where formal education played a comparatively small part in the lives of comparatively few people, the teacher would receive comparatively slight attention. Aside from the primary qualification of religious orthodoxy, little was demanded of the colonial schoolmaster. Under the newer educational proposals outlined above, however, the teacher could hardly be ignored. The school was now to occupy a pivotal position in the maintenance and perpetuation of a healthy American society. The teacher would inevitably occupy a place of first concern and interest to all.

As a matter of fact, educational literature from 1825 to 1865 is virtually crammed with material concerning the qualities of the ideal common school teacher. As might also be expected, the greater part of such material con-

[53] Frank Luther Mott, *A History of American Magazines, 1741–1850* (Cambridge, Harvard University Press, 1930), p. 146.

stituted the ideal teacher in the form of an eclectic saint: the knowledge of Socrates, the patience and kindness of St. Francis, and the economic self-denial of a mendicant friar. The first popular teacher training text in the United States, Samuel R. Hall's *Lectures on School-Keeping* (1829), devoted a whole section to "requisite qualifications of teachers." A schoolmaster must have common sense, uniformity of temper, a capacity to understand and discriminate character, decision of character, an affectionate nature, a sense of moral obligation, and a wide range of knowledge in common school subjects.[54]

Lectures before various teacher groups during these years and articles in the many state school journals begun in the 1850's also gave considerable attention to this problem of teacher qualification. In 1837 the Reverend Charles Brooks of Hingham, Massachusetts, portrayed the ideal American ("for, AMERICAN he should be decidedly and completely") schoolmaster as follows: (1) the American teacher should thoroughly understand the common branches of study; (2) the teacher should be able to communicate ideas with perspicuity and promptitude; (3) he should be able to show practical application of what he teaches; (4) he should be able to govern his school; (5) he should be a good man; and (6) he must have enthusiasm.[55]

Another speaker before the American Institute of Instruction in 1840 made an interesting attempt to tie in his criteria of a good teacher with the distinctive character of American civilization.[56] "Teachers," urged David Mack, ". . . must understand the civilization of the age and country in which they live, or how can they advance its progress?" What, then, were the "leading facts" of American Society in 1840? It was, according to Mack, set within the general movement toward a universal society; it was a Christian civilization; it was a republican civilization of equals; it was increasingly becoming an abundant civilization in which the "means of education are better, more numerous, and more within the reach of all, than at any former period."

What, in the light of this analysis, should be the qualities of a teacher? First: "A practically Christian character, may be regarded as the first and highest requisite." Second: "In an age characterized beyond any other by the accumulation and general diffusion of knowledge, *knowledge* is essential to teachers. . . ." Third: "Amidst this indifference to thorough education, especially to religious instruction in schools,—the conflict of passion and interest with principle—of one interest with another—*true, consistent, en-*

54 Arthur D. Wright and George E. Gardner (eds.), *Hall's Lectures on School-Keeping* (Hanover, The Dartmouth Press, 1929), pp. 65-75.

55 Charles Brooks, "School Reform or Teachers' Seminaries," *The Introductory Discourse, and the Lectures Delivered Before the American Institute of Instruction, at Worcester, (Mass.) August, 1837* (Boston, James Munroe), pp. 169-173.

56 David Mack, "The Claims of Our Age and Country Upon Teachers," *The Introductory Discourse, and the Lectures Delivered Before the American Institute of Instruction, at Springfield, (Mass.) August, 1839* (Boston, Marsh, Capen, Lyon and Webb, 1840), pp. 138-154.

lightened independence of character in a teacher, cannot be too highly prized, too sedulously sought for." In these three demands Mack saw the ideal teacher for 1840 America.

It is interesting to note that generally, the qualifications incorporated in these proposals paralleled the curriculum proposals which grew out of social forces at work in the first decades of the republic. The three great divisions of these curriculum proposals were the common branches of knowledge, the common elements of Christianity (or moral instruction), and the common branches of republicanism (or patriotic instruction). Thus, the three great areas of concern in the ideal teacher gradually became the intellectual or literary, the moral and religious, and the patriotic. While there was considerable disagreement over which of the three was primary, all received extensive treatment in most of the proposals.

Not infrequently, articles or lectures setting forth these high standards for common school teachers offered positive suggestions for attaining such standards. Thomas Cushing, Jr., of Boston, also before the American Institute of Instruction, noted in 1851 that: "No age has probably equalled the present for a theoretical respect for the teacher in the abstract; but deference for the wishes, opinions and feelings of the individual, are not so strongly marked." It would be largely up to the teachers themselves to raise their level in the estimation of the public, and foremost in this respect was the necessity of making teaching a permanent rather than the temporary occupation which it was, of raising the requirements of training and apprenticeship to a point considerably above their level at that time, and of eliminating a good deal of the "quackery" then existent in the schools.[57]

Cushing's recommendations hinted strongly at the keynote of many proposals in this area—the professionalizing of teaching. From every quarter came the suggestion that teachers organize into a strong, self-directing body which would undertake the task of determining fitness and standards. "We must organize as a *profession,* to be regularly recognized. . . ," inveighed a speaker before the Illinois State Teachers' Association in 1858. "From Maine to Iowa, wherever free schools are a part of the public care, come voices for a *teachers' profession.*" [58] A speaker before the Michigan State Teachers' Association in 1854 similarly sought "the cultivation of a professional spirit among the members of the profession, and especially among that portion of it who train the minds of the masses in our common schools." [59] Orville Taylor in his work on teaching, recommended: "Teaching, in our district schools, should be made a distinct profession. . . . The teacher should prepare himself for

[57] Thomas Cushing, Jr., "The Teacher in the Nineteenth Century," *The Lectures Delivered Before the American Institute of Instruction, at Keene, N. H., August, 1851* (Boston, Ticknor, Reed, and Fields, 1851), pp. 71–101.

[58] *The Illinois Teacher: Devoted to Education, Science, and Free Schools.* Vol. 5 (1859), p. 299.

[59] *The Michigan Journal of Education and Teachers' Magazine,* Vol. 1 (1854), p. 145.

his business, and labour as exclusively in his calling as the lawyer does in his." Only as a united profession might teachers gain the power, the deference, and the respectability which they sought and deserved.[60]

Implicit in the demand for a strong profession were proposals that the organized profession take greater responsibility in certifying its own members. "The law," noted the same speaker before the Illinois Teachers' Association, "prescribes what shall constitute a *lawyer,* but, be it observed, prescribes an examination by lawyers. But as for teachers, the State has ordained that a teacher shall be examined, not by his own class, but by some officer who is not required to know any thing of the matters he is to question of." "What blacksmith," he continued, "would not hurl his sledge-hammer at the head of any lawyer who procured a law that no man should shoe horses or make a hay-knife till he had a cerificate from the postmaster?"[61] Here was being raised, of course, the very critical question of public and professional responsibility in the setting up of standards and certification of teacher personnel.

Proposals for Training Common School Teachers

If the common schools were to be of high enough quality to attract pupils of all classes, and if the new methods and educational approaches previously outlined were to enter the schools, it was clear to many that special facilities for teachers were urgently needed. Although the private academies had early taken on the task of teacher training, it soon became evident to many of the educational reformers that something more was necessary in this respect. One of the earliest and most active proponents of teacher training was James G. Carter, Massachusetts educator. His proposals regarding the matter significantly set the pace of those which were to follow in succeeding decades.

Carter's first publications in behalf of public education appeared in the Boston newspapers of 1821 and kept appearing in those media until 1824, when he published a more extensive treatment of his ideas.[62] In this latter pamphlet he saw two principal shortcomings in the New England common schools: incompetent instructors and poor schoolbooks. In the winter of 1824–1825 Carter followed up these observations by publishing a series of "Essays upon Popular Education" in the *Boston Patriot.* Reviewing the many imperfections which he had earlier pointed to in Massachusetts' schools, he launched a plea that the state rectify this condition by reasserting its control over education. Carter also proposed the establishment of an institution designed primarily to train teachers for the common schools. "Our ancestors ventured," he argued, "to do what the world has never done before, in so

---

[60] J. Orville Taylor, *The District School; or, National Education* (Philadelphia, Carey, Lea, and Blanchard, 1835), Sec. VI.

[61] *The Illinois Teacher* . . . , Vol. 5 (1859), pp. 296–297.

[62] James G. Carter, *Letters to the Hon. William Prescott on the Free Schools of New England, with Remarks on the Principles of Instruction* (Boston, Cummings, Hilliard, 1824).

perfect a manner, when they established the free schools. Let us do what they have never so well done yet, and establish an institution for the exclusive purpose of preparing instructors for them. This is only a second part, a development or consummation of the plan of our fathers."

Carter conceived of the institution as both literary and scientific in character —one of its unique tasks resting in the development of a body of materials related to teaching principles and methods. Not only would the institution contribute better teachers to better schools, but also it would greatly stimulate the development of much needed professional spirit among teachers. Vitally important for Carter was the proposal that such an institution be state supported and state controlled. "An institution for this purpose," he stated, "would become by its influence on society, and particularly on the young, an engine to sway the public sentiment, the public morals, and the public religion, more powerful than any other in the possession of government." [63] Thus, only as a teacher training school would be subject to public control did Carter see its potential danger adequately checked.

Carter's proposals came early in what proved to be a flood of demands for teacher training institutions. Numerous visitors to Prussia, with Victor Cousin and Horace Mann foremost among them, praised Prussian teacher training at length. Orville Taylor's *District School, or National Education,* basing its recommendations heavily on Cousin's report of "Public Instruction in Prussia," proposed a teacher education curriculum for New York State to embrace (1) the English language, (2) writing and drawing, (3) arithmetic and bookkeeping (4) geography and history, (5) United States history, (6) geometry, trigonometry, mensuration, and surveying, (7) natural philosophy and elements of astronomy, (8) chemistry and mineralogy, (9) United States and New York constitutions, (10) selected laws, (11) moral and intellectual philosophy, and (12) the principles of teaching.[64] Horace Mann's *Seventh Annual Report* gave extensive attention to this same problem. It is clear from most of these suggestions that what was being recommended was an academy-type or secondary program especially designed for teachers. For all of these proponents, until such institutions were widely established and available, the common schools could never in reality even begin to approach their ideal.

Conceptions of Salary and Status of Elementary School Teachers

In a good deal of the literature there was recognition that high standards would not be met, nor permanent, professional teachers secured until salaries

[63] James G. Carter, *Essays upon Popular Education, Containing a Particular Examination of the Schools of Massachusetts, and an Outline of an Institution for the Education of Teachers* (Boston, Bowles and Dearborn, 1826), p. 46.
[64] Taylor, *op. cit.,* p. 90.

were increased to the point where competent persons could be attracted to and held in teaching. The close relationship between low salaries and incompetent personnel was pointed to again and again. Orville Taylor began as early as 1835 to emphasize the need for higher salaries. *"There is no employment among the American people,"* he observed, *". . . which receives less pay than elementary teaching.* Yes, there is no service so menial, no drudgery so degrading, which does not demand as high wages as we are now giving for that which is the life of our liberty, and the guard of our free institutions." Taylor was clear and direct in urging that only as the well-qualified teachers which higher salaries would bring were employed would the usefulness and character of district schools be brought to an adequate standard.[65]

The plea apparently elicited few results. Twenty-five years later, an editorial in *The Illinois Teacher,* noting a salary of two dollars weekly paid teachers in an Illinois district, responded: "What kind of education do our people expect to get for such a price? They pay muscular girls more for handling inanimate mops and earthen ware. Are children's minds deserving of no more careful handling or skillful treatment than a peach-tree or rosebush? Yet we hardly think these will be properly set and trained by cheap laborers. Let us have teachers fit for their business, and then pay them for their work." [66] Another observer wrote: "The want of adequate remuneration is of itself a sufficient reason why the teachers are generally so miserably qualified for their duties. . . . Many a farmer will much more willingly pay a liberal price to a competent man for shoeing his horse well . . . than to obtain a suitable individual to mould and form the character of his child." [67] It must be remarked that efforts to secure higher salaries were often hampered by the conception that such efforts were undignified and unbecoming to teachers. Yet, for those who favored education, the logic regarding salaries was clear: the life and vitality of the nation depended on common schools; the excellence of a school depended largely on the master (Victor Cousin's statement to this effect was widely cited); good masters could only be secured through good salaries; therefore, good salaries were crucial.

Two principal factors among many produced a somewhat ambivalent attitude regarding the social status of teachers. First, in a society committed to an individualist-capitalist economy and mentality, a low salary would carry with it low social status. When proposals, therefore, were advanced regarding higher salaries and professionalizing of teachers, they carried implicitly the notion of improving the teacher's status in the community. For many, a good job of teaching should have carried with it status comparable to that

[65] Taylor, *op. cit.,* p. 115.
[66] *The Illinois Teacher* . . . , Vol. 6 (1860), p. 229.
[67] J. T. Clark, *Essay on Common School Education in New Jersey* (Trenton, 1865), pp. 21–22.

of the physician or the lawyer. For many, then, the status of the teacher would definitely have to be raised for the common school adequately to accomplish its task.

On the other hand, many of these very same people subscribed to the notion that the teacher, by his every action in and out of school, should be a living example of morality and good living for his students. Add to this the many proposals that young women be employed as teachers (taking account of the more stringent notions of morality applied to women), and it made for the strictest concern with the teacher's private and professional life. Many saw that this encroachment on the teacher's privacy (enhanced by the practice of boarding teachers with different families on a rotating basis) could never allow proper social relationships to develop. One speaker before the American Institute of Instruction observed: "Boards of Trustees and School Committees on the one side, point out the path in which he is to walk, the books he is to use, and even the mode in which he is to use them; while, on the other hand, an unofficial, but by no means unimportant and very numerous board of fathers, uncles, aunts, grandmothers and cousins, claim for themselves authority to form and express opinions upon his qualifications and conduct. . . ." [68] The days of morality and religious orthodoxy as the primary concern of the public regarding its teachers were not too distantly removed for this kind of regulation to be unreal. In many districts these were still the primary and only concerns. Yet the first proposals for professional self-regulation were beginning to point to the dangers of such a situation in keeping promising persons from the field of teaching. As a Connecticut lawyer observed: "So long as teachers show, by their conduct, that they have no profession, from an apparent conscious of demerit, just so long will other professions, at great disadvantage, employ teachers as passive tools, and every man become the teacher's censor." [69] In increasing standards and higher competence proponents of a teaching profession saw the amelioration of these interferences in the private affairs of teachers.

ISSUES FOR STUDY AND DISCUSSION

1. Criticize the following proposition: "In order to make the common school satisfactory to all groups, Horace Mann and his contemporaries set out to build a non-religious elementary curriculum."

2. To what extent has the ideal of the common school as set forth by antebellum educators been accepted as an ideal of contemporary America?

3. Some contemporary educators have taken the position that a public school is one which is supported and controlled by public agencies. Others have argued that a

[68] Cushing, *op. cit.*, p. 76.

[69] J. W. Allen, "The Teacher Is An Agent, Not a Servant," *The Lectures Delivered Before the American Institute of Instruction, at Portland, Me., August, 1864* (Boston, Committee on Publications, 1865), p. 43.

public school is any school which serves the public interest. Which position gains support from our educational history between 1779 and 1865?

4. In what ways did the arguments for and against state control of education between 1830 and 1865 parallel the contemporary arguments concerning the role of the federal government in education?

5. How if at all would you change Jefferson's statement of the purposes of higher education to fit the needs of contemporary America?

SUGGESTIONS FOR FURTHER READING

Brubacher, John S. (ed.), *Henry Barnard on Education,* New York, McGraw-Hill, 1931.

Butler, Vera M., *Education as Revealed by New England Newspapers Previous to 1850,* Philadelphia, Majestic Press, 1935.

Butts, R. Freeman, *The College Charts Its Course,* New York, McGraw-Hill, 1939.

Carlton, Frank T., *Economic Influences upon Educational Progress in the United States 1820–1850,* Madison, Bulletin of the University of Wisconsin, 1908.

Cremin, Lawrence A., *The American Common School,* New York, Teachers College, Columbia University, 1951.

Curoe, Philip R. V., *Educational Attitudes and Policies of Organized Labor in the United States,* New York, Teachers College, Columbia University, 1926.

Curti, Merle, *The Social Ideas of American Educators,* New York, Scribner, 1935.

Culver, Raymond B., *Horace Mann and Religion in the Massachusetts Public Schools,* New Haven, Yale University Press, 1929.

Gordy, J. P., *Rise and Growth of the Normal-School Idea in the United States,* Washington, D. C., Government Printing Office, 1891.

Hansen, Allen Oscar, *Liberalism and American Education in the Eighteenth Century,* New York, Macmillan, 1926.

Honeywell, Roy J., *The Educational Work of Thomas Jefferson,* Cambridge, Harvard University Press, 1931.

Jackson, Sidney L., *America's Struggle for Free Schools,* Washington, D. C., American Council on Education, 1942.

Knight, Edgar W. (ed.), *A Documentary History of Education in the South Before 1860,* Chapel Hill, University of North Carolina Press, 1949–1952, Vols. 1–3.

——— (ed.), *Reports on European Education,* New York, McGraw-Hill, 1930.

Life and Works of Horace Mann, Boston, Lee and Shepard, 1891, 5 vols.

Monroe, Will S., *History of the Pestalozzian Movement in the United States,* Syracuse, N. Y., C. W. Bardeen, 1907.

Tappan, Henry Philip, *University Education,* New York, 1851.

Ulich, Robert, *History of Educational Thought,* New York, American Book, 1945.

Williams, E. I. F., *Horace Mann, Educational Statesman,* New York, Macmillan, 1937.

Woody, Thomas, *A History of Women's Education in the United States,* New York, Science Press, 1929, 2 vols.

Serial publications such as the *Common School Journal* (Massachusetts). *Connecticut Common School Journal,* and the *Common School Assistant* (New York) as well as the annual proceedings of educational groups like the American Institute of Instruction or the Western Literary Institute and College of Professional Teachers are rich resources of educational opinion during this period. The annual reports of state superintendents of common schools are also extremely useful.

8

CHARACTERISTIC EDUCATIONAL PRACTICES

AT THE time of the Revolution the school on the whole continued to occupy a relatively minor place in American life. Horace Mann estimated that even in school-conscious New England perhaps one youngster in ten ever attended a school, and often this youngster attended intermittently and for very brief periods of time. Some did manage to complete the basic instruction of the common school, to weather the rigid classical curriculum of the grammar school, and to stand among the select few who graduated annually from the nine colonial colleges. Yet the average American was far too concerned with the simple fact of getting a living from farm or trade to pay substantial attention to schools. Education was a prize, but a prize which had to wait its turn behind more important things.

The year 1860 presented a vastly different picture. America's great state school systems had definitely taken form, several of them already capped by flourishing state universities. In place of the nine colonial colleges over 200 colleges and universities (182 of them still in operation today) offered instruction to young men and women. Academies established for innumerable purposes and aims offered courses in every conceivable area to all comers. Above all, America had become education-conscious. The school was increasingly viewed as an important social institution by Americans of all classes. Granted that different groups conceived of it as serving different ends. In the last analysis, however, it was becoming more than just a transmitter of knowledge; with it were associated many of the faiths and hopes of the American people.

EDUCATION IN SCHOOL AND COMMUNITY

The Education of Children

Life and learning on the family farm. On the farms which housed well over 90 percent of pre-Civil War Americans, education continued to begin early for the average boy or girl. It continued, as it had in the colonial period, to be largely an apprenticeship education: that is, the young learned largely by imitating adults. The economy was still an economy of scarcity, and every able hand was needed if the family was to make a living from the farm. Thus very early in their lives, children were counted on to help with the innumerable chores on the homestead. Animals had to be cared for, land cleared, crops tended, repairs made—and the boy of seven or eight was already expected to be of considerable aid to his father in these tasks. Similarly, in the cooking, preserving, gardening, and other household tasks, the girl of similar age also contributed—to say nothing of her role in caring for children younger than herself. The boy learned from his father and the girl from her mother; and thereby, the skills necessary for maintaining life on the farm were passed on from generation to generation. To this extent, the school participated little; the job was largely one of informal education.

Economic activities by no means accounted for all of life, however, as important and as primary as they were. The roots of social, religious, and political belief and behavior were inculcated in much the same way. The social life of the family itself, of the neighborhood, of logrollings, house-warmings, prayer meetings, elections, all formed a milieu in which the youngster learned by watching and doing. No special teacher taught these things; they were learned by direct participation in the activities themselves. Society was still simple enough so that the behaviors, attitudes, and values which people were expected to know and use could be learned in this way.

The school takes on certain functions. Even within this framework of learning largely from participation in the community, however, the first half of the nineteenth century witnessed a growing role for the school in the education of children. To be sure the education of farm, family, church, and neighborhood remained primary; the formal education of the school only secondary and supplementary. Yet, signs of growth in the latter's influence were unmistakable. In New England it became very much more the rule than the exception by 1840 for children to have some formal schooling. While the growth of education proceeded at different rates in different sections, it went forward significantly enough to make schooling the rule rather than the exception in the middle and western states by 1850. The southern states, on the other hand, because of their distinctive way of life, showed much less of this development; and while schooling was certainly the rule for upper-class and upper-middle-class children, poorer children seldom enjoyed the opportunity. Negro children, of course, had little opportunity for formal education. The general diffusion of the limited knowledge which formal schooling did impart began increasingly to be noticed after 1830. There seems little doubt, for example, that in states where schools were most numerous, the general level of knowledge was raised accordingly. De Tocqueville noted, for instance, that every citizen in New England received the simple rudiments of knowledge, the doctrines of his religion, the history of his country, and the leading features of the federal Constitution. "In the states of Connecticut and Massachusetts," he remarked, "it is extremely rare to find a man imperfectly acquainted with all these things, and a person wholly ignorant of them is a sort of phenomenon." [1] Although he was fully aware that these generalizations could not be applied to the whole of the nation, he did comment on the "middling" state of knowledge in the country, whereby few were destined to brilliance, but few also, to ignorance. One needs only to view the rise of the penny newspaper and the cheap book and periodical in antebellum America to find ample documentation of these observations.

The Education of Youth and Adults

Early adulthood in early America. For most people during this period—including those who had had some elementary schooling—the responsibilities of full-time employment and family life came early. Marriages of young people in their late teens or early twenties was certainly more common than not, and with marriage came the demand for all the skills which had been learned informally during childhood. For the young lassie—as adolescent women were called—the burdens of caring for a family and keeping a home were considerable; but she was not at all unprepared for them. Years of helping her mother and other women with their households and in the care of younger children had made her familiar with ways of assuming these responsibilities. Similarly, by the time her husband reached his later teens, he had as a rule worked for a number of years on the farm of his family—or that of someone else—or as an apprentice to some tradesman. He too found that he was already familiar with a good deal of what he had to know to make a living.

Both parents had received many ideas on bringing up children both from the large families in which they had been reared and, more often than not, from the church and its minister. Certain conceptions in this realm—many of them carrying Biblical support—such as "Spare the rod and spoil the child" or "Train up a child in the way he should go, and he will not depart from it," were well accepted; and they were handed on from generation to generation as irrevocable truths. If some of the larger seaboard communities entertained Enlightenment notions about man being born good and corrupted by

[1] Alexis de Tocqueville, *Democracy in America*, Phillips Bradley (ed.), (New York, Knopf, 1945), Vol. 1, p. 315.

his environment, the older ideas prevailed in force in the inland rural neighborhoods.

In sum, the young had learned the main business of life by the time they were in their teens. They had learned it by living in their communities, by imitating their elders—in effect, by doing from the earliest age, the very things they would have to do in later life.

Formal schooling in the lives of youth and adults. Not all children managed to get in some elementary schooling before they assumed family responsibilities, but even fewer youths and adults managed to obtain formal education beyond the elementary school. Grammar schools, academies, high schools, colleges, and universities were very specialized schools, and they prepared their students for special social and economic positions in society. There was little that the farmer could learn in any one of them that would help him to be a better farmer, and most people in America during this time were farmers. Thus, these higher schools served a very specialized and definite segment of society.

On the other hand, it is far too easy to underestimate the increasing number who did attend them. The period from 1810 to 1840, for example, has often been called the age of the academy. Literally hundreds of these institutions sprang up all over the United States, and by 1850 there were probably more than 6,000 enrolling over a quarter of a million students. It is important to remember that the academic limits of these private institutions were not at all well defined. Although they are traditionally conceived of as secondary institutions, many offered instruction on the common school level, while others approached college and university levels of excellence.

Obviously, however, if they enrolled this number of students, the lives of many youths were touched in some way by these schools. Young men learned commercial and business subjects there as well as more advanced materials in the rudimentary common branches. Young ladies who attended the "female academies" learned the social graces, a variety of subjects appropriate to their sex, and, of course, some of the cultural subjects. As the most "functional"—that is, having the most practical application to life—of the higher institutions, academies were widely turned to by those seeking to improve their social or economic status in society.

High schools, still in their infancy, were far less widely attended during these years. Only several hundred such institutions were reported by 1860 in the United States, and most were concentrated in New England, New York and a few midwestern states. Being somewhat more conservative than the academies, they had less appeal for practical reasons. Yet being, for the most part, elements of the public school system, they offered youths unable to afford the private academies an opportunity to continue their formal education and perhaps go on to college. The overwhelming majority of college entrants, however, came from the academies.

Colleges and universities also showed a phenomenal expansion during this period. One hundred and eighty-two permanent colleges were founded before the Civil War, and to these must be added dozens which did not last more than a few years. As with the academy, the level of the colleges varied tremendously. Yet, for the most part, they were small institutions offering highly specialized classical curricula. They catered largely to a small group in society and prepared students for a narrow range of professions and occupations. For the vast majority of the American people their program was a foreign, cryptic mystery in which they had little interest.

Nonschool agencies of education in the lives of youths and adults. If higher institutions of formal education still touched the lives of comparatively few Americans before the Civil War, this was far from the case with organized nonschool education. Efforts for the education of youths and adults outside of the regular school and university systems made great gains in early nineteenth-century America. The spread of knowledge among all classes of the population was promoted by innumerable philanthropic and humanitarian agencies as well as by some commercial ventures. The average citizen increasingly had the educational opportunities afforded by mechanics' institutes, workingmen's and merchant's libraries, and lectures for industrial and commercial workers, and as the idea that knowledge gave power gained acceptance, he took advantage of these opportunities.

The Boston Apprentices' Library was formed in 1820, and the idea soon spread to most cities in the country. By 1829 the New York Apprentices' Library had 10,000 volumes, and by the middle of the century it was serving some three quarters of a million people, most of them from the working class. The Boston Mechanics' Institute was founded in 1826 and the Society for the Diffusion of Useful Knowledge in 1829. "Mercantile libraries" for young clerical and commercial workers also became very popular after the 1820's. Many of these organizations sponsored lectures, discussions, debates, and public events of various kinds. Employers and philanthropically minded members of the wealthier classes promoted adult education in such forms as the Lowell Institute in Boston, Massachusetts (1836) and Cooper Union in New York City (1859).

On a larger scale and serving rural and urban communities alike was the lyceum movement. First organized by Josiah Holbrook in Massachusetts in 1826, the lyceum sponsored lectures, public discussion, forums, and reading matter on a vast range of social and scientific subjects. It is interesting to note that public education was itself one of the most oft discussed matters. Beginning as local discussion groups, the lyceums began to command the services of some of the best speakers of the day. By 1830 some 3,000 American communities boasted lyceums. Doubtless, their influence on many persons —young and old alike—was profound.

The growing thirst for knowledge of the American public also expressed itself in other ways. Paralleling the development of public schools was the growth of public libraries. Free public libraries appeared in Boston and other New England towns, and in 1849 New Hampshire passed the first law authorizing publicly supported libraries on a state-wide basis. Improvements in printing techniques made possible all kinds of easily available published materials. The penny newspaper of the 1830's and thereafter brought news to the American home, and cheaply priced books, of varying quality, flowed into the market.

What is important to note here is the increasing scope of organized education in the community which went on outside the school. To be sure, there was infinitely more of such opportunity in the cities than in the more sparsely populated rural areas. Yet more and more, the man or woman who wanted education could get it through these agencies. While not under the control of school authorities, such education undoubtedly played a growing part in shaping the attitudes and outlooks of many American citizens.

THE ORGANIZATION, SUPPORT, AND CONTROL OF EDUCATION

The years between 1779 and 1865 mark the era when the great state school systems of contemporary America took form. In 1779, except perhaps for New England, there was little to foreshadow this phenomenal development. What schools did exist were usually local institutions designed to meet the specific needs of small segments of the community. They still served largely to prepare children for religious orthodoxy, and much of their curriculum was removed from the ordinary, everyday life of the people. Furthermore, they still reflected and perpetuated the great class divisions of Europe, with the vernacular elementary school tending to confine itself to the lower classes, while the Latin secondary school served the upper classes.

Now, in the space of a few decades, some states managed to place a common school within walking distance of almost all their children. Others erected public secondary schools, colleges, and universities for the general education of the people. Everywhere, the "friends of education" pressed their demands; nowhere did they produce results without a struggle. Year after year the great debates over who should pay for schools, who should control schools, and what should be taught in schools echoed through the state legislatures. Communities divided and elections were fought and won on school issues. Often there was rancor, ill-feeling, and bitterness. Yet, almost as if in inexorable response to their changing way of life, Americans during these years forged one of the most revolutionary educational developments of modern times—their public school system.

The Growth of the Common School

The men who fought for common schools. Probably the most significant aspect of the emerging public school system was the public elementary—or common—school. To secure common schools was an unceasing struggle which depended heavily on the leadership of key figures in the various states of the Union. Without these leaders, it is doubtful that the new educational demands for universal schooling would have been realized as quickly as they were. In New England James G. Carter and Horace Mann in Massachusetts and Henry Barnard in Connecticut stand out as giants of the educational scene. In the South such men as Calvin Wiley of North Carolina and Charles Fenton Mercer of Virginia are distinguished for their effort; while the West boasted a host of figures—Caleb Mills in Indiana, Calvin Stowe, Samuel Lewis, and Samuel Galloway in Ohio, Ninian Edwards in Illinois, John D. Pierce and Isaac Crary in Michigan, Robert Breckinridge in Kentucky, and John Swett in California. These men, in combination with friendly public figures and middle-class groups in every state, pointed the way for educational reform. Generally, they employed three means of pressing their demands.

First, these leaders worked through groups and organizations. Among the better known of these were the American Lyceum, the Pennsylvania Society for the Promotion of Public Schools, the Western Literary Institute and College for Professional Teachers, and the American Institute of Instruction. These organizations were only the principal ones. There were literally hundreds of lesser associations of teachers, reformers, and educational enthusiasts. They held innumerable conventions in the several states and generally carried on at a local level the work of the larger bodies.

Second, these leaders, singly and through their organizations, worked through the press. At least two dozen educational journals had been instituted by the year 1840, although few survived more than several issues. The principal periodicals which enjoyed more extended life were the *American Journal of Education* and its successor, the *American Annals of Education;* the *Common School Assistant;* the *Connecticut Common School Journal;* and the *Common School Journal.* These periodicals published materials concerning every aspect of public education and vigorously campaigned for educational improvements of every kind. Moreover, in addition to this regular periodical literature, there were thousands of reports, lectures, pamphlets, brochures, memorials, and petitions. In all, they provided an extensive body of literature to sound the views of the educational leadership of the period.

A third, and perhaps the most powerful, means by which these leaders exerted their influence was through actual positions in state governments or school systems. In this way they were able to serve the double purpose of helping to crystallize public opinion to the point of action, and then shaping the course of that action by administering it. Thus, Horace Mann as secretary of the Massachusetts Board of Education, Henry Barnard as chairman of a similar board of Connecticut, Calvin Wiley as state superintendent in North Carolina, and Samuel Lewis as state superintendent in Ohio, were all influential in their capacity as early makers of educational policy and practice.

European influences. The fact that many of the ideas set forth by the educational reformers had previously been enunciated in Europe has already been pointed out. One is able to trace with very little difficulty, for example, important educational influences from France to the United States, and from the latter back to France again. Jefferson and Franklin both showed profound French influence in their educational thinking, while the ideas developed by Du Pont de Nemours at the behest of Jefferson at the end of the eighteenth century reflected similar influence. As a matter of fact, the whole conception of centralized state systems of education had important origins in French thinking, and the comprehensive educational system established in New York State at the turn of the nineteenth century was directly and profoundly influenced by French ideas. The heritage of universal state education for national ends, of centralized state control and administration, of freedom of thought, and of secular learning was the very heart of this French influence.

France was not the only European nation which exerted such influence on American education during this period. In Prussia, where the notion of universal elementary education dated back to the middle of the eighteenth century, Americans found many stimulating ideas and examples to follow. Prussian methods of organization, administration, and teaching excited profound interest among such educators as Horace Mann, Henry Barnard, Samuel Lewis, and they were the subject of wide discussion after 1825.

The fact that there were European influences on American schools during this formative period in no way implies that America did not develop an indigenous system. On the other hand, to view the picture without these influences ignores an important aspect of the story.

The struggle to secure public support for common schools. One of the most bitter struggles in securing public common schools was the struggle for public support. It was one thing for the "friends of education" to argue logically that common schools could never be truly available to all unless they were free and publicly supported; it was another thing for them to obtain the support. The tradition of schooling as a luxury which a man purchased for his children according to his means was extremely powerful. Those who held property were not particularly interested in being taxed to maintain schools except perhaps as a gesture of Christian charity for poor and indigent children. Even here there was opposition. This was a highly charged issue in this period of intense individualism and weak government; and it was an issue on which much of the public school controversy stood.

A number of things rather quickly become clear on studying this struggle for public support. *First,* there were different rates of progress toward this goal in different states and sections of the country. Generally, New England, with its colonial traditions of publicly supported schools, moved rapidly toward compulsory public support. The middle states, having displayed less interest in education during the colonial period, moved toward public support somewhat more slowly and grudgingly. The western states received tremendous initial impetus from federal grants for schools; yet their movement toward public support seemed dependent to great extent on the traditions which their settlers brought with them. Finally, in spite of herculean and persistent efforts on the part of educational reformers, the South tended to perpetuate older traditions of private and philanthropic support.

Second, there were many different kinds of public support for schools. Taxation, the most controversial form, was only one of these; and this involved both state and local levels. There was income from public lands, a considerable sum in many states. Another widely used source was income from permanent school funds (the revenue of which might accrue from any number of sources—the federal government, fines, license fees, unclaimed estates, certain kinds of taxes, etc.). Finally, many states resorted to public lotteries, the income from which went either to supplement permanent funds or for the direct support of schools.

Third, although these differences stand out very clearly, one is able to note a rather definite general movement toward the adoption of public support for common schools. This movement, as Ellwood Cubberley has clearly pointed out, usually, involved a number of steps. First, education was supported almost entirely by private individuals, churches, and benevolent societies. Then, the state began to aid these efforts with public funds. (In some cities, like New York and Philadelphia, free school societies assumed virtually the entire responsibility for publicly aided education.) Next, the state gave local communities permission to tax for schools, first perhaps schools for the poor only and then schools for all. From here, the next step was usually compulsory legislation requiring certain minimum rates of school taxation. Finally, there was the legislation which made public schools entirely free. By 1865, although different states were obviously at different stages in this movement, enough of a general development had taken place to say that the *principle* of public support for common schools had definitely taken root and that the American people were definitely committed to it. How this struggle was fought and won is one of the fascinating stories of educational history.

Early federal provisions for public support. Among the more important early phases of the struggle was the formulation of a policy of federal aid for schools in the territories and newer states of the Union. It is important not only in understanding the development of school support before 1865, but as material to illuminate the more recent controversies over federal aid.

It would be pleasant to record that the early federal grants for schools grew out of the far-reaching educational vision of leaders in the Continental Congress. This, however, does not seem to have been entirely the case. In fact, the educational policy formulated in the Land Ordinances of 1785 and 1787 was but one aspect of a general, over-all national land policy which had one overbearing purpose—to obtain revenues for a debt-ridden government.

Two principal means for disposing of public lands had been developed in the colonies prior to the Revolution. One, originating in New England, involved the carving of land for sale into townships before it was offered for private purchase. In keeping with New England tradition, grants for the support of religion and education were frequently made as part condition of the township sale. The other system, developing primarily in the South, involved simply the sale of land parcels varying with individual purchases. No grants were made either for schools or for ministers.

When the Continental Congress in 1784 appointed a committee to draft a plan for the sale of public lands, these were the principal alternatives before it. Their deliberations led eventually to the Land Ordinance of 1785, which, although it represented a compromise, carried a provision reserving the sixteenth section of every township (each township was divided into thirty-six equal parcels one mile square called *sections*) "for the maintenance of public schools within the said township." The advantage of such a provision is clear in that public money for schools would make purchase and settlement more attractive to men with families. In any case, when Congress two years later was faced with the problem of establishing a government in the Northwest Territory (an area represented by the present states of Ohio, Indiana, Illinois, Michigan, Wisconsin, and part of Minnesota), it reinforced and restated this policy in the now-famous Article 3 of the Ordinance of 1787: "Religion, morality, and knowledge, being necessary to good government and the happiness of mankind, schools and the means of education shall forever be encouraged."

Although grants under these two ordinances amounted to millions of acres, the federal government extended its liberal policy even further after 1800 by earmarking for educational purposes certain lands in almost every new state. In many sections of the country valuable oil and mineral deposits have since been discovered on these lands, and they have often proved to be lucrative sources of school income.

The above-mentioned grants do not by any means exhaust the story of federal beneficence during this period. Considerable income came from so-called "5-percent funds," which were agreements under which the federal government gave states 5 percent of the proceeds from the sale of public lands within their boundaries if they agreed not to tax federal property. Other school income came from salt lands and swamp lands given to the states for improvement and sale. Finally, the Surplus Revenue Deposit Act of 1836 distributed a surplus of $28 million in federal funds to state governments, and many of the latter devoted the funds to school purposes.

The struggle for public support in New England. As in the earlier colonial period, Massachusetts maintained her educational leadership in the New England area. A considerable body of school legislation had been enacted since the first laws of 1642 and 1647, and the year 1789 witnessed a codification into one law of those practices which had become standard in the century and a half since that time. By its provisions, towns having fifty or more families were required to furnish six months of schooling (distributed among one or more schools) during the course of the year; and towns which had grown to 200 families were also required to support a grammar school. One of the novel principles it also recognized was the school district form of organization, reflecting the decentralization which had come with continued settlement of the rural areas. By granting to the towns the power to create school districts, the law paved the way for the assignment of the tax prerogative to the districts eleven years later. Generally, the law of 1789 stands as evidence that the principle of tax support for schools had been clearly enunciated in Massachusetts before the turn of the century.

Yet the simple presence of the law on the statute books in no way indicated universal assent on the part of the people. Strong opposition to school taxation was forthcoming, especially from the rural population and the upper classes, on the grounds that taxation for education was a deprivation of personal property without just cause. This opposition, nurtured by considerable apathy on the part of many farmers who saw no practical use in "booklarnin," led to a gradual lowering of the quality of public education—to the point where public schools were often deserted by almost everyone who could afford private education. With little state control, local districts managed schools in the interests of local economy, and in doing so they often ignored even the barest standards of instruction. These were the conditions which in the 1820's drew the first sharp criticism from James G. Carter.

Carter, a young Harvard graduate and teacher, published a number of newspaper articles and pamphlets calling attention to the great foresight of Massachusetts' early settlers in founding free schools. Interestingly enough, he ascribed the founding of these early schools to the desire for freedom and equality for all men rather than to the need to perpetuate religious orthodoxy. In any case, he urged that only as more adequate public support be given could this great tradition of free schools be maintained. His arguments were most effective, and in 1827 for the first time in the state's history the legislature made the entire support of schools by taxation compulsory. This pattern of public support was strengthened even further in 1834 with the establishment of a permanent common school fund, the interest of which was also to apply to the maintenance of common schools.

Connecticut's history of school support is somewhat different and worthy of note. It will be recalled that Connecticut's early school legislation strongly resembled that of Massachusetts. At the beginning of the national period, however, instead of following this pattern, Connecticut bolstered its common school fund with a huge grant from the sale of public lands in 1795. Interest from this fund was distributed to districts and towns throughout the state, and legislation soon after permitted communities to maintain schools only as long as these state funds held out. As more and more money was realized from the state fund, ever smaller amounts were raised by local taxation. Finally, in 1821 the state tax was discontinued, and for the next thirty-three years, Connecticut's public schools were supported almost entirely by income from the fund.

Educational conditions under this arrangement were deplorable. At best, schools were maintained for two or three months annually; meager salaries were paid to teachers; and the general quality of educational equipment was extremely low. Under the leadership of men like Thomas Gallaudet and Henry Barnard continuing efforts were made to reinstitute local taxation and to use the interest from the state fund merely to stimulate and supplement local effort. Their efforts, however, met with strong resistance from rural and propertied groups who were vehemently opposed to any form of taxation— especially to school taxation. Not until 1854 did school taxation reappear, and even this legislation did not make the schools entirely free. Small tuition payments made by the students, called *rate bills,* were not finally abolished until 1868.

Of the other New England states, Maine, which had long been part of Massachusetts, and New Hampshire had moved well along toward complete tax support by 1789. Both, however, continued the practice of rate bills into the nineteenth century. Rhode Island, which interestingly enough was the last of the original thirteen states to modify its colonial suffrage policy, did not pass comprehensive school legislation until 1845, and it too continued the practice of rate bills throughout the antebellum period. In general, however, New England had clearly accepted the principle of public support by the time of the Civil War. It remained only to eliminate imperfections in the system of given localities.

The struggle for public support in the middle states. The task of the New England states in securing public support was essentially to strengthen and perfect long traditions stemming directly from the colonial period. In the middle states the job was much more one of changing the traditional pattern of private and philanthropic support into one of public support. The movement was often slow and discouraging. Yet, by the Civil War these states too had largely enunciated the principle of tax support for common schools.

The story in New York is interesting because in the quarter century between 1795 and 1820, she moved from a practically nonexistent school system to one which strongly rivaled that of Massachusetts. Prior to 1795, the pattern of educational support was mostly private, with sporadic attempts by churches and associations here and there to educate small groups of the poor. In the years following the Revolution influences from New Englanders who had settled in the state as well as French influences militated strongly in the direction of a public school system. In response to these demands the legislature in 1784 created the University of the State of New York as a comprehensive body for building a unified school system from the elementary school to the university.

Traditional indifference, the impoverishment caused by the Revolution, and opposition to school taxation combined strongly to block early moves for public schools. A law offering state aid to districts who supported schools through their own efforts was finally secured in 1795, but it was neither adequate nor lasting, expiring five years after passage. The first years of the nineteenth century saw continuing agitation for public schools. Governors' messages, statements of the Board of Regents of the university, pamphlets, and resolutions urged the adoption and extension of principles which had been enunciated in the law of 1795. A partial victory was secured in the establishment in 1805 of a permanent school fund, but the interest from this fund lay unused pending further legislation. Finally, in 1812 a comprehensive school law was enacted providing for an apportionment of interest from the state fund to those districts who raised equal sums by local effort. Districts were also responsible for taxing themselves for the maintenance and repair of a school site and building. Thus, a pattern of support developed where the state subsidized what was principally a local effort to maintain schools.

The law of 1812 was an important victory; yet it too proved increasingly inadequate during the next few decades. A principal shortcoming lay in the fact that the legislature in 1814 had approved the practice of meeting school deficits with rate bill assessments on parents. Although the law had provided that parents unable to defray such expenses might be excused, the taint of pauperism which attached to such excusal prevented many from taking advantage of the provision. Thus, strong efforts to extend the public school system and make it entirely free were continued. A major encounter took place in the constitutional convention of 1846, where the forces favoring free schools attempted to insert a provision requiring the legislature to provide free education for all children between four and sixteen. The proposal, however, failed to secure approval.

The proschool forces continued their efforts. Petitions, memorials, and resolutions flooded the legislature, and finally, in 1849 an act was passed providing for compulsory school taxation and "free and gratuitious education." Paradoxically enough, this law and one which extended it even further in 1851 still provided that school deficits be made up by rate bills, and it was around the removal of these provisions that the "friends of education" directed their efforts during the next years. Finally, in 1867, New York abolished these assessments and made the common schools entirely free.

A word should also be included concerning Pennsylvania's efforts to establish a public school system, for these efforts illustrate the problems connected with removing the taint of pauperism from the public schools. Through constitutional amendment in 1790 and legislation in 1802, 1805, and 1809, Pennsylvania had limited public support to the education of the poor and indigent. This immediately stigmatized any person who took advantage of public schools as one unable to provide for himself and his family. That such legislation did not meet the demands or spirit of education in a republic was quickly realized by governors throughout this period. After 1825 there was growing pressure from workingmen's organizations in the cities, from the Pennsylvania Society for the Promotion of Public Schools, and from other organizations. The establishment of a permanent school fund in the 1830-1831 legislature was a partial victory; the major victory came in 1834 in the form of an act to establish a general system of education. Following the principle of New York, interest from the state fund was to be distributed to districts which raised twice the sum received by local effort. The law was definitely permissive, allowing districts to use these procedures or to continue under the older provisions at will.

The victory of the proschool groups was a perilous one, however, for in the following year there were concerted attempts to repeal the law of 1834. Three groups were primarily responsible for this opposition: the property owners who refused to be taxed for public schools; certain religious groups— the Friends, the Lutherans, the Mennonites, and others—who, although they favored education, preferred to educate their children in their own parochial schools; and the German-speaking residents of the state who preferred to educate their children in the language and customs of their native land. While this group was strongly represented by petitions and memorials, and while it had powerful influence in the legislature, the cause of free schools was saved by an empassioned speech by Thaddeus Stevens, a New Englander who had come to Pennsylvania in 1815. The bill which eventually emerged not only reaffirmed the law of 1834 but strengthened and streamlined its operation and administration. By 1837, 742 out of 987 districts had voluntarily accepted the pattern of tax support, and by the time the state established a universal system of public schools in 1868 the pauper stigma no longer generally attached to these facilities.

Others of the middle states achieved varying degrees of success in their efforts to secure public support. New Jersey had a highly vocal reform group, but there was considerable apathy in the state. A public school system was set up in 1838, but public schools were not entirely free until 1871. Delaware and Maryland, on the other hand, continued the older pattern, and did not secure public school systems before the Civil War.

The struggle for public support in the South. In thinking of the antebellum South as a distinctive region, many persons neglect the fact that it was nevertheless affected by many of the same influences as other parts of the country. The educational revival of the early nineteenth century was not an exception, and its effects may be seen throughout the southern states. Yet the fact remains that by and large, except perhaps for North Carolina, the South only moved partially in the direction of public support for schools. Social, political, and economic conditions in this region tended to favor the continuation of traditional patterns, and although considerable progress was made, the South failed to establish public education systems until after the Civil War.

In general, Virginia's attempts to secure public support exemplify more or less what happened in most of the southern states. Steeped in the English tradition of private and philanthropic support, the state had rejected the broad, humanitarian proposals of Jefferson's education bill. The individualist, laissez-faire tradition was far too strong to secure widespread acceptance of such a bill by those who would have to bear the burden of support. In spite of this, however, there was considerable discussion of the education question in the General Assembly during the first years of the nineteenth century. An important step was taken in 1810 when legislation establishing a Literary Fund was passed. Yet when the next legislature directed the distribution of interest from this fund a year later, it reserved it entirely to the education of the poor.

During the next two decades the struggle for public schools figured increasingly as part of a broader struggle between two major factions in the state. On the one hand there were the eastern property owners. They greatly feared the power of the newly enfranchised groups of small farmers in the West and saw in any extension of public education an invasion of their own rights. On the other hand, there were the western farmers who saw in education the extension of the rights and freedoms which had been guaranteed them in the constitution. A major school law was passed in 1829 in response to these demands, but it was a permissive law which allowed any district to use its portion of the Literary Fund to establish a free school. Except for scattered communities, however, local interests were not willing to levy taxes for education. The sparsity of population in the rural areas made the law even less workable, and even the western sections of the state which had sponsored it failed to avail themselves of its provisions.

Following 1829, Virginia definitely felt the nation-wide agitation for common schools. Education conventions met in many portions of the state, and periodicals threw open their columns to educational debate. Governors requested the legislature to act. However, the only action that was secured took the form of three permissive school acts passed in 1846—legislation which would establish free schools only in districts which voted to support them. These acts represent Virginia's last major attempt before the Civil War to

push through a system involving tax support for education. The unenthu-
siastic response to the permissive clauses clearly demonstrated the continuing
ascendancy of traditional patterns in the state. A "Greek Democracy" could
well afford to leave education to the private efforts of its citizens and provide
publicly, in a spirit of Christian philanthropy, for its poor.

The rapid progress in North Carolina after 1840 deserves brief mention
at this point. When the federal government distributed its surplus revenue by
the act of 1836, the "friends of education" in North Carolina received un-
expected assistance, for most of the state's share of almost $1,500,000 was ear-
marked for educational purposes. The increased interest generated by this
event led to the passage of a comprehensive public school law in 1839. It was
a permissive act which provided that counties choosing to accept its stipulations would receive a share of income from the Literary Fund as soon as they
had built a school to accommodate fifty children and raised half the amount
of their share by local taxation. In 1843 another law was written streamlining
the administrative provisions of the earlier act, and by 1846 every county in
the state had voted to participate in the school program.

In the first years of this new program there were tremendous obstacles to
overcome. Local authorities were lax in their duties regarding taxation; there
was a scarcity of teachers; and the pauper stigma was attached to the public
schools. It was really in the 1850's that the system began to operate with any
success, and this was due largely to the work of a tireless lawyer, editor,
statesman, and educator: Calvin Wiley. Under his superintendency, created
in 1852, North Carolina's schools grew and thrived until in 1861 the state had
some 4,000 public elementary schools serving some 160,000 pupils. It was at
this point that the Civil War literally destroyed North Carolina's schools. ·

In general, the Virginia pattern tended to characterize most of the southern
states. All except South Carolina had established permanent funds by the
time of the Civil War, but most of them continued the practice of supporting
with public funds only the education of the poor. South Carolina's law of
1811, improved slightly in 1835, was based on this principle as was the Georgia
legislation of 1783 and 1822. Laws in Tennessee, Louisiana, Mississippi, Alabama, Arkansas, Florida, and Texas also tended strongly in this direction. In
the last analysis the forces resisting taxation and conceiving of education as
private and philanthropic in nature had successfully opposed the movement
toward common schools.

The struggle for public support in the western states. Two factors seem to
have exercised great educational influence in the newer western states. The
first was the policy of federal aid enunciated in the Land Ordinances of 1785
and 1787 and in the various enabling acts admitting states to the Union. The
second was the traditions which the settlers entering these new states brought
from the societies they left. A brief survey of efforts to secure public support
in Ohio will illustrate how these factors operated in one western state.

Ohio entered the Union in 1803 having come under the provisions of the Northwest Ordinance and with an enabling act ceding the sixteenth section of every township to the support of education. With respect to the cultural background of its settlers, Ohio was provided with two distinct traditions. The northern section of the state was called the Connecticut Reserve and was settled largely by New Englanders. The southern portions, on the other hand, were populated by people from the middle and southern states, Pennsylvania, New Jersey, Delaware, and Virginia. The New Englanders brought with them their traditions of public schools supported by taxation. The immigrants from the middle and upper southern states likewise brought their traditions of private schools and public schools for the poor and indigent. Obviously, these two elements were destined to come sharply into conflict.

A number of factors in frontier life supported one or the other of these conflicting traditions. The rigors of frontier existence, the comparative sparsity of population, and the general disdain for knowledge in a region seeking to throw off all marks of rank and privilege tended to support the forces opposing public schools. On the other hand, the vigorous democracy of the frontier had little use for a system of pauper education to set one class of individuals off from another. Thus, the first Ohio constitution proclaimed that the doors of "schools, academies, and universities shall be open for the reception of scholars, students, and teachers of every grade, without any distinction of preference whatever. . . ."

School legislation during the first two decades of Ohio's statehood dealt mostly with the administration of school lands. In 1821, however, largely through the efforts of four New Englanders in the legislature, a general school law making taxation permissive was passed. Yet the very fact that this was a permissive law caused the "friends of education" to intensify their efforts. Four years later, taxation for education was made compulsory. Although the tax varied from year to year depending on which group had ascendancy in the legislature, it was continued from that time forward. As in New York, a rate-bill system persisted even after compulsory taxation was enacted. Samuel Lewis, as state superintendent of schools from 1837 to 1839, fought tirelessly against these assessments, and they were finally removed when legislation in 1853 made the schools entirely free to the children of the commonwealth.

Depending on the interaction of the factors mentioned above, other western states moved with greater or less rapidity toward the goal of complete public support. Wisconsin provided for free public schools in her first state constitution of 1848. Indiana made her public schools entirely free in 1852, Illinois in 1855, Iowa in 1858, and Michigan in 1869. By the time of the Civil War the common school in these western states had come remarkably close to the ideal enunciated by the reformers—of a school open to all and used by the children of the whole community.

The struggle to secure public control for common schools. The heart of the fight for public control of common schools during this period was really the effort to transfer the schools from the jurisdiction of religious authorities to that of public civil authorities. Two equally important phases of this struggle stand out as central. First, there was the necessity of strengthening the agencies and machinery of public control so that effective schools might be secured. Second, there was the matter of releasing the hold of private and sectarian groups on schools which were to serve and be supported by the public. The latter involved not only replacing private with public control in publicly supported facilities, but it also entailed the withdrawal of public support from institutions which were to continue under private control.

The growth of effective means of local control. Much has already been said about the educational legislation passed by the colonies and states up to the nineteenth century. Unless the results of this legislation are viewed within the context of the life conditions of the time, however, a distorted picture of the educational situation is apt to ensue. In the decentralized rural neighborhoods which made up most of late eighteenth- and early nineteenth-century America, the power of the state could be and was kept relatively distant. Had it not been largely the will of the American people to establish schools, it is doubtful that they would have been established. On the other hand, the phenomenal growth of schools in this period is ample testimony that it was the will of the people to do so. It is this fact that is referred to when the growth of the common school is called a *grass-roots* movement. Tax laws and court records can easily obscure the true picture of a local community setting out to build a school with their own hands, then sharing the cost of employing a teacher for their children, and then supervising the course of this education. Yet this was the true picture of the growth of the common school.

Developments in Massachusetts beginning with and following the comprehensive law of 1789 furnish an excellent description of patterns which eventually came to characterize the American system of school control. The fact that this law included the first legal recognition of the school district has already been mentioned. This recognition merely took account in law of a movement which had been going on ever since the beginning of the eighteenth century when the population had begun to move in large numbers out over the countryside. Inasmuch as their needs could no longer be met by one centrally located town school, some means had to be devised to establish and maintain several schools in the different sections of the township. District schools became the means of satisfying these needs. Second, and equally important, the law gave legal recognition to the town school committee as an agency for controlling and supervising schools. The central tasks of this committee were the two continuing problems of hiring teachers and visiting schools.

Regarding local districts, the permissive provisions of the law of 1789 encouraged most towns which had not previously created them to do so. In 1800 districts were given not only the power to tax, but also to hold meetings, choose clerks, and raise money for school houses and their maintenance. By 1827 their role had expanded to the point where legislation was passed requiring districts to choose a prudential committeeman whose duties would entail the care of school property of his district as well as the selection and employment of a teacher. A significant limitation on the latter function was that the district could employ only teachers who were certified by the town school committee.

It is clear that during the first two decades of the nineteenth century control of common schools passed in large measure into the hands of these local districts. This development brought with it all the strength that resides in direct interest in and control of schools by groups of parents. But it carried with it a number of evils. Inevitably, there was considerable inequality between richer and poorer, or between more and less interested localities. In many districts apathy and extreme resistance to taxation quickly established economy as the chief goal of school policy, and the resultant degeneration of school standards was immediately evident. Here was posed one of the continuing problems of educational control and supervision: the problem of centralization versus decentralization. Essentially, the question was one of how much autonomy to give local communities, of how much power to give larger units of government.

When James G. Carter inveighed against declining standards and educational inequalities in the 1820's, it was largely the evils of this district system that he was attacking. A direct result of his criticisms was the strengthening of town machinery for controlling education, an act accomplished by the law of 1826. By its provisions every town was required to choose annually "a School Committee, consisting of not less than five persons, who shall have the general charge and superintendence of all the public schools in said town. . . ." This committee was charged with the supervision and management of schools by visitation and with the certifying of all public school teachers. Of great interest was the fact that these committees were to be composed of lay citizens rather than either churchmen or professional teachers. Of course, either might serve if elected but only in their capacity as citizens, not as professionals. Moreover, it is important to note that these committees, although related to the town machinery of government, were separate from the agencies charged with the political management of the town. Thus, the tradition was established of separate agencies for control of the schools.

In general, both the New England and the newer western states tended to follow the Massachusetts pattern of town and district supervision and control. In New England the trend toward strengthening the town's powers in order to rectify some of the abuses of the district system was clearly evident. Connecticut in 1856 transferred the powers of local school societies (districts) to town authorities. Vermont, after a brief experience with town committees between 1827 and 1833, established a permanent system of town authorities in 1854; while Maine tended generally to increase the power of town committees from 1821 forward. In the West federal land grants to townships for educational purposes made these communities the logical agencies for control. On the other hand, the decentralized neighborhood settlements made districting extremely necessary. Therefore, the Massachusetts pattern served the West extremely well.

In the southern states where the county had traditionally been the unit of local government, it was logically adopted as the unit of school control. In some of these states counties, as with townships in the northern states, were divided into districts. With the failure of this region to achieve tax support for schools, however, county boards of education remained largely paper organizations with few responsibilities or duties. In the middle states practices varied. Pennsylvania, which before the act of 1834 had used the county system, by that law made each borough, ward, and township in the state a school district with a school committee. New York used the township-district system until the 1830's, when the county board of supervisors and superintendent of schools began to play an increasing role in school affairs. New Jersey tended to follow the pattern of Pennsylvania; while Delaware followed the county pattern of the South. Maryland, while tending toward the county system, accomplished little in the way of school organization before the Civil War.

The assertion and growth of state control. The problem of centralization versus decentralization in school administration was by no means solved by strengthening town as opposed to district control. There were many problems of equalizing educational opportunity which in the eyes of the educational reformers could only be dealt with on the state level. It is true that school legislation from the earliest years had been the province of colonial legislatures. Moreover, the tenth amendment to the federal constitution reserved education to the states inasmuch as education is not mentioned in that document. Much of this power, however, had passed into the hands of local authorities by the beginning of the nineteenth century, and hence one of the great battles of this period was the one in which the state tried to regain this power and authority in the interest of raising standards and equalizing opportunity. Two patterns of strengthening state educational authority appear during the antebellum period, and both come down to the present. One was the state superintendency of education; the other was the state board of education.

New York, under French influence, was the first state really to concern itself with the development of a centralized and unitary school organization. Moreover, New York was also the first state to create the office of superintendent of common schools. His duties, according to the law of 1812, involved the preparation of plans for improving the common school system, the reporting and superintendence of school monies, and the providing of information concerning the schools to the legislature. In the succeeding two decades a few states followed the leadership of New York and created similar offices; but between 1830 and 1850, when every northern state and some of the southern states created similar offices, the practice really took root. Some were merely ex-officio superintendencies—that is, some state official had certain school responsibilities added on to his other duties. Others followed the original New York pattern and created a separate office for a separate incumbent. Still others were secretaries of state boards of education (see below). Generally, the duties of these superintendents closely approximated those of the original one in New York. As the office grew in stature, and as states moved increasingly from ex-officio superintendencies to separate superintendencies, visitation and advisement in local areas were added.

Early boards of education, though perhaps conceived of in broader terms than some of the superintendencies, had much the same function. Once again, as has already been cited, New York had the honor of creating the first such body when the Board of Regents of the University of the State of New York was established in 1784. Although the original legislation, and the law reorganizing this board in 1787, had assigned the regents broad educational responsibilities at all levels, they chose to concern themselves primarily with higher education. Virginia, South Carolina, Vermont, and Missouri created state educational boards in the next fifty years, but it was not until the historic battle over the establishment of the Massachusetts Board of Education in 1837 that the pattern really spread.

Massachusetts had created in 1837 an eight-man board whose principal functions were those of enlightenment through abstracts of school statistics collected from localities and annual reports to the legislature. The law also empowered the board to select and appoint a secretary whose principal duties also involved the collection and diffusion of school information. Though many expected Carter to be selected as the first secretary, Horace Mann was chosen for the post in June 1837.

For twelve years Mann worked tirelessly in the interest of Massachusetts' public schools. In his attempts to carry out his responsibilities, he resorted generally to four agencies: public meetings, county institutes of teachers, annual reports to the legislature, and a biweekly publication he edited called the *Common School Journal*. Through these four media he hoped to reach the groups on which the quality of education would largely depend—the public, the school committees, and the teachers. His success in all of these activities was outstanding. His work with county institutes of teachers, and later in the field of teacher education, set a pattern which spread rapidly to other states. His twelve annual reports to the Massachusetts legislature stand as magnificent testimony to the scope of his vision, efforts, and interests in education.

And the *Common School Journal* was among the most—if not the most—stimulating and creative of the early educational periodicals.

Both the board and Mann, however, were not without adversaries—political, economic, religious, and professional. Serious opposition, for example, was forthcoming from some of the more conservative groups in the legislature and from those who strongly believed in unrestricted local control. The bitter attacks of Reverends E. A. Newton and Matthew Hale Smith, as well as of the Boston schoolmasters, on the religious and educational ideas of Mann and the board have already been discussed. Yet when Horace Mann resigned his secretaryship in 1848 (in order to take the Congressional seat of the late John Quincy Adams), the board had become an established institution in the life of Massachusetts. In slightly more than a decade the agency had vindicated itself in the eyes of the people. Functioning within the bounds of a loosely construed grant of authority, it had served to reassert the educational role of the state. Although by 1865 this power remained principally in the form of powers delegated to towns and districts, the ultimate control of the state and the state's duty to supervise the efficiency and quality of its schools had been enunciated.

The effects of this reassertion of state authority in Massachusetts were by no means confined to that state. They stimulated similar lines of development throughout the North and Northwest. Connecticut created a similar body in 1839, and the work of Henry Barnard as its secretary achieved much the same stature as that of Mann. Yet Connecticut's board succumbed in 1842 to many of the same pressures which had opposed the Massachusetts board, and it was not until 1865 that the board was recreated. Meanwhile in the two decades following 1837 Kentucky, Arkansas, Ohio, and Indiana instituted state boards of education, thereby clearly establishing the state board as a means of asserting state authority in education.

The struggle to remove sectarian control from publicly supported schools. If Americans had not proclaimed the ideals of separation of church and state and of a common school attended by children of all groups, the pattern of a state-controlled common school system might never have taken root. The European practice of dividing public school funds among the various religious groups according to the number of children they educated might have been adopted as a means of providing universal education. Then, as in many European countries, Americans might have had several public school systems. The great division of community loyalties which nineteenth-century Americans saw implicit in such an arrangement, however, precluded its development.

Perhaps the cities, more than other communities, witnessed the greatest struggles to prevent such a division of public school funds. In both Philadelphia and New York, for example, benevolent associations and philanthropic societies as well as religious groups had early turned their attention to educating the poor. Because of the great variety of religious and national groups in such cities, public funds were used to stimulate the work of a number of these societies rather than any one—thus establishing the pattern of a divided school fund. The New York State Act of 1795, for instance, provided that school funds in New York City might be used "for the encouragement and maintenance of the several charity schools as of all other schools." The year 1805 saw the organization in that city of a Free School Society composed of public-spirited citizens interested in securing schooling for poor children. Eight years later the state provided that New York City's share of the common school fund should be paid to the Free School Society, three other existing benevolent associations, and "such incorporated religious societies in said city as now support or hereafter shall support charity schools within the said city who may apply for the same."

The next twenty-five years were a record of continued strife between the Free School Society which, becoming the Public School Society in 1826, gradually took over the task of public education in the city, and various denominational groups. The climax of these controversies came in 1840. In that year, encouraged by the governor's inaugural address urging that public school facilities be expanded even if under the auspices of churches, the trustees and members of a number of Roman Catholic churches made application to the Common Council for a portion of the school fund. They criticized the schools of the Public School Society for teaching Protestantism and essentially took the position that if this continued, Catholic children could not in good conscience attend. Moreover, they argued that if all religion was dropped from the curriculum, Catholic children could not attend either. Obviously, the Catholic groups were pressing for a publicly supported system of their own. In opposing these demands, the Public School Society, supported by a number of Protestant groups, argued that their schools were nonsectarian, that they would be happy to take steps to remove objectionable material from the curriculum, and that any division of the school fund in the city would wreck the public schools. In January 1841, the council denied the proposals of the Roman Catholics.

Having been defeated in the Common Council, the Catholic group carried the struggle to the state legislature. Petitions and memorials were presented urging that the Public School Society, as a private, nonelective organization, had no right to control and supervise the city's public schools. The question rapidly became a state-wide issue, and the whole state election of 1841 was fought around the school question. The Catholic group even went so far as to organize a political faction which gave endorsement to several candidates of the major parties and then nominated several candidates of its own. When the new legislature was seated and turned its attention to the school question, the Catholics achieved one of their aims. In 1842 legislation was passed creating a board of education to control and manage the city's schools and placed the schools of the Public School Society under its jurisdiction. Section 14 of this law distinctly provided that no school "in which any religious sectarian doctrine or tenet shall be taught, inculcated, or practised," could receive a share of the public fund. Although the society's schools continued to exist under this arrangement, the die had been cast, and in 1853 title to these institutions passed to the board.

In spite of their victory in securing a public board, evidences of Catholic dissatisfaction with public facilities persisted. They continued to find in many of the public school texts passages which they felt derogatory to their faith. Even more fundamental, their desire for a curriculum impregnated throughout with Catholic religious teaching had not been fulfilled. Thus, it was probably the results of the controversy of 1840 that gave them the final impetus to go ahead wholeheartedly with the building of their parochial school system.

The struggle in New York well illustrates the twofold problem involved in bringing public control to public schools. First, public funds had to be withheld from schools under private or religious control. This was accomplished in New York by the denial of funds to the various church groups which applied for them. The other problem, however, was that of making the bodies which did control the public schools responsible to the public. To be sure, the Public School Society was far from a private body. On its board of trustees were many of the leading citizens and officials of the city. On the other hand, it was not a representative, public body; therefore, the law of 1842 creating such a body for the city was definitely a concluding step in the struggle to remove private control from public school facilities.

New York's experience was duplicated in dozens of communities and states throughout the Union during the three or four decades after 1830. In Massachusetts continued demands by the Roman Catholics and Episcopalians for public support of parochial schools led eventually to the passing in 1855 of a constitutional amendment prohibiting this practice. In the middle and middle western states not only Catholics and Episcopalians, but also German Lutherans were active in demands for division of public school funds. In isolated cases arrangements were made for public support of parochial schools. In general, however, the movement was definitely in the direction of halting such practices, and they were stopped in principle, either by legislation or by constitutional amendment, in a majority of the states in the decades immediately before and after the Civil War.

The Growth of Academies and High Schools

The academy as a transitional institution. The academy which Franklin had founded in Philadelphia marked the beginning of a significant new movement in American secondary education. The traditional Latin grammar school, with its rigidly classical, college-preparatory curriculum, had increasingly failed to meet the new needs of an expanding commerce and industry. The result was a growing apathy to the latter institution; and although legislation in Massachusetts required Latin grammar schools in larger towns until 1827, many communities refused to comply. Property owners and businessmen were not willing to support an institution in which they saw little practical value or significance.

This slackening of interest in Latin grammar schools, however, in no way indicated a lack of readiness to support a more functional secondary education. Evidence of this is contained in the rapid growth of the private academy following the Revolution. Edgar Knight, in his study of *Public Education in the South,* reports the founding and incorporation of a number of academies in that region in the years immediately before, during, and following the war. In general, they were founded mostly for religious and private purposes; and many of them later became colleges. In New England the founding of the two Phillips academies at Andover, Massachusetts, and at Exeter, New Hampshire, for all intents and purposes marks the beginning of the academy movement. The former, founded in 1778 under a gift from Samuel and John Phillips, was incorporated in 1780, thereby becoming the first chartered academy in New England. Control of the school was vested in a self-perpetuating board of twelve trustees, who, with their successors, were declared to be visitors and governors of the institution. A majority of the board were to be laymen, but the chief instructor at the school was also designated a member. The school, charging a small tuition fee, was immediately successful. The academy at Exeter, endowed by John Phillips, was incorporated with a similar organization in 1781. Opened two years later, it enjoyed much the same success as its predecessor.

The next seventy years saw a phenomenal increase in the number and the influence of academies until a peak was reached some time around 1850. A survey conducted by an English visitor in 1796 mentioned at least fifty academies by name in the original thirteen states and alluded to many others. Certainly, then, by the beginning of the nineteenth century the academy was a well-established aspect of American education. By 1830 there were close to a thousand incorporated (legally chartered as corporate bodies by one of the states) academies in the United States, and many, many others which had been established and were thriving, but which had never been incorporated. By mid-century the number had multiplied sixfold. A list of the states reporting the greatest number of these schools—New York, Pennsylvania, Massachusetts, Kentucky, Virginia, North Carolina, and Tennessee—shows the true universality of the movement.

The character of the student body in these institutions differed markedly from that of the older grammar schools. First of all, they catered to a broader age group. Because of the wide variation in standards and offerings, some academies offered instruction about on a par with the common schools; others provided serious competition for contemporary colleges. In the former case the academies stood as a dangerous threat of a dual school system, for where the common schools were of low quality, richer families able to afford the tuition rates in academies would send their children to these schools, while poorer children went to the publicly supported common schools. Such an arrangement quickly gave the common schools the stigma of pauperism.

A second difference between the grammar schools and the academies was that while the former had excluded young women, the latter quickly began to cater to them. Some of the earliest academies were coeducational; later on, many were established exclusively for young ladies. The latter type of institution really provided the first higher education for women in the United States, and schools like the Troy Seminary (founded by Emma Willard in 1821), Mount Holyoke Seminary (founded by Mary Lyon in 1836), and Hartford Female Seminary (founded by Catherine Beecher in 1828) established important precedents in this area. During the 1830's and 1840's, especially in the South, the female seminary rapidly became the vogue. As in the case of academies in general, many of these institutions were later reincorporated as liberal arts colleges for women.

Private and public support and control for academies. As has already been suggested, the academy was primarily a privately supported and privately controlled institution. Often, as in the case of the Phillips academies, a bequest became the principal initial source of support. Supplementary funds came from tuition rates paid by the students, and later, perhaps, from further bequests. Control was vested in a lay, self-perpetuating board of trustees. Such was the case with a great majority of the incorporated academies. Unincorporated institutions, on the other hand, could be and were often started by a single individual who controlled policy, did the teaching, and supported himself and the school only by tuition fees. Inasmuch as success or failure in these latter cases depended entirely on the number of students who were attracted and stayed, standards were all too often compromised.

It is not difficult to see how in this period of growing state interest in education, the several states would not be long in showing a definite interest in their academies. Such interest was expressed in two forms: first, by direct grants to individual institutions; and second, by attempts to integrate academies into the state system of education. Evidences of the former type of aid were numerous in both the eighteenth and nineteenth centuries. In 1797, for example, Massachusetts made provision for grants of public land to be used for the support of academies, and this policy was also in evidence somewhat later in Vermont and Maine. In the South direct cash grants from Literary Fund incomes were made to numerous schools.

The outstanding example of the latter type of interest occurred in New York

State, where academies were made the concern of the Board of Regents in the original act of 1785 establishing a unified state system of education. For the next twenty years, however, state support was sporadic; it was not until the income of a permanent Literature Fund founded in 1805 was earmarked for academies that support became general. Public support increased as the Literature Fund was built up and as other monies was designated for academies. By 1860 a total of 170 such schools were reported in existence and enjoying this support.

In most of the instances where academies received public support, the schools remained in private hands. The significance of incorporation cannot be underestimated, for although this mechanism was a form of state recognition (and when given by a board of regents as in New York, a form of state educational recognition), incorporation left policy and visitation in the hands of boards of trustees. While certain statistics and information could usually be required in return for partial support, this requirement was a far cry from direct public control. In this respect, then, the academy did retain its private character.

The beginnings of the public high school. Even though the academy moved a long way toward providing useful and practical secondary education, it still failed to meet certain purposes. One was that with all its expansion, and with all the students it did serve, there were still large groups of youngsters whose parents could not afford to pay tuition. Increasingly, arguments pointing to the paradox of a common school system attempting to provide genuine equality of educational opportunity to all and a secondary school system open only to those who could pay began to achieve results.

In 1821, as a result of a highly favorable subcommittee report, the Boston School Committee established a three-year English Classical School which soon after became the English High School. That same year also witnessed the founding of a similar institution in Portland, Maine; Worcester, Massachusetts, and New York City followed suit during the next five years. Boston's first English High School was so successful that in 1826 a high school for girls was established. Finally, in 1827, largely through the efforts of James G. Carter, Massachusetts enacted legislation requiring all towns of five hundred families or more to maintain public high schools.

With a few exceptions, most of the early high schools followed the pattern of the first Boston institution. Gradually, the idea spread to other towns in Massachusetts, south to some cities in the middle states and even to Charleston, South Carolina, and west to the major cities of Ohio, Illinois, and Michigan. The expansion was slow, however, and met with considerable opposition from taxpayer groups and organizations with large investments in private academies. Groups which opposed common schools redoubled their efforts in opposing high schools. Moreover, only larger communities could provide both the funds and the students for such an institution. Inasmuch as America was still very much a rural nation in 1860, this was an important factor in slowing development. In areas where the common school idea had not taken root, public high schools were obviously only dreams for some indeterminate future.

In spite of these obstacles, however, high schools had appeared in significant numbers by the time of the Civil War. A somewhat mistaken picture of this development is often caused by an estimate made by William T. Harris in 1901. In that year, as part of a historical survey of secondary education, he reported forty high schools for the whole United States in 1860. Research in educational history done since that date has established this figure as incorrect. In Massachusetts alone there were over one hundred such institutions by 1860; New York boasted over twenty; while Pennsylvania had approximately forty. Even in a more recently settled state like Illinois, recent studies show over fifty high schools in existence by the beginning of the Civil War. There is considerable support for the contention, then, that although the high school was subordinate to the academy as a pre-Civil War secondary school, it had already shown significant signs of the growth which would eventually lead to its displacing the academy as the American secondary school.

The high school as a publicly supported, publicly controlled institution. The distinguishing mark of the American high school as it emerged during these years was that it definitely stood as a part of the common school system. The high school was supported by public funds in the same way as the common schools. In many communities that meant by taxation. There were numerous instances of tuition charges in the early high schools as well as in the early academies, but these fees could well be regarded as rate bills were in the elementary school—as a last vestige of private support to be removed as soon as practicable. Before the Civil War the movement to abolish these tuition charges was well under way.

Even more important, however, was the fact that the high school was controlled by a board of officials responsible ultimately to the people. In many cases the school committee which managed the common schools assumed responsibility for the high school. Unlike the private, self-perpetuating boards of trustees which managed academies, public boards were ultimately subject, in the making of policy regarding admissions, curriculum, and teacher selection, to the public will.

Finally, the high school, as an institution beyond the common schools, removed the threat of a dual system of education implicit in the private academy. No longer did those who could afford it send their children to one school and those who could not, depend on the public school. Now, in theory at least, everyone was free to avail himself of the public elementary school first, and then, if qualified, of the public high school. If the student were further qualified, the way was open from that point to the public university.

The Growth of Colleges and Universities

The expansion of the private college. The separation of church and state which occurred in the last quarter of the eighteenth century carried important implications for higher education. First of all, the ties which such institutions as Harvard, Yale, and William and Mary had maintained with the colonial governments were drastically weakened. Second, the more popular sects which had been gaining strength since the Great Awakening were now able on an equal footing to turn themselves to the business of seeking converts and training ministers. In this latter task, the college was to play an important role. Taken together, these two factors stimulated a rapid growth of higher education. In fact, no other country had ever tried to establish so many institutions of higher learning in so short a time. Almost every religious denomination was active in founding colleges as a means of spreading its religious doctrines as well as of educating youth in general. As a matter of fact, a healthy—even excessive—rivalry developed in the founding of these schools as the various sects tried to surpass one another in proselyting new territories.

Of the fifteen religious denominations interested in higher education in the pre-Civil War period, the most active were the Presbyterians, Methodists, Baptists, Congregationalists, Roman Catholics, and Episcopalians. Among them, they participated in the establishment of 116 out of the 182 permanent colleges founded by 1861. Working individually and through such group enterprises as the Society for the Promotion of Collegiate and Theological Education at the West, these churches were successful in planting colleges in every single state of the Union.

As for modes of support and control, these private institutions closely resembled the private academies. Support in many cases came from the specific bequest of a religious society—more often than not it was a small one. Often a lottery was held to raise funds for building and other purposes. Tuition and further private bequests were the principal means of further support. Being chartered or incorporated by the state, these colleges were most often controlled by a board of lay trustees which might or might not include faculty representation. These boards retained full power to make general policy, to hire and discharge faculty members, and generally to supervise the institution. In most cases, the board was represented by the president, who more often than not also carried full teaching duties. Interestingly enough, it was these boards of trustees which also granted academic degrees, not the faculties as had traditionally been the case in European universities.

The Dartmouth College case guarantees the rights of private colleges. Despite the dominance of the theory that higher education should be under religious control, a movement for universities controlled and maintained by the state gained increasing momentum during the decades following the Revolution. The movement showed strong influence from the democratic ideas of the French enlightenment and the ideal of a unitary state system of education advanced by Jefferson. Generally, it evidenced itself in two ways: first, in the unsuccessful attempts of state legislatures to make state universities out of the colonial colleges; and second, in the establishment of new state institutions after these earlier attempts had failed.

The end of the former development came with the Dartmouth College decision of the United States Supreme Court in 1819. Twenty years before, when John Wheelock had become president of Dartmouth, he had tried to introduce less conservative political and religious policies than those which had traditionally governed the institution. These Jeffersonian-Republican ideas brought him into sharp conflict with the Federalist board of trustees. The board discharged Wheelock in 1815, whereupon the Republican state legislature passed legislation in 1816 making Dartmouth a state university, enlarging the board of trustees by eleven members, and appointing Wheelock as president of the new Dartmouth University. The old board refused to accede to these changes, and for a strained year or two, two Dartmouths were in existence. Meanwhile, when the old board brought suit in the New Hampshire supreme court to recover control of the college, their plea was denied. At this point they retained Daniel Webster to appeal their case to the United States Supreme Court.

The court's decision, which was written by Chief Justice John Marshall, reversed the decision of the New Hampshire court, and the legislation converting Dartmouth into a state university was declared unconstitutional. The Republican argument that the state support given Dartmouth necessitated a public board of trustees in the interests of free government and education was held less valid than the Federalist argument that the original corporate charter of Dartmouth from the king of England had the force of a contract which the state could not impair. The decision had far-reaching political and economic effects. In the first place, it guaranteed the philanthropic endowments of private colleges from encroachment by the states, thereby encouraging private donors to contribute freely to causes they supported. In the second place, by prohibiting the states from converting established institutions into state universities, it stimulated the founding of new institutions to serve these purposes.

The founding of publicly supported, publicly controlled state universities. In response to demands for free, public universities which would cap state systems of education and provide the leadership necessary to a healthy republic, twenty-one such institutions were established in twenty states between the end of the Revolution and the beginning of the Civil War. Generally, those institutions in the original eastern states evolved from grants of state funds; while those in the fourteen new states were largely aided by federal grants of public land. Interestingly enough, Illinois, Arkansas, Florida, Oregon, and Kansas received federal grants but founded no state universities before 1861.

Opposition to these universities in all states was vigorous. Religious groups waged a continuing battle to prevent the passage of laws establishing these schools and to divert funds earmarked for universities to religious purposes. In the states which failed to establish state universities, it was largely because of the successful agitation of these groups. In other states, even after the establishment of many state universities, religious groups attempted either to limit their funds or to direct their instruction along religious lines.

The agencies for controlling these new state universities varied from state to state. For the majority, a public board of lay persons—called a board of regents or a board of visitors—managed the affairs of the institution. In all cases, either through their appointment or election, the members of the individual boards were in some way ultimately responsible to the people. As with private colleges, these lay boards made policy, appointed and discharged faculty members, and granted degrees.

Mention should be made of the fact that the development of public boards of regents to control state universities gave a double meaning to this name. On the one hand, New York State had established a university with a board of regents, but the university connoted the whole unified state system of education, and the regents really constituted a state board of education. (Moreover, no specific state university was organized in New York until 1951.) In other states the state university was a specific institution and the board of regents was its specific board of control. In some of these latter cases, however, a combination of the two systems led to this board of regents also serving as the state board of education for the whole common school system.

While federal aid in the form of land grants provided the initial stimulus for the founding of state universities, a far more powerful incentive came in the form of the Morrill Act passed in 1862. First introduced into Congress by the Republicans in 1857, the Morrill Bill was vetoed by Democratic President Buchanan on the grounds that it violated states' rights and set up dangerous precedents of federal aid to education. Reintroduced in 1861, however, the bill passed a Republican Congress a year later. By its provisions each state was granted 30,000 acres of public land (or its equivalent in scrip) for each of its Congressmen, the proceeds to be devoted to the establishment of colleges of agriculture and mechanic arts. Considerable opposition from private college interests and groups who feared federal control of education were unable to prevent passage and execution this second time, and "land-grant" colleges became the pattern in every state of the Union. In some states the land-grant college was directly associated with the state university, thus strengthening the latter institution. In other states, where no public university had been established, the land-grant college became the first experiment with public higher education. Needless to say, with their pattern of public support and public control, the land-grant colleges vastly strengthened the state university idea in the United States.

The American System of Education Assumes Its Character

There seems little doubt that by the time of the Civil War, the major outlines of the American school system had emerged clearly enough to warrant some generalizations. That the common school had become an essential feature of American life by that time cannot be debated. By 1866 the conception of this institution had crystallized to a point where a Massachusetts court decision was able to define a common school as one supported and controlled by the local community, open to all children, and teaching the elementary common branch subjects. Though conditions varied considerably from one part of the nation to another, the beginnings of grading systems were already in evidence in the cities, while the work of infant school societies had begun to extend the common school downward. In general, children were able to enter somewhere between the ages of four and six, and could stay from five to eight or nine years, depending on the region.

That the common school was to stand as the first section of an educational ladder stretching all the way through the university was also clear by the time of the Civil War. In many northern and western cities the high school had already begun to displace the academy as the people's secondary school. As has already been mentioned, the fact that the high school came after the common school and was open to qualified graduates of the common school, and embraced both college-preparatory and terminal students, served sharply to distinguish the American system from more traditional European dual systems. With the state universities open to qualified graduates of the high school, the ladder was completed. In some states where rate bills had been entirely removed, a youngster could complete his education from the common school through the university paying little or no tuition. Truly, this was a remarkable development for three quarters of a century.

THE EDUCATIONAL PROGRAM

Of the many conflicting educational aims vying for support during this period of tremendous expansion, traditional ones tended to dominate the schools. While it is true that the curriculum broadened at every level—especially in the more populated areas—and while it is true that dozens of educational experiments and innovations appear in various individual schools or school systems, it was not until after the Civil War that these new influences really began to alter the basic purposes of American education. What, then, were these more traditional aims which continued to provide the guide lines for the American school program?

Perhaps the dominant aim of the whole school system from common school through university was character and moral development. Stemming from the profound influence of organized religious groups in the founding and control of American schools, this stood central in the thinking of most educators prior to 1865. For some, character and moral development could never be separated from instruction in the tenets and doctrines of a particular religious faith. For others, character training could still be central in the program of a nonsectarian common school. Often, the controversy over what kind of school could best provide this training was the crux of the struggle over public education.

Rooted in the European traditions of idealism and rationalism, the ideal of mental discipline was another central aim of early nineteenth-century education, and emphasis upon it increased as the century progressed. Ascribing only secondary importance to the acquisition of knowledge, mental discipline stressed rather the importance of training the faculties and intellectual powers of the mind. Thus, for example, mathematics would be taught not for any practical or theoretical value it might possess, but primarily to strengthen the mind's power to reason logically. This theory was strongly advocated by religious and humanist educators. It was cited most frequently as justification of the continuance of classical studies in the curriculum. It was, therefore, particularly popular in the liberal arts colleges, and was often used to support the college-preparatory functions of the academies and high schools.

A third ideal which held powerful sway, especially at the elementary level, was universal literacy, and through this, the dissemination of information. Traditionally Protestant groups had placed emphasis upon this aim, growing out of their conception that each man achieved salvation by reading and interpreting the Bible for himself. In the nineteenth century the achievement of this goal was increasingly fortified by arguments that a republic could survive only with universal literacy among the electorate. Thus, in those areas which accepted the common school idea the assumption that universal literacy would automatically bolster a people's freedom was commonly acknowledged.

The third aim was quite closely allied with a fourth which had been gaining headway since the European nations had first begun to conceive of education for national purposes in the seventeenth century: namely, education for citizenship. This ideal was certainly powerful in the common schools, where one guiding purpose was to train loyal citizens able to assume their responsibilities. Moreover, it was increasingly evidenced in the establishment of public secondary schools and colleges whose stated purpose was to provide competent leaders for the community. Clearly, education for citizenship furnished considerable support for the inclusion of social studies at all levels of education. Moreover, the programs of Americanization which grew out of it played an important part in welding one nation out of a variety of national and cultural groups.

A fifth aim which began to make headway in the face of traditional opposition was that of vocational or practical competence. This ideal was particularly manifested in the academies, where the claim was most often made that studies would be useful in the "ordinary business of life." In the pre-Civil War period, although there were sporadic attempts at vocational training for manual or industrial positions, most people thought of studies that pertained to the business and commercial world when they thought of these "practical" subjects. This is quite understandable in view of the fact that academies catered principally to the middle classes and the fact that commerce and trade were far more developed than industry before the Civil War. Needless to say, practical and vocational goals were clearly embodied in the agricultural and mechanic arts colleges established under the Morrill Act (1862), but on the whole they did not become powerful factors in the colleges and universities before 1865. As for the common schools, although much was said about practical and vocational competence, little was accomplished during this period.

A final aim tied in clearly with practical competence, namely, the goal of individual success. Nurtured by frontier and capitalist individualism, this end guided many into the school who might not otherwise have attended. For this group—and it was a large one—schooling would help one along the ladder to success. More often than not, just how the school would help was not entirely clear, but the fact that it would help was accepted uncritically. In many cases it was simply a matter of attaining something which over the centuries had traditionally been reserved for small groups among the upper classes. Thus, for example, when Robert Owen in 1830 proposed a special vocationally oriented curriculum for the children of workingmen, his program was vigorously opposed by many of the workingmen themselves. In the spirit of the middle class they wanted for their youngsters what the youngsters of the upper classes had received for decades—a classical education. They were not quite sure of just what advantages would accrue from such an education, but they steadfastly believed that it would help their children along the road to success.

The Elementary School Program

The threefold ideal of the common school curriculum sketched by the educational reformers—subjects providing the knowledge and skills necessary to the responsible exercise of citizenship, subjects providing suitable religious and moral training, and subjects providing loyalty to the republic—formed the major lines of development in the elementary school curriculum during these years. It is all too easy, however, on studying this development to overstate the picture of this broadening. Throughout this section, it should be borne in mind that the great majority of the one-room elementary schools which sprang up over America in the early nineteenth century were simple institutions providing a simple educational fare.

The Reverend Warren Burton, born in New Hampshire in 1800, has left contemporary teachers an excellent account of the instruction in a one-room school during this early period in his book, *The District School As It Was.* Reading, spelling, writing, and arithmetic constituted the principal elements in the offering. The teaching of reading, principally from materials like the *New England Primer,* Thomas Dilworth's *New Guide to the English Tongue,* or perhaps the Bible itself, was largely by rote and imitation, rendering a good deal of the content relatively meaningless to the pupils. "It scarcely never entered the heads of our teachers," wrote Burton, "to question us about the ideas hidden in the great, long words and spacious sentences. It is possible that they did not always discover it themselves." The study of reading was considered important enough to appear in both the morning and afternoon school sessions. Those classes which had mastered the subject sufficiently (i.e., those who were "adequate to words of more than one syllable") also read from the Bible. Reverence for the volume, noted Burton, was not deepened by this constant but exceedingly careless use.

After the middle of the eighteenth century spelling, which had formerly been an aspect of reading, began to assume the role of an independent subject. Movement in this direction was tremendously stimulated by the publication in 1782 of Noah Webster's *First Part of a Grammatical Institute of the English Language,* colloquially referred to by generations of American children as the "blue-backed speller." One of the first effects of the speller, for students and teachers alike, was to make spelling and the spelling bee a fad. "The child," wrote Burton, "cares no more in his heart about the arrangement of vowels and consonants in the orthography of words, than he does how many chips lie above one another at the school-house woodpile. But he does care whether he is at the head or foot of his class. . . ." Undoubtedly, the child's place in the class hierarchy meant far more to him than the meaning of the words he spelled. As with reading and spelling, so with the teaching of writing. Colonial schools had no blackboards or slates so that instruction in writing remained largely at the level of rote copying or imitation. That there was much connection of ideas is to be strongly doubted.

Arithmetic also increasingly began to enter American schools during the latter half of the eighteenth century. Three years after publication of his reader in 1740, Dilworth had published *The Schoolmaster's Assistant,* a textbook in elementary arithmetic. Like many textbooks of its time the *Assistant* was based largely on the catechetical plan of instruction, and it is probable that most teachers followed the method of question-and-answer in working with it. Burton reported that many of his early hours with arithmetic were spent in copying incomprehensible rules into his notebook; examination of student copybooks from this period seems to bear out his observation. Newer textbooks which tended to replace Dilworth after 1790 effected no great improvement in these methods.

The picture recorded by Burton was by no means peculiar to New England. The South, for example, which had left education largely in private hands, showed great similarity in those facilities which did exist at the turn of the century. In general, elementary instruction in reading, writing, arithmetic as well as drill in the Ten Commandments, the Lord's Prayer, and the catechism, comprised the elementary curriculum. In the earliest western schools it is doubtful that even these standards were reached. Throughout the country what schools there were taught this limited curriculum in sessions which were usually short and in facilities which were often tragically inadequate. Attendance of scholars was irregular at best, often sporadic. Techniques of instruction, even at maximum efficiency, were usually incapable of imparting more than a superficial acquaintance with these basic skills. Even so, many pupils were able to gain in a few seasons reasonable proficiency in reading, writing, and ciphering. They must have been if one regards the number who passed on to the higher branches and the professions. While small, this group does present one of the optimistic notes in a general picture of inadequacy.

The expansion of the common school curriculum. Attempts to expand the common school curriculum to meet the new educational needs outlined by the reformers met with different degrees of success in different localities. In general, elementary schools in New England, New York, and some of the cities in other sections tended to expand their curricula significantly before the Civil War. Schools in other areas, particularly in the great rural regions of the country, tended to hew rather closely to the pattern previously described.

As one indication of an expanding curriculum, the first three decades of the nineteenth century witnessed a vast multiplication of available textbooks. In comparing the number of texts offered for sale in the years 1804 and 1832, one writer in the *American Annals of Education* noted that the total had risen from 93 to 407, and that the "number of Spelling Books, Reading Books, and Arithmetics, has increased fourfold; of Grammars, threefold; of Geographies, sixfold; and of Histories, eightfold; while a number of works have been published in branches of study which were then unknown in our schools." The same writer, in turning to the reports of the New York State superintendent of schools, discovered that the texts in general use could be reduced to about twenty. Of these, there were five kinds of spellers, six of arithmetics, three of grammars, five of geographies, ten of readers, and one dictionary.

This latter breakdown fairly well represents the development of the curriculum in New York and New England during the pre-Civil War period. Massachusetts by 1850 had expanded the list of required common school subjects to include orthography, reading, writing, English grammar, geography, and arithmetic. The teaching of good behavior was also required. Moreover, as Horace Mann pointedly noted in his *Eleventh Annual Report,* state requirements set forth only a minimum which any town school committee could enlarge at will. For example, history and bookkeeping were included in a number of town curricula, and music had been introduced into the Boston schools largely through the efforts of Lowell Mason. In the less populated, poorer, rural areas, on the other hand, schools were doing well if they could cover even the required studies.

In other areas, the curriculum tended to remain limited. The schools of Lancaster, Pennsylvania, for instance, in 1852 were teaching spelling, reading, writing, arithmetic, and geography as the primary subjects. Until 1849, when English grammar and geography were added, Ohio required only reading, writing, and arithmetic. In the South reading, writing, spelling, and arithmetic were considered as appropriate to the primary school, while geography, history, and grammar were looked upon as more advanced areas pertinent to academies and high schools. When geography and history did enter the elementary school, they did so in the form of reading matter rather than as separate subjects.

The attempt to build a nonsectarian common school curriculum. In order for the ideal of a universally available, publicly supported, and publicly controlled common school to be at all workable, the teaching of sectarian religion had to be excluded from the classroom. In their attempts to accomplish this by teaching the common elements of Christianity and the Bible without comment, however, the reformers encountered violent opposition from conservative religious interests and the forces allied with them. The idea that morality and character—for many the central purposes of education—could be included in the curriculum apart from the dogma of a sectarian faith was a difficult one for people who had recently lived under religious establishments to accept. Yet the reformers were able, in the space of a half century, to convince a majority of Americans that the plan was practical.

The development of the nonsectarian curriculum in Massachusetts well represents the movement throughout the Union. Interestingly enough, while the general law of 1789 had enjoined teachers to exert their best endeavors to communicate piety, justice, and other virtues to children, it nowhere mentioned the teaching of religion. Although the popularity of the *New England Primer* had begun to wane in favor of newer material, the Bible and the Psalter were in wide use, and the law of 1789 probably represented a more general trend replacing earlier Calvinist teachings with a milder conception of Judeo-Christian ethics and morality. Far from excluding religion, the law merely required the teachng of Christian principles to a Christian community.

When the law of 1827 greatly strengthened the town school committees, the question of sectarian feeling in the selection of school books received important attention. In order to prevent undue sectarian interest in this matter, the following clause was inserted in the law: "That said committee shall never direct any school books to be purchased or used, in any of the schools under their superintendence, which are calculated to favor any particular sect or tenet." Once again, rather than excluding Christian morality from the schools, this provision obviously hoped to bar only sectarian doctrines and tenets.

No particular attention was paid to this provision until the establishment of the Board of Education in 1837 and the appointment of Horace Mann, a Unitarian, as its secretary. When Mann and the board vigorously supported the common elements of Christianity conception, the more conservative religious groups in the state accused him of trying to introduce Unitarianism into the schools. In 1838, in a controversy over school libraries with Frederick A. Packard of the American Sunday School Union, and again in 1844 and 1846, in controversies with Reverends Edward A. Newton and Matthew Hale Smith, respectively, Mann and the board were accused of conducting "godless," immoral schools which bred delinquency and vice. Throughout these continuing struggles, Mann held steadfastly to his position that the common schools were neither irreligious nor nonreligious; they were nonsectarian. If one examines the curriculum of these years, Mann's arguments were entirely borne out in practice, at least to the extent that moral instruction was nonsectarian Protestant in orientation. Very obviously, what his attackers were urging was not that religion, ethics, and morals be taught in the schools, but that their particular sectarian doctrines be taught.

By the time of the Civil War Mann's position enjoyed wide acceptance in most places, and universal acceptance in others. A questionnaire sent to twelve leading citizens of Massachusetts in 1851 revealed general concurrence in the conclusion that the New England system of education, while nonsectarian, was far from irreligious. Had America been entirely Protestant, there seems little doubt that well nigh universal acceptance of this policy might have been achieved by 1865. But this was not the case, and after 1840, their ranks strengthened by the mass immigrations of the 1840's and 1850's, the Roman Catholics raised growing objections. Pointing to the fact that the Protestant version of the Bible was read in schools and that this Bible, contrary to Catholic doctrine, was read without comment or interpretation, this group continued to view the public schools as sectarian. In some places temporary compromises were achieved; in others Protestants refused to heed these complaints; and in still others separate Catholic school systems were established. Suffice it to say that before 1865 the Protestants had no adequate solution to the problem. As far as Jewish groups were concerned, there were few of them to begin with, and in general, they tended to go along with the common school idea in spite of the violence done some of their religious beliefs. At the same time they strengthened their facilities for providing children with religious education during nonschool hours.

The curriculum and political-economic values. The school's commitment to inculcate patriotic values was clearly evident in the work of most American textbook writers by the turn of the century. None of these was more vehement in his nationalistic sentiments than Noah Webster. Believing that citizens of the United States, if they were to feel as a nation, would have to develop a body of distinctive "national prejudices," Webster oriented all of his texts to this end. His spellers sought to develop a uniquely American kind of orthography, while his readers drew on material from American sources in place of the traditional classical orations. Other authors were similarly oriented. The McGuffey Readers, which sold upwards of 100 million copies in the half century after their publication in the late 1830's, also reflected this new nationalism, as did the early geographies of Jedidiah Morse and the early histories and biographies of Mason Weems, Bishop Davenport, and Peter Parley (Samuel Goodrich). Even authors of arithmetic books in the wording of problems found ample opportunity to glorify the nation's past and its heroes.

Inextricably bound up with these patriotic and moral values were the values of economic individualism. In the minds of most Americans the laissez-faire economic system was so intimately related to the republican political system that neither could exist without the other. Therefore, the values of the free capitalistic economy permeated both readers and more formal texts in political economy. Every man, held Professor John McVickar's *First Lessons in Political Economy,* is the maker of his own fortune. The rigid maintenance of industry, economy, prudence, and resoluteness will inevitably produce success. Arithmetic texts spoke of wise men investing their money at 7 percent interest compounded semiannually, and of foolish youngsters letting their money idle or wasting it. Readers loudly proclaimed the glories of resourcefulness and the sadness of indolence. From the spelling bee to the report card, competition was the dominant note of the schoolroom.

Common school methods. The highly formalized methods described by William Burton in *The District School As It Was* were the rule in most early nineteenth-century American common schools. The aim of course after course was the digestion of knowledge embodied in a textbook, and all too often meaning and practical application was subordinated to, if not displaced by, simple memorizing. The typical one-room district school was usually attended by a variety of age groups, running all the way from children of four or five to adolescents in their teens. Needless to say, the discipline problem was often critical, and resort to stern methods of punishment was quite in keeping with the conception of the child as a sinful being. In any case, it was usually the first and last resort of an untrained teacher with few other techniques at his or her disposal.

A good deal of instruction was on an individual basis. Because of the great diversity within each such group, the teacher would have to deal with each student separately. Therefore, the early district schoolroom was most often a picture of a teacher seated at a central desk with one child after another approaching, reciting from text or memory, being rewarded with a smile or a blow depending on the effectiveness of the recitation, and returning to his seat. On occasion, perhaps, the loud voices of spelling or reading of the Scriptures in unison would issue from the window. On other occasions this was replaced by the loud raucous noise of an undisciplined crowd of young-sters or the cries of one or more being disciplined by the teacher. As if to add to an already difficult situation, inadequate facilities only increased the dis-comfort of all concerned. Many a schoolroom was dangerously cold in the winter and vice versa in the summer; while an insufficient number of seats or an uncomfortable supply aggravated discomfort.

One method of instruction which gained wide acceptance during this period, and which played a large part in the expansion of school populations, was the *monitorial,* or *Lancasterian,* system of instruction. Originating in England under the sponsorship of Andrew Bell and Joseph Lancaster, it was a method whereby one teacher taught a packaged lesson to a group of older, brighter students, and these students, called monitors, in turn each taught a group of younger students. In this manner one teacher was able to minister to one or two hundred children instead of the several dozen which were his usual maximum. It is not difficult to see how this method, imported into the United States in the first years of the nineteenth century, was instrumental in rapidly expanding the number of children that could be handled in one school and at a very moderate proportional increase in cost.

Another development which began to appear in the larger cities in the decade before mid-century was the division of students into classes, or grades. The evolution of school grades was a gradual process which began when different school buildings were built to house older and younger children and quite naturally progressed to the point where many groups of children attended concurrently in one building. Patently, division of children by age group greatly simplified the problems of teaching and discipline. Although the actual dividing points differed in different places, the movement itself was in evi-dence in many parts of the Union by 1860. Greatly stimulated by Horace Mann's observations of grading in the Prussian elementary schools [as set forth in his *Seventh Annual Report* (1843)], the movement had progressed most rapidly in the New England area at that time.

The Higher School Program

The expansion of secondary studies. The dominant, often the only, pur-pose of the traditional Latin grammar school was to prepare young men for college education. The curriculum, therefore, was geared entirely to the aca-demic needs of youngsters seeking to enter and complete succssfully the college course. Through the end of the eighteenth century, Latin, Greek, and arithmetic were the only subjects required for admission to the leading American colleges. In the years between 1800 and the Civil War five new ones were added to this list: geography, English grammar, algebra, geometry, and ancient history. Within the scope of these eight areas, then, lay the curriculum of the Latin grammar school.

The academies, on the contrary, were bound by no such limitation of purpose. As a matter of fact, they arose for the very purpose of offering a broader program for persons not contemplating attendance at college. The latter institutions, bound by tradition and conservative values, were little responsive to the needs of a new and expanding America. Moreover, catering as they did in 1800 to the upper classes, there was little necessity for them to take account of these needs. On the other hand, the early academies were for many the people's colleges. There, the common man could receive the benefits of a further education which would, along with other values, prepare him for the lively business and commercial world.

In response to these new needs, the academies developed what came to be known as the "English course" as opposed to the "classical course" of the grammar schools. The difference in names indicates what was perhaps the most central difference in character between the two programs. The heart of the earlier classical course had been Latin grammar and the study of such texts as Caesar's *Commentaries,* Cicero's *Orations* and Vergil's *Aeneid*—or perhaps Greek grammar and some elementary Greek texts (although Greek never gained the stature of Latin in American classical curricula). The heart of the newer English course was the study of English grammar and literature. With the publication of Lindley Murray's grammar in 1795 and a score of others in the first decades of the nineteenth century, the study of English quickly took over the formalized structure of the earlier work with Latin. In addition to grammar, English masterpieces by such men as Milton, Pope, and Cowper entered the English curriculum in place of Caesar, Cicero, and Vergil. Taken along with the American readers stressing patriotic material, these formed the body of the new study of grammar. Needless to say, traditional subjects like philosophy, debating, and declamation fit neatly into the developing English course.

It was probably in reflecting the newer scientific interests of the nineteenth century that the academy made the greatest advances. Natural philosophy, a kind of pot-pourri of all the natural sciences, made rapid headway in the curriculum, as did astronomy, chemistry, and botany. The increasing emphasis given mathematics, especially algebra and geometry, was doubtless closely related to the scientific movement. The work of such a man as Newton received considerable attention, while the chance to combine patriotic hero worship with scientific instruction made the study of Franklin's experiments popular. Although most schools maintained little or no scientific equipment, individual institutions here and there began to bring together the material to perform laboratory demonstrations of natural phenomena.

In the social sciences the academies experienced much the same development as the common schools. With the publication of Morse's text, geography became a popular subject, while American history enjoyed tremendous interest as part of growing nationalism. Documents such as the Declaration of Independence and the Constitution were studied with almost the same fervor as religious materials had received in the earlier period, and the biographies of national heroes rapidly became common knowledge.

The effort to introduce practical subjects of use in the business and commercial world accounted for another large block of the academy curriculum. In a number of cases astronomy and arithmetic were combined to make a course in navigation. In others arithmetic and geometry combined to form a course in surveying. A large number of academies included courses in bookkeeping; while others directed the subject matter of penmanship toward business letter writing. Some even turned the highly traditionalized subjects of declamation into a public speaking course of benefit in the business world. It must be borne in mind, however, that these commercial subjects were by no means the only ones looked upon as practical. The whole area of scientific studies was regarded as a highly useful body of information.

Closely allied with attempts to make the secondary curriculum more practical was the manual labor movement. Stemming from the work of Pestalozzi and Fellenberg in Europe, it gained wide popularity in the United States under the leadership of men like William Maclure and Joseph Neef. To stimulate the movement, the latter two men organized the Manual Labor Society for Promoting Manual Labor in Literary Institutions in 1831. Many academies took up the idea and tried to combine farming or industrial work with regular study. The character-forming aim, as well as social aims, were involved in the habits of industry, independence, health, and cooperation which enthusiasts of this plan saw developing in youngsters. The strength of academic tradition was too great, however, and the movement declined rapidly in the 1850's. Its importance lay principally in its indication of a willingness among the people to move secondary education in more practical and useful directions.

Although the academy pioneered in the development of the English secondary course, it by no means confined its activities to this program. What actually happened was that most academies began to offer two parallel courses: the classical course and the English course. Thus, opportunity was provided both for those who wished to continue on to college, and for those who were merely rounding out a common school education and considered the academy as an educational terminus. This obviously was an important step in the democratizing of secondary education, for it brought together in one institution both youngsters who would and would not go on to college. Thus, it removed many of the aristocratic tendencies of the earlier Latin grammar schools.

One major point of interest is the way in which academies moved toward a nonsectarian curriculum. Unlike the common schools, academies catered to students from a variety of distant communities—thereby leading to a heterogeneous group of students who were compelled to board at the schools. Moreover, even though many academies were founded by specific denominational groups for the purpose of furthering specific religious doctrines, the scarcity of advanced students in any one sect soon forced these groups to broaden their entrance requirements to include children of all denominations. Otherwise, there were rarely enough youngsters of a single denomination in the area served by the academy to warrant its continuance. Very much as in the case of elementary schools, the attempt to include children of many sects rapidly led to the necessity of offering nonsectarian religious instruction. To be sure, most of the academies were vitally concerned with some kind of Christian education, but most of them soon adopted the teaching of the common elements of Christianity. As one might well expect, opposition to this pattern developed from conservative religious interests, especially in academies under denominational auspices. But the movement toward nondenominationalism was too strong for such groups to stymie the development of nonsectarian instruction more than temporarily or in specific cases.

This presentation of a kind of composite picture of the average American academy during this period must not be allowed to obscure the great variety of special institutions which developed. In fact, the private character of the academy was itself a factor making it an ideal institution to serve special purposes. For example, although the nonsectarian pattern was widespread, the growth of religious academies sponsored by given denominations must not be ignored. Particularly in the case of the Roman Catholics, the academy was an important phase of the parochial school system. Teaching orders such as the Jesuits, the Brothers of the Christian Schools, and the Sisters of Notre Dame de Namur established and conducted a number of thriving institutions during this period. As a matter of fact, the convent schools established by the Catholics were an important incentive for Protestant groups in promoting women's education. Among the Protestants, too, in spite of nondenominationalism, there was considerable sectarian activity, and the Protestant Episcopal Church expended considerable energy in this direction.

The founding of the United States Military Academy at West Point in 1802 began another interesting movement in secondary education, that of military academies. This took root rapidly, particularly in the South. Similarly, the beginning of special seminaries for young women introduced the development of still another kind of specialized curriculum, one which gave important emphasis to home economics and domestic science. Final mention should be given to the wide use of academies as teacher training institutions and the concomitant development of subject materials appropriate to this task.

Inasmuch as the high school first emerged as an attempt to provide the academy's education at public expense to all who were qualified, one would expect the high school curriculum to resemble closely that of the average academy. This was clearly the situation. In Boston, where the Boston Latin School continued to provide the classical college-preparatory course, the new English High School offered only the English curriculum. Candidates for entry into the latter institution had to be twelve years of age (thus making them two or three years older than entrants into the Latin school) and proficient in reading, writing, English grammar, geography, and arithmetic. The school itself was organized into three classes, the programs of which were as follows:

THIRD CLASS (Lowest)
1. Intellectual and written arithmetic
2. Ancient and modern geography
3. General history and history of the United States
4. Elements of arts and sciences
5. Reading, grammar, and declamation
6. Bookkeeping
7. Sacred geography

SECOND CLASS (Middle)
Items 1 through 7 continued
8. Algebra
9. Rhetoric and composition
10. Geometry
11. Natural Philosophy
12. Natural theology

FIRST CLASS (Highest)
Items 5, 8, 9, 10, 11, and 12, continued
13. Chronology
14. Moral philosophy
15. Forensics
16. Criticisms on English authors
17. Practical mathematics (navigation, surveying, etc.)
18. Experimental lectures on natural philosophy
19. Evidences of Christianity

Except for the addition of philosophy of history, chemistry, intellectual philosophy, linear drawing, and logic (all at the discretion of the masters) and trigonometry, French, and the Constitution of the United States, the course remained unchanged until 1852, when a very similar four-year curriculum was introduced.

English courses in most high schools established before the Civil War tended to follow the above pattern. Doubtless, there were countless minor variations. In those high schools where a classical course existed parallel to the English course, it was limited rather narrowly to those subjects which made up the college entrance requirements. In general, some combination of the two tended to constitute the average high school curriculum up to 1865. **The expansion of the college and university curriculum.** If an American who attended Harvard College in 1650 had returned to the institution in 1800, the curriculum would have been highly familiar. Latin, Greek, and mathematics were its core, while some philosophy perhaps entered in the final year. He would have found many of the texts he had used still in use, and most of the class exercises much the same.

In the first decades of the nineteenth century, however, a significant expansion took place at this level, too. Probably the most conspicuous of the new additions came in the field of the natural sciences. Of these, chemistry, appearing first as part of the professional medical curriculum, was the earliest to gain a foothold. William and Mary appointed a professor of chemistry and natural philosophy as early as 1774, as did Princeton in 1795. Columbia, Yale, and a number of other colleges followed suit soon after the turn of the century. That the subject did not enjoy a universally enlightened reception is well illustrated, perhaps, by the fact that one of the first of the college laboratories, built for Benjamin Silliman at Yale, was constructed fifteen feet below the ground. The architect, undoubtedly believing that the new science had some relation to medieval alchemy, thought a subterranean room entirely appropriate. In any case, it was this early work in chemistry which paved the way for the growth of scientific departments in colleges, and physics, botany, and scientific astronomy (as opposed to the earlier religious astronomy) entered soon afterward. The whole movement was no doubt greatly stimulated by the founding of scientific schools such as the independent Rensselaer Polytechnic Institute in 1824 and the special scientific institutions established at Harvard, Yale, and Dartmouth by 1860. Quite appropriately, the field of mathematics also enjoyed growing interest during this period, and new translations of pioneering European texts in this area stimulated a good deal of creative thought.

The social sciences, which had previously enjoyed only an incidental place in the curriculum, also underwent considerable expansion. Traditionally, history had been considered an aspect of philosophy or religion. William and Mary again pioneered by founding a professorship of history in 1822. By the end of the Civil War similar chairs had been established at Harvard and Yale, and at the former institution the first incumbent, Jared Sparks, made a highly influential early contribution to the field. Yet, as one writer has appropriately observed, "the teaching of history remained dormant in American colleges until America itself was engaged in making history." Therefore, it was not until after the Civil War that this subject really spurted forward. The fields of politics, economics, and law tended to follow a similar course of development.

The establishment of a professorship in the modern languages of Europe at Bowdoin in 1826 marked the beginning of another significant new area in the college curriculum. Devoted primarily to the study of French and Spanish, this chair was first occupied by Henry Wadsworth Longfellow. The modern languages, generally, had been enthusiastically advocated as part of the curriculum by such men as Thomas Jefferson, Benjamin Franklin, and George Ticknor. To be sure, there was considerable opposition. French, for example, had traditionally been considered as a mark of elegance rather than a language of scholarship, and it is reported that many of the students who took the extracurricular course in French at Harvard did so for pleasure rather than for instruction. Moreover, inasmuch as French teachers were usually natives of France, they were ordinarily not regular members of the faculty. In spite of such hindrances, however, the modern languages, particularly French and German, made considerable progress by the time of the Civil War.

One point worthy of mention in bringing out the increasingly secular character of this expanding curriculum was the steady decline in the proportion of college graduates who entered the ministry. Although Harvard and other colonial colleges had not been founded solely for the training of ministers, this had become their primary function. It has been estimated that during the first century of American higher education, approximately 70 percent of all graduates entered the ministry. In the period following the Revolution it had dropped to 20 percent, and despite the vigor of church groups in establishing colleges to train ministers, it remained at 10 percent or less following 1840. As has often been noted, the change itself was not so much an indication of decreased needs for ministers as it was testimony to increased needs for other professionals. In any case, this profound change was just one further reflection of the increasingly nondenominational and secular character of American higher education.

Another important point to note is that in spite of the expansion of the curriculum in some of the larger and older colleges, the movement was by no means universal. As in the case at all school levels, there was considerable variation between urban and rural areas and between older and newer institutions. Thus, for example, small frontier colleges would usually do well if they taught the more traditional curriculum with any moderate effectiveness. Many did not even meet the standards of the better Latin grammar schools in the East. The shortage of texts in the frontier areas only aggravated this situation, and in this age of the establishment of many new smaller colleges, it is probable that the older, more traditional curriculum prevailed in most places.

The beginnings of the elective system. In the colonial period when most people were agreed that a certain limited body of material was appropriately the college program, the average student was able to master the whole of it during the three or four years of his attendance. With the vast enlargement after 1800 both of the field of knowledge itself and of the curriculum, it was obviously no longer possible for every student to traverse it all. As a consequence, what came to be known as the elective system began to make rapid gains after the 1820's.

The earliest evidences of this plan came in the course of study as eventually set up at the University of Virginia in 1825. The program well illustrates Jefferson's conception of higher education. The university embraced eight separate "schools," each entirely independent of the others, covering the ancient languages, the modern languages, mathematics, natural philosophy, natural history (later chemistry only), medicine, moral philosophy, and law. Students were allowed to choose which schools they would enter, but to qualify for a diploma from a school, the student had to take all the prescribed subjects of that school and pass its final examination. Thus, the student was allowed freedom of choice among schools and as far as the order in which he took the prescribed subjects in his chosen school, but he was not allowed actual choice among subjects.

At Harvard, largely under the influence of George Ticknor and the men around him, there was significant progress toward actually allowing students to choose their own subjects. The modern languages (Ticknor's field), however, were about the only studies which might be used as substitutions for the standard curriculum. The principle grew until at the beginning of the 1840's, there were probably more elective subjects than at any previous time. When the faculty was polled by incoming President Everett in 1846, they divided about evenly in their views on election, and in that year the system was reduced to three electives each in the junior and senior year out of an otherwise prescribed curriculum. Similar attempts to introduce election at Brown University, under the leadership of President Francis Wayland during the 1850's and 60's met with partial initial success, and then succumbed to retrenchment.

While election remained in the experimental stage before the Civil War, the "choice among schools" idea of Jefferson did reveal itself in three types of development which began to take root. Two have already been mentioned: the independent technical school, represented by institutions like Rensselaer, Worcester Polytechnic Institute and Massachusetts Institute of Technology; and the scientific schools established in association with Yale, Harvard, and Dartmouth. A third development which closely resembled a similar movement in the secondary schools, was that of *parallel courses*. Established within the framework of the traditional colleges (Brown under Wayland, and the University of Michigan under Henry Tappan are examples), these courses gave students a chance to study scientific and "literary" (meaning English or modern languages as opposed to the classics) subjects leading either to no degree or to a degree other than the traditional B. A. As an example of the latter, the catalogue of Brown University in 1850–1851 announced the regular B. A. program of three years work in the usual subjects and an alternative Ph. B. (Bachelor of Philosophy) program of three years work with emphasis in the new scientific studies. This movement toward parallel courses was destined to great expansion following the Civil War, when traditionalists in higher education, unable to prevent both new subjects and election, sought to preserve the "sanctity" of the B. A. degree.

TEACHERS AND TEACHING

One key to the efficiency of any educational system is always the teacher. This was especially true prior to the many educational improvements of the contemporary era. During the eighteenth and nineteenth centuries there were few of the well-planned texts, the workbooks, the reference guides and libraries, the play equipment, and the comfortable physical facilities which today lighten the burden of the average teacher. Almost everything which went on in these earlier classrooms was in some way concerned with the immediate and direct teacher-student relationship. Then as always—but even more so —a good teacher meant a good school, and a poor teacher a poor school. Obviously, with the tremendous expansion of the facilities and scope of formal education during this period, the problem of securing adequate teachers would become central. Even more important is the fact that many of the precedents established during that early period—although they represented temporary measures to meet emergency situations—have continued to form the basis of public policy regarding the American teacher ever since. It is of considerable moment then to analyze some of these precedents and the way in which they developed.

The Pre-Civil War Elementary School Teacher

The increasing use of unskilled women as teachers. The practice of using college students, college graduates without professional posts, and lesser trained men as elementary school teachers seems to have continued for at least a few decades after the Revolution. In addition, the women who had conducted the "dame schools" during the colonial period continued to teach the very young children. After 1820, however, a distinct change came about in the character of teachers in the elementary school, and increasingly, the common school teacher became a young, unskilled woman.

At least two factors seem to have been largely responsible for this change when it took place. The first might roughly be referred to as the Jacksonian conception of democracy. According to this conception, any citizen of the community had the qualifications for any public office in the community. If this was not the case, it was the office which was at fault, not the citizen. As public school systems rapidly grew after 1830, a large number of public offices in the form of teaching positions came into being. It followed quite logically from the Jacksonian conception, that anyone could be a teacher as long as he was a loyal American, and under the spoils system teaching positions could also be given to reward loyal party workers.

The second factor stimulating the increasing use of young women as teachers grew out of district control of the public schools. All too often local districts were concerned with one thing in the management of schools—economy. During the first part of the nineteenth century women earned considerably less money than men for the same job. Since the teacher's salary was the principal item in the school budget, a saving there would reduce school costs appreciably. When these two factors combined—the feeling that no special qualifications were necessary for teaching and the desire to keep school budgets at a minimum—they were highly conducive to the use of women teachers. Whether the urgings of the educational reformers regarding the use of women as teachers were sincere efforts to improve the schools or simply recognition of practical realities is not known. In any case, these urgings met with definite response, and by the Civil War the American teacher was female. The war too affected teaching. As has every war since, it forced many men out of the profession into military service or higher paying industrial and business jobs, and unskilled women entered the schools to take their places. When the war ended, the men did not return.

The conditions of public elementary school teaching remain poor. Despite continued efforts to better education by providing better teaching conditions, these conditions remained generally poor during this period. Salaries remained low, although the years after the 1840's show steady improvement. While reliable or complete statistics are difficult to obtain for these years, the following table indicates fairly well the progress of teacher salaries during the two decades preceding the Civil War:

Table 3—Average Weekly Salaries of Teachers, 1841–1861 [2]

Year	Rural		Urban	
	Men	Women	Men	Women
1841	$4.15	$2.51	$11.93	$4.44
1846	4.03	2.53	11.53	4.18
1851	4.43	2.95	14.10	4.87
1856	6.07	3.85	16.76	6.10
1861	6.30	4.05	18.07	6.91

Obviously, these wages cannot be evaluated against present ones because of great changes in the value of the dollar. On the other hand, comparison with

[2] W. Randolph Burgess, *Trends of School Costs* (New York, Russell Sage Foundation, 1920), p. 32.

other pre-Civil War salaries reveals that teachers were earning just about enough to get by on, certainly no more. Their salaries were a bit above those of skilled labor, but far from the professional salaries envisoned by the reformers. For many the problem was shrugged off by pointing out that the young women who taught lived at home and therefore did not need as large a salary. Others regarded teachers as misfits anyway—persons who could not succeed in the business world and who therefore did not deserve better salaries.

In a society with as strong an emphasis on individual economic success as nineteenth-century America, it is not difficult to see how low economic remuneration would go hand in hand with low social status. Once again, a number of factors combined to keep the teacher from occupying a place of great respect in the community. One of these was a practice which had come down from the colonial period—that of "boarding round." By this arrangement a community paid part of its teacher's salary by boarding the teacher with different local families for stated periods of time. What reminiscences are available show the practice to have been arduous and demanding on teachers. They had no private lives of their own and were subjected to every possible hardship—always being strangers and "extras" in the households where they stayed.

This procedure was strongly reinforced by a tradition of "genteel respectability" which had gradually grown up around the teacher. Like the minister, the teacher was ever to provide a good and healthy example for the children under his care. Therefore, the community was continuously interested in the behavior of its teachers both in and out of school. Inasmuch as communities were interested in the conduct of their young, unmarried women to begin with, such supervision of the teachers was not difficult. Thus, special rules regarding smoking, drinking, courting, church going, teaching Sunday school, leaving town, etc., increasingly were applied to teachers, and the latter had little recourse when conservative community leaders made inordinate demands.

Two other factors operated to keep the teacher from high social status in the American community. One was the youth of teachers in general; the other was their rapid turnover. For many persons teaching was a temporary, stop-gap job until marriage, business, or some other more permanent career was possible. More than anything else, perhaps, the inferior social status of the American teacher during these years was reflected in stereotypes which began to develop. The best known of these was Washington Irving's character Ichabod Crane. Here was an eccentric, ugly old man, sour, tempestuous, and unable to succeed in anything except teaching. On the female side, in spite of the youth of teachers, they were pictured as prim spinsters-to-be, entirely unapproachable by any ordinary human male. It is not difficult to see how many shied away from teaching as a permanent career.

Public Teacher Training

The tradition of schoolkeeping. With the prevalence of the Jacksonian conception of public office, little or no training was thought necessary for the post of teacher, and after 1830 this was increasingly the case. Quite often the teacher was simply the daughter or some other unmarried female relative of the local district prudentialman. She had completed the common school, and in a very limited number of instances she had attended a local academy for a short period of time. The tradition of schoolkeeping rather than schoolteaching was strongly implanted. The teacher's job was to keep order—to keep the class intact. In the upper grades, as often as not, this meant that the teacher had to be able physically to subdue the larger members of the class. In general, good moral character was the principal—often the only—qualification for the post.

The beginnings of teacher training. The rising demands for facilities to improve the above situation by more adequate teacher training began to yield results in the 1820's and 1830's. The influence of European methods cannot be underestimated, for the training of teachers was a central element in the French and Prussian state systems. When Americans such as Horace Mann, Henry Barnard, Calvin Stowe, and Charles Brooks went abroad to study European education, they came back and published enthusiastic descriptions of these teacher training facilities. Their reports were an important stimulus for the establishment of similar facilities in America.

These appeared in America in the form of the normal school. (The word "normal" came from the Latin word meaning a model or rule, connoting that the object of the institution was to provide teachers with the rules for teaching.) The first normal schools in America were private schools such as those promoted by Samuel R. Hall at Concord, Vermont, in 1823 and by James G. Carter at Lancaster, Massachusetts, in 1827. They were graded at the academy level and offered a course much like the English one in the academies, adding several subjects in teaching methods, discipline, and the management of children. These first private schools were of great importance, for they influenced the course of teacher training in the private academies which trained the great majority of American common school teachers before 1865.

Of even greater import, however, was the founding of the first public normal schools. It will be remembered that an important plank in James G. Carter's efforts to improve the Massachusetts public schools was the establishment of public normal schools. He began direct agitation for the establishment of such an institution as early as 1827, and when the American Institute of Instruction was organized in 1830, he was instrumental in turning its attentions to the same matter. When the Massachusetts Board of Education and its secretary took office in 1837, they too joined in the effort. Finally in

1838, stimulated by a grant of funds from Edmund Dwight, a member of the board, the effort was successful. The first public normal school in the United States was opened at Lexington, Massachusetts, in July 1839 and a second at Barre, just two months later.

Considerable opposition to these institutions developed in the state legislature from groups who thought they were an attempt to "Prussianize" the schools. Many others thought that the academies were doing an excellent job of teacher training, and that there was no need for the newly founded normal schools. The opposition was unsuccessful, however, and a third school was opened at Bridgewater in 1840. The successful establishment of these institutions in Massachusetts paved the way for similar schools in other states, and by the Civil War twelve such schools had been founded in eight different states. As the private normal schools, these public institutions gave primary attention to the subjects in the English course of the academy. Much time was devoted to advanced training in the common branches, and some attention was given to problems of method using such texts as Samuel Hall's *Lectures in Schoolkeeping* and David Page's *Theory and Practice of Teaching*.

Brief mention should also be given to teacher institutes, which expanded rapidly in the later 1840's and 1850's. The idea seems entirely American in origin, and credit for their origin is usually given to Henry Barnard for conducting the first such gathering in Connecticut in 1839. At that time he brought together twenty-six men for a six-week session during which methods of teaching the common branches and other pertinent topics were intensively reviewed. Barnard had a number of prominent educators as guest lecturers, and the Hartford schools were made available for visitation by the group.

The idea rapidly spread to New York and Massachusetts, and in the latter state teachers' institutes began to enjoy public support in 1845. Within the next five years at least nine other states in the North and Northwest made similar arrangements. For many the less formal arrangements of the institutes had to suffice in place of normal schools. Yet, all too often, these gatherings of teachers took on a highly formal atmosphere. Whereas the original purposes had been to improve teaching by group discussions of methods, it was not long before they became simply teaching situations in which further information in the common branches was imparted.

A final word should be said about evidence of the beginnings of teacher training in established colleges and universities. Although this movement must be thought of largely as a post-Civil War development, lectures on the "art of teaching" and pedagogy began to appear at Washington College (Pennsylvania) in 1831, at Brown in 1850, and at the University of Michigan in 1860. New York University announced a chair in education to instruct "teachers of common schools" in 1832, but there is no evidence as to whether the lecture series was ever given.

The beginnings of professional organization.   With teaching as a temporary, stop-gap job, requiring little or no training, it is not difficult to see how little of an occupational consciousness or *esprit de corps* would develop among teachers. The evidence shows that although the beginnings of professional organization were in evidence before the Civil War, no vigorous and unified professional group of teachers developed.

The work of the early school pressure groups has already been mentioned. Such organizations as the Pennsylvania Society for the Promotion of Public Schools, the Western Literary Institute and College of Professional Teachers, the Lyceum, and the various state groups of "Friends of Education" played a tremendously important role in winning the battle for free public schools. On the other hand, they were not teacher organizations as much as they were pro-school lobbying groups. Also included in the membership were hundreds of professional and other people who had never taught but who were interested in the cause of public education. A high point was reached with this form of organization with the formation in 1849 of the American Association for the Advancement of Education, with Horace Mann as president.

Somewhat different were the first local, state, regional, and national organizations of teachers. Local teacher groups are known to have existed in New York and Boston from the turn of the nineteenth century, and they soon became common in the larger cities. One of the most interesting of the early regional teacher associations was the American Institute of Instruction. A powerful voice in educational affairs, its membership represented a selected elite in New England school affairs, and it was controlled largely by scholars and college educators. In 1845 Rhode Island, Massachusetts, and New York organized state teachers' associations, and by 1856 fourteen other states had followed suit. Although women had been excluded from membership in the American Institute of Instruction, they were welcomed in most of the state associations. Rarely, however, did they play any significant role before the Civil War. The tradition of deference among women was far too strong in nineteenth-century America to permit otherwise.

The founding of local and state teacher organizations reached a kind of culmination in the establishment of the National Teachers Association in 1857. Membership was confined to members of the educational profession, and the avowed aim of the association was "to elevate the character and advance the interests of the profession of teaching, and to promote the cause of popular education in the United States." In general, the organization closely resembled the state associations in interests and efforts; and though national in scope, it enrolled only a small number of teachers during the early years of its existence.

Made up overwhelmingly of elementary classroom teachers, these associations devoted themselves primarily to the problems and needs of teachers and teaching. Representative speakers treated problems of method, discipline, school management, relations of parents and teachers, and the necessity of including this or that subject in the curriculum. By and large, they directed their attention to the problems of the classroom proper and kept away from the often thorny questions of salaries, tenure, and controversial social issues. This type of neutrality was both demanded and expected of teachers during this period, and their associations tended to respect such boundaries.

ISSUES FOR STUDY AND DISCUSSION

1. Which techniques used by the early educational reformers to win public support for their cause would prove useful to present-day American teachers in their efforts to improve education?

2. Why do you think that elementary education reacted to the great changes in American life between 1779 and 1865 far more quickly and radically than did higher education? Does elementary education in the present period seem more receptive to innovation than higher education?

3. It is clear that the youngster of the mid-nineteenth century American learned most of what he needed to know from out-of-school agencies of education and a comparatively small proportion from the school itself. Has this situation persisted or changed in contemporary America?

4. If you had been a judge passing on the Dartmouth College Case in 1819, would you have agreed or disagreed with the decision of Chief Justice John Marshall?

5. How far has the traditional pre-Civil War stereotype of teacher persisted in the American mind? To what extent has it been modified? What factors have been associated with its modification?

SUGGESTIONS FOR FURTHER READING

Beale, Howard K., *A History of Freedom of Teaching in American Schools,* New York, Scribner, 1941.

Boas, Louise, *Women's Education Begins: The Rise of the Women's Colleges,* Newton, Mass., Wheaton College Press, 1935.

Brown, Elmer E., *The Making of Our Middle Schools,* New York, Longmans, 1903.

Brown, Samuel W., *The Secularization of American Education,* New York, Teachers College, Columbia University, 1912.

Burns, James A., *The Growth and Development of the Catholic School System in the United States,* New York, Benziger, 1912.

Burton, Warren, *The District School As It Was,* Clifton Johnson (ed.), New York, Crowell, 1928.

Caldwell, Otis W., and Courtis, Stuart A., *Then & Now in Education,* Yonkers-on-Hudson, World Book, 1924.

Cremin, Lawrence A., *The American Common School,* New York, Teachers College, Columbia University, 1951.

Ditzion, Sidney, *Arsenals of a Democratic Culture,* Chicago, American Library Association, 1947.

Elsbree, Willard S., *The American Teacher,* New York, American Book, 1939.

Goodsell, Willystine (ed.), *Pioneers of Women's Education*, New York, McGraw-Hill, 1931.

Grizzell, Emit Duncan, *Origin and Development of the High School in New England Before 1865*, New York, Macmillan, 1923.

Hayes, Cecil B., *The American Lyceum: Its History and Contribution to Education*, U. S. Office of Education, Bulletin 12, Washington, D. C., Government Printing Office, 1932.

Johnson, Clifton, *Old-Time Schools and School Books*, New York, Macmillan, 1917.

Kiefer, Mary Monica, *American Children Through Their Books: 1700–1835*, Philadelphia, University of Pennsylvania Press, 1948.

Knight, Edgar W., *Public Education in the South*, Boston, Ginn, 1922.

Monroe, Paul, *Founding of the American Public School System*, New York, Macmillan, 1940.

Mosier, Richard D., *Making the American Mind*, New York, King's Crown, 1947.

Swift, Fletcher Harper, *A History of Public Permanent Common School Funds in the United States, 1785–1905*, New York, Holt, 1911.

Taylor, Howard Cromwell, *The Educational Significance of the Early Federal Land Ordinances*, New York, Teachers College, Columbia University, 1922.

Tewksbury, Donald G., *The Founding of American Colleges and Universities Before the Civil War*, New York, Teachers College, Columbia University, 1932.

Woody, Thomas, *History of Women's Education in the United States*, New York, Science Press, 1929, 2 vols.

Henry Barnard's *American Journal of Education* is a goldmine of materials relating to education in antebellum America. The numerous school textbooks published before 1865 also offer excellent guides to the actual school program of the period. A series of articles by Alton D. Mayo in various reports of the United States Commissioner of Education during the 1890's is highly useful, as are the many state histories of education and histories of individual academic institutions.

PART 3

THE EXPANSION OF AMERICAN EDUCATION (1865-1918)

9

THE EMERGENCE OF
INDUSTRIAL AMERICA

THE YEARS between 1865 and 1918 mark the transition from an old to a modern America. In roughly half a century a vigorous, young agricultural people healed the wounds of a disastrous Civil War and became a leading industrial world power. A keynote of the antebellum period had been territorial expansion, and the keynote of post-Appomattox years was greater and faster expansion in all areas of life. The frontier, ever present as a democratizing force in early America, was declared officially closed in 1890. Arizona and New Mexico were admitted to the Union in 1912, thereby completing the process of state making in the territories between the Mississippi and the Pacific. Swelled by the tremendous immigrations of the late nineteenth and early twentieth centuries, the population grew from just over 30 million in 1860 to well over 100 million by 1920. Representing almost every nation of the world, this population had by the latter date proved itself among the most vigorous and creative in history.

It was in the development of industrial production, of course, that the most phenomenal expansion took place. Spurred on by favorable governmental policies, a vast supply of cheap labor, and a continent of virtually untapped resources, the barons of American industry—the Goulds, the Carnegies, the Rockefellers, and a hundred others—built their gigantic empires. By the turn of the century the first billion-dollar corporation—United States Steel—had been organized; by the outbreak of World War I the United States was producing roughly one half of the total mechanical power of the entire world. American manufactured goods literally flooded both home and foreign markets, opening up new vistas of plenty to the peoples of the world. Yankee ingenuity with machines made real what a few decades before had existed only in the minds of visionaries.

The new machines did not bestow their benefits, however, without exacting their penalties. Exploitation of children and workingmen was widespread, and it was common practice in the cities for immigrants to labor sixteen hours daily in intolerable sweatshops. The industrial giants devoured thousands of small businessmen in their growth, while roads to success were often paved with dishonesty, deceit, and fraud. The corruption in local, state, and federal government was unspeakable, extending all the way from petty district functionaries to Congressmen and cabinet members. Increasingly, Americans began to realize that the unrestricted freedom with which they had conquered a continent could not forever remain unrestricted, and that government, which had traditionally been their enemy, might well become their friend.

Politically, control of the national government passed largely into the hands of the Republican Party. With the exception of the two terms of Grover Cleveland, the party held the presidency between the end of the Civil War and the inauguration of Wilson in 1913. Generally, they were able to maintain their ascendancy by advocating high tariffs, free land, civil-service reform, and "sound money." All were distinctly favorable to the business, industrial, and commercial classes of the nation. When the federal government emerged from the Civil War stronger than ever, these groups attempted to turn its financial and political support to their own ends.

Needless to say, there was considerable discontent with these policies among the agrarian and unpropertied classes. More and more, their dissatisfaction was expressed in the formation of new political parties. The latter may have secured minor support themselves, but they often forced support for their proposals from the major parties. A number of labor reform parties came into existence during the 1870's; and agrarian and labor groups organized the Independent Party—known as the Greenback Party—in 1874. Several such groups coalesced into the Populist Party, which polled a million votes in 1892, and when the Populists joined with the Democratic Party in 1896, their candidate, William Jennings Bryan, polled 6.5 million votes to 7.1 million for William McKinley.

In the midst of all their busy expansion, Americans turned the briefest glance at the world about them. In a spirit of high Christian morality they "liberated" Cuba from Spanish rule, but then proceeded economically to exploit Latin America. They maintained a friendly "open-door" policy in Asia but closed American doors to Chinese and Japanese immigrants. When, in a spirit of righteous indignation, they entered World War I to make the world safe for democracy, their economic might quickly subdued the enemy. Wilson's Fourteen Points carried a spirit of magnanimity which in theory had characterized American international policy since the declaration of war against Spain. Yet, throughout it all, Americans were woefully naïve in their foreign policy. Above all, perhaps, they failed to see that the technology they were advancing so rapidly was quickly shrinking the oceans which for three centuries had kept them free of European conflict. Thinking that the oceans were still there, they renounced the League of Nations and turned their attention to further expansion and the Jazz Age. It took only twenty years for them to experience the full impact of their tragic error.

RECONSTRUCTION AND THE BUILDING OF A NEW SOUTH

The South in Ruin

The Civil War left the South in ruin, physically, economically, and politically. Its destruction was paralleled only by that of the major wars of history, leaving much of the Confederacy as a huge battlefield strewn with the flotsam and jetsam of military operations. What had formerly been the rich farming areas of the Shenandoah Valley and the Georgia tidelands had been rendered wasteland. Buildings, bridges, and railroads had been systematically destroyed; crops had been burned; livestock had been slaughtered; and plantations had been pillaged. The few southern cities fared no better. Charleston, the cultural center of the Old South, was, according to one northern observer, a city of "vacant houses, of widowed women, of rotting wharves, of deserted warehouses, of weed-wild gardens, of miles of grass-grown streets, of acres of pitiful and voiceless barrenness." Of Mobile another writer noted, "Torpor and decay reigned on every hand." Richmond, Columbia, Atlanta, Vicksburg, and Galveston fared little better.

Economically and politically, the story was the same. With the plantation destroyed agricultural production was at a standstill, and as late as 1870 the region was only producing one third to one half as much as it had in 1860. Land values had depreciated to the point where ten dollars an acre could purchase the best farms in many regions. Factories were almost completely destroyed, and businesses and banks were largely insolvent. Needless to say, both the bonds and currency of the Confederacy were worthless, and there was neither money to support government functions, nor means of obtaining it. With the breakdown of civil authority marauding bands stole and pillaged at will, stimulating other bands to take the law into their own hands. Lynch law rapidly filled the vacuum left by nonexistent courts, judges, and sheriffs. Families were separated, and starvation was common. Negroes and whites suffered alike.

Among the most potent factors in the social situation, of course, were the 4 million Negro citizens of the South. In many ways they constituted a group completely unprepared for the leadership into which they were suddenly thrust. Plunged into the insecurity of a totally new way of life, some rose to the situation; many more died or were broken by it. For the majority traditionally low standards of living continued to prevail as formerly. For a decade the story of their new-found political freedom was one of exploitation, manipulation, and abuse by outside interests—a far cry from the idealistic visions of the early abolitionists.

The Reconstruction Period

With the surrender of Lee and Johnson in 1865, the United States became a military victor. The cessation of hostilities brought to a climax a controversy which had long been smoldering in the ranks of northern politicians—how to treat the South in defeat. Certainly the spirit of Lincoln's *Proclamation of Amnesty and Reconstruction* (1863) and *Second Inaugural Address* (1865) indicated a readiness to accept the eleven defeated states back into the Union with the least possible malice. His position, however, by no means enjoyed universal acceptance, especially among his fellow Republicans. A radical group among them vehemently favored more rigorous terms which would guarantee the former confederate states re-entering with governments supporting Republican policy. It is interesting to speculate on what might have happened had Lincoln lived to complete his second term. The fact is, of course, that he did not.

The years following Lincoln's assassination saw an ever more intensive struggle between his successor, President Andrew Johnson, and the radical Republicans in Congress. Johnson tended to favor the milder policy of his predecessor, while Congress, controlled by the radical group after the election of 1866, advocated the harsher policy. The struggle between them eventuated in President Johnson's impeachment but not in his dismissal from office. In any case, controlling enough votes to override a succession of presidential vetoes, the radical Republicans made reconstruction policy for a decade.

Even though the Negro had been emancipated, the southern states were determined to preserve white ascendancy. They attempted to do this in the form of "Black Codes," laws which limited the rights and freedoms of Negroes in varying degrees. In some states, such as Georgia, they were lenient; in others, such as Mississippi and Louisiana, they were severely harsh. In general, they made penal codes more rigorous for Negroes, punished vagrancy, regulated their right to keep and bear arms, and placed on them certain economic limitations. Congress responded with the Civil Rights Act (1866) conferring the full rights of citizenship on the Negroes, and then, doubting the constitutionality of this act, with the Fourteenth Amendment (proposed in 1866 and ratified in 1868). The amendment gave constitutional guarantee to the rights of Negroes, barred southern leaders from holding public office, validated the northern debt, and invalidated the southern debt. When the southern states refused to ratify the amendment, Congress responded with the First Reconstruction Act of 1867.

This Act set the tone of reconstruction for the next ten years. According to its provisions, the South was divided into five military districts, each under the direction of a military commander. Each state would continue under this occupation until it held a constitutional convention chosen by universal suffrage, established a new government according to the same principle, and ratified the Fourteenth Amendment. Upon satisfying these conditions, individual states might return to the Union. As with most military occupations, conditions tended to be harsh. Although in some places discrimination was abolished by edict, compensation came in the form of other edicts proclaiming military law, summarily removing local officials, and modifying local legislation. As might be expected, northern politicians (called carpetbaggers) and southerners with northern sympathies (called scalawags) enjoyed their heyday under these arrangements.

Under the military commanders voters were registered and conventions were held. That constitutions were framed and legislatures elected favorable to the Republican point of view might well have been expected. In addition to the numerous carpetbaggers and scalawags at work (especially among the newly enfranchised Negroes), a number of other factors turned elections toward the North. The Freedmen's Bureau, established in 1865 for the relief, guardianship, and education of Negroes, had acted since that time as a powerful political force favoring Republican ideals. Needless to mention, the presence of a northern army of occupation strengthened these ideals in no small way. Finally, the Union League, a secret organization to further Republican Party interests in the South, had been extremely active among the freedmen. By 1868 seven of the former confederate states had set up reconstruction governments, and the others followed suit soon afterward.

Government under these reconstruction legislatures was in large measure an unfortunate chapter in American history. In spite of some constructive enactments reforming the tax system, furthering political democracy, and advancing relief and education, the coalitions of carpetbaggers, scalawags, and freedmen showed little competence for their task. The public debts of some states trebled and quadrupled, taxes increased appreciably, and there were evidences of blatant corruption in politics. Money was spent foolishly and extravagantly, and public appropriations were often diverted to private purposes. It should be borne in mind, however, that much of this maladministration was by no means confined to the South. The machinations of private industrial interests in Congress and the gigantic swindles typified by the Tweed Ring in New York City often dwarfed the perversions of southern politics.

The reconstruction governments had no support from the former ruling groups in the South. Resistance of the latter took the form of such organizations as the Ku Klux Klan and the Knights of the White Camelia. For several years after 1867 these groups attempted unofficially to preserve order and some vestiges of the older southern way. All too often they represented simple white supremacy and turned to lawlessness themselves. Both organizations incurred the wrath of the radicals in Congress, and legislation combined with military force soon curbed their power.

By 1869 and 1870 there were increasing demands in the North for an end to the southern problem, and gradually, the whites began to recapture the southern state legislatures. Only three states of the former confederacy by 1875 were under radical control, and two years later President Hayes removed the Union army of occupation. Meanwhile, the new legislatures repudiated state debts, together with a large part of their reconstruction costs, and turned their attentions to building a new South maintaining considerable continuity with the old.

The New South

In 1886 Henry W. Grady, editor of the Atlanta *Constitution,* delivered a speech entitled *The New South* before the New England Society of New York. In it he enunciated a bold policy of reconciliation with the North as well as a program of economic and racial readjustment by which the South might achieve an ever higher standard of living. Central in the speech was the need for improvements in agriculture, for an expansion of manufactures, for a more effective exploitation of local natural resources, and for a reasonable settlement of the interracial problem.

It was in the industrial realm, perhaps, that Grady's new South was most rapidly coming into being. Whatever manufacturing had existed in 1860 had been largely destroyed by the war. However, by the 1880's a combination of cheap labor and the energy provided by abundant water power and Alabama coal had produced a growing number of textile mills in the region. Paying piece wages and widely utilizing child labor, these plants soon began effectively to challenge the ascendancy of New England's textile industry. The rapid expansion of the southern mills is well illustrated by the increase from 600,000 spindles in 1880 to 13,000,000 by 1915. The latter figure accounted for well over a third of the entire number of spindles in the nation during that year. Similar growth was evidenced in a number of other important industries. The manufacture of tobacco products boomed in North Carolina and Virginia, as did the lumbering industry in Arkansas. The steel mills of northern Alabama grew so rapidly that they were soon second only to the Pittsburgh area, and Birmingham came to be known as the Pittsburgh of the South. Likewise, the development of the oil industry in Texas and Oklahoma placed those regions among the top oil producers of the world. Clearly, the industrial South was a reality by the time of World War I.

As far as agriculture was concerned, progress was slower and far less certain. The immediate effect of the Civil War was the breakup of large prewar plantations which could no longer be maintained, thereby greatly increasing the number of individual farm owners. In the beginning white owners had tried to maintain the form of the old plantation system by organizing Negroes into the traditional supervised gangs and paying them for their labor. These attempts were largely unsuccessful, however, because of the Negro's lack of familiarity with and responsibility under the wage system.

Although the increase in individual farm owners was a part result, the development of farm tenancy and crop liens was far more widespread. By the former a tenant worked a piece of land for a landlord, gave a stipulated part of the yield to the landlord as rent, and kept the remainder for himself. By the latter an independent farmer gave another man a mortgage on his future crops in return for immediate funds advanced. Both systems clearly grew out of the lack of capital in the postwar South. If a man had no capital, he either had to farm someone else's land or borrow with his prospective crops as guarantee in order to farm his own. In the latter situation crop failures often reduced him to tenancy in any case. Credit was advanced by southern merchants and bankers who in turn secured it from their northern counterparts. The latter were eager to lend at exorbitant rates of interest.

The economic effects of the farm tenancy and crop lien systems were in most cases harmful. Creditors, anxious to guarantee their loans, insisted that debtor farmers raise the one crop for which the market would be certain—cotton. Thus, needed rotation of crops was hindered. Moreover, farmers themselves were interested in high returns with minimum expenditures and thereby ignored the long-term good of the land. In spite of this, however, by 1879 the southern cotton crop had surpassed that of 1860, while by 1900 it had more than doubled. In general, though, southern agriculture at the turn of the century was far from the scientific industry which Grady had envisioned.

With the decline of the reconstruction governments, political power quickly slipped back into the hands of former Confederate Army men. The latter, bitterly opposed to the Republican Party, laid the foundations of the solidly Democratic South and proceeded through frugality, state control, and repudiation of debts to lead the region up from postwar ruin. By means of the poll tax, literacy tests, and other educational qualifications, they rapidly took away from the Negro the franchise guaranteed him by the Fifteenth Amendment, thereby insuring white supremacy. Politically, the new South rapidly integrated into the Union; spiritually, it remained apart in the glorification of an ideal old South that really never was. If by 1918 much of the new South envisioned by Henry Grady had never come to be, a new South was, nevertheless, in existence.

AMERICA BECOMES AN INDUSTRIAL NATION

The Civil War was at heart a struggle between two alternative ways of life—the decentralized agricultural way of the South and the centralized industrial way of the North. The victory of the North has been called by Louis

Hacker the triumph of industrial capitalism. Through it the way was paved for America to become an industrial nation. By 1890 the value added to products by manufacturing already exceeded the value of agricultural products; by 1920 the number of persons engaged in manufacturing exceeded the number in agriculture and the gross value of American manufactures far exceeded that of any other nation. In truth, this enormous development changed the entire face and mind of America, and with it, the character of American education.

The Growth of Manufacturing Industry

A number of important factors combined to render possible this tremendous industrial growth. The first was America's fabulous wealth of natural resources. Forests estimated at over three quarters of a billion acres in their virgin state provided the raw materials for a thousand wood products. Of the nine major known iron deposits in the world, the United States had two. These were supplemented by an abundance of copper, silver, sulfur, phosphates, zinc, lead, and other industrial minerals. In the matter of energy, the nation was also particularly favored, possessing somewhere around half the world's supply of coal, billions of barrels of oil, trillions of cubic feet of natural gas, and a waterpower potential conservatively estimated at thirty-eight million horsepower. A large number of well-situated waterways even further enhanced this favorable picture.

A second factor stimulating the growth of industry came in the form of considerable Congressional aid during and following the Civil War. Tariffs protecting American goods from the competition of cheaper European imports were levied; a national system of banking allowing for tremendous expansions of unregulated credit was legislated; laws allowing the importation of indentured labor from Europe were passed; and direct stimulation in the form of huge monetary land grants was awarded. In effect, American businessmen controlled the national government in their own interest during the decades following 1860.

There were other highly important factors. The flood of immigrants who came to our shores between 1870 and 1910 provided a continuing source of cheap, unskilled labor to serve the machines. American creativity made continuing improvements as evidenced by the fact that over a million patents were issued between 1860 and 1910. The increase of population and its concentration in cities provided a ready market for manufactured goods. Finally, a long tradition of laissez-faire capitalism allowed unprecedented freedom to the captains of industry in building and expanding.

A primary aspect of the growth of industry during these years was the growth of transportation and communication; and probably the outstanding feature of this in the decades following the Civil War was the building of the railroads. Whereas in 1860 there were just over 30,000 miles of track in the nation, by 1900 there were some 200,000. In the twenty years after 1865 the transcontinental lines had reached the Pacific coast, and the main outlines of the country's railroad network has been completed. The history of federal, state, and local grants for the building of these roads is one of profiteering and misappropriation. It has been estimated that by 1870 the federal government had given the various railroad companies land equal to the combined areas of New England, New York, and Pennsylvania. In any case, the roads were built and served as important stimuli not only to industrial development, but also to the populating of the Far West. The expansion of postal, tele-graph, telephone, and finally wireless service served similarly to spur expansion.

The production of machinery and the energy to run it also underwent an enormous growth during the latter decades of the nineteenth century. With the adoption of the Bessemer and open-hearth processes for making steel production of the latter metal soared. A rising supply of iron and steel from the Pittsburgh and Lake Michigan regions fed the busy machinery industry, and by the turn of the century the value of machinery alone was equal to half the total of all manufactures in 1860. Coal, oil, and electricity in increasing amounts provided the energy for these machines, and the result, of course, was a vast rise in the production of consumer goods. In the forty years between 1860 and 1900 the number of factories and shops rose from 140,000 to over 500,000, while their output increased from less than $2 billion to $13 billion. Food products, textiles, clothing, rubber goods, building supplies, household supplies, and office equipment rapidly reached American and world markets and began to change the entire complexion of American life.

The Growth of Large Corporations

In 1860, although some corporations were in existence, most American business was carried on by single proprietors or partnerships. Even many of the large iron and textile mills of the East tended to take the form of unincorporated enterprises. This picture changed considerably during and following the Civil War, however, and the growth of the large corporation paralleled the phenomenal growth of industry. The corporate form, with its independent and continuing existence, limited liability, and possibility for wide distribution of ownership, was admirably suited to the bigness of these new enterprises, and the number and size of corporations increased rapidly in the decades after 1865.

In many cases, however, huge corporations became the means by which businessmen swindled one another and the public. Numerous railroad companies, for example, became the means by which federal subsidies were channeled into private coffers. Other companies stood as giant inflated balloons on flimsy foundations of watered stock. Manipulations, secret price fixing, and plain fraud were common practices in the free competition which existed within and among concerns. Moreover, from single multi-million dollar corporations, it was a short step to trusts and holding companies, in a sense mergers of corporations designed to remove all competition from a given field. The first large trust in America was the Standard Oil Trust, organized by John D. Rockefeller and others in 1882. Trusts in other fields such as steel, beef, sugar, and lead followed closely on the heels of Standard Oil, and the pattern of monopoly rapidly established itself in American industry. When John Moody in 1904 published his book *The Truth About the Trusts,* it listed 318 monopolies representing mergers of 5,300 formerly competing companies.

Undoubtedly, the immensity of these enterprises helped produce a good deal of the efficiency and growth of American industry. On the other hand, it produced a number of glaring abuses. Laissez-faire competition became cut-throat competition. Rate wars, secret agreements, and pooling robbed the public with high prices and uncertain business conditions. Thousands of honest businessmen were ruined as monopolies sought to crush all competition. Gradually, Americans who had traditionally feared the power of government began to look to the government for help. Various states during the 1870's passed Granger Laws regulating freight and passenger rates, and when the railroad companies complained that their rights under the Fifth and Fourteenth Amendments had been violated, the Supreme Court declared the legislation constitutional. In 1887 Congress passed the Interstate Commerce Act further regulating railroad abuses and paving the way for a number of other important railroad acts during the next thirty years. A more comprehensive step was taken in 1890, with the passage of the Sherman Antitrust Act. This law declared illegal every contract, combination in the form of trust or otherwise, or conspiracy in restraint of trade or commerce among the several states. While its provisions were not enforced at first, the Sherman Act provided the whole basis of Theodore Roosevelt's program of "trust busting," and during the twenty-five years after its passage it was continually strengthened by a line of legislation which culminated with the Clayton Antitrust Act of 1914.

The Continuing Growth of Cities

The movement to the cities which had begun well before the Civil War continued and accelerated in post-Appomattox years. By 1890, 30 percent of the American people lived in cities, and New York, Chicago, and Philadelphia had passed a million in population. Drawing their people from the rural areas and from the waves of immigrants, these communities rapidly became what Arthur Meier Schlesinger has called the nerve centers of the new industrial order. By the census of 1920 well over half the population of the United States lived in places classified as urban.

The cities themselves were tremendous pictures in contrast. In them were concentrated the banks, the distributors, the factories, and the armies of middle-class people and workingmen to serve them. The grossly overdone mansions of the newly emerging upper-middle and upper classes stood side by side with tenements and slums in which crowded immigrant families lived among unspeakable conditions. All of the problems which had traditionally come to be associated with teaming urban communities beset these new centers of population. Organized crime spread by leaps and bounds, and small, newly founded police departments could do little to prevent it. Disease was rampant and fed avidly on the unhygienic conditions of the slum neighborhoods. A combination of concentrated wealth and vast building projects, public and private, led the corruption in urban politics to dwarf lawlessness in other parts of the country. It has been estimated, for example, that the Tweed Ring in New York City looted the public of something between $20 and $200 million dollars during the 1860's and 1870's. Its counterparts in Philadelphia, Washington, St. Louis, Minneapolis, and San Francisco were equally successful. Urban politics during the fifty years following 1865 was truly "the shame of the cities."

In spite of this glaring maladministration, significant improvements did take place in urban life during these decades. Professional fire and police departments were organized; sewerage and sanitation facilities were constructed; streets were paved and lighted; and electric and cable cars began to provide speedy public transportation. On the whole, city dwellers undertook to face their new problems experimentally and creatively, and they rapidly built a new American way of life.

The Revolution in Farming

Pre-Civil War agriculture in America was a picture of crude techniques, simple tools, and wasteful methods. Vast stretches of cheap fertile land had always been readily available to the West, and such advanced principles as crop rotation, the use of fertilizer, and intensive cultivation held no attraction to the men exploiting the virgin continent. Inventions such as McCormick's reaper were available as early as the 1830's, but little use was made of them. By 1860 enough progress had been made for the census report of that year to note that in nearly every department of rural industry mechanical power had wrought a revolution. Yet, it was not until the decades after 1865 that farm machinery came into general use. During that era, as one major aspect of the general industrializing of America, agricultural mechanization proceeded at an astounding rate. Spurred on by a myriad of inventions—twine binders, harvesters, combines, grain drills, etc.—the old agricultural order rapidly took on the character of a modern industrial economy.

Between 1860 and 1890 the value of farm machinery in the nation doubled, and in the thirty years after 1890 it increased some 700 percent. When this is combined with the fact that in the thirty years after 1870 more land was added to America's farms than all the farming acreage developed since the earliest settlements, the phenomenal increase in agricultural yields begins to be explained. Moreover, although the percentage of farm workers in the United States decreased during these years (because of the vast rise of city populations), in actual numbers the farm population increased by some 5 million persons. A further stimulus to farm production, especially after 1890, came from the application of scientific knowledge and techniques to agriculture. From the land-grant colleges and from newly established agricultural experiment stations came a steady stream of information on soil analysis, fertilizers, cattle breeding, control of pests, etc.

Stimulated by these favorable factors, phenomenal yields came from American agriculture in the decades after 1860. The production of wheat, for example, rose from 173 million bushels in 1860 to nearly 500 million in 1880 and to a phenomenal 1 billion bushels in 1915. Similarly, corn production rose from nearly 839 million bushels in 1860 to over 3 billion in 1920. Other major crops as well as livestock production also showed unprecedented increases during these same years. It is little wonder that during World War I America was the granary of Western Europe.

The plight of the farmer.   Strangely enough, one of the most widespread results of this revolution in farming was the gradual ruination of the farmer. As production figures mounted, prices began a steady fall. The price of wheat, for example, went from $1.05 per bushel between 1866 and 1875 to $.66 between 1896 and 1900. Similar drops occurred in prices of other crops and livestock. When this situation was aggravated by physical phenomena such as droughts, windstorms, and insect plagues, the financial plight of the farmer became ever more acute. The extent of the situation is illustrated in the fact that by 1900, thirty-one percent of the nation's farms were mortgaged (with a high proportion of these in states like Wisconsin, Iowa, Nebraska, and the Dakotas) and large numbers of formerly independent farmers had slipped into tenancy.

Farm organization.   Increasingly, the farmers began to turn to organization and political action in the hope of ameliorating their condition. In 1867 the National Grange of the Patrons of Husbandry was organized, and less than a decade later boasted 800,000 members. During the years after its founding the organization was extremely active in agricultural and domestic education, in fostering social activities in rural regions, and in stimulating the growth of cooperatives. Needless to say, it was vigorously opposed by private business interests in this latter activity. In the 1880's the work of the Grange was supplemented by a far more militant organization, and one with a far more politically oriented program—the Farmers' Alliance. Organized into a northern and a southern group, the Alliance worked for a number of ends with which farmers had become identified: regulation of railroads, modifications in the banking system (which would allow greater expansion of farm credit), a government controlled currency more favorable to a debtor group, and a number of political reforms.

Paralleling the rise of these organizations was the growth of farmers' political parties. Appearing during the early years of the Grange, and often closely connected with it, these parties elected a number of candidates to office in agricultural states like Iowa and Kansas. Both the Grange and these parties were partly responsible for securing legislation like the Interstate Commerce Act and the Sherman Antitrust Act. Growing activity in the political arena culminated with the formation in 1891 of the Populist Party, which represented the first real and major challenge to the ascendancy of the business and industrial interests in American national politics. Of the many diverse interests which went to compose this party, the farmers were at all odds one of the strongest and one of the most powerful determinants of policy.

The Labor Movement

Another of the strong elements in the Populist Party was organized labor. The warnings which an earlier generation of labor leaders from 1830 had given the American workingman had rapidly become reality. Increasingly, the laborers who tended the fires and machines of America's new industry began to realize that individually they were helpless against their employers. Without organization they could not resist the exploitation and abuse which so often characterized industrial policy. In 1860 labor unions enrolled a pitifully small percentage of American workers and wielded commensurate power. By 1918, although a long and bloody struggle for organization remained ahead, they had secured a firm foothold in American life.

The organization of the National Labor Union a year after the end of the Civil War represented the first attempt of workingmen to create such a group on a national basis. It was a short-lived effort, however, going out of existence six years after its founding. In spite of this, it managed to enroll over 600,000 workers during that period. The 1870's marked a stormy period for American labor. During those depression years numerous disturbances broke out in industrial areas, and there were dozens of violent encounters between workingmen and police. Terroristic groups, such as the "Molly Maguires" of the Pennsylvania coal fields, considerably aggravated this strained situation.

It was in this period of tension that an organization destined to dominate the labor scene in the 1880's was slowly increasing its membership. Founded as a secret society in 1869, the Knights of Labor worked "to secure to the toilers a proper share of the wealth that they create; more of the leisure that rightfully belongs to them; more societary advantages." Attempting, as did its predecessor, to organize all American workers into one national union, the group directed a principal appeal to the increasing group of unskilled laborers.

The successful conduct of a strike against Jay Gould's railroad greatly strengthened the union's stature in 1884, but two years later an unfortunate incident undermined their status with the public. The Knights, in concert with a number of independent unions, struck for an eight-hour day in Chicago. When police fired on a number of demonstrators outside the Chicago McCormick Harvester works, a mass protest meeting was held in Haymarket Square the next day. As the police arrived at the latter meeting, a bomb was thrown, killing seven of the demonstrators and wounding a number of others. Although responsibility was never traced to the Knights of Labor, public reaction opposed them, and the organization began a steady decline after that year.

Concurrent with the downfall of the Knights, a new workingmen's organization appeared on the scene—the American Federation of Labor (A.F. of L.). Organized on a craft basis, and disavowing all radical doctrines, the federation attempted to work within the framework of the capitalist system as it then existed. In addition to strikes and collective bargaining, this group also embarked on a political policy of "rewarding its friends and punishing its enemies." The years of the 1890's, however, were difficult years for labor organizations. Many of the larger industrial concerns set out on a vigorous campaign to crush unionism. There was continuing violence between police, militia, and workingmen. In 1904, with the organization of the radical International Workers of the World, the labor movement in general had to fight charges of socialism, communism, and disloyalty. In spite of this, however, the membership of the A.F. of L. increased to 500,000 by the turn of the century and 2 million by the outbreak of World War I.

Brief mention should also be made of the successful organization and growth of the railroad brotherhoods by the end of the nineteenth century. Founded as independent groups, the Locomotive Engineers, the Railway Conductors, the Locomotive Firemen and Enginemen and the Railroad Trainmen were all in existence by the 1870's. Devoting themselves extensively to benevolent purposes as well as union activity, they gradually achieved importance in the development of American transportation.

THE CHANGING AMERICAN POPULATION

The New Immigration

The year 1882 marked an important transition from an old American immigration to a new one. During the years before that time the bulk of the immigrants had come from northwestern Europe, particularly from England, Ireland, Germany, and Scandinavia. Except for the Irish, they had generally pushed inland, settling the rich fertile territories of the middle, northwestern, and middle western states. The decade from 1850 to 1860 had witnessed a remarkable rise in this immigration, with more than 2.5 million arrivals.

Despite the Civil War, almost as many came during the 1860's, while over 2.8 million braved the depression years of the 1870's. In the 1880's, nineteenth-century immigration reached a peak when more than 5 million newcomers reached American shores.

It was during this latter decade that the character of American immigration began to change significantly. Instead of the northwestern parts, the southern and eastern portions of Europe began to supply the newcomers, with Italy, Austria-Hungary, and Russia contributing by far the greatest numbers. In England, Germany, and Scandinavia, commercial and industrial development had reached the point where the economic lure of America, while ever present, was by no means as great proportionately. In Austria-Hungary, on the other hand, many of the peasants were still living under semifeudal conditions; in Italy there was a vast oversupply of labor constantly stimulated by a high birth rate; and in Russia of the 1880's pogroms and harsh restrictions made conditions increasingly untenable for the Jewish population. It is little wonder, then, that immigrants from these latter countries continued to view America as a promised land, and flocked there by the hundreds of thousands.

While in the year 1882 itself, the vast majority of immigrants still came from the older sources, the years immediately following saw a pronounced shift to the newer sources. By 1900 the balance had moved in favor of the southern and eastern European nations, and in the first decade of the twentieth century some 8.8 million persons, largely from these latter sources, reached America's shores. Apart from nationality, these newcomers differed from the older immigrants in a number of other ways. First of all, in contrast to their predecessors who settled on farms, the new arrivals remained largely in the new cities of the Northeast. There they served as a reservoir of unskilled labor for rapidly expanding industries, laboring at wages far below the acceptable minimum for native American workingmen. Differing from the earlier Anglo-Saxons far more than the latter nationalities had differed among themselves, the new immigrants tended to settle in self-contained communities that perpetuated the language, customs, practices, and standards of their homelands. Furthermore, whereas the older immigrants had come with their families, a far higher proportion of this new immigration was made up of single men who hoped at some future date to return to their homelands with their earnings. Finally, a far higher rate of illiteracy was evidenced among these later immigrants than among the earlier, thereby causing political and educational problems of the first magnitude in the cities where they settled.

As with the earlier immigrants, the post-Civil War newcomers were by no means universally welcomed. Many Protestants feared the increasing number of Roman Catholic arrivals, and some of the former organized the American Protective Association in 1887 to promote a spirit of nativism. Vigorous opposition to the immigrants came from organized labor whose

Table 4—American Immigration, 1860–1920

Period	Total	North and West Europe		South and East Europe	
		Number	Percent	Number	Percent
1861–1870	2,314,824	2,031,624	87.8	33,628	1.4
1871–1880	2,812,191	2,070,373	73.6	201,889	7.2
1881–1890	5,246,613	3,778,633	72.0	958,413	18.3
1891–1900	3,687,564	1,643,492	44.6	1,915,486	51.9
1901–1910	8,795,386	1,910,035	21.7	6,225,981	70.8
1911–1920	5,735,811	997,438	17.4	3,379,126	58.9

aims were challenged by the competition of lower standards of living. The combination of such forces procured a number of laws which, although they themselves did not actually do so, foreshadowed a substantial change in American immigration policy. In 1882 legislation was passed excluding convicts, lunatics, idiots, and others likely to become public charges. In that same year Chinese were excluded for ten years, a period which was made indefinite in 1902. By arrangement with the Japanese government immigration from Japan for all intents and purposes ceased in 1907. Finally, in 1917 the passing of a literacy test in some language was required of all newcomers. The virtual ending of immigration in large numbers was to come but a few years later.

The Changing Characteristics of the Population

The composition of the American population in general evidenced a number of highly important changes by the beginning of the twentieth century. Although accurate statistics are not available, there is little doubt that both the birth rate and the death rate decreased steadily during the nineteenth century. As far as the former was concerned, it has been roughly estimated that the crude birth rate per 1,000 white population fell from 55 in 1800 to 41 in 1860 to 30 in 1900. Concerning the death rate, most progress seems to have been made during the last quarter of the century, and the death figure in the registration area in 1900 stood at 17.6 per 1,000 population. Closely related to the latter was the increase in life expectancy for the average adult —a figure which is estimated to have gone from under thirty-five years at the close of the eighteenth century to around forty-five years at the beginning of the nineteenth. Regarding family size, a decrease was also in evidence, with the figure dropping from 5.7 persons on the average in 1790 to 4.6 in 1900.

A combination of these factors brought about a gradual change in the age composition of the American people. The crux of this change—one with important educational implications—seems to have been a reduction in the proportion of young people, an increase in the proportion of older people, and an increase in the median age. The following graph will serve well to illustrate the course of this development:

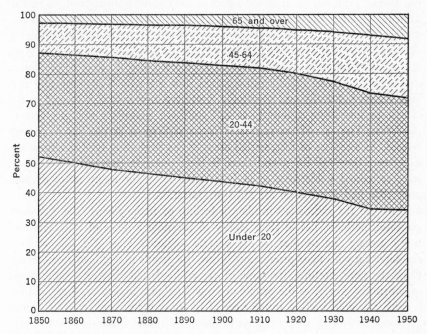

Proportion of population in each age distribution of total population, 1850–1950. [Based on U. S. Department of Commerce, Bureau of the Census, *Historical Statistics of the United States, 1789–1945* (Washington, D. C., Government Printing Office, 1949), p. 28, and *1950 Census of Population, Preliminary Reports,* Series PC-7, No. 1, p. 6.]

NATIONAL AMERICA BECOMES A WORLD POWER

The movement toward nationalism so clearly seen during the first half-century of the Republic continued with accelerated speed in the decades following the Civil War. Of the many factors which helped to foster national spirit—and which in turn were affected by it—three seem to have stood out as primary: the growth of communications, the coming of centralization and "bigness" to American life, and America's participation in two major wars by 1918. The latter indicated only too well that this newly powerful and unified America could no longer shun participation in world affairs in spite of a traditional determination to do so. Thus, the years before 1918 also witnessed growing American influence in the political and economic life of Europe and Asia, a fact which was ultimately destined to change the power structure of the world.

The Growth of Communications

The tremendous expansion of transportation and communications after 1860 has already been discussed as one aspect of the rise of industrialism. Its role in knitting together the various sections of the country was none the less important. One of the prime forces in uniting the West with the North during the Civil War, for example, had been the railroads built before 1860. With the rapid rebuilding and expansion of southern railroads after Appomattox, that region too was rapidly reintegrated into the whole, economically perhaps before politically and spiritually. Southern raw materials flowed to the North in increasing amounts, as did southern manufactured products to the West. The role of the railroads in the settlement of the Far West was crucial. As a matter of fact, settled areas at the beginning tended almost entirely to follow rail lines, and there is little question that the West would have remained wilderness, or at best range land, for many more decades after 1880 had it not been for rail transportation.

How did the railroads stimulate a feeling of nationalism? The principal response, perhaps, lies in their ability to promote a sense of sameness and unity among the peoples of the various regions. They did this well in combination with mass production. Thus, the people in California could purchase the same clothing, the same processed foods (in effect, the same range of consumer goods) as the people of New England. Moreover, they paid for it with the gold bullion much needed by eastern business interests. Thus, the maintenance of common ways of doing things, of common business procedures, of a common monetary exchange, and of common laws was of advantage to all concerned.

No less important was the increasing interchange of ideas during these years. By the 1870's the telegraph had effectively connected the major communities of the country, and news of a given event could be disseminated in a matter of hours. Rapid improvement came in succeeding decades with the advent of the telephone, and later, the wireless. A rising literacy rate, fed by growing numbers of newspapers, periodicals, and books, further enhanced the similarity of ideas. Little by little, and without ignoring significant regional differences, the later years of the nineteenth century witnessed an ever increasing sameness in the habits, the values, and the attitudes of the American people. What with the vast material progress of the nation and a long tradition of national pride, it was a short step to thinking this way of life superior to all others.

The Increasing Centralization of American Life

The "bigness" which industrialism brought to American life affected not only the business world, but other important areas as well. The advent of national labor and farmer organizations has already been alluded to. Similarly, veterans' and various professional groups also organized on a country-wide basis. Even the churches began to coalesce into national units. In effect, what was happening was a new organization of power in the American economy and society. Businesses discovered that large concerns, through mass operations, streamlining of processes, standardization of procedures, and often by sheer use of the power of size, were able to crush competition and dominate industries. The same large concerns wielded tremendous powers in legislatures and with other political agencies. It was not long before workingmen realized that to meet this power, they too would have to organize on a large scale. The National Labor Union, Knights of Labor, and American Federation of Labor are ample testimony to this point. Once this movement toward the concentration of power through organization had thus begun, it spread rapidly to other groups who also realized that only in this manner might their voices be heard and their policies given attention.

Perhaps the most interesting documentation of this trend toward centralization was its presence in national politics and government. By the 1880's Henry Grady's forward-looking spirit of conciliation with the North was already achieving widespread acceptance. For a new generation of Americans the hatreds of the 1860's had far less meaning, and therefore far less vitality. Communication and common problems brought an increasing feeling of unity to the two regions, and twenty years after Appomattox northern and southern veterans' organizations were holding meetings together to exchange reminiscences of the conflict.

The Thirteenth, Fourteenth, and Fifteenth Amendments clearly illustrated growing ascendancy of the national government in internal affairs. The latter two spoke of "citizens of the United States" and prohibited the several states from abridging certain rights of these citizens. Such provisions represented merely one manifestation of the imposition of federal power over state power—a movement which was strengthened considerably twenty years later when the Supreme Court (in the Wabash and Minnesota Rate Cases) took on the responsibility of passing judgment on state legislation.

Interestingly enough, as far as business interests were concerned, bigness in government proved a two-edged sword. From the early nineteenth century forward a powerful central government had consistently been to the distinct advantage of commercial and industrial groups. Such a government could serve well in effecting internal improvements (for example, Henry Clay's American Plan), keeping protective tariffs high, donating vast grants of land, and managing the currency to the advantage of businessmen. That the government played this role well has already been pointed out in the treatment of the rise of industrialism; that it has continued to play this role to greater or lesser extent down to the present is unquestionable.

The other edge of this two-edged sword began slowly, but surely, to sharpen during and after the 1870's. Taking a good lesson from the way in which the industrial groups had used the power of government to their advantage, labor and farm groups turned to the same source to redress their grievances. Once again, it was a question of bigness. If business groups had the power of the federal government behind them, and if some of these groups represented hundreds of millions of dollars worth of economic power, then labor and farm groups could ill afford to turn to local or state governments for succor. More and more, they too demanded favorable legislation of the national government. Their demands eventually produced the succession of laws regulating monopoly, interstate commerce, and business practices in general. If the enforcement of these laws was not general during the closing years of the nineteenth century, they did provide the legislative springboard for the extensive use of national power that characterized the "trust-busting" efforts of President Theodore Roosevelt.

One final point is worthy of mention here: the dramatic shift in public opinion implicit in these changes. In roughly a hundred years since the founding of the republic the federal government had changed in the minds of the people from an enemy to a friend. No longer did "that government which governed least govern best." The question now was, which interests and groups the government was best serving. Increasingly, then, politics became not the effort to maintain freedom from government, but rather to secure with the support of government this or that view of society. Arising slowly, this concept of government did not reach its culmination in America until the New Deal came to power on a platform of using the resources of the government to pull the nation out of the worst economic depression in history.

The Growth of Nationalism During the Spanish-American War and World War I

Throughout history wars have been a means of removing the differences and cementing the bonds of loyalty and common purpose within the societies which fight them. The two major wars which America fought between 1865 and 1918 were no exception. Although one of the most important foreign policy debates in American history emerged out of the second, their role in stimulating the growth of nationalism was profound.

Interestingly enough, nationalism itself was probably among the most, if not the most, significant causes of the Spanish-American War. The conflict itself originated out of the Cuban Revolution of 1895, the latter insurrection having occurred at just about the time when a circulation war between Joseph Pulitzer and William Randolph Hearst, publishers of the New York *World* and *Journal,* respectively, reached its peak. The Cuban conflict, therefore, provided a superb source for the kind of atrocity stories so valuable in attracting readers, and the appearance of a number of such articles spurred American sentiment for the Cuban cause. The whole affair came to a head in February 1898 when the *Journal* printed a letter written by the Spanish minister in Washington which attacked the personal qualities of President McKinley. Fiery anger was fed even further when six days later the United States battleship *Maine* blew up in Havana harbor. The newspapers were quick to attribute the incident to Spain, and the slogan "Remember the Maine" echoed from New York to San Francisco. Although the matter might have been settled amicably, the United States declared war two months later, a conflict which Hearst was happy to acknowledge as "the *Journal's* war."

In spite of the dubious origins of the war, Americans rallied to support their cause. All were convinced that they were fighting to liberate the Cubans and grant them the blessings of self-government. Spain was the Goliath who had to be conquered in the cause of freedom. Though the war was short, it engendered a high degree of national spirit. The bond issues floated to support it were heavily subscribed. Commodore Dewey's crushing defeat of the enemy fleet in Manila Bay and the successful charge of the "Rough Riders" under Teddy Roosevelt during the Battle of San Juan rapidly joined Bunker Hill and Saratoga in the folklore of the people. Four months after its commencement the war ended in the defeat of Spain and her relinquishment a few months after of almost her entire colonial empire.

America's participation in World War I, less than twenty years later, can scarcely be conceived of on the same scale as that of the earlier conflict. In this twentieth-century conflict it was no longer a matter of a small professional army fighting the war while the majority of the civilian population went about its business as usual. The whole people fought this war, financially, industrially, and militarily. As in the case of the Spanish-American War, national honor and a sense of waging a world-wide battle for democracy were powerful factors in bringing America into the struggle. As late as 1916, Woodrow Wilson was elected President on the strength of his having kept the nation out of war. In a little over a year the German policy of unrestricted submarine warfare plus a continuing flow of atrocity stories and effronteries to America's sense of righteousness had reversed this earlier policy, and in April 1917 America entered the war on the side of the allies.

The scope of America's response to the declaration was enormous. Through Selective Service the armed forces rose from under 400,000 in April, 1917, to 4,800,000 when the armistice was signed some nineteen months later. The inevitable standardization of army life rapidly promoted feelings of unity among urban Americans who had lived in the country for less than a year and midwestern Americans whose ancestry went back to the early settlers. Twenty-one billion dollars was raised in four Liberty Loans and one Victory Loan—all of them subscribed to by the great body of the American people. With mobilization the national government assumed vast powers and used many of them to produce industrial efficiency through further standardization. Under groups like the Committee on Public Information, established by Congress not only to inform the public but also to "sell" the war, national spirit was stimulated through every available medium of communication, pamphlets, newspapers, motion pictures, and posters. In effect, every aspect of the nation's life became permeated with the will to win the war—and unfortunately, the spirit of nationalism was carried so far that it all too often resulted in the suppression of legitimate criticism. In any case, for a year and a half the American people showed a unity of purpose and a common will equaled in few of the previous periods of their history.

America Becomes a World Power

An unprecedented provision was included as part of the American declaration of war on Spain in 1898. It read: ". . . the United States hereby disclaims any disposition or intention to exercise sovereignty, jurisdiction or control over said Island [Cuba] except for the pacification thereof, and asserts its determination, when that is accomplished, to leave the government and control of the Island to its people." In spite of this resolution, however, the conflict and victory which ensued actually changed the policy of the United States from one of complete isolation to one of growing interest and participation in world affairs.

With the Treaty of Paris, which concluded the war with Spain, America acquired control of Cuba temporarily and of Puerto Rico, Guam, and the Philippine Islands. In addition, 1898 saw America's annexation of the Hawaiian Islands as a territory, while the next year witnessed the addition of a number of smaller Pacific islands. These acquisitions marked the first major additions to United States territory since the purchase of Alaska in 1867 and posed immediately the vital question of world policy for the American people. The latter were far from ready to meet the problems implicit in imperialism. The business interests were anxious to expand their markets by adding underdeveloped areas to America's sphere of influence. Witnessing the glutting of local and even national markets with an increasing flow of manufactured supplies, they saw in these underdeveloped areas the same advantages as other industrial powers had recognized decades before: important sources of raw materials and important outlets for manufactured products.

The policy of imperialism, however, posed many important problems. What about trained personnel to administer these new possessions? What would be the status of the new peoples? Would they be citizens or colonials? Would the new territories be allowed statehood? Would diverse peoples with widely varying ways of life be able to assume the ways of democracy? Although answers to some of these questions were quickly settled by the Supreme Court (such as in the Insular Cases which held that America might possess territories outside the continental limits of the United States and that the inhabitants of these territories did not necessarily have the rights of citizens), responses to others were long in coming.

Once this policy of expansion had begun, it proceeded steadily. One of the great engineering feats of history was accomplished with the completion of the Panama Canal in 1914. With it the United States was able to protect interests in both the Atlantic and Pacific Oceans with one navy. Once built, the canal became one of the most important links in America's chain of defense and its protection a major aspect of foreign policy. American interests were further expanded when President Roosevelt proclaimed the Roosevelt Corollary to the Monroe Doctrine, by which America enjoined European nations from *economic* as well as political penetration in the affairs of Latin America. The first two decades of the nineteenth century saw the growing power of the United States in Caribbean affairs, as well as the attempt to organize hemispheric cooperation under the Pan-American movement. Finally, the expansion of American interest and power to the Far East marked another step in the development of a world policy. Friendly relations between the United States and China led to a number of favorable treaties and in 1899 to American leadership in securing an Open-Door Policy of equal trading rights for all nations in Chinese ports. When China became a republic in 1912, America took the lead in aiding the infant nation to remain on its feet. By literally opening up Japan to Western influences the United States vitally affected the life of that nation.

In view of this growing interest and power in world affairs, one might well have expected overwhelming support for President Wilson's League of Nations idea after World War I. The results of the struggle over ratification of the Treaty of Versailles, however, attest to the great power of isolationism among the people. Under Senators Henry Cabot Lodge and William Borah the League went down to defeat in Congress in spite of President Wilson's herculean attempt to organize public opinion in favor of passage. When separate treaties were completed with the defeated Central Powers in 1920, America stood in the paradoxical position of a nation who refused to take the reins of a world leadership made inevitable by its political and economic might.

PROBLEMS OF HUMANITARIANISM AND DEMOCRACY

The Social Problems of an Industrial Civilization

The American social reformer, so much a part of American life during the antebellum period, increasingly turned his attention to the ills of industrialism and urbanization in the years after 1865. In the teeming slums of the cities poverty, disease, vice, and crime annually took their toll in human misery. Much influenced by similar movements in England, a number of social settlements began to appear in American cities during and following the 1880's. The most famous of these was Hull House, founded by Jane Addams and

Ellen G. Starr in Chicago in 1889. In this and other such settlements social workers lived among their charges and organized a multitude of activities designed to enrich the living of slum residents. Other individuals and groups worked in a hundred other ways and directions to alleviate these social evils. The efforts of Jacob A. Riis of the *New York Sun* to improve housing standards will long be remembered. Others turned their attention to the problems of "children's rights." The organization in New York of the Society for the Prevention of Cruelty to Children attests to the widespread interest in this movement. Closely allied with this latter effort was the growing interest in the problems of child delinquency and punishment, and innovations like the special reformatory for younger offenders, the indeterminate sentence, and the parole system soon appeared in penal practice. Health problems were attacked by state boards of health; by the 1880's the latter agencies were fairly common. Local authorities were quick to follow suit. Needless to say, the findings of scientists and physicians in no small measure were responsible for the ever declining death rate.

While a majority of the social reformers were content to work at these problems within the framework of the society as it then existed, a small but significant group saw the only hope resting in drastic alteration of America's social and economic structure. Many of the radical social and political ideas of Europe found their way into America, and socialism, communism, anarchism, nihilism, and innumerable other social philosophies were preached to America's bourgeois workingmen. Soon after the Civil War, socialist parties appeared in the major industrial centers of the East, and they grew to the point where a unified Socialist Party under Eugene V. Debs polled a little short of 1,000,000 votes in the election of 1920. Anarchism gained a far smaller number of adherents, and the rather drastic measures of the anarchists rapidly brought public disdain for the movement, to a point where just after the turn of the century all anarchists were excluded from immigration by law.

As might be expected, both the less and the more extreme movements mentioned above produced a considerable body of literature of social protest. This involved at least two types of writing: the utopia and the criticism. Of the first, there seems little doubt that Edward Bellamy's *Looking Backward, 2000–1887,* was the most popular and widely read. Its vision of a perfect society of plenty, a society devoid of crime, want, and poverty, carried great appeal for a people who had traditionally combined a belief in inevitable progress with a faith in their own manifest destiny. Doubtless, Henry George's *Progress and Poverty* awakened similar aspirations. Throughout both ran an optimism which had characterized the American mind since the early years of the republic. On the heels of these utopias came a flood of "muckraking" literature exposing and criticizing the sordid conditions of industrial life. Ida Tarbell's *History of the Standard Oil Company* was among the first of a long series of publications exposing and documenting the seamy side of American business growth. Upton Sinclair's novel *The Jungle* sharply awakened Americans to the problem of sanitation in the meat packing industry, as well as the sordid quality of immigrant life in the new world. Another area of interest was exhibited by Lincoln Steffens and others who turned their probing eyes toward the corruption in local and national government and politics. These and hundreds of other materials increasingly turned the interest of the people to the pressing problems they treated.

The Movement Toward Women's Suffrage

The movement to give women the vote, one which had been powerful in the antebellum period, revived with growing force after 1865. Two women's suffrage associations were organized in 1869, and both proceeded to work earnestly for local and national reform. In spite of support from organizations such as the Knights of Labor and the American Federation of Labor, none but local progress was made before the twentieth century, and it was principally in the Midwest that these innovations appeared. What actually happened was that women began to achieve the vote first in specific areas (such as school elections) and in specific localities. Full equality was first granted when Wyoming entered the union in 1890, and Wyoming's example was followed by a few other states.

In spite of these very real beginnings, however, the major political parties tended to ignore the issue. It was not until the extremely widespread participation of women in World War I provided overwhelming testimony as to the justice of their demands that federal action universalizing the practice was forthcoming. Wilson, who had earlier chosen to leave the matter to the states, now saw it as a means of demonstrating America's belief in democracy to the world. Accordingly, Congress approved a proposed women's suffrage amendment to the Constitution in 1919; a little over a year later enough states had ratified it to enable women to participate as a group in the national elections of 1920.

Color and the Civil Rights Question

Of profound importance during these years was the development of a body of legal principles bearing on the civil rights of non-Caucasian persons, particularly Negroes. The Thirteenth Amendment to the Constitution had abolished slavery; the Fourteenth, after conferring citizenship on all persons born or naturalized in the United States, had prohibited states from abridging the privileges and immunities of citizens or from denying equal protection of the laws; and the Fifteenth had prohibited the states from abridging the right of citizens to vote because of "race, color, or previous condition of servitude." Congress had also enacted a number of laws designed to enforce the spirit and the provisions of these amendments. Of these, probably the most significant was the Civil Rights Act of 1875, guaranteeing to all persons "the full and equal enjoyment of the accommodations, advantages, facilities, and privileges of inns, public conveyances on land or water, theaters, and other places of public amusement; subject only to the conditions and limitations established by law, and applicable alike to citizens of every race and color, regardless of any previous condition of servitude."

With the withdrawal of federal troops from the South in 1877, however, many of the changes introduced by the reconstruction governments were quickly reversed. Laws prohibiting intermarriage, mixed schools, and social intercourse quickly appeared. In 1875 Tennessee gave legal permission for hotels, railroads, and theaters to discriminate against persons of color; while six years later, this was reaffirmed by a "Jim Crow" law permitting separate railroad cars or compartments for Negroes. Other states followed suit soon afterward, and when the trend was challenged in 1883 before the Supreme Court on the basis of the Civil Rights Act of 1875, those sections which the state legislation seemed to contravene were declared unconstitutional. Congress did not have the power, held the court, to regulate by law the social associations of persons. The way was left clear for state action in this realm.

One of the most interesting doctrines which was applied to the question of segregation was the one of "separate but equal" facilities. Curiously enough, the principle was first enunciated in the Supreme Court of Massachusetts in 1849. A Negro named Benjamin Roberts had attempted to enter his five-year-old daughter Sarah in one of the public white primary schools of the Boston district in which he resided. When the application was rejected by the school committee solely on the grounds of color, Roberts brought suit against the city for damages. He retained Charles Sumner, later to be prominent in the Reconstruction Congress and an ardent opponent of slavery, as counsel. Sumner argued eloquently for the equality of all human beings before God and before the law. He argued that separate facilities could never be equivalent because of the stigma of caste they imposed. Nevertheless, the court ruled unanimously that Boston in providing separate schools for colored children was not violating their equal rights to education.

Although Boston six years later abolished separate schools for Negroes, the principle enunciated in the Roberts case persisted. It appeared in a number of state supreme court decisions, and finally figured prominently in a United States Supreme Court decision in 1896. In the highly influential case of *Plessey* v. *Ferguson,* the Roberts decision was cited as a major precedent for the right of the state to require segregation of colored and white persons in public conveyances. Thus the "separate but equal" doctrine became a support for legal segregation.

Going further than simple segregation, a succession of laws virtually destroyed the political rights of southern Negroes in the last decades of the nineteenth century. Some states passed "grandfather" clauses which made one qualification for voting the fact that one's grandfather had done so previously. Naturally, this excluded most Negroes who had gained citizenship under the Fourteenth Amendment. Other states enacted vague literacy requirements by which local authorities could disbar Negroes on technical grounds. Even worse than these denials of right were the extra-legal crimes committed against Negro persons. Between 1880 and 1900 some 2,000 lynchings were reported, with Mississippi, Georgia, and Louisiana as the worst offenders.

While the problem was most pressing in the case of Negroes because of their number alone, similar denials of civil and political rights were carried out against Americans who were members of the red and yellow races. In spite of efforts to secure equality of right for these minorities, discrimination and segregation was the rule in most communities where they appeared in substantial numbers.

RELIGION AND THE CHURCHES

The Growth of Non-Protestant Groups

One of the most striking facts about American church groups after 1865 was the steady increase of non-Protestant organizations. While the character of American religion remained largely Protestant, the growth of other denominations exercised a profound effect on American life and education. The Roman Catholic Church, for example, grew rapidly with the large Irish, German, and Italian immigrations of the nineteenth century. Inasmuch as many of these immigrant families tended to settle in the larger cities, the Roman Catholic Church became particularly strong in urban communities. Often, in the latter places, religious affiliations thereby assumed ascendancy in local politics.

Among the most important problems with which Americans concerned themselves during the latter half of the nineteenth century was that of primary loyalties among these Catholic groups. The problem was framed most widely as one of loyalty to the nation or loyalty to the Pope in Rome. Much of the earlier nativism which had been directed toward Roman Catholicism as a "foreign influence" continued during this period, and there was mounting criticism of Catholicism on this account. On the other hand, it is impossible to deny the significant Americanizing of the Catholic Church in the United States. In spite of the Syllabus of Errors, by which Pope Pius IX condemned many of the liberal institutions and ideas which enjoyed favor in America, a number of prominent Catholic churchmen like Cardinal Gibbons and Archbishop Ireland espoused liberal ideas both in the United States and in Rome, and it is known that the former was influential in persuading the Roman authorities that it would be a mistake to condemn the Knights of Labor in 1887. On the other hand, in the matter of education, which will be discussed later, the Church was adamant on the question of having and operating its own parochial school system.

The growing Eastern-European immigration after 1890 led to a concomitant increase in the Jewish population of the United States. While there had been a few Jews in America during the eighteenth century, and while their number had increased significantly with the German immigrations of the later 1840's and early 1850's, they had not exercised a particularly important influence on religious, educational, or social thought. Now, as their numbers grew, there were effects both on Judaism itself and on American life as a whole. Just as there was an Americanizing of the Roman Catholic Church, so might Reform Judaism be viewed as a kind of Americanizing of the Jewish religion, although Reform Judaism was by no means confined to America. Jewish leadership was also prominent in the founding of the Ethical Culture Society, a group which sought to make ethics rather than theology the heart of religious experience.

A study of state constitutions, statutes, and court decisions reveals that the increasing heterogeneity of American religious life only reinforced the determination to support the separation of church and state. For some, to be sure, separation was simply a protection against control by Roman Catholic interests and doctrines; for others separation was the attempt to attain true governmental neutrality toward the various religious groups. In any case, from 1876 onward all new states added to the Union were required by Congress to include in their basic laws an irrevocable ordinance guaranteeing religious freedom and the principles of the First Amendment. Inasmuch as education was one of the central problems involved in separation, it is worthwhile to note that both the prohibition against using public funds for sectarian schools and the prohibition against teaching sectarian religions in public schools were almost universally expressed in principle by 1900.

Increased Social Awareness Among American Churches

Just as the minister on the frontier had to make his religion far more practical and meaningful to his parishioners if he wished to interest them than did the more established minister of the eastern states, so did all of the churches face the problem of practicality at the end of the nineteenth and beginning of the twentieth century. Increasingly, ministers, priests, and rabbis found that the theological wranglings which had been so much at the heart of religious life earlier in American history attracted little or no interest among both urban and rural populations. Both were beset by too many problems of pressing and real nature to pay much attention to metaphysics, and only as the churches began to turn their attention to social problems did their attention and interest return.

By the turn of the century, however, this new interest in social affairs was noticeable. In general, churches seem to have taken two lines of approach to these questions: the first involved making Christianity a living phenomenon in everyday life instead of the rather sterile concept that it all too often became. Churches began to draw up "social creeds" setting forth their positions on controversial problems of the time. Second, this movement began to be reflected in the drive for legislation to curb some of the social evils. Increasingly, church groups demanded restrictive laws on liquor, gambling, and divorce in an effort to control these practices. Even more evident was the attempt of the church to play a significant part in the lives of its communicants. Thus, the turn of the century also saw the organization of luncheon clubs, young people's groups, and numerous other enterprises designed to make religion a living part of everyday life.

ISSUES FOR STUDY AND DISCUSSION

1. If you were a school superintendent in a moderate-sized community at the turn of the century and viewed the statistics on the changing character of the American population, how would you modify your educational offering to take account of the changes?

2. Advances in technology between 1865 and 1918 rapidly began to alter the whole character of American life. What were some of the ways in which technological advances (e.g., the invention of the automobile) began directly to affect the school program?

3. The teacher in the sprawling urban tenement districts between 1880 and 1920 faced herculean problems in the attempt to introduce millions of immigrants to the American way of life. What were some of the most pressing of these problems? Do teachers in some American cities face similar problems today?

4. The turn of the century saw the United States becoming increasingly involved in world affairs. Nevertheless, schools were doing little, if anything, to prepare citizens with the outlooks and understandings necessary to comprehend this new national role. To what extent does this same problem, magnified considerably, face contemporary American educators? Are contemporary educators of a single mind regarding its solution? Is the American public?

SUGGESTIONS FOR FURTHER READING

Adams, Henry, *The Education of Henry Adams,* Boston, Houghton, 1922.

Bailey, Thomas A., *A Diplomatic History of the American People,* 3d ed., New York, Appleton-Century-Crofts, 1946.

Beard, Charles A., and Beard, Mary R., *The Rise of American Civilization,* New York, Macmillan, 1936.

Bryce, James, *The American Commonwealth,* New York, Macmillan, 1907, 2 vols.

Clark, Victor S., *History of Manufactures in the United States,* Washington, D. C., Carnegie Institution, 1916–1928, 2 vols.

Commons, John R., and Associates, *History of Labour in the United States,* New York, Macmillan, 1918–1935, Vols. 2–4.

Coulter, E. Merton, *The South During Reconstruction, 1865–1877*, Baton Rouge, Louisiana State University Press, 1947.

DuBois, W. E. B., *Black Reconstruction*, New York, Harcourt, 1935.

Faulkner, Harold Underwood, *The Quest for Social Justice, 1898–1914*, New York, Macmillan, 1931.

Hacker, Louis M., *The Triumph of American Capitalism*, New York, Simon & Schuster, 1940.

Hansen, Marcus L., *The Immigrant in American History*, Cambridge, Harvard University Press, 1940.

Harris, Herbert, *American Labor*, New Haven, Yale University Press, 1938.

Moody, John, *The Truth About the Trusts*, New York, Moody, 1904.

Nevins, Allan, *The Emergence of Modern America, 1865–1878*, New York, Macmillan, 1927.

Schlesinger, Arthur M., *The Rise of the City, 1878–1898*, New York, Macmillan, 1933.

Shannon, Fred A., *The Farmer's Last Frontier: Agriculture, 1860–1897*, New York, Farrar & Rinehart, 1945.

Steffens, Lincoln, *Shame of the Cities*, New York, McClure, Phillips, 1904.

Strong, Josiah, *The Twentieth Century City*, New York, Baker and Taylor, 1898.

Tarbell, Ida M., *The Nationalizing of Business, 1878–1898*, New York, Macmillan, 1946.

Wittke, Carl, *We Who Built America*, New York, Prentice-Hall, 1939.

Woodward, Comer Vann, *Origins of the New South*, Baton Rouge, Louisiana State University Press, 1951.

10

RESHAPING THE AMERICAN MIND

IN THE fifty years between the Civil War and World War I the intellectual life of America underwent a vast revolution. Within a period no longer than the span of a single lifetime radical changes were wrought in the fundamental conceptions of the universe, the outlooks upon man and his relation to nature, and the conceptions of knowledge and learning as they affected education. Basic to these changes in intellectual frames of reference was the appearance of new world views made necessary by wide ranging investigations in the physical and biological sciences. Above all, the theory of evolution produced a shattering effect upon inherited beliefs and stimulated thoroughgoing revisions of philosophy, psychology, and the social sciences. Bitter controversies between science and religion were set off as new scientific views challenged the traditional views of man's origin and destiny. Masses of scientific data confronted the authorities that had appealed to revelation, theology, or traditional philosophy for the fundamental answers to life's riddles.

THE IMPACT OF EVOLUTION

The battle of authorities in its simplest terms took such forms as these. Supernatural religion had long stated upon authority of the Bible and the Christian churches that God had created the world out of nothing at a specified time in the past, that He had created all the species of living things, that these species have not changed substantially since their creation by God, and that God had created man at a specific time, endowing him with distinctive spiritual characteristics of soul, mind, and conscience. The publication of Charles

Darwin's *Origin of Species* in 1859 threw a bombshell into the intellectual scene.

Now the doctrines of biological evolution and the physical sciences of geology, paleontology, and astronomy came along to challenge the supernatural authorities and to put naturalistic explanations in their place. Building upon the earlier work of Linnaeus, La Place, Erasmus Darwin, Charles Lyell, Lamarck, and especially Charles Darwin, evolutionists like Thomas Huxley and Herbert Spencer pictured the world as a natural product of natural forces that had been at work for at least 2 to 5 billion years or more. The world was not created in a few days or nights; many eons were involved. Similarly, the living species had not been created at one specific time in history by supernatural intervention, but they too had slowly emerged by natural processes over countless eons of time. Through a process of interaction between the various organisms and their environments the simplest organisms had gradually changed into more complex forms by means of adaptation and selective adjustment. Thus, according to the theory of evolution, the species of life are not fixed and changeless but have been growing, changing, and evolving as the result of changes in the environment and of adaptive changes in generation after generation of organisms.

At the climax of the evolutionary process man appeared, also within the natural process of adjustment and evolution. Man has evolutionary roots along with all other species of life in the common trunk of life. Man achieved his human nature in the process of interaction with his environment rather than receiving it as a special gift or act of creation. Not only did man's bodily structure gradually emerge from a common form of life, but also man's mental and spiritual nature was a product of an interactive experience in a physical and social environment. Studies in chemistry, morphology, and physiology supported the findings of biology that man's physical structure and functioning link him with other living forms in a continuous process of nature. Darwin explained this process by arguing that those species survived which could adapt themselves most successfully to changed conditions. "Survival of the fittest" and "natural selection" thus became by-words in the explanation of human social institutions as well as of the lower species. Despite inadequacies of particular explanations of the evolutionary process, the main doctrines made their way into almost all realms of thought in the later nineteenth century. Outstanding exponents and popularizers of such views were Thomas Huxley, Herbert Spencer, Edward L. Youmans, John Fiske, Chauncey Wright, John W. Draper, Robert Ingersoll, and Andrew D. White.

The concept that growth, change, interaction, and process were inherent in a world of nature which encompassed man as well as the physical and animal world was one of the most radical and influential ideas that ever was produced. It burst upon an intellectual world that had assumed for centuries that fixed species were created by divine intervention and that man was absolutely different from animals by virtue of his permanent spiritual faculties of reason, will, and conscience. To have it suggested that man's faculties appeared in the natural process of evolution caused a great outburst of intellectual activity that paralleled in some respects the immense intellectual ferment among Christian thinkers of the twelfth and thirteenth centuries when Aristotle's philosophy and science were rediscovered in Western Europe. Every major outlook in America in the later nineteenth century had to reckon with the evolutionary theory. Some religious fundamentalists rejected evolution and reasserted traditional supernatural faiths based upon revelation and a literal interpretation of the Bible. On the other hand, many liberal theologians and philosophers worked out reconciliations with evolution but held on to a basic belief in the reality of the spirit of God and of man. Still others deliberately set about to build a conception of man and of education based upon the fundamental assumptions and findings of evolution.

Three principal intellectual orientations can thus be identified at work in America in the period under consideration. Each developed a distinctive conception of man, of his essential characteristics, of his processes of thinking and learning, and of an education appropriate to man as thus conceived. One view saw man as a reflection of God. In their various ways Christian fundamentalist theism, liberal theology, the philosophy of idealism, and a new dualistic humanism appealed to the authority of the spiritual. They saw man essentially as a spiritual being. A second view saw man as a reflection of the natural world. In their several ways an empirical philosophy of mind, a realistic philosophy of knowledge, and an objective psychology of learning (known in later days as connectionism) appealed to the authority of the natural sciences. They saw man largely as a complex biological organism. The third view saw man as a reflection of human society. Here a social conception of mind and a new and distinctively American philosophy of pragmatism and experimentalism appealed not only to the authority of the natural sciences but also to the social sciences. They viewed man as primarily a social and cultural being.

THE SPIRITUAL CONCEPTION OF MAN

Despite the impact of the new geological evidence concerning the origin of the world and the new biological evidence concerning the origin of man, the traditional views of creation and of man's spirituality maintained their hold upon the great majority of people in general as well as upon those who dominated American schools and colleges. The sway of supernaturalism was being narrowed and limited, but it probably continued to be the dominant view held by teachers in the schools and professors in the colleges. Appeal to the authority of a spiritual element in man and beyond man took several forms that ranged from a reassertion of Christian fundamentalism to a philosophical idealism and dualistic humanism.

Fundamentalism

A fundamentally theistic view of God and a Calvinistic view of man were maintained and reasserted in many of the colleges and divinity schools of the country in opposition to the naturalistic views of the new science. Strong theological cases were made by such eminent educators as Charles Hodge of Princeton, Enoch F. Burr of Amherst, Andrew P. Peabody of Harvard, and William G. T. Shedd of Union Theological Seminary. In general, they boldly rejected the evolutionary doctrines either as bad theology or as bad science and continued to appeal to the authority of the Scriptures as revealing the only true description of the origin of the world, God's creative spirit, and man's origin in sin. The world *was* created by God whose essence is spiritual and infinite; man *was* created by God with a body that tempts him to evil and a soul that gives him the possibility of salvation through faith and the sacrifice of Christ. Man may be linked to nature by his body, but he is linked to God by his spirit and thus is set off by an impassible gulf from the rest of nature. Growth and change in God's nature, or in man's nature, or in truth and knowledge were rejected in favor of belief in the eternal and unchangeable nature of God, of man's spirit, and of religious and moral truths created by God.

Whatever the differences among the several fundamentalist churches, they swept new thousands into their folds. Evangelical Protestantism appealed to great numbers of Americans through the preaching of such influential evangelists as Dwight L. Moody and of countless preachers in the popular denominations of the Protestant churches. Thousands of others were affected by the new religious evangelism of the Salvation Army, the Mormons, and Christian Science. The Roman Catholic Church grew rapidly from some 9 million in 1890 to nearly double its size by the end of World War I.

Despite the decline of specific sectarian doctrines in the schoolbooks for children in the common schools, the basic supernaturalistic underpinnings of many, if not most, school texts of the later nineteenth century continued to be Christian theism. Spellers and readers continued to refer to God and to man's soul. Books on history and geography attributed differences in peoples and climates to God's will. Science texts found God at work guiding the course of physical laws and the actions of the atoms. Even new books on physical education found the external manifestations of physical activity to be expressions of the inner soul of man.

Liberal Theology

A second major response to the findings of the newer sciences of geology, biology, and history was the attempt to reconcile evolution with Christian theism. The continuing accumulation of scientific evidence led many liberal theologians to try to do more than simply deny the validity of the scientific investigations. They either had to soften the rigid fundamentalist authority of the Bible as a literal description of the origin of the world, or they had to incorporate in some way the idea of growth and evolution into the Christian epic. Both of these efforts became important movements in religious thought of the later nineteenth and early twentieth centuries.

Some Americans looked to the developing scholarship in Europe for help in the "higher criticism" of the origins of the Bible itself. The historical analysis of the Scriptures began to reveal that the Bible was not of one piece written at one time by divinely inspired persons who had directly heard the voice of God. Rather, it was shown that the Biblical stories had been written over a period of hundreds of years by a large number of human beings who had written historical and human reports of events and activities of a great ethical and spiritual movement. In this respect the Bible was comparable to the writings of other great religious documents. Thus, the studies of history, archaeology, philology, and comparative religions were brought to bear upon the Judeo-Christian story as contained in the Bible. Outstanding in this movement in America were the scholarly writings of Philip Schaff of Union Theological Seminary, Orello Cone of St. Lawrence University, and James Freeman Clarke of Boston. In the light of such higher criticism it became more and more difficult for fundamentalists to claim that the Bible was the one and only authoritative, indisputable, and literal word of God.

On the other hand, many theologians set out to incorporate the findings of evolution into Christian theology and to argue that there was no essential conflict between evolution and Christianity. The heart of this argument was that God used the process of evolution in his act of creation. Or, to put it another way, the findings of evolution simply reveal the thought and actions of God on this earth. In various ways this new gospel was preached with great effectiveness by such outstanding liberal ministers as Henry Ward Beecher and Lyman Abbott in Brooklyn, Phillips Brooks in Boston, and Washington Gladden in Ohio.

Even some of the more conservative Calvinists went to great lengths to show that evolution did not destroy the Calvinist views of God and of man. James McCosh at Princeton and George Frederick Wright at Oberlin argued that Darwin's conception of gradual and spontaneous adaptations in nature was really the plan and design for man introduced into nature by God. Whereas Darwin thought that the fitness of the species to survive was a spontaneous, accidental, or arbitrary affair of natural selection, fitness was really achieved as a result of the supernatural intervention of God's design. What a few Calvinist Presbyterians could do, a great many Unitarians and liberal Congregationalists likewise could do. If the Calvinists could use Darwinism to prove that adaptations and survival revealed the operation of God's selection among the elect and the damned, the Unitarians could argue that evolution proved that evil would gradually disappear and that salvation, love, and virtue were gradually evolving in the scheme of human life as a result of God's presence in man and nature.

Still farther to the "left" in liberal religious circles were those who found in evolution a new religious faith devoted to the spiritual manifestations of God in the cosmos and in man, but a faith divorced from a specifically Christian theology. Outstanding spokesman for this kind of view was John Fiske who spent his life popularizing the view that evolution was God's plan for achieving His divine purposes. The world itself was viewed not as a static order created whole from the beginning by God nor was it a machine obeying mechanical laws, but the world itself was a moving, progressive organism. God himself is an infinite force or energy, eternally motivating the cosmic processes of change and revealing Himself not only in the processes and growths of nature but also in the spiritual processes of man's consciousness. Not only is the cosmos itself theistic, but also man's spiritual fulfillment is the goal of all evolution from all time on this earth.

Similar views were expressed by Francis Ellingwood Abbot and Octavius B. Frothingham, leaders in the organization of the Free Religious Association in 1867 which devoted itself to the promulgation of a new religion of humanity based upon freedom of thought, historical criticism of the Bible, and evolution. Abbot edited for years the *Index* which was the journal of the Free Religious Association and which preached for a religion devoted to the perfection of man as a progressive being, freed from the constraints of traditional doctrinal authorities and resting upon faith in man's abilities to achieve continual betterment through education. Felix Adler, also involved in the Free Religious Association, moved to implement his ideas in education and in society by the organization in 1876 of the Society for Ethical Culture which remains today a vital ethical and educational movement based upon a humanistic religion divorced from traditional theologies. These latter movements revealed the growing effort of many Americans to maintain a stout allegiance to the spiritual qualities of human life and to translate man's spiritual achievements into a positive moral and religious program of social betterment. They thus carried forward the effort to create a nonsectarian or secular, yet spiritual, religious orientation toward the world and man.

The Philosophy of Idealism

A third kind of approach to the authority of the spiritual was represented in the various forms of the philosophy of idealism. We have already indicated something of the effect of German idealism as it was first taken up by the American transcendentalists during the first half of the nineteenth century (see pp. 168–171). After the Civil War, however, transcendentalism as such grew less and less effective, but the attention to the philosophy of idealism grew by leaps and bounds. It is probably not too much to say that idealism became the most influential academic point of view taught by the professional philosophers in the colleges and universities of America in the latter part of the nineteenth and early twentieth centuries. The philosophies of Fichte, Schelling, and Hegel were probably the most popular as several variations or "schools" of idealism were formulated in American departments of philosophy.

One of the most important points about this movement is that it helped to replace the sectarian orthodoxies of the early nineteenth century in American higher education with a kind of nonsectarian reliance upon spirituality. In this way the hold of the churches and sectarian clergy upon higher education gave way to a nondenominational outlook that was nevertheless congenial to Christian outlooks. Specific sectarian theologies tended to give way to idealistic philosophy. As transcendentalism prepared the American mind outside of higher institutions for this transition from orthodoxy to a nonsectarian religious orientation in the early nineteenth century, so did idealism provide a transition from orthodox sectarian theology toward a nondenominational spiritual orientation *within* the colleges and universities after the Civil War. This was an important intellectual revolution that had far-reaching effects upon American education. It meant that the interest in religion in general would remain strong but that specific sectarian control of education for doctrinal purposes was greatly weakened. This trend can be seen in the way that many church-related colleges and universities which had originated in denominational effort began to become "nondenominational" as the nineteenth century drew to a close.

The heart of idealism, despite its many variations, was an affirmation that the essence of the universe was spiritual and not material. The whole cosmos is in essence motivated and moved by spirit rather than by mechanical or natural laws. Whether the name assigned to this spirit was God, or the Infinite, or the Absolute, the moving force of the universe is spirit. In philosophical terms, reality was not made up of material or physical substances; reality is spiritual or mental. Idealism might even better be called idea-ism, for it held that the enduring and real nature of the universe is an expression of ideas or mind rather than matter. Although the world of physical things seems to exist and persist in our experience, the physical world could not exist except as the expression of some mind or intelligence. Usually this universal mind or intelligence was identified as God. Therefore, the world is simply an expression of God's mind. As a result, the whole movement of the world and the universe is shaped by the moral and spiritual purposes of God or the Infinite Spirit, or the Absolute Mind.

Similarly, the essence of man is spiritual and not material. The most important thing about man is his spiritual self or his personality, not his bodily characteristics. Man is simply a finite spiritual expression of the infinite spirit and must therefore be treated as such. Many of the idealists worked out a way to incorporate the evolutionary concept into their systems by emphasizing that the universe is going through an evolutionary process of growth and movement in time which is a progressive realization of God's spirit. So, also, man's spiritual nature reveals a similar process of growth and unfolding. This was a particularly important outlook for educational theory, for it put stress upon respect for the child's self and personality and care in providing the optimum conditions whereby the child's spiritual nature could grow and unfold itself. This underlying assumption should be remembered as a part of the educational theories of Pestalozzi and Froebel which were so influential in America in the later nineteenth century.

Detailed study of idealism is, of course, impossible here, but something of its major forms may be mentioned. There were several germinal educational centers of philosophic idealism in America. One such center was St. Louis where William T. Harris, Henry Brokmeyer, Denton J. Snider, and Thomas Davidson were active in popularizing German idealism. One expression of their effort was the *Journal of Speculative Philosophy* begun in 1867 and long edited by Harris who was Superintendent of Schools in St. Louis and later United States Commissioner of Education. Another expression was in the form of a number of adult education efforts that took shape as philosophical clubs or discussion groups not only in the Middle West but also in the East. A Plato Club, an American Akademe, the Concord School of Philosophy and Literature, and the Summer School of the Culture Sciences were all efforts to turn men's activities away from material things and toward a more spiritual life of speculation, virtue, the fine and literary arts, and in general "the better things of life."

Several colleges and universities were also germinal centers for various schools of idealism. An early center was Amherst where Laurens Perseus Hickok, Julius Seelye, and Charles Edward Garman preached the gospel of German idealism and helped to turn Christian theology toward a critical and rational idealism. At Boston University Borden Parker Bowne developed his personalistic idealism in which he stressed personality as the seat of all value. At Cornell Jacob Gould Schurman and James E. Creighton developed an "objective idealism" and organized the American Philosophical Association in 1902. At Johns Hopkins and later at Michigan George Sylvester Morris developed his "dynamic idealism" which had such an early influence upon John Dewey. At Harvard George Herbert Palmer began an idealistic trend that culminated in Josiah Royce and his "absolute idealism."

In their various ways Creighton, Morris, and Royce began to stress the *social* character of idealism. Creighton stressed the fact that thought is the product not of an individual mind but of a community of minds and that individuals cannot exist apart from society. Morris emphasized the growth and development of human experience and the creative activity of minds in the process of achieving knowledge in contrast to a static or merely passive or receptive role of mind in acquiring knowledge. Royce argued that reality and knowledge are social products of the human community achieved as individuals communicate with each other and interpret themselves.

Thus, idealism in various ways promoted outlooks that were to have important influences upon American education. The stress upon human personality as an end in itself, the emphasis upon respect for the growth and unfolding of the child's personality as a pedagogical method, and the vision that individuals were inextricably related to other individuals in a social and spiritual community were important ingredients of a new philosophy of education. Strangely enough, however, it was not the idealists themselves who were most effective in translating these views into a philosophy of education or a theory of pedagogical method. It was John Dewey who drew upon these outlooks for their emphasis upon the social and creative role of persons in education, but he went on to develop quite a different basic philosophy.

Classical Humanism

Although the idealists of the nineteenth century seldom spelled out the educational implications of their philosophy, we have a clear definition of educational philosophy in a position that came to be known as dualistic or classical humanism. Resting upon the historic philosophy of idealism and the traditional faculty psychology, dualistic humanism received increasing attention in the early decades of the twentieth century at the hands of such scholars as Charles Eliot Norton, Irving Babbitt, and Paul Shorey of Harvard, James Rowland Angell of Yale, Paul Elmer More and Andrew F. West of Princeton, and Nicholas Murray Butler and Albert Jay Nock of Columbia. In a reaction against the growing emphasis upon science, industrialism, and naturalistic philosophies, a growing chorus of voices reasserted the idealistic and dualistic basis of human nature as the groundwork upon which to build a sound humanistic education.

These humanists reaffirmed the essential dualism between man and nature, the absolute difference between the spiritual nature of man and the material basis of the physical world. Man has certain distinctive and permanent qualities of reason, moral conscience, esthetic taste, and religious faith that set him poles apart from the animal and natural world. Dualistic humanism set its face resolutely against the evolutionary conceptions of continuity, change, and growth. It hearkened back to the faculty psychology that put consciousness at the heart of the spiritual faculties of man and elevated intellect as the primary instrument of acquiring knowledge. Values, knowledge, and truth are unchangeable and absolute and exist in a realm that is above and beyond nature. Learning is not a matter of sense perceptions received from the external world but is a matter of disciplining the intellectual faculties and developing the moral and spiritual and esthetic faculties of the mind. The best studies for these purposes are found in the classical languages and literatures of ancient Greece and Rome, in mathematics, in philosophy and religion, and in the fine arts. In other words, the humanities are the prime studies of education, far superior to the sciences, the social sciences, and immeasurably above the practical, technical, or vocational studies.[1]

There is a direct line of descent from the disciplinary and classical position of the orthodox sectarians of the early nineteenth century through the idealisms of the late nineteenth century to the humanists of the early twentieth century. From the days of the inaugural address of James McCosh at Princeton in 1868 and Noah Porter at Yale in 1871 innumerable college educators echoed their arguments that the chief aim of college education was "to draw out and improve the faculties which God has given" or to "aim at intellectual culture and training rather than at the acquisition of knowledge." Idealists such as William T. Harris publicly stood in favor of mental discipline and the formal training of the spiritual powers of the mind. By the end of the century the meetings of the National Educational Association were even resounding with the plea that the mind and will would be trained more effectively if the tasks set for the student were hard and unpleasant rather than interesting and pleasant.

After the turn of the century the most vigorous exponents of the doctrine of discipline were the classical humanists who marched out all the traditional arguments for the continued study of the classics as the best and even the only real studies for an educated man. Irving Babbitt's *Literature and the American College* (1908), Francis W. Kelsey's *Latin and Greek in American Education* (1911), Andrew F. West's *The Value of the Classics* (1917), and the speeches, annual reports and books of Nicholas Murray Butler are but a few samples of the vast outpouring that echoed the Yale Faculty Report of 1828 (see pp. 178 *ff.*). They argued that the study of the classics would do the following things: discipline the mind and the character of students; train the intellectual faculties so that such training would transfer to other subjects and other activities; cultivate a sense of duty and moral obligation; cultivate the imagination and sense of esthetic taste; and provide a broad basis for a generous liberal education that would serve students well no matter what occupation they might later follow.

Conversely, they thundered against the inroads upon education of the physical sciences, the social sciences, and practical studies; they decried the specialization of the elective system and Thorndike psychology; they belittled the attention to the interests, needs, and freedom of students; and they deplored the general decline of morals, hard work, and discipline. In general, they attributed much of the evil of American life and education to the growth of philosophies and psychologies that rested upon modern science rather than upon traditional religion and idealism. But they were fighting a rear-guard

---

[1] For a full account of the humanist position and its underlying assumptions see R. Freeman Butts, *The College Charts Its Course* (New York, McGraw-Hill, 1939), Chaps. XV–XXII.

battle. New psychologies and new philosophies began to make serious inroads upon American education, especially at the elementary level, but also somewhat at the secondary, college, and university levels.

THE BIOLOGICAL CONCEPTION OF MAN

Despite the hold of religious and idealistic views upon the American mind and American education, the new scientific outlooks began to produce a radically different conception of man's nature, his mind, his learning process, and therefore his education. In these views man came to be viewed as a reflection of the natural world describable by the methods of science. A biological conception of the human mind and learning was one of the results of the influence of Darwinism upon American thought. The impact of evolution led to the view that man was an essential part of nature; that his intellectual and moral achievements were developed in the natural processes of biological adaptation and adjustment to his environment; that man's mind as well as his body emerged as a product of a long period of growth from simple beginnings to more complex forms through natural selection, survival, and gradual variation. Since man is continuous with the rest of nature, the development of his mental behavior is subject to the same kind of history and scientific analysis as is his physical body and behavior. Supernatural explanations for the origin of man and his development are not necessary; natural explanations will suffice.[2]

Stemming from these fundamental assumptions of naturalism and grounded in one way or another upon the findings of the biological sciences, several new outlooks in philosophy and psychology were formulated in the later nineteenth and early twentieth centuries, all of which tended to contribute to produce a radically different conception of human nature. Most important for our purposes were an empirical philosophy of mind, a realistic philosophy of knowledge, and an objective psychology of learning.

Empirical Philosophy of the Mind

In the decades following the Civil War an increasing number of American philosophers began to look upon the mind as a *process* rather than as an entity or substance. In various ways mental activity was seen not as a spiritual faculty that has an existence independent of the body and that thinks its own thoughts but rather that mental activity is a *function* of the behavior of the individual whereby the organism can adapt itself more suitably to its environment. Mind in man is simply a way of behaving and adjustment that is more complex than the adjustive mechanisms of the lower animals.

---

[2] For an excellent short statement of Darwin's contribution to psychology as seen by E. L. Thorndike in 1909, see E. L. Thorndike, *Selected Writings from a Connectionist's Psychology* (New York, Appleton-Century-Crofts, 1949), Chap. XXII.

As early as 1864 Francis E. Abbott was saying that the mind was not merely a passive receiver of external impressions nor an active creator of ideas but was a form of action and reaction in relation to external objects. Chauncey Wright argued that man's consciousness emerged gradually in the process of evolution and that his development of signs, language, memory, imagination, and reason arose as necessary for survival when environmental conditions changed. Similarly, John Fiske argued by inference that in the process of natural selection consciousness arises when the nerve paths can no longer handle the increasing number of undulations along the nerve channels; when the nerve paths become congested, tension arises and the individual begins to sort out the impulses by conscious effort. Edward D. Cope, biologist at the University of Pennsylvania, found that in lower forms of life the process of sensation and memory formed the basis of simple judgments; in man this process became a complex adapting and judging mechanism called mind. Experience thus produces mind as man exerts conscious effort to improve his ways of dealing with the environment. Edmund Montgomery pushed still further the attack upon idealism by arguing that man's consciousness emerged by natural means as the highest form of the process of evolution. In various ways a genetic and naturalistic conception of man gave to experience the prime role in developing man's unique nature. Here was an appeal to experience (empiricism) rather than appeal to man's spirit (idealism).

It was thus no news to some but a great shock to many when William James at Harvard really began to fasten a biological and evolutionary framework upon the study of mental behavior. Through the influence of his personality as a speaker and teacher and the influence of his writings James was a great popularizer as well as a germinal thinker. His book *Principles of Psychology* published in 1890 set the philosophical and academic world by the ears and elicited great antagonism as well as great enthusiasm. The study and exploration of the mind had long been considered the exclusive province of philosophy, but now James proposed that psychology should become a natural science based upon evolutionary biology and physiology. The idealists, of course, argued that this effort to make psychology a natural science was a denial of all that is known about the spiritual and intellectual qualities of human nature. What a ridiculous thing to profess to reveal something about human nature by scientific methods that are appropriate only to inanimate objects and lower forms of life and that neglect the only really significant element in human life, man's moral, religious, and intellectual nature.

But the biologists, the geneticists, the physiologists, and a new generation of objective psychologists picked up James' challenge with enthusiasm. They were impressed by his argument that consciousness should be viewed as a functional type of behavior that arose out of a trial-and-error effort to achieve better adjustments in a changing world of variation and struggle. Mind was viewed as an active rather than a passive form of behavior and closely related to the emotional and feeling aspects of behavior. No longer, said James, could we speak, as the faculty psychologists spoke, of separate faculties of thinking, feeling, and willing. They were all integral forms of behavior of the functioning organism as it tried to adjust its behavior to a changing environment. The study of the mind must be a study of behavior, not an introspective classification of ideas or of an entity known as consciousness. Here was a frontal attack upon idealism and faculty psychology that was picked up and pursued by a whole new school of objective psychologists who applied their findings to educational practice. The most eminent was E. L. Thorndike at Teachers College, Columbia University (see pp. 338-339).

A Realistic Philosophy of Knowledge

Another kind of attack upon idealism that came from within the field of philosophy itself was known as realism. It represented an effort to build a philosophy of knowledge upon strictly scientific foundations. As a movement in American thought in the early twentieth century, realism received great impetus from William James. His article "Does 'Consciousness' Exist?" in the *Journal of Philosophy* in 1904 marked an upswing of interest in realism. Besides many articles in the professional journals two cooperative efforts were written by six realists as summaries of their views. One was a "platform" summarizing their views on realism in 1910 and the other was *The New Realism* published in 1912.[3] The formulation of the realistic position was a protest against the current idealism of the day in general and against the absolute idealism of Josiah Royce in particular. The theoretical intricacies of these views are so many that we can only mention a general position that seemed important for education.

Idealism had given prior status to the realms of spirit, ideas, and thought by arguing that reality itself consisted of ideas or spiritual selves. Nature and the physical world have no reality in themselves; they are dependent for existence upon the conscious mind of personal selves or of an infinite or universal Mind or God. The external world is simply an expression of God's mind, and all that we can know about the external world comes to us through our thoughts or ideas of it.

Now, the realists turned most of these propositions around. They argued that the real objects studied by the physical sciences are not mental objects or mere ideas; physical objects are real, and their existence does not depend upon their being known by conscious beings. The physical world will exist whether human beings have any knowledge of it or not. There will be objective relations among external objects that will exist apart from the know-

3 See Edwin B. Holt, Walter T. Marvin, W. P. Montague, Ralph Barton Perry, Walter B. Pitkin, and E. G. Spaulding, "The Program and First Platform of Six Realists," *Journal of Philosophy*, Vol. 7 (July 21, 1910), pp. 393-401; and *The New Realism* (New York, Macmillan, 1912).

ing minds, and these relations are to be determined only by the empirical methods of science and will not be altered simply by being perceived by the observer or the scientist. Physical things may pass in and out of knowledge without being altered, and the existence of a thing is not dependent upon its being experienced or perceived by anyone. Knowledge of things is not made up of "ideas" that are substantially different from the things themselves. Objects of physical nature may be directly present in consciousness and may be responded to through the reflex nervous system, but the presence of things in the field of consciousness does not alter the things themselves.

The point of this analysis is that the realist argument put great authority in the external world of nature and in the description of nature by scientific methods. Speculation about spirit and mental substances cannot be very fruitful. Knowledge of real things of the external world is the most authoritative knowledge. Painstaking study and analysis by scientific means will enable us to gain accurate, dependable, and authoritative knowledge so long as it corresponds accurately with the real existence of things which it purports to describe. The external world operates according to discoverable laws in a regular and uniform manner. What we need to do is to discover those laws by painstaking analysis, and we will have arrived at the truth. Once we have found the truth and organized it into systematic form, we have authentic bodies of knowledge that can be acquired by students in schools and colleges.

The process of education, according to the realists, is thus the acquisition of verified knowledge and the adjustment of students to the realities of the external world. The realistic view of knowledge relied upon science as a method and upon the acquisition of tested bodies of knowledge as the chief goal of education. Much of modern education rests implicitly upon such assumptions as these, although few of the academic philosophers of realism carried their implications directly into the educational field. Their outlook was carried into education largely by the new psychologists and the scientific study of educational tests, curriculum, and methods (see pp. 438–439).

Objective Psychology of Learning

A third attack upon the reigning idealism in American thought and education came from the development of an objective psychology that set out to study human nature and human learning with the experimental and laboratory methods of science. The most influential form of this objective approach to human behavior came to be known as connectionism or stimulus-response psychology, recognizable most clearly in the work of E. L. Thorndike and Robert S. Woodworth.

Several streams of influence flowed into the connectionist psychology in addition to the evolutionary and biological conception of mind and the realistic assumptions of modern science. One such influence was the "associationism" of British philosophy that stemmed back to Thomas Hobbes and

John Locke in the seventeenth century, to David Hartley and David Hume in the eighteenth century, and to James Mill, John Stuart Mill, Thomas Brown, Alexander Bain, and Herbert Spencer in the nineteenth century.[4] Through a long period of introspective philosophy and psychology these men had emphasized the importance of the association between ideas as a significant element in learning and the development of the mind itself. In various ways they hit upon the notion that the more recently and the more frequently ideas or sensations were associated together the more they will tend to continue to be connected in experience. Some even speculated on the role of the nervous system in this process.

In Germany the philosopher Johann Friedrich Herbart had developed a full-blown introspective theory of associationism which had great influence upon American education (see pp. 381–382). Herbart argued that the mind itself was nothing but a set of perceptions and ideas that had been linked together as the individual received impressions from the external world. Simple perceptions and simple ideas became associated and were built up into more complex combinations known as the "apperceptive mass" which was the mind. When two or more ideas have been closely related by frequent, or recent, or vivid association, they will be more likely to continue to be related in future similar experiences. Thus, teaching must take account of the association of ideas by making sure that new subject matter is related in the student's mind to his former ideas.

Although associationism hinted at some of the conclusions that objective psychology was to verify by actual experimentation, associationism had a mentalistic basis which was to be less useful to the psychologists than a second kind of influence that came to America from Europe. This was the scientific study of physiology, neurology, genetics, and heredity. A growing number of scientists began to take "consciousness" into the laboratory and to make careful observations and measurements of the way the human organism behaved under controlled conditions. They measured sensory and motor nerves; they studied how the five senses responded to various stimuli; they tested eyes, ears, tactile impressions, speech, and all kinds of reflex movements of the body. Wilhelm Max Wundt at Leipzig analyzed sense perception; Francis Galton studied hereditary factors in genetics; animals as well as humans were subjected to many kinds of experiments and tests; and Ivan Pavlov in Russia built a theory of conditioned reflexes as fundamental to learning on the basis of his study of animals. Alfred Binet in France began to test the functions of association, memory, motor skill, attention, and intelligence of children as a means of arriving at normal mental ages for children of various chronological ages. He thus helped to prepare the ground for the development of standard-

[4] For a brief resume of these views on associationism, see National Society for the Study of Education, *The Psychology of Learning,* 41st Yearbook (Bloomington, Ill., Public School Publishing Co., 1942), pp. 102–111.

ized intelligence tests. As a result of the experimental trend in psychology, a whole generation of American psychologists threw themselves into the task of creating an objective educational psychology. Among these were Thorndike, G. Stanley Hall, Joseph Jastrow, James McKeen Cattell, Lewis Terman, and many others.

On the basis of a vast amount of experimentation a definitive statement of the stimulus-response psychology was ready before World War I in the three volumes by E. L. Thorndike entitled *Educational Psychology*. In these volumes and in a vast amount of other writings Thorndike began the task of demolishing the assumptions of idealism about consciousness, faculty psychology, mental discipline, and transfer of training. The intellectual faculties are not inherited as a spiritual bequest of man, but intelligence is built up out of the biological action and reaction system of the organism which *is* inherited. The reflex arc based upon an afferent nervous system leading from perceptors to the brain and an efferent or motor nervous system leading from the central nervous system to the muscles or glands is the inherited unit of behavior. Sensations and ideas are built up as connections are established in the reflex arc between a situation S and a response R. Learning is thus not a matter of training unformed and potential "faculties" but is a process of forming a series of bonds or connections between stimuli and responses.

On the basis of these assumptions Thorndike enunciated the famous laws of learning, the law of effect, the law of exercise, and the law of readiness. Of these, the most fundamental to the whole system was the law of effect which stated that a modifiable bond is strengthened when accompanied by a satisfying effect and it is weakened when accompanied by an annoying effect. Connections will tend to be learned better when satisfaction or pleasure results, but annoyance or pain will tend to prevent learning. The law of exercise stated that a modifiable bond between a stimulus and response will be strengthened when it is used and it will be weakened when it is not used. The more frequent and recent is the use, the stronger will be the learnings. The law of readiness stated that when the action system is ready to act, satisfaction will follow action, but failure to act will result in annoyance.

Armed with this basic conception of the nature of the learning process an attack was made upon the theory of mental discipline in general and the role of the classics in American education in particular. Thorndike insisted that no one study would be likely to result in general improvement of the mind any more than any other study, but rather "the intellectual value of studies should be determined largely by the special information, habits, interests, attitudes, and ideals which they demonstrably produce." [5] Transfer of training may occur; but it will not be because of the inherent disciplinary value of the classics, but only because there may be a common content or

[5] E. L. Thorndike, "Mental Discipline in High School Studies," *Journal of Educational Psychology*, Vol. 15 (February 1924), p. 98.

method of study appropriate to the desired activity. In other words, learning is more specific than it is disciplinary. If students are to be prepared for a particular activity or purpose, then they should study those subjects that can be shown to lead directly to the desired goals.

Psychological justification was now given for opening the doors of the schools and colleges to the sciences, the social sciences, and the technical studies that had been clamoring for acceptance on a basis of equality with the traditional classics and humanistic studies. Virtually every subject in the school curriculum was now to be examined, analyzed, and tested by the connectionist psychologists in order to find the most satisfactory methods of teaching those subjects. Vast improvements were thus made in the methods of teaching reading, spelling, arithmetic, writing, and most of the other subjects in the school curriculum.

THE SOCIAL CONCEPTION OF MAN

A third major intellectual orientation appeared in America in the decades prior to World War I, and it too proved to be very influential in education. It centered upon a social conception of human nature, thinking, and learning. Whereas idealism had found the distinctive element in man to be spiritual and objective psychology had found it to be in man's biological action system, a whole series of philosophers and psychologists began to find the distinctive nature of man in his social relationships with other human beings. Fundamental ingredients for this view came from a new concern in philosophy that emphasized social psychology and from a new movement in philosophy known as pragmatism. The convergence of these movements in the work of John Dewey produced a view that came to be known variously as experimentalism or experimental naturalism. The ramifications of the development of this story are too involved to permit an adequate discussion in the space available here, but some of the broad outlines may be sketched in, particularly as they culminated in Dewey's conception of educational method.

Social View of Mind and Self

The latter decades of the nineteenth century witnessed a growing concern to apply the evolutionary concept to the growth and change of social institutions as well as to individuals. Sociologists, social historians, and social philosophers began to find profitable interpretations in the application of the evolutionary idea to society. Herbert Spencer's *Sociology* set the trend for a vast amount of study, investigation, and speculation about the relation of the individual to society. Some sociologists like William Graham Sumner at Yale followed Spencer's lead and found Darwin's survival of the fittest in the animal world to be paralleled in the human world by a struggle for existence and survival of the fittest in the competition of the economic and political institutions of laissez-faire capitalism. Others used the techniques of social analysis of human institutions to find just the opposite, that social cooperation and common undertakings were at the heart of human social institutions in contrast to the competitive struggle for existence in the animal world.

Thus, for example, Lester F. Ward found that human society was an antithesis of animal life. Whereas natural selection was characteristic of purely biological processes, the human society produced intelligence as a means of control in order to achieve a higher level of human welfare. Similarly, James M. Baldwin at Princeton and at Johns Hopkins argued that by virtue of his life in society man achieves a social self that is not the result of a simple Darwinian process of natural selection on the biological level, but rather that the human mind emerges only at the social level of interaction. Similar views were being expressed at the University of Chicago by Albion Small, James H. Tufts, W. I. Thomas, and especially by George Herbert Mead and John Dewey. All of them arrived at some version of the notion that the interactions of a human individual in relation to society were qualitatively different from the adaptations made by biological organisms in their interactions with a physical environment.

Peculiarly significant in their own right and in their influence upon Dewey were the theories of the social nature of the human self produced by George H. Mead from about 1890 until his death in 1931. The dominant motif of idealism and humanism was that the human self is a spiritual entity or a set of faculties that man possesses prior to his social relationships or social experiences, and it is this quality that sets man immeasurably above the animals. In somewhat similar terms supernatural religion defined the self in terms of a pre-existent soul. Realism and biological psychology did not speak of a self or a soul but defined the distinctively human in terms of an inherited biological action system which also exists prior to the experiences that man has and which produces the basic motives and drives that help to determine his behavior.

Mead, however, viewed the self and mind as products of the social interaction of the individual with other human beings or other selves. The newborn child does not have a self or a "mind" at birth. He develops a self and a mind as he learns to communicate with others. The self does not exist first and then gradually enter into relationships with others, but the self emerges as the individual learns to distinguish between himself and others and as he takes on the common attitudes and outlooks of others. Mead's basic thesis was that the individual develops a conception of him*self* as he learns to use the symbols of communication that are common to others. Mind exists as a set of functioning significant symbols. At first, the baby does not distinguish between himself and others about him. He does not recognize his own body as belonging to himself in contrast to other objects that belong to others. As he learns by gestures, signs, and symbols to distinguish what belongs to himself as distinguished from what belongs to others, he develops a consciousness of self. He learns that *this* toy is *mine* and belongs to *me* but *that* toy is *his* or *yours*. He learns to adopt an attitude toward him*self* that others have adopted toward him.

The principal means of becoming a self is thus the attainment of common meanings through the acquisition of significant symbols. A symbol is a word or a sign that has a common meaning among two or more people. When an individual uses a symbol with the intention of calling out the same response in another that he calls up in himself, he is using significant symbols; at that point he is developing his mind. A symbol is something present that stands for something else that is not present. The word "dog" is not the dog; it is a symbol that stands for the dog. As a child learns to use the word "dog" to refer to the dog and as he *intends* for his mother to realize that he is referring to the dog, the child and his mother come to have that symbol in common. They understand each other; they have meanings in common. The child is learning to become a self; he is developing a mind; and he is entering upon the task of thinking by employing symbols to deal with events either before or after an event takes place.

The significant symbol is a social learning, and thus mind is a social learning. An individual has to be a member of a social group that has symbols in common in order to become a self. The human community is the only social group that has developed these significant symbols to a very great extent, and this largely through language; it is thus the social activity of communication through significant symbols that distinguishes man from animals. Communication is the heart of community.

Thus the relation of the human being to his social environment is somewhat analogous to the relation of the biological organism to its physical and biological environment, but there is a vast difference in the amount of control over the environment. An *individual* human being could never have attained any more control over the environment than other animals have done. Control over the environment has been achieved by human beings because they are social beings who have been able to achieve social speech and language, social thought, and social institutions. Through this emphasis upon social control Mead and others moved naturally into looking upon thought and intelligence as essentially a means whereby man not only adapts himself to his environment, but also adapts the environment to his own purposes and goals. By means of the scientific method man has devised an instrument of control over the physical environment and an instrument of reconstruction of the social environment. Social action and social reform thus became a natural extension of the philosophy of thought and mind as social processes. This is one of the reasons why the development of the social conception of the self became so important in redefining the character of the educational process as a social affair, especially in the hands of John Dewey.

The Pragmatic Philosophy of Knowledge

A second major trend in later nineteenth-century philosophy that became most important in a new outlook on education was the development of the philosophy of pragmatism. The outstanding and creative personalites in the philosophy of pragmatism have been recognized to be Charles S. Peirce, William James, and John Dewey as well as Mead. Pragmatism became one of the most influential of the attacks upon idealism and classical humanism. It, too, absorbed the outlooks of evolution and of modern science and applied them principally to the development of a distinctive theory of knowledge based upon empiricism in opposition to the idealism and rationalism of the dominant academic traditions of the day. It somehow seemed distinctively American in its emphasis upon change, uncertainty, growth, and practicality.

Whereas the traditional outlooks on the world had emphasized order, finality, and comprehensiveness and had looked upon truth as essentially fixed and permanent, pragmatism began to stress incompleteness, contingency, novelty, and change as real aspects of the world of nature and man and to look upon truth and knowledge as achievements of human experience. It thus came into conflict not only with the idealistic and rationalistic views of knowledge as determined largely by an act of thought but also with realism and its emphasis upon the validity of knowledge apart from the creative act of the thinker. Pragmatism held that knowledge arises out of the consequences of human experience; ideas may change as they are tested by human experience; and truth is determined in the light of the consequences of the testing of ideas.

As early as 1871, Charles Peirce began the attack upon idealistic conceptions of knowledge and truth. Although not very well known in his day, he is coming to be recognized as having made important contributions that were influential upon James and Dewey. Peirce argued that the only genuine road to knowledge was the scientific method; therefore, philosophy ought to imitate the sciences in proceeding only from premises that can be tested carefully by the empirical methods of science. All knowledge must be based upon experience, and verifiable knowledge will arise only by careful observation and experimental testing of theories. Conceptions of an object do not exist apart from experience of those objects. Indeed, the whole meaning of an intellectual conception consists in the formation of what practical consequences might follow from acting upon that conception, and the totality of the consequences or practical effects will constitute the meaning of that conception.

Thus, theories must be *tested* in practice to see what their consequences are; truth arises from this process of experimental testing. If an idea does not work out the way it purports to work out, the idea is not true. The test of ideas is in their practical consequences. The term pragmatism, derived from the Greek word πρᾶγμα, means literally a thing or a deed well done. Peirce went on to affirm that the test of ideas is in the last analysis a social test, for verification of an idea is based upon the belief that the true idea will be the one that is eventually agreed upon by an infinite community of observers and knowers. A statement of fact or of truth is thus a statement of belief that is relatively stable because of the continuing agreement of competent observers.

William James was important in the history of pragmatism because of his great ability to popularize and attract attention to pragmatism as a philosophy of revolt against the traditional philosophies. He had a more individualistic conception of pragmatism than did Peirce, but he agreed with the basic proposition that ideas must be defined in terms of what differences they would make if they were acted upon. If no practical difference among ideas can be found, then they are not different ideas. To arrive at the meaning of an idea, we should determine what conduct or action will result.

James was also influential because of his insight into the application of the pragmatic method to all realms of life, not merely to the abstractions of philosophy. His great achievement was the effort to apply philosophy to the practical affairs of men in ethics and conduct, in religious experience, in art and science, in law and government. In all these realms our inherited ideas should be critically examined, should be tested to see what effects they produce in practice, and should be revised or changed until they produce the results deemed desirable. The rationalists had said, in effect, that if there is a conflict between practice and a true idea as they conceived it, then it is too bad for the practice. James reversed the order and said that if there is a conflict between a supposedly valid idea and what it actually produces, then the idea should be re-examined and perhaps reconstructed.

James was thus a wide-ranging and stimulating thinker whose influence fanned out in several directions. His biological conception of mind influenced Thorndike's objective psychology; his criticism of the idealists and his challenges to the realists stimulated them to dig deeper; and his pragmatism prompted John Dewey to go on to develop his theories of experimentalism.

Dewey's Experimentalism as Philosophy of Education

Perhaps more than any other American thinker of the period before World War I John Dewey responded creatively to the currents of thought that were sweeping in and about the American educational scene. He began his professional training and career under the influence of philosophic idealism as a student of George S. Morris at Johns Hopkins. He soon began to break away from the mentalistic and spiritual assumptions of idealism, but he held on to that aspect of the Hegelian thought which looked upon ideas as a product of a community of minds. He picked up the evolutionary and biological conception of man as an organism that lives in a process of interaction with his environment, but he rejected the assumptions that the primary impulses to behavior come from physiological and neurological sources. So he differed from the behavioral psychology of Thorndike and the connectionist psychologists. He adopted the empirical and scientific assumptions of the pragmatism of Peirce and James and developed further the pragmatic philosophy of knowledge, but he fitted them into the social conception of mind and self that was being expressed by Mead and others.

This is not to imply that Dewey was merely eclectic in his approach. Rather he was reworking the basic problems, seeing new avenues of constructive formulation of theory, and above all he saw an integral connection between education and the operating beliefs about human nature, mind, self, knowledge, learning, and intelligence. Philosophy for Dewey was not simply a pleasant exercise with abstract symbols and intellectual generalizations. Philosophy properly understood should be a general theory of education. Unless philosophy made a difference in educational practice, philosophy was a useless though entertaining enterprise. Pragmatism had said that ideas must be tested in practice. Dewey insisted that the most important realm for the testing of ideas was in the arena of education.

For a period of some twenty years prior to World War I one of Dewey's primary concerns was to make the application of philosophy to the theory and practice of education. In addition to conducting his Laboratory School at the University of Chicago Dewey formulated the main lines of his educational philosophy in a series of important documents. These included "Interest as Related to Will" (first published in 1896 and later issued as *Interest and Effort in Education* in 1913), "Ethical Principles underlying Education" (first published in 1897 and later elaborated as *Moral Principles in Education* in 1909), *My Pedagogic Creed* (1897), *The School and Society* (1899), *The Child and the Curriculum* (1902), *The Educational Situation* (1902), *How We Think* (1910), and *Democracy and Education* (1916).

It is, of course, impossible to try to describe or analyze this set of writings here. Millions of words have been written and spoken in their defense and in attack upon them. Whole courses in the philosophy of education could be and are devoted to them. Only three points will be made to relate them to the discussion of this chapter. Dewey's social conception of mind led him to look upon education as basically a social process. His pragmatic theory of knowledge led him to look upon thinking as an educational method of problem solving. His whole philosophic and educational outlook was based upon a conception of experience that led him to affirm that education should be grounded firmly upon moral commitments to a democratic way of life. For more than fifty years John Dewey stood for such ideas as these in American life and education.

Dewey criticized both the idealistic views of faculty psychology and the realistic views of a purely biological psychology because of their neglect of the social character of intelligence. The learner, according to faculty psychology, was conceived to possess a ready made set of intellectual faculties that simply needed to be unfolded or sharpened by the discipline of certain studies, especially the classics. Since the intellectual faculties were formal in character, that is, they gave form and order to the content of knowledge, it did not matter so much what specific content a student learned. The important thing was to cultivate or "form" his intellectual powers by a rigid discipline, hence the term "formal discipline." Learning was an individual matter for the learner to undergo. On the other hand, the biological view of mind opposed this formal nature of learning and stressed the learning of specific content by a process of fixing a series of stimulus-response connections in the organism's habit system. In both cases the emphasis was upon the individual as a separate entity, though acting in different ways.

In contrast Dewey insisted that learning and education were essentially social in character because nature, experience, and mind were themselves essentially social in character. Nature is not a settled or immobile thing: nature is made up of movement and interaction of bodies in time and space, and human experience is a part of the transaction of events that goes on in nature. Mind is a natural activity that appears when human beings begin to give new directions to experience by observing events, anticipating consequences, and striving to reconstruct future events. But mind is not the product of individuals behaving in isolation from one another; it is a social affair because interaction includes human interaction—the influence of some people upon others. So, in Mead's terms, the self and mind appear in this process of interaction. Education thus becomes a deliberate effort to provide a situation conducive to desirable self-development. This means constant emphasis upon both terms in the process of experience, the active self and the active social environment. If we neglect either term, we miss the point of the social nature of the individual.

Hence, from the beginning, Dewey emphasized the necessity of studying both the psychological nature of the individual and the social nature of his environment. In applying these doctrines to the educative process, Dewey insisted that the child is inherently an active being with impulses to communicate with others, to construct things, to investigate, and to create. These impulses should be recognized in the school, and opportunity given to the child to develop these impulses by engaging in such activities as language, manual and household arts, nature study, dramatics, art, and music. Hence, the origin of the "activities" program.

Interest is a moving, active, and dynamic element that children have when they become identified with certain events or tasks or projects and when the goals seem important to them. Interest is not something to be added to formal subjects. Effort is not something that is extraneous to interest; it is the achievement required to attain goals in the face of obstacles or difficulties. Effort will be expended when interest is present, as it is present inherently in physical, constructive, intellectual, and social activities. Mistakes are made when interest is viewed as a purely internal matter of an individual mind or when effort is viewed as a purely external pressure that must be elicited from the outside. Both interest and effort are integral parts of an on-going process of interaction.

So also Dewey stressed the social nature of learning as well as the psychological. The school must be a social institution in vital connection with the society of which it is a part. Education is a moral and social enterprise; the school should provide better conditions for social goals to be realized by the child. Therefore, the school must carry forward the life of home, neighborhood, and community which are the local sources of the child's experience. It must also lead him into the far wider community of ideas, customs, and beliefs of his larger society. Education is properly conceived as a process of helping the child to participate with others in increasingly desirable social relationships. The emphasis upon the ethical, the moral, and the social runs throughout Dewey's writings.

A second approach to education that was revolutionary in its impact was Dewey's conception of thinking as problem solving. Thinking is not a matter of "disciplining the mind" as the classical humanists said, nor is it a matter of manipulating verbal symbols or arriving at knowledge of pre-established truths as the rationalists claimed. Basically, Dewey argued, thinking is the application of the scientific method to all kinds of problems, from the simplest everyday kind of problem to the most complex social problem or abstract intellectual problem. In his book *How We Think* Dewey set forth his conception of the scientific method as a generalized statement of human thinking and intelligence.

Building upon the pragmatic conception that truth is achieved as a process of testing ideas by their consequences, Dewey stated that the complete act of thought consisted of five steps: (1) *defining the problem* that is raised by some upset or difficulty or disturbance in the smooth flow of experience. This defining or locating may be easy to do in a simple problem, or it may be a long and involved step in a complicated situation. (2) *Observing the conditions* surrounding the problem, taking into account the whole situation and carefully studying its origin and all the pertinent factors that may be involved. This is a stage of gathering data pertinent to the problem. (3) *Formulating hypotheses* that may possibly solve the problem. These hypotheses are ideas or alternative plans of action that might be followed to solve the problem. (4) *Elaboration of the possible consequences* of acting upon the several alternative hypotheses. (5) *Active testing* to see which alternative idea best solves the problem. This last stage of experimental testing is required to make sure that knowledge and action are kept in close relationship. The idea that solves the problem when put to the test is the true idea; it is validated by its ability to produce the consequences desired.

Dewey argued that this conception of the thinking process should lie at the heart of the educational process. The students should be involved in an active situation in which they are genuinely concerned and interested. A disturbance or difficulty will produce a genuine problem for them to solve. They will then put forth the effort required to define the problem, make the necessary observation and conduct the necessary study that will lead to creative suggestions (hypotheses or ideas) for solving the problem. A good school situation will aid the students in obtaining the relevant knowledge and ideas as instruments for solving the problems and for developing them in an orderly way so that they can be put to the test to see if they are valid for solving the present problem.

Students will learn genuinely to *think* if they are genuinely at work in solving problems of concern to them. Here is the basis for the "project method" in which students engage in activities that require thinking as well as doing. But mere doing is not necessarily thinking. Genuine thinking and genuine education should have the ingredients of the complete act of thought. Here was a great lever to pry loose the encrusted regime of formal subjects and logically organized subject matters that characterized most of the schools of the late nineteenth and early twentieth centuries.

A comparison of Dewey's *Democracy and Education* (1916) with *The Value of the Classics* (1917) and Thorndike's *Educational Psychology* (1913-1915) (cited on pp. 332 and 338) will illustrate the great and startling contrast between three major educational points of view that were competing for the loyalties of educators in America as World War I began. The very title of Dewey's book with its emphasis upon democracy was a new theme that had received relatively little attention in the prewar period. In a day when the interest of educators revolved around such concepts as mental discipline, value of the classics, scientific method, scholarship, the elective system, adjustment, liberal education, apperceptive mass, individual differences, original nature, and the law of effect, a new and prophetic note was struck when Dewey made the democratic ideal and the democratic way of life the fundamental framework for his whole conception of education. He believed that democratic values should permeate the whole life of the school and the society in which the school functions. Democracy with its emphasis upon respect for the individual and the welfare of the group is the only kind of social framework in which his conception of learning and intelligence could find fulfillment. As democracy is the social process whereby man may most desirably shape things to his higher purposes, so education is democracy's way of teaching people to become deliberate and thoughtful about the direction of social change. Dewey's plea for democracy received increasing if belated attention among educators as world events moved into the critical stages of the middle decades of the twentieth century.

EXPANSION AND SPECIALIZATION OF ORGANIZED KNOWLEDGE

The problems posed for American educators prior to World War I stemmed not only from the conflicts among intellectual outlooks but also from the vast and rapid extension in the amount of organized knowledge. The process of specialization attendant upon the additions to knowledge was greatly accelerated as the nineteenth century drew to a close and the twentieth century began. Research, stimulated by the application of scientific method to nearly all fields of knowledge, produced an amazing mass of information that could have been scarcely imagined a century before. Educators were constantly pressed with the problem of what to do with the new knowledge in colleges and schools. This was especially true with respect to the physical and natural sciences and the social sciences. Spurred on by the ideals of research that came out of the German universities and by a faith in the power of knowledge, scholars in all fields plunged into their tasks with renewed vigor. The results were staggering. Only a bare mention of a few of the developments is possible here.

One outstanding characteristic was clear. Knowledge broke its subservience to theology, philosophy, and religion and become increasingly secularized. Reliance upon the methods of science and upon human investigation replaced in large part a reliance upon supernatural faith and purely introspective methods of inquiry. Evolutionary and naturalistic ideas of growth were applied to virtually every field of knowledge, and human reason became the test for the validity of knowledge rather than agreement with revelation or supernatural authority. Sanctions became increasingly secular and human and social rather than religious. This trend in knowledge and education paralleled similar trends in American political, economic, industrial, and social life.

Knowledge came to be looked upon as useful for practical purposes in life rather than as a discipline for the mind or as a road to salvation. Knowledge was recognized as useful for improving the production and distribution of goods, raising the level of welfare, or achieving better social arrangements for the happiness and well-being of the masses of people. Utilitarian ideals for knowledge became increasingly popular among those who desired improvement in the welfare of the nation, in business enterprise, or in the spread of democracy. They were opposed by those who felt that spiritual and intellectual values were being sacrificed in the name of efficiency, or success, or humanitarianism. But the trend was unmistakable and undeniable. By World War I the "genteel tradition" was on the defensive and the ideal of social responsibility for knowledge was moving from victory to victory.

The Physical and Natural Sciences

What had formerly been lumped together as "natural history" was split up into botany, zoology, paleontology, physiology, and a number of other "natural sciences." What had formerly been thought of as "natural philosophy" was broken up into astronomy, physics, chemistry, geology, mineralogy, meteorology, and a number of other "physical sciences." A vast company of scientists in the universities, in government, and in business and industry explored the whole range of physical phenomena in the universe and in the world. The Newtonian conception of a fixed universe and a "billiard ball" conception of the atomic world gave way to evolutionary views that described the underlying constitution of matter in terms of change, development, growth, relativity, force, and energy. Although Darwinism was met with scepticism at first by many scientists, they soon were being convinced of its importance as a result of their own investigations and the constant persuasion of such men as Spencer, Huxley, A. D. White, and Edward L. Youmans, editor of the *Popular Science Monthly.* The number of professional and scientific organizations rapidly increased as an important means of stimulating and criticizing the findings of the scientists.

The Social Sciences

Perhaps the greatest single fact about those studies that had been concerned with investigation of society is that they became in this period social *sciences.* The success of the scientific method and scientific ideal in studying physical and natural phenomena led a large number of scholars to try to make sciences out of their studies of man in society. As the physical scientists began to look for natural laws to explain their findings rather than to rely upon supernatural explanations, so the social scientists began to look for natural and human explanations for human behavior rather than divine intervention in man's affairs. What had formerly been treated under "moral philosophy" now was subdivided into such subjects as history, political science, economics, sociology, and anthropology. Of great influence in all of the social sciences was Herbert Spencer, who argued that human society should be viewed in Darwinian terms of a struggle for existence and survival of the fittest. "Social Darwinism" had great effect upon the social scientists in directing their attention to change and evolution and the genetic approach to human society.

In the field of history two principal "schools of thought" appeared. One was the scientific approach represented by the great German historian Leopold von Ranke, who argued that history should be a purely scientific discipline aimed at describing past events exactly as they actually happened. The historian should thus divest himself of all prejudices and simply look for the facts by painstaking study of original sources, careful sifting of records, and constant testing for valid information. This approach had great influence upon the development of graduate study in history in American universities, led by such outstanding scholars as Herbert B. Adams at Johns Hopkins and John W. Burgess at Columbia.

About the turn of the twentieth century, however, a revolt against this structural view of history took place that somewhat paralleled the revolt of the pragmatists against the realists in philosophy. Frederick Jackson Turner at Wisconsin, James Harvey Robinson, and Charles A. Beard at Columbia, and Carl Becker at Cornell began to preach a "new history" that would make history more functional and useful in the process of making better public and private decisions. They argued that history could not be purely scientific but would be inevitably related to some conception of a desirable society.

In political science, economics, and sociology the vogue of social·Darwinism became very popular. It was taken to mean that the struggle for existence and survival of the fittest justified the economic system of laissez-faire capitalism and individualism that was dominant in American life. William Graham Sumner at Yale, Franklin H. Giddings at Columbia, and John Bates Clark generally took this view. But they were opposed by others who argued that the social sciences should contribute to the possibilities of cooperative effort to control the processes of social change in the direction of social reform and improvement of the welfare of all. In various ways this ideal was represented by Richard T. Ely at Wisconsin, Simon Patten at Pennsylvania, Thorstein Veblen at Chicago, Lester F. Ward, E. A. Ross at Wisconsin, and Charles H. Cooley at Michigan. Whatever their political or economic assumptions, most social scientists began to look at society with outlooks steeped in the conceptions of evolutionary change. Even more was this true of the anthropologists who studied primitive societies and found evidences of a cultural evolution that paralleled the biological evolution of plant and animal life. Notable here were Charles L. Brace, Lewis H. Morgan, and Franz Boas. The evolutionary and pragmatic view of the law as a reflection of historical and social development was elaborated especially by Oliver Wendell Holmes.

The Humanities and Arts

Functionalism and realism began to challenge the great tradition in the humanities and the arts, but gains in these fields were considerably less marked than in the physical sciences and in the social sciences. After carrying on a running battle with the modern foreign languages and literatures in the early part of the nineteenth century, the classical humanities found they had to team up with their former enemies to try to hold their positions against the physical and social sciences. Even so, the scientific methods of critical analysis invaded the literary fields with a new emphasis upon the study of philology and literary criticism. Then the humanists of the early twentieth century not only reacted vigorously against the more useful studies of science but also recoiled from the newer realistic trends in literature represented by the reformism and utopianism of such men as Edward Bellamy, Hamlin Garland, William Dean Howells, Frank Norris, Theodore Dreiser, and Upton Sinclair.

The classical revivals in art and music resulted in increased attention to traditional forms imported from Europe. Music of the opera, symphony, and the concert stage was dominated by adherence to "classical" music despite some attempts to break away and produce a modern American music. Architecture of the "Gilded Age" looked principally to the "gingerbread" motifs of the Victorian era or to the classic forms of Greco-Roman styles as models for public and private buildings. This trend was reinforced by the Columbia Exposition in Chicago in 1893, but gradually some architects were won over to the pleas of Louis Sullivan and Frank Lloyd Wright for more modern and functional designs.

Few of these newer trends in art or music that were struggling to find expression appropriate to a new age found their way into the academic halls of schools or colleges. By the beginnings of World War I the sciences had won their way fully into the educational system, the social sciences were on their way to a full status, but the expressive arts lagged far behind. It was symptomatic that art and music were usually not given full credit in the fulfillment of college entrance requirements or full status in bachelor degree requirements. They were often classed with physical education and the vocational studies as distinctly inferior to the languages, the sciences, and the social sciences.

DEMOCRACY VERSUS ARISTOCRACY IN SOCIAL THOUGHT

American education was caught up in the swirl of social forces described in Chapter 9, the intellectual orientations described in this chapter, and a set of social ideas whose main currents are now to be mentioned. On one side was a growing tide of argument that looked to greater democratic control of affairs as a means for social reform. On the other side was a rising chorus that individualism and business enterprise were truly representative of the American spirit. American educational thought and practice responded to both of these outlooks as will be described in Chapters 11 and 12.

Progressivism and Social Reform

Three major democratic movements appeared in the latter part of the nineteenth century and early twentieth century. One was a drive to improve and extend the working of political democracy; a second was to extend the degree of governmental control over a runaway business economy; and the third was a series of movements toward social reform. These ideas were fed by several grass-roots groups in America, including farmers in their Granges and Alliances, workingmen in their labor unions, middle-class intellectuals in their humanitarian associations, and a number of liberal religious groups. Politically, these forces fed into the several Populist parties, into the Progressive revolts within the Republican Party led by such men as Theodore Roosevelt and Robert M. LaFollette, and into the popular movements within the Democratic Party led by William Jennings Bryan and Woodrow Wilson.

In various ways these groups tried to reform political democracy and bring it closer to the control of the people, remove it from dominance by big business, and prevent crime and corruption in public offices. To these ends efforts were made to improve the machinery of government by instituting such devices as civil service, the secret and short ballots, direct election of senators, the initiative, referendum, and recall, direct primaries, woman suffrage, and greater political equality for Negroes. Every success along these lines and most of the arguments in their favor required an extension and improvement in education if the people in general were to have more to say about the control of government. So the arguments for providing a universal education were tied closely to this current of thought.

Another line of argument was that government, both state and federal, was the only agency that could control the excesses of monopoly and overcome a blatant disregard for the public interest. So farm groups, labor groups, and middle-class intellectuals argued long and late for state legislatures to increase their control over railroads, natural resources, factory inspection, working conditions and hours, housing conditions, public utilities, and especially over price fixing by huge corporations and monopolies. Political leaders like James Baird Weaver of the Populists, William Jennings Bryan in the Democratic Party, Robert M. LaFollette in the Progressive Republicans, and writers like Henry Demarest Lloyd, Thomas Nast, and E. L. Godkin hammered away for greater public control. When it became apparent that state legislatures could not adequately control business enterprises that encompassed the whole country, it was only natural that more and more people began to look to the federal government as an agency of public control in the interests of greater democracy. Movements in this direction begun by Theodore Roosevelt and the Progressive Republicans culminated in the ideals of the "New Freedom" expounded by Woodrow Wilson within the Democratic Party. Here again, in the demands for greater public control over the political and economic conditions of life, was a setting appropriate to the demands for greater public control over education as an institution that would promote democratic humanitarianism.

Social reform not only took these political forms, but also became involved in many kinds of voluntary associations ranging from temperance and prohibition movements, peace movements, and women's rights to alleviation of the dreadful slum conditions that bred crime, poverty, and delinquency in American cities. Here again education was seen as an agency that could be enlisted to aid in improving social conditions.

Some reformers argued that reform could not genuinely be achieved within the inherited framework of individualistic democracy but would require a movement toward socialism. Marxist socialism had some adherents but made relatively little dent upon American loyalties. Much more attractive were the non-Marxist socialists represented by Utopian Socialism and Christian Socialism. Chief among the Utopians was Edward Bellamy whose writings had great popularity in turning men's ideals to brotherhood rather than to competition. Even more widespread was the influence of the Social Gospel movement spearheaded by such Protestant leaders as Horace Bushnell, Theodore Munger, Washington Gladden, and Charles Sheldon. They rejected the class struggle assumptions of the Marxists and argued that if Christian love were actually put to work in the everyday lives of people our social institutions would be revolutionized and men would move toward human brotherhood and social justice. Some religious leaders even tried to implement these ideals in such political and economic organizations as a Christian Labor Union.

Conservatism and Individualism

The basic line of argument in reaction against reform was that our society is dedicated to preserving an individualism that would permit the able to rise to the top and the unfit to sink to the bottom. This can best be achieved when the government does not interfere with free competition in any sphere of activity. Various sanctions were appealed to in justification of this view. The natural laws of economics were favorite authorities, interference with which would destroy the basic institutions of government, law, family, and religion. Here, Social Darwinism was used as justification and reinforcement of the laissez-faire economics of Adam Smith. Such prominent educators as William Graham Sumner, Theodore Woolsey, and William T. Harris argued persuasively for the maintenance of free competition, individual effort, and the rights of private property as fundamental elements in nature and as expressions of human nature itself.

Appeal was also made to the results that had been achieved under individual enterprise. Capitalism had preserved equality of opportunity, a high standard of living, and an open road for the best individuals to achieve success through their own efforts. The rise to power and to fortune achieved by poor boys became a favorite theme to illustrate the American dream in practice. The earlier ideals of success described by Benjamin Franklin and John McVickar were restated in popular form by such writers of novels as Horatio Alger and by such school books as those of William McGuffey. Others appealed to the inherent inequality of people as justifying an open competition so that the most able could exert their natural rights to superiority. Sometimes this view was bulwarked with religious sanctions by preachers like Henry Ward Beecher and by educators like Mark Hopkins and James McCosh who argued that God's gift of freedom to man resulted in divine authority for inequality of wealth and property.

Still others argued that men were basically unequal in their intellectual endowments and that therefore an intellectual aristocracy has the right to rule by the very laws of human nature. Prominent in this group were classical humanists like Paul Elmer More of Princeton and Irving Babbitt of Harvard who insisted that the effort to educate everyone was doomed to failure. The proper road to education was to select those few who by nature were intended to be leaders and to give them a humanistic education which would insure that they would be heroes of good and not heroes of evil. So was education torn by the basic struggle between democratic and aristocratic forces that permeated much of American life.

ISSUES FOR STUDY AND DISCUSSION

1. Why did the different conceptions of man's nature arouse such intense controversy in the late nineteenth century? Do they still produce such controversies today? Must educators develop defensible positions on these questions, or is it better to leave them alone?

2. Why have the philosophies of idealism and humanism been so popular among educators for the past 100 years? Can you find in your own educational experience any effects of the humanist philosophy at work? If so, do you think its influence upon you was on the whole beneficial, harmful, or neutral?

3. Why did the various biological conceptions of man begin to attract the attention of so many scholars? Do any aspects of this point of view make sense to you, or does it seem to be a harsh and materialistic outlook?

4. Do you respond positively or negatively to the various social conceptions of man's nature? Why do you suppose there have been recent attacks upon the philosophy of pragmatism? Are there aspects of Dewey's philosophy of experimentalism that appeal to you? Do you find any aspects of it that do not appeal to you?

5. Do you think it was justifiable for the philosophers, scientists, and scholars to take the theory of evolution so seriously? Did some of them go too far in applying the evolutionary concepts to human and social life? Is there any turning back from the theory of evolution today?

6. Can you find any influences in your own educational experience from the increasing specialization of knowledge that characterized the late nineteenth century?

SUGGESTIONS FOR FURTHER READING

Babbitt, Irving, *Literature and the American College,* Boston, Houghton Mifflin, 1908.
Blau, Joseph L. (ed.), *American Philosophic Addresses, 1700–1900,* New York, Columbia University Press, 1946.
———, *Men and Movements in American Philosophy,* New York, Prentice-Hall, 1952.
Butts, R. Freeman, *The College Charts Its Course,* New York, McGraw-Hill, 1939.
———, *A Cultural History of Education,* New York, McGraw-Hill, 1947.
Cargill, Oscar, *Intellectual America: The March of Ideas,* New York, Macmillan, 1941.

Commager, Henry S., *The American Mind*, New Haven, Yale University Press, 1950.

Curti, Merle, *The Growth of American Thought*, 2d ed., New York, Harper, 1951.

Dewey, John, *Democracy and Education*, New York, Macmillan, 1916.

——, *How We Think*, Boston, Heath, 1933.

Gabriel, Ralph H., *The Course of American Democratic Thought*, New York, Ronald, 1940.

Hacker, Louis M., *The Shaping of the American Tradition*, New York, Columbia University Press, 1947.

Hofstadter, Richard, *Social Darwinism in American Thought*, Philadelphia, University of Pennsylvania Press, 1945.

James, William, *Pragmatism, A New Name for Old Ways of Thinking*, New York, Longmans, 1907.

Mead, George H., *Movements of Thought in the Nineteenth Century*, Chicago, University of Chicago Press, 1936.

Mumford, Lewis, *The Brown Decades: A Study of the Arts in America, 1865–1895*, New York, Harcourt, 1931.

Nevins, Allan, *The Emergence of Modern America, 1865–1878*, New York, Macmillan, 1927.

Parrington, Vernon Louis, *Main Currents in American Thought*, Vol. III, *The Beginnings of Critical Realism in America, 1860–1900*, New York, Harcourt, 1930.

Robinson, James Harvey, *The Humanizing of Knowledge*, rev. and enl., New York, Doran, 1926.

Robinson, James Harvey, *The New History*, New York, Macmillan, 1912.

Schlesinger, Arthur M., *The Rise of the City*, New York, Macmillan, 1933.

Schneider, Herbert W., *A History of American Philosophy*, New York, Columbia University Press, 1946.

Smith, Bernard, *The Democratic Spirit: A Collection of American Writings from the Earliest Times to the Present Day*, New York, Knopf, 1941.

Spitz, David, *Patterns of Anti-Democratic Thought*, New York, Macmillan, 1949.

Tarbell, Ida M., *The Nationalizing of Business, 1878–1898*, New York, Macmillan, 1936.

West, Andrew F., *The Value of the Classics*, Princeton, Princeton University Press, 1917.

White, Morton G., *Social Thought in America—The Revolt Against Formalism*, New York, Viking, 1949.

Wiener, Philip P., *Evolution and the Founders of Pragmatism*, Cambridge, Harvard University Press, 1949.

Wish, Harvey, *Society and Thought in Modern America: A Social and Intellectual History of the American People from 1865*, New York, Longmans, 1952.

11

CONFLICTING CURRENTS OF EDUCATIONAL THOUGHT

THE AMERICAN ideal of a common, ladder system of education had been clearly enunciated by the time of the Civil War. While it was far from realized, there can be little doubt that by 1865 its broader outlines had already appeared in practice. Yet major shortcomings and inequalities were everywhere evident. In spite of elaborate legislation, many states in 1865 still failed to provide school facilities for every child. The fact that one section of the nation lay in the ruin of war obviously aggravated this situation considerably. In other states public high schools were confined to cities, or at best sporadically scattered through richer districts. State universities, in ideal established for the people, in practice continued to cater to a small group who could afford the luxury of a higher classical education.

In many respects, these conditions posed the most important educational problem for the generations following the Civil War: to extend and perfect the ideal of universal educational opportunity, and to realize it more effectively in practice. Around these two concerns revolved much of the educational controversy of this period. Furthermore, the attempt to extend the common school ideal soon instigated challenges to the ideal itself, and from an increasing number of sources came questions concerning the state's right to educate at all, its power and responsibility to tax for universal education, and the educability of people in general. Even more so than in the antebellum period, the public school had become a threat to the values of certain groups, and they lashed out bitterly in their opposition to it.

While such problems stimulated much of the controversy, it was excited no less by questions concerning what and how the schools should teach their steadily expanding student bodies. In the minds of many the simple curricula proposed by the early school reformers could no longer meet the demands of an industrial society. For others the "fads and frills" of a "new education" could lead only to worthless instruction. Traditional problems concerning the teaching of moral, ethical, and religious values multiplied and were argued with growing fervor as America became even more religiously heterogeneous than before. Needless to say, continuing demands for more functional education on the higher levels also intensified, and the resultant controversies were made no less sharp as warring factions claimed the support of a newly developing "educational science."

CONTINUING DEMANDS FOR EQUAL EDUCATIONAL OPPORTUNITY

The Drive for Universal Elementary Education

Compulsory attendance. Although Massachusetts passed compulsory attendance legislation as early as 1852, the whole issue of compulsory education quite properly belongs in the post-Civil War period. It was during these years that the great debates on this matter were carried on throughout the nation and major decisions reached.

It is not difficult to see how the common school ideal (viewing the school as crucial in the perpetuation of a republican society) might be extended to the point where it embraced compulsory education for all children. If education alone could provide the intelligent electorate and leadership necessary for republican government, if education alone could prevent crime, provide for the general happiness, and secure the rights of persons and property, then the state had the right to compel it for the general welfare. Moreover, a government which had already established the power to tax for public education certainly had the right to enforce school attendance. Finally, the argument ran, true parental freedom could only be based on the parent discharging his full responsibilities to his child. Clearly, the child had a right to education. If governments are instituted among men to secure to all the enjoyment of their rights, then what objection could be raised to the government compelling parents and guardians to send their children to school?

Doubtless, the argument was a persuasive one in a society which placed such great faith in education. Yet it was not without its opponents, most of whom urged that it represented an unjustified trespass on parental rights. Illustrative was an article by a Roman Catholic clergyman writing in the *American Ecclesiastical Review* for April 1892.[1] One must distinguish, wrote Father Messmer, between free cooperation of the citizens in the cause of education and state compulsion. While the former was entirely acceptable to him, the latter drew his unqualified objection. "What right has society," he queried, "to force me to learn reading, if I do not want to? or writing, if I

[1] S. G. Messmer, "Compulsory Education," *American Ecclesiastical Review,* Vol. 6 (1892), pp. 279-298.

can get along without it? or numbering, if I will know enough of it by the practical schooling of hard life? or geography, if I can make my way through life without the maps?" The great majority of those who would compel education, he continued, rest their arguments on exaggerated claims and false suppositions. One of these is that "a man cannot be honest and industrious without having passed through a primary school. . . ." Another is that substantial bodies of parents, native and especially foreign, will neglect the education of their children unless it be made compulsory. Both for Messmer were forcefully disproved by actuality. In sum, he urged: "Universal education of all classes would be very useful . . . and most desirable. But mere utility does not justify compulsion. Few political writers, except socialists, to whom the state is omnipotent and sole owner of original rights, would allow the doctrine that the Government has the right and power to *compel* its citizens to whatever promotes the common welfare." Evidently the central point at which Messmer's arguments conflicted with those favoring compulsory attendance concerned the extent of the state's right to promote the general welfare.

The demand for Negro education. As is perfectly obvious, the 4 million Negro citizens of the South posed a tremendous educational problem for that region and for the nation as a whole. Once the initial emergency appropriations for relief and education had been exhausted, the southern states were faced with the necessity of determining long-range policy with regard to Negro education. The question invoked considerable argument. Was the Negro capable of learning at all? Many urged simply and directly that he was not. Others, more convinced of his ability to learn, were faced with the question of how and what to teach him. Was the Negro to attend the common school? Was he to receive the same education as his fellow white citizens, or a special one? Here, too, major controversies arose.

One might well begin by turning to the Negro leaders themselves for opinions on these weighty problems. Probably the outstanding among them was Brooker T. Washington, notable principal of the newly established Tuskegee Institute in Alabama and acknowledged educational leader of his race. Throughout his work in behalf of Negro education, Washington seemed continually to urge two things. The first was that the education of the Negro, by improving his purchasing power and social responsibility, would benefit white man and black man alike. The second was that the Negro in no way sought through education the domination of southern life. "The Negro in this country," he emphatically stated, "does not seek as a race to exercise political supremacy over the white man, nor is social intermingling with any race considered by the Negro to be one of the essentials to his progress." [2] On

---

[2] Booker T. Washington, "The Education of the Southern Negro," National Educational Association *Proceedings* (1904), p. 134. (The National Educational Association *Proceedings* became the National Education Association *Proceedings* beginning with the 1907 volume.)

all occasions Washington maintained the position that the race question must be *lived* down rather than *talked* down. In the great linguistic, religious, and other cultural similarities between white and Negro Americans, he saw the bases of unity.

One must not get the idea that Washington was the only Negro to urge universal education for his race. Other powerful voices were heard. For example, at the 1903 convention of the National Educational Association (NEA) a northern Negro pastor from New York City outlined a three-point program to meet the educational needs of Negroes in the South: *first*, a better system of public schools; *second,* an expanded program of trade and technical training for the masses; and *third,* high-grade normal schools and colleges for the training of teachers, leaders, and professional men. Adopting much the same approach as Washington, he concluded that the black men in the South, with well-regulated public schools in the rural districts and with protection to life and property, could easily become an important factor in the economic regeneration of that region.[3]

It goes without saying that the white people of the country found themselves bitterly divided on these questions. One of the most important problems involved the struggle over whether Negroes and whites would attend a common school. As early as 1847, there had been a definite ruling in the Masachusetts State Supreme Court holding "separate but equal" facilities for Negroes to be legal. Yet by the latter decades of the century, there was pretty much of a North-South split on the problem. White southerners were virtually unanimous that only separate schools for Negroes could meet the problem. So strong was their belief that many held that the region's whites would sooner give up public education entirely than allow intermingling of races in one common school. Thus, for example, Gustavus Orr, State School Commissioner of Georgia, in a speech before the Florida Chautauqua in 1886,[4] held that the two races in the South were no nearer to intermingling socially upon terms of equality than they had been when the freedom of the slave was first decreed. "I know whereof I affirm," he maintained "when I say that vast multitudes of our best white people would keep their children out of the schools altogether and trust to giving them such home instruction as they might themselves be able to communicate, or to such private teaching as they might be able to procure, rather than place them in daily contact in the common schools with children coming from such homes as have been described." Not only did Superintendent Orr attribute these attitudes to the white race, but he also felt that they were universally and properly shared by Negroes.

Northern opposition to Orr's conception of a dual public school system

---

[3] Charles T. Walker, "The Educational Needs of the Southern Negro," *National Educational Association Proceedings* (1903), pp. 123–129.

[4] Gustavus J. Orr, *The Best School System for a Southern State* (Atlanta, J. P. Harrison, 1886).

was considerable. A key figure among the northern critics for many years was Reverend William Hayes Ward, editor of the New York *Independent* and descendant of early New England settlers. His remarks before the National Educational Assembly held in New Jersey in 1883 exemplify his position.[5] While Ward was ready to grant that the dual system was deeply rooted in southern life, and that some system was better than none at all, he vehemently attacked it as "unchristian and bad, terribly expensive, and one that perpetuates, because it is based upon, the spirit of caste." Ward had little but contempt for a system that was born in and tended to perpetuate a slave society.

Final mention must be made of outright opposition to schemes of raising the level of the Negro through education. Such opposition was rooted in a number of positions, ranging all the way from the idea that the Negro *could* not learn to the idea that the Negro *should* not learn. Embodying a kind of synthesis of both was an address by Paul Barringer of the University of Virginia to a meeting of the Southern Educational Association in 1900.[6] Picturing the southern Negro as an incapable, ignorant, vengeful person scheming to obtain political power in the South, Barringer envisioned education in his hands largely a tool to obtain political mastery over the whites. Not only this, but the educated Negro was also pictured as an economic menace to the long suffering white yeomanry. Thus, it was not difficult for Barringer to encourage his countrymen to "go back to the old rule of the South and be done forever with the frauds of an educational suffrage." Clearly, Barringer embodied and exemplified the position of "white supremacy" and all that it implied for education.

Restatements and extensions of the common school ideal. One of the most impressive things about post-Civil War educational thought is the extent to which educators restated the previously enunciated ideal of the American common school. At association meetings, in pamphlets, and through a variety of other media, one speaker after another dealt with the traditional arguments supporting common education. The halls of NEA conventions still resounded to proposals that universal education would bring enlightenment to the republic, that it would minimize social cleavage and keep equality of opportunity open, that it would serve to induct an increasingly heterogeneous and growing immigrant population into American society, that it would prevent crime, and that it would generally contribute to the material and spiritual welfare of the American people.

In light of these many restatements, and of the movement for compulsory attendance, the question of including groups traditionally excluded from the

---

[5] William Hayes Ward, "The Danger Line in Negro Education," in J. C. Hartzell (ed.), *Christian Educators in Council* (New York, Phillips and Hunt, 1884), pp. 67–71.

[6] Paul B. Barringer, "Negro Education in the South," *Report of the Commissioner of Education for the Year 1900–1901*, Vol. I, pp. 517–523.

common school gained in importance. As early as 1886, the NEA gave over a complete section of its annual convention to a discussion of "The Problem of Race Education in the United States." [7] In a series of speeches three qualified men spoke of the necessity for educating the American Indian, the Chinese immigrant, and the Mexican immigrant for their places in American life. "Let Congress," urged Robert L. Owen, former secretary of the Cherokee Board of Education, "increase tenfold the present appropriations for the education of the wild men, who unlike the civilized tribes have not the means to educate their children, and out of these people will grow in a few years a class of intelligent and useful citizens, as many have already become. They will then be absorbed into the great body of American citizenship, where all the races of men can and do meet on the level of common right and equal justice." Similarly, the speaker on the Chinese, a former missionary in China, pointed proudly to the long tradition of Chinese learning and urged that "the gates of education be opened wide to these strangers in our midst. . . . It is not desirable that they should have special schools by themselves." The speaker on the education of the Mexican was no less vigorous in his demand for free, state-controlled schools for these people. In effect, all of these men were picturing the public school as the great "melting pot" of American society. Into it would go people of every foreign nationality, creed, and loyalty; out of it would emerge Americans.

Another movement grew out of the increasing concern with the education of defective children. This concern had grown to a point by the end of the nineteenth century where a separate department of the NEA annually turned its attentions wholly to problems in this area. Generally, in the early years of its work, this group tended to the position that while the state had a responsibility to defective children, this responsibility did not involve a common school education in concert with normal children. On the other hand, it did involve liberal endowment of special schools which would train such youngsters to the limit of their capacities.

Opposition to the common school ideal.   Opposition to the common school ideal during this period generally stemmed from two sources, and it is difficult to determine which of the two carried more weight with the American public. The first group comprised those people who were unequivocally opposed to universal education and who urged that it was bringing only harm to the American people. The second group, largely Roman Catholic but inclusive of other denominations, continued to support universal education, but they objected to having it carried on in common schools. Quite possibly the latter, arguing within the framework of friendship for education in general, was more palatable to the American people. Notwithstanding this fact, both served seriously to challenge the cause of public education.

Despite the numerous examples of spirited opposition to the whole idea

[7] National Educational Association *Proceedings* (1886), pp. 192–232.

of universal schooling that may be cited, two will have to suffice at this point. The first came in a series of essays by Zach. Montgomery, an attorney active in both California and national politics, collected in 1886 under the title *The School Question from a Parental and Non-Sectarian Stand-Point*.[8] Actually, Montgomery was a Roman Catholic, but his own statements and careful study of his position reveal that he was not taking a stand generally identified with most American Roman Catholic authorities at that time.

Montgomery's attack on universal public schooling was direct and unqualified. Referring to the common schools as a "crime and pauper-breeding system of public instruction," Montgomery cited long pages of statistics from the federal census to demonstrate that Massachusetts, with a well-perfected system of universal public education, had an alarmingly higher rate of crime than Virginia, who had traditonally maintained only schools for the poor at public expense. Suicide too, he argued, increased directly as the amount of public education in different states. Interestingly enough, Montgomery did not infer from these conclusions that education itself caused crime or suicide. On the contrary, he was much in favor of education, but only an education properly bestowed and wielded by parents. It was in a public school system which had broken down the bonds of parental authority that crime and suicide were rooted. Montgomery concluded his arguments with an extensive list of recommendations. In effect, they proposed that parents assume primary and principal responsibility for the education of their children and that no citizen be taxed to support education for children whose parents could afford it. The state's role was merely to assist children whose parents did not meet these responsibilities (and then only in a program entirely acceptable to the parents) and to encourage and supplement the activities of private educational enterprise.

Even more vehement and concerted was the attack on the schools made by Francis B. Livesey of Sykesville, Maryland. Livesey, self-styled reformer, "self-made man" according to one of his pamphlets, founder, president, and general manager of an organization known as the American Press Writers Association (allegedly numbering some 300 editors, authors, poets, correspondents, ministers, lecturers, reformers, lawyers, businessmen, farmers, and others), was rabid in his denunciation of everything that public education had brought to the American commonwealth. He published literally thousands of pamphlets, leaflets, and news releases, and his views appeared in dozens of newspapers throughout the country.

According to Livesey, public schools were associated with most of the ills of the time. In a single leaflet he laid at their feet the "negro problem, the servant problem, the labor problem, the tramp problem, the unemployment

---

[8] Zach. Montgomery, *The School Question from a Parental and Non-Sectarian Stand-Point* (Washington, Gibson, 1886).

problem, the divorce problem, the eyesight problem, the juvenile problem, the bribery problem and the pure food problem." These were not the only shortcomings of public education. One leaflet argued that "Education Has Brought the Negro to Crime and Revolution!" Another blamed the alarming increase in Massachusetts divorce to the "much vaunted schools of Massachusetts." Others protested against the education of Indians, Chinese, and foreigners. Still another accused the schools of breeding revolution. ". . . the very same schools," cried Livesey, "are primarily responsible for the production of classes of citizens who have had drilled into them the discontent, the lassitude and the covetousness which go to make up the genuine revolutionist." Some pamphlets accused the schools of breeding "criminals, tramps, and sharpers," while still others accused them of fermenting "strikes and socialism." In every one was the same conclusion: the public school must be abolished at all costs. "I must tell you," wrote Livesey to county school commissioners, "that in both this country and England there are now bands of able men and women who see the public school devastation, and who have set themselves resolutely at work in demand for its abolition." From the number of his statements which found their way into reputable newspapers, one should not underestimate Livesey's audience and, therefore, effect.

The other brand of opposition to the common school, coming from that group which approved of universal education but objected to public schools, was quite as vigorous as that outlined above. Although a number of Protestant educators joined with them in their objections, the leading exponents of this opposition were the Roman Catholics. Roman Catholic attitudes toward public education had precedents in the earlier objections of men like Bishop John Hughes to the "nonsectarian" education of New York City's public schools in 1840. Their fundamental basis had not changed. Roman Catholic doctrine taught that no education could be complete unless it was permeated throughout with the teachings of Roman Catholicism. This obviously was impossible in a common school supported by the state and embracing children of many religious denominations. Thus, since its inception, Roman Catholic authorities had been objecting to the common school. In its early phases they objected to the fact that it taught the common elements of Protestant Christianity. Following the Civil War, when the common school curriculum had been even further secularized, they objected to it because it was religiously neutral.

A long series of pastoral letters to the clergy and the faithful in the United States began to urge with increasing vigor that Roman Catholic parents educate their children in Roman Catholic parochial schools. In few places, however, was church policy stated as directly as in the pronouncements of the Third Plenary Council of Bishops, presided over by Cardinal James Gibbons, and held at Baltimore in 1884. The sections on education are clear and forceful.[9] ". . . not only out of paternal affection but also by whatever authority we are invested, we urge and enjoin Catholic parents to provide their beloved children . . . an education which is truly Christian and Catholic. Further, that they defend them throughout infancy and childhood from the perils of a purely secular education and place them in safekeeping; that they therefore send them to parochial schools or other truly Catholic schools, unless in particular cases the Ordinary judges that some alternative may be permitted." To implement their injunctions, the bishops enjoined each parish priest to provide, within two years of their pronouncement, a parochial school for the children of his parish. Further sections urged the establishment of Roman Catholic higher education for the training of teachers and other professional men.

By and large, this was the position taken by most Roman Catholic writers from that time forward. Many bishops were rigid in their rulings concerning the sending of children to parochial schools, and some went so far as to refuse absolution and penance to parents who continued to avail themselves of public education when parochial schools were available. When the NEA gave a panel over to the theme "Denominational Schools" at its annual convention in 1889, Cardinal Gibbons forcefully reiterated the position of the Baltimore conference. His and other addresses in this symposium achieved wide circulation in many parts of the nation through reprinting and free dissemination.

Demands for Equality of Higher Educational Opportunity

"There is one educational principle that is peculiarly American," wrote Dean James Earl Russell of Teachers College, Columbia in 1908. "It is that every man, because he is a man and an American citizen, should be liberally educated as far as circumstances permit."[10] The common schools, he continued, had made a good beginning in providing American youngsters with a basic preparation for life. But the common school was only a beginning. It left off at the age of thirteen or fourteen—for Dean Russell one of the most critical periods in the youngster's life. This was the time when the average boy had to learn means of self-support and when the average girl had to fit herself for domestic duties. This was the time, too, when technical training was vital. In light of this, Russell contended "that every American boy and girl is entitled to practical help in this time of greatest need—and at public expense, too, if the state maintains high schools, universities, and professional schools for those who aspire to leadership in professional life." Actually, in reiterating the ideal of equal educational opportunity, the dean was summoning the heart of the American educational ideal—the educational ladder. In doing so, he was

[9] Frederic E. Ellis (ed.), "Parochial and Public Schools: A Point of View. Selections on Education from the Pronouncements of the Third Plenary Council of Baltimore," *Educational Forum*, Vol. XIV (1949), pp. 21–37.

[10] James E. Russell, "Democracy and Education: Equal Opportunity for All," National Education Association *Proceedings* (1908), pp. 155–158.

pointing to one great task of educators in the post-Civil War period: the extension and expansion of this ladder to meet the changing needs of American life.

Secondary education.   It was at the 1885 convention of the National Educational Association that John E. Seaman, a New Orleans schoolman, delivered an address under the title "High Schools and the State." [11] For two generations, since the establishment of the first public high school in Boston in 1821, Americans had watched with interest this new secondary school they had created. In the beginning there were relatively few of them, and therefore they excited comparatively small interest. Americans were busy building their much vaunted common school systems. Yet for many, the upper reaches of this common school system—the public high school and the state university— were to evoke the greatest interest. Gradually, especially in the years following the Civil War, both the demands and the opposition grew sharper until in the 1880's and 1890's the problem became one of wide discussion in and out of educational circles. Here, then, was Seaman, exemplifying a growing interest in the role and functions of this new institution in American life. What were to be its purposes and the groups it would serve?

Seaman's argument was most noteworthy perhaps for its comprehensiveness. It began syllogistically. If in all governments the source of power must be educated, and under a republican government the people are the source of power, then the people must be educated. It was a syllogism which would assuredly evoke wide acceptance at the time it was proposed—and yet so very much hinged on the meaning of "education." For some, it meant simply instruction in the rudiments of learning—reading, writing, arithmetic, and perhaps some moral and patriotic instruction. For Seaman it meant a great deal more. "We contend," he argued, "that the circumscribed course of rudiments taught in the lower schools is not education. They are the tools only. . . . If the ultimate object of a public school education is to lift up man to the dignity of a reflecting, self-guiding, virtuous member of society, then the instruction, scrupulously limited to the three R's, is a lamentable failure. . . . A moment's reflection will satisfy us that the high schools in this age are as important as the primary schools a century ago. They are imperatively demanded by the progress of the sciences, arts and inventions, and their application to the commercial and domestic uses of life." Clearly, Seaman was incisively pointing to the fact that an ever more complex, industrial America was demanding skills of the people which some decades ago had been demanded only of a few. Only through the widest dissemination of education beyond the primary grades could a wise citizenry cope with the problems of the new age.

Seaman saw numerous other roles for this remarkable institution. An im-

---

[11] J. E. Seaman, "High Schools and the State," National Educational Association *Proceedings* (1885), pp. 173–180.

portant one was the training of teachers and other professional men, particularly to serve America's growing public school system. Another was a political one: by detecting and exposing "the fallacies of socialism," the high school could contribute to the stability of the republic by lessening the antagonism of classes. In providing for the association of youngsters from all social classes in a common quest for knowledge, it could—as the common school before it—serve as a continuing wellspring of the spirit of democracy. Finally, the high school would undeniably raise the level of common school instruction; for in providing an ever present goal for elementary students, it would constantly stand as "the stimulus and great reward of grammar schools."

A variety of statements contemporary with and following Seaman's analysis elaborated and extended one or another of his points. The president of the NEA's Department of Secondary Education in 1891 placed great stress upon the high school's role as a "people's college." [12] Such an institution must stand as a friend of the laboring man, he held, "for he is coming to know that this is the institution which shall level the distinction between the rich and the poor, as far as power and place are concerned." Here again was allusion to the leveling function of the American public school—this time in the secondary rather than the elementary realm.

The relationship Seaman drew between the high school and the growing demands of American industrial life was another which received considerable mention. By and large, most of those concerned with this problem maintained that with the increasing complexity of American industrial life, more and more children would be attending the high school. But this would be so, they cautioned, only if the high school continued to modify its program in terms of the needs of the times. Thus, for example, an inspector of the New York State Education Department wrote in 1907: [13] "Today the three greatest industrial interests, commercial, manufacturing, and agricultural demand a share of attention from the high school. Their demands are not only just, but they have a compelling power behind them. Properly heeded, these demands may save the high school from becoming a caste school."

Many educators took pains to point out that the high school was really a combination of the more practical academy with the older Latin grammar school. For example, Professor W. H. Payne of the University of Michigan, in a speech to the "School-Masters' Club" of Ann Arbor in 1887, made much of the fact that man is more than a "bread-earning" animal.[14] "Public education," maintained Payne, "should have no lower aim than to endow every son of toil with a kingly spirit, to raise every son and daughter of earth into

[12] Frank E. Plummer, "The Future High School," National Educational Association *Proceedings* (1891), pp. 620–631.

[13] E. W. Lyttle, "The Relation of High Schools to Industrial Life," National Education Association *Proceedings* (1907), pp. 698–700.

[14] W. H. Payne, "The Functions of the High School," *The Academy*, Vol. II (1887), pp. 398–403.

spiritual companionship with the elect of the race." He saw the liberal studies which would accomplish this for the great body of the people as the just domain of the high school or people's college.

Other educators came at the problem as one of the relation between the high school and the university. As it became increasingly clear that the high school for many would serve as preparation for the university, such educators occupied themselves not only with the former's effect on the latter, but the latter's effect on the former as well. The great majority realized that one of the most important functions of the high school would be the linking of the common school with the university, providing the middle rungs in the educational ladder for the great body of the people.

Colleges and universities. The ideal of genuine equality of educational opportunity for many did not stop with equal secondary education. As with Presidents Lindsley, Wayland, and other liberals of the antebellum period, many saw grave inequality unless every American with the necessary desire and ability was afforded the opportunity to progress through the higher reaches of the university without economic or social discrimination. (It is interesting that few educators discussing equality in the higher schools gave any attention to discrimination based on color or creed.) Among those who maintained this position were some of the towering intellectual figures of late nineteenth- and early twentieth-century America.

One of the clearest demands for equality of higher educational opportunity was embodied in a commencement address by President James B. Angell of the University of Michigan in 1879.[15] Angell set forth the theme of his address as follows: *"That it is of vital importance, especially in a republic, that the higher education, as well as common school education, be accessible to the poor as well as to the rich."* In support of his proposition, he advanced numerous cogent arguments. Hearkening back to the Jeffersonian tradition, he held that higher education was the just due of youngsters as human beings in order that they might develop as far as possible both talent and character. Moreover, it was to the benefit of a republican society to place such education within the reach of all, for no society could afford to ignore the potentialities which God has bestowed "with impartial hand equally on the rich and the poor."

Angell also proclaimed with deep faith the amalgamating and leveling possibilities of the college. Restating the ideals of men like Robert Dale Owen, Samuel Lewis, and Horace Mann, he pointed to the "democratic atmosphere" of the college, where men were judged not according to wealth or ancestry, but according to "brains and character." Moreover, insofar as it distributed the power of knowledge among different classes and sections of the community, he saw the college contributing powerfully to the prevention of

---

[15] James B. Angell, *The Higher Education: A Plea for Making It Accessible to All* (Ann Arbor, Mich., Published by the Board of Regents of the University of Michigan, 1879).

despotism. Finally, he saw equality of educational opportunity as the guarantee of a Christian community to its citizens. Anything less would be a denial of Christianity's great moral and ethical principles of the brotherhood of man.

Another compelling argument widely advanced in support of all levels of higher education was that there was no justifiable upper limit to the common school system. Once the state had decided to see to the education of the people, no limited effort would suffice. The common school idea was recognized as an integral one—one in which the aspect of universal education could not be divorced from equality of further educational opportunity.

Mention should also be made of the continuing agitation and demand for a national university carried on during these years. Literally hundreds of letters, speeches, memorials, and pamphlets appeared urging the establishment of such an institution. Many were included in a rather comprehensive pamphlet entitled *Memorial in Regard to a National University* [16] and published in 1892 by the United States Government under the authorship of John W. Hoyt, former governor of the territory of Wyoming and then president of the University of Wyoming. Although his conclusion could by no means summarize the rich range of arguments represented by the materials in his pamphet, they are indicative of the major lines. Hoyt forcefully urged that a national university could complete an American system of public education, coordinate the schools of the states, and most effectively cultivate patriotic sentiment in the minds of the people. A body of representative citizens from all parts of the country calling themselves the George Washington Memorial Association actually organized in 1897 for the express purpose of implementing similar ideas.

Opposition to equality of higher educational opportunity. Just as in the case of the common schools, considerable opposition to the notion of equality of educational opportunity managed to crystallize during this period. Even more so than in the lower schools, opposition here was rooted in traditional conceptions of the purposes of secondary and higher schools. It is not difficult to see how all of the arguments resisting the spread of universal education would also be turned against the idea of equal educational opportunity. It is hard to imagine a man like Livesey, for example, throwing his support behind public high schools and universities after reading his sentiments on elementary schools. There were other arguments of a very different order, however, and many of these came from people who were highly favorable to universal elementary education. It was these latter arguments that probably constituted the most telling opposition to equality of higher educational opportunity.

One of the most important—if not the most important—arguments advanced against equality of higher educational opportunity maintained that to secure such equality, secondary schools, colleges, and universities would have

---

[16] John W. Hoyt, *Memorial in Regard to a National University* (Washington, Government Printing Office, 1892).

to be publicly supported and that public support of such institutions was not within the right and power of the state. Common schools, the argument ran, were vital to the life of the state. As such, they were deserving of public support. Higher education was a luxury. The health of the state did not depend on it. As such, it was clearly not deserving of state support and should be left to private effort. Moreover, inasmuch as only a few people went on to higher schools anyway, to provide such education at public expense would be taxing the multitude for the benefit of a few. Such taxation was patently unjust. The close, even inextricable, relationship between problems of support and control on the one hand and attendance on the other is obvious at this point.

An excellent example of this argument was embodied in a pamphlet published in 1894 by Charles E. Taylor, calling himself "A Citizen of North Carolina." [17] Taylor in the first pages of his work took pains to point out his unequivocal support of elementary education. On the very next page, however, he was quick to note that this had nothing to do with state sponsorship of high schools, colleges, or universities. With respect to these latter institutions, very different principles applied. Primary instruction was a natural requisite for citizenship. Higher education was patently a private luxury. "People must not starve, but the public purse may not be drawn upon to feed them on turtle soup and plum pudding. The key to knowledge has been put into their hands by the public schools. If they have taste or aptitude for greater things, they may be left to make their way up." Clearly, the central point of conflict between this position and one supporting equality of opportunity was a definition of what exactly was the basic education demanded of citizens in a republic. Actually, as will be pointed out in Chapter 12, it became the crux of the famous Kalamazoo controversy in Michigan which eventually led to a state supreme court decision legalizing public support of high schools.

On the question of taxation without benefit, Taylor was equally clear and direct. There could be no justification for taxing the great body of the people to support institutions which only a privileged few could ever attend. It is interesting that this notion of the "people" paying for public higher facilities while the "rich" enjoyed them was strongly implanted in the thinking of labor following the Civil War. The Knights of Labor, for example, while proclaiming strong support for the common school, believed that the boys and girls of workingmen did not need a higher education. Rather, the Knights urged, such youngsters should be steered along the course of good and productive citizenship. In view of American labor's long and continuous record of support for public education, this early distrust of the "people's colleges" is noteworthy.

Another argument which found considerable expression during these years vehemently attacked higher education because of its traditional preoccupation

---

[17] C. E. Taylor, *How Far Should a State Undertake to Educate? Or, A Plea for the Voluntary System in Higher Education* (Raleigh, N. C., Edwards and Broughton, 1894).

with classical and humanistic studies. Why should the public support such institutions, it was maintained, when they contributed very little that the public could really use? A rather extreme, but nevertheless interesting, example of this position is found in the writings of Richard T. Crane, a Chicago businessman at the turn of the century. A contemporary of Livesey, Crane penned a number of pamphlets attacking the purposes and existence of colleges and technical schools. His principal argument was that a college education, because of its classical and literary emphasis, was a worthless undertaking for any young man who wished to succeed in the business world. Even more vitriolic was his contention that Harvard, Princeton, and other noted colleges were dens of iniquity where students loafed, learned drunkenness, and practised immorality.[18] While Crane's arguments were attacked by a wide variety of people, he produced enough evidence of support for his views to merit attention.

THE HEIGHTENING CONTROVERSY OVER SUPPORT AND CONTROL

As has been indicated, problems of support and control for education are so completely intertwined with conceptions of educational opportunity that it is difficult to separate the two even for analysis. So many arguments against the state's right to tax for education grew out of the notion that most people are uneducable. On the other hand, so many arguments concerning the state's right to control education stemmed from conflicting conceptions of the ultimate aim of education, be it religious, secular, or otherwise. In spite of these difficulties, one is able to isolate a number of problems in this area which were foci of contention during the decades following the Civil War. One of these problems concerned the role of the federal government in education, particularly as an agency of support. When local districts, because of varying abilities, had been unable to equalize educational opportunity throughout a state, the state stepped in to do so. Could the federal government do the same? Another major problem concerned the role of the state in education. There were those who claimed that the state was all-powerful in this realm. Others saw a limited role for the state; while still others saw any state activity whatever as an encroachment on church and parental rights. It is these two centers of controversy that this section will consider.

The Struggle for Federal Aid to Education

The Hoar proposal for federal participation in education. With the end of a war which liberated 4 million slaves, laid waste to the educational facilities of the South, and stimulated greatly the desire for national unity, considerable

---

[18] R. T. Crane, *The Utility of an Academic or Classical Education for Young Men Who Have to Earn Their Own Living and Who Expect to Pursue a Commercial Life* (Chicago, 1903). See also *The Value of Higher Schooling* (Chicago, 1911).

pressure developed for some form of federal participation in education. The first major legislative proposal for federal aid came before Congress during the period of radical Republican control. On February 25, 1870, Representative George F. Hoar (Republican, Massachusetts) introduced into the House a bill "to establish a national system of education." "The purpose of this bill," wrote Hoar, "by which it is for the first time sought to compel by national authority the establishment of a thorough and efficient system of public instruction throughout the whole country, is not to supersede, but to stimulate, compel, and supplement action by the State." [19] As he remarked later in Congress, it was to compel states to do what they would not do by themselves, and to do for them what they could not do for themselves.[20]

The provisions of the bill were as follows: Whenever any state slipped below a minimum of education, the President of the United States was empowered to designate it a "delinquent state." Upon doing so, the President would also appoint a federal superintendent of schools for that state, while the Secretary of the Interior would appoint school inspectors for each Congressional and local school district. The federal authorities would have the power to erect schoolhouses, and to supervise the production of textbooks. The operation would be financed by a tax of fifty cents per inhabitant on the delinquent states, supplemented by interest from a proposed permanent school fund. Patently, the bill was a harsh one, and this was made even further apparent by Representative Hoar's later remark that: "I do not believe, if we should pass this law, that it will ever be necessary to put it in force." [21] He evidently assumed that the penalties of educational delinquency would serve as an adequate threat to the poorer states.

The Hoar Bill never came to a vote in either house of Congress. While considerable support did come from within the Republican Party, public opinion was almost uniformly in opposition. Professional educators, led by the NEA, were vehement in their denunciation. Their sentiments were well expressed, perhaps, in a speech by James P. Wickersham, Superintendent of Common Schools of Pennsylvania, before the association in 1871.[22] Wickersham called the establishment of such a system (1) in opposition to the uniform practices of the national government, (2) contrary to the views of the founding fathers and the leading statesmen of the nation, (3) of doubtful constitutionality, and (4) in opposition to a sound, republican political philosophy. While he was thoroughly sensitive to the needs of the southern states, he was firmly convinced that such a compulsory system would never work. Rather, he urged, let the federal government grant aid to encourage local support. The power of educating children, Wickersham concluded, must be

[19] *Congressional Globe,* 41:2, p. 478.
[20] *Ibid.,* p. 485.
[21] *Ibid.,* 41:3, p. 1042.
[22] James P. Wickersham, "A National System of Compulsory Education," National Educational Association *Proceedings* (1871), pp. 16–25.

left in the hands of the people. To show their support of this position, the association adopted a resolution favoring any plan that would grant "pecuniary aid to the struggling educational systems of the South."

In addition to opposition from the profession, there was strong opposition from the Roman Catholic Church. Answering Republican support for the bill, the *Catholic World* in 1871 bitterly condemned its proposals.[23] The article saw the plan as a great design "to suppress Catholic education, gradually extinguish Catholicity in the country, and to form one homogeneous American people after the New England Evangelical type." The federal government, the article continued, had no business in education, since the latter was primarily a local and state concern. Interestingly enough, there was a hint that Catholics would be willing to accept a national system which provided public support for parochial schools. "We hold state authority is the only constitutional authority under our system to establish schools and provide for them at the public expense; but we could manage to get along with national denominational schools as well as others could." Thus, although squarely opposed to the Hoar Bill, the Catholic group evidenced willingness to qualify its objection in this respect.

The Blair proposals for federal participation in education. The years following the controversy over the Hoar Bill saw the increasing crystallization of public sentiment for and against federal aid. The remainder of the 1870's saw two bills, the Perce Bill introduced into the House of Representatives in 1872 and the Burnside Bill introduced into the Senate in 1879 aiming at federal grants to education. Both of these bills sought to apply the proceeds from the sale of public lands to educational purposes. Both passed in their respective houses. Yet neither managed to win the approval of both houses of Congress. During the 1880's, however, the heightening struggle really reached a climax in the great debates over the Blair Bills. So great was the interest manifested that it was probably not until the years immediately following World War II that public and Congressional concern again reached this level. Moreover, it was around these bills that the arguments of the opposing camps were most clearly and forcefully drawn.

Senator Henry W. Blair (Republican, New Hampshire) proposed his bill "to aid in the establishment and temporary support of common schools" at five different times during the 1880's. It secured passage in the Senate in 1884, 1886, and 1888 and failed of passage in 1882 and 1890. While there were variations in the several versions of the measure, the bill as introduced in 1884 substantially represents Blair's proposals. This provided that $77 million be divided in specified amounts over a period of eight years among the several states and territories "in that proportion which the whole number of persons in each who, being of the age of 10 years and over, can not write, bears to the whole number of such persons in the United States. . . ." In order to become

23 "Unification and Education," *Catholic World*, Vol. 13 (1871), pp. 1-14.

eligible for receipt of federal funds, a state had to meet the following conditions: *first,* maintenance of a common school system for all its children of school age (separate schools for whites and Negroes were countenanced if equal support was accorded both); *second,* a willingness to supply school statistics and information to the Secretary of the Interior; *third,* a curriculum to include "the art of reading, writing, and speaking the English language, arithmetic, geography, history of the United States, and such other branches of useful knowledge as may be taught under local laws . . . ;" *fourth,* the provision that no funds received under the act be spent on school rental or construction (except as provided for in special authorization) and that funds be used only for common, nonsectarian schools. Further sections held that the several states and territories would have to match at least the amount of their federal grant through local initiative and that portions of federal money might be expended for teacher training. Grants were to be administered by state and local officials within the bounds of certain general federal requirements.

As has been indicated, there was considerable public response to the Blair Bills by both individuals and organizations. In the case of the latter, as always, it is difficult to judge how far the official pronouncements represented the views of the membership. Then too, American society in the 1880's, while beginning to organize in response to industrialism, had achieved far less complex an organization than in the contemporary period. Thus, the question is not only one of the extent to which an organization spoke for its membership, but the extent to which it spoke for the total group it purported to represent. Even with these limitations in mind, however, it is useful and informative to survey the alignment of forces for and against the Blair proposals.

In general, farm and labor groups during this period were far too busy with immediate economic concerns to give extensive attention to educational matters. On the other hand, a number of favorable statements were made. For example, at its first convention in 1887, the Southern Alliance of farmers demanded of Congress "That as upon the intelligence of the people depend the stability and perpetuity of our own free government, we demand for the masses a well-regulated system of industrial and agricultural education." [24] Organized labor too was primarily concerned with better working conditions. Yet in 1886 the Knights of Labor resolved that "the cause of education would be promoted by the passage of the Blair educational bill" and sharply criticized Congress for its failure to do so. [25] As a matter of fact, the Knights actually maintained a lobby in Washington during these years, and one of its principal purposes was support of the federal aid bills. Similar support

---

[24] W. A. Dunning, *The Farmers' Alliance History and Agricultural Digest* (Washington, D. C., Alliance, 1891), p. 76.
[25] Henry W. Blair, *The Education Bill* (Inside of rear cover).

in the form of resolutions came from the American Federation of Labor following its organization in 1886.

The attitude of organized business is also of interest. While once again there was not too much concern with education, those few statements which were put forth were generally favorable. The Union League Club of New York City, for example, heartily approved the Blair Bill in its resolutions of 1882. It was joined in its support by the Boston Chamber of Commerce and Board of Trade. The lack of interest of the Grand Army of the Republic, the most important veteran's organization, was complete, and there is no record of any pronouncement either way.

The educational profession, while extremely interested in the measure, was itself gravely divided. The NEA, the most vocal group of professional educators, was consistently behind the proposal. Support also came from the National Education Assembly, a group which convened in Atlantic City in 1882 and 1883 for the express purpose of arousing public opinion to the need of federal aid, and the Inter-State Educational Convention, which represented a group of southern state governors and convened in 1883. In spite of this significant affirmation, however, most college and university officials, as well as private school leaders, found themselves opposed. In addition, the opposition of such educational journals as *Academy,* catering largely to high school and private school administrators, was pronounced.

The churches too were divided in their stand. While some Protestant journals such as the *Andover Review* (Congregational) were notable in their support of the measure, others such as the *New Princeton Review* (Presbyterian) were vehemently opposed on grounds of unnecessary centralization of education and irreligion. The Roman Catholic Church was unalterably opposed to the measure, and the *American Catholic Quarterly Review* labeled it an unconstitutional scheme to destroy the Catholic Church and its educational system in the United States.

As for the two major political parties, although there was much conflict *within* them, in general, the Republicans supported the measure while the Democrats opposed it. Gordon Lee's analysis of these extensive congressional debates on the Blair Bills is thorough and exhaustive, and summarizes well the varying arguments for and against federal aid.[26] Generally, the supporting contentions ran as follows:

1. A literate electorate, hence an adequate, effective school system throughout the nation is essential to the maintenance of democratic government.
2. Federal aid to education is unquestionably constitutional.
3. There is ample historical precedent for federal aid to education.
4. The legislation is the logical consequence of the winning of the Civil War and the enfranchisement of the Negroes.

[26] Gordon Canfield Lee, *The Struggle for Federal Aid: First Phase* (New York, Bureau of Publications, Teachers College, Columbia University, 1949), pp. 149–155.

5. Although the greater part of the bill's benefits accrue to the South, it is designed to meet the educational needs of the whole nation.

6. The bill is designed so that initial financial requirements on the states (matching federal grants) are small, and rise gradually as the life of the bill progresses.

7. Any bill of this nature would necessitate the imposition of certain requirements by the federal government on the states.

8. The bill involves only a temporary commitment of the federal government.

9. Public opinion definitely supports the bill, and Congress must respond to it.

On the other hand, the general course of the opposing arguments was as follows:

1. Legislation of this sort will undermine the foundation of the government by causing the states to be dependent on the federal government.

2. No constitutional authority exists for legislating on the matter of education.

3. The historic precedents of land grants for education do not hold in this case.

4. Federal participation in education will inevitably introduce party politics into the schools.

5. The need for federal aid to education is nonexistent. The South is slowly but surely developing the ability to meet its own educational needs.

6. Unless states receiving federal money match these grants from the beginning, local initiative will be destroyed.

7. The proposal imposes too many conditions on the recipient states.

8. The idea of this measure as a temporary one is unrealistic. There will be tremendous pressure for its continuance.

9. The public has not expressed itself in favor of this measure sufficiently to warrant its adoption.

The debates on the Blair Bills in Congress were brilliant and thorough. Despite the fact that the measures were at no point enacted into law, they helped a great deal to clarify many of the issues concerning the role of the federal government in the American educational system.

Controversies Concerning the Role of the State in Education

One of the most bitterly fought controversies during the decades following the Civil War concerned the role of the state in providing and controlling education. In general, one is able to distinguish three positions which vied for acceptance. The first held the state responsible for providing whatever educational facilities would meet the complete needs of the people. This position usually saw the state as sponsor of schools ranging from the earliest grades through the university; some who argued it even saw the eventual elimination of private facilities through lack of need. A second position urged a limited role for the state. The state had the right to furnish and control schools up to a certain level or for certain special groups like paupers or orphans. Institutions above that level should be left to private endeavor. A third position saw no role for the state at all in education. Any attempt of the state to sponsor and control schools was a violation of the most fundamental rights of parenthood, and an obvious overextension of state power. Within the scope of these three proposals fell most of the arguments dealing with the problem of educational control. ⌐

The state as sponsor of all levels of education. One of the finest and clearest arguments for state sponsorship of all levels of education made during this period was advanced by President William Oxley Thompson of the Ohio State University in his commencement address of 1900.[27] Taking a positive conception of the state as guarantor of all needs of the people, Thompson saw education as a vitally important domain of state activity. As such, it was the responsibility of the state to provide every phase of schooling needed by society. In earlier times, higher education had been a luxury; but with the growing complexity of industrial America, many luxuries had become necessities, and higher education was one of them. To the objection that the state had no business training men to be tradesmen, or professional men, because this would be of profit to individuals, Thompson retorted that the result of such argument would be "to rob education of all ordinary utility." This would oppose the very purpose for which the education was being offered—the maximum development of the individual as a useful member of society.

In answer to the question of whether the state's right and duty were exclusive, Thompson was decidely in the negative. It was perfectly clear to him that the state had a right to supervise all educational work to insure its character and quality. But the right of churches and benevolent associations to engage in education could not be denied. "The field of education seems therefore to be fairly and honestly open to both church and state," he concluded. "The extent to which either will engage in the work or the character of the work to be undertaken are not questions to be settled by any *a priori* method. It is purely a question of duty and wisdom to be judged in the light of past experience and present needs."

The same question had been raised during the 1880's by Professor Henry S. Frieze, Acting President of the University of Michigan. Frieze was much more direct in his approach to the problem, and his words brought considerable criticism from private school educators. "Every educational want," held Frieze, "shall be provided for here at home just as perfectly as if no other State nor any private institution were in existence." [28] In other addresses he maintained that the state might as properly consign its judiciary to a private corporation of lawyers, or its financial affairs to a syndicate of bankers, as to leave its educational work, or any part of it, to private corporations. It is easy

[27] William Oxley Thompson, *Annual Address at the Commencement Exercises of the Ohio State University* (Columbus, The Ohio State University, 1900).

[28] University of Michigan, *The President's Report to the Board of Regents for the Year Ending June 30, 1880* (Ann Arbor, Published by the university, 1880), p. 20.

to see where, even though it is not directly stated, many would interpret these remarks as an argument against the right of private schools to exist. While it is difficult to say, there was probably an element of hope in Frieze's message that the need for private schools would in time vanish. Such was undoubtedly the ideal of a substantial group who embraced the common school ideal. In many respects it was but an extension of the objections to private schools advanced by Orville Taylor, Horace Mann, and a number of other antebellum reformers.

An obvious correlary of the demand for state control and sponsorship of education was the demand for adequate machinery for the administration of this task. Before the Department of Superintendence of the NEA, and through numerous other channels, this demand received increasing voice. Only through the strengthening and enlargement of state authority in education could waste be eliminated, compulsory attendance laws properly enforced, and efficient uniformity brought about. In a majority of cases this would involve an extension of the powers exercised by state superintendents and boards of education, and the placing of professional educators rather than loyal politicians in state educational positions.

The state as a limited sponsor of education. Enough has been said previously about the argument that the state should only support education up to a given point to justify only passing attention here. The argument was essentially that while universal elementary education was necessary for the health and perpetuation of the state, higher education in all forms was a luxury. Being enjoyed by a few only, it should be sponsored by a few only, namely, by private endeavor. For some who were even willing to see secondary education sponsored by the state, public higher education was still an encroachment on individual rights.

It should be borne in mind that in some cases, even state sponsorship of universal elementary education was regarded as a trespass. Thus, for example, a Jesuit priest wrote in the *American Catholic Quarterly Review* in 1877:[29] "The only educational taxes that can be reasonably defended are those which go to the support of orphans and helpless children. . . ." Here was the old English philanthropic tradition being reasserted with vigor. Education was completely a private undertaking except in the case of destitute children. Their education was a state responsibility.

Opposition to state sponsorship of education. Coming primarily from Roman Catholic sources, this argument became extremely powerful during and after the last decades of the nineteenth century. Essentially, it was little different from the arguments used by Roman Catholics since Bishop Hughes and his followers had set forth their position in New York City during the 1840's. The public schools, urged the Catholics, were sectarian. Either they had a

---

[29] P. Bayma, "The Liberalistic View of the Public School Question," *American Catholic Quarterly Review*, Vol. II (1877), pp. 1–29 and 240–270.

definite bias toward Protestantism or were completely neutral and secular. In either case they were offensive and inadequate for Catholic children. Education is primarily, fundamentally, and ultimately a religious undertaking. As such, it is a matter for parents and the church. The state can aid these agents in their duty; but it can never replace them.

An excellent statement of this position is embodied in an article which appeared in the *Catholic World* for September 1904. "It is beyond question," wrote the author, "the exclusive right and duty of the parent to provide his children with all those aids which are necessary to their physical, intellectual, and moral life—subject to the special right and duty of the church to add thereto a training in the Christian faith." [30] The parent cannot surrender this right; therefore, the state has no direct role in education. Its only prerogative is to compel parents to educate their children and to assist them to the most efficient and economical performance of the task. The issue was put even more directly, perhaps, by a chief justice of the Supreme Court of Arizona speaking on behalf of a group of Roman Catholics in that state: "We, that is, those for whom I now argue maintain—*First*— That the State has no right to teach religion. *Second*— That the State has no right to teach irreligion. *Third*— That the State has no inherent right to teach at all." [31]

It is important to note that in the minds of many Roman Catholics the state did have one important function to fulfill. Moreover, this was the positive clue to their solution of the school problem. Rather than one single public school system, these Catholics urged, why not have several public school systems? "On our part," maintained a writer in the *Catholic World,* "we are willing to be taxed for unreligious schools for the children of unreligious parents, if such parents are willing on their part to be taxed for religious schools for our children." [32] Arguing that even compulsory attendance would be acceptable under such a scheme, this writer continued: "If some citizens wish to maintain schools exclusively secular let the state help them. If other citizens wish to have denominational schools let the state help them also; and let the state aid in every case be in proportion to the numbers benefited and the success obtained in such instruction as the state judges necessary to form good citizens."

Although the overwhelming majority of articles taking the Roman Catholic point of view tended to agree with the above arguments, it is noteworthy that there was controversy among some of the Catholics themselves. One of the most significant of these, concerned with the right of the state to educate, has been called the "Bouquillon Controversy" after its central figure. The con-

[30] Thomas F. Woodlock, "American Principles Versus Secular Education," *Catholic World,* Vol. 79 (1904), pp. 711–718.

[31] Edmund F. Dunne, *Our Public Schools: Are They Free or Are They Not?* (New York, Thomas Egan, 1875).

[32] [Walter Elliott], "The School Grievance and Its Remedy," *Catholic World,* Vol. 36 (1882–1883), pp. 713–718.

troversy began in 1891 with the publication of a pamphlet by Reverend Thomas Bouquillon, Professor of Moral Theology at Catholic University, entitled *Education: To Whom Does It Belong?* In it, he maintained that the state had a proper and special right to education. ". . . civil authority," he argued, "has the right to use the means necessary for the diffusion of . . . knowledge, that is to say, to teach it, or rather to have it taught by capable agents." [33] Bouquillon even extended his argument to include approval of compulsory education, provided that such education did not necessarily take place in state schools.

Needless to say, the pamphlet stirred up a storm of controversy. Two Jesuit priests, Reverend R. I. Holaind and Reverend James Conway, published extensive rebuttals reaffirming the right of the Church and the parent to educate. A visit by Cardinal Satolli as papal legate in 1892 failed to quiet the controversy. As a matter of fact, in many ways the visit fanned it to new intensity. However, in May 1893 Pope Leo XIII in a letter to Cardinal Gibbons reiterated his approval of the position taken by the Third Plenary Conference of 1884 and called for an end to the controversy. For all intents and purposes, the letter accomplished its purpose, and Bouquillon, continuing at Catholic University, gave up the fight.

THE HEIGHTENING PROBLEM OF THE CURRICULUM

In the realm of the curriculum one senses a period of ferment during these years—of men thinking out on new frontiers and of other men opposing their departures. Much of this ferment may be seen as a response to the increasing complexity of American life. A host of new educational demands appeared in the emergence of industrial America, and schoolmen heatedly debated the proper response of the school. From Europe came an influx of new ideas as the thought and writings of Pestalozzi, Herbart, Froebel, and others were interpreted in America. They found a favorable milieu in the new and beneficent conceptions of the child which were increasingly associated with American democratic thought. Obviously, this growing respect for the individual child posed herculean problems for a rapidly expanding school system. What was the happy balance between the educational claims of society and the educational needs of individuals? Were they at variance? These were questions which received extended treatment in the councils of the day.

At the secondary level the question of serving diverse social and economic groups in one public school was always central. Should the high school build its curriculum to meet the needs of college-bound students, or of the great majority for whom the high school was an educational terminus? The problem at the college level was somewhat similar. Should an individual student have the right to pursue a curriculum tailor-made to his own needs and aspirations; or was enough known about the heritage of the race and the nature of a liberal education to warrant demanding the same of all? At every level one is struck with the sense of urgency in the various arguments. Above all, one cannot but be impressed with the way in which many of the problems which have continued to plague contemporary educators were delineated, sharpened, and debated.

The Influx of European Educational Thought

The ideas of Johann Heinrich Pestalozzi. Mention has already been made in Part II of the early influence of Pestalozzi's ideas on American education. It was in the period after 1860, however, that the thinking of the great Swiss educator really made itself felt in school theory and practice. While it is beyond the scope of this volume to treat Pestalozzi's ideas at length, a brief consideration of his basic educational principles is vital to an understanding of post-Civil War educational thought.

Much of Pestalozzi's fame doubtless stemmed from the fact that he not only wrote about educational theory, but he also conducted schools putting his theories into practice. Above all, perhaps, it was his conceptions of learning that appealed to educators who were looking for new ways to teach the children of the common people. Looking upon the child as a unity made up of separate faculties of moral, physical, and intellectual powers, he believed that education should consist in the natural, progressive, and harmonious development of all the child's powers and faculties. He insisted that the natural instincts of the child should provide the motives for learning rather than external prodding and compulsion. Cooperation and sympathy, he believed, would achieve discipline far more readily than physical punishment. In this way the natural powers of the child could develop and be freely and naturally expressed. Moreover, since it is nature that gives drive to life, the teacher's task is one of adapting instruction to the individual child accordingly as his nature unfolds in the various stages of natural development.

Pestalozzi held with the sense realists that "sense impression is the absolute foundation of all knowledge." Therefore, in the education of children it was necessary to rely at the earliest stages upon observation of actual things and natural objects rather than upon books and reading. Thus, Pestalozzi devised a whole series of "object lessons" in order to give full play to the child's natural desire to develop his senses of sight, touch, and sound. Plants, animals, special methods, tools, drawing, modeling, music, and geography were important items in Pestalozzi's program for developing the perceptive faculties. Throughout, there was emphasis on the child as an active being engaged in the process of experiencing. Unlike the earlier sense realists, Pestalozzi did not view the young mind as a passive receptor of sense impressions. Rather it was an active mind, perceiving, discriminating, analyzing, and selecting.

The ideas of Friedrich Froebel. Another towering figure of European education whose ideas bear mention at this point is Friedrich Froebel. Froebel was impressed not only by the sense realism of Pestalozzi, but also by the semimystical idealistic philosophy of his day. He looked upon the child as an agency for the realization of God's will in human nature. Through education the child's spirit could become linked with the spiritual unity of the Absolute.

Froebel felt that the educative process should start with the small child of three or four years. He called the institution appropriate to young children the *kindergarten,* a garden where children grow. Inasmuch as play is the characteristic method of growth and learning for young children, it is as appropriate for young children as work is for adults. Froebel called it "the highest phase of child-development." This new respect for the child, for his individuality, and for the dynamic and active qualities of his nature obviously involved a lessening in the traditional rigidity and formality of school atmosphere. The emphasis upon manipulation of objects and freedom to explore and to express one's self produced a greater accent on activity in place of constant intellectual pursuit. Furthermore, his notion of group activity as a natural means of expression led to a realization of the importance of good social relationships as a desirable outcome of school and community life.

The ideas of Johann Friedrich Herbart. A third profound influence on American education following the Civil War was the work of Johann Friedrich Herbart, famous German philosopher and psychologist. The moral end of life, character, was for Herbart the central aim of education. Character could be attained only by analyzing the social interests of men to discover the ideal ones for an educated man, and then to develop these in the individual by means of instruction. The first step in realizing character was "many-sidedness of interest." It is important to note, however, that although he used "interest" in its contemporary meaning as a *stimulus* to learning, Herbart employed it far more fundamentally to mean a *result* of learning. Thus, he noted in his *Outlines of Educational Doctrine:* "The word *interest* stands in general for that kind of mental activity which it is the business of instruction to incite . . . ; he who lays hold of his information and reaches out for more, takes an interest in it." [34] Herbart saw the study of history and literature as peculiarly adapted to this purpose. Moreover, he even urged that these subjects should form the core of the curriculum, around which other studies were *correlated* (i.e., explicitly related) and *concentrated* (i.e., related, but with emphasis at the core). Correlation and concentration for Herbart and his followers led to *unity* in a curriculum. The tragedy of traditional education for them was the failure to achieve unity, namely, *isolation.*

Despite his insistence on the social and moral aims of education, Herbart believed that these aims could best be achieved by an intellectual approach

[34] John Frederick Herbart, *Outlines of Educational Doctrine* (New York, Macmillan, 1913), p. 44.

to the learning process. His whole psychology of associationism stressed the importance of developing clear ideas in students. He reduced emotion, will, and feeling to secondary qualities dependent upon the association of ideas in the mind. The teacher should therefore direct his attention primarily to the processes by which ideas are formed from perceptions and sensations. Above all, the teacher must concentrate upon the problem of interest. Inasmuch as consciousness is made up of ideas associated in many ways, the teacher must see to it that new ideas are presented in such a way that they are vitally associated with ideas already part of the experience of the learner.

Herbart's followers made his insistence upon association and interest a rather rigid pattern that came to be known as the *five formal steps* of teaching and learning. These were (1) *preparation*, in which old ideas useful in learning the new material are called to the learner's mind; (2) *presentation*, or the actual statement of the new material; (3) *association*, in which the new material is related to, compared with, and connected with the old; (4) *generalization*, in which rules, definitions, or general principles are drawn from specific cases; and (5) *application*, in which general principles are given meaning by reference to specific examples and practical situations. At a time when reading, memory, and student recitation were the principal methods of teaching, these ideas found extremely fertile soil in American educational theory.

The "New Education" Challenges the Traditional Elementary Curriculum

The child-centered conception. The educational conceptions set forth by Neef, Maclure, and others of the early American Pestalozzians matured significantly during and after the Civil War period. Perhaps the most ardent and outspoken exponent of this "child-centered" approach during the 1860's and 1870's was Edward A. Sheldon, President of the State Normal School at Oswego, New York. Conceiving of education as "all the influences that go to develop the human being," Sheldon saw the earliest education of the school as directly continuous with that of the home. The whole work of the school, as that of the home, "should be *so* to help the child that when he becomes a man, he can help himself." The teacher, therefore, should bring into the schoolroom all of the objects of nature and art necessary for the child to continue his active investigations into the world about him. In this way, the child himself can build an education adapted to his individual tastes, needs, and capacities.

Obviously influenced by Pestalozzi, Sheldon saw the curriculum built largely around object lessons. These were to be appropriately divided into lessons involving numbers, magnitude, form, drawing, color, weight, sounds, places, animals, plants, minerals, and liquids. Herein lay the clue to a new organization of the curriculum. Rather than given subjects to be taught to the youngsters the emphasis was on having them undergo certain kinds of learning experience. A curriculum built on this principle would have subject matter, to be sure, but this matter would be drawn upon only as the child's investigations led him to it, not as foreordained by adult teachers.

Another of the more active proponents of the new education was Colonel Francis W. Parker, Principal of the Cook County Normal School in Illinois. Parker's definitive work, *Talks on Pedagogics,* is literally a gold mine of materials concerning the new view of the child. Interestingly enough, it may well be said that Parker took the best from Pestalozzi, Froebel, and Herbart in the formulation of his educational position—taking from the former two the centrality of the child in the educative process and from the latter his principles of correlation and concentration in the organization of the curriculum. "The centre of all movement in education," argued Parker, "is *the child.* We must grant that human beings are absolutely governed by immutable, ever-acting, all-efficient laws of growth and development, and that all development means conformity to the laws of being; nonconformity is decay, degradation, and death." [35] Indeed, the diagrammed chart at the beginning of Parker's work illustrating his theory of concentration placed the child at the center of an education which consisted in an ever expanding sphere of experience. Obviously, such a conception would lend great support to the scientific study of children which moved forward so rapidly during the latter years of the century. Throughout, their needs, interests, capacities, and concerns remained all important determinants of the curriculum.

Inasmuch as a good bit of the stimulus for the child-centered position grew out of the thought of Pestalozzi and Froebel, one might expect growing concern with hand or manual education. Accordingly, the years after 1875 witnessed rising interest in manual training as an aspect of general education. The movement was given great stimulus by the Russian Exhibit at the Philadelphia Exposition in 1876, and under the leadership of Professor Calvin M. Woodward of Washington University in St. Louis, it grew rapidly in popularity during the 1880's. What is extremely important is that manual training in the minds of its progenitors was vastly different from technical instruction. While the latter was specific training for a specific trade, the former was a general education in and systematic study of the motor skills associated with common tools. It was general *preparation* for later specific technical activity. Moreover, it was felt that manual training aided the development of intellectual capability quite as much as symbolic material improved and directed motor activity. Needless to say, as proponents of the "new" education sought to provide a well balanced education for the growing child, they paid increasing heed to the claims of this new area.

The subject-centered conception. While many felt that the child-centered education could contribute much to an understanding of the educational process, they were loath to give up the subjects which had formed the school

35 Francis W. Parker, *Talks on Pedagogics* (New York, E. L. Kellogg, 1894), p. 383.

program for generations. When the National Educational Association appointed a Committee of Fifteen in 1893 to study the problem, the issue was considerably sharpened, for part of their report delivered two years later undertook clearly to set forth in liberal terms the values of the more traditional subjects.

The report viewed the elementary curriculum entirely in terms of content areas. The primary studies of the first eight years were grammar, literature, arithmetic, geography, and history. In effect, these were seen as the "five branches upon which the disciplinary work of the elementary school is concentrated." Of course, other areas were definitely to be included. Industrial and esthetic drawing, natural science (to train habits of observation), physiology, hygiene, vocal music, physical culture, algebra, and morals all had certain just claims upon a student's time. The committee took these subjects and wove them into a rather elaborate eight-year program, with a definite time allotment and sequential order for each. Clearly, what they had done was to draw a blueprint deemed suitable for every child and independent in organization, content, and sequence of the children who studied it. President Nicholas Murray Butler of Columbia University characterized it as "an elaborate defense of the *status quo*" which faced backward rather than forward and which completely ignored individuality in education.

John Dewey recasts the educational problem. It was into this seemingly irresolvable conflict between child-centered and subject-centered views of the curriculum that Profesor John Dewey first projected the light of his analysis. Quickly realizing that cast in the either-or terms of child or subject, the question could never be resolved, Dewey devoted his first efforts to reconstructing the problem—a task which he undertook in his monograph *The Child and the Curriculum* published in 1902.[36]

Taking as the fundamental factors in the educative process the immature human being on the one hand and the social aims, meanings and values incarnate in adult experience on the other, Dewey saw the educational controversy as a problem of emphasis. One school placed the emphasis on the subject matter of the curriculum as over the contents of the child's own experience. The latter, they maintained, was narrow and crude; the purpose of education was to substitute for this superficiality the well-ordered, objective realities of the former. *Discipline,* according to Dewey, was their watchword. The other school placed emphasis on the child—as "the starting-point, the center, and the end." With his individual development as ideal and standard, all studies become subservient, "instruments valued as they serve the needs of growth." Self-realization, rather than simple knowledge or information, is the goal of education. Rather than discipline, *interest* was the watchword of this group.

Granted this dichotomy, Dewey posed the problem: "It is just to get rid

[36] John Dewey, *The Child and the Curriculum* (Chicago, University of Chicago Press, 1902).

of the prejudicial notion that there is some gap in kind (as distinct from degree) between the child's experience and the various forms of subject-matter that make up the course of study." The solution of the problem, then, lay on the one hand in abandoning the notion of subject matter as fixed and outside of the child's experience, and on the other, in abandoning the notion of the child's experience as something "hard and fast." If the latter is viewed as something "fluent, embryonic, vital," then "we realize that the child and the curriculum are simply two limits which define a single process." Thus Dewey concluded: "Just as two points define a straight line, so the present standpoint of the child and the facts and truths of studies define instruction. It is continuous reconstruction, moving from the child's present experience out into that represented by the organized bodies of truth that we call studies." Once the problem was thus viewed, as Dewey himself pointed out in *The Educational Situation,* it became one of providing the external machinery and pupil-teacher relationship where education in its totality might be carried on, rather than an irresolvable conflict over two emphases within a single process.

Criticism of the "new" education. As for criticism of the newer educational ideas cited above, it was sharp and plentiful. As early as 1866, Frederick A. Packard, former secretary of the American Sunday School Union, published a stinging denunciation of contemporary elementary education.[37] Surveying the public schools of Massachusetts, New York, Pennsylvania and Ohio, Packard concluded they had failed miserably. Nine in ten pupils, he observed, were unable to "read properly a paragraph in a newspaper, to keep a simple debt and credit account in a mechanic's shop, or to write an ordinary business letter in a creditable way, as to chirography, orthography or a grammatical expression of ideas." His suggestions were simple and direct. Every youngster should be taught to read a newspaper, to write a grammatical and well-spelled letter on a common subject, to work an ordinary arithmetic problem, and to know the geography of his own country and neighborhood. This, together with suitable training in Christian principles, should be the scope of public education. Anything higher and broader should be left to private enterprise.

A writer in *Gunton's Magazine* was even more critical than Packard.[38] "The object of the public-school teacher," he wrote, "is to develop an English-speaking, self-respecting, self-supporting American citizen." "To accomplish this simple and noble purpose," he continued sarcastically, "she has vast and varied means at her command: abundance of manual training, such as cooking, wood-carving, sewing, carpentering, paper-cutting, clay-modeling, drawing and painting; dabs of science, such as physiology, botany, mineralogy, geology; driblets of French or German; proportionately plenty of musical

[37] Frederick A. Packard, *The Daily Public School in the United States* (Philadelphia, J. B. Lippincott, 1866).
[38] Lys D'Aimee, "The Menace of Present Educational Methods," *Gunton's Magazine,* Vol. 19 (1900), pp. 257–267.

sight-reading and part singing; a fair amount of arithmetic; some history and geography; touches of English composition and grammar, and odd moments of English reading." In general, three reasons were cited for the utter failure of public education: *first,* a curriculum full of frills like art and music which detracted from teaching of the essentials; *second,* "the absolute decadence of the study of English"; and *third,* "the tendency of modern education to make study too easy, too entertaining." "The mental nourishment we spoon-feed our children," he concluded, "is not only minced but peptonized so that their brains digest it without effort and without benefit and the result is the anaemic intelligence of the average American school-child." As may be obvious, his answer was simple—a return to a curriculum which demanded of the students practice and skill in the essential subjects of language and arithmetic.

The Conflict Over the Role of Religious Instruction

Another problem which received even more attention and discussion than it had in the earlier period was the problem of what, if any, religious instruction ought to be given in the common school. While there were many variant positions on this highly charged question, most of them tended to fall under three headings: (1) the view favoring sectarian religious instruction, taken principally by the Roman Catholics, (2) the view favoring nonsectarian instruction and Bible reading, and (3) the view rejecting both Bible reading and religious instruction per se.

The Roman Catholic point of view has been treated previously, and will be given only the briefest attention at this point. Essentially, it maintained that religious instruction was the heart of education and that consequently no education could be complete, or even worthy of the name, without it. Nonsectarian instruction and Bible reading without comment was entirely unacceptable. Both were essentially Protestant in content and character. Moreover, a completely neutral school was equally unacceptable. "Secular education cannot be neutral," noted a writer in the *Catholic World,* "—it will at least make men indifferent; and religion is a thing too important to have men indifferent about it." [39] Hence, the only position that most Catholic writers could accept was that education should be carried on in denominational rather than common schools.

The second view, calling for Bible reading and nonsectarian religious instruction in the schools, was the one which affirmed the traditional position of the common school reformers on this question. It was widely urged in most Protestant quarters. Generally, proponents of this position viewed the Bible as a completely nonsectarian document which, although subject to different interpretations by different men, would have inspiration for all of them. In light of this, no one could fairly object to using this volume in a

[39] *Catholic World,* Vol. 44 (1886–87), p. 155.

school attended by children of many faiths. Its great lessons would certainly be a telling force in binding them together in a spirit of Christian love and charity. Such a spirit of Christianity was at the heart of and vital to the maintenance of American civilization.

Yet a third position began to claim increasing attention during these years. This one maintained that religion was not within the province of the state, that nonsectarian Christian instruction tended to give offense to non-Christian denominations which, though in the minority, were entitled to freedom of conscience, and that therefore, all religious instruction ought to be excluded from public schools. An excellent illustration of this view was embodied in a sermon preached by the Reverend Samuel T. Spear, a Presbyterian minister of Brooklyn, New York, in 1870.[40] Objecting to Judge Story's oft-cited argument that the American government rested on Christianity, Spear held that the Constitution established not a *Christian* government but a *republican* government—one in which men of all faiths enjoyed equal rights. In view of this, Spear took the position that: "The State, being democratic in its constitution, and consequently having no religion to which it does or can give any legal sanction, should not, and cannot, except by manifest inconsistency, introduce either religious or irreligious teaching into a system of popular education which it authorizes, enforces, and for the support of which taxes all the people in common." To introduce the Bible, he continued, was sectarianism—against those who "reject its divine authority in any version." The government and the Constitution had left the way open for each man, in his own way, to worship *privately*. To introduce any religious view into public, state-supported schools, was a clear violation of this sacred freedom.

The Attempt of the Secondary School to Serve a Variety of Purposes

From its earliest days, the high school was inextricably involved in a conflict of purposes. Some were attending it as a preparatory school for college and university study. Others sought from it a general education beyond that of the elementary school which would prepare them for life in the American community. Still others sought from it some kind of specialized, technical, or vocational instruction. When secondary education was extremely limited and catered to but a small percentage of the population, these problems, although present, were not pressing. When secondary education became public, however, and began to expand by leaps and bounds at the end of the nineteenth century, these conflicts assumed an urgency comparatively new to the secondary scene.

Certainly the college-preparatory function of the high school was early and often stated. Those who did so pointed always to the need for close articu-

[40] Samuel T. Spear, *The Bible in Public Schools* (New York, Wm. C. Martin, 1870).

lation between secondary and higher education. Only through such an articulation might the university be guaranteed a continuing supply of well-trained, qualified students. Many went further to add that while private secondary facilities might well continue to provide the new state universities with students, it was the public high school which would really to great extent determine the future of higher education.

Even as these pleas for closer articulation between high school and university were being made, however, considerable attention was being attracted to the other functions of the secondary school. Many argued that only as it broke with tradition and turned its attention to the wants of the people could it fulfill its role as a "people's college." Into the determination of ways of doing this most effectively went much of the frontier curriculum thinking of the period.

The growing demand for more practical secondary education. Just as the years after 1875 saw a heightening interest in manual training for elementary school children, so did they also witness a growing demand for manual, industrial, and commercial education on the secondary level. All three obviously stemmed from the increasingly commercial and industrial character of the American economy following the Civil War. In the cities, there was a continuing need for trained personnel. In the rural communities, too, with the growing mechanizing and commercializing of agriculture, the skilled man was at a premium. Moreover, since most people apparently agreed that the elementary curriculum during the early years should remain fairly general, and since colleges and universities had both a powerful tradition of intellectual pursuit and a small clientele, the American secondary school seemed the obvious point at which to address these demands.

The turn of the century witnessed intensifying pressure for this more practical kind of secondary curriculum from a wide variety of sources. The National Society for the Promotion of Industrial Education, for example, was a persistent advocate. The National Association of Manufacturers went on record year after year in its favor, and the report of its Committee on Industrial Education in 1908 furnishes evidence of such sentiments. ". . . it is genuine, practical industrial education we stand for," noted the report, "an industrial education which will make of the American boy an all-around, full-fledged, skilled mechanic, able to take his place and hold his own alongside of the skilled mechanic having learned his trade in the skilled industries of this or any other country. . . ." [41] The National Education Association warmly endorsed the establishment of public trade and industrial schools.[42] Organized labor, while it consistently opposed and cautioned against flooding the labor marked with "half-baked journeymen" graduated from inadequate industrial curricula, was also in favor of "genuine industrial education." The

[41] *Report of the Commissioner of Education* (1909), Vol. I, p. 153.
[42] National Education Association *Proceedings* (1908), p. 34.

American Federation of Labor, for instance, at its twenty-ninth annual convention in 1908, proclaimed that "organized labor has the largest personal and the highest public interest in the subject of industrial education, and should enlist its ablest and best men in behalf of the best system, under conditions that will promote the interests of the workers and the general welfare. . . ." [43] A year later, John Golden, president of the United Textile Workers of America, maintained: "Organized labor realizes just as keenly as anybody else that this movement in the interest of industrial education is not a fad, but a stern reality and an absolute necessity." [44]

Just as there was increasing interest in industrial secondary education during these years, so was there growing demand for business and commercial as well as agricultural instruction on the secondary level. Proponents in all camps argued the lasting benefits of such education for the American public in general and for the high schools themselves. By being thus responsive to the needs of the people, the high schools would insure for themselves continued and substantial support. It is interesting to note that as also in the case of industrial education, those urging business and agricultural training viewed it only within the framework of liberal understanding. What was desired was technician citizens who would serve society well. Thus would society realize return on its educational investment.

The continuing restatement of the traditional values of classical secondary education. This heightening demand for more "practical" studies on the secondary level met with a continuing restatement of the cultural and practical values of classical education. While many of these arguments contented themselves with pointing to the traditional ends of the classics, the most interesting, perhaps, were those which sought to point out their practical use. Such was the theme of a pamphlet *Latin in the Secondary School* written in 1910 by the president of the University of New Mexico.[45] The traditional arguments on Latin's cultural value, maintained Gray, were wholly ineffective before twentieth-century Americans. Rather, he continued, why not turn to the eminently practical value of the subject? As far as he was concerned, this was twofold: Latin was practical because it helped students to acquire facility and correctness in English usage, and Latin was practical because it demanded "clarity of and definiteness in statement." Traditionally, Gray admitted, the subject had been poorly taught. With improvement in teaching by competently trained teachers, however, he felt that the subject would have no trouble in assuming its former primary place in the secondary curriculum—justified this time on its essentially practical merit.

The reports of two NEA committees attempt to achieve standardization.

[43] *Report of the Commissioner of Education, op. cit.,* p. 154.
[44] *Ibid.,* p. 156.
[45] E. D. McQueen Gray, "Latin in the Secondary School," *Bulletin University of New Mexico,* Educational Series, Vol. I, No. 4 (1910).

During the 1890's a considerable effect on secondary education was exercised by the work of two major committees appointed by the National Educational Association. The first was the Committee of Ten on Secondary School Studies, appointed in 1892 and reporting in 1893; the second was the Committee of Thirteen on College Entrance Requirements, appointed in 1895 and reporting in 1899. Both were composed of prominent educators, principally college people and administrators, and both reports were widely read and commented upon.

Of the two, the report of the Committee of Ten was probably the more discussed. By and large, it determined the course of American secondary education for a generation following its publication. Interestingly enough, the report itself was highly paradoxical. It stated rather forthrightly its recognition that the secondary school was a terminal rather than a college-preparatory institution for most of its students. Yet, in spite of this realization, the report then proceeded to recommend a series of studies oriented almost completely toward preparing the college-bound student.

The assumption throughout was that those courses which best prepare for college entrance also best prepare for the duties of practical life. Thus, most of the report was devoted to a proper organizing and harmonizing of traditional college-preparatory subjects. Moreover, the recommendation was that every subject be taught the same way, whether in preparation for college or as part of a finishing course. Throughout, the committee assumed and implied adherence to the theory of mental discipline. After recommending the regrouping of certain subjects, for example, the report argued: "Every youth who entered college would have spent four years in studying a few subjects thoroughly; and, on the theory that all the subjects are to be considered equivalent in educational rank for the purposes of admission to college, it would make no difference which subjects he had chosen from the programme—he would have had four years of strong and effective mental training." [46] Finally, the principle of election was recognized, but election from among four curricula rather than from among a variety of subjects. From its major recommendations the report was clearly dominated by the more conservative spirit of the colleges and universities of the time.

The appointment of the Committee of Thirteen grew out of a discussion in the 1895 meeting of the NEA on what action ought to be taken by the universities and secondary schools to put into practice the recommendations of the Committee of Ten. Their report,[47] handed down four years later, was

[46] Report of the Committee on Secondary School Studies Appointed at the Meeting of the National Educational Association July 9, 1892, With the Reports of the Conferences Arranged by the Committee and Held December 28–30, 1892 (Washington, D. C., Government Printing Office, 1893), p. 53.

[47] "Report of the Committee on College-Entrance Requirements," National Educational Association Proceedings, 1899, pp. 632–817.

couched within an acceptance of the prior committee's conclusions. Specifically, they proposed that a number of *constants* (four units in foreign languages, two units in mathematics, two in English, one in history, and one in science) be required of all college entrants, and that these programs be supplemented by a number of acceptable electives. The scope of the latter for all intents and purposes was confined to the major studies recommended by the Committee of Ten.

Proposals for new organization of secondary instruction. No discussion of the major demands on secondary education during these years could be complete without some attention to the problems of reorganization. If any one beginning point of these discussions may be indicated, it was probably a speech of President Charles W. Eliot before the NEA's Department of Superintendence in 1888 entitled "Can School Programs Be Shortened and Enriched?" [48] In this address, Eliot directed attention to the rising average age of entering freshmen at Harvard as a problem generally acknowledged in American higher education. The problem had forced Eliot to review elementary and secondary curricula. There he saw a tremendously crowded secondary program usually extending over four years, succeeding a rather narrow elementary curriculum which usually extended over eight years. Although President Eliot made no concrete suggestions, he raised questions that were destined to excite considerable discussion during the next two or three decades.

Eliot's address was one of the more important stimuli to the appointment of the three major committees of the National Educational Association during the 1890's. The most influential of these, the Committee of Ten, while it assumed the traditional eight-four division between elementary and secondary studies, did turn brief attention to the reorganization of secondary education: "In preparing these programmes," the report noted, "the Committee were perfectly aware that it is impossible to make a satisfactory secondary school programme, limited to a period of four years, and founded on the present elementary school subjects and methods." [49] The solution, they concluded, lay either in assigning some of the secondary school subjects to the elementary school, or in extending the secondary period down two years, leaving six for the elementary curriculum.

The Committee of Fifteen on Elementary Studies gave further attention to the problem and found considerable division among educators on six versus eight years of elementary training. Many feared that shortening the elementary program would cause children to leave school earlier. In the final report the committee stood in favor of retaining the eight-year program. On the other hand, the Committee on College Entrance Requirements, re-

[48] Charles William Eliot, *Educational Reform* (New York, Century, 1898), pp. 149–176.
[49] *Report of the Committee on Secondary School Studies* . . . , p. 45.

porting in 1899, recommended "a unified six-year high-school course of study beginning with the seventh grade." [50]

These discussions at the conclusion of the nineteenth century paved the way for numerous proposals during the opening years of the twentieth. Generally, they argued that the elementary school wasted much time on endless repetition, that a break after six years would more closely parallel mental and physical changes of adolescence than one after eight, and that such a shortening of the elementary program would allow for more vocational differentiation and preparation in the last two years of the secondary school. A standing committee of the NEA was appointed in 1905 to consider the question, and its three reports, handed down in 1907, 1908, and 1909 respectively, all vigorously urged the shift to a six-year elementary school followed by a secondary program of equal length.

The Sharpening College Controversy

As on the lower levels, college and university curricula during these years also became the scene of sharpening conflict and controversy. Some of the questions bore close relation to those of elementary and secondary schools; others were peculiar to higher education. Many were the fruits of controversies that had started decades before. The question of whether or not colleges ought to expand into universities was one which provoked considerable discussion. So did the problem of the extent to which students should be free to choose their own studies. Many of the struggles raged around the conflict between the "cultural" and the "practical" subjects— much as they did on the secondary level, and, of course, intimately related to this latter question were all the problems over mental discipline as a theory of learning. In many ways these controversies reflected the growing differences in philosophical orientation among the American people; in others, they simply reflected the growing demands of American society upon its institutions of higher learning.

Proposals for University-Level Instruction. One of the most characteristic movements of the decades following 1865 was the attempt to extend American collegiate instruction to the university level. While many of the greatest men of the time—Charles W. Eliot of Harvard, Andrew Dickson White of Cornell, and Frederick A. P. Barnard of Columbia among them—were involved in this movement, no more representative thinker can be cited than President Daniel Coit Gilman of Johns Hopkins. Working initially at Yale and as president of the University of California, Gilman was instrumental in establishing Johns Hopkins as the first all-graduate American university modeled after the traditional European type. His program there was to exercise profound effect on the course of American higher education.

[50] "Report of the Committee on College-Entrance Requirements," *op. cit.*, p. 659.

In his inaugural address as president of Johns Hopkins,[51] Gilman indicated a sharp distinction between college and university work. He defined a *university* as a place for advanced and special instruction of youth who had been prepared for their freedom by the discipline of a lower school. The *college,* on the other hand, was an institution which stood *in loco parentis,* implying restriction instead of freedom, tutorial rather than professorial teaching, and residence within college halls. As for Hopkins, it would be most definitely a university aiming at "the most liberal promotion of all useful knowledge; the special provision of such departments as are neglected elsewhere in the country . . . the encouragement of research; the promotion of young men; and the advancement of individual scholars, who by their excellence will advance the sciences they pursue and the society where they dwell." Throughout the program, freedom of teaching and research would be watchwords of the faculty.

The attempt to preserve the traditional college.   While the demand for university-level instruction was widespread, it by no means went unchallenged. As in the antebellum period, there was considerable evidence of conservatism at Yale in opposition to the more radical ideas of its traditional rival, Harvard. One finds in the volume *The American Colleges and the American Public,*[52] written by Noah Porter, President of Yale from 1871 to 1886, a glowing defence of the traditional college and its values. Porter extolled the English type of communal college which had spread through America because he felt that such an institution had exercised a more rigorous supervision over its students and made possible the continuing religious character of higher education. "The consideration of the common life of the college," noted Porter, "is essential to a just estimate of its importance. Without it the college can neither be understood nor appreciated." The heart of this common life consisted in its varied intellectual, social, ethical, and religious influences on the student—influences which were quite as valuable as the intellectual and moral instruction imparted in formal classes. None of these dimensions could be excluded from a balanced college program.

Porter believed that the college as it had thus evolved had adequately met the needs of the American public, and he was confident that this public was satisfied and not desirous of radical changes. Thus, he consistently opposed the introduction of university ideals into undergraduate institutions. Porter was joined in his views by many other leading educators of the period, not the least of these being President Franklin Carter of Williams College and Chancellor Alexander Winchell of Syracuse University. It might also be added that, in general, those who supported the continuance of the tradi-

---

[51] Daniel Coit Gilman, *University Problems in the United States* (New York, Century, 1898), pp. 1–41.

[52] Noah Porter, *The American Colleges and the American Public* (New Haven, Charles C. Chatfield, 1870).

tional college form also tended to remain conservative in other questions such as the introduction of newer practical studies into the curriculum and the use of the elective system.

The growing demand for the elective system. The demand for *Lernfreiheit* —or freedom of learning—which had been enunciated so forcefully by George Ticknor in the antebellum years, received increasing voice during the later decades of the nineteenth century. At Harvard the elective system found fertile and rich soil for growth, and it is to the writings of Charles W. Eliot, President of Harvard from 1869 to 1909, more than anyone else that one must turn for the continued formulation of the idea.

Eliot's view of the elective system was securely rooted in a threefold conception of reform for higher education: *first,* an ideal of a university; *second,* an ideal of a liberal education; and *third,* an ideal of freedom of learning. Concerning the first point, Eliot was particularly broad. A real university, he felt, would include all subjects—both liberal and technical—which could be taught in the most advanced manner. His contention was that the distinction between liberal and technical subjects was not a matter of subject matter, but of aim. Both aims belonged in a university. Moreover, a genuine university would include not only an undergraduate college, but a variety of coordinate schools for technical, graduate, and professional training. These ideas led right into Eliot's second conception—that of a liberal education. Here he definitely stood with those who believed that the traditional notion of a liberal training should be expanded to include the modern studies. Hence, the significance of the bachelor of arts degree—the usual evidence of a liberal education—should be enlarged to embrace them. In considering the several subjects, Eliot urged that English language and literature, French and German, history, political economy, and the natural sciences be placed on a par with the ancient classics and mathematics. When taught properly, he argued, all were "liberal" and all promoted mental discipline.

It was at this point that Eliot came to his third point—a conception of election, or freedom of learning. A corollary of widening the circle of equivalent subjects, he indicated, must be a greater amount of freedom for the student to choose his subjects. One person could not possibly encompass all of these areas and acquire a thorough knowledge of any, so the student must be allowed to select those to which he would devote himself. Moreover, such a scheme would make proper allowance for individual differences in ability and preference. After the boy had dipped into the major fields of human knowledge in elementary and secondary school, he would know as a youth of eighteen or nineteen what he liked best and what he was best fitted for. Through the active application of *Lernfreiheit,* the college might carry out its task of education more effectively than it ever had before.

Opposition to the elective system. Needless to say, there was spirited opposition to the ideas of Eliot and his camp. Basing their arguments on traditional values of mental discipline, breadth of study, and common pursuit, these opponents offered sharpening resistance to election in the closing years of the nineteenth century. Much of this opposition was located at Yale and Princeton, and a prominent leader was Andrew F. West, for many years graduate dean of the latter institution. West was particularly active in defending the high place accorded to the ancient classics in the college curriculum, and he made his position clear in a specific criticism of Eliot's annual report of 1884-1885 which described the elective system at Harvard.[53] West was frankly skeptical that the system was accomplishing all that Eliot claimed for it, and he reaffirmed his faith in the disciplinary college. Among other things, he claimed, election offered "heavy temptations to higher students to become premature specialists without gaining a liberal education and general intellectual training," caused students to "avoid the severer and flock into the easier studies," and led to "the disintegration and dissipation of meaning" which had traditionally attached to the B. A. degree.

The demand for more practical subject matter.   In his crusade to widen the scope of liberal education, Eliot was running up against one of the most impregnable strongholds of liberal education. Yet this stronghold was under increasing attack from those who saw value in the growing practical and utilitarian studies. One of the earliest and most active proponents of more practical education was Professor W. P. Atkinson of the Massachusetts Institute of Technology. In an address before the NEA in 1873,[54] Atkinson urged the inclusion of the physical sciences on an equal par with traditional classical studies. He cited a number of influences leading to a modification of older theories and a "new idea of liberal education." Among them were the findings of the new psychology, the attempt to give opportunity for a liberal education to the whole people rather than to a small privileged class, the advent of the physical sciences, and the growing perception of the value of art and esthetic culture. Only as higher education responded to these new demands did Atkinson see the emergence of the "one homogeneous system of free schools" which lay at the heart of republican institutions.

Another example—one which gained a good deal of notoriety—is the Phi Beta Kappa address of Charles Francis Adams in 1883 entitled *A College Fetish*.[55] Adams came from outside the ranks of professional educators to attack the purely cultural emphasis of a liberal education. His address was a stinging denunciation of the traditionally limited classical curriculum. To maintain it in the face of newer and more practical demands was "fetish-worship, pure and simple." ". . . I am practical and of this world enough," he argued, "to believe, that in a utilitarian and scientific age the living will

---

[53] Andrew F. West, *A Review of President Eliot's Report on Elective Studies* (New York, J. K. Lees, 1886).

[54] W. P. Atkinson, "Liberal Education of the Nineteenth Century," National Educational Association *Proceedings* (1873), pp. 141–163.

[55] Charles Francis Adams, *A College Fetish* (Boston, Lee and Shepard, 1883).

not forever be sacrificed to the dead." Inevitably, he concluded, the more use-ful modern languages and natural and social sciences would assume their rightful place in higher education in place of the time-honored but un-practical classics.

Defending the traditional meaning of liberal education. The defenders of the traditional curriculum vigorously defied this invasion of their redoubt. Most of their arguments tended to follow three or four definite lines: that traditional classical education was the "best expression of the eternal spirit of man"; that true liberal education must be sought for its own sake and would be destroyed if pursued for utilitarian values; that a liberally educated man ought not to specialize before acquainting himself with the principal fields of thought; and that the traditional meaning and integrity of the bachelor of arts degree must be preserved.

Once again, Dean Andrew F. West figured in the leadership of the con-servatives. For over forty years he labored to keep Latin and Greek as prescribed studies in the course that led to true liberal education. In 1884, for instance, he wrote an article entitled "Must the Classics Go?" [56] in which he argued that Greek as well as Latin be kept alive in the college curriculum. West cited at least seven types of men who objected to the classics: men of action; those who had never studied the classics; those im-bued with the spirit of money-making; those who disliked a severe mental training; those who believed the modern languages were more adequate; those who advocated the physical sciences; and those who had suffered from poor teaching in the classics. West countered by arguing that the classics inspired literary culture and provided mental discipline. He concluded in favor of Greek as well as Latin because the two together were better than just one, because Latin would be hurt by the separation, and because there was ample time for both in a four-year curriculum. In another address before the NEA some nineteen years later West viewed with alarm "The Present Peril to Liberal Education." [57] In the spirit of "commercialism," the "ignorance of good literature," the "disposition to do the pleasant rather than the hard thing, even when the hard happens to be the best thing," and the prevalence of the elective system, West saw the virtual destruction of liberal culture in America.

Proposals for the junior college. One of the most interesting discussions of the turn of the century involved the proper length of the baccalaureate course. With the improvement of secondary education at the end of the century, and the parallel raising of standards in professional education, col-leges found themselves increasingly caught in a squeeze between the two.

---

[56] Andrew F. West, "Must the Classics Go?" *North American Review*, Vol. 138 (1884), pp. 151–172.

[57] Andrew F. West, "The Present Peril to Liberal Education," National Educational Association *Proceedings* (1903), pp. 54–60,

What then would be a proper adjustment? One prominent debate on the question took place before the NEA's Department of Higher Education in 1903, with Presidents Eliot of Harvard, Harper of Chicago, Butler of Columbia and Dean West of Princeton participating.[58] Eliot very much in the spirit of his 1888 address "Can School Programmes Be Shortened and Enriched?" spoke in favor of a three-year bachelor's course. With the improvement of secondary education, he argued, there was no reason why the average American boy could not finish the required work in this time. Butler tended to agree with Eliot, especially for young men going on to professional school. He even suggested a pre-professional course of two years' duration. Dean West and President Harper, on the other hand, opposed the suggestion. If it were a question of reducing a four-year course of elective studies to a three-year prescribed one, noted West, he would be all in favor of it. "But if the proposal be to reduce the other type of four-year course to three years, then the loss is not only unnecessary, but is in every way undesirable. . . ." Harper thought it would work havoc with the educational system and offer comparatively little if any benefit in return.

There was one note in the arguments of West, Harper, and Butler, however, that was central. All of them proposed the junior part of the college as a separate two-year course of liberal study. For Butler, it would "enable intending professional students to spend this time as advantageously as possible in purely liberal studies." For West, this "natural break" would allow the departure of men called by "hard necessity"; while for Harper, who had been instrumental in putting the plan into effect at the University of Chicago, it would meet "the need of many who cannot take a longer term of residence, and likewise of many who ought not to take a longer course." Undoubtedly, within such discussions lay the seeds of the American junior college.

THE CONTINUING DEMAND FOR THE PROFESSIONALIZING OF TEACHING

Even the most cursory glance at the educational literature of this period reveals the persistence of the principal pre-Civil War problems concerning the teacher. If there was any major difference, it lay merely in their intensification. By and large, educators were even more concerned with the professionalizing of teaching—with questions of how to obtain better personnel, train them, keep them in the profession, and raise the quality of their work. In general, two major factors contributed to the increasing importance of such problems. First, the extremely rapid increase in the number of children in elementary and secondary schools made the question of adequate personnel more critical than it had ever been before. Often, it degenerated into a

---

[58] "The Length of the Baccalaureate Course and Preparation for Professional Schools," National Educational Association *Proceedings* (1903), pp. 489–516.

problem of simply getting one teacher, however qualified, to each classroom. If the early common school reformers had quickly recognized the intimate connection between universal public education and the necessity for adequately trained teachers, it was the educational leaders of 1890 who were really faced with meeting this necessity. In many ways their situation paralleled that of a battle commander whose initial joy in victory was quickly tempered with a realization of the prodigious responsibilities it imposed. A second factor associated with the movement to professionalize was the influx and growth of new educational aims, curricula, and methods. Pestalozzi's methods were so intricate, for example, that considerable training was indicated if teachers were properly to employ them. If education was intimately concerned with the "natural development" of youngsters, then teachers would need to study the nature of children in order properly to guide their development and adjust instruction to their needs. Much the same was true of the newer ideas associated with Herbart and Froebel. Especially did the tremendous body of theory advanced by such Herbartians as DeGarmo, the McMurry's, John Hall and E. E. Brown contribute to the need. In effect, school teaching had now reached a point where special professional preparation was required. Less than ever before was it merely a task for some incompetent who could do little else. It was clearly a job for a well-chosen, well-trained, well-organized profession.

Securing Adequate Personnel

Just as the problem of securing adequate personnel had been uppermost in the minds of many educators before the Civil War, so did it remain primary as the school expanded. As always, the problem was a twofold one—that of securing adequate personnel and that of paying them adequate wages to hold them in the profession. While the first of these two questions received far more attention than the second before 1918, both were of critical importance.

One of the persistent areas of concern for many was the actual process of certifying teachers. The traditional procedure, wherein a lay committee of citizens performed this duty at annual examinations, had come under increasing attack as a method of really determining an applicant's fitness. It was simply a matter of competence to judge; and the question of the postmaster's competence to judge the blacksmith's work, asked in the 1850's by *The Illinois Teacher,* was raised again and again with respect to teaching. John Swett, for example, who pioneered in obtaining common schools for California, vehemently attacked the system of lay certification before the NEA in 1872.[59] Swett described this traditional process from his own experience. Finding that his letters of recommendation from New England were not valid

[59] John Swett, "The Examination of Teachers," National Educational Association *Proceedings* (1872), pp. 71–82.

for certification in California, he submitted himself to an examination in the latter state. "It was the same old rigmarole of 'readin', 'ritin' and 'rithmetic,' with never a question to test education, culture, or power to teach." After a half-day's examination, explained Swett, he received a certificate and someone else with "influence in the board" got the position.

Swett felt that the system described above was simply perpetuating the disastrous system of "school-keeping"—a system in which young girls anticipating marriage, young men working their way through college, and traveling Ichabod Cranes *kept* school rather than professional teachers *teaching* it. The only possibility of remedy, in his estimation, lay in establishing a well-organized state system of examinations managed by efficient city, county, and township boards of examiners. The latter would be composed of superintendents and professional teachers, themselves holders of high-grade certificates. They would have the power to issue, on actual written examinations, certificates of different grades, valid for periods of time ranging from two to ten years, according to grade. Moreover, these boards would be paid for their services, and should be made up exclusively of practical teachers, "for the same reason that only lawyers can legally examine law students applying for admission to the bar, that only physicians can legally examine medical students, and that only clergymen pass on the fitness of theological students to enter the ministry." Only in such a system did Swett see the public schools protected against "charletans, ignoramuses and humbugs generally. . . ."

Although it has been stated that speakers generally tended to avoid the question of salaries, the topic was not entirely neglected. In the latter years of the nineteenth century it was more often than not treated in passing during some treatment of the place and function of the profession. Yet as early as 1894, a Colorado high school principal was willing to argue before the NEA that only when teaching offered salaries and security commensurate with other professions would men of strong capability be attracted to it.[60] When interest continued to rise after the turn of the century, the National Council of Education in 1903 appointed a committee to study the whole salary, pension, and tenure problem, and this committee reported several times during the next few years. Needless to say, the salary problem provided a vital factor in the organization of the American Federation of Teachers in 1917.

Achieving effective organization. The continuities between the antebellum and postbellum period are also evident in the continued demands for organization of the profession. Once again, just as Orville Taylor and others of the earlier reformers had seen in an organized profession the key to school and teacher improvement, so did educators of this generation. Just as the problems of salary and tenure, however, remained secondary to the more spirited con-

---

[60] Ida B. Haslop, "How May a Professional Spirit Be Acquired by the Secondary Teachers of America," National Educational Association *Proceedings* (1894), pp. 758–764.

siderations of method and training, so were those of organization. Weak at
the turn of the century, these demands increased in vigor until by the period
of World War I, the problem of what kind of organizations might best serve
teachers was one of paramount interest and heated discussion.

An address which encompassed both discussions—the demand for organization in general, and the question of what kind of organization—was one
by Margaret A. Haley, President of the National Federation of Teachers,
before the NEA in 1904.[61] Her theme was that teacher organizations might
well benefit teachers, but their far greater benefit lay in their educating the
public to educational needs. Quoting John Dewey's claim that the profession
had no official arrangement whereby teachers might submit pressing educational questions for group discussion, Miss Haley suggested that "organization
is the method of all intelligently directed effort." In organization alone would
teachers find effective means of improving the school system, and with it,
their own lot.

In the course of her discussion, she pointed to two kinds of teacher groups
—those organized along professional lines and those organized for the improvement of conditions. Both, she held, were vital for the profession and for
the good of the schools. Moreover, both were vital for the furtherance of
democracy against organized interests which were throttling it. Teachers,
she concluded, had come to a critical crossroads. The nation and the profession critically needed intelligent classroom teachers, informed about school
techniques and school needs, who would "successfully engage in the work
of securing better conditions for themselves, and for the schools, through
organization." It remained for the teachers themselves to decide on the character of such an organization and then to build and support one to the
best of their ability.

Building an adequate professional education. Certainly it was in the area
of what constituted an adequate education of teachers, and how to provide
it, that much of the discussion concerning the teacher was located. Victor
Cousin's classic remark about the teacher making the school loomed large
in the minds of late nineteenth-century schoolmen; and they searched with
vigor for effective means of training the large number of personnel needed
to staff America's rapidly growing school system.

One of the most active groups concerning itself with this question was
the American Normal School Association, which later affiliated itself with
the NEA as its Normal School Department. In 1872 a committee of this group
appointed to study the question of normal training schools urged as its thesis
that "unless we can raise up whole generations of able, skillful, devoted teachers, we can not educate." [62] Only as Americans rapidly expanded their teacher-

[61] Margaret A. Haley, "Why Teachers Should Organize," *National Educational Association
Proceedings* (1904), pp. 145–152.
[62] "Report of the Committee on 'The System of Normal Training Schools Best Adapted to
the Wants of our People,' " *National Educational Association Proceedings* (1872), pp. 28–38.

training facilities and made education a study in all institutions of higher learning could the need be met. With these propositions in mind, the committee submitted five recommendations for facing these needs: *first,* "That in each university throughout the country there be established a school or faculty of education, in which the nature, ends, means, history and literature of that subject shall be thoroughly taught"; *second,* that in every college and high school there be a professorship of education and didactics; *third,* that in every state there should be established one or more higher normal schools to train high school teachers, elementary normal school instructors, and city and county school superintendents; *fourth,* that these higher normal schools be supplemented with county elementary normal schools wherever possible; and *fifth,* that county institutes be held annually in all parts of the country for the in-service training of teachers. While the committee admitted that it was proposing nothing startlingly new in character, they felt that such a coordinated plan could meet the pressing demands for trained teachers.

While the committee's recommendations were widely supported at the time they were advanced (the NEA adopted them in substance in 1872), there was also considerable opposition. Public normal schools, for example, had been under attack ever since the first three had opened in Massachusetts in 1839 and 1840. They were expensive, and many felt that the expense was not justifiably public. Further opposition came from colleges who took issue with the committee's suggestion that they take on the work of training teachers. A speaker before the New England Association of Colleges and Preparatory Schools, for example, in 1889 steadfastly maintained that no pedagogical training could justly be imposed on college curricula.[63] The liberal education there provided by high-quality teachers was in itself the best possible training for teaching.

If the development of special normal schools and university departments for the training of teachers was a first demand of the schoolmen, a second phase of it was the demand for a specialized professional body of materials to constitute the heart of this new training. There seemed to be growing argument that only as professional curricula remained closely articulated with public school programs and needs would their pursuit be worth while for the prospective teacher. "The university professor," maintained Minnesota's State Superintendent of Public Instruction in 1882, "may have his chair, and from it satisfy a well-established demand; but the normal-school professor must live in his saddle in the field and on the march." In line with this belief came demands for greater emphasis on *professional* rather than *general* education for the teacher. As early as 1871, Professor William F. Phelps of a Minnesota normal school noted that the "true office of a normal

---

[63] J. B. Sewall, "The Duty of the Colleges to Make Provision for the Training of Teachers for Secondary Schools," New England Association of Colleges and Preparatory Schools *Proceedings* (1889), pp. 22–27.

or training school for teachers is to impart professional, rather than general instruction; to make good teachers rather than profound scholars." A year later, the state school commissioner of Ohio urged that all academic instruction be removed from the normal school curriculum and professional instruction in methods, administration, and educational history and philosophy substituted.

While spirited disagreement continued, proposed curricula during these years were more and more representative of these aims. While there were almost as many variations as there were proponents, the general lines of these programs became fairly clear during the 1890's. Most included *first*, some professionalized treatment of the academic subject matter the teacher was to teach, giving particular attention to method and to the relation between various areas of knowledge; *second*, the history and philosophy of education; *third*, the organization and administration of school systems; *fourth*, child study and development; and *fifth*, general study of teaching methods. While there was considerable agreement concerning these five areas, continuing disagreement characterized the function of practice teaching and the role of preparatory academic work.

It goes without saying that out of these suggestions was emerging a new professional study known as *education*. While sharp ridicule was forthcoming from those who continued to see research training in the traditional disciplines as the heart of teacher preparation, the new area increasingly won commitment from those engaged in the actual work of training teachers. In the minds of leaders like William Payne at Michigan, Commissioner William T. Harris, and Dean James Earl Russell of Teachers College, Columbia, it quickly became the heart of a rigorous graduate program ultimately destined to be the common property of every well-prepared member of the profession.

ISSUES FOR STUDY AND DISCUSSION

1. Do the various pressure groups in America today maintain positions on the question of federal aid to education consistent with their positions during the 1880's? Have the two major political parties remained consistent?

2. How does an understanding of the vitriolic attacks on public education at the turn of the century condition your attitude toward some of the more recent attacks of the early 1950's?

3. Some educators today identify John Dewey with the conception of a curriculum built principally around the felt needs and immediate interests of children. Is this justified in the light of your understanding of Dewey's writings?

4. Some contemporary educators argue that the professional preparation of a teacher should be largely practical and should come only after four years of rigorous undergraduate liberal arts education. Others argue that professional education should begin in the freshman year of college and continue as part of an integrated program throughout the preservice period. To what extent does this controversy

reflect some of the major conceptions of teacher education vying for support during the 1880's? Which in your mind is the more conservative conception?

5. Review the several positions of the late nineteenth century concerning the role of the Bible in the school program. How many of these positions are still alive in contemporary America? To which position do you think the majority of Americans subscribe?

SUGGESTIONS FOR FURTHER READING

Butler, Nicholas Murray, *The Meaning of Education*, New York, Scribner, 1915.

Butts, R. Freeman, *The College Charts Its Course*, New York, McGraw-Hill, 1939.

Curti, Merle, *The Social Ideas of American Educators*, New York, Scribner, 1935.

DeGarmo, Charles, *Herbart and the Herbartians*, New York, Scribner, 1895.

Dewey, John, *The Child and the Curriculum*, Chicago, University of Chicago Press, 1902.

———, *The Educational Situation*, Chicago, University of Chicago Press, 1904.

———, *The School and Society*, Chicago, University of Chicago Press, 1899.

Eliot, Charles W., *Educational Reform*, New York, Century, 1898.

Flexner, Abraham, *The American College: A Criticism*, New York, Appleton-Century, 1908.

Gilman, Daniel C., *University Problems in the United States*, New York, Appleton-Century, 1898.

James, Henry, *Charles W. Eliot*, Boston, Houghton Mifflin, 1930, 2 vols.

Lee, Gordon C., *The Struggle for Federal Aid: First Phase*, New York, Teachers College, Columbia University, 1949.

McMurry, Charles A., and McMurry, Frank M., *The Method of the Recitation*, New York, Macmillan, 1911.

Mathews, Basil, *Booker T. Washington, Educator and Interracial Interpreter*, Cambridge, Harvard University Press, 1948.

Monroe, Walter S., *Teaching-Learning Theory and Teacher Education, 1890–1950*, Urbana, University of Illinois Press, 1952.

Parker, Francis W., *Talks on Pedagogics*, New York, Kellogg, 1894.

Porter, Noah, *The American Colleges and the American Public*, New Haven, Charles C. Chatfield, 1870.

Thursfield, Richard E., *Henry Barnard's Journal of Education*, Baltimore, Johns Hopkins Press, 1946.

Washington, Booker T., *Up from Slavery*, Garden City, Doubleday, 1927.

Woody, Thomas, *History of Women's Education in the United States*, New York, Science Press, 1929, 2 vols.

There is a comparative lack of good monograph literature in this period indicating vast areas in need of specialized study. The enterprising student will therefore do well to turn to such rich serial publications as the *American Journal of Education, Education,* the annual proceedings of the National Education Association, of the American Institute of Instruction, and of the various associations of colleges and secondary schools. The many reports and documents issued by the United States Commissioners of Education during this period are also extremely useful and revealing.

12

TYPICAL PATTERNS
OF EDUCATION

THE YEARS following the Civil War witnessed a phenomenal expansion of the American educational system. In effect, schools grew from an uncertain infancy in 1865 into a young maturity by 1918. Checked somewhat by a Civil War which had ruined the South and heavily taxed effort in the North and West, educational development continued anew after Appomattox. It proceeded modestly at first in the face of continuing resistance, and once overcoming this resistance, blossomed into a renaissance which compared favorably with the one of the 1830's and 1840's. By 1918 the vast majority of American children attended elementary school for some shorter or longer period of their youth. High schools of 1865, confined largely to the cities and richer rural areas, had been more an ideal than a reality for most American communities. By 1918 they were a recognized part of American life and education. Much the same might be said for colleges; and graduate and professional facilities, largely nonexistent during the earlier period, were becoming increasingly available throughout the country. Everywhere, the educational ladder was strengthened and bolstered to bear its increasing flow of citizens.

The scope of this education broadened immeasurably. Groups which had formerly been largely excluded from public elementary facilities—Negroes, Indians, Chinese and Mexicans, or the physically and mentally handicapped, for example—were increasingly provided for as a matter of *right* rather than *charity*. Moreover, the school assumed responsibilities which had formerly been alien to its purposes. Active training for self-expression and citizenship entered the halls of an elementary school which had formerly devoted itself largely to transmitting knowledge and moral precept. Preparation for trade and vocation increasingly became a part of high school and college programs.

New institutions such as the junior high school and the junior college were established to meet the needs of specific groups of individuals. More and more, in practice as well as in theory, the ideal of universal education was acknowledged.

At the heart of these developments was a profession ever more conscious of its great heritage and worthy purposes. America's outstanding philosophers —William James and John Dewey among them—increasingly turned their attention to the school, and their writings spirited a growing body of educational theory that slowly made itself felt in practice. Experimental schools, utilizing the findings of psychologists, philosophers, and a growing number of educational scientists, put into practice advanced theories which decades before would assuredly have remained dreams. Teacher organizations, their membership expanding, provided an interested arena for the struggle of educational ideas, while teachers themselves, granted training facilities and the tools for their task, began to demand of the public compensation commensurate with their responsibilities. Attempting to answer the needs of an expanding nation with expanding world interests, American education by 1918 had become a "big business." Its plant was valued at close to $2 billion; it employed over 650,000 teachers; and it enrolled over 25 percent of the American people. In sum, these teachers had translated the educational "faiths and hopes" of 1860 Americans into a going reality which by 1918 had excited the interest of civilized peoples the world over.

EDUCATION IN SCHOOL AND COMMUNITY

The Education of Children and Youth

In 1866, Packard in his book *The Daily Public School in the United States* devoted considerable attention to a discussion of the school's role in the total education of the child. The school was for Packard a comparatively subordinate influence. By far the largest share of a child's education came from the home and community. Moreover, even a major share of this was incidental rather than intentional. "No one can look back upon his own childish days, however happy his home, without being reminded of a multitude of instances in which some paragraph in a book or a newspaper; a picture, an anecdote, or a song; a conversation overheard in a shop, a bar-room, or at the street corner; a scene or a suggestion of mischief—made a far deeper impression upon the mind and character than a month's, nay, perhaps a year's schooling." [1] By and large, Packard was sketching an educational situation which faithfully characterized early agrarian America. In some communities, particularly in rural ones, it continued to describe the job of the school with children. In others, however, particularly in the thriving cities

[1] Frederick A. Packard, *The Daily Public School in the United States* (Philadelphia, Lippincott, 1866), pp. 15–16,

of young industrial America, profound changes were wrought in the school's task.

Hamlin Garland describes the life of a youngster in late nineteenth-century agricultural America in his delightful book *Boy Life on the Prairie.* The volume tells the story of Garland's own experiences in Wisconsin as a boy. In vivid pictures, he outlines a world of ploughing, harvesting, herding, camping, threshing, and a hundred other activities. It is a picture in which youngsters always have important tasks and important responsibilities. Significantly, too, they were not tasks which were learned in school. True, Garland does mention schooling, but principally in connection with reading and intellectual activity. But these were secondary in the rich variety of experiences on that Wisconsin farm. Garland, as did the pre-Civil War youngster, learned the major part of what he had to know by doing it, by actually participating in the life of the community. And on the family farm, he had an ever present body of teachers—the other members of his family as well as neighbors with whom there was always considerable contact.

A vastly different picture of life is given in the writings of Jacob A. Riis, ardent exponent of urban social reform. In volumes like *The Children of the Poor* and *The Battle with the Slum* are sketches of squalor, of poverty, of intolerable living conditions, and of a thousand degenerating influences on the youngsters inhabiting the bleak tenements of the city. There are gangs, appealing always to the youngsters' desire to conform, to be tough and adult. There is idleness, the fertile soil for unhealthy influence to reap its harvest. There is gambling, the trashy novel, the cheap show. All of these prove continuing educational influences on the child. Only through a concerted educational effort by a variety of agencies does Riis see the problem mitigated. The school, the church, the boy's club, the voluntary agency—all have a role to play in combating the unhealthy influence of the street.

The educational problem of Riis' slum was obvious. Yet in many ways it was undergirded by the far deeper educational problem of urban life. The cities, growing by leaps and bounds, presented an entirely different, far more complex way of life from that of the earlier rural community. The close, well-knit relationships of the small agricultural neighborhood gave way to the multitude of informal relationships characterizing the city. The home, for instance, was a very different phenomenon. Often, all of the adult members in a family toiled long hours every day in different parts of the city, leaving little opportunity for the group activities so important in the general and moral education of the young. As well-knit family ties were weakened by this new economic situation, so were formerly powerful ties to church and Sunday school. At least part of the problem lay in a lack of church facilities to accommodate the tremendous influx of population. Another major reason, perhaps, lay in the inability of the churches to view the problem as a social and environmental one rather than a simple case of human depravity.

The new immigrants from Southern and Eastern Europe posed another profound educational problem. If the task of Americanizing had been a difficult and necessary one in the antebellum period, it became even more so as the religious, linguistic, and national backgrounds of the immigrants became increasingly heterogeneous. The clannish immigrant settlements of the cities threw added burdens on the school, for it was working against a host of educational influences tending to perpetuate the life and ways of European cultures. If Italian, or Russian, or Yiddish was spoken in the home, in shops, in the neighborhood, and in local newspapers, it was difficult for the school to teach English; the same was true of customs, of values, of dress, and of traditions. Here again was increased responsibility for the school.

Finally, there was the growing complexity of urban social and economic life in general. In a small, well-knit, face-to-face rural community the necessity to read was secondary in the ordinary course of everyday existence. In the large city it was virtually a requirement. Merely to go from one place to another, one had to negotiate street signs and perhaps various forms of public transportation. The public press offered a wealth of necessary information which in the rural community might just as well be transmitted by word of mouth—news, public announcements, government business, election notices, etc. Whereas in the rural neighborhood many of the necessities such as clothing were manufactured by the family on the homestead proper, the specialization of city life demanded increased trade, buying, and selling. More so than anything, perhaps, the commercial and industrial life of the city demanded formal education. Available employment increasingly demanded skills. Record keeping demanded the ability to read and write. Bookkeeping and commercial activity demanded a knowledge of arithmetic and of formal accounting. Many jobs in the factories demanded trade or industrial skills which, although they could be learned by apprenticeship, might be mastered in far less time with formal instruction. More and more, the man with schooling "got the job" in favor of the unschooled man. And thus, formal education, while still only one of many educative influences, became more of a social and individual necessity than it had ever been before.

Of course, from the discussion in Chapter 9, it would be clear that many of these educational demands were also present in the agricultural community. The mechanization of the farm and the application of scientific knowledge to agriculture proceeded rapidly in the last decades of the nineteenth century. Obviously, it demanded the same skill to manage farm machinery as it did to cope with industrial machinery. Moreover, there was in many of the rural areas a definite migration from farm neighborhoods to small rural towns and villages. As this movement proceeded, many of the complexities of urban life appeared (on a much smaller scale, of course), and the same weakening of primary home and church ties took place. Thus, in agricultural areas, too, there were signs of a growing need for formal education.

In response to these demands one finds more and more children in an ever expanding school system between 1865 and 1918. Whereas in 1870 some 57 percent of American children between five and eighteen were enrolled in schools, by 1918 the figure had passed 75 percent. Of the group between seven and thirteen, the census of 1920 reported over 90 percent in school. Moreover, these children remained considerably longer than their predecessors a generation before. Whereas the average number of days attended was just under forty-five in 1870, it had risen past ninety by 1918. School mortality, while still high, was steadily decreasing, and the holding power of the school is illustrated by the fact that in 1870, roughly 1 percent of the school enrollment was in high schools, while by 1918 this had risen to just under 8 percent. Further evidence of expansion lay in the total expense for each child in attendance which stood at $15.55 in 1870 and had risen to $49.12 in 1918.

As for the effectiveness of these schools, once again it is difficult to judge. Certainly, one is safe in assuming that there was considerable variation from one section of the country to another, and from rural areas to urban communities. One of the most indicative figures attesting to educational effectiveness is the steadily rising literacy rate between 1870 and 1920. While in the former year 20 percent of the population over ten years of age was judged illiterate, this had fallen to just under 11 percent by 1900 and to 6 percent by 1920. As in the antebellum period, foreign travelers continued to show deep interest in American schools. Visitors such as Emily Faithfull and James Bryce were particularly favorable; and the latter noted that because of the schools, "the average of knowledge is higher, the habit of reading and thinking more generally diffused, than in any other country." [2] Certainly, the school was particularly effective as an Americanizing institution in the teeming cities of the East, and the continuing plaint of the immigrant elders that youngsters were falling away from old values and loyalties is ample testimony to this effectiveness. Generation conflict among these peoples was the constant price of education and assimilation.

The Education of Youth and Adults

In the life of youth and adults both school and nonschool agencies of education continued to play an increasingly important role. With new and varied courses offered in a variety of secondary schools—regular comprehensive high schools, manual training high schools, industrial schools, trade schools, and commercial schools—more and more youths remained in school after the eighth grade. The census of 1920, for example, reported almost 80 percent of the population between fourteen and sixteen years of age as well as 42.9 percent of the group between sixteen and eighteen as still attending school. Furthermore, well over a million persons eighteen years of age and over were similarly listed; just under half of these were in colleges, universities, technical

2 James Bryce, *The American Commonwealth* (New York, Macmillan, 1907), Vol. II, p. 284.

schools, and independent professional schools. Certainly, schooling at this level had undergone a phenomenal expansion.

Of equal interest was the rapid development of nonschool agencies of formal education. The Young Men's Christian Association, introduced into America from England during the 1850's, expanded rapidly until by 1874 it claimed nearly 1,000 branches and 100,000 members in the United States and Canada. Together with its counterpart, the Young Women's Christian Association, this organization carried on a vast program of social, recreational, and educational activities in communities throughout the country. The Boy Scout movement, originating in England in 1908 and taking root in America soon thereafter, was quickly successful as a new generation of urban Americans sought some of the lost out-of-door pleasures of their predecessors. By the beginning of World War I, the organization boasted some 300,000 members and a large variety of youth activities. Similar organizations for girls, like the Girl Scouts and the Camp Fire Girls, continued to attract membership and interest.

Among adults, considerable enthusiasm developed for the religiously motivated Chautauqua movement. Originated in 1874 by an Ohio manufacturer, Lewis Miller, and a Methodist minister, John H. Vincent, it began as a summer training course for religious workers at Lake Chautauqua, New York. The movement quickly developed broader educational functions, however. Local Chautauquas eventually appeared in hundreds of communities. In 1878 the Chautauqua Literary and Scientific Circle was formed to provide a four-year reading course in literary, social, scientific, and religious studies. Fourteen years later, the circle had an enrollment of 100,000 students, with half of them between thirty and forty years of age. Other Chautauqua activities included publication of the *Chautauquan,* a monthly magazine established in 1880, and the founding of the Chautauqua College of Liberal Arts in 1888, which granted a bachelor's degree for a four-year program of resident, correspondence, and extension study. Formal and informal series of lectures attracted similar enthusiasm. One interesting example was the establishment of the Ford Hall Forum in Boston in 1908 under the leadership of George W. Coleman. Local series including entertainers, humorists, and inspirational speakers were also widespread and popular.

The public library movement, begun in the Northeast before the Civil War, also received considerable impetus. By 1900 thirty-seven different states had authorized the expenditure of public funds for libraries, and in 1895 New Hampshire took the lead in making public libraries compulsory. The founding of the American Library Association in 1876 provided considerable momentum to the movement. The huge bequests of Andrew Carnegie and other philanthropists made possible tremendous expansion. Carnegie alone gave over $31 million to this cause, while gifts to American libraries between 1892 and 1902 totaled over $46 million. By 1900 the Commissioner of Education reported over 9,000 free circulating libraries possessing 300 or more volumes. Few areas existed, except perhaps in the South, where there was not access to free library service of some sort.

The improvement in printing methods brought a flood of cheap newspapers, books, magazines, and periodicals of all kinds before the American people. The Hearst and Pulitzer press fed the popular demand for human interest and popular scientific stories. By the turn of the century there were some 1,800 monthlies and well over 200 quarterlies in existence, and magazines such as *Harper's Monthly,* the *Atlantic,* and *Scribner's Monthly* (which became the *Century* in 1881) were unrivaled for literary and artistic quality. Others like the *Ladies' Home Journal* and *McClure's* catered particularly to women's tastes and problems and increasingly achieved significance in shaping opinion among the middle- and upper-class "female" group.

In general, although these influences tended to concentrate among the groups which could afford even their modest cost, they had broad educational appeal and effect. The eagerness for improvement reached all levels—the upper- and middle-class women's clubs as well as the settlement houses for the underprivileged, the scholarly and professional societies as well as the mechanics' institutes, the Chautauqua as well as the Metropolitan Museum of Art (1870) and the American Museum of Natural History (1869), the county fairs as well as the Metropolitan Opera Company and the New York Philharmonic Society. In these and a multitude of other ways, the education of American youth and adults outside of school went forward along with the extension and expansion of the schools themselves.

THE ORGANIZATION, SUPPORT AND CONTROL OF EDUCATION

The Organization of Public Education in the South

With the termination of hostilities in 1865, the educational problems of the South again became matters of national concern. The needs of the region were vast; the resources to meet them inadequate. There was little capital, and with the land and factories laid waste, little means of producing capital. In the effort to reorganize responsible government there was fraud, extravagance, misappropriation, and maladministration. Often, the scant funds actually available for schools were diverted to other less useful purposes. In many communities an aristocratic educational tradition still held that schooling was a luxury to be purchased by those who could afford the leisure and expense it demanded. Public education was something for the poor, and as a matter of Christian charity, it was justly the province of churches and benevolent societies. When the victorious North attempted to force acceptance of free public schools, state-sponsored education was even further opposed as a heinous fruit of the reconstruction.

In spite of these overwhelming difficulties, a slow and steady advance was seen in the South—an advance which accelerated into a genuine educational revival after the turn of the century. Philanthropic support from the Freedmen's Bureau and the Peabody and Slater Funds provided early stimulus. Scattered but heartening results stimulated optimistic legislation which, while rarely completely realized, furnished excellent precedent for later activity. With the organization of the Conference for Education in the South in 1898 and the Southern Education Board in 1901 a concerted campaign for educational improvement got under way, and while by 1918 the region as a whole lagged considerably behind the rest of the nation in educational accomplishment, enough progress had been made to justify hope and optimism for the future.

Early philanthropic and national aid.   The problem of caring for the destitute and homeless, especially among the Negroes, faced the North as soon as victorious Union commanders began to occupy large areas of the Confederacy. Initial military efforts to relieve suffering were soon supplemented by northern religious and benevolent agencies which sought to meet immediate needs, particularly among the Negroes, for food, clothing, education, housing, and employment. While much of this early aid was perhaps ineffective because of the lack of coordination and long-range planning, it did provide some cushioning against the initial hardships of reconstruction.

Supplementing this early benevolent activity was the work of the Bureau of Refugees, Freedmen, and Abandoned Lands (usually called the Freedmen's Bureau). Established by Congress in March of 1865 to aid in the work of rehabilitation, the bureau a year later was authorized to cooperate with voluntary organizations in providing school facilities. Under its able administrator, General O. O. Howard, the agency undertook to afford "unity and system" to the many uncoordinated efforts at Negro schooling, pouring over $5 million into southern education between 1865 and 1871. Interestingly enough, while the bureau represented a clear instance of federal participation in education, at no time did it replace local and private effort. Throughout its existence the benevolent societies continued to bear a large share of educational expenses, and with its demise private effort and local taxation took over the task completely.

In spite of the bureau's efforts, a good portion of this early work was comparatively blind and misdirected. With much of the administration falling to northerners there was often little understanding of local conditions, values, and feelings. Even the best of intentions sometimes failed to take account of community sentiments, and all too often the hand of aid was met with ill-feeling, indifference, and even rebuff. It remained for the pioneering work of the Peabody and Slater Funds to stimulate a concerted local drive for educational improvement.

The education funds.   The story is told that George Peabody, at a dinner party with Johns Hopkins, was once asked which he enjoyed more, making money or giving it away. While Hopkins "cocked up his ears," Peabody noted that he had always had a struggle, but that after seeing the happiness of the children in some London tenements he had remodeled, he began to find out that "it was pleasanter to give money away than it was to make it." Forty-eight hours later, the story continues, Hopkins, who had always resisted the making of a will, was designating his great fortune to the founding of a university and a hospital. It was this same George Peabody who was through his philanthropy to spark the revitalizing of southern education.

Peabody's gift was the sum of $2 million to be used "for the promotion and encouragement of intellectual, moral, or industrial education among the young of the more destitute portions of the Southern and Southwestern States of our Union. . . ." The grant was placed in the hands of sixteen distinguished men representing all sections of the nation, to use as they saw fit for the accomplishment of the above-stated purpose. In 1867, encouraged by almost unanimous approval from the public press, and by appreciative resolutions from Congress, the trustees began their momentous undertaking.

Under the leadership of Barnas Sears, first general agent, and later under J. L. M. Curry, the Peabody Fund literally breathed life into southern education. The policy was early accepted that aid would be confined to public common schools, that it would be dispensed where its influence might be most widespread, that a few schools would be supported well rather than many at low standards, that state systems would be improved, that state normal schools would be encouraged, that Negro teachers would be trained, and that the professional activities of teachers would be strengthened. In every one of these areas the fund managed to encourage significant advances. When the trustees decided to liquidate the fund they established in 1905 the George Peabody College for Teachers at Nashville, Tennessee, an institution which has since led in the effort to improve southern education. The services of the Peabody Fund throughout its existence cannot be overestimated. Without its support it is doubtful that the South would have achieved even the limited advance evidenced by the turn of the century.

The Peabody bequest set the pattern for a number of other great funds which were similarly important in stimulating educational improvement. In 1882 a Connecticut businessman named John Slater donated $1 million to assist in the education of southern Negroes, and his grant was instrumental in providing teacher training and industrial education for Negroes. Another grant of $1 million in 1907 by Anna T. Jeanes created a fund which greatly raised the quality of Negro rural education. Two years later the Phelps-Stokes Fund was established to aid Negro education generally, and in 1917, after five years of experimentation, Julius Rosenwald created a fund bearing his name which was active in all realms of southern education during the next three decades. Often, aid from these funds meant the difference between unfulfilled plans and that little starting push which enabled active workers to translate these plans into reality.

The growth of southern education. The actual growth of southern education during these years may properly be divided into two periods, with the turn of the century as the dividing point. During the earlier period considerable legislation was passed, but actual progress was slow. Under presidential reconstruction a number of constitutional and legislative provisions for education were enacted. Nearly all were concerned with some system of state administration, and provision for a state superintendent or state board of education was frequent. The question of mixed versus separate schools quickly entered the picture. The Alabama Constitution of 1865, for example, provided only that: "The General Assembly shall, from time to time, enact necessary and proper laws for the encouragement of schools and the means of education. . . ." On the other hand, the Texas Constitution of 1866, after proclaiming a general diffusion of knowledge as essential to the preservation of the rights and liberties of the people, provided that taxes "collected from Africans, or persons of African descent, shall be exclusively appropriated for the maintenance of a system of public schools for Africans and their children. . . ." The southern states were by no means agreed on the question during the first years of the reconstruction, and several actually made provision for mixed common schools. By 1895, however, every state of the Confederacy (South Carolina, Mississippi, Florida, Alabama, Georgia, Louisiana, Texas, Virginia, Arkansas, North Carolina, and Tennessee) had provided by law or constitutional provision for separate schools for Negroes. They were joined by the District of Columbia in 1862. Kentucky in 1866, Maryland in 1868, West Virginia in 1872, Delaware and Missouri in 1875, and Oklahoma in 1907.

With the inception of the congressional plan for reconstruction, education was advanced on paper, but it was increasingly hindered by southern resistance to what the paper provided. In every one of the former confederate states either constitutional or legislative provision or both was made for schools. In many, especially in South Carolina, Florida, Mississippi, and Louisiana, the determination of carpetbaggers to secure mixed schools immediately wrecked any hope for educational advance. Where such schools were actually put into operation, they were generally avoided by whites. By and large, even scalawags, with their pro-northern and pro-Negro sentiments, were opposed to the plan. There was even considerable division among the Negro community itself. In light of southern traditions one is not surprised to learn that in no part of the region was the mixed school particularly successful.

Continuing hindrance to school success came with the widespread misappropriation and maladministration of school funds. Often, money which had been collected and earmarked for educational purposes was simply appropriated in other directions. Other funds were mismanaged and found their way into private hands. In many respects, inexperienced, often ignorant, school officials unwittingly aided and abetted this fraud. Both misadministration and the mixed school quickly became identified in the minds of many southerners with the public school of Yankee reconstruction, and thus was resisted. When this resistance was added to traditional apathy toward public education, it formed a spirited opposition to southern progress.

While the South had made some advances along educational lines by 1900, it still lagged considerably behind other regions in enrollments and expenditures per pupil. More and more, southern leaders called the attention of their countrymen to these educational shortcomings. A number of changing conditions served to strengthen their cause. The older caste-like system of the South was rapidly giving way to a rising middle class by the end of the nineteenth century. Materially, the "new South" was coming into being as industrial and commercial growth ushered in rising prosperity. The return of a sense of belongingness to the Union, coupled with the spread of traditional American ideas concerning universal schooling, strengthened the cause of education in the minds of a new generation of southerners. All of these forces paved the way for an educational renaissance at the turn of the century.

Much of the early spirit behind this reawakening stemmed from a group of men who came to be known as the Conference for Education in the South. Little realizing the eventual effect of their actions, this group of northern and southern ministers and educators began in 1898 to hold annual meetings addressed to ways and means of improving Southern education. Growing largely out of their early deliberations, a Southern Education Board was established in 1901 to conduct a "campaign of education for free schools for all the people by supplying literature to the newspaper and periodical press, by participation in educational meetings, and by general correspondence." A bureau of information and advice on legislation and school organization was also founded. A year later the General Education Board was formed in New York "for the receipt and disbursement of money for educational purposes." Having somewhat broader purposes than its predecessor, the latter board envisioned a large measure of its work being carried out in the South.

The effect of these agencies was powerful and immediate. Campaigns for school improvement were held in many of the southern states during the first decade of the twentieth century. Enrollment, attendance, school budgets, length of sessions—all evidenced steady improvement. Local interest as well as local taxes showed remarkable increase. Yet in spite of all these improvements, the South in 1918 still showed many shortcomings when compared with the rest of the United States. South Carolina, Mississippi, Arkansas, and Alabama stood at the bottom of the Union in educational attainment, with the other southern states close behind. High school populations were lower; teachers were more poorly paid and trained than in other regions. In general, while there had been much advance, much remained to be done before the South reached the level of other states.

The Continuing Growth of Elementary Education

Elementary education, firmly rooted in the American tradition by 1865, expanded rapidly in the decades following the Civil War. Compulsory attendance requirements, established by two states prior to the Civil War, were universal by 1918. Kindergartens, an interesting experiment before 1865, were common throughout the nation fifty years later. Members of the non-Caucasian races, as well as the mentally and physically handicapped, were increasingly embraced by public facilities. By and large, the public elementary school was beginning to affect the great majority of American children. In spite of continuing opposition, the American people were firmly committed to its preservation and extension to all parts of the nation.

Movement toward universal elementary education. Strongly indicative of the increasing commitment to universal schooling was the growth of compulsory attendance legislation between 1865 and 1918. While it is true that Massachusetts had passed a compulsory attendance measure as early as 1852 and that New York had followed suit a year later, the real extension of the idea awaited the end of the Civil War. By 1900 thirty-two states, embracing most of the North and West, had passed such laws, and with Mississippi's acceptance of the principle in 1918 the idea became universal. Needless to say, there was considerable variation in the provisions of different states. The required length of annual attendance, the compulsory age period, the means of enforcement—all differed from state to state as well as from region to region.

Compulsory attendance brought a host of new problems to the public school. Thousands of recalcitrant or slow-witted children, who in former times would have dropped out of school in the normal course of events, now became the responsibility of the school for the minimum attendance period. Moreover, the school was now forced to enroll many new groups of children for whom the traditional program had no particular meaning, use, nor appeal. In effect, the burden of compulsory attendance really tended to force differentiation of school purposes and curricula in order that the many different educational needs of a heterogeneous population might be met.

Furthermore, although the new laws did much to secure increased school attendance, their mere existence by no means guaranteed compliance. Especially in the cities, and in spite of an increase in child labor legislation, one finds a growing number of children working, often slaving, in factories and shops for inordinately long hours at abysmally low wages. The census of 1920, for example, reported a million children between the ages of ten and fifteen as gainfully employed. The importance of this child labor problem was clearly reflected in the growing attempt to secure regulating legislation at the national level after 1906—an attempt which secured enactments in 1916 and 1919 later to be declared unconstitutional.

One of the most interesting aspects of steadily rising elementary school populations during this period was the comparatively rapid expansion of non-Caucasian attendance. The census of 1920 reported over 70 percent of all Negro children between seven and fifteen as in attendance, as well as over 67 percent of the Indian children and 85 percent of the Chinese and Japanese children in the same age bracket. Also of great interest was the rapid building of public facilities for the handicapped. Clearly, large groups of special children formerly considered ineducable were now deemed potentially useful members of society. The early seeds of education for the blind, the deaf, and the mentally defective, planted by men like Gallaudet before the Civil War, began increasingly to bear fruit. By 1918 there were literally hundreds of special public schools to care for such youngsters, and their attendance numbered in the thousands.

The growth of the kindergarten. In light of its origination by the German, Froebel, one is not surprised to learn that the kindergarten idea was brought to America by Germans—principally German intellectuals forced to flee Europe after the abortive revolutions of 1848. Apart from an unsuccessful experience in Boston, the first great experiment with public school kindergartens came in the St. Louis school system under the superintendency of William T. Harris. Harris had recommended the innovation to the board as early as 1870, but it was not until Susan Blow, a native of St. Louis who had completed a course in kindergarten methods, offered to teach the group in 1873 that the idea was adopted. It was so successful that Miss Blow soon organized a training school to educate co-workers, and as fast as the school produced graduates, the public kindergartens of St. Louis expanded. In doing so they attracted nation-wide interest, and it was really the successful prosecution of this experiment that paved the way for similar innovations all over the country.

Once the success of the movement had been demonstrated, it rapidly took root. To be sure, because of wealth and the higher number of children, they appeared more quickly in cities. Yet the movement was by no means confined to them. By 1918 the kindergarten had clearly been accepted as the first rung of the American ladder system, and the biennial survey of education carried out in that year reported 10.5 percent of the estimated 4.5 million American children between the ages of four and six enrolled in kindergartens of one sort or another.

The continuing role of the private elementary school. In spite of the fact that the greatest expansion in elementary education came in public, state school systems, one should not ignore the continuing role of the private school in American education. Generally, this role involved the serving of special interests or purposes in the community. Thus, for example, there was schooling of exceptional children—deaf, dumb, blind, feeble-minded, bright, etc.— which, although increasingly undertaken by public systems, was still provided in large measure by private facilities. Furthermore, there were the "class" schools—institutions which catered rather exclusively to the youngsters of the upper socio-economic brackets. In many cases, these were "prep" schools— the preparatory elementary departments of private secondary schools or academies.

By far the greatest proportion of the private school population, however, was enrolled in private religious—or parochial—schools. Of these, those of the Roman Catholic faith were far and away the most numerous. By 1910, a quarter century after the promulgation of the Third Plenary Council at Baltimore, close to 1.25 million children were reported as enrolled in the parish schools of this church. Of the Protestant sects, the Lutherans, perhaps, were probably the most active in founding parochial schools; and especially in the Midwest, one sees a rising number of their institutions.

Against an ideal of a common school which would embrace all children, the existence of these private systems posed a multitude of problems for American educators. In 1918 about 1.5 million youngsters were reported as enrolled in private and parochial elementary schools. Doubtless, such schools provided many advantages. Often, innovations which were impossible in public school systems were easily introduced into private institutions. Special religious, creedal, or linguistic instruction which parents desired was more easily provided. Greater freedom tended to provide an incentive for better and more highly qualified teachers.

With these advantages, however, came a number of compelling shortcomings. Among them, perhaps the most significant was the feeling of separatism engendered in students of different systems. Among Catholic writers the public school was increasingly called "your system" and the parochial school "our system." It is probable that such sentiments permeated down to the youngsters. Needless to say, these attitudes, coupled with hostility often generated by struggles over public funds, created divisions in the American community. Often, too, the private "class" schools created just the kind of snobbery predicted by the early common school advocates. Foreign-language schools also stimulated their share of mutual suspicions. While some might justifiably argue that the preservation of such heterogeneity was healthy for an American community increasingly tending toward standardization, the question of building a common working framework of values and attitudes for adult life remained ever present. Certainly, it was not a question that had been solved to any degree by 1918.

The Growth of the Public High School

As has been pointed out, America entered the latter decades of the nineteenth century firmly committed to public elementary schooling. While this policy was not without its opponents, it gained rapid headway between 1865 and 1918. On the secondary level the problem was a very different one. For those who envisioned a unified public school system embracing all levels from the elementary school through the university, the struggle for the public high school still lay ahead. This struggle was a fascinating one, for the free secondary school, embracing both college-preparatory and terminal students, was truly a distinctively American creation. By 1918 there was little doubt but that the struggle had been conclusively won. Public high schools of every kind existed throughout the Union. There were comprehensive high schools —by far the most common—vocational high schools, manual training high schools, industrial, trade, and commercial high schools. High school populations were clearly rising, and although controversy continued, public secondary education had wide support among the American people.

The struggle to secure public high schools. The actual struggle for free secondary education was somewhat different from the earlier fight for free elementary schools. In the case of elementary schools it was a struggle before state legislatures to secure passage of laws authorizing or compelling their establishment. In the case of high schools these earlier enactments were already on the books, and the central problem was whether or not they furnished legal basis for secondary education. In other words, if prior state enactments had given districts the right to tax for public elementary schools, did these same districts have the right to "extend the elementary school upward" and establish public high schools? While the struggle for high schools was not entirely removed from legislatures, much of it was fought in the courts over such matters of interpretation.

In the years immediately following the Civil War, the expansion of the high school was vehemently opposed by taxpayers' groups and religious organizations with large investments in private academies. Added to this opposition was the financial difficulty following the Panic of 1873. Yet the 1870's saw a series of judicial decisions in the state courts of Michigan, Illinois, and elsewhere which finally laid a sound legal basis for the public secondary school. Most famous of these was the Kalamazoo decision, handed down by the Michigan Supreme Court in 1874.

The case involved the attempt in 1872 of certain citizens of Kalamazoo's School District No. 1 to prevent the board from collecting school taxes for the support of high schools. It was very obviously a move to determine the right of school authorities in general to support free high schools and to offer appropriate secondary studies in them. The complainants had no argument with the right of the state to support and maintain public common schools. Rather, they were arguing that secondary instruction as it was then conceived embraced largely the classics and foreign languages. These, they held, were by and large an acomplishment of the few rather than the many, and they should, therfore, be paid for privately. There was nothing in such a curriculum which justified its support at public expense.

The decision, written by Justice Thomas M. Cooley and concurred in by his three colleagues, came out squarely against the complainants. Reviewing the educational history of the Northwest Territory and of the state of Michigan, Cooley maintained that from the very beginning the state had intended to furnish not only the rudiments of education but also equal opportunity for all to proceed on to higher studies. Having specifically provided for free elementary schools and a state university, Cooley concluded, the state would be highly inconsistent if it forced parents to secure private secondary instruction. Based on this, the legal right of the school board to levy taxes for public high schools was clearly affirmed. Moreover, having legalized classical education at public expense, the court had closed one more door on the opportunity for a dual system to develop; for not only useful and practical studies, but cultural, college-preparatory studies as well were now the just province of the public secondary school. Four years later, in the case of *Richards* v. *Raymond,* the Illinois supreme court similarly held constitutional a law providing for the establishment of high schools to be operated under special charters.

With the legal basis thus clarified, local school boards began to feel free to establish high schools as the demand arose. State legislatures were also encouraged to pass laws permitting local boards to establish high schools, to offer aid to those districts which did so, and finally actually to compel high schools to be established in certain larger and more populous districts. To be sure, such legislation came slowly at first. Minnesota began to aid high schools financially in 1878. Maine passed a high school law in 1873, while Wisconsin enacted similar legislation in 1875 and appropriated $25,000 for the assistance of high schools. However, it was during and after the 1890's that the avalanche of high school legislation really came, and by the end of World War I the number of public high schools had spiraled to 25,000 with an attendance of over 1,600,000 youngsters. Quite obviously, the middle rungs of the American educational ladder had been securely bolted in, and an increasing number of children were using them to climb to higher educational and social positions.

Differentiated and comprehensive high schools.   Most public high schools tended to offer at least two programs: a more practical one for terminal students as well as a classical one for college-preparatory students. The simple fact was that those communities which could afford a high school at all could as a rule only support one high school. Thus the *comprehensive* high school—the high school offering many parallel programs under one roof—soon became the standard American secondary school. It is not difficult to see also how this comprehensive pattern would be a suitable continuation of a common elementary school in which students of many different social classes tended freely to associate.

In noting this general pattern, however, one cannot ignore the movement toward special schools serving special purposes which was increasingly evidenced in larger communities. Actually, it was much closer to the older European pattern of secondary education than was the comprehensive high school. In Germany, for instance, as the need developed for more practical secondary education, the tendency had been to establish the *realschule*—a separate school—rather than to integrate the practical studies into the *gymnasium*—the traditional classical secondary school. Inasmuch as many leading American educational theorists of this period were steeped in European thought and philosophy, it is not difficult to see why they would support a movement toward differentiation.

One of the first such schools was the manual training high school developed by Professor Calvin M. Woodward, Dean of the Polytechnic School at Washington University in St. Louis. Students in Woodward's school were to "divide their working hours, as nearly as possible, equally between mental and manual labor," thereby mastering the fundamentals of mechanical as well as intellectual processes. Other manual training high schools soon appeared in public systems. A Baltimore Manual Training School was opened in 1883, while Eau Claire, Wisconsin, and Toledo, Ohio, established similar institutions a year later. By 1894 Massachusetts had required all cities of 20,000 or more to provide high school manual training courses.

Growing interest in manual training schools brought interest in other specialized high school programs. The turn of the century also witnessed the founding of a number of successful commercial and agricultural high schools. Clearly, although the comprehensive high school tended to remain the pattern, these special high schools were becoming more and more frequent. Nevertheless, there was something about keeping all of the children in a single high school which appealed strongly to the American people; and the burden of their support went principally to the comprehensive schools.

The development of the junior high school. The pressure for some change in the eight-year-elementary–four-year-secondary organization has already been alluded to in Chapter 11. A response came in the form of the junior high school. The actual determination of when the first American junior high school was established remains a matter of controversy. As early as 1895 an institution was founded in Richmond, Indiana, embracing the final two years of the elementary school. It did not, however, have a separate organization or separate housing. Therefore, it has been viewed primarily as a precedent for later developments. The principal claimants of the first genuine junior high school are Columbus, Ohio, and Berkeley, California. According to the reports of the Columbus Board of Education, an institution called a junior high school, "consisting of the seventh and eighth grammar grades and the first grade of the high school," was established on August 31, 1909. For many, however, the Columbus junior high school accomplished more of a physical reorganization than anything else. They hold that not until the establishment of the Berkeley junior high school under Superintendent Frank Bunker in January 1910 was a physical reorganization accompanied by genuine changes in program and orientation. The decision between the two claimants probably goes to Columbus, with the Berkeley program being a decided improvement and extension of the junior high school idea.

Regardless, the appearance of these early schools definitely gave headway to the junior high school movement. After 1910, many systems proceeded to reorganize on an elementary school, junior high school, senior high school basis—with 6-3-3 the most common but also with 6-2-2 and 6-6 organizations in the picture. By 1918 the Bureau of Education estimated 557 junior high schools with over 116,000 students in the United States, and the rate of increase at that time was rapidly accelerating.

Private secondary schools.   As on the elementary level, the continuing role of the private secondary school between 1865 and 1918 should not be underestimated. It is true that in 1890 only 61 percent of all high schools in the country were under public control, while in 1918 over 87 percent of the high schools reporting to the Bureau of Education were public. On the other hand, these are but relative figures. Generally, both public and private secondary school enrollments tended to rise. Thus, the number of private secondary schools rose from 1,632 in 1890 to 2,058 in 1918; while the number of pupils in these institutions rose from 95,000 in the former year to 159,000 in the latter. These 2,058 private secondary schools in 1918 served a variety of purposes. The great majority—over two thirds—were under denominational control; of these, the Roman Catholics maintained 940 with an enrollment of 62,000 students. Among the nonsectarian institutions were a variety of special purpose schools—academies, military schools, etc. By and large, private secondary schools tended to break themselves down into the same categories as private elementary schools, and many served purposes which were not within the scope or possibility of publicly managed systems. As also in the case of the elementary school, the advisability of placing youngsters in separate schools to serve separate purposes remained very much a moot issue.

The Expansion and Extension of Higher Education

The tremendous expansion of elementary and secondary school populations in the decades following 1865 is reflected in a definite, but considerably smaller, increase in college, university, and professional school enrollments during the same years. By far the more significant development in higher education came in the actual development of new organizational forms. The university, which had existed in name alone prior to 1865, became a reality by 1918. Professional instruction—theological, legal, medical, educational, and agricultural—was increasingly embraced by the university. The junior college came into existence at the turn of the century to serve special purposes, and by 1918 the number of such institutions was clearly on the upswing. Equally interesting were the organizational modifications designed to enlarge the extent of the university's public service. Extension courses carried the benefits of higher education to groups and areas hitherto unserved. Summer sessions allowed teachers and other professional workers to avail themselves of in-service training. Agricultural experiment stations worked with farmers in the effort to improve techniques and methods. Finally, one notes a steady increase in the number of women availing themselves of higher education. In a field in which they had formerly been oddities, they now became familiar—and often outstanding—figures. While a sharp expansion of enrollments in higher education had to await a later period in American history, certainly the foundation of a fitting capstone for America's educational system was clearly laid during these years.

The development of American universities.   The founding of colleges, which went ahead so rapidly in the second quarter of the nineteenth century, continued with unabated speed following the Civil War. If anything, it accelerated. In the thirty years after 1865 over two hundred colleges were founded, of which the great majority survived permanently. This more than doubled the number of colleges existing in 1865, and as one might well expect, the number of enrollments rose accordingly.

Along with this expansion in the number of colleges came an extension of their scope and role. Throughout the nineteenth century it remained difficult to tell a university from a college simply by its name. There were many titular "universities" which were merely colleges, and some whose instruction barely qualified for the high school level. On the other hand, Bryn Mawr College, opened in 1885, offered under a faculty of philosophy truly graduate instruction leading to a master of arts or doctor of philosophy degree. A Yale professor in 1899 took the pains to point out that: "Any one possessed of the requisite information knows at once what is meant by the university of France, the English university, or a German university; but no one can become so conversant with facts as to tell what an American university is." [3] In spite of this seeming confusion, however, there was clear evidence of a definite movement toward university organization under way by 1900.

One of the most important steps in this direction was the founding of Johns Hopkins University. The novelty of this institution, incorporated under a large grant by Hopkins in 1867, was that its primary emphasis lay in work beyond the bachelor's degree. President Daniel Coit Gilman placed heavy accent on the German ideal of research, and accordingly, the seminar and lecture techniques figured prominently in the institution. In 1885, nine years after Johns Hopkins actually went into operation, Bryn Mawr College, pat-

[3] George Trumbull Ladd, *Essays on the Higher Education* (New York, Scribner, 1899).

terned closely after its predecessor, admitted its first classes of women. In addition to the regular undergraduate course, a faculty of philosophy admitted only holders of the bachelor's degree and offered graduate instruction leading to the master of arts and doctor of philosophy. Two years later Clark University was founded, organized purely on the graduate level with no college, technical schools, or professional schools contemplated. Under President G. Stanley Hall, former professor of philosophy at Johns Hopkins, the institution strongly reflected German practices of seminar organization, research specialism, the granting of fellowships, etc. Similarly, Catholic University began instruction in 1889 also as an institution primarily for holders of the bachelor's degree.

Spurred on by these innovations, traditional colleges and universities began slowly to move in similar directions. Thus, for example, Harvard by the turn of the century embraced two undergraduate schools, a graduate faculty, and six professional schools. Yale, the first American institution to grant a Ph. D., also moved toward university status. By 1900 it had organized instruction into four general departments: philosophy and the arts, theology, medicine, and law. Columbia by the same date included, in addition to the college, faculties of philosophy, political science, pure science, and applied science, and professional schools of medicine, law, mines, chemistry, engineering, and architecture (the last four under the charge of the faculty of applied science). State universities such as Michigan, Minnesota, Wisconsin, and California also were moving in very similar directions by the turn of the century.

The growth of professional education. As with higher education in general, one finds following 1865 a gradual expansion of professional facilities. As colleges became universities, new professional schools were organized. Formerly independent professional schools, in an effort to improve their facilities and obtain the benefits of affiliation, sought institutional arrangements with the new universities. As increasing attention was given to the role of the professions in American life, the quality of the work at these schools improved considerably, and with this improvement, students flocked to them for instruction. By 1918 the Commissioner of Education reported close to 150 schools of theology, enrolling over 9,000 students; over 100 schools of law enrolling close to 11,000 students; 72 medical schools enrolling close to 14,000 students; 19 schools of veterinary medicine with over 1,000 students; 36 schools of dentistry with over 8,000 students; and 55 schools of pharmacy with some 4,000 students. Because the reports of the commissioner only included those schools which responded to questionnaires, there were doubtless other schools and students in every area.

Although government reports tended to regard technical and agricultural higher education apart from professional education, one might well group them together. Here too, there was significant expansion. Public support of agricultural and mechanical colleges was given tremendous stimulus by the Morrill Act of 1862; and most of the states established "A and M" colleges in connection with their state universities. Others created separate institutions in fulfillment of the federal provisions. In addition, schools of technology and/or agriculture were established in many of the older private institutions. Following the examples of Harvard and Yale—both of whom established scientific schools in 1847—other colleges organized departments or schools of science, technology, or engineering. After the establishment of the Michigan State Agricultural College, the first of its kind, and the rapid founding of institutions under the Morrill grants, many private institutions also incorporated colleges of agriculture.

The founding of the junior college. One of the most interesting developments in the field of higher education at the end of the nineteenth and beginning of the twentieth centuries was the junior college movement. The concern of prominent educators with reorganizing the traditional college course has already been discussed in Chapter 11. Actually, the first real separation of the junior college from the total program came with the opening of the reorganized University of Chicago under President Harper in 1892. Under this reorganization the freshman and sophomore years of the college course were designated the *academic college,* while the latter two years were designated the *university college.* Four years later they were redesignated the *junior* and the *senior* colleges. Upon conclusion of the junior division the student at the University of Chicago was granted the Associate in Arts degree.

Quite independent of this development, and yet related to it, was the attempt to organize a junior college program around an extended secondary school. Possibly the first work of this kind was done in Michigan under the stimulus of the state university there. During the early 1890's the university was accepting for credit one year of college work done under the auspices of the better high schools in that state. Quite naturally, this development soon led to the founding of public junior colleges as capstones of local public education systems. The first such institution to continue for any length of time was the public junior college organized not in Michigan but at Joliet, Illinois, in 1902. It seems rather evident from available documents that President Harper was highly influential in the founding of this school. Probably his friendship with J. Stanley Brown, Superintendent of Schools in Joliet, plus the fact that both were Baptists and met often in connection with religious activities, was the leading factor in stimulating its establishment. Two years later Superintendent Brown reported a similar development in eighteen institutions in different parts of the country.

For an actual picture of the early development of such institutions, one must, however, turn to California. Largely under Professor A. F. Lange of the University of California—often called the father of the junior college—

and President David Starr Jordan of Stanford University, the movement rapidly spread through the state's public school system. As early as 1907, California passed a law permitting district boards of education to "prescribe post graduate courses of study for the graduates of such high school, or other high schools, which courses of study shall approximate the studies prescribed in the first two years of university courses." By 1917 there were sixteen junior college departments of secondary schools in existence in California and a number of other institutions which offered post-graduate secondary instruction.

In other states, too, the junior college idea went forward. Illinois, Michigan, Minnesota, Iowa, and Missouri were among the leaders. A study conducted on a nation-wide basis for the Bureau of Education revealed at least seventy-six institutions by 1917 calling themselves junior colleges. Although a proportionately tremendous expansion of these institutions took place in the decade following this study, the study itself clearly revealed that the junior college was by 1918 already serving an important function in American life.

The Growth of Federal Participation in Education

The increasing tendency toward centralization in American affairs following the Civil War has already been noted. Much of this was reflected in the growth of federal power in the last decades of the nineteenth century, and, inevitably, this federal power touched education. Although the Constitution had clearly left educational matters to the states and local communities, one is easily able to distinguish a gradual assumption of certain educational functions by the national government. The land ordinances of 1785 and 1787 as well as the land and monetary grants during the first half of the nineteenth century were all steps in this direction, as was the Morrill Act of 1862. Even more so, however, did the Morrill Act usher in a period of increasing federal *participation in* as well as aid to education. The establishment of the Federal Department of Education in 1867 attested to this, as did the heightened agitation for federal aid to common schools between 1870 and 1890.

While these early efforts to obtain federal aid were unsuccessful, a number of smaller and more specific acts exemplified a continuing policy of support and interest. These acts in a sense were climaxed by passage in 1914 of the Smith-Lever Act and in 1917 by the Smith-Hughes Act. Both provided for large grants of aid to specific vocational programs in the various states. Finally, the role of schools during World War I clearly indicated that while education continued to remain a local and state affair, the national prerogative in some areas—especially those concerning the national safety—by 1918 had been well established. Already by then, the problem had become one of *how* the federal government might best aid education rather than *whether* the federal government should aid education at all. It was a reconstruction of the problem, however, that far too few persons actually realized at that time, or, as a matter of fact, for several decades thereafter.

The creation of a federal department of education. The attempt to commit the federal government to the collection and diffusion of useful educational statistics and information dates back to 1837, when Henry Barnard tried to interest Washington authorities in such a proposal. His efforts in this direction, although unsuccessful, ushered in similar proposals from numerous prominent individuals and organizations during the following thirty years. In spite of considerable support in educational circles, these proposals drew spirited opposition, much of it coming from men who believed such a department would bring federal control and supervision of education. Others opposed the idea on religious or constitutional grounds. Nevertheless, a measure was finally passed and signed by President Johnson in 1867.

By its provisions a Department of Education was created "for the purpose of collecting such statistics and facts as shall show the condition and progress of education in the several States and Territories, and of diffusing such information respecting the organization and management of schools and school systems, and methods of teaching as shall aid the people of the United States in the establishment and maintenance of efficient school systems, and otherwise promote the cause of education throughout the country." The legislation provided for a Commissioner of Education to direct the department, for clerical assistance, and for an annual report to the Congress. In spite of this seeming victory, however, opposition and hostility to the department continued even after its establishment, and in 1869 it became the Bureau of Education within the Department of the Interior. Although its functions and organization remained in large measure unchanged, its prestige and budget were accordingly reduced.

As in the case of many of its state predecessors, the federal Department of Education had no direct powers of control, supervision, or disbursement of funds. Whatever influence it exerted came principally from the power of knowledge and the personal efforts of the commissioner and his staff. Yet even within these limitations, the department, later the bureau, exerted important influence. The first six men who held the commissioner's post—Henry Barnard, John Eaton, Nathaniel Dawson, William T. Harris, Elmer Ellsworth Brown, and Philander Claxton—were indefatigable in their efforts on behalf of education. Their addresses at national and local educational meetings were always considered and wise. Their writings were widely circulated and instrumental in crystallizing opinion and making policy. Their annual reports were, and remain, a gold mine of educational information. These reports maintained a breadth of interest that was refreshing for their time, embracing subjects ranging from reindeer schools in Alaska, to elementary schools in Europe, to university problems in the United States. The *Bulletins* published by the bureau, as well as other papers, stimulated a wealth of significant research in all aspects of education. Continually hampered by low budgets and secondary status in the government, these commissioners and their staffs did superb jobs. Moreover, as also in the case of Horace Mann, the very breadth with which they conceived their function and the tact with which they discharged it more than anything made the bureau the force that it has been in American education.

Continuing legislation for limited federal aid. The failure to secure passage of a general aid bill between 1870 and 1890 (see Chapter 11) in no way precluded further measures granting federal aid for more specific educational purposes. As a matter of fact, more than at any previous time, the agitation during these twenty years crystallized both the need for federal aid and the issues involved in getting it. In 1887, for example, Congress passed the Hatch Experiment Station Act, providing for a $15,000 annual grant to each state and federal territory to finance agricultural experiment stations in connection with Morrill land-grant colleges. (See p. 266.) General supervision was vested in the Commissioner (later Secretary) of Agriculture, and in many ways the act brought the federal government into a tremendously important educational domain—that of research and experimentation in agricultural and conservation problems. In 1906 the annual appropriation to each state and territory was raised to $20,000 with the provision that it would increase $2,000 a year until the annual appropriation reached $30,000. Another act in 1890 provided for annual federal appropriations of $15,000 to land-grant colleges. Known as the Second Morrill Act, it also provided for increments of $1,000 a year until the annual sum reached $25,000.

During the first decade of the twentieth century a renewal of interest in federal participation in general common school education was apparent. There was pressure for a national university, for a Department of Education with an officer of cabinet rank at its head, and for aid to vocational instruction. It was in this latter area that the pressure became most significant. Numerous bills were introduced providing for appropriations to aid agricultural and industrial education in secondary schools, to train agricultural and industrial teachers in normal schools, and to extend the work of the agricultural experiment stations. Finally, Congress in 1914 appointed a Commission on National Aid to Vocational Education to study the problem, and the commission's report was highly instrumental in securing legislation some three years later.

In 1914 another significant move came in the passage of the Smith-Lever Act. This law provided for federal grants to the states for "diffusing among the people of the United States useful and practical information on subjects relating to agriculture and home economics, and to encourage application of the same." County agricultural agents were authorized to work with farmers and housewives to improve their practices and raise the levels of farm life. Lectures, meetings, classes, conferences, publications, and demonstrations were provided by federal funds, to be matched dollar for dollar by those states which elected to participate in the program. In many ways the Smith-Lever Act followed closely in the traditions of former federal aid provisions. Some writers have pointed out that it was simply a tremendous expansion of the idea behind the Hatch Experiment Stations. Fairly extensive latitude was given to local authorities to execute the general purposes of the act. While approval of the Department of Agriculture was involved in programs, much freedom was left to officials of state agricultural colleges and other local agencies. On the other hand, the matching principle, whereby states matched federal grants dollar for dollar, was an innovation in federal policy. Although it had appeared in some of the defeated federal aid bills of the 1870's and 1880's, this was the first time it had been put into effect on a large scale in education.

Building on the precedent of the Smith-Lever Act, and stimulated by the recommendations of the Commission on National Aid to Vocational Education, Congress in 1917 enacted the Smith-Hughes Act. By its provisions the federal government was to cooperate with the states "in paying the salaries of teachers, supervisors, and directors of agricultural subjects, and of teachers of industrial subjects, and in the preparation of teachers of agricultural, trade and industrial, and home economics subjects." In effect, it was to provide vocational education in these areas in secondary schools. A Federal Board of Vocational Education and corresponding state boards were organized to administer the federal funds. As with its predecessor, federal funds were to be matched dollar for dollar by state funds. The money was to be used to pay the salaries of agricultural teachers in the proportion that the rural population of a state bore to the total rural population of the nation; to pay salaries of home economics, trade, and industrial arts teachers in the proportion that the state's urban population bore to the total urban population of the nation; to help states prepare teachers in these subjects in proportion as the state's total population bore to the nation's total population; and to conduct research in these various fields. In addition to the actual educational work, an appropriation of $200,000 a year was made to carry on the work of the board.

Although many provisions of the Smith-Hughes Act were similar to those of its forerunners, there were some notable innovations. Principal among these was the specificity of the bill. While former enactments had left considerable latitude to the states, this one specifically outlined many details of the program. Instruction was to be in certain areas, of a vocational character, to persons over fourteen years of age and in schools or classes of less than college grade. The federal board was assigned broad powers of inspection, evaluation, and acceptance or rejection of state plans. In other areas, the law was equally direct and specific. More than any former federal act aiding education, then, the Smith-Hughes Act laid the groundwork for effective federal definition and supervision of its principles.

Centralization and School Administration

It has already been stated that education quickly became "big business" following the Civil War. Budgets which had formerly been small soared, the Commissioner of Education reporting total educational revenues in 1918 at over three quarters of a billion dollars. Public school property in that same year was valued at $2 billion. With this tremendous increase came a prodigious growth in the techniques and agencies of school administration. Nowhere was this better illustrated than in the 27,000 administrative and supervisory officers reported by the end of World War I.

Even more important, however, in light of this vast expansion, was the continuing problem of reconciling state and local authority in education. That the states, more than ever before, were exercising their powers of over-all policy making was attested to by a flood of constitutional pronouncements, legislation, and state judicial decisions. This was also clearly reflected in the rapid development of state educational administration. On the other hand, the picture is distorted if one does not also take account of the numerous continuing local forms of school management. School districts, as well as township and county units, continued to play a major role in carrying on the actual business of education, and in the majority of communities, the people continued to make immediate decisions within a framework of state policy. Needless to say, while the two levels of authority often worked smoothly together, there were innumerable instances of conflict where local residents resented state encroachment, or where state authorities were dissatisfied with local initiative or achievement.

One also notes a number of new administrative forms—outstanding among these the highly complicated city school system. Managing as they did huge enterprises involving large staffs and appropriations, these systems encountered many problems that called for more efficient administrative approaches. The effort to solve these problems gave rise to a scientific study of administrative procedures which resulted in considerable crystallizing of desirable methods by the early 1920's. The latter movement did much to stimulate the professional character of educational work.

The continuing growth of centralization. State influence in education, vehemently reasserted by Horace Mann, Henry Barnard, and others of their contemporaries, continued to grow after the Civil War. State constitutional provisions regarding education, especially in the case of the South during reconstruction, became far more detailed and specific than they had been before, giving extensive treatment to local responsibility for school maintenance, to school finances and upkeep, to teacher certification, and to other matters of general policy. Acting under the mandate of these constitutions, state legislatures began to pass lengthy and highly technical laws governing the rights and responsibilities of smaller administrative units. When litigation inevitably arose over interpretation of these laws, or when individuals or corporations challenged their constitutionality, state courts rendered significant decisions which also affected over-all policy.

One of the most concrete illustrations of state power in the educational realm was the increase in scope and function of state educational administration. A study carried out in 1880,[4] for example, indicated some chief educational officer in every one of the thirty-eight states then in the Union. He was elected by the people in twenty-one, appointed by the governor in eight, elected by the legislature in three, and appointed by a state board of education in six. In most states his duties by then included official visits and the apportionment of school revenues in addition to the collection and diffusion of school information. In some states he granted teaching licenses; in others he prescribed recommended textbooks. In still others he took on judicial functions such as the interpretation of school legislation and the editing of school laws.

One might think that by 1880 such duties were already becoming burdensome; but they went right on multiplying. With the growth of high schools in succeeding decades, with the vast expansion of the curriculum to encompass new vocational and industrial subjects, with the extension of school functions to include many new welfare services for children, and with the increasing tendency toward centralization in school affairs, the duties of the state superintendent became ever more important and ever more demanding.

Paralleling the growth of the state superintendency was the development of the state board of education. Both, in effect, embodied the power of the state in education. Twenty-four states had such boards by the time of the 1880 survey. In about half they were composed chiefly of professional educators; in the other half, chiefly of state political officers. There was considerable variation in their powers, ranging from the appointment of administrative officers on lower levels, to the making of qualifying examinations, to the issuance of state teaching licenses. As in the case of the state superintendent, the powers and responsibilities of such boards tended to multiply as educational systems became more and more complex.

On the local level, county, township, and district agencies continued to represent the people in immediate decisions regarding education. At the turn of the century the district form still prevailed in most states; in many the actual number went into the thousands. Much was written about the role of the local district in bringing the schools and the people closely into touch with one another. On the other hand, the glaring inequalities of the district system

[4] *Circulars of Information of the Bureau of Education* (1880), No. 2 (Washington, D. C., Government Printing Office, 1880), Appendix B.

had stimulated considerable movement toward consolidation by the turn of the century. Massachusetts as early as 1869 had passed legislation permitting two districts to consolidate, and thirteen years later the district system was abolished. By 1890 the movement had gained enough force in other states to bring about pressure for similar laws, and by 1910 a majority had authorized consolidation. Yet, as with many permissive statutes, actual accomplishment varied. In some states, like Ohio, Colorado, or North Carolina, results were comparatively good. In others, such as California, Kansas, or Wisconsin, progress was relatively poor. Where consolidation did take place, results were quickly evident in the form of larger schools with better instructional services. Where the autonomous district persisted, the trying conditions associated with the one-room rural school continued to plague educational efforts.

In many instances state and local authorities worked extremely well together in raising educational standards and increasing educational opportunity. On the other hand, conflicts were bound to appear. Where they did, judicial authorities ruled that ultimate power rested with the state; that is, that education was a state undertaking. An illustrative decision in New York State in 1897 clearly enunciated this policy. Because of divisions in the local board, the city of Watervliet had failed to open its schools for the regular September session. Acting under his legislative powers, the State Superintendent of Public Instruction had moved to open the schools and employ the necessary personnel to do so. The state Supreme Court upheld his authority in doing so and refused to issue an injunction to prevent the continued operation of the schools. It should be pointed out, however, that very rarely did the conflict between state and local authorities actually come to such a head. Rather, it was often a matter of continuing friction infused all too frequently with personal difficulties. In spite of such friction, the power of states did grow, and with it, responsibilities.

One final problem of educational centralization came with the mushrooming of urban communities after the Civil War. They brought an entirely new problem to school affairs: the administration and supervision of school systems ministering to thousands of children. By and large, city school organization followed the traditional pattern of a board of education with powers delegated by the legislature, and a city superintendent as chief local school officer. The boards themselves varied considerably. In a study completed in 1885, John D. Philbrick, Superintendent of Boston's public schools, found boards ranging in size all the way from six to over a hundred members.[5] Considerable variation of powers also occurred, with cities like Pittsburgh having rather well-defined and restricted educational powers as compared with the broad—almost absolute—power of cities like New York or St. Louis.

[5] *Circulars of Information of the Bureau of Education* (1885), No. 1 (Washington, D. C., Government Printing Office, 1885).

It goes without saying that in light of these developments, the city school superintendency also grew in stature and complexity. The incumbent was often responsible for millions of dollars, thousands of students, and hundreds of teachers. Often, too, he was the center of struggles between organized pressure groups for control of the schools. Obviously, the position called for men of high character, intellect, and training. While one has good reason to be impressed with the number of such men who did fill the city superintendencies during this period, he is often equally appalled with the alarming number of untrained, and sometimes even corrupt, incompetents.

Partisan versus professional administration. Particularly in the cities, but certainly at every level and phase of the school administration program, the problem of building a professional orientation toward the job and its incumbent was a continuing one. In many states, for example, the chief state school office was a political plum, to be handed out after election along with other lucrative posts. This fact, together with short terms of the office and generally inadequate pay scales, tended to keep the best educators from considering state positions. City administrative positions, with higher salaries and better working conditions, were far more attractive to the career schoolman. On the other hand, the opportunity really to influence the course of public education in a single state and in the nation drew many to the position in spite of its shortcomings. Much the same might be said for administrative positions at the county level. Here too, the danger was far too prevalent that the post would be either a political reward or a convenient sinecure for retired party men.

For many the clue to solving this problem was the professionalizing of administrative positions. It was all too obvious that state and county officers would not be able to fulfill their educational responsibilities until their positions were lifted above the realm of partisan politics, given the prestige and power necessary and appropriate, and freed from the baser forms of partisan interference. Moreover, educational qualifications would have to be introduced in order that competency always remain a prime criterion. One began to see movement in this direction sporadically in various states in the early twentieth century. Some states required extensive experience of a candidate. Others removed the traditional residence requirement in order that the best professional educator might be secured. Some states introduced special elections for the superintendency apart from the ordinary November elections. Some placed the office in the hands of a state board of education, or of the governor or legislature in the hope that they would be less partisan than the electorate. While the question was a hotly debated one by 1918, it had in many ways been clarified, and while much remained to be done, a good deal of sensitivity to its importance was evident.

Of great interest in this attempt to professionalize school administration was the movement to develop scientific tools for evaluating school progress. One of these which gained increasing acceptance especially in the second decade of the twentieth century was the school survey or research movement. The idea behind it, of course, was to use scientific measurement in assessing educational practice, and its popularity is readily understandable in light of the interest in scientific evaluation throughout American affairs. Rochester, New York, for example, began research in its school accounting and finance as early as 1911, and by 1920 over fifty cities had established similar services. Such activity was a significant prelude to the extensive school survey techniques developed during the succeeding decade, especially under George D. Strayer and Nickolaus Engelhardt at Teachers College, Columbia.

THE EDUCATIONAL PROGRAM

Educational Aims

It is one thing to theorize on desirable educational aims, and clearly, a good deal of such theorizing went on in America after 1865. It is quite another thing, however, for theory to be realized in practice. While one is able to find numerous examples of fundamentally new school programs here and there before 1918, and while modifications slowly entered most curricula, by and large, traditional aims continued to dominate education. Those who built educational programs continued to assume that education is something which goes on in school for a certain period of time each day, that education is something done in the early years of life and *preparation* for the real business of living which comes later, that education is something to be derived primarily from words and numbers provided by books and teachers, and therefore, that the school curriculum consists largely of a body of previously discovered facts and principles which must be communicated to the young.

In spite of growing attacks on traditional conceptions of human nature and learning, religious-moral development and mental discipline remained paramount aims well into the twentieth century. Therefore, the intellectual activities which supposedly would achieve these ends continued to hold primary places in the course of study. To be sure, stated aims at all levels paid tribute to the goal of good citizenship. Yet when this aim was further analyzed and broken down, it became evident that in the minds of most educators, the good citizen was the man who could read and write, whose mind had been disciplined, and who had received appropriate character education. Obviously, then, notions of citizenship education were intimately bound up with moral development and mental discipline. Insofar as this was true, the situation closely paralleled that of antebellum America.

With these facts in mind, however, one should not ignore the increasingly powerful practical aim in education. The "cash value" of schooling was a principle which educators sought increasingly to justify in practice. Forceful evidence of this was the steady growth of the vocational dimension. While it is true that preparation for business and commercial life had been important in the early academies and high schools, the vocational aim in the latter half of the nineteenth century tended to affect all levels of schooling and to include preparation for trades, industry, business, and the professions. As the practical temper of American life deepened, so did its counterpart in education; especially in the minds of high school students did this aim loom ever larger after the turn of the century.

Mention should also be made of the newer "progressive" aims which were being demonstrated in a variety of experimental schools. In many such programs, as schoolmen began to take account of individual differences, growing attention was directed to the cultivation of particular talents and potentialities in youngsters. In some of these schools, especially in those committed to the philosophy of John Dewey, conscious attention was devoted to training in the skills of democratic living. Inasmuch as Dewey was giving heed to the common as well as the individual needs of a democratic society, these schools stressed group activities which would equip youngsters to participate in the sharing of power and responsibility which was the essence of democracy. Such goals, while new and far-reaching, were by no means in vogue by 1918. They should be regarded simply as early evidence of aims which were destined in succeeding decades to play a much more influential role in the conduct of American education.

Finally, the goal of individual success remained paramount in the minds of many. American society, while losing some of the vertical mobility of earlier years, was still flexible, and many saw in education the social elevator which would carry them to higher prestige positions. Especially among the immigrant groups was this true. Immigrant parents sacrificed comforts and even necessities to allow their offspring to attend school. The school, in addition to acting as an assimilating agency, assumed for them a much broader and more inclusive function. It was the principal means of making a life for their children better, richer, and happier than any they had ever known in Europe. For immigrants and natives alike, the school remained a symbol of individual success. It provided a unique opportunity for social and political advancement.

Curriculum and Method in the Elementary School

The continuing expansion of the elementary school curriculum. The elementary school curriculum continued slowly to expand during the decades immediately following the Civil War. Nevertheless, by the turn of the century the program still reflected much the same emphasis that it had in earlier years. A study of curricula in city school systems for 1888–1889 documents well this latter assertion.[6] In New York City in 1888, for example, reading,

[6] *Report of the Commissioner of Education for the Year 1888–89* (Washington, D. C., Government Printing Office, 1891), Vol. I, pp. 373–410.

spelling, and grammar accounted for over 40 percent of class time, writing over 15 percent, arithmetic over 25 percent, while geography, history, music, and drawing filled out the remainder. Thus, roughly 80 percent of the youngster's time in the elementary school was spent in direct study of the three R's. Boston's elementary curriculum was much the same with the addition of elementary science and physical training. With variations that might be expected, all of the eighty-two city curricula surveyed revealed similar emphases, and while later studies done after 1900 show the increasing entry of subjects like manual training, physiology, hygiene, nature study, science, cooking, and sewing, this emphasis on the three R's continued.

Of considerable significance were important changes in the content and outlook of the subjects themselves. Reading, for example, tended to move away from the rote memorization of which Warren Burton spoke in 1830 toward concern with understanding. Moreover, one notes a growing attempt in all fields to write textbooks in a manner which would be of interest as well as comprehensible to children. In arithmetic textbooks attacks on the theory of mental discipline led to a diminishing concern with training the mind and a growing concern with practical problems and principles. This was reflected in the increasing substitution of everyday problems for the long lists of rules and generalizations characteristic of earlier texts. Grammar, too, tended to apply increasingly to everyday language; while geography and history, traditionally concerned with the memorizing of details, turned ever so slightly toward the meaning of and relationship among facts and bits of information.

Despite these changes, one is still able to find spellers consisting of nothing more than lists of words, readers with passages discussing things and events totally outside a child's experience or comprehension, histories and geographies with long lists of questions concerning names, dates, and places, and grammars which were nothing more than compilations of rules. While one cannot fail to note the growing concern with making subject matter meaningful to children, he cannot also ignore the conspicuous failure to do so in these countless cases.

Bible reading as a subject for the elementary school. It seems evident that the principle of separation of church and state in education was increasingly accepted in constitutions, legislation, and court decisions toward the end of the nineteenth century. Involved in this, however, was the continuing problem of whether Bible reading in public schools violated this principle. The various opinions which vied for acceptance have already been outlined in Chapter 11. What actually happened in practice is what might well be expected given the variety of educational and religious conditions in the several states: there was considerable difference. Some courts ruled that the Bible was not sectarian instruction provided it was read without comment and students who objected were excused from taking part. Such decisions obviously reflected the feeling that nonsectarian religious teaching was essential in a school program and that Bible reading without comment did not violate the commitment to separation. Usually, the King James—or Protestant—version of the Bible was involved in such decisions. As can readily be seen, they merely reaffirmed the course decided upon in the last decades before the Civil War.

Other courts, however, held that reading the King James Bible—a sectarian version in the eyes of Catholics, Jews, and non-believers—violated freedom of conscience, was thereby unconstitutional, and should therefore be pro-hibited. Clearly, such decisions were a departure from traditional practice. One of the earliest and most important of them came in Ohio with respect to religious instruction in the Cincinnati public schools.[7] A group of tax-payers were bringing suit to enjoin the Cincinnati board of education from implementing a resolution prohibiting "religious instruction and the read-ing of religious books, including the Holy Bible. . . ." Citing the Northwest Ordinance in support of their case (see pp. 244-45), they argued that the public schools were not only permitted but also required to provide religious instruction.

Ohio's Supreme Court, however, pointed out that the defendants were really urging not that "religion" be taught but that the *"Christian* religion" be taught. This interpretation was held unconstitutional because it would establish Christianity as the law of the state. "United with government," the court maintained, "religion never rises above the merest superstition; united with religion, government never rises above the merest despotism; and all history shows us that the more widely and completely they are separated, the better it is for both." Obviously, when the court emphasized the neutrality of a government based on *human* experience, it was defining a *secular* basis for public education, a basis specifically neither antireligious nor irreligious, but upon which the several religions might pursue their own activities free from government interference.

This and similar decisions represented significant changes in policy. They clearly stated that any religious teaching and/or Bible reading in the public school was an infringement on the rights of conscience and thereby uncon-stitutional. Needless to say, this view by no means gained universal accept-ance in practice. In many places, Bible reading without comment from the King James version continued and was approved in the courts. In Penn-sylvania superintendents were given permission to use either the King James or the Douay version. There were several instances in New York and Minne-sota of Roman Catholic parochial schools being integrated into the public school systems of local communities and the nuns who taught in them being given leave to choose the version of the Bible to be studied. Doubtless, the Douay Bible was used in a number of such instances. Generally, the American

[7] *Board of Education* v. *Minor*, 23 Ohio 211 (1872).

people remained divided among the several positions. For some the practice was unconstitutional; for others it was not. While no clear-cut resolution in law or practice was reached during this period, there were definite moves to exclude all religious instruction and Bible reading from the schools and to relegate such teaching entirely to home and church.

The appearance of new methods. One might well assume that the new conceptions of method advanced after 1865 would have their effects in practice, and such was the case. Yet in viewing these effects, it should be remembered that such changes were slow in developing and were often introduced only after herculean efforts by some capable leader. Nevertheless, unmistakable signs of progress were apparent by the beginning of the twentieth century.

Object teaching, after the example of Pestalozzi, was certainly in evidence before 1850. Between 1809 and 1813 at Joseph Neef's school in Philadelphia lessons were taught almost completely orally. The surrounding environment of fields, gardens, streams, animals, and the like furnished the objects for a rich program in the languages, natural science, and mathematics. In spite of the fact that numerous New England educators took up similar ideas during the second quarter of the nineteenth century, it was largely through the work of Edward A. Sheldon at the Oswego State Normal School that the method became popularized. Diffusing out from Oswego, it was enthusiastically taught in other normal schools, such as New Jersey and Michigan, and served to enrich teaching in a multitude of schools. Yet, as more and more teachers were trained in object teaching, it rapidly took on a formalism of its own, and all too soon it assumed the proportions of a fad. From the traditional notion that everything could be learned by reading a textbook, far too many teachers now moved to the extreme that everything could be taught by object method. In many cases the true principles of Pestalozzi—of inducing learning through direct experience with objects—were obscured by strict, formal adherence to a sequence of steps. Nevertheless, even as a fad, object teaching presented a sharp challenge to time-honored notions of method.

Toward the end of the century object teaching began increasingly to give way before Herbartian principles. More and more, teachers began to organize lessons along the five formal steps of preparation, presentation, apperception, generalization, and application. The method enabled many teachers to go a long way toward providing instruction which was far more meaningful to students. On the other hand, formalism once again all too rapidly set in; and for every teacher who used the method creatively, there were probably ten who slavishly organized a lesson along Herbartian steps and rigidly refused to depart from them. It goes without saying that many of the latter used the method rather mechanically and with little understanding of its psychological bases. Yet, the Herbartians did go a step further in challenging the traditional formal approach. Their very concern with the problem of method was itself a good thing for teaching.

Of great interest toward the turn of the century were the educational experiments of numerous innovators. In laboratory schools and in individual school systems these innovators stimulated a sense of experimentalism in the realm of teaching which closely paralleled the practical experimentalism in other realms of American life. One of the most outstanding of these innovators was Francis W. Parker. Parker had taught and been a school principal even before he was twenty, and after service in the Civil War and travel abroad (during which he observed at firsthand the outgrowth of Pestalozzi's, Herbart's and Froebel's work), he became superintendent of schools at Quincy, Massachusetts, in 1875. Eight years later, he was made principal of the Cook County Normal School at Chicago. At Quincy Parker introduced many of the essentials of Pestalozzian method. Throughout the work of the schools functionalism became an important criterion. The geography of the local terrain stood more important than that of unknown, faraway lands. The solving of everyday problems in arithmetic stood more important than abstract principles and abstruse rules. Language, too, was seen as a tool for communication rather than as lifeless material for study and analysis. Arts and crafts were introduced, as well as elementary science. Individual children were seen as important, the traditional rigidity of the schoolroom gave way before the bustle of lively, intent, and occupied youngsters. When the usual criticisms that "children were not learning the three R's" were leveled, the Massachusetts Board of Education was persuaded to visit Quincy's schools, and their findings vindicated Parker. Quincy's youngsters actually stood ahead of the majority of Massachusetts schoolchildren. At the Cook County Normal School, Parker for sixteen years continued to develop and teach his method. Through his efforts and the philanthropy of Mrs. Emmons Blaine, the Francis W. Parker school was opened in 1901. Under Principal Flora J. Cooke, a former student of Parker, the school excelled as an experimental center of progressive education.

Very similar to the experimentation of Parker was the early school work of John Dewey. Largely through his efforts, The Laboratory School at the University of Chicago was founded in 1896 to implement his progressive ideas. Out of this early work came the *activity program* through which Dewey sought to train youngsters "in cooperative and mutually useful living." Self-expression, cooperation, activity, experimentation, construction, play, and contact with nature became the watchwords of the new school. In it educational principles with far-reaching consequences were tested exactly as in a physical or chemical laboratory, and findings were diffused in writings and through observation by teacher trainees.

Other significant developments came in the field of testing. The experiments of Joseph Meyer Rice, editor of the *Forum,* showed as early as 1897 that the amount of spelling learned by 30,000 children was not in direct proportion to the amount of time they spent studying the subject. While such early findings were widely ridiculed, they were the beginning of a measurement and evaluation movement which got well under way during the first two decades of the nineteenth century. Through the work of Binet, Simon, Cattell, Terman, Goddard, and Judd, intelligence testing made rapid headway in the United States. In the years after 1900 Edward Lee Thorndike and Charles Judd began to develop a vast scheme of scientific measurement and quantitative investigation into every phase of the school curriculum, and they and their co-workers quickly developed the first achievement tests in spelling, handwriting, arithmetic, composition, and other areas. Their work was so profoundly influential that by the end of World War I the scientific movement permeated every aspect of education.

A combination of the growing concern with the individual student implicit in the newer methods and these newer measurement devices led quickly to some attempt to tailor programs more effectively to diverse groups of students. The movement was known as *differentiation*. Thus, for example, some schools or school systems attempted to provide slightly different programs for retarded, average, and superior youngsters. Colonel Parker was interested in the idea at Quincy, while somewhat later, it was spelled out more specifically under Superintendent John Kennedy in the Batavia, New York, schools. Under the latter plan an assistant teacher was used to give special coaching to retarded children, thereby enabling them to achieve promotion with the average youngsters. Just before the turn of the century similar plans for parallel courses of study designed for groups of varying mental abilities were developed in Baltimore and in Santa Barbara, California. By the first decade of the twentieth century such parallel plans were becoming fairly common, as were special classes conducted for mentally superior or inferior groups of children.

Much more might be said about innovation during the years under consideration, especially in the latter decades. Such discussion, however important, should not obscure the fact that while this progress was becoming ever more common, the greater part of the nation did not feel its influences for another few decades. In the average American elementary school, rural or urban but especially rural, traditional methods persisted in great force, and rote or textbook learning was much the rule. While educational experimentation went on in large cities or in connection with new faculties of education, most teachers were content to continue with the methods under which they and their predecessors had learned. And while much of the groundwork for later progress was being laid, one might still look to the descriptions of Warren Burton in the 1830's to get a picture of many late nineteenth- or early twentieth-century American schools. Unfortunately, it remained far too adequate a description.

Curriculum and Method in the Secondary School

The expansion of secondary education. The American secondary school between 1865 and 1918 became increasingly responsible for two distinct groups of students—those who were preparing for college and those for whom high school was to be an educational terminus. Yet as one views secondary curricula during these years, the dominance of the college-preparatory program is clear. While clerical, business, and even industrial subjects assumed an ever more important place in the curriculum, on the whole it remained heavily weighted in favor of linguistic, verbal, and book-centered education. By 1918 the problem of reorganizing curricula to suit the overwhelming proportion of terminal students still loomed as a primary one for secondary educators.

Extensive evidence of the expansion of high school programs may be gleaned from John Elbert Stout's excellent study: *The Development of High-School Curricula in the North Central States from 1860 to 1918*.[8] While the study deals only with one region of the country, it seems possible on the basis of other more limited investigations to generalize on a number of Stout's conclusions. For example, it is clear that mathematics, English, foreign languages, some science, and even less of the social sciences comprised most secondary curricula during the 1860's. Of the more practical subjects from academy days, only bookkeeping seems to have held an important place. Forty years later, the situation had changed appreciably. In the study of English, grammar, composition, rhetoric, and literature appeared most often, while language and word analysis—important in 1860—had declined significantly by 1900. Of the mathematical studies, algebra, arithmetic, and geometry were by far the most frequent; while of the sciences, it was physiology, physical geography, chemistry, physics, botany, astronomy, and natural philosophy—a course now closely resembling physics. History and government were the social sciences most frequently offered; Latin and German were dominant among the languages. Mental and moral philosophy—traditionally strong in college curricula—were prominent in 1860, but they had practically vanished by 1900. Except for bookkeeping, commercial subjects were not significantly present until the turn of the century.

It was during the first two decades of the twentieth century—particularly after 1910—that many late nineteenth-century tendencies apparently ripened. By 1918 the broad outlines of the secondary curriculum had expanded to include mathematics, English, science, social studies, foreign languages, physical education, commercial subjects, and the fine and practical arts. The latter areas enjoyed a rapid increase between 1900 and 1918, with subjects like typewriting, stenography, bookkeeping, commercial law, domestic science, industrial arts, and manual training fairly common by 1918.

[8] (Chicago, University of Chicago, 1921).

Equally interesting, especially after 1900, were changes in the actual content of the subjects themselves. The influences of commercialism and industrialism appeared throughout the curriculum. Commercial and business arithmetic, for example, began to receive extensive attention in the mathematics curriculum. Textbook authors, although all too often unsuccessful, worked at bringing out the "practical phases" of their subjects, and a growing number of problems from the business world appeared. In many cases authors also made concerted attempts to break down traditional boundary lines between arithmetic, algebra, geometry, and trigonometry. Much of this apparent change, however, took the form of reorganization rather than of any fundamental revision of subject matter.

In the study of English, time-honored boundary lines were also attacked. One text announced that its purpose was "to unify the teaching of English in the high school." [9] The subject, its authors contended, embraced more than grammar, or composition, or literature; it was rather "a judicious combination of these three component parts." Courses in business and commercial English also frequently appeared as the demand grew for persons trained in the terminologies and forms of the business word. Although American literature began to receive increasing attention toward the end of the century, the traditional emphasis on English authors persisted.

In the realm of foreign languages, although the ancient tongues retained a central place in college-preparatory programs, French and German made headway against the foreboding outcries of classicists. In spite of considerable discussion concerning the streamlining and modernizing of methods, emphasis on grammar, technical analysis, and the reading of great classics continued to constitute the heart of language study—evidencing conservative resistance to growing demands for greater usefulness.

In the sciences the great proliferation of courses actually began to disturb some educators, and one notes numerous attempts to bring about unification. Thus, for example, a popular text in *First Year Science* [10] published in 1914 took pains to treat "all the subjects of elementary school science—physics, chemistry, meteorology, botany, zoology, astronomy, physiography, forestry, and agriculture" so that pupils might decide for themselves directions of their further study. Other books, it should be noted, rejected this position. With the rapid development of knowledge in the various sciences, a multitude of specialized treatments of one or another of the various fields also appeared. In general, separate courses in physics, biology, botany, chemistry, and geology remained the prevailing pattern. Needless to say, the desire to relate science teaching to the "things of everyday life" was widespread in all these areas.

Although traditional history courses continued to dominate the social

[9] A. R. Brubacher and Dorothy E. Snyder, *High School English, Books One and Two* (New York, Merrill, 1912).
[10] William H. Snyder, *First Year Science* (Boston, Allyn and Bacon, 1914).

science field, one notes the early beginnings of civics and problems courses in response to demands for "citizenship training." However, chronological treatments stressing political and military events remained in vogue, to the exclusion of social, economic, and cultural materials. Questions in textbooks and on examinations tended overwhelmingly to support this emphasis. Although the continuing development of nationalism encouraged the further growth of American history, concern with ancient and European history persisted. While subjects such as geography and government expanded slowly in scope and content, they continued to occupy secondary status.

The move toward practicality had its greatest effect, perhaps, in the evolution of the vocational subjects themselves. While manual training, industrial arts, and commercial education had early attempted to inculcate a kind of generalized training and competence, they now leaned toward specific preparation for positions in business and industry. Similarly, courses in domestic science developed more and more into opportunities for girls to build the actual skills necessary for family care and home management.

Rural and urban high schools. One of the most interesting conclusions of Stout's intensive study was that little outward difference appeared between urban and rural high school programs. Throughout the period under consideration, he noted that "neither the size of a school nor its location seems to have much influence except that schools in the larger centers of population offer a wider range of subjects." Commercial and industrial education, for example, was by no means confined to business and industrial localities. Agriculture was taught in urban as well as rural communities.

One might well ponder the reasons for this phenomenon. Of course, one factor which Stout did not consider was the quality of teaching; he took only the course listings from catalogs and bulletins. There seems little doubt that urban communities were often able to afford better teachers and better facilities because of their greater taxable wealth. On the other hand, although there was much talk in educational circles about "relating the high school to life," there was actually little of such relation. In a sense, people "knew" what a secondary education was, and they all too often "knew" it apart from the specific needs of their students and their communities. If, for example, contemporary educational thinking held the more practical subjects to be of great value, then they were included where a community sought to be progressive. The idea that some of these newer practical subjects might not be of particular benefit in a given community rarely dawned on innovators.

In view of this, one is not surprised to find secondary schools much alike wherever they appeared. As yet, they catered to a small percentage of the population, and they were much in the hands of the intellectuals, the educators, and the upper classes. That their instruction, in spite of major changes toward practicality, should remain apart from the everyday life of the community was not at all difficult to understand.

The differentiation of secondary curricula. As with the elementary school, another interesting development in the secondary curriculum was the growing adaptation of programs to the varying needs of students. Among the two broad groups of students served by the high school, there was an infinite variety of academic and vocational needs. With the tendency toward election in colleges, students preparing for higher education found that they could depart from formerly rigid classical preparatory curricula and exercise more choice among high school subjects. English and scientific programs, for example, vied increasingly with traditional Latin programs for the attention of college-bound students. Among the terminal students there was even greater differentiation of purposes. Any number of vocational aims hitherto deemed "unrespectable" for the secondary school now appeared as the bases for organizing new curricula.

In response to these efforts, one notes a rapidly increasing number of program designations, especially after 1910. Stout found in a survey of sixty schools between 1915 and 1918 that although a fourth still maintained only one program, over a fourth offered seven or more. Moreover, there was one school which offered nineteen separate curricula. While programs designated "college preparatory," "commercial," "English," "general," "manual training," "science," and "teacher's" appeared most frequently, Stout found seventy-seven separate curricula exclusive of two-year programs. Many of them reflected the growing vocational and industrial needs of the period: viz., "industrial arts," "engineering," "course in needle arts," "stenography," etc. Others, such as "domestic-science," "industrial course for girls," and "home economics" obviously reflected the attempt to cater to the specific purposes of female students.

The great number of public high schools in which two or more programs were offered attests to the strength of the comprehensive high school idea in the United States. It was by far the most popular form of secondary institution after the turn of the century.

Attempts at standardization. The increasing variety of acceptable high school programs along with the great diversity of college entrance requirements soon directed the interests of educators to the problem of accrediting in college admissions. Moreover, implicit in the problem of accrediting was the related problem of standardizing quality and course work. Beginning in 1870, when President Frieze of the state university recommended certifying the graduates of selected high schools for admission without examination, Michigan gradually laid the foundations of an accrediting plan. In 1873 the University of Indiana established a similar admissions policy for graduates of high schools certified by the state board of education. The practice was well received, and by 1900 it was employed by over forty state colleges and numerous other institutions.

The kind of cooperation stimulated by such arrangements was deemed highly beneficial to high schools and colleges alike, to say nothing of the advantages accruing to students. The attempt to formalize the lines of such cooperation and establish them on some sort of permanent basis led to the founding of several major standardizing associations at the end of the nineteenth century. In 1885, growing out of a series of conferences on college entrance requirements, the New England Association of Colleges and Preparatory Schools was formed for "the advancement of the case of liberal education by the promotion of interests common to colleges and preparatory schools." Seven years later, a similar organization—the Association of Colleges and Preparatory Schools of the Middle States and Maryland—was founded to serve that region. Regional associations of colleges and secondary schools in the north central and southern states were also established before 1900, and the picture was completed with the establishment of the Northwest Association of Secondary and Higher Schools in 1918.

Another institution of permanent value was the College Entrance Examination Board founded at the turn of the century through the efforts of Presidents Nicholas Murray Butler and Charles W. Eliot. Although established initially under the auspices of the Middle States Association, it soon became an independent organization and extended its scope well beyond the national limits of the United States. The efforts of the board undoubtedly enhanced the general movement to establish standard criteria for college entrance.

The work of the Committee of Ten has been discussed in Chapter 11; its importance in developing norms for the secondary curriculum was tremendous. The committee's work was carried forward in 1895 with the appointment of a Committee on College Entrance Requirements (also of the National Educational Association) "to study the question of college entrance requirements, for the purpose of harmonizing the relations between the secondary schools and the colleges." The fourteen resolutions which this latter committee reported in 1899 were widely accepted, and they served as a foundation for subsequent work by the Carnegie Foundation for the Advancement of Teaching in evaluating college standards and requirements for admission.

Methods in secondary schools. While one can report numerous experiments with teaching method in the elementary schools during this period, a comparable picture for secondary education cannot be drawn. It is true that laboratory methods in the sciences and practical arts were pushed with great vigor, especially after 1900. In the natural sciences the chemistry and physics laboratory in which students actually performed guided experiments gained a more established place in the curriculum. In manual training and industrial arts courses practical instruction in shop work stood as a regular part of the curriculum. Well-equipped rooms in which youngsters actually learned by performing specific tasks were built in many of the newer schools. Girls in stenography and typing classes actually took shorthand and typed on machines; other girls in domestic science classes actually cooked and sewed. At least in these senses, functional instruction moved forward.

Moreover, it must be acknowledged that the early studies of G. Stanley Hall and his associates on the developmental stages of adolescence revealed and organized much knowledge concerning the youngsters who were attending secondary schools. Pioneer curriculum thinkers used these materials as the bases for new recommendations regarding teaching in the secondary school. By and large, however, actual teaching closely resembled traditional college and university methods. The lecture and recitation, the exposition and memorization of texts, the use of the examination to measure symbolic understandings—all retained their former place in the secondary school. The curriculum remained inextricably tied to the college program, and it is not difficult to see how methods as well as content would remain very similar.

Curriculum and Method in Higher Education

The expansion of the course of study. In spite of numerous changes which occurred in the antebellum period, the year 1865 saw the classical languages, mathematics, and philosophy as still very much the heart of a liberal higher education. The newer subjects had gained, to be sure, but they had not yet challenged the supremacy of these primary three. The modern languages, for example, had secured a foothold in higher education; but their importance was slight when compared with the classical tongues. English, especially in the form of literature, had begun to assert itself increasingly at mid-century, especially as related to philosophy and the social sciences. While the sciences received much attention in educational meetings, their role also was slight. Chemistry, physics, zoology, and geology were taught, but only in elementary forms and in a few courses. The place of the social sciences was even less significant, and chairs of history, the most popular, were comparatively infrequent. Political economy and political science remained in their infancy as subjects. While it is true that there had been experiments with election and with alternate or parallel courses, scholars and intellectuals of the Civil War period were in general agreement that a liberal education contained the three primary requisites.

After 1870, however, and even more rapidly after 1910, a number of critical changes came about in this curriculum. A principal difference came in the widening of the traditional conception of liberal education to include such new studies as English, the modern languages, the natural sciences, and the social sciences. Much of this change was embodied in the movement to include "practical" sciences and laboratory subjects on a par with the "cultural" subjects. The many obvious applications of scientific and technical knowledge in business and industry as well as the vast increase in scientific knowledge lent great support to the scientific studies in their bid for recognition. Slowly the stature of scientific departments grew. A similar expansion took place in the social sciences. The chairs of history which had been scarce during the 1870's were common by 1900 and virtually universal by 1920. Political science and economics were rapidly gaining footholds by 1900, and sociology was strongly bidding for entrance. Psychology, traditionally one phase of the study of philosophy, was profiting from the pioneering experiments of Wundt and his students, and it too was making a powerful demand for independent recognition. The functional uses of English and the modern foreign languages were also increasingly urged as these subjects too were more frequently acknowledged. Finally, physical education, building on roots going all the way back to the manual labor schools of the 1830's, was also making its claim for time in the college program.

The obvious outcome of this movement was the tremendous multiplication of course offerings in individual institutions. This is well illustrated by any simple tallying of such courses in representative liberal arts colleges between 1900 and 1920. Even a cursory glance reveals a trebling or even a quadrupling of courses in many such schools.

The kinds of courses involved in this great expansion also give evidence of two other significant changes. First, it seems clear that the traditional disciplinary notion began to give way to the conception that it is important to know the actual content of the materials studied. The importance of physics, for instance, lay not in its ability generally to strengthen this or that faculty of the mind but rather to impart useful knowledge of physics. More and more, studies were required to justify their retention on the basis of direct rather than generalized value. Second, it seems obvious that the traditional religious orientation of the college curriculum continued to yield to a growing secularism. The aim of the new curriculum was to prepare mature, responsible citizens and individuals rather than to nurture Christian loyalties. This is not to imply that the college was no longer concerned with character. Rather, it indicated a growing awareness that character development was bound up with an individual's ability to build his own livelihood, to enrich his own personality, and to contribute to his own community. To enhance an individual's ability to do these things was to nurture character.

The growth of the elective system. Another obvious corollary of this proliferation of courses lay in the fact that no student could hope adequately to master all areas of knowledge. Moreover, in the complex society of industrial America a great variety of aims and purposes were present among college students. When these facts were joined with the growing knowledge of the differing capacities, capabilities, and interests of youngsters, they presented for some an overwhelming argument in favor of the elective system.

A survey of practices at the turn of the century reveals that the continuum of acceptance of the elective system in American colleges was complete. At one end was Harvard College under the presidency of Eliot. There, a student might receive a bachelor's degree for virtually an entire program of elective work. Contrary to popular criticism, it must be pointed out that the system did involve considerable advisement from the faculty in the building of programs. On the other hand, students were given the greatest possible freedom on the grounds that only then would resulting curricula be fully suited to individual purposes. At the other end of the continuum was the group of colleges where virtually the complete four years of work was prescribed and uniform for everyone. By far the most common pattern, however, was for an institution to fall somewhere between the two extremes. As the popularity of the elective system spread, most colleges made some adjustment in their programs. A widely used plan was to prescribe a certain portion of the curriculum and then to allow election for the remainder, usually in the senior year. In this way it was thought students could be given the fundamentals of a liberal education and at the same time allowed to prepare for work along more specific lines.

It is extremely interesting to note that the granting of elective privileges, while they undoubtedly provided some with the opportunity of an easy, uncoordinated, and purposeless bachelor's program, did not bear out the dismal fears of conservatives. For example, the number of students who availed themselves of the opportunity to give up the classics in their programs varied considerably from year to year. At Harvard 8 percent abandoned them in 1889, and the number rose to 47 percent in 1898. A year later, however, it was down to 15 percent and in 1900 up to 45 percent again. Similar variations were present in the percentages who dropped mathematics, although the fluctuation was by no means as great. It is also interesting to note that the intense specialization predicted did not materialize to the alarming degree prophesied. For example, in 1886 only 13 percent of the students, after their freshman year, took more than half of their work in one department. In 1900 it was only 28 percent. On the contrary, the number of students who actually built purposeful, coordinated programs was encouragingly high. Even in light of these figures, however, many educators by the time of World War I were deeply disturbed by the progress of the elective system. Harvard had moved to the plan of program concentration, and other institutions had moved to the major-minor system. In the discontent with the fact that election guaranteed no common education for all lay the roots of the general education movement.

Methods of teaching in colleges and universities. Although a long traditionalism pervaded the area of methods in the college and university, certain changes began to gain ground during the years in question. In the study of languages, particularly the classics, there was comparatively little change. Time-honored procedures continued with little other excuse than the fact that they were time-honored, and it is interesting to note that criticism of these methods came from the pro-Classicists as well as the anti-Classicists. One exception to this was the study of English, with its increasing accent on literature. Formerly, grammar and rhetoric—the ability to analyze the structure of language and speak it well—were the heart of English study. Now, a growing number of English instructors turned to the great writings of the English language as their material of instruction. The study of English soon took on a richness and vitality which it had not formerly possessed.

It was in the sciences, however, that the most significant changes occurred. When the sciences first entered the curriculum, most teaching had been in the form of lectures. Students rarely observed the phenomena which the lecturer described unless they either saw the one or two demonstration experiments performed in class or worked out their own experiments outside the classroom. In the last decades of the nineteenth century chemistry and physics laboratories rapidly became standard equipment in institutions where the subjects were taught. More and more experimental procedures were undertaken by the student himself, and work in the laboratory became a definite part of the course. In geology the field trip assumed a primary place. In the teaching of agriculture it was the use of the demonstration farm that actually revolutionized agricultural instruction. In the early years agricultural colleges had enjoyed comparatively little interest from the farmers they served. Those who attended agriculture classes usually heard lectures about subjects which had little direct relation to the actual business of farming. Now, the radical change of technique created widespread interest in the work of these institutions. Through demonstration farms, agriculture students learned the techniques which were to revolutionize American agriculture, and state A. and M. colleges quickly became centers of progressive scientific thought.

Granted these changes, however, one must not overestimate their actual scope. The overwhelming majority of instructors, as in secondary institutions, remained committed to the lecture methods used by their predecessors. For every one enthusiast of the German university who introduced the seminar method, there were a hundred who continued to analyze texts in class. While enthusiasm may be justified over the progress in given places, one should not ignore the over-all picture in assessing the adoption of newer methods.

THE TEACHER AND TEACHER EDUCATION

By 1900 American society had heaped vast responsibilities on its teachers. Yet, although modest beginnings were in evidence, this same society had offered little in the way of equipment or compensation. To be sure, teacher education facilities were rapidly growing. On the other hand, an overwhelming number of teachers had no professional training whatever. One could point to gradually rising pay scales. Nevertheless, teachers' salaries were woefully below professional salaries, and often they were below those of tradesmen. Orators spoke of the tremendous role of the teacher in the community; yet, teachers were often granted little status and many times supervised more rigidly than the children they taught.

In spite of this continuing paradox, however, one senses throughout this period the efforts of a profession to better its work in the face of tremendous obstacles. Memoirs of teachers reveal a devotion which easily overcame the many drawbacks of the teacher's role. The efforts of the profession to establish facilities to educate itself are well nigh remarkable considering the opposition it encountered. One notes continuing self-pressure for high standards, more qualified personnel, and more adequate compensation and working conditions. One is even more impressed with the effort to organize for the struggle to obtain these things. Throughout it all, one senses that the teaching group remained singularly loyal and singularly unselfish in the face of opposition and adversity. As in every paradox, there was a dark side and a bright side, and one is impressed with the fact that the bright side faced toward the future.

The Development of Teacher Education

In spite of the existence of numerous normal schools by 1860, one cannot fail to realize immediately their glaring inadequacies. Their instruction was almost entirely on the secondary level and was closely similar to that given in contemporary academies and high schools. There were few entrance qualifications, and few were denied admission. Most entering students had only the elements of a district-school education to their academic credit. The semesters were short, and the whole normal course was usually only one or two years in length. Even so, the great majority of students attended for only part of the course—many for only a few weeks. The courses themselves were often simply reviews of elementary school subjects with some emphasis on teaching problems. Texts such as Orville Taylor's *The District School,* Samuel Hall's *Lectures on Schoolkeeping,* and Jacob Abbott's *The Teacher: Or Moral Influences Employed in the Instruction and Government of the Young* continued in wide use. As one author has remarked, the institutions generally were more important for what they were to become than for what they were.

The growth of the normal school idea. That this last statement was true is illustrated by the development of the normal school just before 1900. In every state of the Union there were forces similar to those which battled for the first normal schools in Massachusetts and New York. In the great majority of them the attempt was successful. By 1900, although all states had not yet established state normal schools (Ohio was a notable exception), all of the forty-five then in the Union had public normal schools of one sort or another. Probably the highest general standards were maintained in Massachusetts, where students were required to have completed high school or an equivalent education. The general two-year course for elementary school teachers embraced: (1) history of education, psychology, principles of education, general methods of instruction, school organization, and the laws of Massachusetts; (2) methods of teaching English, mathematics, science, vocal music, physical culture, and manual training; and (3) observation in the model school and in other public schools. The Bridgewater school had in addition a four-year course directed primarily toward high school teachers and potential principals. The additional subject matter was academic material of a more traditional variety. Normal schools in other states, while they tended to be similar to those of Massachusetts, evidenced considerable diversity. Most of them accepted entering students with two years of high school, and the courses themselves varied from one to three years as a rule, thereby providing a total of four years beyond elementary school for many teacher trainees.

Most of the graduates of these normal schools went into elementary school work. One might look with pride at the 167 public normal schools reported in 1898 and predict a great lessening of the critical supply problem. Such was by no means the case. Massachusetts, for example, with the third largest number of public normal schools at the turn of the century, reported during the school year 1897–1898 that only 38.5 percent of the teachers in its public schools had received normal school instruction and that only 33.5 percent had graduated from a normal school course. In most places in the United States the figure was infinitely smaller. The remaining group may have included some with college training or other kinds of academic preparation. It seems safe to assume that the overwhelming majority were appointed to teaching with little regard for their academic or professional training.

The evolution of the teachers college. The growth of normal schools by no means ceased in 1900. If anything, it continued rapidly. Yet in view of later developments, it is of interest to turn attention to one particular phase in the growth of the normal school—the beginnings of its development into the teachers college. A number of factors were involved in the beginnings of this movement. The increasing "respectability" of education growing out of its entrance into university programs was undoubtedly one. Another lay in the rapid increase in high school graduates after 1890. Still another came as an increasing number of persons gave attention to the *quality* as well as the quantity of school facilities. During the early establishment of universal education communities pressed for teachers were prone to assume the attitude that any teacher was better than none at all. In the early staffing of schools it was often more important to secure a teacher of any kind in order simply to get the school moving. This began to change as school systems became more secure, and boards of education turned attention to the kind of education they were providing. Yet another factor was the rapidly growing demand for high school teachers possessed of a bachelor's degree.

One stimulus for this new movement was the growth of the normal school curriculum itself. Like the public school systems they served, normal schools had comparatively rude beginnings. As the task of teacher training progressed, there was a vast extension in the course offerings of the typical institution—to the point where some were actually offering four-year curricula by 1900. A final factor lay in the rise of accrediting associations. Increasing attention was given through these bodies to the quality of public school instruction, and often the problem of teacher education was paramount as a criterion of instructional quality. It is not difficult to see where lack of accreditation would lead many a reluctant school board to seek qualified, professionally trained personnel in place of lower-salaried untrained teachers.

All of these factors stimulated the growth of college-level teacher training. Gradually, institutions which had moved in the direction of four-year curricula —often without much planning—began to reorganize these offerings according to some sort of design. The inclusion of many courses with no direct application to the work of teaching gave rise to the conception that the teacher, like other professionals, had to be liberally educated. In other words, the kind of *person* the teacher was mattered quite as much as his professional competence. Actually, although the state normal school at Albany, N. Y., was reorganized as a teachers college in 1890, the first normal school to become a teachers college in the modern sense was the Michigan State Normal College at Ypsilanti. In order to recognize the fact that the school was providing instruction on the college level, the Michigan legislature in 1897 designated it a Normal College. Under subsequent action of the legislature in 1903, the state Board of Education organized courses at the college leading to the B. A. degree, and the first such degree was granted in 1905. While the progress of the movement was slow, it was also definite. In 1913 there were only nine such colleges, but by 1920 there were forty-six. The number thereafter grew quickly.

University instruction in education. Another interesting development in teacher training was the growth of the university department of education. As has been pointed out in Chapter 8, such work was begun well before the Civil War. Nevertheless, it received its principal stimulus from the demand for college- and university-trained high school teachers after 1865. The first permanent university chair of education seems to have been established at the University of Iowa in 1873. Actually, the chair developed out of the specific provision for a normal department made in the founding legislation of the university. Iowa built on the beginning to the establishment of a school of education in 1907. With the establishment of a permanent Chair of the Science and Art of Teaching at the University of Michigan in 1879, the idea of university instruction began to move forward; and increasingly institutions created similar chairs or departments to attract potential secondary teachers or candidates for principalships. The actual establishment of such chairs literally mushroomed after 1890, and the number jumped from a mere handful in that year to almost 250 at the turn of the century. Liberal arts colleges also took on the work of teacher training, and by the turn of the century, over one fourth of them were offering regular courses in education.

Needless to say, the founding of these chairs was profoundly important in raising the stature of education as a subject for serious academic consideration. The movement was not, however, without its opponents. Professors of education were often looked down upon by their colleagues in the older disciplines. As is understandable, the feeling was strong that pedagogy was traditionally a secondary school subject and had no place in higher education. Others criticized the new study for its lack of a well-defined body of content. In spite of this resistance, the benefits were apparent, and many who had formerly refused to deem teacher training a serious problem were now far more inclined to view it with concern.

Other agencies of teacher education.   While normal schools, teachers colleges, and university departments of education increasingly took over the education of teachers, one should not ignore numerous other agencies of considerable import. The teachers institute, for example, continued to grow after the Civil War much along the original Massachusetts pattern. In many states it remained the prime, if not the only, means of educating rural teachers. Another educational arrangement which grew in prominence was the university summer session. Its great advantage was the contact it offered with the faculties and facilities of major colleges and universities. Nevertheless, it drew much criticism on the grounds that teachers needed their vacations for social and intellectual recreation. A third development was the university extension. Once again, its advantages centered largely in contact with regular faculty members of higher institutions. On the other hand, critics maintained that standards were low in these classes, that library facilities were necessarily inadequate, and the instruction often had little direct application to teaching.

Education as a subject of study.   One significant change which has been alluded to above was the growth of a serious academic discipline called education. As one might anticipate, the first developments in this field came in the areas most closely related to traditional subjects. Thus, for example, study of the philosophy of education or the history of education was considered "respectable" by scholars earlier than the study of methods or materials of teaching. These years witnessed genuinely pioneering work in the history and philosophy of education. William Payne, B. A. Hinsdale, Paul Monroe, Ellwood P. Cubberley, Henry Suzzallo, and Elmer Ellsworth Brown accomplished a great deal of their study and writing before 1918, while John Dewey, William C. Bagley, Nicholas Murray Butler, and William H. Kilpatrick were during the same period laying the foundations of a new philosophy of education. As psychology itself broke away from philosophy and was established as an academic discipline, so did educational psychology under the leadership of E. L. Thorndike, James McKeen Cattell, and others begin to achieve stature in the university. With the beginning of graduate study of education, particularly at Teachers College, Columbia University, the University of Chicago, and Stanford University, a new body of scholars began to apply the latest scientific techniques and methods to the processes and materials of education; and among them, they began to build the foundations of a new disciplined study of the field.

The Beginnings of Improved Teaching Conditions

Teacher certification. In response to concerted and frequent demands for some sort of certification for teachers, there was considerable improvement of procedures and criteria. The principal phase of this movement, perhaps, was the tendency to centralize certification in the hands of larger administrative units. Toward the end of the century the increasing centralization of educational control began to affect traditional local autonomy, and by 1911 a majority of the states had passed certification laws. In that year fifteen had arrangements whereby the state issued all certificates, two had arrangements whereby the state prescribed rules and examinations, but county authorities issued some certificates, while ten had arrangements where the state made regulations and examination questions with the county as administrative agent and certifying authority. Ten years later, there were twenty-six states in the first category, seven in the second, and ten in the third. Clearly, local control of certification was rapidly being replaced by state authority.

Another phase of this moment involved the general upgrading of requirements and prerequisites for certification. During the decades following the Civil War, the most general manifestation of this movement was an increase in the number of students granted teaching certificates on the basis of normal school diplomas in lieu of examinations. During the first decade of the twentieth century a number of states began to require high school graduation for an elementary school teaching certificate. Indiana passed legislation to this effect in 1907, and Utah followed suit in 1911. Other states began gradually to increase the number of years of secondary instruction required from one to two, three, or four. By 1921 four states already required high school graduation and some professional training of their teachers; fourteen states required four years of secondary school but made no stipulation concerning professional training; and the remaining thirty made no definite academic requirements. The pattern of increasing certification requirements, however, had been definitely set, and the decade following 1921 witnessed continuing movement in this direction.

Brief mention should be made of special requirements in education or pedagogy courses as part of the certification requirements. As the study of education came into its own, more and more states saw it as necessary to the training of a teacher. By 1910 more than three-quarters of the states mentioned education courses in the requirements of one or more certificates. Others had elaborated regular programs of required education courses such as history of education, principles of teaching, educational psychology, school law, theory and practice of teaching, etc. Here, too, the pattern had definitely been set, and succeeding decades saw primarily its further elaboration.

Teacher salaries. It will be remembered that an important area of contention for those interested in raising the status of the profession was the salary question. It was urged on many sides that the profession would never attract the personnel needed to accomplish its momentous tasks unless adequate compensation could be provided. Studies reveal that although some progress was made between the years 1865 and 1920, much remained to be desired.

W. Randolph Burgess' investigation of school costs provides excellent data on the question. In spite of fluctuations over short periods of time, his figures show a rather general increase in the actual wages of teachers between 1865 and 1918. They also reveal that women's salaries tended to increase more rapidly than men's, thereby lessening somewhat the traditional distance between male and female salaries. As might be expected, traditional differences between urban and rural salaries persisted.

Table 5—Average Weekly Salaries of Teachers, 1865–1918 [11]

	Rural		Urban	
	Men	Women	Men	Women
1865	$ 9.09	$ 5.99	$23.15	$ 8.57
1870	10.88	7.53	35.42	11.88
1875	11.46	8.00	36.63	12.69
1880	9.73	7.46	31.36	12.20
1885	10.95	8.23	33.15	13.24
1890	11.30	8.55	32.62	13.16
1895	11.70	8.91	31.63	13.40
1900	12.13	8.93	31.54	13.88
1905	14.39	10.15	33.79	14.86
1910	17.11	12.15	36.42	17.38
1915	18.61	13.63	37.15	21.06
1918	20.75	14.35	40.06	23.90

It is also interesting to note that these actual increases in compensation were by and large real increases. A comparison of teachers' wages with the cost of living reveals that while the latter figure increased less than 30 percent between 1865 and 1915, salaries increased two- and threefold. After 1915, however, with the sharp inflation set off by the war, the situation reversed, with costs rising far more rapidly than salaries.

Comparison of trends in teachers' salaries with trends in the wages of laborers and artisans is also of interest. Burgess found that although the former had tended to increase more rapidly between 1865 and 1915 than the latter,

[11] W. Randolph Burgess, Trends of School Costs (New York, Russell Sage Foundation, 1920), pp. 32–33.

this trend, too, had been reversed during the war, when artisan and laboring wages shot forward while teacher salaries remained fairly constant. In looking at his statistics, Burgess noted that while requirements of training for artisans had remained fairly constant since 1865, requirements for the urban teacher had increased many fold. Yet, he found that the reward of the teacher had advanced at about the same rate as that of the artisan. In light of this, he found the financial position of the latter "much less desirable."

Pensions and retirement provisions. Closely related to the salary problem was that of pensions and retirement. Teachers' salaries in that period were not such as to allow extensive savings for retirement. Little, however, seems to have been done before 1869—a fact which is entirely understandable in view of the strong individualism of the period. Most people, including teachers, believed that provision for old age or retirement was an individual problem and that if one was unable to make such provision, it was his own misfortune. It seems, however, that it was necessary several times during the year 1869 to circulate requests for contributions to the burial funds of New York City teachers who had died without making such provision. The collections led to the formation of the New York City Teachers Mutual Life Assurance Association—an informal agency to provide for death benefits to teachers through voluntary contributions at irregular intervals. Other cities soon followed suit with similarly informal organizations to provide death and sick benefits. Some even moved to retirement systems. It was not long before public arrangements were made for such benefits, and between 1905 and 1914 sixty-five cities established public retirement plans. Some states, too, moved toward state-wide retirement schemes, but the movement was slow. By 1910 only four states—Maryland, New Jersey, Rhode Island, and Virginia—had so moved. Clearly, the local movement was to retain the greater vitality for some time to come.

Teacher tenure. A brief word should also be devoted to the problem of teacher tenure so closely related to economic problems. As was brought out in Chapter 8, the tradition in this respect was one of unlimited freedom for local boards of education to hire and fire personnel who had met what meager state requirements were in existence. Even the latter were all too often ignored. Toward the turn of the century, however, and especially in the several teachers associations, it was increasingly urged that only as teachers received some sort of tenure would professional status be enhanced. At least two reasons were cited for this argument: first, only with tenure would teachers feel reasonably free of pressures and interests in the community; and second, only with some sort of tenure arrangement would qualified persons feel the security to make teaching their life's work. Once again, however, individualism was strong. Local boards complained that their hands would be tied by such legislation and sought to assert the doctrine that free competition in hiring and firing would bring the best quality to teaching.

In the face of considerable opposition, there was a slow and steady development of state tenure legislation before 1918. Seven states and the District of Columbia had acted by that time. The most distinguishing feature of the legislation seems to have been its loose organization and wording. Generally, it provided for tenure for teachers as long as good service and behavior were offered. As a rule, however, inadequate service and behavior were so loosely defined that considerable independence still remained with local authorities. Once again, the legislation was extremely important for the fact that it introduced the concept of tenure into teacher affairs, thereby providing a foundation on which to build in later years.

Professional Organization

Many of the early school reformers had pointed time and again to the need for strong professional organizations of teachers to secure professional ends. The period between 1865 and 1918 is marked by a steady growth of teacher organizations of various kinds; yet one is impressed by the fact that as of 1918, teachers still had no one powerful professional organization which could speak out on matters of importance.

The National Teachers Association which had been founded in 1857 became the National Educational Association in 1870; and sixteen years later, it was incorporated under the laws of the District of Columbia. In 1906 the organization became the National Education Association of the United States by special act of Congress. In terms of the organization's influence and scope during the present period, it is easy to overestimate its effect during the last decades of the nineteenth century. Its membership between 1870 and 1900 varied considerably—never reaching 15,000 and falling as low as 625 in 1885. For much of this period the organization was in financial difficulty or debt, and at least once during the 1880's, it was necessary to induce a patron to make up certain deficits.

Given these facts, however, it also becomes easy to underestimate the effect of the group. In spite of changing membership, one notes that some of the most influential men in American education used the organization as a sounding board for new ideas between 1870 and 1900. Such distinguished names as Francis W. Parker, William T. Harris, E. E. Brown, Henry Barnard, Susan Blow, Charles DeGarmo, Nicholas Murray Butler, Charles W. Eliot, William Rainey Harper, Charles McMurry and Frank McMurry—college presidents, school superintendents, professors of education, and classroom teachers—all played an active role in the conventions and affairs of the association. The proceedings of the NEA during the years in question furnish a superb entree into the latest thought and the most significant educational controversies of the period. In other words, even though the organization had comparatively little effect, perhaps, on legislatures or boards of education, it was highly instrumental in aiding the development of a self-conscious profession with a philosophy and a program of its own.

The period is also marked by the growth of state and local teachers associations. The former, gradually increasing their membership, were able to hire paid executive secretaries and to undertake numerous activities for the improvement of teaching. As for local associations, the establishment of well over 100 individual ones is reported between the years 1870 and 1920. Although many were not permanent, they too dealt with immediate problems of teaching and teachers and enabled members to exchange ideas and practices to their mutual benefit. Social and cultural activities often rounded out the professional programs of local associations.

Finally, although it was organized at the very end of the period under discussion, one might take note of the founding of the American Federation of Teachers. A significant body of American educators sincerely felt that the National Education Association with its grouping together of teachers and administrators could never possibly play a militant role for the improvement of American education. Only, they felt, as educators allied themselves with labor organizations and other powerful groups could teachers really fulfill their purposes. Accordingly, the American Federation of Teachers was organized in April 1916, and it affiliated with the American Federation of Labor a month later. Previously, there had been a small number of local unions, but now they merged into one organization. Nine such locals gave the new organization a membership of 2,800 teachers in 1916.

ISSUES FOR STUDY AND DISCUSSION

1. In spite of the antipathy they drew from antebellum educational reformers, private schools continued to increase after 1865. What are some of the important values these schools have served in American life? What have been some of their principal shortcomings? Do the values outweigh the shortcomings in your mind?

2. In what ways was the "G. I. Bill of Rights" of 1944 a continuation of traditional federal policy with respect to education? In what ways was it a reversal?

3. Between 1857, when it was organized, and 1918 the NEA enrolled only a small percentage of America's teachers. What factors do you think influenced most teachers not to affiliate with their national professional organization? Are these factors operative today?

4. Compare the relation between teachers' salaries and other professional and trade salaries today with the same relation in the period 1900–1920. What conclusions do you draw?

5. The late 1940's saw a rapid growth in the number of local citizens' organizations concerned with developing more effective school programs and activities. What does this mean for the strong tradition of state control so firmly established by 1918?

SUGGESTIONS FOR FURTHER READING

Beale, Howard K., *A History of Freedom of Teaching in American Schools,* New York, Scribner, 1941.

Bond, Horace Mann, *The Education of the Negro in the American Social Order,* New York, Prentice-Hall, 1934.

Bunker, Frank Forest, *The Junior High School Movement—Its Beginnings,* Washington, D. C., W. F. Roberts, 1935.

Burgess, W. Randolph, *Trends of School Costs,* New York, Russell Sage Foundation, 1920.

Burns, James A., *The Growth and Development of the Catholic School System in the United States,* New York, Benziger, 1912.

Butler, Nicholas Murray (ed.), *Education in the United States,* Albany, J. B. Lyon, 1900, 2 vols.

Dearborn, Ned H., *The Oswego Movement in American Education,* New York, Teachers College, Columbia University, 1925.

Ditzion, Sidney, *Arsenals of a Democratic Culture,* Chicago, American Library Association, 1947.

Elsbree, Willard S., *The American Teacher,* New York, American Book, 1939.

Ensign, Forest C., *Compulsory School Attendance and Child Labor,* Iowa City, Iowa, Athens Press, 1921.

Flexner, Abraham, *The American College, A Criticism,* New York, Appleton-Century, 1908.

Harper, Charles A., *A Century of Public Teacher Education,* Washington, D. C., National Education Association, 1939.

James, Henry, *Charles W. Eliot,* Boston, Houghton, 1930, 2 vols.

Kandel, Isaac L. (ed.), *Twenty-Five Years of American Education,* New York, Macmillan, 1924.

Knight, Edgar W., *Fifty Years of American Education,* New York, Ronald, 1952.

———, *Public Education in the South,* Boston, Ginn, 1922.

Koos, Leonard V., *The Junior College Movement,* Boston, Ginn, 1925.

Leidecker, Kurt F., *Yankee Teacher: The Life of William Torrey Harris,* New York, Philosophical Library, 1946.

Pangburn, Jessie M., *The Evolution of the American Teachers College,* New York, Teachers College, Columbia University, 1932.

Payne, Bruce Ryburn, *Public Elementary School Curricula,* New York, Silver, Burdett, 1905.

Pierce, Paul Revere, *The Origin and Development of the Public School Principalship,* Chicago, University of Chicago Press, 1935.

Rice, J. M., *The Public-School System of the United States,* New York, Century, 1893.

Stout, John Elbert, *The Development of High-School Curricula in the North Central States from 1860 to 1918,* Chicago, University of Chicago, 1921.

Todd, Lewis Paul, *Wartime Relations of the Federal Government and the Public Schools, 1917–1918,* New York, Teachers College, Columbia University, 1945.

Woody, Thomas, *A History of Women's Education in the United States,* New York, Science Press, 1929, 2 vols.

The serial publications mentioned in the note to the bibliography following Chapter 11 are useful, as are the many state histories of education and histories of individual academic institutions.

PART 4

AMERICAN EDUCATION IN THE CONTEMPORARY WORLD

WORLD

(1918-Mid-Century)

13

THE INCREASING TEMPO
OF SOCIAL CHANGE

AMERICA AFTER World War I was like a strong adolescent boy on the verge of maturity. He had demonstrated vast power, economically, politically, and militarily. His armies had helped to conquer one of the greatest nations of Western Europe. His power was undoubtedly adult. But like any adolescent, his mind was often childish, often confused. In an increasingly interdependent world, many Americans preached isolationism. Others sought to preserve high tariff walls between nations whose economies were more and more tied together. Still others sought to preserve the spirit of the small entrepreneur in an economic world of giant corporations and cartels. By and large, the transition was from a childhood of agrarianism to an adulthood of industrialism, and more than anything else, this painful transition reflected the spirit of the age.

In the economic realm, production figures which twenty years before would have gone "off the graph" became accepted standards. American technology led the world and American "know-how" became legend. Americans ate better, dressed better, and lived better than had any of their predecessors or contemporaries in history. Yet, the upheaval of all of this was the greatest challenge to contemporary America. Contradictions in this economic system were glaring. Literally, within potential abundance there was starvation. In 1929, growing out of a variety of causes, the worst depression in modern times struck America and quickly spread to the corners of the earth. Millions were out of work; agriculture and industry came to a standstill.

Within the context of the depression, the 1930's saw greater and deeper changes in American life than in any other period in history. Organized labor, having increased its numbers and strength slowly during the past half

461

century, now mushroomed into power under the stimulus of the Wagner Labor Relations Act. Under the Roosevelt administrations the whole political face of America was reshaped as the government moved slowly toward a welfare conception of the state. The range of local, state, and federal services increased sharply, and whereas in 1930 just over $10 billion were spent on all kinds of government services, this figure had risen to $23 billion by 1941. A people who had traditionally argued that any government which governed least governed best now turned to their government for aid and succor in times of economic distress.

Changes on the world scene were no less disturbing. Powerful totalitarian nations began to recast the political structure of Europe, bringing to the fore the antidemocratic philosophies of fascism and communism. As much as Americans attempted to avoid the clash of these giants, they were inextricably involved in the struggle. World War II, frought at an alarming cost of lives and materials, altered the complete power structure of the Western world and left two great nations: the Soviet Union and the United States. Much against their will, the American people were thrust into an uneasy seat—that of leading half the world. Equally disturbing to them was the tremendous appeal of communism all over the world. Traditionally, the underprivileged and depressed peoples of the earth had looked to America for leadership and haven. Now Americans all too often were cast as "imperialists," "exploiters," or "reactionaries." Much of this undoubtedly was the result of skillful Communist propaganda. Much of it also stemmed from ultra-nationalist movements in the underdeveloped areas of the world. Some of it, to be sure, resulted from the acts and attitudes of America herself.

This uneasy role of world leadership, coupled with the critiques of American democracy inherent in communism and fascism, led many Americans to take stock of their own situation. Increasingly, they came to realize that there was much to be done. In the area of race relations the role of the Negro citizen was scrutinized with an eye to correcting time-honored prejudices and inequalities. Nationality and religious groups which had traditionally been discriminated against in social and economic life moved more and more toward equality. In relations between the sexes one also noted a considerable drive toward equality. In the realm of social class, too, Americans gradually became aware of the gulf between idea and reality in the meaning of their democracy.

Thus, the middle of the twentieth century saw America facing the greatest challenges of her history. As Franklin D. Roosevelt had so lucidly expressed it, this generation had a rendezvous with destiny. The problem was clear—whether democratic civilization as the West had known it could preserve its traditional freedoms and moral commitments while adjusting to the new demands of industrial life. Cast in the system of the great historian, Arnold Toynbee, the question was one of whether or not Western civilization—with

America as part of it—could meet the challenge of the age. While no one could predict the answer with certainty, one thing did seem clear: that education as a social force would play a major part in the ultimate decision.

THE AMERICAN ECONOMIC GIANT

The Continuing Increase in Production

The continuing perfection and application of a variety of techniques—among them the use of mass production, interchangeable parts, and new forms of energy and control—led to the steady growth of American industry and production after 1918. With minor fluctuations and variations, the story was one of rising industrial output and diminishing hours of labor. The following chart, taken from a survey of the Twentieth Century Fund during the middle 1940's, reveals this trend: [1]

	Employed workers	Average weekly hours worked	Net output per man-hour 1940 prices	Total national income in 1940 dollars
	(in millions)		(in cents)	(in billions)
1920	41.8	51.9	43.1	48.6
1930	45.0	47.2	52.3	57.8
1940	46.9	43.0	74.0	77.6
1944	63.2	46.7	79.3	121.7

To be sure, this table ignores the dips in production which came during the height of the depression in the 1930's. Nonetheless, it clearly indicates the extent to which technology helped to produce more income with each man-hour. The national income more than doubled between 1920 and 1944, increasing by a third between 1930 and 1940 alone. Moreover, the wartime effort actually brought a 55 percent increase in the total output of goods and services between the years 1940 and 1944. Needless to say, this represented a near fantastic accomplishment which put American production far out in front of any other nation in the world, and in many cases far out in front of the entire remainder of the world. Instead of the sharp decline predicted by many for the post-war years, the expansion continued, with the national income rising from $180 billion in 1946 to $239 billion in 1950.

What is perhaps even more startling is that study after study revealed these production figures to be only a portion of the nation's total capacity. As early as 1921, a group of engineers under the leadership of Herbert Hoover undertook a comprehensive study of American economic efficiency. Their report, entitled *Waste in Industry,* found the American economy only 50

[1] J. Frederic Dewhurst and associates, *America's Needs and Resources* (New York, Twentieth Century Fund, 1947), p. 23.

percent efficient on the basis of actual achievement. In 1934, under the auspices of the Brookings Institute, another study revealed as its most conservative estimate that America's economy was 19 percent inefficient. That same year, the Columbia University Commission on Economic Reconstruction predicted that a 70 to 80 percent increase was possible. Certainly, these findings were borne out by America's war production experience.

Contradictions in the American Economy

Against this picture of America's growing economic might appeared certain great contradictions between the promises of individual enterprise capitalism and the actual conditions of economic life. Perhaps the most striking discrepancies concerned the production of goods and the distribution of income. Capitalism had promised to secure greater production than any other economic system in the world. Yet, the great depression of 1929 and the 1930's clearly revealed a situation of want among plenty. The studies of economic waste and inefficiency told only part of the story. A far greater contradiction lay in the losses of the depression years when vast areas of the American economy lay idle. In the depression year of 1932 production had fallen to between 50 and 60 percent of capacity. An economy which ten years later proved that it could produce enough goods to give Americans the highest standard of living ever enjoyed and still feed millions of men and machines in all parts of the world, allowed 11 million persons to remain unemployed and countless families to live in abject poverty.

Actually, the distribution of income during the depression was ample testimony to certain inadequacies in the distribution system of laissez-faire capitalism. The reports of the National Resources Committee for the year 1935–1936, for example, revealed that 27 percent of American families had received less than $750 per year; 42 percent, less than $1,000 a year; 64 percent less than $1,500 a year; 83 percent less than $2,000 a year; and 91 percent less than $3,000 per year. In startling contrast was the concentration of income in the higher brackets. Three percent of the families at the top of the scale received an aggregate income of about 21 percent of the total income of the nation—roughly as much as the lowest 50 percent of the population received. One percent at the top received almost as much as 40 percent at the bottom. In truth, there was widespread poverty in the midst of potential plenty. One might well have had reason to fear that the great differences of wealth and station which the early labor leaders had seen implicit in early American industrialism had really come to pass.

More recent studies indicate that these years were probably the peak of such concentration. Certainly, there is considerable evidence that income taxes, inheritance taxes, and corporation taxes, as well as the general prosperity of the war years, have tended to level the scale off somewhat. On the other hand, the very fact that income and production jumped so tremendously during both of the World Wars led many Americans to wonder why some sort of consolidated effort might not be applied to peacetime production and consumption. The nub of the problem was to achieve full production through coordination and yet maintain all-important personal liberties in the economic and political spheres.

It became increasingly clear, too, that the promises of constantly expanding employment inherent in capitalism had also not been met. Investigators found that the number of unemployed became greater with each depression and reached an apex in 1933 when 12 million persons found themselves out of work. Advocates of laissez-faire capitalism argued that depressions were simply a part of the natural business cycle, and they were to be expected. As the Lynds pointed out in their classic studies at Muncie, Indiana, this notion was widely accepted by all classes, and well after the collapse of the economy in 1929 owners and workers alike were seeking the prosperity that was just around the corner. The business cycle had hit its nadir, and it was bound to swing upward. As unemployment rolls mounted on into the 1930's, however, many began to doubt the "naturalness" of the depression, and employers and employees alike turned to the government for succor. Laissez-faire capitalism had traditionally preached against a government role in the economy, but this depression was so uniquely disturbing that even industrialists turned to the government for help. Whereas capitalism had traditionally put faith in the profit motive and private property as the essential economic ingredients of a sound economy, it became increasingly clear that the quest for security was dominating the nine tenths of American people who were not property owners.

The traditional theory of free competition in the open market had also largely given way to the actual practice of price fixing and regulation of production by large corporations and monopolies. More and more, Americans began to feel that if these practices were to continue it would be preferable that prices, production, and wages be regulated by the joint efforts of government, labor, and management rather than leaving such matters entirely in the hands of private owners and mangement. Whereas advocates of free enterprise had traditionally proclaimed that planning was alien to the American way of life, many began to see that a great amount of economic planning went into the management of huge corporations, and they began to insist that government and labor should have a larger share in planning to ensure that the benefits of planning would accrue to the general welfare.

Finally, whereas individualistic capitalism had traditionally identified itself with the growth of democracy and insisted that freedom of opportunity and enterprise could exist only under private auspices, many Americans began to suggest that an unmodified capitalism was a threat to the continued freedom and welfare of a majority of the people. The latter, it was increasingly pointed out, had less and less chance to rise unaided as individuals in the economic scale. All these doubts and questions led to increasing support for social legislation by the government and culminated in the New Deal. Increasingly, the pattern of the mixed economy—one partially undertaken by government and partially by private industry—took form. Gigantic corporations such as the TVA (Tennessee Valley Authority) carried on vast enterprises under the control of the government. Public and private power companies worked along with the TVA, as did innumerable individual entrepreneurs. Each had a place and an optimum role in the newly emerging pattern. The industrial and technological trends that had begun in the nineteenth century had now progressed so far that technical efficiency could produce a higher standard of living for all. The rub, however, was to keep the economic system functioning smoothly. The whole problem was aggravated and intensified by the vast increases in technical knowledge and efficiency achieved during the war years. The harnessing of atomic energy, the automatic factory, the growing use of the electronic machine—all increased more than ever before the promise of American life. The solution of adequate harnessing became the principal political and economic problem for American democracy to solve in the postwar era.

The Mushrooming of the Labor Movement

One of the most significant developments of the period between 1918 and 1950 was the growth of organized labor. As economic power became more and more concentrated in the hands of the industrial owning group, the unpropertied worker increasingly saw his only recourse in solidarity and organization. The movement obviously appeared as a threat to the power of the owning group, and in many areas it was fought with all the force that the industrialists and managers could muster. Yet, by the time the 1930's had passed labor unions had secured for themselves an accepted place in American social and economic life.

With the prosperity created by World War I, American unions had prospered. In order to avoid the disrupting influence of strikes and labor shortages, both government and private industry had allowed union leaders a comparatively free hand in organizing formerly unorganized groups of workers. As a result, many unskilled or semiskilled workers in fields where unionism had not formerly made headway—for example, the textile, packing, or clothing industries—were organized, and by 1920 total union membership was just under 5 million. The return of peacetime conditions, however, marked the real test of this extension of unionism, and by and large, the movement lost ground. With the prosperity and pressures of the war years a thing of the past many industries sought a return to prewar conditions such as the open shop, the company union, and lower wages. In spite of a few strong moves by unions, the labor movement declined in power, and by 1923 it embraced only 3,700,000 American workers. In the face of growing prosperity between 1923 and 1929 the movement made little headway. The initial counter-attack of industry during the first years of the decade had crushed some of the new unions in packing and textiles. By 1930 total union membership had fallen to just over 3 million, of which over 80 percent were affiliated with the A.F. of L.

The New Deal marked the beginning of a new era. The situation during the early 1930's had become perilous and desperate. In a milieu marked by extensive unemployment, starvation, unspeakable hardship, and dissention, radicalism flourished. The coming of the Democratic administration represented a landslide victory of a comparatively liberal program. Moreover, it indicated the willingness of some of the more conservative to embark on reforms that might avoid more drastic changes. Out of this combination of factors grew labor's new power. Labor's bill of rights was written into the legislation establishing the NRA (National Recovery Administration). This legislation (the NIRA) undertook to create employment, improve working conditions and wages, and guarantee the rights of collective bargaining and organization. Section 7(a) of the National Industrial Recovery Act safeguarded these rights with the provision: "That employees shall have the right to organize and bargain collectively through representatives of their own choosing, and shall be free from the interference, restraint, or coercion of employers of labor, or their agents, in the designation of such representatives or in self-organization or in other concerted activities. . . ." In August 1933 a National Labor Board was established as an administrative agency for mediating, conciliating, and arbitrating disputes arising out of the above provisions. When the NRA was declared unconstitutional by the United States Supreme Court in 1935, some of the labor provisions of the earlier legislation were enacted in the same year in the Wagner-Connery Act. The latter legislation established the National Labor Relations Board to administer and supervise controversies growing out of its provision, and the work of the board was sustained by the Supreme Court in a five-to-four decision in 1937.

Given this mandate from the government, labor proceeded to recoup its losses since 1923 and to expand beyond all previous records. By 1936 enrollments approached the all-time high of 1920, and a year later they reached 7,300,000. Although new industries such as the automobile and rubber industries were rapidly organized, most of these gains were made in older unions such as the soft coal workers, the teamsters, and the textile workers. It was at this point that differences within the labor movement which had been evident for some time came to a head. Many of the younger and more radical leaders felt that the older, more conservative group had cooperated too freely with industry. Moreover, they felt that unionism had too often represented skilled labor and the exclusion of non- or semi-skilled workers. In 1935 a group of eight unions maintaining industrial organization (i.e., an organization in which *all* workers of a given industry participated along

industry-wide lines rather than along craft lines) broke away from the
A.F. of L. contending that the parent organization had been dominated by
craft unions. When the A.F. of L. tried to counter the move by organizing
new unions to compete with those which had seceded, the schism widened,
and late in 1938 the CIO adopted a permanent organization and became
the Congress of Industrial Organizations. Although both factions seem to
have continually claimed membership far in excess of the actual facts, both
experienced growth during the ensuing years of an expanding war economy;
and the year 1950 saw a total number of about 15 million organized workers
of which 8 million belonged to unions affiliated with the A.F. of L. and
somewhere between 5 and 6 million belonged to unions affiliated with the
CIO.

MOVEMENT TOWARD THE WELFARE STATE

Republican Normalcy

The three administrations which followed Wilson's after World War I represent in many ways the temper of America during the 1920's. While it is
not possible to find any one consistent position running through the Harding-
Coolidge-Hoover era, certainly the groups in power hewed fairly closely to the
dictum of a weak, noninterfering central government. Harding characterized
his administration as a return to normalcy, and normalcy, of course, meant a
rather consistently laissez-faire conception of government except, perhaps,
when government was aiding business. Coolidge placed his stamp of approval
on his predecessor's policies by proclaiming that the business of the United
States is business. During his administration high tariffs, low taxes, and government subsidies to business continued to enjoy the seeming vindication of
prosperity and generally increasing standards of living. Hoover too proclaimed
that traditional business individualism was at the heart of the American way
of life and continued the direct and indirect aid to business described above.
In spite of growing agricultural depression and discontent, the country generally enjoyed business prosperity after 1923, and this prosperity provided
a fertile context for the successful continuance of these policies.

Granted the dominance of "normalcy" and laissez-faire Republicanism,
however, the spirit of reform was not entirely absent. In the 1924 presidential
campaign a number of farm and labor groups joined with socialist elements
to nominate the elder Senator Robert La Follette on a Progressive-Republican
ticket. Quite clearly, the third party was an expression of discontent with the
conservative lines around which the traditional two parties had drawn their
platforms. In spite of the Coolidge victory, the Progressives polled nearly 5
million votes—ample testimony to the fact that this dissatisfaction was neither
local nor the monopoly of a single group or class.

Although the Progressive movement failed, one does note the beginnings of certain practices later to be associated with the New Deal. First, the effort to plan and coordinate the bigness of American economic life had definite beginnings during this period. American business was opposed to the kind of government planning and restriction that had prevailed during World War I. But organized business, on the other hand, could not help but be impressed with the prodigious results of wartime planning. Actually, the position of businessmen who remonstrated vigorously against any government interference in economic life was that it was perfectly all right for business itself to undertake such planning and coordination. Thus, the growth of monopoly and other forms of corporate combinations was much enhanced during this period, leading to greater concentration than ever before. Actually, when the concerted business attack on the NRA came during the 1930's, it was little more than businessmen objecting to the government doing much the same thing that they themselves had been doing for much more than a decade.

Other seeds appeared in what social legislation did manage to pass a reluctant Congress and President. While a proposed child labor amendment to the constitution did not succeed, Coolidge was known to have favored it. Half-hearted attempts to relieve agricultural distress during the Coolidge administration met with consistent vetoes, but laws were passed protecting farmers against fraud in the transportation of livestock, grain, and perishable farm products. In 1929 Hoover favored an agricultural marketing bill designed to give relief to farmers through a farm board which would stabilize prices and keep down production. Labor was further reinforced in its struggle for collective bargaining by an anti-injunction bill of 1932 sponsored by two Republicans: George Norris and Fiorello LaGuardia. In 1928, the authorization of the construction of the Hoover Dam put the government into the water and electrical power business. While both Coolidge and Hoover vetoed plans for government ownership of Muscle Shoals, the Hoover operation did foreshadow the TVA.

For seven years—between 1922 and 1929—America enjoyed the greatest "boom period" in her history. The heavy importation of gold from abroad, the increasing inflation and extension of credit, the growth of mass production and new industries, the concomitant expansion of construction and real estate trading, and the virtual craze for speculation in stocks and bonds all contributed to the "boom." But ultimately, the prosperity of these seven years rested on flimsy foundations, and like the Biblical fat years, they were followed by at least seven lean ones. Unsound economic conditions abroad, many of them connected with the aftermath of the war, high tariffs, underconsumption of goods caused by the poor distribution of wealth (a factor all too often called overproduction), the collapse of the farm market, and a combination of inflation and speculation all combined to destroy even these flimsy foundations, and in October 1929 came the collapse in the American market which ushered in the great depression.

The effects of the crash were immediate and far-reaching. Savings were wiped out; banks closed or failed; farms formerly mortgaged passed into the hands of banks and insurance companies. Evictions and breadlines were all that awaited many middle- and working-class people. Any measures that the Hoover administration did take were largely temporary and geared to tide both business and labor over until the health of the economy could be restored. Labor leaders were urged to check strikes; businessmen were urged to maintain production and employment; consumers were urged to maintain purchasing levels. When these measure failed miserably, the Hoover administration took legislative steps to stimulate business. An attempt to stabilize farm prices through the Agricultural Marketing Act of 1929 failed, and the Federal Farm Board was unable to raise prices or reduce production. In 1932 Congress established the Reconstruction Finance Corporation to lend money to banks, business, and other financial institutions in an effort to avoid growing collapse, and in that same year federal reserve policies were liberalized to allow loans to banks and prevent failure. Other measures authorizing the use of federal funds to alleviate financial difficulty proved hopelessly inadequate, and the Hoover administration increasingly lost the confidence of the public. By 1932 the national income was halved; 11 million were unemployed; over 6,000 banks had failed; and values in all parts of the economy had tumbled. Even in the face of this economic disaster, the Hoover government steadfastly refused to take radical governmental action. It was this impasse which led to the overwhelming victory of the Roosevelt administration during the elections of 1932.

The New Deal

The Democratic Party was swept into power in 1932 with a popular majority of 7 million and with 472 out of 531 votes in the electoral college. Rarely did a political party have such a clear mandate from the people and such great power to accomplish change. For over twelve years Franklin D. Roosevelt remained in office, smashing all traditions against a third term and achieving the unparalleled distinction of being elected for a fourth term. Taking office in the dark days of 1933, he set out to restore confidence, relieve suffering, prime the pump of business, alleviate agricultural distress, and introduce social reform on a broad front. His boldness was expressed in one of his great statements to the American people: "The only thing we have to fear is fear itself." Many New Deal reforms had precedents and roots deeply imbedded in American culture. They were taken so vigorously, however, that many believed the country was undergoing a political revolution. Actually, the political institutions of the country were being reshaped and reconstructed in directions which had long been familiar to the democracies of Europe—in fact, which were often accepted in Europe by conservative and liberal parties alike.

What were some of the foundations and assumptions of the New Deal program? Much of the program grew out of a conception of the ills of the American socio-economic system. There had been, in the minds of the New Deal economists, an overexpansion of production; prices had been manipulated by corporate monopolies; labor had been denied an adequate share of the national income and adequate bargaining powers; public utilities under private ownership had failed to grow in line with the expanding needs of the American people; the insecurity of old age, invalidity, child dependence, etc., could no longer be met by private resources and philanthropy; inadequate living conditions demanded government action; banking completely in private hands demanded federal regulation; and the traditional policy of high tariffs throughout the world was hamstringing much needed trade and exchange among nations. The program indicated was clearly set forth by the New Dealers. By and large, the government would have to assume powers which had formerly remained with private individuals or organizations. The government, through loans and regulations, would undertake the responsibility of restoring prices. Individual debts would be amortized by government aid; government aid would also restore and expand credit which private facilities had been unable to furnish; labor, with government encouragement to organize, would have to have expanded purchasing power; the relief of the needy and social security would have to be undertaken; the improvement of homes and living conditions would be a government function, as would protection of the saver and investor; electric power would have to be partly under private, partly under public auspices; foreign trade would have to be stimulated by government measures reducing tariffs and extending credit to potential foreign purchasers; and finally, government funds generally would have to create the work and the production which would set industry on its feet again. This last function was known as "pump-priming."

The story of how the New Deal administration worked at these problems is a fascinating one and demands great detail. Needless to say, that story cannot be told here. Extensive measures for control and regulation of the banking, currency, and credit structure were enacted to prevent bank failures and fluctuations in the value of money. Vast sums were loaned to all sorts of institutions and individuals through the Reconstruction Finance Corporation, Home Owners' Loan Corporation, Federal Housing Authority, Federal Farm Credit Administration, and other such agencies. Many and varied efforts were made to stimulate employment and regulate the relation of prices and production of goods by means of the Agricultural Adjustment Act for farm goods, the National Industrial Recovery Act for industrial goods, the Securities Exchange Commission for stocks and bonds, and the Federal Communications Commission for certain public utilities.

The attack on unemployment took the form not only of pump-priming by loans to business but also of direct aid to less privileged Americans. The Federal Emergency Relief Administration helped states to finance their ever mounting relief rolls; the Civilian Conservation Corps and the National Youth Administration secured the dual advantages of needed relief and effective conservation of natural resources. The Civilian Works Administration, the Public Works Administration, and the Works Progress Administration provided millions of jobs for the unemployed in building, in art, and in public improvement. The Tennessee Valley Authority carried on a revolutionary transformation of a region taken as a whole and provided a chance to experiment with regional planning on a broad scale. The Soil Conservation Service, the Rural Electrification Administration, the Resettlement Administration, and the National Housing Authority also dealt on a broad scale with persistent problems of economic and social life. Direct aid to the unfortunate as well as the principle of a minimum security level were involved in the Social Security Act, which provided a wide range of benefits for the unemployed, the dependent, the handicapped, and the aged. In addition, there was the highly positive policy toward labor discussed earlier in this section.

The changes which four successive Roosevelt administrations brought to American life were vast and numerous. Spiritually, the firm and spirited attack on the problems of 1933 bred in Americans a confidence and assurance which had been significantly lost between 1929 and 1933. Institutionally, this spirit was undergirded by equally far-reaching achievements. Obviously, a primary consideration in the establishment of the many agencies mentioned above (and the hundreds of others unmentioned) was the strengthening and expansion of government authority beyond any other time in American history. American government began to match the "bigness" of American industry and economic life—much as it had begun to do in the latter decades of the nineteenth century. It was apparent that in a great variety of vital services—labor, agriculture, health, banking, education, and the arts—the government had stepped in with the hope of furnishing a broad minimum that private activity had been unable to furnish. Increasingly, the concept was that the government would initiate where private industry failed to do so, would coexist where private industry was not doing a completely effective job, and would coordinate in areas where planning and design were necessary in the public interest. Gradually, but more and more evidently, the government acted as a friend to a formerly hostile American people. The powers of the executive were strengthened to the point where many cried "dictatorship," but, by and large, controls were established so that these powers would be used in the public interest. Perhaps the full hope of the plan was expressed by Roosevelt himself when he said: "The only sure bulwark of continuing liberty is a government strong enough to protect the interests of the people, and a people strong enough and well enough informed to maintain its sovereign control over its government." Here, within a broad and genuine commitment to the values and processes of democracy, was the heart of the political changes of the New Deal.

The Fair Deal Continues the New Deal Tradition

With the sudden death of Roosevelt in 1944 many wondered if the New Deal program could be continued with a lesser personality at the helm. It was obvious to all that much of the drive behind the New Deal—in fact, the principal force in effecting its realization—lay in the personality of Roosevelt himself. With his death the work of continuing the program fell to President Harry S. Truman.

Truman's speech to the Congress in September 1945 clearly displayed his intention of carrying on the work of his predecessor. Among his proposals were a federally supported program of unemployment insurance, an increase in the minimum wage, the maintenance of full employment through government projects, the creation of a permanent Fair Employment Practices Commission to prevent racial and religious discrimination by business and labor unions, gradual lifting of wartime controls, compulsory military training, federal slum clearance, public works, conservation programs, and finally, federal social security, health insurance, and aid to education. Obviously the Truman program, called the Fair Deal, was very much a continuance of the New Deal. The opposition, however, which had been mobilizing since the accession of Roosevelt to power was strong, and many of the above-mentioned points were hamstrung in Congress. Within Mr. Truman's own party more conservative congressmen, especially from the southern states, found themselves unwilling to go along with such measures as the proposed FEPC or federal health insurance. In spite of a show of power in the 1946 elections which gave Congress to the Republicans, the reelection of Truman in 1948 along with a Democratic Congress revealed a clear mandate from the American people for the continuance of the Fair Deal.

Events during the second Truman administration were to accelerate with unrelenting speed the expanding role of the government. Whereas the American people had looked forward to a return of peacetime conditions and a concomitant reduction of government power and spending following the end of World War II, they found themselves in a "cold war" which grew increasingly warm after 1946. When North Korea attacked South Korea in June 1950, the United States took the lead in the United Nations attempt to stem the aggression. Huge forces in men and material were committed in an effort to support the UN action. Moreover, the Korean aggression stimulated the American people to redoubled effort in creating an adequate defense for Europe and the West against possible Soviet aggression. Clearly, the end result of all this military effort was an even further strengthening of federal powers. Curbs on the economy, on wages and prices, on employment, and in dozens of other areas were forthcoming in an effort to meet America's international obligations.

With the victory of President Dwight D. Eisenhower and a Republican-controlled Congress in the national election of 1952, it was clear that a fundamental review of New Deal and Fair Deal reforms in American life was indicated. Yet, it was equally clear from Eisenhower's campaign that many of the great innovations of these programs had become accepted elements in Republican as well as Democratic thinking. It remained for the future to determine how far and how rapidly extensions would be made, and in what places retrenchments would be sought.

INTERNATIONALISM AND THE CHALLENGE OF TOTALITARIAN GOVERNMENTS

Isolation and the Failure of Wilson's Peace Program

During the closing years of the nineteenth century and the first decades of the twentieth America had reluctantly assumed an expanding role in world affairs. The attempt to remain neutral in World War I had been unsuccessful, and during the last months of that conflict the United States had committed vast forces of men with comparable sums of money and equipment. For many the traditional policy of isolation was untenable. The forces of industrialism were increasingly shrinking the world, and America was too big and too powerful not to play a part in its affairs. President Wilson undoubtedly realized this when he proposed his Fourteen Points to Congress early in 1918. Not only did he suggest international action to reduce armaments, remove trade barriers, and adjust colonial problems, but he also proposed the formation of a League of Nations which would afford "mutual guarantees of political independence and territorial integrity to great and small states alike." The United States was to have a central role in the League as conceived by Wilson.

The story of the heated struggle over Wilson's proposals and the tragic failure of the United States to assume these crucial world responsibilities is a familiar part of American history. Powerful opposition to the League developed in the Senate from a group of isolationists led by Senators Henry Cabot Lodge and William Borah. It was attacked as an arrangement whereby the United States would become inextricably involved in the conflicts and wars of Europe. Wilson dramatically took his case to the people in a tour across the nation and in doing so ruined his already failing health. The Treaty of Versailles was finally defeated in the Senate on March 1920, and during the Harding Administration the United States concluded separate peace treaties with Germany and Austria.

This rejection of the League of Nations set the stage for and colored America's participation in world affairs for the next two decades. Although the United States did join in a number of international deliberations during the 1920's and 1930's, the effort, by and large, was to remain discreetly apart from what were thought of as "foreign" political struggles. It is true that America was most active in the peace and disarmament movement. Both in the conferences for the limitation of armaments—particularly of naval power —and in the construction and signing of the Kellogg-Briand Peace Pact American leadership was evident. Interestingly enough, these ultimately were to prove the least effective in actually preserving peace, and the affairs in which America failed to participate were the most decisive. As for the League itself, the Senate persisted in its opposition, but the increasing realization that the United States could not remain aloof led to the practice first of sending "unofficial representatives" to League conferences, and eventually to official representation and cooperation on certain issues. Nonetheless, the failure of America to assume a leading role in League affairs was a powerful detriment to effective world action and undoubtedly contributed to the League's eventual decline and demise.

The Challenge of World Communism

Meanwhile, as America attempted to perpetuate isolation from world affairs, a powerful challenge to Western democracy was developing in the Soviet Union. Having seized power in 1917, the Soviets proceeded to begin the shaping of a nation according to the political philosophy of Bolshevism. For many, the new Soviet experiment held out vast potentialities for social planning and betterment. As the experiment progressed through the 1920's and into the 1930's, however, it became increasingly clear that the Russian people were paying a terrible price for their tremendous economic and social advances—they were paying with their political liberties. In spite of this price, the great promises of communism along with the security which the Russian state had been able to provide were immensely attractive to peoples both in the West and the underdeveloped Eastern parts of the world.

To understand the nature of this great world movement, one must realize that Bolshevism drew both on Marxism and the Russian tradition for its principles. From the former it took the dialectical and materialistic conception of history. All history for the Marxian was a record of the struggle of economic classes. The state, education, religion, and the mass communication media—in effect, all social agencies—were tools of the dominant economic class for the exploitation of the oppressed classes. In capitalist-industrial society they were the tools of the owning classes for the exploitation of the workers. Only as the working class organized, disciplined itself, and seized power from the ruling classes did the Marxian see the end of the oppression. The ruling classes would never give up their power without a struggle; so violent revolution was necessary. Once the revolution was accomplished and the workers controlled the tools of production, all of the great hopes of mankind would be fulfilled. There would be economic security and plenty for all. There would be an end to warfare—formerly a tool of capitalists for guaranteeing a market. And there would be an end to race exploitation, for all men would be brothers. Needless to say, these promises captured the fancy of disillusioned Europeans as well as exploited colonial and colored peoples throughout the world. The Marxian conception of their inevitability—often referred to as the communist apocalypse—only added to their enchantment.

What did Bolshevism draw from the Russian tradition? Even the briefest glance at Russian history will reveal that the autocratic techniques of the movement were clearly drawn from nineteenth-century Russian revolutionary thought. The Communist Party, as organized in the Soviet Union, probably most closely resembled a military organization. There was the Politburo of fourteen, the central committee of seventy-two, and then the actual party membership of several million. Actually, all decisions were made by the high command, and these decisions were passed down to the rank and file through a hierarchical organization. Close examination reveals a remarkable similarity to the political preachings of Paul Pestel, the foremost revolutionary in Russia of the early nineteenth century. The concept of autocracy was certainly at the heart of Russian politics under the czars, as were the alternate swings between cosmopolitanism and provincialism. Clearly, one fails to understand the Bolshevik movement if one ignores its major roots in the Russian tradition.

The Challenge of Fascism

Communism as a movement had a rational philosophy with roots going all the way back to the ancient Greek period. The term fascism, however, did not even appear in the dictionary before World War I. As such, fascism has no great historical body of literature, or theory, or doctrine. It emerged largely as a reaction to communism, but inasmuch as both embody totalitarian conceptions of the state, they have a number of important resemblances. The most important similarity, perhaps, lies in the fact that both negate the foremost commitments of Western democracy. Rather than placing communism at the extreme left, fascism at the extreme right, and democracy in the middle of a political continuum, it seems far more useful to regard democracy as a radical form of government with the despotism of both communism and fascism at the other end of the political scale.

Central in the political theory of fascism are the principles of regimentation and leadership. The ultimate reality and good is the state, and it is the leader's task to regiment society and lead it for the good of the state. The whole Western conception that the state and other agencies exist for the benefit of the individual is turned about by the fascist, and in its place is inserted the opposite. "The relations . . . between state and citizens are completely reversed by the Fascist doctrine," maintained Alfredo Rocco, noted Fascist theorist, in 1925.

Instead of the liberal-democratic formula, "society for the individual," we have, "individuals for society" with this difference however; that while the liberal doctrines eliminated society, Fascism does not submerge the individual in the social group. It subordinates him, but does not eliminate him; the individual as a part of his generation ever remaining an element of society however transient and insignificant he may be.[2]

Given this transcendent conception of the state, the fascist constructed a conception of history, which, like the Marxist, employed struggle for its dynamic. The struggle, however, was not between classes; it was between peoples, nations, and races for possession of the earth. Because of the inherent inequality of races and peoples, history foreordains that the most powerful and the purest shall win. It is not difficult to see how the fascist would then glorify war as a means of facilitating the course of history. It is only in war that history can effect true judgments. Little wonder that the noted historian Hans Kohn has referred to fascism as "The cult of force." It used force to organize society internally and to subjugate individuals to the will of the state as formulated by a select group of leaders, and it then built a state committed to the use of force in international relations.

The Rise of the Popular Dictatorships

The popular despotisms which arose following World War I were known as totalitarian dictatorships. Their marks have since become familiar: the single political party closely identified with the state, the leader or dictator at its head, the complete suppression of political liberty, the crushing of opposition, control of the media of communication and of cultural and educational agencies, the secret political police, the large military force, and the assertion of vigorous nationalist sentiments.

Such a government came to power in Russia in 1917. A provisional democratic government had seized power from the czar in March 1917, and for less than a year Russia knew the only democratic government and free elections in her history. In November of that same year, under the leadership of Lenin and Trotsky, the Bolsheviks seized power from the provisional government and established the first "proletarian" state in history. In spite of vigorous opposition from conservatives, from White Russians, and from outside powers, the Bolsheviks quickly consolidated power and proceeded to the industrialization and rebuilding of Russia. In 1922 the Union of Soviet Socialist Republics was established as a "free Socialist society of the working people of Russia." While the government purported to rule according to the principles of Marx, actually, they had complete political control, a secret police, a one-party system, and all other earmarks of a dictatorship.

In 1922 the second of the great modern totalitarianisms was born in Italy.

[2] Alfredo Rocco, "The Political Doctrine of Fascism," *International Conciliation*, No. 223 (October 1926), p. 402.

Under the leadership of Benito Mussolini and his Fascist Party; and ostensibly to save the nation from communism, the Fascist movement first helped to create internal disorders, and then came to power on a platform of restoring political, economic, and social stability. Once again, the keynote of the movement was regimentation and leadership. Mussolini abrogated the old constitution, instituted complete centralization in the government, and organized the economic life of society to a vast corporate body. In place of the former free trade unions, there were Fascist trade unions, and likewise with other organizations. The suspension of civil liberties was quickly effected, and a military sort of discipline soon gripped Italy. Increased efficiency was secured, to be sure (it was often noted that Mussolini made the trains run on time), but at a terrible price in human suffering.

The third of the great modern dictatorships in the West came to power under Hitler and the National Socialist Party in Germany. Appealing to the German sense of shame at the defeat of 1918 and the Treaty of Versailles and capitalizing on the economic, social and political unrest of the depression, the Nazi movement was actually voted into power. Making tragically effective use of the Jews as scapegoats for Germany's troubles, Hitler, too, quickly consolidated power. Within six months after his appointment as chancellor in January 1933, he and his confreres were absolute rulers of Germany. Moreover, all of the techniques and principles of dictatorship were carried to their ultimate form in what had been one of the most creative and freest democracies in Western Europe.

World War II

International affairs deteriorated rapidly during the 1930's. In 1931 the Japanese occupied Manchuria in China, and created a puppet state of Manchukuo. Although the League of Nations sent an investigating commission and sought to negotiate the difficulty, Japan rejected its proposals and its authority. When Italy invaded Ethiopia in 1935, the League applied economic sanctions, but the half-hearted cooperation of the member nations coupled with Italy's resignation from the League in 1937 made the move of little avail. When Civil War broke out in Spain, there was active aid to the forces of fascist-minded General Franco, but no aid from the democracies to the Loyalist-Republican forces—a situation which quickly led Communist Russia to extend aid and thus prejudice the Loyalist cause. Once again, the League was virtually powerless to halt this preliminary to a more dreadful conflict.

During the first years of the 1930's the United States vigorously attempted to preserve neutrality, an almost impossible decision to implement. Very soon, however, increasing numbers of Americans realized that while the United States refused to aid democracies in trouble, the totalitarian nations were happy to aid aggressions which served their purposes. Gradually, a shift of policy appeared. In his famous "quarantine speech" in Chicago Roosevelt in

1937 declared that nations of good will must cooperate against would-be aggressors. Reciprocal trade treaties were signed with many countries through the efforts of Secretary of State Cordell Hull, and in 1938 the President requested bigger appropriations for the navy. When general war came to Europe, the isolationist issue came to a head. Very soon, however, events strengthened the interventionist cause. Neutrality provisions were relaxed; naval and air bases were leased from Great Britain in exchange for fifty overage destroyers; the Selective Service Act was passed in 1940 and the Lend-Lease Act in 1941. Yet public opinion remained divided, and when the Selective Service Act came up for renewal in 1941, it passed Congress by only one vote. On the other hand, when the Japanese actually struck at Pearl Harbor in December of that year, the question was to all intents and purposes resolved, and the United States turned its attention to the most costly war in its history.

The course of the war itself is not within the province of this volume. Needless to say, it virtually put an end to arguments against international cooperation in the United States. Much of the problem shifted to the extent of this cooperation rather than to its desirability. Many of the foundations were laid during the war itself. Numerous international conferences set the stage for later peacetime cooperation. A liaison committee between the State Department and the Senate and House Foreign Relations Committees went to work in 1943, and House and Senate resolutions, as well as both the Democratic and Republican platforms in 1944, expressed the intention of the United States to join an international organization. By and large, the end of the war brought a more internationally minded American people than had ever before existed.

The Postwar Scene

The steppingstones to a United Nations had been many and varied. One can certainly look to the League of Nations—as unsuccessful as it had been— as a precedent for the world cooperation. In August 1941 when the future of the democratic world looked bleak indeed, England and the United States signed the Atlantic Charter declaring their anticipation of the establishment of a "wider and permanent system of general security." By 1945 forty-six nations including Britain and the United States had signed the "Declaration by the United Nations," thereby supporting this principle of the Atlantic Charter. These and other steps were clear indication of the world's will to have an organization that might effectively deal with international problems. The Moscow and Teheran Conferences of 1943, the Dumbarton Oaks Conference of 1944, and the Yalta and Washington Conferences of 1945 were ample testimony to this fact. Finally in 1945 the United Nations came into existence as an international organization to deal with world problems.

But the optimism and happiness of that period was destined to draw quickly to a close. At the heart of a new struggle gripping the world was a phenomenon called "the cold war." Beginning in 1946, and increasing in the following years, the world saw move after move evidencing the intent of the Soviet Union to hamstring effective world cooperation. Once again, the inconsistencies between totalitarianism and democracy became increasingly apparent, and in this case the former took the role of Russian expansionism. Little by little, the world divided itself into two armed camps—one associated with the Soviet bloc and one with the American. Efforts to control atomic energy, to settle the political and economic problems of the war, and to work out differences were ever more unsuccessful. Tension mounted as military power was brought to bear in Europe and Asia either to accomplish or to hinder Soviet expansion. Four years after the end of World War II the world once again felt itself standing on the brink of catastrophe.

A climax came in June 1950 when North Korean troops invaded South Korea in an attempt to unify the country under Communist rule. Within a week the United Nations had declared the move a violation of the peace and an act of aggression, and led by the United States, the international organization took steps to consider it. The decision marked the beginning of a long and costly "police action." By January 1952 the United States alone had suffered over 100,000 casualties, with many times that number suffered by South Korea. On the opposing side, vast casualties were borne by North Korea and Communist China, who had entered the war on her side. Yet, in many ways, the Korean war had wakened the free world to the dangers it faced. Under the provisions of the North Atlantic Treaty Western countries joined themselves with the United States to bring about a common defense. While the UN itself had been slow and perhaps indecisive in acting, its police action was a show of strength which had never been demonstrated by a previous international organization. Whether or not the Korean war would prove the undoing or the strengthening of the UN was at the beginning of 1953 a matter of conjecture.

GROUP RELATIONS IN THE AMERICAN COMMUNITY

The Corporate Character of American Society

The increasingly corporate character of American industrial society has already been discussed in Chapter 9. There it was pointed out that with the development of industrialism after the Civil War came a large number of organizations in every realm of life representing a vast variety of purposes. By 1950 the *World Almanac* listed some 1,200 of these voluntary groups—most of them national—and this listing did not include churches, political parties and organizations, and corporations. One could find amongst this great array a group to support virtually any cause he might espouse—or its opposite for that matter. There were business and labor groups, veterans groups, civil and moral groups, professional groups, service groups, racial and religious groups, women's groups, and educational groups of every kind. Each had its particular interests which it supported in a variety of ways. Even more significant, many had definite conceptions of the *common* good. In other words, whether expressed or implied, many had some notion of a future program which would be good not only for their own members but also for all American citizens. This varied from a more limited view of the American Automobile Association that good roads would benefit drivers and nondrivers alike, to the all-encompassing programs of groups like the National Association of Manufacturers or the American Federation of Labor.

The place of these groups in American life has been a topic of great interest and discussion. For political scientists and educators their role is crucial. For example, of the many different federal-aid-to-education bills presented in Congress during the latter 1940's, some were drafted by the National Catholic Welfare Conference, some by the American Federation of Teachers, some by the National Education Association, and some by the National Association of Manufacturers. Clearly, these groups played a role that involved far more than simple lobbying. They were actually serving to articulate the views and opinions of large segments of the American public—or, as John Dewey pointed out in *The Public and Its Problems,* they were representing diverse American publics. Nevertheless, it was principally through unofficial means that their influence was felt. The problem of what groups to recognize, of which were truly representative, and of which ones to listen to remained ever present. In effect, new ways were needed to recognize through law the contribution of organized groups to the American democratic political process. They seemed the inevitable product of industrial democracy; they seemed to have an important role to play. Just what this role was to be remained unanswered.

The Need for Improved Group Relations

One of the critical problems facing America at mid-twentieth century was the need for improved group relations. American ideals had traditionally proclaimed the values of human brotherhood, freedom, and equality, and America, in spite of great discrepancies at a number of points, had come a long way toward fulfilling these ideals. If for no other reason than their complete fulfillment, Americans had reason to work tirelessly to eradicate all sorts of racial, ethnic, and religious discriminations. But in the world of the 1950's there was even another equally compelling reason to do so. The eyes of the rest of the world were on America. They were the eyes of a divided world. The forces of Bolshevism were proclaiming the great promises of racial equality and freedom; they promised that Bolshevik triumph would bring an end to persecution, discrimination, and colonialism.

Western democracy, it is true, had made the same promise. The historic ethic of democracy also proclaimed the values of liberty, equality, and fraternity as well as the dignity of the individual human being. As the world looked to the United States, however, they still saw the signs of discrimination. To be sure, this discrimination was lessening year by year, but the Communist press made capital of every instance it could discover. Discrimination remained a cancer which sapped the very vitality of America, and American leaders increasingly realized that in the last analysis the world would judge America by her ability to cut it out and cure it.

The Drive for Equality of Citizenship

That the cancer continued to persist should not lead to the belief that nothing had been done to eliminate it. On the contrary, the years following 1930 had witnessed a concerted effort to uncover and deal with problems of discrimination on every front. To combat the anti-Semitic, anti-Catholic, and anti-"foreigner" campaigns of groups like the Ku Klux Klan and individuals like Gerald L. K. Smith, organizations like the National Conference of Christians and Jews and the Federal Council of Churches of Christ were formed. Other groups like the American Civil Liberties Union redoubled their efforts in legislatures and the courts; and on local, state, and national levels lawmakers, citizens commissions, and public spirited businessmen and labor leaders took positive steps to promote religious and ethnic amity and to prevent discrimination.

On the question of race the drive was equally, if not more, intense, for World War II had brought many race and color problems to a head. The outbreak of war with Japan meant hardship and internment camps for the Japanese-Americans of the west coast. Mass movements of Negroes from the South to war industry centers brought violence to many industrial communities, and race riots in Detroit and New York were among the ugliest internal incidents of the war years. On the other hand, many gains were made in industrial relations through the efforts of the Fair Employment Practices Committee and of progressive employers and unions. Through the Supreme Court decision in the Texas primary case, political gains were made against the poll tax and for the freedom of Negroes to vote in Democratic primaries of the South.

As the war progressed, the armed services were forced to reassess traditional policies toward racial groups, and in the first years after the cessation of hostilities, sweeping changes were introduced integrating Negro troops into regular units on an equal basis. A number of groups like the National Association for the Advancement of Colored People and the National Urban League redoubled their efforts for better interracial relations, and a flood of literature and proposals for action came under public consideration. The Democratic Party made civil rights a central plank in its platform, and although the resistance of southern congressmen prevented any measure from passing during the Truman administrations, the issue remained a heated one. In 1952 both the Republican and Democratic platforms included sections on civil rights in their platforms. While the Republicans seemed willing to leave much responsibility to the states, they did see a role for "supplemental action" by the federal government. The Democrats, on the other hand, favored federal legislation effectively to secure to all the rights of equal opportunity for employment, security of person, and full and equal participation in the nation's political life.

Social Class in America

Another grouping which caused growing concern to Americans—particularly with reference to school programs and organization—was their social class system. While most people cherished and voiced time-honored ideals of equality, they were well aware of social inequalities. In fact, they were fond of stating that anyone with proper initiative and capabilities could "reach the top." The paradox was at the heart of the American tradition.

A good deal of light was thrown on the changing character of the class structure in a study published by Lewis Corey in 1945. In it, he compared the social class divisions in 1870 and 1940, with the following results:

Table 6—Class Divisions in the United States, 1870–1940 [3]

	1870	1920	1940
Farmers	27.2%	——	10.2%
Working class	52.8	——	57.1
Industrial	30.0	37.0	31.0
Other	22.8	——	26.1
Middle class	20.0	——	32.2
Old entrepreneurs	13.4	——	7.5
New salaried	6.6	——	24.7
Upper bourgeoisie	——	——	.5

One of the more important items which Corey's analysis pointed out was that the Marxian prediction that society would increasingly divide between industrial proletarians and owners had not been fulfilled. The industrial class reached a peak about 1920 and has declined in proportion ever since that time. A second interesting phenomenon was the rise of a new middle class composed not of businessmen, enterprisers, and independent professionals, but of technical-managerial persons, clerical workers, professional workers, salespeople, and public service employees. Corey ascribed the rapid growth of this class to (1) the expanding need for technically competent employees in the complex industrial machine, (2) the increased amount of goods and production creating more leisure and consequent demand for

[3] Lewis Corey, *The Middle Class* (Yellow Springs, Ohio, Antioch Review, 1945), p. 3.

services, and (3) the increased need for administrators to plan, regulate, control, and coordinate public and private affairs.

Another more subjective approach to the social class problem was made during the 1940's by W. Lloyd Warner and his associates at the University of Chicago.[4] While Corey took the data for his study from the census reports on occupation, Warner's group went into American communities and talked with average Americans about the problem of social stratification in their communities. While the subjects vigorously denied the existence of classes, they seemed in every case ready to rank the persons they knew into hierarchical social groupings. Throughout his studies in different regions Warner tended generally to acknowledge five social classes: an upper class (which sometimes split into two classes) composed of a small group of high-income families; an upper-middle class composed of professional men, salaried executives, and owners of well-established businesses; a lower-middle class composed of small businessmen, skilled and white collar workers, and other wage earners; an upper-lower class composed of wage earners in local factories and small business; and a lower class composed of unemployed and low-income families. Warner, although he found considerable mobility, discovered that people tended to remain with the class into which they were born. Seeing democracy as an open class system, he was therefore concerned with keeping class lines fluid. It was at this point that he saw education most prominently involved. Although important criticisms have been levelled at Warner's methods and findings, the problems which he posed for education were real ones and pressed for intelligent solution.

ISSUES FOR STUDY AND DISCUSSION

1. List some of the more powerful pressure groups today interested in the program of public education. Granted the important place in American life which these groups have acquired during the past fifty years, what would be your policy regarding their demands if you were a school superintendent in a local community?

2. If the United States is to participate in the United Nations, it will undoubtedly be necessary to develop in future citizens the attitudes and knowledge necessary for continued support of such a world organization. How can these be provided in a school program dedicated to the nurture of patriotism and loyalty in American children?

3. What role do you see for the public schools in preserving equality of opportunity within a framework of the social class system described in Chapter 13? Does the nineteenth-century common school ideal still have pertinence in this respect?

[4] W. Lloyd Warner, Marchia Meeker, and Kenneth Eells, *Social Class in America* (Chicago, Science Research Associates, 1949). See also August Hollingshead, *Elmtown's Youth* (New York, John Wiley & Sons, 1949); W. Lloyd Warner, et al., *Democracy in Jonesville* (New York, Harper & Bros., 1949); W. Lloyd Warner, Robert Havighurst, and Martin B. Loeb, *Who Shall Be Educated?* (New York, Harper & Bros., 1944).

4. Has the vast extension of federal power since 1918 rendered desirable a concomitant increase in federal control over education?

5. Granted the important challenge to democracy inherent in communism and facism, do you think that penetrating knowledge about these totalitarian movements should be provided by American public schools?

SUGGESTIONS FOR FURTHER READING

Baldwin, Leland D., *The Stream of American History,* New York, American Book, 1952, Vol. 2.

Beard, Charles A., and Beard, Mary R., *America in Midpassage,* New York, Macmillan, 1939.

——, *The Rise of American Civilization,* New York, Macmillan, 1936.

Burns, Emile (ed.), *A Handbook of Marxism,* New York, International, 1935.

Cochran, Thomas and Miller, William, *The Age of Enterprise: A Social History of Industrial America,* New York, Macmillan, 1942.

Counts, George S., *Education and American Civilization,* New York, Teachers College, Columbia University, 1952.

——, *The Social Foundations of Education,* New York, Scribner, 1934.

Dumond, Dwight Lowell, *Roosevelt to Roosevelt,* New York, Holt, 1937.

Faulkner, Harold Underwood, *From Versailles to the New Deal,* New Haven, Yale University Press, 1950.

Kohn, Hans, *The Twentieth Century,* New York, Macmillan, 1949.

Lindley, Ernest K., *Half Way with Roosevelt,* New York, Viking, 1936:

——, *The Roosevelt Revolution, First Phase,* New York, Viking, 1933.

Lynch, David, *The Concentration of Economic Power,* New York, Columbia University Press, 1946.

Lynd, Robert S., and Lynd, Helen M., *Middletown,* New York, Harcourt, 1929.

——, *Middletown in Transition,* New York, Harcourt, 1937.

Mitchell, Broadus, *Depression Decade, 1929–1941,* New York, Rinehart, 1947.

Myrdal, Gunnar, *An American Dilemma,* New York, Harper, 1944.

President's Research Committee on Social Trends, *Recent Social Trends in the United States,* New York, McGraw-Hill, 1933.

Rocco, Alfredo, "The Political Doctrine of Fascism," *International Conciliation,* No. 223 (1926).

Schapiro, J. Salwyn, *The World in Crisis,* New York, McGraw-Hill, 1950.

Slosson, Preston W., *The Great Crusade and After, 1914–1928,* New York, Macmillan, 1930.

Smith, B. Othanel and others, *Readings in the Social Aspects of Education,* Danville, Ill., Interstate, 1951.

Stokes, Anson Phelps, *Church and State in the United States,* New York, Harper, 1950, Vols. 2–3.

Temporary National Economic Committee, *Final Report and Recommendations of the Temporary National Economic Committee Transmitted to the Congress of the United States,* Washington, D. C., Government Printing Office, 1941.

——, *Technology and Concentration of Economic Power,* Washington, D. C., Government Printing Office, 1940.

United States National Resources Committee, *Consumer Incomes in the United States: Their Distribution in 1935–36,* Washington, D. C., Government Printing Office, 1938.

———, *The Structure of the American Economy,* Part I: *Basic Characteristics,* Washington, D. C., Government Printing Office, 1939.

Wallace, Schuyler C., *The New Deal in Action,* New York, Harper, 1934.

Wecter, Dixon, *The Age of the Great Depression,* New York, Macmillan, 1948.

14

INTELLECTUAL STRESSES AND STRAINS

ACCUSTOMED TO the relatively leisurely pace of the early decades of the twentieth century, educators not only found their tasks exceedingly complicated by the new forces described in Chapter 13, but they were also subjected to an increasing number and variety of conflicting educational views. During the period between World War I and the mid-century the chorus of voices that made their claims upon education increased in range and volume until the conscientious professional educator could no longer afford to ignore them or fail to develop a defensible point of view of his own. Outlooks formulated in earlier times were restated with increased clarity and vigor, and distinctively new outlooks were formulated in a way that demanded the educator's attention. It is impossible to mention adequately the range and quality of intellectual points of view that have swept over America in recent decades, but a few of those that found their way into the educational arena can be mentioned here. Any educator who would deal fundamentally with these problems should study at much greater length than is possible here the philosophical, psychological, and social foundations of his educational credo.

The modern American educator had to make up his mind with regard to at least four kinds of orientation that laid claims upon his basic view of man's most cherished values, his conception of knowledge and learning, and his outlook on the nature of society. First, he had to reckon with the religious view of man and values, especially as stated by various branches of the Christian faith, Protestant and Roman Catholic. Secondly, he had to consider the several dominant philosophic views of man and knowledge, especially as defined by such "schools of thought" as idealism, realism, humanism, and experimentalism. Thirdly, he had to make up his mind about several psychological points of view, represented by such methods of approach as those of connectionism, behaviorism, field psychology, psychoanalysis, and social psychology. And, finally, he was engulfed by a vast increase in organized bodies of knowledge all of which asserted their claims to a place in the schools, colleges, and universities of the nation. To find his way among these competing views, to say nothing of taking some leadership in them, posed a new and sobering and challenging task for the American educator. It required a whole re-orientation concerning the task of education and a corresponding conception of the professional preparation required of those who would venture into the vast educational enterprise of our times.

RELIGIOUS VIEWS OF MAN

The strength and vitality of the several religious traditions are among the outstanding factors of the recent period in America. It is well to remember, also, that they represent one of the oldest strains in the American heritage, making their influence felt from the very day when European settlers touched these shores. Some of the ways they have affected American education have been revealed, we hope, in the pages of this book. Although it looked for a time in the latter part of the nineteenth century as though the religious forces in American life were on the run, it is now clear that there has been a vital and aggressive reassertion of religious claims since World War I which American educators cannot ignore.

There are many ways that the issue posed by religion for American education could be stated, but one of the most suggestive is this: Must public and private morality be based upon religious sanctions, or may conduct rest upon the common agreements of a secular morality? This issue is crucial for education because it has become increasingly clear that education has a fundamental moral task to perform in American society. Thus, educators have been forced to look to the bases upon which the moral task of education can be built in a society of divided religious loyalties. The most insistent voices to claim that both public and private education must rest upon religious sanctions have come from both Protestant and Roman Catholic sources.

Protestantism

Within the general Protestant orientation three major points of view were discernible in the period after World War I. They may be described loosely as fundamentalism, liberalism or modernism, and a neo-orthodoxy. The clash between fundamentalism and modernism marked the 1920's and 1930's, and the neo-orthodoxy added a third orientation, especially in the 1930's and 1940's. Many within the religious field feel that neo-orthodoxy or neo-Protestantism is a movement that will not be denied in the 1950's.

Fundamentalism was the oldest of the Protestant traditions in America (see pp. 172, 326). It rested primarily upon a literal interpretation of the Bible as the divinely revealed word of God and thus to be believed implicitly by the faithful. It reasserted itself with great force in the 1920's as a reaction against the upsetting views of biological evolution and modern science. Whether based upon a belief in the potential salvation of all souls by means of their own effort or by faith alone or by the grace of God or whether based upon a belief in the original sin of all and the election of a certain few to be saved, fundamentalism viewed man as created in the image of God as revealed in the Bible. The moral commandments required obedience of man to God's will at peril to his eternal soul, and the possibility of salvation was present only through faith in Jesus Christ as the savior of all men. Good conduct was thus impossible unless based upon obedience to God's will; in other words, morality must rest upon religious faith.

Armed with this belief many Protestants responded to the plea that the public schools of America should give more attention to religious instruction as a means of developing better moral standards among youth. They thus turned, in many ways, to reinsert the religious instruction into the public schools which had tended to be reduced if not disappear during the nineteenth century. Under this pressure local school boards and state legislatures moved in two major ways. One was to authorize more Bible reading in the public schools. Many states passed laws to this effect (see pp. 549), and some accompanied these laws with other laws prohibiting the teaching of evolution because it conflicted with the Biblical story of the creation of the world and of man. The trial of a high school teacher of science, John Thomas Scopes, in Tennessee focused the limelight of the whole nation in 1925 upon the legal contest between William Jennings Bryan representing the fundamentalist view and Clarence Darrow representing the scientific. A second effort to insert more religious instruction in the public schools was the program of released time which gained great popularity especially in the years after World War II (see pp. 547–548).

After the Scopes trial fundamentalism continued to remain a great force in American life, but it lost much of its hold among the educated and intellectual groups within the Protestant fold. Flat rejection of the overwhelming accumulation of scientific evidence could no longer satisfy those who were cognizant of the movements of modern science. The liberal theology of modernism which had begun to appear in the nineteenth century (see pp. 326–328) gained considerable headway in the decades between the two world wars. Several kinds of attempts to find a rational meeting ground between the claims of Christianity and the claims of modern science were formulated, the details of which cannot be enumerated here.

In general, however, some of the modernists began to look upon the Bible as a great resource for ethical and moral guidance rather than the literal revelation of the word of God that must be obeyed word for word. Greater emphasis was put upon interpreting God in spiritual but nontheistic terms or upon interpreting Jesus as the greatest of the ethical teachers of all time but not stressing his divine character as the son of God. These views looked upon religion as a quality of experience that elevated man and brought out his better nature rather than as an adherence to a fixed and orthodox creed that was unchangeable in form or content. Many modernists agreed, however, that religious instruction in the public schools of a nonsectarian kind would be desirable. They thus supported an increased attention to Bible reading or released time, not as the revelation of divine authority so much as ethical guides to better conduct that could be followed by all sectarian groups in common. Other modernists of Protestant persuasion argued that genuine religious faith could not be achieved by these means but must come from greater effort by home and church.

Then with the impact of two world wars, a world-wide depression, and the evident cruelty of man to man, a demand for a return to a new Protestant orthodoxy appeared with increasing force during the middle decades of the twentieth century. This was an effort to avoid the literal orthodoxies of fundamentalism which tried to deny the realities of modern science and man's social evolution and also to avoid the "soft" modernism that had developed a too easy faith in man's unaided powers to achieve salvation either in this world or in the next. Here was a reassertion of faith in the Bible as a revelation of God's power and sovereignty and of man's weakness and sin. Evil in the world was seen as a result of man's gift of freedom which he had been given by God. Man has an inherent tendency to deny God's power and grace, a tendency which leads man to sin. Salvation can thus be reached only by a recognition of man's sin, his repentence, and his renewal of faith in God's sovereignty and in his power to save by the fact of the life, death, and resurrection of Christ. Moral conduct and social betterment can be achieved only by a reassertion of the fundamental tenets of a traditional Protestant Christianity that recognizes the power of modern science but does not put faith in it. Neo-orthodoxy gained strength from a disillusionment and pessimism arising out of the dreadful alternatives that faced men of good will in the middle of the twentieth century. An increasing number of Americans began to feel that they needed more help than they could count on from man's own intelligence and effort alone. Thus the movements toward a revival of religious instruction in the public schools gained considerable momentum from these sources.

Roman Catholicism

One of the outstanding facts of the recent period is the great extent to which Roman Catholic theology and philosophy have become aggressive, effective, and consistently stated. For nearly 300 years most Protestants could assume that they held certain beliefs in common despite their outward differences and their often devastating conflicts. In effect, they could merely look over their shoulders at the growth of the Catholic Church. But in the twentieth century the power and influence of the Catholic Church made itself increasingly felt in political, economic, and social affairs, not least of which was its claim to recognition in the field of education. It added a powerful and insistent voice to the demand for a return to orthodoxy in the intellectual realms that could not be ignored by the educator.

Stimulating the attention of American Catholic writers to educational matters was the appearance in 1929 of an encyclical letter of Pope Pius XI on *The Christian Education of Youth*. This declaration of policy set the framework within which a large number of Catholic educators renewed their campaign for public approbation. It added enormous stimulus to the general movement toward intellectual and religious orthodoxy. Statement after statement plied the public mind with the argument that morality must rest upon religion. Many Protestants could nod agreement with this view and with much of Catholic theology. God is a personal being, infinitely powerful, wise, good, and just. Man has a spiritual soul and a physical body created by God for his purposes and whose end is salvation. Man has an intellect and a free will which set him immeasurably above and beyond the rest of created nature. Despite man's fall, his supernatural nature, the grace of God, and the sacrifice of Christ enable man to hope for salvation as revealed in the Scriptures.

But when Protestants looked more closely at Catholic doctrine, they found that the argument that morality must rest upon religion seemed really to say that morality must rest upon the Catholic religion. They found claims that the Catholic Church was divinely ordained by God to be the custodian of the whole of faith and morals as revealed in God's will. They found Catholics arguing that all persons are born into three societies. Two societies are of the natural order, namely the family and the state, and the third society is of the supernatural order, namely the Roman Catholic Church. All three societies have been given a distinctive task by God, the family to generate offsprings and care for them, the state to care for the temporal welfare of the community, and the Church to care for the eternal salvation of men's souls. Thus the family has priority of rights over the civil state in matters of education, and the Church has priority of rights over both the family and the state, for the Church deals with supernatural affairs and the family and state deal only with natural affairs.

Although the Catholic doctrine argued that these views applied only to Catholics and not to all persons, difficulties arose when the Church instituted campaigns to induce state governments to enforce its conception of faith and morals through law. Here Protestants often backed away and contested the Catholic conception of the relation between church and state. Many Protestants agreed with many Catholics on the general formula that went something like this: Morality must rest upon religion. This is a Christian nation.

Christianity promotes good citizenship, nay good citizenship is not possible unless it rests upon Christianity. Therefore, the state in its proper goal of promoting good citizenship should also promote Christianity by a free "co-operation" between the state and the churches.

But when these doctrines came down to practice, many Protestants found that they disagreed with the Catholic outlook on the right of the state to send an ambassador to the Vatican, to prevent by law the dissemination of birth control information, to prohibit sex instruction in the schools, or to censor books, magazines, and movies on the grounds that they were sacrilegious. Many Protestants could agree with Catholics that released time in the public schools was desirable as a means of promoting their respective sectarian religious doctrines, but when it came to the Catholic demand that public funds be used to support Catholic parochial schools, most Protestants drew back and wondered whether the theory of "cooperation" between church and state was as desirable as the long-struggled-for principle of separation of church and state. This issue provided the setting for one of the most difficult and bitter controversies that swept over American education in the twentieth century. (See pp. 528-534 and 547-551).

PHILOSOPHIC VIEWS OF MAN

Just as the religious views of man were more clearly defined in the recent period, so did several philosophic formulations become more insistent in their claims upon education. Educators were torn by competing philosophies and found difficulty in responding to their demands. There are many possible ways to define the different philosophical outlooks. There was general agreement that at least four philosophies were important, but little agreement as to which ones were most valid. Each had roots in earlier periods. In the long view it seemed apparent that while idealism was still present, it no longer could claim a dominant position in American intellectual or educational thought. Similarly, realism continued to be a concern of a growing number of professional philosophers but was seldom translated into systematic educational terms. Much more influential in their direct appeals to educators were humanism and experimentalism, both of which enlisted considerable attention and the loyalties of a growing number of educators either explicitly or implicitly. Idealism and humanism seemed closer in spirit to the religious orientations already mentioned, whereas realism and experimentalism strove to find moral sanctions in a secular view of man.

Idealism

The great popularity enjoyed by philosophic idealism in the latter half of the nineteenth century had declined so much that by the 1930's it was no longer the leading philosophy in America. A few creative centers remained in the twentieth century, represented by such outstanding names as William E. Hocking and Josiah Royce of Harvard, Hartley Burr Alexander at the University of Nebraska and Scripps College, Ralph Tyler Flewelling at the University of Southern California, and A. C. Knudsen and Edgar S. Brightman at Boston University. The differences in their views cannot be considered here, but in general the interests of idealism began to shift from a concern with the infinite Absolute toward a concern with the finite personality of man and from the problems of man's relation to God to a concern with man's relation to nature and human society. In either case, however, the predominant concern was with the spiritual significance and reality of human values and human personality. Many idealists gravitated toward a view known as "personalism" in which the supreme reality was assigned to persons and personality. They quarreled as to whether all human persons were finite or all persons were infinite, and whether God as a person was infinite or finite, but they were likely to agree that the spiritual self was the most important source of values, knowledge, and freedom.

Similarly, idealism as a philosophic basis for education came to be on the defensive, despite some important and recent efforts to translate idealism into educational philosophy by such men as Herman H. Horne of New York University, Michael Demiashkevich at George Peabody College for Teachers, Boris B. Bogoslavsky of the Cherry Lawn School in Connecticut, Robert Ulich of Harvard, and Rupert C. Lodge of Manitoba. Little can be done here to describe the details of an idealistic philosophy of education, but it is apparent from the temper and character of the writings that much was made of study of the essentials of the Western literary, intellectual, religious, and moral tradition as the best means for development of the student's self and personality. There is close sympathy with a religious, and especially a Christian, orientation. Whereas creative activity and interest on the part of children is prized, the goals are likely to be set by the teacher who should try to represent the best of the heritage of Western civilization. Science and practical activities should have a place definitely subordinate to language, literature, and religion insofar as these latter reveal concern with God, the spiritual, and the absolute values of truth and right. The fundamentals of skill, knowledge, and information as a basis for the acquisition of social, moral, and scientific truths are to be insisted upon. A well trained and disciplined mind is requisite to achieving the proper conceptions of the universe, man's civilization, and one's own self.

Realism

The realistic reaction in philosophy against academic idealism continued to grow in the period after World War I as several attempts were made to reformulate the realistic position. One of the centers of interest in the 1920's was a movement known as "critical realism" which arose to criticize the "new realism" of the earlier decade. Outstanding names here were those of Arthur O. Lovejoy of Johns Hopkins, George Santayana of Harvard, and Roy Wood Sellars of Michigan. The details of their criticism were never fully worked out into an influential philosophy of education and thus need not delay us here, but it is entirely possible that much could be done by creative philosophers of education if they became concerned to work in this area and go on to consider the educational bearings of such philosophical positions as those of Bertrand Russell and Alfred N. Whitehead. The fundamental premise of realism that objects exist independently of knowledge about them raises fundamental questions about the content and processes of education.

Another and still more recent interest in the empirical and realistic orientation has come to be known since the 1930's as logical positivism or logical empiricism. The concern of the logical empiricists is primarily with the careful and systematic analysis of language as the road to clarity of meaning and thinking. They reject too much reliance upon deductive forms of logic and transcendental forms of metaphysics and insist that truth must rest upon a necessary logical relation between theory and fact as defined within a rigorous system of definitions and rules of logical analysis. They borrow a great deal from the formal properties and rules of mathematics as suggestive in the analysis of valid knowledge. Again the logical empiricists have as yet done little in formulating a thoroughgoing philosophy of education; therefore, they have had little concrete effect upon educational theory or practice.

A few educators tried to make explicit some of the implications of the general realistic philosophy for education. Among these are often included Henry C. Morrison and Frederick S. Breed of Chicago, William C. Bagley of Teachers College, Columbia University, and Ross L. Finney of the University of Minnesota. They have in common a respect for the stubborn facts of the physical and social sciences which provide the necessary subject matter which students must acquire. The conservative function of education is emphasized. The schools must pass on the accepted truths and values of society as well as the realities of scientific fact. Students must not only acquire this information by whatever method is most appropriate; they must learn to adjust themselves to it. The teacher's role is to see that children do acquire the essential knowledge by whatever discipline and authority is necessary.

The realists have little faith in a "soft" pedagogy that relies extensively upon the interests of the child. After all, valid knowledge is relatively stable. Consequently, there is a relatively stable content to knowledge that should be required of students and that can be measured objectively by the development of scientific tests. We have overemphasized interests, individualism, and freedom; we must now reassert the values of discipline, authority, truth, and the tradition. This view, deeply rooted in American educational practice, had a vogue in the 1930's under the name of "essentialism." Its practice has remained vitally present, but the name had a relatively short life except in the textbooks of educational philosophy.

Humanism

Closely akin to the religious orientations and to the philosophy of idealism in spirit and temper, humanism attracted an increasing audience in the decades following World War I. Appealing to the reaction against the optimistic faith in success that followed the war and boom years, humanism was represented by proponents who were particularly adept in intellectual argument, rhetorical debate, and literary skill. Two branches of the humanist orientation were identifiable. One stemmed directly from the literary and classical humanism of the earlier twentieth century (see p. 331) and was represented by such advocates as Nicholas Murray Butler and Mark Van Doren of Columbia, Paul Elmer More of Princeton, Norman Foerster of the State University of Iowa, and Abraham Flexner. A second branch which stressed the rational and intellectual character of man was most popularly represented by Robert M. Hutchins and Mortimer Adler of Chicago. They spoke less of the religious, spiritual, and supernatural nature of man but stressed rather his distinctively human faculties as guides to the moral and intellectual goals of education.

The literary humanists reacted vigorously against the role of modern science and social science in modern life. They stressed the importance of selecting a few able students for advanced education as a means of training an aristocratic elite to become the leaders of the masses of men. They repudiated the humanitarian ideal of democracy and spoke longingly of the cultural and liberal education of the past when little thought was given to the effort to educate everybody. Freedom was really only within the competence of a few who by dint of hard discipline in a liberal education could become worthy of freedom. The masses of people could profit only from a trade, or technical, or vocational training, not from a genuinely liberal education.

Most literary humanists argued that man had certain distinctive qualities or faculties that made him absolutely different from the animals. These characteristics consisted of the faculties of reason, moral conscience, esthetic taste, and a religious instinct. These faculties were not a product of evolution, nor were the values of truth, goodness, and beauty a matter of evolution. They are absolute, permanent, and unchanging, not creations of a natural experience. The principal repository of these values is the great tradition of Western civilization, especially the classics of Greece and Rome. Thus, the goal of education is the well-rounded development of the intellectual, moral, esthetic, and religious capabilities of man through study of the humanities which include the traditional arts and sciences of a liberal education. Priority, however, belongs to the linguistic and literary arts.

The rational humanists or intellectualists had much in common with the literary humanists, but they tended to give top place in the hierarchy of human values to man's rational nature, his reason or intellect. They argued that the distinctive job of education was to develop the faculty of intellect, and therefore they paid less attention to the moral, the esthetic, and the religious aspects of human experience. Intellect was to be cultivated best by discipline in the liberal arts of grammar, rhetoric, logic, and mathematics and through the medium of reading the great books of the Western tradition. Appealing to the philosophy of Aristotle, St. Thomas Aquinas, and Cardinal Newman, the intellectualists claimed to be in the main line of rationalistic philosophy which to them was the only true philosophy. Anything else was not considered to be philosophy; it was merely science, or art, or practical technology.

Following Aristotle, the intellectualists claimed superiority for the theoretical reason over the practical reason. The theoretical reason was concerned with first principles, ultimate causes, final truths; whereas the practical reason was merely interested in how to do things and make things. The only true education would thus be concerned with the cultivation of the higher intellectual virtues and would leave matters of moral and social conduct, physical well being, and earning a living to other agencies but would not include them in a general education to be offered by schools and colleges. In their belief in a permanent human nature and in a permanent set of truths and values the intellectualists were close to the religious, idealistic, and classical humanist views.

The intellectualists were especially close to the Roman Catholic position because of their espousal of neo-Thomism as a philosophy of man and knowledge, but they did not argue for the theological underpinnings that Catholics insisted upon as essential to a truly Christian education. They all agreed, however, that education must serve only the higher nature of man and avoid traffic with the useful, the practical, the scientific, the empirical, or indeed the interests and needs of the students. Since we know what human nature is like and what permanent truth is, we should formulate a prescribed curriculum that contains those truths and that will cultivate the intellectual virtues by a rigorous system of mental discipline. Only by these means could a person be considered to be educated. The affinity for the nineteenth-century faculty psychology runs throughout the humanist positions.

Experimentalism

One of the most influential views of man, and certainly one whose implications for education were carefully worked out in recent decades, came to be known as experimentalism or experimental naturalism. Building upon the earlier social conceptions of self and a pragmatic conception of mind and knowledge, experimentalism broadened and deepened after World War I. John Dewey continued to be the outstanding and creative spokesman for this view.[1] It is patently impossible to deal satisfactorily in short space with a whole philosophy here as elsewhere, but one or two outstanding conceptions that are peculiarly important for education may be mentioned. The whole discussion of the social conception of mind and the pragmatic conception of knowledge should be regarded as pertinent here (see pp. 339-347).

Basic to the experimentalist philosophy is the conception of *experience* as *interactive* and as *continuous* with nature. The other views looked upon the distinctively human in human nature as something *given* to man; the religious and idealistic views defined it as a soul or a self; the humanists as a set of moral and intellectual faculties; the realists as a peculiarly complicated nervous system. But the experimentalist view defines human nature as a *product* or a result of experience. This is thus a cultural conception of man, for experience is viewed as the interaction between an individual and his culture. The individual brings to experience his biological equipment, and the culture brings to experience the group ways of doing, believing, thinking, and behaving. If either term is entirely lacking, there is no experience and thus no human nature; if either term is inadequate or defective, then by so much is experience and human nature inadequate or defective. Different cultures and different individuals will give rise to differences in experience.

The interactive process of human experience is analogous to but not identical with the interactive process in the rest of nature. The primary distinction is the presence of a more complicated biological organism known as man *and* a cultural environment produced by human society. But this whole process of human experience is an achievement *within* nature, not created prior to or located outside of nature. The principles of continuity and of interaction thus are placed over against other views that stress a dualism between man and nature, between mind and body, between the supernatural and the natural, between individual and society. The reality of the spiritual is affirmed by experimentalism, but it is seen as a product of man's experience when he deals with the deepest and most cherished values of self and society. Values arise out of human experience; they are not imposed upon experience from some supernatural or nonnatural source above or beyond experience.

A second key conception in experimentalism is faith in human *intelligence* as the best hope for man to solve his problems and achieve his values. The religious and idealistic views looked upon intelligence as subordinate to faith, and the humanists looked upon intelligence as a rational means of achieving permanent and theoretical truths that are superior to experience. In contrast, the experimentalist looked upon faith, loyalty, commitment, and values as integral to the process of intelligence, not in a separate realm; he

[1] Outstanding philosophical works by Dewey included *Essays in Experimental Logic* (Chicago, University of Chicago Press, 1916); *Human Nature and Conduct* (New York, Holt, 1922); *Reconstruction in Philosophy* (New York, Holt, 1920); *Experience and Nature* (Chicago, Open Court, 1925); *Logic, the Theory of Inquiry* (New York, Holt, 1938); and *Art as Experience* (New York, Minton, Balch, 1934).

sees the theoretical not as separate from the practical but as a means of better solving practical problems. Experimentalism turns the Aristotelian hierarchy on its head. The primary goal of human intelligence is to improve conduct and to solve the practical problems of life from the most lowly and simple problems to the most elevated and complex. Theory is not an intellectual virtue to be valued for its own sake, but theory and ideas are to be highly valued for the aid they give in improving human experience. As intelligence operates within experience and is not external to it, intelligence is empirical and not rationalistic as the intellectualists defined it.

Most experimentalists thus looked to the scientific method of problem solving as the generalized method of intelligence appropriate to the solution of practical problems of social conduct as well as the theoretical problems of science and knowledge. Scientific method is applicable to problems of morality and society as well as to problems of fact and information. Other experimentalists became restless with the application of the scientific method of problem solving as a generalized method of intelligence to all spheres of experience. They began to make much of the distinction between judgments of fact and judgments of practice. Judgments of fact can and must be achieved on the basis of the scientific method of inquiry much as Dewey defined it. This is man's best resource for achieving warrantable knowledge and information concerning what *is*. But they argued that the scientific method cannot produce adequate guides to what *should* be. A more inclusive process must be undertaken in order to achieve adequate guides to *desirable* goals for human conduct.

These normative judgments must be achieved in a process of deliberation, discussion, and consensus free of coercion and must be made by all those concerned with the judgment. The desired goal must be projected; the relevant facts must be ascertained by the scientific method; and then a plan of action must be formulated that will guide action from the present state of affairs to the desired goal. The test of a wise decision lies not in the scientifically ascertained facts of what *is* but in the uncoerced consensus of those concerned; the ultimate resource of human intelligence lies with the eventual agreements of a democratic community. Fact and value must be kept in close relationship, but they must be treated differently in the process of intelligence.[2]

Whatever their differences about the nature of intelligence, experimentalists agreed that the cultural conception of man and experience and faith in intelligence are fundamental for education. The educative process is basically a moral task. The sanctions for morality rest not exclusively upon religion but upon the common agreements of human experience achieved by a process of human intelligence. As education must face up to the most demanding moral

[2] For differences among experimentalists on this issue see, for example, John L. Childs, *Education and Morals* (New York, Appleton-Century-Crofts, 1950) and R. Bruce Raup, *The Improvement of Practical Intelligence* (New York, Harper, 1950).

problems of the society in which it operates, so the school must be closely related to this society. Its content, processes, and organization must be based upon an interpretation of a desirable society to be determined in the light of a study of our historical tradition, our deepest moral values, and the most urgent social and intellectual problems that face our society. Along with commitment to human experience and human intelligence must go a commitment to a democratic society and a democratic way of life as the only setting in which human intelligence can work freely to elevate and improve the quality of human experience.

PSYCHOLOGICAL VIEWS OF MAN

The range and scope of psychological views of man were as complex and controversial in their claims upon education as were the religious and philosophic views. Little can be done here except to point to three or four clusters of psychological orientations that swept American thought from the period of World War I to the present. Connectionism continued to be a dominant position that was refined, expanded, and solidified through the work of a large company of experimental and scientific psychologists. Beginning in the World War I period and reaching its height in the 1920's and early 1930's a more extreme version of associationism, known as behaviorism, engaged the loyalties of many scientific psychologists. Three other viewpoints came rapidly upon the scene to criticize the associationist assumptions of connectionism and behaviorism. One view stressed the structure and "field" of the situation in which experience operates. These "field" psychologies attracted considerable attention in the 1920's and continued to grow in popularity and importance in the 1930's and 1940's. Somewhat slower to achieve academic respectability in the colleges were the approaches to human nature represented by psychoanalysis and the "depth" psychologies. Drawing from many sources in psychology and in the social sciences, a new emphasis upon social psychology gave promise of giving needed insights into the relation between individual and group behavior. The over-all result was to broaden enormously the view of man and thus to complicate the task of educators as they faced children in the classroom and adults in society.

Connectionism and Behaviorism

Connectionism continued to place emphasis upon the stimulus-response bonds or connections set up within the individual as the best explanation for most forms of human behavior. The connection between the external situation and the response that the individual makes is the important thing. These connections result from inherited tendencies to respond instinctively or automatically to certain stimuli. Upon these biologically inherited tendencies can be built countless other connections through the process of learning.

As noted earlier, learning centered around the laws of effect, exercise, and readiness (see p. 338). In recent years the connectionist view tended to put less stress upon trial and error learning and mere repetition or drill as the keys to the law of exercise. Instead, much more emphasis was placed upon the role of insight, problem solving, reasoning, and motivation as roads to effective learning. The law of readiness was interpreted in such way as to put more stress upon purposes, goal-sets, motives, and drives rather than merely random trial and error. Throughout these changes the connectionists seemed to find little reason to modify their central emphasis upon the law of effect.

One other thing the connectionists did was to drop their emphasis upon the neurological basis of learning. Whereas early connectionists had inferred that their laws of connection were based upon a physical bond in the synapse between two nerves in the nervous system, later connectionists began to give less emphasis to neurophysiological explanations and more emphasis to overt behavior and the operation of behavior. Stung by the attacks of field psychologists and psychoanalysts, the connectionists began to insist that behavior is much more complex than might be inferred from earlier and more simple explanations of stimulus-response connections. They gave more and more attention to the processes by which concepts are formed, meanings are acquired, and understanding is achieved. Reliance upon passive receptivity gave way to belief in the active and dynamic character of learning. And it was agreed that learning must take into account emotional and attitudinal factors in behavior along with motor and verbal responses. Thus incentives, motives, purposes, and goals become more central as subjects for study and inquiry.

Connectionism continued, however, to put considerable emphasis upon the inherited elements in human nature as important explanations for differences in ability, motivation, and achievement. Many connectionists tenaciously attributed more potency to the inherited qualities of individuals than to the effects of environment. They were likely to insist that intelligence was largely an inherited quality and could not be changed much by changes in environment. Thorndike came to the conclusion in 1939 that behavior was much more the result of heredity than it was the result of environment. Thus, if social improvement is desired it would be better to induce the wise and able to have children of their own rather than to take in boarders. Not all psychologists agreed, nor indeed did all connectionists agree. Studies of identical twins separated at birth showed that significantly superior differences in intelligence appeared in children who had been placed in favorable homes in comparison with those placed in homes where inferior opportunity for education and cultural achievement was present.

The quarrel over heredity and environment was heightened in the years following World War I by the appearance of an extreme associationist view known as behaviorism. Whereas it could be inferred that many connectionists approached a materialistic view of human nature, there could be no doubt about the behaviorists who openly proclaimed that they would not be concerned with explanations of human behavior that rested on such mysterious concepts as mind, soul, consciousness, will, or ideas. They were not content to be concerned with "internal" evidences of thinking or mental activity but would be concerned only with outward overt behavior. They would not attempt to "explain" behavior by referring to some internal factor but would describe only what they could observe from the outside. As early as 1914 John B. Watson at Johns Hopkins University urged that physical explanations would be enough to explain all human behavior. Watson, Max Meyer, A. P. Weiss, and others endeavored to build a science of human behavior that would be just as scientific as the physical sciences and that would produce scientific laws as certain, as valid, and as accurate as the scientific laws of physics and chemistry.

At the center of the behaviorists' conception of behavior and learning was the process of conditioning. Drawing upon the animal experiments of Pavlov, the behaviorists argued that the conditioned reflex was the primary basis of all learning. Pavlov had discovered that the presentation of food to a dog would bring out a response marked by an increase in salivary flow. Then he controlled the conditions by ringing a bell every time the food was presented to the dog. He then discovered that he could produce the salivary flow in the dog simply by ringing the bell even though the original stimulus of the food was not present. Thus the secondary stimulus (bell) became so closely associated with the primary stimulus (food) that the secondary stimulus could call out the original reflex or response. The response had thus been conditioned or associated or attached to a new stimulus.

The behaviorists felt that this process of conditioning through associated stimuli was the fundamental process of all learning and all behavior. All children are born with certain inherited, unlearned, and unconditioned reflexes which could be reduced to the simple responses of fear, rage, and love. Removal of support or threat of dropping the child could elicit responses of fear such as crying; excessive restriction of the child's actions could produce reactions of rage such as rejection or struggling against the stimulus; and caressing and kissing could produce reactions of love such as laughing, smiling, and movement toward the stimulus. Watson argued that all learned responses are built upon these inherited action tendencies by the process of conditioning whereby thousands of new and more complicated stimuli are associated with the earlier and simple reflexes. Habits, attitudes, and the most complicated processes of thinking and learning are built up in this way.

Watson further set the psychological world by the ears by proclaiming that the process of conditioning meant that the character of responses could be manipulated by controlling the stimuli that were presented to the individual. Carried to its extreme this view would mean that all children are virtually identical at birth; differences arise because of the different stimuli that are presented to them by their environment; therefore the character and quality of human beings could be determined to the extent that the environment could be controlled. Watson virtually argued that he could produce any kind of person that was desired if he could be given complete control of the environment.

The extreme materialism and environmentalism of the behaviorist position attracted many in the generation of younger psychologists of the 1920's, but the same ingredients repelled a growing number of psychologists after about 1930. The quarrels over heredity and environment began to soften somewhat, but the issue is still alive and continues to be one way in which psychologists tend to be divided in their approaches to behavior, learning, and education. Together the connectionists and behaviorists represent one of the dominant psychological outlooks in academic circles in psychology and educational psychology today. However, the sharp lines of controversy of the 1920's and 1930's do not seem to be as clearly present as they were. The appearance of still newer psychological orientations began to attract attention away from the older controversies.

Field Psychologies

From several quarters came criticism of the connectionist and behaviorist conceptions on the grounds that they concentrated too exclusively on analyzing behavior into its smallest or most specific elements. For purposes of discussion these critical views are joined together here under the heading of field psychologies. They had this much in common: they argued that every situation of learning is a total "field" that includes the surrounding situation, the learner, and his reactions. They held that every situation of experience has a character or structure or organization that dominates the field, and thus it is a mistake to try to analyze any situation into its specific elements. This effort will result in an atomistic approach that will neglect the all pervading character of the situation. Behavior can only be properly viewed when the *whole* organism of the individual and the *whole* situation in which the individual finds himself are considered as esssential ingredients in the total learning process. These theories thus came to be known as field theories or organismic theories.

The notion of a "field" was brought into psychology from the physical and mathematical sciences where fields of force were being talked about. The rotation of the earth in space cannot be understood apart from the gravitational field in which it operates or in relation to the gravitational pull of the sun; similarly, the movements of the moon cannot be understood apart from the gravitational field that includes the earth. In like manner, the notion of the individual human being as an "organism" was borrowed from the studies in biology and physiology that showed the interrelations of physical functioning, physiology, emotion, feeling, and thinking all as integral parts of a behaving organism. Thus, by analogy with fields of force and by direct application of the organismic view of human behavior, a new emphasis was given to American psychology.

One such emphasis came from Germany in the 1920's in the form of Gestalt psychology. Such leaders as Max Wertheimer, Kurt Koffka, and Wolfgang Kohler began to criticize the analytical methods of connectionism and associationism. They began to say that learning does not arise from a specific response to a specific stimulus, but rather that it arises as the individual sees the whole pattern (or Gestalt) in a situation and changes his behavior in accordance with the pervading character of the situation. The learner is a whole organism and he responds as a whole; he does not respond automatically or mechanically through specific reflexes. The Gestaltists thus emphasized learning by insight into a situation; drill and repetition are useless unless the learner "sees into" the problem that faces him. Thus, purposes, goals, and motivations become more important in the learning process, and the purposes and goals must be "seen" by the learner as important to him and not merely as something important to the teacher.

Much of the concern of the Gestaltists was with the process of perception, and their examples were often taken from the field of visual perception. It was easy and dramatic to show how the context of an item or a letter or a word could take on different meaning when placed in a different context or "field." Thus, for example, the item "1" which is printed with exactly the same accuracy in a number of cases will mean one thing when it is the first figure in "1952" and something quite different when printed as the second letter in "election." It is the pattern or form of 1952 which gives meaning to "1" in one case and the pattern or form or field of "election" which gives meaning to "1" in the second case. They thus argued that it is the *structure* of the situation which is important; not the mass of separate or specific details or items that make up the situation. Learning to read by whole sentences and whole words rather than by building up one letter after another was an application of the Gestalt approach to reading skills. Learning in general was thus defined as a process whereby the learner sees himself in a situation confronting a problem and sees the way to solve the problem in relation to his purposes and goals.

More recently influential in America has been another variety of field psychology that has come to be associated with Kurt Lewin and is often called topological psychology. It is less concerned with perception in experience and more concerned with motives, drives, and purposes in human behavior. The individual is seen as behaving in the "field" of psychological forces that are acting upon him at a given time. His behavior can be described and predicted only as we realize what his goals are that impel him forward, what barriers that stand in his way, and what threats may operate to thwart or deflect him from his goals. This group of "forces" can be plotted in diagrams as a physical field of force can be computed. The goals have positive valence or power; threats have negative valence; and barriers have no valence or power. When the total field of forces is computed, the behavior of the individual will be better understood.

The term topology (study of places or regions) comes from that phase of mathematics where the zones to be traversed are more important than the direction or distance between two points. Although often confusing in its terminology, the topological psychology has been important for its emphasis upon goals and for its implications for social psychology where threats and barriers are seen to arise from the psychological forces of social groups that affect individuals. Lewin became well known for his work in showing that group learning is often better than individual learning. Since attitudes and prejudices are the result of the surrounding social atmosphere, we all live according to group standards, and no one person can depart very much from the standards of the group. But if a group changes, then the individual can change with the group and feel a part of it. For example, a group of six farm mothers learned to care for their children much more effectively than a single individual learned the same things. Thus, in order to increase the power of positive valences to overcome negative threats and neutral barriers to learning, group methods are often superior to individual methods. Here was a new and attractive approach to learning and behavior that occasioned a good deal of attention at the mid-century.

Psychoanalysis

A third conception of man that came to have great influence upon education stemmed from the work of Sigmund Freud and others in Vienna in the late nineteenth and early twentieth century. Whereas connectionism and behaviorism tended to make the study of human behavior more scientific and more objective and the field psychologies tended to look upon the interrelations of the individual with his social and physical setting, the psychoanalytical approach emphasized some of the dimensions of human behavior that were relatively untouched by the other views.

Much concerned with the motivations, drives, and instincts of people, the Freudian psychoanalysts looked upon each individual as a battleground of conflicting urges which could be revealed only by deep introspective methods. Some of these urges were primitive blind drives that stemmed from the instincts of sex and aggressiveness; these were summed up in the term *id*. Other tendencies were centered in the desire to preserve, protect, and advance the individual and maintain his status in the face of the realities of the outside world; these negotiating and conscious tendencies were called the *ego*. As the blind primitive urges struggle to force their way into outward behavior they must pass from the unconscious arena of the *id* into the conscious arena of the *ego*. Here the *ego* has the help of the *superego* which represents the demands of morality and acts as a social conscience to keep unwelcome or dangerous urges below the level of consciousness by the mechanism of repression.

The mental apparatus of the individual is thus made up of three realms or regions: (1) The *superego* represents the conscientious demands of parents, of society, and moral authority. (2) The *ego* tries to mediate between the external world and the *id;* it receives stimuli from the external world and tries to protect the organism from being destroyed by introducing thought processes between desire and action and using memory as an aid. (3) The *id* is the obscure, inaccessible part of personality, a seething cauldron of excitement, energy, impulse, and desires with no logic, no organization, no good or evil, no values or morality.

The poor *ego* thus must serve three masters, the external world, the *superego,* and the *id*. The *ego* is driven and goaded on by the *id,* blocked and rebuffed by the external world, and hemmed in by the critical, watchful, and severe eye of the *superego*. The *ego* tries to give synthesis and unity and organization to life by using conscious thought, deliberation, and intelligence. But when the ego finds that it cannot serve all three masters satisfactorily and must acknowledge its weakness, it breaks out into various forms of anxiety: fear of external events in the face of the external world, guilt and inferiority in the face of the *superego,* and neurotic anxieties in the face of the internal passions of the *id*.

Anxiety is produced as the *ego* tries to reconcile the forces playing upon it. So anxiety causes the *ego* to try to repress unwelcome or dangerous urges and push them back into the unconscious; they are not driven away, but continue to work, possibly to reappear in some other less recognizable form. Freud put great stress upon the urges of sex as the origin of desires that emerged in other forms when suppressed or repressed. Alfred Adler located the basic drives in a desire for power in the face of a sense of helplessness and a feeling that the community is against the lone individual. Carl G. Jung identified the basic drive as a desire to find a way to express one's own unique individuality in the face of the pressures of society for conformity.

No matter what desire may be thought of as the central urge, the Freudians threw a bombshell into the dominant psychologies of the early twentieth century. Their emphasis upon the unconscious determination of behavior, the emotional drives, the role of the irrational, and especially the importance of sex in behavior meant that their point of view would meet great opposition. But gradually the psychoanalytical approach won adherence from psychiatrists and from the new guidance movement in psychology despite a continuing opposition from scientific and objective psychologists, from intellectualists, and from religious groups. Nevertheless, it became apparent that much control over behavior could be achieved by the process of introspective psychoanalysis whose purpose was to strengthen the *ego,* make it more independent of the *superego,* widen its vision, and enable it to extend conscious and intelligent control over external reality, the *superego,* and the *id.*

In recent years many modifications have been made in the original Freudianism. Much of the superstructure of nineteenth-century terminology and dualistic conception of human nature has been dropped. Furthermore, the almost exclusively biological approach of Freud, who neglected the role of the culture in behavior, has been modified by greater attention to the culture as a source of the dynamics and desires of behavior. Such persons as Karen Horney, Erich Fromm, Harry Stack Sullivan, Lawrence K. Frank, Abraham Kardiner, and many others have begun to stress the social nature of the individual. They tend to look for the origins of anxiety and frustration in the pressures and conflicts that arise in society and find a focus in individuals rather than to look for their origins wholly within the individual himself. The psychoanalytical approach has been the stimulus of much of the mental hygiene movement and the study of the psychology of adjustment and personality which have become so important in education in recent decades.

The mental hygiene approach has had great influence in focusing attention upon the irrational or nonrational motivations in behavior and learning. It has been of enormous value in directing attention upon the need for guidance and counseling for normal children and for psychiatric care for abnormal children. Above all, it has made educators aware of the importance of the early years of the child in his home, family, and schooling. These early years are now seen as crucial in the formation of maladjustments that tend to shape personality development throughout the later years of childhood and adulthood. Study of the mechanisms of adjustment used by children and adults as they face problems and conflicts that prove to be too much for them is invaluable in helping people to lead happy and wholesome lives.

Some of these mechanisms of adjustment have been found to include: adjustment by compensation, whereby the individual tries to make up for deficiencies in one trait by excelling in another; rationalization, whereby an individual gives "good" reasons for what he does or wants to do instead of the "real" reasons; sublimation, whereby the individual channels his socially unapproved desires into socially approved activities; withdrawal from the scene of reality by retreat into fantasy, daydreaming, seclusion, apathy, or negative reactions; repressions that appear in diverse forms of fear, inferiority, worry, or compulsion; ailments that are real to the individual but have no direct basis in physical origins; blaming others for doing what the individual himself wants to do; and dozens of others. Increased attention to such behavior problems enabled educators to be better prepared to deal with the whole child or the whole person rather than simply with his "mind." Personal adjustment became a concern of educators along with their concern with learning and acquisition of knowledge.

Social Psychology

Another psychological development that was growing in importance at mid-century was the appearance of social psychology as a distinctive approach to the understanding of human behavior. It is perhaps still too new to assess fully, but thirty years of development reveal contributions that are worthy of more full historical treatment than is possible here. Several sources can be seen. One was the social conception of the self that appeared in philosophy in the works of George Herbert Mead, John Dewey, and others. A landmark in this development was Dewey's *Human Nature and Conduct,* which appeared in 1922 and carried the subtitle *An Introduction to Social Psychology.* Another source was the growing emphasis upon social attitudes in sociology as represented by the work of Charles H. Cooley. Another was cultural anthropology as represented by such writers as Ralph Linton, Margaret Mead, Ruth Benedict, Melville J. Herskovits, and others. The field psychologies and the neo-Freudians made their contributions, and there were undoubtedly still other sources.

But the important thing is this. Forty years ago educational psychology was almost exclusively a matter of the psychology of the individual. Today the individual is seen in many of his relations as a member of many groups. His attitudes, his motivations, and his learnings are seen as related to the role he takes as a member of these social groups. The individual takes on attitudes and motives that are expected of him by the group to which he belongs and by the role he plays in his family, in his occupation, in his social class, in his school, and in many other positions related to his age, sex, or voluntary association groups. The individual finds that he must live up to the norms of behavior or expectations that are assigned to the position he holds. The attitudes one develops toward oneself and toward others are shaped by the hierarchy of positions and behaviors expected in any society. Personality itself is a result of the predispositions and attitudes that are organized and structured by the individual as he behaves in his various social groups.

Such assumptions as these have led social psychologists to be concerned with study of the culture and the society as a means of arriving at better understanding of individuals. They have studied race relations, minority-majority attitudes and prejudices, group tensions, the effect of social class and status upon the individual, religious motivations and prejudices, the effects of family, neighborhood, and community upon individual behavior, delinquency, crime, and crowd behavior. The whole study of intergroup and intercultural relations with their bearings upon individual personality became an important theme in social psychology. Furthermore, since group life is so important to the individual, it became important to give special study to improving the way informal groups behave when they are trying to reach group decisions by joint action. This movement came to be known as group dynamics. Recognizing that decision making by groups was increasingly important in every sphere of life from the intimate family group to the United Nations, the techniques and methods of improving group decisions became an interesting and useful approach. Other approaches and uses of group methods were represented by the techniques of role playing or the sociodrama in which participants have a chance to take various roles in situations that resemble lifelike experiences and thus gain direct insight into the attitudes and motives that prompt or interfere with effective group behavior.

SOCIAL ROLE OF ORGANIZED KNOWLEDGE

In addition to making decisions about the conflicting claims of religious, philosophic, and psychological views of man, the twentieth-century educator was faced with conflicting outlooks concerning the role of knowledge in society. Whatever else the educator had to deal with he had to deal with people and with knowledge. One fact overshadowed all others as American educators turned their attention to devising the best kind of education they could for the children and youth of the land. They were staggered by the sheer weight and mass of knowledge that was being accumulated in nearly every field of inquiry. We have more information in the fields of science, social science, and the humanities than ever before. What to do about it in education? There were several kinds of answers.

One form the problem took was in the quarrel between the advantages of specialization versus the advantages of integration and synthesis. No one doubted that knowledge was becoming ever more specialized as thousands of scholars delved deeper and deeper into narrower and narrower problems. The demands of graduate and professional schools for persons competently trained in one field of knowledge led many to say that scholars cannot be trained adequately unless they are highly specialized. It was argued, for example, that no one can become competent as a nuclear physicist unless he begins his scientific and mathematical training early in his educational career and keeps at it in a concentrated way for years on end.

This view led others to say that such specialization will be disastrous for individuals and for society. If the ideal becomes to "know more and more about less and less," how can we achieve the general intelligence and breadth of outlook required in a complex society? Many began to say that we have amassed so much unrelated knowledge and information in various fields that we ought to call a moratorium on new investigation for a while so we can digest and assimilate what we have already discovered. Thus, the plea arose for more integration and synthesis of knowledge rather than more specialization. The problems we face are so vast and so complicated that we cannot rely upon the methods of only one academic discipline; we must try to see interrelations among various bodies of knowledge by an interdisciplinary approach. The demand for integration and synthesis lay behind the movements for various kinds of "general education" at the secondary and college levels and for cooperative efforts in teaching and research among scholars representing related fields of knowledge at the graduate and professional levels of education.

A second form that the problem of knowledge took for educators was an old one. Is knowledge primarily valuable for its own sake, or is it primarily valuable for its usefulness in helping us to solve the pressing problems of life? The tradition of knowledge for its own sake as developed in Europe and especially in the German universities of the nineteenth century continued strong. It received explicit statement as a desirable goal for universities by such spokesmen as Abraham Flexner, Robert M. Hutchins, and Norman Foerster, and it continued to be an implicit goal of thousands of teachers who saw the acquisition of information as the chief goal for their students.

On the other side, an increasing number of voices began to say that the primary or even the only purpose for acquiring knowledge is to *use* it in the solution of problems. Applied research and the application of knowledge to the problems of government, industry, agriculture, labor, and society in general are the true goals of knowledge. Unless this is done, they argued, the resources of scholarship and of knowledge will be cut off from the mainsprings of power and activity in a society which will result in the divorce of intelligence from action and of knowledge from moral conduct (as actually happened to the German universities under the Nazis). The writings of John Dewey, Alexander Meiklejohn, and Robert S. Lynd are simply a few examples of the plea that social responsibility and usefulness should be the goals of knowledge. They were no less interested in truth, but they felt that truth should be used to guide conduct rather than simply acquired for its own sake.

A third kind of issue that concerned the intellectual world of America had to do with the problem of objectivity in knowledge. One view insisted that the scholar must remain completely aloof from the social problems of his time; he must remain neutral, impartial, and indeed indifferent to social concerns if he is to achieve accurate, authentic, and objective knowledge. If the scholar allows his predilections or preferences to interfere with his work, he will become no better than a political propagandist; Nazi Germany, Fascist Italy, and Communist Russia could be pointed to as horrible examples of the way political ideologies can pervert science and scholarship.

On the other side, many scholars argued that objectivity should not mean neutrality or indifference to the critical social problems of our time. They argued that preferences are always at work in the mind of the scholar who cannot divorce himself completely from the cultural and social values of his times. The objective scholar will be one who will recognize his assumptions and predilections, make them explicit for all to see and to judge, and adhere to the most rigorous canons of accuracy, fairness, logic, and scientific method. But the objective scholar must be concerned with the pressing problems of society and must be concerned to promote the values of free inquiry and a free society which are necessary for the free pursuit of authentic knowledge. They, too, argued that knowledge should not be perverted by the pressures for nationalistic, partisan, sectarian, or class propaganda, but scholars must be as concerned as anyone else for the maintenance of the kind of society that will promote freedom. They pointed to the dreadful results that occur when scholars in Nazi, Fascist, or Communist orbits tried to maintain a spurious objectivity in the face of power forces that liquidated them, drove them into concentration camps, or in a few cases permitted them to escape as refugees to America or to other free nations. The problem of freedom of objective inquiry thus became a vital problem for American education.

A fourth question that American educators had to face was whether knowledge should be confined to the few or widely disseminated among the many. The outlook of the Genteel Tradition remained strongly in favor of concentrating upon the education of an intellectual elite or an aristocratic leadership of quality and intellect. This view rested on the assumption that most people did not have the intelligence or ability to acquire knowledge or to make decisions for themselves. This view would thus concentrate educative efforts upon the most able.

On the other side, there was a growing concern that the widest dissemination of knowledge was the only proper goal for a democratic society which must rest upon the assumption that the vast majority of people not only have the ability to acquire more knowledge than was formerly assumed, but also that they could be trusted to make sound decisions if they had access to sound knowledge. This divergence of opinion cut right across the whole educational world and found its most obvious counterpart in the attitudes concerning who should go to college. The former outlook continued to say that college attendance should be confined to the most able or else our "culture would be spread too thin." The latter outlook was at the basis of the view that far larger numbers of youth could profit from a college education than we had ever suspected. The success of the veterans who poured into our colleges and universities after World War II with the help of the educational benefits of the G. I. Bill of Rights seemed to confirm the latter outlook.

The Sciences and Mathematics

The rapid developments in modern science continued to stagger the imagination of those who knew what was going on or who became sensitive to the profound changes in intellectual outlooks and in the social and physical environment that science was producing. The traditional conception of the universe based upon Newtonian physics was further weakened by the developments in astronomy, physics, and astrophysics. Astrophysicists even began to take kindly to theories that envisioned the universe not as having been created suddenly in a dense mass at some point in prehistory and has been expanding or running down ever since but rather as a continuing series of creations that would continue to go on in the future. Scientists envisioned a cosmos of universes, stars, suns, and galaxies in which our own solar system became only a relatively small speck in space. The hard and fast laws of Newtonian gravitation and cause and effect gave way to theories of relativity. Physical matter gave up its hard and rigid appearance in the face of the view that matter is a system of organized energy and electromagnetic fields of force. Investigation of the atom which had been the province of a few mathematical physicists burst upon the public consciousness with incredible impact when the atomic bombs were set off beginning in 1945. Then the public became dimly aware of theories of quantum physics, electromechanics, radioactivity, electronics, and the mathematical theories that made the new physics possible. Similarly, work in biology, physiology, and chemistry led to new views of the growth of living organisms and of human beings and their relation to the physical environment.

Anyone who had lived through the forty years from World War I to mid-century could not help but become aware of the vast technological changes that rested upon scientific knowledge. A mere catalog of such changes would fill volumes. The most obvious surface evidences showed up in the changes in communication as we moved from the horseless carriages to the streamlined automobile, from the first shaky airplanes to the huge round-the-world airliners and jet bombers, and from the "wireless" to radio and television. Air conditioning, synthetic products, plastics, prefabricated houses, anesthetics, wonder drugs, X-rays, blood banks, vitamins, vast networks of flood control with power production and irrigation as by-products, production of food from the sea and from artificial chlorophyll, and plans for travel through interplanetary space were but a few of the vast changes that staggered the imagination but were becoming the ordinary accompaniments of an advanced technological society. No wonder that government, industry, labor, and agriculture turned to private laboratories and to the universities for even more aid in exploring the new frontiers envisioned by the scientists. If educators were still unaware of the importance of science in nearly all the affairs of war and peace, they had only to look about them. An educational system that neglected science in the twentieth century could mean the difference between life and death for vast numbers of people, indeed for civilization itself.

The Social Sciences

In the face of the new kind of world created by the scientists and the technologists new tasks were posed for the social sciences to find ways of ordering man's social institutions in order that they might promote the welfare of humanity rather than its destruction. The problems of world peace, of race relations, of class conflicts, and of competing political, economic, and social systems began to be faced more boldly by the social scientists. The impact of two world wars and of world-wide depression stimulated social scientists to delve into the complicated social issues that faced the world.

Anthropology came up with a concept of "culture" that looked upon man as the bearer of values and ideals as shaped by his institutions and his groups. Sociologists, political scientists, economists, and historians began to study realistically the way our social institutions actually worked and to enlist their disciplines in the task of creating social institutions that would serve human welfare by bringing to bear the best knowledge and planning of which man was capable. The social scientists came out of their ivory towers to serve government, business, and industry, labor and agriculture, and the political parties. As in the field of science, the range and scope of investigation in the social sciences began to accumulate at an ever accelerating rate. When faced with this vast accumulation, the educator could either throw up his hands in dismay or resolutely set out to answer the question "What shall we teach about man and society in our schools and colleges?"

Humanities and the Arts

The creative artist was by no means idle. Modern literature, drama, dance, poetry, architecture, and the several arts were describing the realities of the new society and trying to find a new synthesis of values in the face of what they found. The romantic and the sentimental continued to find expression in popular forms, but serious students of the creative arts tried to find formulas of security, escape, or acceptance of the new kind of world that confronted man. Social reform was a theme of much of modern literature and drama, while architecture, art, and music were concerned with modern themes and functional forms. Much attention was given to the question "How can modern man find personal integrity and self-expression in a world of mass production and forces that make for group conformity?" The humanities and the arts urged educators to become aware once more that they must not only deal with people and with knowledge but with the aspirations and hopes, the fears and faiths of individuals.

ISSUES FOR STUDY AND DISCUSSION

1. Do you think that religious differences are greater or less than they were in colonial times? Do you think that education would be benefited more if religious differences were sharpened or if they were softened? Do you think they may be more reconciled than they are now? If religious differences cannot be softened, what kinds of things can Americans agree about as a basis for unity of action and belief?

2. Why do you think that experimentalism has become so influential in the philosophy of education for public schools in recent years? Why do you think humanism

has remained so strong in the philosophy of education for college educators? Do you think that the philosophies of idealism or realism should play a larger role than they do now in the philosophy of education?

3. Which of the psychological outlooks seems to make most sense to you as you think of the fundamental tasks of education? Is it helpful to say that they all have some contribution to make? Or is it better to follow one view consistently as an educator?

4. In your own educational experience do you find evidences that the teaching you know about was based upon a belief in knowledge for its own sake or for its use in solving problems? Do you feel the need for greater integration in your learning or teaching experiences? If so, how do you think it could best be brought about? Do you think your loyalties should be devoted to promoting a superior education for the few or to the best education possible for the many? Is there a better way to define these issues?

SUGGESTIONS FOR FURTHER READING

Blau, Joseph L., *Men and Movements in American Philosophy*, New York, Prentice-Hall, 1952.

Boas, George, *Our New Ways of Thinking*, New York, Harper, 1930.

Burtt, Edwin A., *Types of Religious Philosophy*, New York, Harper, 1939.

Butts, R. Freeman, *The College Charts Its Course*, New York, McGraw-Hill, 1939.

Childs, John L., *Education and the Philosophy of Experimentalism*, New York, Appleton-Century, 1931.

Commager, Henry S., *Living Ideas in America*, New York, Harper, 1951.

Conant, James B., *On Understanding Science*, New Haven, Yale University Press, 1947.

Counts, George S., *Education and American Civilization*, New York, Teachers College, Columbia University, 1952.

Curti, Merle, *The Growth of American Thought*, 2d ed., New York, Harper, 1951.

Dewey, John, *A Common Faith*, New Haven, Yale University Press, 1934.

———, *Human Nature and Conduct*, New York, Holt, 1922.

Edman, Irwin, *Arts and the Man*, rev. ed., New York, Norton, 1939.

Gabriel, Ralph H., *The Course of American Democratic Thought*, New York, Ronald, 1940.

Grattan, C. Hartley (ed.), *The Critique of Humanism: A Symposium*, New York, Brent, Warren and Putnam, 1930.

Hacker, Louis M., *The Shaping of the American Tradition*, New York, Columbia University Press, 1947.

Hogben, Lancelot, *The Retreat from Reason*, London, Watts, 1936.

Hook, Sidney, *Reason, Social Myth, and Democracy*, New York, Day, 1940.

Johnson, F. Ernest, *The Social Gospel Re-examined*, New York, Harper, 1940.

Kilpatrick, William H., *Selfhood and Civilization*, New York, Macmillan, 1941.

Krikorian, Yervant H. (ed.), *Naturalism and the Human Spirit*, New York, Columbia University Press, 1944.

Linton, Ralph, *The Cultural Background of Personality*, New York, Appleton-Century, 1945.

Lynd, Robert S., *Knowledge for What?* Princeton, Princeton University Press, 1939.

Maritain, Jacques, *True Humanism,* New York, Scribner, 1938.

Mead, George H., *Movements of Thought in the Nineteenth Century,* Chicago, University of Chicago Press, 1936.

Morris, Charles W., *Paths of Life,* New York, Harper, 1942.

Nash, Arnold S. (ed.), *Protestant Thought in the Twentieth Century,* New York, Macmillan, 1951.

National Society for the Study of Education, *Psychology of Learning,* 41st Yearbook, Part 2, Bloomington, Ill., Public School Publishing Co., 1942.

Newcomb, Theodore, *Social Psychology,* New York, Dryden, 1950.

Niebuhr, Reinhold, *The Nature and Destiny of Man,* New York, Scribner, 1941–43, 2 vols.

————, *Moral Man and Immoral Society,* New York, Scribner, 1932.

Otto, Max, *The Human Enterprise,* New York, Crofts, 1940.

————, *Things and Ideals,* New York, Holt, 1924.

Randall, John H., *The Making of the Modern Mind,* Boston, Houghton, 1940.

Roback, A. A., *History of American Psychology,* New York, Library Publishers, 1952.

Schneider, Herbert W., *A History of American Philosophy,* New York, Columbia University Press, 1946.

Smith, Bernard, *The Democratic Spirit; A Collection of American Writings from the Earliest Times to the Present Day,* New York, Knopf, 1941.

Thorp, Willard, Curti, Merle, and Baker, Carlos, *American Issues; The Literary Record,* Vol. II, Philadelphia, Lippincott, 1941.

Thompson, Clara, *Psychoanalysis, Evolution and Development,* New York, Hermitage, 1950.

Thorndike, Edward L., *Human Nature and the Social Order,* New York, Macmillan, 1940.

Werkmeister, W. H., *The History of Philosophical Ideas in America,* New York, Ronald, 1949.

Whitehead, Alfred North, *Science and the Modern World,* New York, Macmillan, 1925.

Williams, Daniel Day, *What Present-Day Theologians Are Thinking,* New York, Harper, 1952.

Wish, Harvey, *Society and Thought in Modern America: A Social and Intellectual History of the American People from 1865,* New York, Longmans, 1952.

15

THE CLASH OF
EDUCATIONAL IDEAS

THE PERIOD from World War I to mid-twentieth century has seen a vast outpouring of ideas dealing with educational problems. Countless books, magazine articles, speeches, debates, and discussions of all kinds have come from interested public groups and individuals as well as from professional educators. They reflect the social, political, and economic issues described in Chapter 13 and the intellectual, philosophical, and religious outlooks described in Chapter 14. This chapter will attempt to point to the highlights of a few of the conflicting educational points of view that have been stated in America during the past thirty-five to forty years.

The difficulties of selecting materials for this chapter are enormous. As the historian comes closer to his own times, the task of deciding what is important is greatly complicated by the great amount of material available and by the intensity of feeling surrounding present controversial issues. Entire books have been written and entire courses are taught dealing with only one or parts of one of the problems to be discussed here in a single short chapter. It is not assumed that the discussion of any one issue will be adequate, but it is hoped that attention will be directed to some of the educational issues that are likely to require the best thought and most careful consideration by educators in the years immediately ahead. It is assumed that the conscientious educator will need to continue to give time and attention to such problems as these as he pursues his professional preparation, whether in formal courses in college or university or in his active work with his colleagues on the job.

Four clusters of educational problems and issues have been selected for mention. They have been chosen on several bases: they have deep roots in our traditions and thus represent a continuity with the past as described in the foregoing chapters of this book; they are issues that have received a great deal of public attention in recent years and are currently among the most controversial and therefore the most difficult to solve; they are issues of concern not merely to the educational profession but also to the public at large; and they represent issues upon which the American public and the profession are most sharply divided both among and within themselves. There are many other problems of academic or professional interest to the profession that could be discussed, but *these* are the ones that seem to be most closely related to questions of public policy and whose solutions will depend in large measure upon public decisions. If the profession is to take a role of leadership in helping to shape the answers to these questions of educational and public policy, the profession will need to be sure of the grounds of its position.

The first set of educational issues deals with the problem of providing equal educational opportunity for all Americans. Here the most controversy in recent years has centered upon a conflict between the ideal of equal opportunity and the practices of segregation and discrimination against minority or underprivileged groups.

A second set of issues revolves around problems of control and support of education. Here are such problems as the conflict between public and private control of schools, the conflict between church and state in the control and support of schools, and the conflict over federal aid to education.

A third set of issues has to do with the nature of the educational program in schools and colleges. Here a wide range of problems has stirred the public and professional mind to debate the relative merits of traditional subject matter versus the needs and interests of the child, the advisability of teaching about controversial issues in the schools, the debate over whether the schools should try to take leadership in social change or should follow the accepted customs of society, and the merits of religious instruction in the public schools.

Finally, a fourth set of issues focuses upon the social role of teachers and the teaching profession. Here the most difficult and controversial issues have centered upon the nature of academic freedom, the merits of special loyalty oaths for teachers, the methods by which Communist and subversive teachers should be weeded out of the profession, and the proper role of teachers in political action.

THE STRUGGLE OVER EQUAL EDUCATIONAL OPPORTUNITY

We have noted from the very first chapter of this book that class, sectional, and ethnic differences have had great influence upon education. In colonial times the class distinctions produced a dual system of schools: secondary classical schools for the upper classes and elementary vernacular schools and apprenticeship for the lower classes. From the beginning urban sections have demanded more extensive educational facilities than the rural areas. In the nineteenth century the democratic ideal of a common school open to all children and supported by public funds was largely realized. Most states established a single-track system of free schools from the elementary level upward through the college and university. Great gains were thus made in many states toward achieving the principle of equal opportunity for all children in public schools.

Following the Civil War, however, a severe modification of the principle of a single system of public schools was fastened upon the southern states where a dual system of public schools and colleges was set up, one system for white children and one system for Negro children. A segregated school system was made mandatory by constitution or by law in seventeen southern states (Alabama, Arkansas, Delaware, Florida, Georgia, Kentucky, Louisiana, Maryland, Mississippi, Missouri, North Carolina, Oklahoma, South Carolina, Tennessee, Texas, Virginia, West Virginia) and the District of Columbia. The segregated school systems were defended in the South on the basis of the "separate but equal" doctrine. According to this doctrine, it was argued that separate school systems for whites and Negroes were necessary for the social welfare of all and that equal opportunity as required by the Fourteenth Amendment to the Constitution could be preserved so long as the separate facilities were equal in quality. Since World War I more and more people in both the North and the South began to argue that genuine equality could not in fact be achieved while segregation was sanctioned by law.

A second breach in the principle of equality of opportunity was noted in the discrimination against certain religious and ethnic groups as well as racial groups who found it more difficult to gain entrance to private and even to public schools and colleges than did majority groups. Particularly affected were those of Jewish and Catholic faith as well as those of Mexican, Asiatic, and Central and Eastern European background. Here was operating not only religious discrimination but also social class discrimination against those of more recent immigration to the United States and those of a less privileged social status. Equality of opportunity was being denied not because of individual deficiency or ability but because of unavoidable membership in certain religious, nationality, or racial groups.

A third way in which the ideal of equality of opportunity seemed to be inoperative was increasingly made evident by the economic inability of large groups of people to afford advanced education. An insufficient number of schools or colleges was no longer the problem; it now was rather the problem of large numbers of people denied the opportunity of attending schools and colleges because of inadequate funds. The feeling grew that the democratic ideal of equality should be extended by means of scholarships or aid from government as well as from private sources in order to permit the intellectually able but economically handicapped persons to attend educational institutions, especially higher institutions. Few publicly opposed this principle of aid to the needy, but many opposed the idea that higher education should be made more easily available to a vastly increased number of youths.

Since World War I these have been the three most controversial issues in the persistent problem of providing equal opportunity in education. Each has many facets of which only a few can be given brief mention here.

Segregation and Discrimination in Education

Agitation for breaking down the system of segregated Negro schools and colleges where it existed paralleled somewhat the general state of race relations in the country. After World War I the new freedom found by many Negroes in war work led to violent reactions in many parts of the country. The Ku Klux Klan reached its height of power in the 1920's, and it looked for a while as though few gains could be made. Then with a rise in social consciousness, which developed in the depression years, an increasing awareness of the sorry plight of millions of Negro Americans, the spectacle of racial persecution exhibited by German Nazism and Italian Fascism in the 1930's, and finally the call for achievement of better democratic relations that accompanied World War II, notable gains began to appear in the 1940's. Leadership was initiated by President Roosevelt in the New Deal attack upon discrimination in employment and was carried considerably further by President Truman, who appointed the President's Committee on Civil Rights which issued an important report in 1947. Upon the basis of this report, entitled *To Secure These Rights,* President Truman formulated a civil rights program which he urged upon Congress and which became one of the most controversial political issues of the elections of 1948 and 1952.

The report of the President's committee urged that civil rights legislation be enacted on a broad front both by Congress and by the several states. Among its proposals were these: (1) Law enforcement by federal agencies and by states should be strengthened by reorganizing the Civil Rights Section of the Department of Justice and the Federal Bureau of Investigation and the establishment of permanent civil rights commissions in the Executive Office of the President, standing committees in Congress, and permanent commissions in the states. (2) The right to security of person should be strengthened by enactment of several laws by Congress, especially an anti-lynching law making lynching a federal offense. (3) The right to citizenship and its privileges should be strengthened by legislation outlawing poll taxes and guaranteeing participation by all persons in federal primaries and elections regardless of race or color and removing segregation and discrimination in the armed forces. (4) The right to equality of opportunity should be strengthened by eliminating in general all segregation based on race, color, creed, or national origin from American life, especially in employment, housing, health services, public services, and education. This would mean a federal Fair Employment Practices Act to prohibit discrimination in private employment, state laws to forbid segregation and discrimination in public and private health facilities, state laws prohibiting legal enforcement of restrictive covenants in housing, laws prohibiting segregation and discrimination in hotels, travel facilities, and other public places, and "Enactment by the state legislatures of fair educational practice laws for public and private educational institutions, prohibiting discrimination in the admission and treatment of students based on race, color, creed, or national origin."

Spurred on by this general program and the attendant arousal of public opinion, efforts were redoubled to try to break down the walls of segregation in education in the South. Two major frontal attacks were made, one through legislation and one through court cases to require public educational institutions to admit Negroes. In general, more progress had been made by the court decisions by the early 1950's than by legislation. Spark-plugged by the National Association for the Advancement of Colored People, the Urban League, the Southern Regional Council, and other groups, several court cases were brought to gain admittance of Negroes to the graduate and professional schools of the higher institutions in the South under the doctrines of the Fourteenth Amendment that all citizens shall be entitled to equal rights before the law. As early as 1938 the Supreme Court in the Gaines case required the University of Missouri to provide a Negro student with a law school education equal to that for whites. But this did not touch the "separate but equal" doctrine; it meant that segregation was still possible.

Much more influential were two unanimous Supreme Court decisions in June 1950. In the Sweatt case the University of Texas was required to admit a Negro to its law school and could not make him attend a new institution that had been set up for Negroes because it was far from equal in quality to the University of Texas Law School. In the McLaurin case the University of Oklahoma was prohibited from making a Negro graduate student in the School of Education sit in a special part of the classroom or be set apart in the library, cafeteria, or other facilities of the university.

Thus, the Supreme Court made it clear that southern states must provide equal educational opportunities for Negroes in their state institutions, but it did not face squarely the "separate but equal" doctrine and did not say flatly that any legal separation or segregation was thereby automatically a denial of equality. But considerable gains were made at the college level in the South. Negro students by 1950 were being admitted to colleges and universities in Arkansas, Virginia, Missouri, Kentucky, Maryland, and Delaware as well as in Texas and Oklahoma. Less progress had been made in the southern states of the Southeast. A survey by the *New York Times* in October 1950 estimated that more than 1,000 Negro students were attending classes with white students in southern colleges, and the prospect was that the number would increase.

Encouraged by the gains made against segregation in higher education, efforts were turned toward the segregated school systems of the elementary and secondary level. The two most publicized court cases were in Georgia and South Carolina. In 1949 a suit was filed in federal court in Irwin County, Georgia, alleging that Negro children were not receiving an equal education and asking that segregation be permanently prohibited under the equal rights provisions of the Fourteenth Amendment. A similar suit was brought in Clarendon County, South Carolina, in 1951. An interesting aspect of this case was the argument that segregation results in such psychological injury to the personality of the Negro child that feelings of inferiority and unequal status in society are inevitably produced. The court in Clarendon County found that segregation in itself was not unconstitutional, but that the freely admitted inferior conditions in the Negro schools must be made equal and the school officials must report back on the improvement within six months. The case went up to the United States Supreme Court which began to hear arguments in December 1952 along with cases from Virginia, Delaware, Kansas, and the District of Columbia. The constitutionality of the "separate but equal" doctrine was at stake in these cases as the Supreme Court was being asked to declare segregation itself unconstitutional even if equal facilities were provided separately to the races.

These inroads upon segregation in education were not made without opposition, but public opinion seemed to be growing in their favor. Several southern governors and public leaders both in and out of higher institutions expressed their satisfaction with the gains. Most students in the colleges took the new regime as a matter of course, but many college educators and not a few public school officials, especially in Georgia, Alabama, and Mississippi, were fearful that the frontal attack on segregation would hold back the gains that were being made to improve Negro schools. Many white southerners were fearful that the legal approach was perhaps too hasty and would provoke unnecessarily too vigorous reactions.

The reaction was not long in coming. Governor Herman Talmadge of Georgia vigorously opposed the court case in 1949 and insisted that Georgia would never permit the breakdown of segregation in the public schools. By January 1951 a constitutional amendment was introduced into the Georgia House of Representatives by followers of Governor Talmadge providing that separate schools for white and Negro students must be preserved, and, if necessary, the state could turn over the state schools and property to private individuals and could give financial grants to individuals for their use in attending schools and colleges of their choice. A law was passed taking away public funds from any white school or college that admitted Negroes. Similarly, in South Carolina Governor James F. Byrnes announced early in 1951 that he would urge the state to abandon its public school system and turn it over to private or religious agencies rather than adhere to any federal court requirement that segregation be prohibited. On November 4, 1952 the voters of South Carolina approved a proposed amendment to the state constitution which, if adopted by the legislature, would abolish the state's public school system. Thus the issue was joined, the results were in doubt, and the prospects were that bitter conflicts would ensue before the issue was settled.

Although the problem of segregation was most pronounced in the South, it was not confined to the South. Court cases were fought in California to prevent school boards from segregating children of Mexican parentage in separate schools. In Cairo, Illinois, violence flared over the attempt to enter Negro children into the white schools of Cairo, which still maintained in early 1952 segregation of Negro children despite the laws of Illinois prohibiting segregation on the basis of race or color and denying state funds to any school system that violated the law. A federal district court in Topeka, Kansas, refused to outlaw segregation in the elementary schools of Topeka because the separate facilities were found to be substantially equal. This case was also to be reviewed by the United States Supreme Court late in 1952 along with the Clarendon County case and the others mentioned above.

Much more difficult to deal with in some respects was the widespread practice of districting in cities of mixed population which sometimes produced all white schools and all Negro schools because the school district lines followed the residential lines of color. Many localities faced such problems as these with greater or lesser difficulties for parents, children, and school officials. Professional educators became increasingly aware of the principle of equality and of civil rights at stake for all Americans. Sharp controversy appeared in the National Education Association because the convention of 1950 was scheduled to be held in St. Louis where Negroes were not permitted to occupy hotel sleeping rooms. As early as 1943 the NEA had resolved not to hold its meetings in cities where discrimination existed. In 1952 the National Society of College Teachers of Education and the Philosophy of Education Society resolved not to return to St. Louis so long as the hotel situation went unchanged. Consciousness of the race problem had made great strides by mid-century.

In addition to the growing concern for enabling students of minority racial groups to take advantage of equal educational opportunity, a new interest in reducing discrimination against minority religious and ethnic groups developed momentum, especially in the 1940's and 1950's. This again was a part of the larger movement to make public services, housing, and employment more equally available to all Americans. Moral pressure and campaigns to educate public opinion to want greater equality and to reduce prejudice were promoted by such groups as the National Conference of Christians and Jews and many religious agencies of all faiths. A great public interest was developed in the 1940's among professional educators and the public generally in the problem of intergroup, intercultural, and interpersonal relations. Courses and activities designed to promote better human relations were introduced into many schools, colleges, and teachers colleges.

Similarly, the campaign against discrimination took legal form, especially with respect to employment, housing, and education. From 1941 to 1950 nine states passed laws designed to prevent discrimination in employment and six states passed laws to prevent discrimination in public housing because of race, color, creed, or national origin. Bills were introduced into many other states, and the prospect was that the number would grow. New York State's Anti-Discrimination Commission reported each year that public opinion, conference, and discussion resulted in the satisfactory settling of many cases of alleged discrimination. The possibility that court action could be used to enforce the decisions of the commission seemed enough to help settle differences along with the increased desire of employers, labor unions, and employees themselves to see that greater equality was achieved. The federal government reversed its earlier policy of 1935 to 1947 and moved to prevent discrimination in public housing that was aided by federal funds, and in 1948 the United States Supreme Court ruled that enforcement of restrictive covenants through the use of court action was unconstitutional.

The President's Commission on Higher Education reflected this trend in its forthright and extensive arguments that racial and religious discrimination in college entrance was a violation of the American principle of equality of opportunity.

> If education is to make the attainment of a more perfect democracy one of its major goals, it is imperative that it extend its benefits to all on equal terms. It must renounce the practices of discrimination and segregation in educational institutions as contrary to the spirit of democracy. Educational leaders and institutions should take positive steps to overcome the conditions which at present obstruct free and equal access to educational opportunities. Educational programs everywhere should be aimed at undermining and eventually eliminating the attitudes that are responsible for discrimination and segregation—at creating instead attitudes that will make education freely available to all.[1]

The general impression that many colleges had "quota systems" whereby they restricted the number of Jewish or Catholic students was borne out by a study of 15,000 high school seniors made under the direction of the American Council on Education from 1947 to 1949. It was found that only 63 percent of Jewish seniors were accepted by the college of their first choice in comparison with 71 percent of Catholic students and 82 percent of Protestant students. A higher proportion of Jewish students was admitted to *some* college because they kept trying by applying to several colleges, but it was clear that it was most difficult for Jewish students to gain admission to the privately controlled institutions located outside the applicant's home town, especially the small liberal arts colleges of the Northeast. Whether or not these figures represented accurately the situation throughout the country, there was little doubt that Jewish people felt they were victims of discrimination.

---

[1] President's Commission on Higher Education, *Higher Education for American Democracy,* Vol. I, *Establishing the Goals* (New York, Harper, 1948), pp. 38–39.

The survey of opinion about higher education conducted by Elmo Roper and reported in *Fortune* in September 1949 showed that 78 percent of Jewish persons believed that it was more difficult for a Jewish student to get into most colleges than for a non-Jewish student with the same high school marks. The public and the colleges were more alert at mid-century to the problem of religious discrimination and the need for greater equality than at any other period in our history.

Extending Educational Opportunity to All Classes

Besides segregation on the basis of race and discrimination on the basis of religion, the inability of many young people to gain an education because of financial difficulties gained increasing attention. The problem was at least twofold. At the elementary and secondary level the main problem was to make sure that public schools were just as available and just as high in quality in those districts and states that had poor financial resources as they were in those areas of greater financial ability. (This problem as it relates to federal aid to education is treated on pages 534 to 538). The other problem was how to make it possible for less privileged young people to take advantage of higher education when they had insufficient funds.

Here again the President's Commission on Higher Education argued that many more young people could profit from going to college than were able to do so as a result of economic barriers. The commission argued that virtually 50 percent of the population has the ability to complete fourteen years of schooling, that is, through junior college, and that nearly one third has the ability to complete a college course in liberal arts or professional training. It thus maintained that the minimum goal for enrollment in higher institutions by 1960 should be 4,600,000 or virtually double what it was in 1947. To achieve this goal the commission recommended a vast expansion of educational facilities at the level of the thirteenth and fourteenth grades, especially to be made available in junior colleges or, as they preferred to put it, in community colleges. This would require, too, a great program of scholarship aid to be supported by the federal government for students who had the requisite ability but lacked adequate financial resources.

American public opinion seemed in general to support the idea that large numbers of college age youth should attend college. The *Fortune* survey showed that 83 percent of the people thought that there are many young people not now in college who should be there. Similarly, 83 percent of the people said that they would want a son of theirs to go to college and 69 percent want their daughters to go to college. Interestingly enough, those in the upper classes were much more unanimous in their opinion: professional men and executives, white collar employees, and business proprietors were considerably more enthusiastic about the idea of college for their children than were farmers and wage earners. The same difference in level of expectation was shown by the American Council on Education study of high school seniors. A total of 35 percent of high school seniors in 1947 actually applied for admission to college; another 23 percent said they hoped to go *sometime;* and another seventeen percent said they would like to go if they were sure of admission and scholarship aid, making a total of 75 percent. Of those who actually applied, the proportions were greatest among those whose fathers had had the greatest amount of education themselves, were executives or professional men, and came from the larger cities, whereas the lowest proportions were among those students who lived in smaller towns and whose fathers had had the least education and were factory workers. Class and financial considerations were obviously at work in the expressed desires to go to college.

With respect to the question of scholarship aid, 56 percent in the *Fortune* survey said they approved the idea that the federal government should provide money for qualified high school graduates who could otherwise not afford to go to college. Interestingly enough, the poorer the respondents the more they favored the plan (up to 60 percent), whereas the more prosperous the respondents the more they opposed the plan (58 percent). But the most telling argument in favor of the plan was that there are a great many qualified high school graduates who cannot afford to go to college but who should have the chance, a clear expression of the belief in equality of educational opportunity despite economic handicap.

College educators were by no means as overwhelmingly in favor of a vast expansion of educational opportunity for American youth as were the President's commission and much of the public. Many college educators argued that there were already too many students in college who should not be there, that ability to do college work was not nearly so widespread as the President's commission claimed, and that our culture would be spread too thin if great numbers of students flooded into our colleges. Those who held typically to the humanistic conceptions of higher education (see p. 495) and some who held to conservative religious conceptions of education were likely to be most outspoken against the idea that virtually "everyone should go to college." [2] They were likely to affirm that college education was primarily for leaders, that intellectual attainment and scholarship or religious and moral values are the chief goals of college, and that the practical ideals of vocational preparation will seriously hinder the development of a good higher education. Furthermore, the nation can ill afford to spend the vast amounts of money that would be required to fulfill the goals of the President's commission. Whereas elementary education and perhaps even secondary education are desirable for all people, higher education should be reserved for the rela-

---

[2] See, for example, the criticisms of the President's commission in Father Allan P. Farrell (ed.), *Whither American Education?* (New York, America, 1948), a symposium by prominent Roman Catholic educators.

tively few who can profit from it. Thus, the issue was drawn over extending educational opportunity, much as it had been drawn for decades, but the forces in favor of extension seemed to be gaining.

CONFLICTS OVER THE SUPPORT AND CONTROL OF EDUCATION

A second great cluster of problems which elicited sharp controversy among professional educators and the public alike centered upon fundamental issues of educational support and control. This book has tried to trace the background and development of the most pressing of these issues, many of which overlap and bear upon each other but which will be distinguished into three types of issues for purposes of discussion.

Public versus Private Control of Education

From colonial days Americans have been trying to determine the relative merits of public education in relation to private education. The origins of public authority for the control of education are deep in our colonial tradition of the seventeenth century; the rise of private control by delegation of authority from the state was a marked feature of the eighteenth century; and the decision to give preference to public education as an agency of national unity was a characteristic of the long controversies of the nineteenth century. Now in the twentieth century the problem is still with us and is marked by a heightened controversy. The question in effect is "Should America continue its experiment to maintain public and private systems of schools side by side, or should we give still greater emphasis to public education, or should we encourage private institutions to become the major factor in American education?"

Two very important Supreme Court decisions in the 1920's high-lighted the issue following World War I. Between 1917 and 1921 some thirty-one states passed laws requiring all instruction in the public schools to be given in the English language. This was obviously a result of nationalistic and patriotic fervor that grew out of World War I and threatened the existence of private schools conducted in foreign languages. In 1919 Nebraska passed a law prohibiting instruction in any language but English in private or religious as well as in public schools. In *Meyer* v. *Nebraska* (1923) the United States Supreme Court declared this law unconstitutional on the grounds that the Fourteenth Amendment protected the liberty of teachers to make contracts to engage in the common occupations of life (teaching German) and the liberty of parents to educate their children as they saw fit (the right to send their children to private and religious schools).

The Supreme Court argued that the state can compel children to attend *some* school, that it can establish reasonable regulations for all schools, including the giving of instruction in English, and that it can prescribe a curriculum for public schools which it supports, but it cannot prohibit instruction that interferes with the religious and private rights of parents to seek the kind of instruction they wish. Justices Oliver Wendell Holmes and George Sutherland dissented on the grounds that the state had the right to take appropriate measures to maintain the common welfare through education for unity.

In 1922 the state of Oregon adopted a compulsory education act requiring, with certain exceptions, that all normal children between the ages of eight and sixteen years must attend a public school and that any who attend a private school or teacher must obtain the permission of and be examined by the county superintendent of schools. Fearful that the law if enforced would destroy the private and parochial schools in Oregon, a Roman Catholic teaching order brought suit to have the law declared unconstitutional. The United States Supreme Court did so in *Pierce* v. *Society of Sisters* in 1925, commonly known as the Oregon decision.

Those who favored the law hearkened back to the arguments used in building the common school ideal of the early nineteenth century. They claimed that the demands of citizenship required the state to see to it that all potential citizens be given appropriate training for their responsibilities; that the increase in juvenile delinquency followed upon an increase of numbers attending nonpublic schools; that attendance at a common school would prevent religious hostility and prejudice; and that instruction in American government and institutions for immigrant children could best be done when children of all classes and creeds attended school together. The crowning argument was made that loyalty to America could best be taught in public schools and that if the law were declared unconstitutional the state would have no means of prohibiting the teaching of subversive doctrines by bolshevists, syndicalists, or communists in private schools.

The Supreme Court was impressed by some of these arguments but not by all of them. It reaffirmed the right of the state to regulate schools, private as well as public, and to compel attendance for the public welfare at *some* school, but it ruled that the state had no right to require all children to attend a public school and thereby destroy the property of private schools or infringe the rights of parents to guide the upbringing of their children. The nub of the Supreme Court decision was as follows:

> No question is raised concerning the power of the State reasonably to regulate all schools, to inspect, supervise and examine them, their teachers and pupils; to require that all children of proper age attend some school, that teachers shall be of good moral character and patriotic disposition, that certain studies plainly essential to good citizenship must be taught, and that nothing be taught which is manifestly inimical to the public welfare.
>
> The inevitable practical result of enforcing the Act under consideration would be destruction of appellees' primary schools, and perhaps all other private pri-

mary schools for normal children within the State of Oregon. These parties are engaged in a kind of undertaking not inherently harmful, but long regarded as useful and meritorious. Certainly there is nothing in the present records to indicate that they have failed to discharge their obligations to patrons, students or the State. And there are no peculiar circumstances or present emergencies which demand extraordinary measures relative to primary education.

Under the doctrine of *Meyer* v. *Nebraska,* 262 U. S. 390, we think it entirely plain that the Act of 1922 unreasonably interferes with the liberty of parents and guardians to direct the upbringing and education of children under their control. As often heretofore pointed out, rights guaranteed by the Constitution may not be abridged by legislation which has no reasonable relation to some purpose within the competency of the State. The fundamental theory of liberty upon which all governments in this Union repose excludes any general power of the State to standardize its children by forcing them to accept instruction from public teachers only. The child is not the mere creature of the State; those who nurture him and direct his destiny have the right, coupled with the high duty, to recognize and prepare him for additional obligations.[3]

The Oregon decision was thus taken as a charter of privileges for the continuance of private and religious schools on the American educational scene, but the controversy over the role of private schools did not diminish. Following World War II it reached another crescendo. The drive by religious groups, especially Roman Catholic groups, to expand their schools and to demand not only their continuance but also public funds for their support caused considerable concern among those who desired to see the public school system continue to serve the majority of American youth. Many public school educators feared that a vast expansion of private schools would create divisiveness and disunity in America at a time when it needed unity and strength.

For example, in 1949 Professor John L. Childs of Teachers College, Columbia University, argued that the Oregon decision needed reconsideration and that if children were to learn to cooperate with other religious and cultural groups, they could do it best if they all learned to live, work, study, and play together in a common school. He therefore proposed that all children should spend at least half of their school lives in a public school.[4] In 1952 President James B. Conant of Harvard University, speaking before the American Association of School Administrators in Boston, reaffirmed his belief that unity in our national life and equality of opportunity could best be achieved where all youth attend the same schools irrespective of social class, religious belief, or cultural background.[5] He did not question the right of parents to send their children to private schools, but he feared that a great expansion of private education would create a dual system that would have the effect of

[3] *Pierce* v. *Society of Sisters,* 268 U. S. 510 (1924), pp. 534–535.

[4] John L. Childs, "American Democracy and the Common School System," *Jewish Education,* Vol. 21 (1949), pp. 32–37.

[5] See *The Saturday Review of Literature* (May 3, 1952), p. 11. Also the reply by Archbishop Richard J. Cushing and Allan V. Heely, headmaster of Lawrenceville School.

creating sharp cleavages and perpetuating stratifications in American society along class or religious lines. Also in 1952 Dean Hollis L. Caswell of Teachers College, Columbia University, argued that American unity could only be preserved if the vast majority of American parents continued to send their children to the common public schools, while at the same time affirming their right to maintain private and religious schools at their own expense.[6]

On the other side, proponents of religious and private schools extolled the merits of private schools and expressed fear of state monopoly in education. Most outspoken of these were Roman Catholic educators who conduct the largest of the private school systems in the United States. At their convention in St. Louis in April 1952 the delegates to the National Catholic Educational Association took issue with President Conant and insisted that Catholic schools were not divisive but rather reenforced the American conception of freedom in education, promoted cultural diversity in society, and formed a bulwark against the totalitarian conceptions of a state monopoly of education. Thus, from the Oregon Act of 1922 to the present, the running battle over the relative values of public and private education showed no signs of abatement at mid-century. At the heart of much of the controversy was the religious question which gives another perspective to the problem of control and support of education.

Church and State in Educational Control and Support

In the conflict of educational ideas in the 1920's the religious issue was incidental to the struggle between private and public education as just described. But in the 1930's and 1940's the tempo of controversy increased, and the religious issue came to the forefront. The basic question was, "Shall public funds be used for the support of religious schools, and, if so, for what purposes?" As we have seen in the earlier chapters of this book, the struggle between church and state has had a long history. By and large, the American people had moved away from direct public support for religious schools and had generally agreed that the best interests of the nation and of religion alike would be served if public funds were not granted to religious schools. This was one of the accepted meanings of the principle of separation of church and state at the end of the nineteenth century. Now, however, the whole question of the meaning of separation of church and state has been reopened, and at mid-century several well-defined positions were being stated, especially as they referred to the question of public funds for religious schools. (The question of the role of religious instruction in the public schools will be dealt with on pages 547–551.) Three positions were being taken on this subject.

First, it was argued that public funds should be granted to religious and parochial schools as a recognition of their role in serving the public welfare

---

[6] Hollis L. Caswell, "The Great Reappraisal of Public Education," *Teachers College Record,* Vol. 54 (1952), pp. 12–22.

and in meeting the requirements of compulsory attendance laws on a level of equality with the public schools. The most outspoken advocates of this position were members of the Roman Catholic Church. They argued that as a matter of justice the parochial schools should share with public schools in tax funds, for it was unfair to tax Catholic parents for the public schools and then expect them also to pay for their Catholic schools which they felt were needed for their children. They also argued that constitutional provisions for the separation of church and state permitted "cooperation" between church and state so long as the state aided all religious schools without showing preference for any one religion or denomination. The only thing the First Amendment prohibits is the granting of privileges to one church that are not granted to others.

The basic policy statements on this issue were clear. Pope Pius XI said in his important encyclical of 1929:

> [In some countries] the school legislation respects the rights of the family, and Catholics are free to follow their own system of teaching in schools that are entirely Catholic. Nor is distributive justice lost sight of, as is evidenced by the financial aid granted by the State to the several schools demanded by the families.[7]

In interpreting this passage from Pope Pius XI for American Catholics the Reverend Gerald C. Treacy, S. J., had this to say in the discussion club outline that follows the encyclical letter in the pamphlet cited:

> Even in a nation where there are different religious beliefs there is no need for the neutral or mixed school. Each religious group can have its own schools aided by the state as is done in Canada and in England. Distributive justice calls for the state to do this. In countries where this is not done the Catholic and other religious groups desiring their own schools labor under the injustice of double taxation. Be it said to the credit of our Catholic people that they bear the unjust burden cheerfully whatever its cost, alive to their responsibility to see "Catholic education in Catholic schools for all Catholic youth." [8]

In November 1948 the American bishops and archbishops who comprise the Administrative Board of the National Catholic Welfare Conference criticized the growing secularism in American life and asserted that the authentic tradition in American education was one in which government should promote "impartial encouragement of religious influence on its citizens" through the schools:

> We feel with deep conviction that for the sake of both good citizenship and religion there should be a reaffirmation of our original American tradition of free cooperation between government and religious bodies—cooperation involving

---

[7] *Christian Education of Youth*, Encyclical Letter of Pope Pius XI (New York, The Paulist Press, 1930[?]), p. 31.

[8] *Ibid.*, p. 46. A neutral school is defined as a school from which religion is excluded; a mixed school is one in which separate religious instruction is given but in which Catholic students receive their other lessons from non-Catholic teachers in common with non-Catholic students.

no special privilege to any group and no restriction on the religious liberty of any citizen.[9]

In this statement the bishops did not spell out what their belief in "impartial encouragement" and "cooperation" meant for public funds for parochial schools, but many took it to mean what the Papal Encyclical meant, namely, distributive justice by financial aid for their religious schools from public funds. In a later statement published in the *New York Times* on November 16, 1952, the Catholic bishops clarified their view by stating that ". . . if religion is important to good citizenship—and that is the burden of our national tradition—then the State must give recognition to its importance in public education. The State, therefore, has the duty to help parents fulfill their task of religious instruction and training."

A second general position on this issue held that even though *direct* aid for the support of religious schools by public funds was contrary to good policy and the constitutional separation of church and state, it was nevertheless justifiable for the state to use public funds for *indirect* aid to the parochial schools. This could be achieved under the "child benefit" theory that public funds for certain auxiliary services to parochial school children were aiding the child to take advantage of the welfare services of the state and were not aiding the school. Under this doctrine the state could not give financial aid to pay salaries of teachers or build buildings or help maintain parochial schools, but it *could* use public funds to pay for transportation of children to parochial schools, give them free textbooks, pay for health and medical services, and furnish free school lunches. The United States Supreme Court affirmed this doctrine as early as 1930 in the Cochran case over free textbooks in Louisiana and in 1947 in the Everson case concerning free bus transportation for parochial school children in New Jersey.[10]

Many Protestants joined many Catholics in upholding the belief that the separation of church and state did not prohibit certain kinds of aid to the parochial schools or to the children who attend parochial schools. In words that paralleled closely the Catholic bishops' statement a group of well-known Protestant leaders spoke thus:

> We favor the separation of Church and State in the sense which we believe to have been intended by the first amendment. This prohibited the State from giving any Church or religious body a favored position, and from controlling the religious institutions of the nation. . . . Cooperation, entered into freely by the State and Church and involving no special privilege to any Church and no threat to the religious liberty of any citizen, should be permitted.[11]

[9] *New York Times* (Nov. 21, 1948).

[10] For a discussion of these cases and several others see R. Freeman Butts, *The American Tradition in Religion and Education* (Boston, Beacon, 1950), Chap. 6.

[11] See "Statement on Church and State" in *Christianity and Crisis,* Vol. VIII, No. 12 (July 5, 1948), p. 2. See also letter of the National Council of the Churches of Christ in the U. S. A. in *New York Times* (Dec. 13, 1952).

Several Protestant church bodies affirmed similar statements. The Oberlin General Council of the Congregational Christian Churches in June 1948 favored "functional interaction" and "cooperation" between church and state so long as religious liberty was protected. The Lutheran Church–Missouri Synod, meeting in Milwaukee in June 1950, urged the state to cooperate with the churches whenever the welfare of the nation demands such cooperation. Thomas B. Keehn, writing for Congregationalists, approved the Supreme Court's action in the Everson case in upholding public grants for transportation of children to parochial schools:

> In short, the Supreme Court here approved reasonable cooperation between state and religion through aid to children attending non-public (including parochial) schools. The purpose was a limited welfare service. Any other decision would have endangered the entire welfare function of government in the fields of health, welfare, social security and education. The decision did not violate religious freedom or organic separation of church and state.[12]

Most explicit and most persistent in their demands for "auxiliary services" or indirect aid to parochial schools were Roman Catholic leaders. In his controversy with Mrs. Eleanor Roosevelt in July 1949 Francis Cardinal Spellman of New York insisted that he merely wanted public aid for health and transportation benefits and the distribution of nonreligious textbooks to children in parochial schools as a recognition of justice for the parochial schools, but he did not seek or expect funds for parochial school construction, maintenance, or teaching services. In a series of articles on federal aid to education beginning in *America* on January 7, 1950, Father Robert C. Hartnett made the same claim, but many critics felt that the *ultimate* goal of Catholic leaders was full public support of Catholic schools.

The third general position on this issue, stated simply, is that direct aid from public funds to religious schools is unconstitutional and that indirect aid in the form of "auxiliary services" is also unconstitutional. Aid to parochial school children for free transportation, free textbooks, and free health and medical services is a form of indirect aid to the religious schools and thus unsound and unwise as public policy. These beginnings may eventually lead to direct aid and a reversal of 175 years of American effort to separate church from state. Aiding all religions or churches equally is just as unconstitutional and unwise as aid to one church in preference to others. The history of separation of church and state in the United States shows that multiple establishment of religion was outlawed as well as single establishment. (For the origins of multiple establishment, see pages 22–29.)

The proponents of this position point to the Everson decision as the constitutional basis for adhering to complete separation rather than cooperation between church and state. The majority opinion stated:

12 See *Social Action*, Vol. XIV, No. 9 (Nov. 15, 1948), pp. 35–36. See also "The Public Schools and Protestant Faith," *ibid.*, Vol. XIX, No. 3 (Dec., 1952).

The "establishment of religion" clause of the First Amendment means at least this: Neither a state nor the Federal Government can set up a church. Neither can pass laws which aid one religion, aid all religions, or prefer one religion over another. . . . No tax in any amount, large or small, can be levied to support any religious activities or institutions, whatever they may be called, or whatever form they may adopt to teach or practice religion.[13]

The majority of five went on to say, however, that the state of New Jersey could use tax funds for free transportation because this was a welfare service to the children and not an aid to the religious school. Proponents of this third position felt that the majority had stated the principle of separation correctly but had not applied it correctly in practice to transportation. The minority of four on the Supreme Court felt the same way and argued that the use of public funds for transportation should have been prohibited.

Many Protestant groups, most Jewish groups, and many educational and nonreligious groups adhered to this position. An active and militant group was organized in 1947 called Protestants and Other Americans United for the Separation of Church and State. The growing political power of the Catholic Church and the gains made in obtaining public funds for parochial schools as signalized by the Everson decision were among the reasons for its organization. Prominent leaders among the Presbyterian, Baptist, Methodist, and other large and small Protestant denominations were among its founders and supporters. Its manifesto issued on January 10, 1948 announced the following platform for action on the issue of funds for religious schools:

> To work for the repeal of any law now on the statute books of any State which sanctions the granting of aid to church schools from the public treasury.
> To invoke the aid of the courts in maintaining the integrity of the Constitution with respect to the separation of church and state, wherever and in whatever form the issue arises, and, specifically, to strive by appropriate constitutional means to secure a reconsideration of the two decisions of the Supreme Court upholding the use of tax funds (a) for providing the pupils of parochial schools with free textbooks and (b) for the transportation of pupils to parochial schools.[14]

The majority position of the Jewish community in America was just as clear. It is represented by the National Community Relations Advisory Council whose constituent organizations included the American Jewish Committee, American Jewish Congress, B'Nai Brith, Jewish Labor Committee, Jewish War Veterans, the Union of American Hebrew Congregations, and some twenty-four local, state, and regional agencies. Their statement of principles in 1948 included the following:

> We are opposed to governmental aid to schools under the supervision or control of any religious denomination or sect, whether Jewish, Protestant, or Catholic, including outright subsidies, transportation, text-books and other supplies. We

---

[13] *Everson v. Board of Education,* 330 U. S. 15 (1947).
[14] See the text as quoted in the *New York Times* (Jan. 11, 1948).

are not opposed to the use of any school for the provision of lunches, medical and dental services to children.[15]

A similar statement was adopted by the Central Conference of American Rabbis in 1949.

The American Federation of Teachers, an affiliate of the American Federation of Labor, finally came to the same conclusion at its Boston convention in 1947 when it approved federal aid to the states for improvement of the public schools at all levels, but with no obligation for government to give aid to religious schools. It specifically would deny transportation funds for nonpublic schools but would grant health and welfare services to all children in nonpublic as well as public schools.

After considerable debate the largest organizations of American educators came to a similar conclusion as a matter of policy. Virtually identical resolutions were adopted at their annual conventions in 1950, 1951, and 1952 by the National Education Association and its most powerful affiliate, the American Association of School Administrators:

> We believe the American tradition of separation of church and state should be vigorously and zealously safeguarded. We respect the right of groups, including religious denominations, to maintain their own schools so long as such schools meet the educational, health, and safety standards defined by the states in which they are located. We believe that these schools should be financed entirely by their supporters. We therefore oppose all efforts to devote public funds to either the direct or indirect support of these schools.[16]

As the National Education Association took its stand against public financial aid to parochial elementary and secondary schools, so did the President's Commission on Higher Education take the same stand with respect to higher education:

> Federal funds for the general support of current educational activities and for general capital outlay purposes should be appropriated for use only in institutions under public control . . . any diversion by government of public funds to the general support of nonpublicly controlled educational institutions tends to deny the acceptance of the fundamental responsibility and to weaken the program of public education.[17]

Monsignor Frederick G. Hochwalt of the National Catholic Welfare Conference and one other member of the commission made a vigorous dissent to this principle arguing that private institutions should also receive federal grants.

Thus were the lines drawn on a very complicated and controversial issue

[15] National Community Relations Advisory Council, *Report of the Sixth Plenary Session* (New York, the Council, 1948), p. 41.

[16] *School Administrator,* Journal of the American Association of School Administrators (April 1950), p. 2.

[17] President's Commission on Higher Education, *op. cit.,* Vol. V, *Financing Higher Education,* p. 57.

that required the best thought of the public and the profession. In the political arena it came to a head most prominently over the question of federal aid to education in which other extremely difficult problems were involved.

Federal Aid to Education

During the 1920's and 1930's the issue of general federal aid to education was relatively quiescent. Significant gains for grants to special forms of education had been achieved under the Democratic administration of President Woodrow Wilson through the Smith-Lever Act of 1914 for agricultural extension service and the Smith-Hughes Act of 1917 to aid vocational education. But the drive for federal aid to improve general education in the states gained little headway under the Republican administrations of the 1920's despite their support by the National Education Association.

The dominant view of both the Democratic and Republican parties in the 1920's and 1930's was that education was largely a matter for state and local control. This followed the traditional view that decentralized control and support of education was the democratic American way. The Republican Party platforms maintained this view throughout the 1930's and 1940's either by omitting mention of the problem of federal aid entirely or making very vague statements in favor of equality of educational opportunity and freedom of the states. The Republican platform of 1952 made very brief mention of education and simply subscribed to the principle that responsibility for sustaining popular education has always rested upon the local communities and the states.

The Democratic Party, however, gradually began to change its stand. It made no mention of education in its platform of 1932, but in 1936 and 1944 it approved the role of the federal government in aiding youth through the NYA and CCC, through public grants for the construction of school buildings, and through increased aid for vocational education and rehabilitation. Finally in 1944, 1948, and 1952 the Democratic Party platform explicitly came out for federal aid to education to be administered by the states without federal control. The Democratic platform of 1952 went still further and urged the adoption of the legislative proposals of the President's Commission on Higher Education, including federal scholarships. President Truman actively urged Congress to pass a federal-aid-to-education bill and also federal aid for scholarships. He carried amounts for these purposes in his proposed budgets of the late 1940's and early 1950's. Thus, the two major parties had made a complete reversal of policy from the 1870's and 1880's when the Republican Party was the strong advocate of federal aid to education (see pp. 370-375).

Meanwhile several professional education organizations and advisory commissions to the president (in 1931 and in 1939) began to recommend more forcefully in the late 1930's and 1940's the need for federal aid to education.

For example, the Educational Policies Commission of the National Education Association and the Problems and Policies Committee of the American Council on Education issued a joint statement on federal-state relations in education in March 1945 which well summarized the dominant view of the profession. They deplored centralization of *control* of education by the federal government and pointed to its dangers, but they just as vigorously asserted that the federal government should participate in *support* of education in the states in order to equalize educational opportunity among American youth. Prevailing control of education should be at local and state levels, but the federal government should aid the states to achieve a minimum level of quality of education and aid should be granted according to wealth, ability to tax, and need of the several states for help.

With the policy so well stated, the problem then became one of achieving the policy in practice by persuading Congress to pass a federal aid bill. The details of this struggle cannot be told here, but all would agree to two points: the struggle increased in intensity and in public debate in the late 1940's and early 1950's; and the main stumbling block was the issue over whether or not federal funds should be available for parochial school children in any form. Success seemed within sight when a federal aid bill was passed by the Senate in 1948 and again in 1949, but in both cases it died in the House of Representatives amid wide public clamor over the religious issue. Especially bitter were the feelings in 1949 when charges of bigotry were leveled at Mrs. Eleanor Roosevelt by Cardinal Spellman for her stand against aid to parochial schools. Similar charges were made in 1950 against Representative Graham A. Barden of North Carolina for his efforts to gain support for a bill that would give federal aid only to public schools and would rule out transportation and health services for parochial schools. Federal aid to education had become a bitter political issue at both the national and state levels. For example, it was prominent in the campaign for the Senate in New York in 1949 when former Governor Herbert H. Lehman favored federal aid on the Democratic-Liberal ticket and Senator John Foster Dulles opposed it on the Republican side.

By 1952 three types of federal aid bills had been introduced into Congress. The Taft-Thomas Bill (S. 246) provided for $300,000,000 a year to be paid to the states for use in bringing their elementary and secondary schools up to a minimum expenditure of about $55 per pupil. By the formula involved every state would receive at least $5 per child of school age each year, and some states would receive as much as $25 per child. Two other provisions were especially controversial. One required that those states which maintain segregated schools must allocate a just and equitable proportion to the schools of the minority race. The other provision would allow states to use federal funds for any purpose of current school expenditures (not buildings, interest, debt, or health services) for which the state used its own funds. This meant that any state that permitted use of state funds for transportation or textbooks for parochial school children could also use federal funds for those purposes, but where states prohibited such use of state funds, there also federal funds could not be used. This was the bill that passed the Senate in 1948 and 1949 but foundered in the House on the religious issue.

A second type of bill was represented by the one known as the Barden Bill (H. 4643) which was somewhat similar in financial amounts to the Taft-Thomas Bill, but it specifically provided that federal funds could be used only for public schools. It was not nearly so specific on the issue of equal distribution of federal funds to segregated schools where they existed.

The third type of bill was represented by the Murray-McMahon Bill (S. 947) in the Senate and the Fogarty Bill (H. 915) in the House which had some provisions directly opposite to those of the Barden Bill. These bills would require that some federal funds be used for auxiliary services to non-public as well as to public schools. The obvious intent was to make sure that parochial school children would receive such benefits even if the federal government must pay these funds directly to the parochial schools and with-hold their payment to state authorities wherever state laws prohibit the use of state funds for such purposes. Members of the Catholic Church testified to their preference for this type of bill and to their opposition to the Taft-Thomas and the Barden bills. Notable among these was the Reverend William E. McManus, assistant director of the Department of Education of the National Catholic Welfare Conference.

After 1949 when it saw what was standing in the way of passage of federal aid bills, the National Education Association became more vigorous in its campaign for passage of a federal aid bill and more explicit in its opposition to the use of federal funds for parochial schools. In 1949 the Legislative Com-mission of the NEA explicitly labeled the following groups as roadblocks to federal aid: the National Catholic Welfare Conference, the United States Chamber of Commerce, the Daughters of the American Revolution, the Friends of the Public Schools, and the Committee on Constitutional Govern-ment.[18]

The National Education Association also grew more active in attempting to marshall the support of other organizations for a federal aid bill. It claimed that as many as sixty prominent national organizations were ranged on its side.[19] Such groups as the following were among those that were in favor of federal aid legislation of either the Taft-Thomas or the Barden type: Amer-ican Farm Bureau Federation, Farmers Educational and Cooperative Union, National Grange, American Federation of Labor, Congress of Industrial Organizations, Brotherhood of Railroad Trainmen, American Legion, Amer-ican Veterans of World War II, Jewish War Veterans, Veterans of Foreign Wars, American Association of University Women, General Federation of

---

[18] National Education Association, *Journal* (October 1949), p. 494.
[19] *New York Times* (Mar. 29, 1949).

Women's Clubs, League of Women Voters, National Council of Jewish Women, National Federation of Business and Professional Women's Clubs, Baptists, Methodists, Evangelical and Reformed Church, Congregational Christian Church, Central Conference of American Rabbis, United Council of Church Women, American Library Association, National Congress of Parents and Teachers, National School Boards Association, United States Conference of Mayors, and dozens of professional education associations.[20]

Opposition to federal aid for education unless it provided for considerable amounts of aid for parochial school children as well as for public school children was most consistently expressed by the National Catholic Welfare Conference, National Catholic Educational Association, National Council of Catholic Men, and National Council of Catholic Women as well as by many members of the Catholic clergy.

Some groups continued outspoken in their opposition to federal aid for education of any kind. These included some business groups and patriotic organizations, notably the National Economic Council, the United States Chamber of Commerce, the Council of State Chambers of Commerce, the Junior Order of United American Merchants, the Wheel of Progress, the Daughters of the American Revolution, the Sons of the American Revolution, and the Ladies of the Grand Army of the Republic. Their arguments ranged from the fear of heavier taxes, the fear of centralized control, fear of education being thrown into politics, extolling of states' rights and local control, fear of standardized education, fear of subversive influences in education, and fear that schools would cost too much money. It should not be inferred that American business as a whole was opposed to improved finances for public schools. Important business interests were represented in a very active organization formed in May 1949 and called the National Citizens Commission for the Public Schools under the chairmanship of Roy E. Larsen, President of Time, Inc. Similarly, the board of directors of the Standard Oil Company (New Jersey) adopted the following statement:

> The importance of our public school system to the growth, prosperity, peace, and security of our country can scarcely be overestimated at any time. Its significance is never more apparent than in times of emergency. At times like these the relationship between freedom and a literate and educated population is thrown into clear focus.
>
> American business enterprise is aware of its great debt to the public school system of this country, because that system is essential to the survival and growth of business.
>
> The right and duty of the individual to support our public school system is clear. One such duty is, of course, that of paying taxes. But it seems to us clear that the obligation of each of us as an individual runs beyond mere payment of taxes.
>
> Over the years many Jersey Standard employees have participated actively in

20 NEA, *Journal* (March 1950), pp. 180–181.

their local school programs. The company would like to see more of its people take an active interest in the problems and opportunities facing the public schools in their own communities. Obviously, the conditions affecting the individual's ability to participate in school activities will vary, but our company encourages its employees, as good American citizens, to undertake this important work.[21]

Thus were the lines drawn. Federal aid for education at mid-century had once again become a major political and economic issue. Whether they liked it or not, professional educators were in the middle of a critical issue of public policy in which they would increasingly be expected to stand up and be counted if not take an active part. Some educators and laymen kept on the alert to find new ways to increase general funds for education. For example, it was proposed in February 1952 that revenues from the submerged oil lands that lie in the tidelands off the coasts of several states should be devoted to federal aid for elementary, secondary, and higher education. At hearings in Senate committee strong support was given to the proposal by spokesmen for the American Council on Education, the American Federation of Labor, Congress of Industrial Organization, the National Grange, National Farmers Union, American Federation of Teachers, and some thirty other organizations. If such a proposal should be achieved, it would revive the earliest type of aid for education granted by the federal government, namely, the income from public lands beginning with the Land Ordinances of 1785 and 1787, and extending through many other nineteenth century grants to the Morrill Act of 1862 for the land-grant colleges (see p. 244). It remained to be seen, however, what the Republican victory in 1952 would mean for this or other proposals for federal aid to education in the coming years.

CONTROVERSIES OVER THE EDUCATIONAL PROGRAM

In addition to the deep-seated clashes of opinion over the issues of equal educational opportunity and the elements of sound educational control and support, educators and the public alike became increasingly concerned about what went on in the public schools. One who reads many of the books and articles written during the last thirty-five years might gain the impression that few people were satisfied with the educational program of the public schools. This would be a hasty judgment, but certain it is that the amount of criticism represented genuine differences of opinion about the aims, curriculum, and methods of American schools. So widespread had the criticism become that Dean Hollis L. Caswell of Teachers College, Columbia University, appropriately termed it "The Great Reappraisal of Public Education" in his Steinmetz Memorial Lecture in May 1952.[22]

Much of the criticism of public schools was genuinely made and pointed to

[21] National Citizens Commission for the Public Schools, *The Stake of Business in Public School Education* (Jan. 12, 1951), p. 11.
[22] Caswell, *op. cit.*

glaring weaknesses; some of it, however, seemed ill-considered and unfounded. The latter type of criticism seemed to grow in volume in the 1940's and 1950's to such an extent that educators and citizens of good will became seriously disturbed about the ulterior motives of the "attacks upon the public schools." The tempo and temper of such attacks required educators at mid-century to try to evaluate and to distinguish carefully the motives of critics of the schools; to take seriously those criticisms that were given in good spirit and intended to express legitimate complaints made in the effort to improve the schools; and to expose and oppose those criticisms that were made with the motive to harm or even to destroy the public schools.

Legitimate and well-intentioned criticisms of the educational program stemmed from differences of value and of interest of several kinds. These differences grew out of several orientations to which people turned for authority as they set forth their claims concerning the emphasis in education that seemed most desirable to them. At least six such orientations may be mentioned, several of which rested upon or drew from the general points of view described in Chapter 14.

Religion. There were those who appealed to a religious orientation. Catholic, Protestant, and Jewish alike, they argued that the paramount claims in education must rest upon religion. The development of religious faith, devotion to ethical principles, and concern for moral character were the major elements determining their attitudes concerning whether education was serving its proper purposes or not. Those of a religious orientation were deeply divided, however, as to just what role religion as such should play in the public schools.

Discipline. There were those who stressed intellectual discipline as the chief goal of education. This concern ranged from a desire for the learning of systematic subject matter in the basic three R's and other academic subjects in the elementary school to the strong emphasis upon the traditional liberal arts in college. The ideal of a disciplined mind was often stated as the most cherished outcome of the educative process.

Scholarship. There were those who put major emphasis upon scholarship and acquisition of systematic knowledge in the several scholarly disciplines, with special devotion to science and the scientific method as the prime instruments for education. They were likely to be impatient with religious or disciplinary outlooks and to stress the importance of rigorous acquisition of subject matter, especially in the sciences and the social sciences, and the rigorous application of the scientific method as the best evidence of an educated person. Acquisition of sound knowledge and information and application of the analytical methods of science to the problems of men are most to be sought after in teaching.

Vocation. A persistent claim, and a growing one, came from those who demanded that, whatever else an education did, it should be practical enough to give the individual a satisfactory preparation for some vocation or profession. All the other high sounding goals for education will go for naught unless the student comes out of school or college able to do something practical, able to earn a living, and prepared to be economically useful to himself, his family, and his society.

Individual needs. More recently appearing on the educational scene but quickly influential have been those who would direct the teacher's attention to the individual student, his needs, his development, and his interests. They argued that the educational program and educational methods must grow largely out of a study of the individual child. The aims of education are largely to be determined from a knowledge of the way the learner grows and develops, physically, emotionally, and mentally. Adherence to traditional subject matters and to traditional methods will stand in the way of genuine education and the enrichment of personality through a wide variety of educative experiences.

Society. Finally, there were those who insisted that the demands of a democratic society are paramount in education. They argue that the social situation in America and in the world is so critical that education must concentrate on promoting the democratic ideal through education for citizenship and world-mindedness. The curriculum should thus grow out of a study of the deepest trends, values, and conflicts in our culture. The schools should devote much more direct effort to preparing youth to deal intelligently and constructively with the basic social problems of our time. This requires a content and a method devoted to improving the process of making sound decisions.

Curriculum makers at all levels of the educational system were torn by these several orientations.[23] Obviously they were not mutually exclusive categories, but they were, however, centers of emphasis. When educators responded to one claim, they were likely to be criticized by proponents of some of the others. Such conflicting claims as these beset education on all sides; they were made by the colleges upon the lower schools; by public groups upon the schools and colleges; by parents upon the teachers; and by the teachers colleges upon the school systems. Experts in the social and philosophical foundations of education, in curriculum development, in methods of teaching, and in educational psychology in our institutions of teacher education devoted whole courses and many books to the problems raised by such orientations as these. Only a sample of the resulting issues can be discussed, especially those that have historical bearings on the present. Interestingly

[23] See, for example, two recent studies of curriculum development: Florence B. Stratemeyer, Hamden L. Forkner, and Margaret G. McKim, and others, *Developing a Curriculum for Modern Living* (New York, Teachers College, Columbia University, 1947); and B. Othanel Smith, William O. Stanley, and J. Harlan Shores, *Fundamentals of Curriculum Development* (Yonkers, World Book, 1950).

enough, proponents of the several orientations listed above were likely to line up differently in opposition to each other, depending upon the particular issue at hand.

Traditional versus Modern Programs

One great cluster of criticisms that marked the recent period had to do with the nature of the curriculum and the methods of learning, particularly in the elementary and secondary schools. One group thought that the traditional ways of teaching as represented in the older and well-established subject matters were the best. They stood generally for insistence upon a relatively narrow curriculum of the three R's and the accepted subjects of English, grammar, mathematics, history, and science. They were likely to deplore the addition to the curriculum of such "fads and frills" as the arts and music. They stressed the acquisition of information and logically organized bodies of knowledge as the chief goal of education. They asserted belief in traditional methods of memorizing, drill, and skill with major emphasis upon learning from books. They assumed that education was likely to be hard and disagreeable but that strict application and exertion of effort was the best training for learning to meet the demands of adult life. They seemed to rely upon theories of learning that stemmed from the faculty psychology and the disciplinary theories of the nineteenth century. Many citizens and educators who felt loyal to the religious, disciplinary, and scholarly orientations mentioned above were likely to feel drawn to such traditional views.

On the other hand, another group stressed modern or newer or progressive approaches to the curriculum and the educative process. They criticized the narrow "lifeless" curriculum of the three R's and argued that a much wider range of experience should be brought into the schools to enrich the curriculum by means of creative, expressive, physical, handcraft, and social activities. Thus, they were more likely to find educative value in play activities, in recreation and physical education, in the several art forms and dramatics, in instrumental and vocal music, in manual arts, in home economics, and in social studies. They were likely to argue that social attitudes, personal habits, and personality development were as important as, if not more important than, the acquisition of facts and subject matter or the development of skills by memorization and drill. They insisted that learning was best when the learner was interested in what he was doing and that learning could be promoted by active experiences as well as, if not better than, by reading. They argued that the learner must be helped to live his life in family, neighborhood, and community by relating these activities to his school life while he was still in school. They believed that much greater freedom for the individual child to learn at his own rate and to develop his interests was preferable to a standardized system of class learning and promotion or failure by rigid grade levels.

Very often those who held to the claims of child needs, vocation, and society (as cited earlier) found themselves allied together in the camp of modern or progressive education.

In the 1920's and 1930's the advocates of a modern educational program seemed to be most aggressive and vocal in their criticisms of "old-fashioned" and "out-worn" methods of the traditional program. They hit hard at almost every phase of practice that had come down from the nineteenth century, and some of them went to extremes in devaluing learning from books, the fundamental skills of the three R's, and the acquisition of factual information. But their views continued to gain acceptance from more and more professional educators. In the 1940's and 1950's, however, it appeared that something of a reaction was setting in, for it was clear that many of the attacks made upon the schools charged a neglect of the three R's, a "soft pedagogy" of excessive coddling of students, and catering to their whims and fancies. Sincere critics of the schools felt there was an unjustifiable neglect of achievement of high standards of knowledge and skills. Carping critics complained that progressive methods actually produced bad manners, insubordination, undermining of parental and home influence, undisciplined ruffianism, and even juvenile delinquency.

By mid-century professional educators were noticeably distressed by the criticisms of the schools, and they found much of it to be unjustified. Whenever they turned for evidence to the careful research of psychologists, sociologists, curriculum experts, and guidance specialists, they found that the weight of evidence favored sound modern methods of teaching. Children learned more in quantity and quality with modern methods than with traditional methods. They were also learning much better personal and social attitudes toward themselves and their bodies. Their relationships with others and their understanding of their physical surroundings and the society in which they lived were also superior. Whether the profession could convince the public of the superiority of modern methods remained a question. Much depended upon their ability to gain the confidence and respect of their communities as well as to produce the evidence, to help children to develop satisfactorily, and to correct some of the extremes that had undoubtedly developed. Increasing public interest in the program of the schools could be turned to a great asset if educators displayed the courage and the sensitiveness to meet the challenge.

The Social Role of the Educational Program

One of the most difficult of the issues posed for American education in the modern period concerned its function in aiding students to develop valid ideas about American society and world affairs. Virtually everyone agreed that the schools had some kind of role to play in developing good citizenship, but there was deep disagreement about what was and was not proper for the schools to do. The problem took its sharpest form when the question was asked, "How should the schools deal with the controversial social issues of our time upon which the public itself is divided in their outlooks?" Obviously, the teaching of the social studies was directly involved, but the problem applied to all fields of endeavor of the schools in greater or lesser degree. The conditions changed considerably in the period under consideration, but in general there were several persistent points of view among educators and the public.

One view held, either explicitly or implicitly, that schools should not deal directly with current controversial social issues. This view was likely to be held by many of those who believed, as mentioned above, that the school was primarily a place for teaching the accepted scholarly subject matters, or disciplining the mind by acquaintance with the great tradition of the past, or developing the interests of individual children, or teaching them a vocation. It was believed that the school fulfilled its social role if it concentrated on one or the other of these functions and left the individual student to make up his own mind about the pressing problems of his time under the guidance of his family, church, or other community groups.

This view appealed to those educators who were glad to avoid being plunged into controversy or who feared the consequences of social pressures on the schools or who were so busy with their own specific jobs that the wider social implications of what they were doing did not occur to them. This position, resting upon indifference or unconcern with social issues, became increasingly difficult to maintain as the march of domestic and world events through world wars, depressions, and international tensions increased the pressures upon the schools from many directions. But it had its attractions for the harassed teacher and busy administrator.

A second view held that it was the duty of the schools to inculcate patriotic loyalties to the American way of life and to teach the commonly accepted moral, ethical, political, and economic values upon which the American tradition is based. This view assumed that there were dominant themes in American life that were so commonly accepted that they should not be questioned. Many religious, patriotic, veteran, and business groups as well as many educators considered that such teaching would include understanding and appreciation of the great moments in American history, the development of the American constitutional forms of government, the ideals of individual liberty, and, often, the basic assumptions and great achievements of the system of competitive free enterprise. The principal social function of the school was thus to conserve the commonly accepted values of the past, to avoid questioning the dominant trends in our history, and to avoid dealing directly with the controversial issues of the present. Therefore, it was deemed proper by such groups that they should be alert to condemn any teaching or any textbooks, especially in the fields of history and the social studies, that raised questions about these inherited values or attempted to deal with them critically pro and con.

A third position held that the schools should properly deal directly with current controversial issues as well as to look critically at the successes and failures of our history. Advocates of this position argued that good citizenship in a democracy rested upon the development of a critical intelligence and ability to deal with different points of view. They asserted, however, that it was not the prerogative of the schools or of the teachers to take sides on any controversial issue but simply to present the facts on both sides of an issue and let the students make up their own minds without influence from the teacher. The school, therefore, should deal with controversial issues, but it should remain neutral. It should teach students "how to think but not what to think." For the school to do anything less than this was to fail in its social function of preparing citizens for a democracy; to do anything more was to become an indoctrinating agency that went beyond its neutral function.

A fourth position agreed that controversial issues should be dealt with fearlessly and critically in the schools and that the best resources of scholarship and authenticated evidence should be the basis of all instruction. But advocates of this position believed that it was impossible for the serious teacher to conceal or withhold permanently his own position. He should observe all the democratic canons of logic, scholarly evidence, fairness to all sides, and respect for the traditional values of democracy, but the requirements of intelligent discussion and academic freedom not only permitted but also obligated him to state clearly his own position on the controversial issues under discussion in his field of competence.

They argued that it is not the business of the teacher to tell his students what they should think nor merely to give both sides of the issue. The teacher's job is to promote the process of getting students to move toward soundly based convictions of their own on the basis of study, discussion, and evidence. The teacher should present his own point of view at that point in the educative process when the forming of sound convictions will be best promoted. Such outspoken taking of a position, when resting upon considered judgment and careful study, is the right of all citizens in a democracy and should be no less the right of a teacher, so long as students are free to criticize and reject the teacher's position with no pressure or detriment to them as students. Only by such mutual study and discussion can students themselves learn to develop a critical intelligence and arrive at considered judgments of their own. It was argued that if it was the right of all other kinds of organized groups to participate in such discussions, it was no less the right of teachers, whose training and scholarship should have prepared them for just such activities.

A fifth position argued that the school not only had the right and obligation to deal with controversial issues but also that teachers ought to take an unequivocal stand in favor of a positive social outlook that looked toward a radical reconstruction of American life and institutions in the interests of the masses of the people. This would mean definitely taking sides on controversial issues that would promote attitudes in youth favorable to the welfare of the great majority of Americans and intolerant of the privileges and vested interests of wealth and power. While concerned with fair treatment of all sides of an issue, the "reconstructionist" teacher would know quite clearly in which direction he would prefer society to move, and in general he would find that he should ally himself with those agencies that represent the most people, especially organized labor. The school thus should frankly take a positive role in seeking social changes and exerting leadership in moving from an individualistic society based upon free competition toward a collectivistic society based upon greater social and public control.

A brief analysis such as this cannot possibly do justice to the important positions represented among the lay public and professional educators, but it may serve to stimulate further inquiry and study by the reader.[24]

Public and educational controversy on these issues seemed to be reaching a peak of intensity in the period following World War II. Examples of pressures upon the schools could be found throughout the recent period in all parts of the country and over many kinds of issues. Just one example can be mentioned to illustrate the point. On one hand, organized educators were increasingly alerted to the attacks upon the public schools. They pointed to the efforts to censor textbooks which had the effect of making teachers increasingly afraid to deal with controversial issues. In 1951 the Committee on Tenure and Academic Freedom of the National Education Association issued a report entitled *The Freedom of the Public School Teacher* in which it was pointed out that teachers tended to avoid such controversial issues in the classroom as those having to do with sex, criticism of prominent persons, separation of church and state, race relations, and communism. A year later the pressures and attacks had grown in scope and intensity until the NEA was convinced that they were often the work of dishonest racketeers and professional agitators hoping to make a profit by playing on fears and prejudices. Especially disconcerting was the growing opposition to study of the United Nations and of UNESCO in the schools. Patriotic and religious groups professed to fear that such international organizations were subversive and that study about them would diminish loyalty to America.

[24] For differing approaches and critical summaries of various conceptions of the social role of education, see, for example, Smith, Stanley, and Shores, *op. cit.*; John S. Brubacher, *Modern Philosophies of Education* (New York, McGraw-Hill, 1950); John L. Childs, *Education and Morals* (New York, Appleton-Century-Crofts, 1950); Theodore Brameld, *Patterns of Educational Philosophy* (Yonkers-on-Hudson, World Book, 1950); and George S. Counts, *Education and American Civilization* (New York, Teachers College, Columbia University, 1952). See also the ten volumes of *Social Frontier* (1934–1939) and *Frontiers of Democracy* (1939–1943).

A nation-wide survey in the spring of 1952 by the *New York Times* showed that prominent educators all over the country were much concerned about the efforts to censor textbooks, especially by patriotic organizations. Textbooks were being "screened" by many voluntary groups in order to ban those books that contained "subversive" teaching. Pressure was exerted upon libraries and school authorities to have such books removed from the schools. Outspoken resistance to these attacks upon the freedom of teachers was stated by such prominent persons as the Librarian of Congress, the United States Commissioner of Education, the president of the American Association of School Administrators, the director of the National Education Association's Commission on the Defense of Democracy through Education, and the director of the Public Education Association.[25]

On the other hand, a typical response to this emphasis by educators upon freedom was a statement published a few weeks later in the *New York Times* stating the case for public criticism of the schools by community groups. Representatives of several voluntary organizations criticized the schools for permitting study of any social ideas that might raise questions about the profit motive or competition in a free enterprise economy. They criticized the neglect of "traditional standards and basic courses in fundamental subjects" as well as the consolidation of history courses into "social studies" for fear they would lead to indoctrination in a new social order. The goals of education as they saw them should consist of a return to the values that were being neglected by modern schools:

> Many of the courses and practices of this "new" or "progressive" education tend to undermine faith of the child in time-tested and established standards of success, loyalty, nationalism, authority, discipline, competition and the value of work or sustained effort, and other attributes of character which the experience of the ages has proved of value.[26]

This was a good illustration of those who adhered to the second point of view mentioned above (p. 543). They criticized indiscriminately all the other four points of view on the social role of education. Many educators began to feel that such uncritical criticism of anything labeled "new" or "progressive" came in the category of unfair and unjustified attacks upon the public schools. The National Education Association became so aroused over this issue that its convention at Detroit in July, 1952 passed a special resolution deploring the appearance of an article in the June issue of the American Legion magazine and condemning it as an unfair and unwarranted attack.

[25] "Textbook Censors Alarm Educators," *New York Times* (May 25, 1952).
[26] "Subversive Education," *New York Times* (June 15, 1952), Letter to the Editor signed by representatives of Child Education Foundation, National Society of New England Women, The American Coalition, Daughters of the American Revolution, Guardians of American Education, and Sons of the American Revolution.

Religious Instruction in the Public Schools

A third aspect of the educational program that elicited continuing and intensified controversy in the public mind and in professional circles following World War I had to do with the role of religion in the public schools. By the end of the nineteenth century the general principle had been established that sectarian religious instruction should not be promoted by the public schools if freedom of religious conscience and the separation of church and state were to be preserved. But since the end of World War I the demand has grown more widespread that some sort of religious instruction should be given in public schools. The public schools have been labeled as Godless and secularist, and it was charged that the neglect of religion has promoted not only indifference to religion but active irreligion, both of which have contributed to a decline of moral and spiritual values and indeed to positive juvenile delinquency.

Three general points of view have received considerable attention. One view, promoted largely by Protestants and Catholics, has urged a revival of sectarian religious instruction, notably through a plan of released-time religious instruction whereby public school children could be released from their regular school work for a certain period of time each week in order to receive instruction in the principles of their own particular religious faith. A second view, promoted almost exclusively by Protestants, has urged more attention to nonsectarian religious instruction through such plans as reading selected passages of the Bible or reciting nonsectarian prayers. A third position, promoted largely by educators, argues that the public schools should not promote specific instruction in matters of religious faith but should promote objective study about religion and its role in American culture. Opposition has been expressed to all three of these forms of instruction as dangers to the principle of separation of church and state and possible infringements upon religious freedom.

Released time.   The spread of released-time programs has led to a whole series of court cases. One New York court prohibited the practice in Mount Vernon in 1925; another New York court permitted it in White Plains in 1927. State courts permitted it in California and in Illinois in 1947. When the Illinois case was appealed, the United States Supreme Court ruled in 1948 that the released-time plan in Champaign, Illinois, was unconstitutional because it violated the First Amendment and was in effect "an establishment of religion":

> The foregoing facts, without reference to others that appear in the record, show the use of tax-supported property for religious instruction and the close cooperation between the school authorities and the religious council in promoting religious education. The operation of the State's compulsory education system thus assists and is integrated with the program of religious instruction carried

on by separate religious sects. Pupils compelled by law to go to school for secular education are released in part from their legal duty upon the condition that they attend the religious classes. This is beyond all question a utilization of the tax-established and tax-supported public school system to aid religious groups to spread their faith. And it falls squarely under the ban of the First Amendment (made applicable to the States by the Fourteenth) as we interpreted it in *Everson* v. *Board of Education,* 330 U. S. 1.[27]

The religious classes in Champaign had been taught by religious teachers and had been held inside the public school buildings; it thus remained uncertain as to whether a plan in which children left the school buildings and went to their own churches would likewise be unconstitutional. A court in St. Louis in 1948 held that such a plan would be unconstitutional under the McCollum decision, whereas courts in New York in the same year held that the New York plan was enough different to be permissible, because the children left the school buildings.

The New York case was taken to the Supreme Court and was decided in April 1952.[28] By a six to three decision the Supreme Court decided that the New York system was unlike the Champaign plan and was therefore permissible because the schools did not aid the religious groups to promote their religious instruction in school buildings and did not spend public funds for the purpose. The majority opinion, written by Justice William O. Douglas argued that no coercion was exerted in the New York plan, but that the plan would be unconstitutional if coercion were present. The majority opinion reaffirmed the McCollum principle of separation of church and state, but it stated that government and religion need not be unfriendly or hostile to each other. They can "cooperate" to the extent that students are enabled by the schools to take part in religious instruction offered by the churches.

The minority of three justices (Robert H. Jackson, Hugo L. Black, and Felix Frankfurter) argued in effect that there was no esssential difference between the New York plan and the Champaign plan and that therefore the New York plan was unconstitutional because it violated the separation of church and state and used the power of the state to secure the attendance of children at religious classes. The dissenters made it clear that they would have little objection to allowing *all* children to leave school to go to religious classes or not as their parents chose, but that the refusal of religious groups to accept this "dismissal plan" was evidence that they really wanted the compulsion of the school system to work in their favor. The question remained as to whether the practices of released time would spread in view of the decision or whether the controversy would be shifted to the state and local levels and fought out on grounds of the educational desirability of the programs rather than their constitutionality.

[27] *McCollum* v. *Board of Education,* 330 U. S. 203 (1948), pp. 209–210.
[28] *Zorach and Gluck* v. *Board of Education,* 343 U. S. 306 (1952).

Bible reading and prayers.   Under the stimulus of Protestant groups at least twelve states have enacted laws requiring that passages from the Bible be read in the public schools. At least twenty-five other states permit Bible reading either by permissive legislation, by court decision, by rulings of attorney generals or state education departments, or by local custom. Despite the fact that twelve states have constitutional provisions prohibiting sectarian instruction in the public schools and twenty-four states have similar laws, most states have ruled by court decisions that Bible reading is *not* sectarian instruction and is thus permissible. But at least six state courts have ruled that the Bible *is* a sectarian document in the eyes of Catholics, Jews, and nonbelievers and is thus unconstitutional. These latter states include Wisconsin, Illinois, Ohio, Louisiana, South Dakota, and Washington. Many of the cases on Bible reading have been brought in behalf of Roman Catholic and Jewish plaintiffs who argued that the King James version of the Bible was actually Protestant sectarianism and thus should be prohibited as violating the religious conscience of Catholics and Jews.

One of the most recent of such cases was a test of New Jersey's law that requires the daily reading of at least five verses from the Old Testament in the public schools. A lower court and the Supreme Court of New Jersey ruled in 1950 that the law was constitutional on the grounds that, although the Bible reading was religious, it was not sectarian. The courts ruled that the Bible was not sectarian when read without comment because of its age, its content, and its wide acceptance by Jews, Roman Catholics, and Protestants alike. The case was appealed to the United States Supreme Court whose majority of six ruled in March 1952 that the appellants, Anna E. Klein and Donald R. Doremus, had not shown enough direct injury by the law and that therefore the constitutional issue could not be decided.[29] Justices William O. Douglas, Stanley Reed, and Harold H. Burton dissented on the grounds that the constitutional issue should have been decided. In any case the decision had the effect of permitting the law to remain in effect. Roman Catholics have long argued that reading of the Bible by a non-Catholic without comment is in effect a Protestant use of the Bible to say nothing of the fact that the King James version is not the authorized Roman Catholic version. Jews have also long objected to Bible reading because it does not hold the same place in their religion that it does for Christians, and they oppose all sectarian religious practices, observances, and festivals in the public schools.

Typical of other demands that the public schools recognize some sort of nonsectarian religious instruction or observance in the public schools was the proposal in November 1951 by the New York State Board of Regents urging that a nonsectarian prayer be recited in the public schools.[30] The regents

---

[29] *Doremus* v. *Board of Education,* 342 U. S. 429 (1952).

[30] See *New York Times* (Dec. 1, 1951). By January 1953 only 300 of 3,000 school districts in the state had followed the regents' proposal; see *New York Times* (Jan. 16, 1953).

argued that public acknowledgment of dependence upon God would be one of the best methods of achieving security against the dangers of these difficult days. Similarly, the International Council of Religious Education has been urging that faith in God and the teachings of a theistic religion should be promoted in the public schools. This would amount to a common core of religious faith that could be agreed upon by all the major religions and thus taught in the public schools. Proposals such as these and that of the New York Board of Regents were opposed by many religious as well as educational groups on the grounds that they would use the public schools to promote religion in violation of the principle of separation of church and state as defined in the Everson and McCollum cases.

Study about religion. In the effort to find a way through the conflicting opinions about religious education, more and more educators were trying to find a method of promoting moral and spiritual values without the dangers of sectarian religious instruction. For example, the Committee on Religion and Education created in 1944 by the American Council on Education argued in its report of 1947 that the secularization of public schools had gone too far. The committee opposed sectarian instruction in specific creeds and it opposed the efforts to find a common core of nonsectarian religious creed that should be taught in the public schools. The committee proposed that the schools undertake an objective study of the values of our great religious traditions and treat religion wherever it naturally occurs in the study of history, sociology, psychology, economics, philosophy, literature, music, and the fine arts. In other words, the curriculum of schools and colleges should be extended to include religious subject matter just as it treats other great elements in our culture. In this way the schools could overcome a growing religious illiteracy, could provide the groundwork for an intelligent understanding of the role of religion in our culture, and could promote a positive appreciation of religion among students who may thus be brought to realize the necessity of vigorous personal reaction to the values of religion.[31] Somewhat parallel in its outlook was a major statement by the Educational Policies Commission urging increased attention to the moral and spiritual values of American life through cooperation of home, church, community, and school.[32]

Such proposals as these were met with wide interest and acclaim. They met with difficulties, however. Those in favor of sectarian and nonsectarian religious instruction feared that emphasis upon objective study of religion or "vague" moral and spiritual values would not solve the problem of a revival of religious faith among the American people. Those who favored separation of church and state were afraid that such middle-of-the-road measures would

[31] American Council on Education, Committee on Religion and Education, *The Relation of Religion to Public Education—The Basic Principles* (Washington, D. C., the Council, 1947).

[32] Educational Policies Commission, *Moral and Spiritual Values in the Public Schools* (Washington, D. C., the Commission, 1951).

open the way for vast religious and sectarian influence upon the public schools under the guise of an objective study that might become actually religious indoctrination. Despite these difficulties more and more educators were stimulated to look again at the educational program of the public schools to see if appropriate measures could be taken to avoid excessive secularism as well as excessive sectarianism.

THE PROFESSION IN PERIODS OF TENSION

In periods of domestic crisis, or war, or international tension the role of the educational profession is likely to come under close scrutiny and public debate. The people have been concerned about the orthodoxy of teachers from the earliest colonial period, when religious principles were paramount, down to the present time, when political and economic views of teachers seem to cause the greatest concern. In the recent period three kinds of proposals have been set forth as methods designed to protect students and society from the dangers assumed to emerge from the ideas or actions of unorthodox teachers. Teachers have been required to subscribe to special oaths of loyalty to the government; legal measures have been undertaken to discover and oust teachers who belong to the Communist Party or other subversive organizations; restrictions have been put upon freedom of teaching, of writing, and of speech by teachers in their classrooms or on the campus; and measures have been taken to restrict the political activity of teachers outside the classroom. Such measures seemed to be on the increase from World War I to mid-century.

Loyalty Oaths for Teachers

One of the most common measures designed to keep the teaching profession clear of subversive teachers was the passage of state laws requiring teachers to take special loyalty oaths. By 1952 a total of thirty states had enacted such legislation. So extensive had this movement become that most of the influential teachers' organizations had taken stands against such measures, including the National Education Association, the American Association of University Professors, and the American Federation of Teachers. These and other professional organizations were supported in their views by the American Civil Liberties Union and other organizations concerned with academic freedom in a democratic society.

One of the most notable of the controversies arising about this problem took place at the University of California when the board of regents in 1949 passed a resolution requiring the members of the university faculty to take a special non-Communist oath as a condition of their employment. Those who refused to sign were to be discharged. As a result of great opposition on the part of the faculty, the board of regents rescinded its rule in 1951. Meanwhile the Third District Court of Appeal in Sacramento ruled in April 1951 that the special oath was an unconstitutional infringement of speech and action and that the highest test of loyalty that can be exacted from public employees is a regular oath to uphold the constitution of the nation and the state. In October 1952 the Supreme Court of California unanimously upheld this principle.

On December 15, 1952 the United States Supreme Court declared an Oklahoma oath law for teachers to be unconstitutional as a violation of freedom of thought, action, and association as guaranteed by the First and Fourteenth Amendments (*Wieman* v. *Updegraff*).

Opposition to special loyalty oaths for teachers rested on two principal grounds: they discriminated against teachers and gave them less than the civil rights of freedom of speech accorded to all other citizens; and they were useless and ineffective in their purpose because no genuinely subversive person would hesitate to sign such an oath. Loyalty oaths were thus deemed an affront to loyal teachers and ineffective in discovering disloyal ones.

Communist Teachers

Much more difficult for the profession to decide was whether or not teachers who belonged to the Communist Party should be permitted to teach in the schools and colleges of the nation. Here the profession was divided not so much as to the desirability of such teachers but as to the methods and grounds upon which decisions should be made. In this case the educational organizations were divided. None approved the hiring of disloyal teachers nor the retaining of incompetent teachers.

After considerable discussion over a period of years the National Education Association came to the conclusion that members of the Communist Party should not be permitted to be teachers or members of the NEA. At its convention in July 1949 the NEA delegates affirmed the position taken by the Educational Policies Commission in its statement on international tensions:

> *Members of the Communist Party of the United States should not be employed as teachers.*
>
> Such membership, in the opinion of the Educational Policies Commission, involves adherence to doctrines and discipline completely inconsistent with the principles of freedom on which American education depends. Such membership, and the accompanying surrender of intellectual integrity, render an individual unfit to discharge the duties of a teacher in this country.
>
> At the same time we condemn the careless, incorrect, and unjust use of such words as "Red" and "Communist" to attack teachers and other persons who in point of fact are not Communists, but who merely have views different from those of their accusers. The whole spirit of free American education will be subverted unless teachers are free to think for themselves. It is because members of the Communist Party are required to surrender this right, as a consequence

of becoming part of a movement characterized by conspiracy and calculated deceit, that they should be excluded from employment as teachers.[33]

The American Federation of Teachers was more divided in its outlook. In 1948 its National Commission on Educational Reconstruction decided that the conspiratorial and disciplinary nature of the Communist Party did not permit its members the freedom and intellectual integrity required of teachers in a free and democratic society. Membership in the party is a form of action that repudiates freedom and scholarship; thus to prohibit such members from holding teaching positions is not to find them merely guilty of association but guilty of a definite act of disloyalty:

> The commission believes that membership in the Communist Party is not compatible with service in the educational institutions of the United States. It holds that we misconceive the real nature of the Communist movement in this country when we regard it as a political party organized in accordance with the basic principles of the democratic system of government. The Communist Party has demonstrated by its deeds over a period of years that it functions as a disciplined and conspiratorial agency to advance the interests and the policies of the Soviet Union. Membership in this authoritarian political movement necessarily involves each Communist in practices that are hostile to the fundamentals of our democratic way of life, and that also negate devotion to truth and to those principles of disinterested inquiry which are the essence of scholarship.
>
> The commission recognizes the right and the obligation of our government at this time to take due steps to assure itself of the loyalty of those engaged in public service, including education. It believes, however, that the public interest as well as justice to individuals requires that all such investigations be undertaken with a real regard for the high values at stake, and under procedures that will adequately safeguard the rights of individuals. In our effort to remove from positions of public trust those whose first loyalty is to a foreign power, we must not introduce a reign of terror which will not only injure individuals but will also interfere with the effective operation of our own political and educational institutions.[34]

In August 1949, however, the convention of the American Federation of Teachers subscribed rather to the majority report of its Committee on Civil and Professional Rights of Teachers in which it was declared that membership in an organization or in a legal political party is not in and of itself sufficient grounds for the dismissal of a teacher. The federation had been one of the first to outlaw Communist as well as Fascist party members from its own membership, but its convention was not disposed to apply this principle to all teachers. The grounds for dismissal should be individual competence rather than membership in an organization as such, and wherever Com-

---

[33] Educational Policies Commission, *American Education and International Tensions* (Washington, D. C., the Commission, 1949), pp. 39–40.

[34] John L. Childs, "Communists and the Right to Teach; the Case Against Communists in the Schools," *Nation* (Feb. 26, 1949), pp. 230–233.

munist teachers violated the right of students to learn in an atmosphere of freedom and impartiality, their competence is affected and dismissal should be on those grounds. By August 1952 the AFT convention changed its mind and decided that party membership was grounds for dismissal from teaching just as it was grounds for exclusion from the AFT. (See *The American Teacher,* October 1952, pp. 19–20.)

On the other hand, a consistent policy was maintained by the American Association of University Professors which upheld the doctrine that individual competence should be the determining factor rather than guilt by association. The association continued to reaffirm its 1940 Statement of Principles on academic freedom and to interpret them in such way that party membership as such was not automatically grounds for dismissal:

> Members of the Committee have followed with interest the discussion in the press on the question of whether or not members of the Communist Party should be permitted to teach in colleges and universities in the United States. Nothing has been brought to light that seems to indicate that the presence of members of that party on our college and university faculties has thus far constitued a substantial danger to the maintenance of our ideals and our institutions. When we consider the comparatively small number of the members of the Communist Party in the United States as compared with the total population, and when we further consider the character of those entrusted with the management and administration of our universities and colleges, we are inclined to doubt that the presence of members of the Communist Party on the faculties of these institutions is now, or is likely to be in the near future, a present danger. In the degree that a member of the Communist Party is an incompetent teacher because of his dogmatism and conspiratorial behavior he will naturally not be appointed to a faculty where scholarship is a primary criterion of appointment, nor should he be retained as a permanent member if appointed.
>
> The members of the Committee have been concerned and are still concerned lest in a laudable desire to protect ourselves from dogmatists and conspirators we forfeit the freedom that has made us strong and embrace in some measure the evils we seek to avert. We have an abiding faith in the ability of a group of free scholars in the long run to detect error and to persist in the pursuit of truth. Lacking this faith, we should have little hope for our profession or for the world. We cannot feel that a citizen of the United States who has long held a position of trust should be summarily dismissed from it solely because he has at some time or other been a member of an organization which contains conspirators and dogmatists. We believe that it is the right of such a man to be judged on the merits of his own behavior. . . .
>
> We repeated the same statement more briefly in our report last year. We did not then nor do we now urge that colleges and universities appoint to their faculties or retain on them undesirable members. We specifically stipulated that persons with the undesirable qualities commonly alleged to be characteristic of all members of the Communist Party are in fact unacceptable members of the

faculty of an institution of learning. We take it for granted that no institution is apt knowingly to appoint persons with these qualities. We assume that if an institution has unwittingly made such an appointment, it will take steps in an appropriate manner to establish the fact of its mistake and, using due process, dismiss the appointee.

We treasure, however, as a most precious heritage, the right to be judged on the basis of one's own behavior as an individual, the right not to be condemned unheard or solely for association with others who may be appropriately condemned. We are unwilling to join in proscribing all members of any lawful party or group. We think that such a precedent of wholesale proscription might prove to be the beginning of the end of our liberties.[35]

In April 1952 the Academic Freedom Committee of the American Civil Liberties Union issued a statement on academic freedom and academic responsibility in which it aligned itself with the position of the AAUP.

Thus the profession was divided about membership in the Communist Party as disqualifying for teachers, but the profession was quite united in opposing repressive witch hunts and limitations on genuine academic freedom in the name of finding subversive teachers. Much fear was expressed that "subversive" would be so broadened as to include any kind of criticism or genuine intellectual inquiry that might offend anyone. Considerable controversy was waged, for example, over the Feinberg Law passed by the New York State Legislature in April 1949. It authorized the state Board of Regents to make a list of organizations which it deemed subversive and then to make regulations whereby membership in such organizations shall be prima facie evidence of disqualification for holding a teaching position in the public schools of the state. Subversive groups were defined as those that "advocate, advise, teach, or embrace the doctrine that the Government of the United States, or of any state, or of any political sub-division thereof, shall be overthrown or overturned by force, violence or any unlawful means." The Board of Regents drew up regulations whereby boards of education and school administrators were empowered to conduct continuing investigations of all school personnel and to prefer charges against those for whom evidence justifies dismissal. Passage of the Feinberg Law was fought by the American Federation of Teachers, and it was later opposed by the Committee on Academic Freedom and Tenure of the National Education Association in its report of 1952.

The Feinberg Law was taken to court, was declared unconstitutional by a district court in Albany in November 1949, but was upheld as constitutional by the New York Court of Appeals in November 1950 and also by the United States Supreme Court by a six to three decision in March 1952. The arguments of the majority and minority opinions represent excellent statements of the

[35] American Association of University Professors, *Bulletin* (Spring 1950), pp. 41–43.

conflicting views among educators. Stressing the right of the state to protect its schools Justice Sherman Minton stated the case for the majority in upholding the Feinberg law:

A teacher works in a sensitive area in a schoolroom. There he shapes the attitude of young minds toward the society in which they live. In this, the state has a vital concern. It must preserve the integrity of the schools. That the school authorities have the right and the duty to screen the officials, teachers, and employees as to their fitness to maintain the integrity of the schools as a part of ordered society, cannot be doubted. One's associates, past and present, as well as one's conduct, may properly be considered in determining fitness and loyalty. From time immemorial, one's reputation has been determined in part by the company he keeps. In the employment of officials and teachers of the school system, the state may very properly inquire into the company they keep, and we know of no rule, constitutional or otherwise, that prevents the state, when determining the fitness and loyalty of such persons, from considering the organizations and persons with whom they associate.

. . . If, under the procedure set up in the New York law, a person is found to be unfit and is disqualified from employment in the public school system because of membership in a listed organization, he is not thereby denied the right of free speech and assembly. His freedom of choice between membership in the organization and employment in the school system might be limited, but not his freedom of speech or assembly, except in the remote sense that limitation is inherent in every choice. Certainly such limitation is not one the state may not make in the exercise of its police power to protect the schools from pollution and thereby defend its own existence. . . .

Membership in a listed organization found to be within the statute and known by the member to be within the statute is a legislative finding that the member by his membership supports the thing the organization stands for, namely, the overthrow of government by unlawful means. We cannot say that such a finding is contrary to fact or that "generality of experience" points to a different conclusion. Disqualification follows therefore as a reasonable presumption from such membership and support.[36]

In contrast, stressing the rights and values of academic freedom, Justice William O. Douglas stated the case against the Feinberg Law:

The present law proceeds on a principle repugnant to our society—guilt by association. A teacher is disqualified because of her membership in an organization found to be "subversive." The finding as to the "subversive" character of the organization is made in a proceeding to which the teacher is not a party and in which it is not clear that she may even be heard. To be sure she may have a hearing when charges of disloyalty are leveled against her. But in that hearing the finding as to the "subversive" character of the organization apparently may not be reopened in order to allow her to show the truth of the matter. The irrebuttable charge that the organization is "subversive" therefore hangs as an ominous cloud over her own hearing. The mere fact of membership in the organi-

[36] *Adler* v. *Board of Education of City of New York*, 72 S. Ct. 380 (Mar. 3, 1952), pp. 385–386.

zation raises a prima facie case of her own guilt. She may, it is said, show her innocence. But innocence in this case turns on knowledge; and when the witch hunt is on, one who must rely on ignorance leans on a feeble reed.

The very threat of such a procedure is certain to raise havoc with academic freedom. Youthful indiscretions, mistaken causes, misguided enthusiasms—all long forgotten—become the ghosts of a harrowing present. Any organization committed to a liberal cause, any group organized to revolt against an hysterical trend, any committee launched to sponsor an unpopular program becomes suspect. These are the organizations into which Communists often infiltrate. Their presence infects the whole, even though the project was not conceived in sin. A teacher caught in that mesh is almost certain to stand condemned. Fearing condemnation, she will tend to shrink from any association that stirs controversy. In that manner freedom of expression will be stifled.

But that is only part of it. Once a teacher's connection with a listed organization is shown, her views become subject to scrutiny to determine whether her membership in the organization is innocent or, if she was formerly a member, whether she has *bona fide* abandoned her membership.

The law inevitably turns the school system into a spying project. Regular loyalty reports on the teachers must be made out. The principals become detectives; the students, the parents, the community become informers. Ears are cocked for tell-tale signs of disloyalty. The prejudices of the community come into play in searching out the disloyal. This is not the usual type of supervision which checks a teacher's competency; it is a system which searches for hidden meanings in a teacher's utterances. . . .

What happens under this law is typical of what happens in a police state. Teachers are under constant surveillance; their pasts are combed for signs of disloyalty; their utterances are watched for clues to dangerous thoughts. A pall is cast over the classrooms. There can be no real academic freedom in that environment. Where suspicion fills the air and holds scholars in line for fear of their jobs, there can be no exercise of the free intellect. Supineness and dogmatism take the place of inquiry. A "party line"—as dangerous as the "party line" of the Communists—lays hold. It is the "party line" of the orthodox view, of the conventional thought, of the accepted approach. A problem can no longer be pursued with impunity to its edges. Fear stalks the classroom. The teacher is no longer a stimulant to adventurous thinking; she becomes instead a pipe line for safe and sound information. A deadening dogma takes the place of free inquiry. Instruction tends to become sterile; pursuit of knowledge is discouraged; discussion often leaves off where it should begin.

This, I think, is what happens when a censor looks over a teacher's shoulder. This system of spying and surveillance with its accompanying reports and trials cannot go hand in hand with academic freedom. It produces standardized thought, not the pursuit of truth. Yet it was the pursuit of truth which the First Amendment was designed to protect. A system which directly or inevitably has that effect is alien to our system and should be struck down. Its survival is a real threat to our way of life. We need be bold and adventuresome in our thinking to survive. A school system producing students trained as robots threatens to rob a generation of the versatility that has been perhaps our greatest distinction.

The Framers knew the danger of dogmatism; they also knew the strength that comes when the mind is free, when ideas may be pursued wherever they lead. We forget these teachings of the First Amendment when we sustain this law.

Of course the school systems of the country need not become cells for Communist activities; and the classrooms need not become forums for propagandizing the Marxist creed. But the guilt of the teacher should turn on overt acts. So long as she is a law abiding citizen, so long as her performance within the public school system meets professional standards, her private life, her political philosophy, her social creed should not be the cause of reprisals against her.[37]

Following the Supreme Court's decision the Board of Regents began the process of defining its list of subversive organizations by opening hearings on the Communist Party in December 1952. When the list was complete, membership in any listed organization would be grounds for dismissal from teaching. Meanwhile New York City discharged several public school teachers and city college instructors who refused to answer questions concerning whether they had been, or were, members of the Communist Party.

Academic Freedom of Teachers

Of growing concern to educators was the whole problem of academic freedom as a fundamental pillar of a democratic society. Under the stress of criticism of schools and colleges for being subversive the profession responded in two ways. Some felt that it was wise to be cautious and prudent in what they said and did. Others felt it was more important than ever to reaffirm the values of freedom of thought and action.

The first reaction was represented in the findings of a survey of seventy-two colleges and universities undertaken by the *New York Times* in the spring of 1951. The survey revealed a decided tendency on the part of faculty members to avoid controversial issues and unpopular ideas, to accept passively the status quo in order to avoid suspicion by boards of trustees, legislators, colleagues, and community groups, and to avoid taking public stands on social issues or joining organizations devoted to political or social causes. Similarly, students were tending to fear the "pink" or Communist label if they joined student organizations interested in humanitarian or political matters or if they spoke out in class on any such issues. All this meant an avoidance and even an exclusion of topics or organizations to which the terms "liberal," "peace," or "freedom" could be attached. The close investigation of one's activities by government, private industries, and the armed forces also led students to be afraid that such activities would make it more difficult for them to get jobs. All in all, the survey found "a subtle, creeping paralysis of freedom of thought" attacking college campuses.[38] The Committee on Academic Freedom and Tenure of the National Education Association similarly

[37] *Adler v. Board of Education of City of New York,* 72 S. Ct. 380 (Mar. 3, 1952), pp. 393–394.
[38] Articles by Kalmen Siegel in *New York Times* (May 10, 1951; May 11, 1951).

found in 1952 that the academic freedom of American teachers was more threatened than at any time in the last 100 years. More and more voices were being raised to define the values and legitimate bounds of academic freedom.[39] More and more professional organizations became alert to the growing dangers and mobilized their forces to oppose the forces that would limit the freedom of teaching, but at mid-century the issue was in doubt.

One final point remains to be made. It concerns the right of teachers to engage in political activities. One example must suffice. It grew out of a situation in Grand Prairie, Texas, in the spring of 1949, when the board of education refused to renew the contract of five teachers despite the recommendation of the superintendent that their contracts be renewed. Although the board gave no reasons for the dismissal of the teachers, it was assumed by many in the community that the reason was that the teachers had expressed opinions about the candidates in a school board election. As a result the National Education Association's Commission on the Defense of Democracy through Education reaffirmed the right of teachers to engage in political activity in general and their right in particular to participate in public discussion and elections that involve policies of public education:

> The position of the NEA is clear as to a teacher's right to assume fully the responsibilities of citizenship, including the right to give constructive criticism and participate in schoolboard elections. This position has been taken not only to preserve the constitutional rights of teachers, but in recognition of the fact that such participation is essential to proper citizenship training of the nation's youth.
>
> It is necessary to defend this right and urge its exercise. American public schools are dependent upon the understanding and loyalty of our citizens for their financial support and their development and improvement. Very often questions involving the welfare of the schools are issues in political elections. Sometimes candidates who are enemies of education run for public office. The integrity and often the very existence of schools depends upon the political activity of members of the teaching profession. It is part of their professional obligation to keep the needs and problems of the schools before the public.
>
> Support for this position has not come from members of the teaching profession alone. It was endorsed by the Congress of the United States in 1942 when the question was squarely presented in the form of a proposed amendment to the Hatch Act, which had been construed so as to prohibit many teachers paid in part from federal funds from taking any active part in political campaigns. On the theory that in the public interest teachers should have the right and be encouraged to participate to the fullest extent in public life and school affairs in particular, the Hatch Act was amended by unanimous vote in the Senate and a voice vote in the House so as to exclude teachers from its operation.
>
> The controversy in Grand Prairie raises a dual problem of major importance to the profession; namely, the civil rights of teachers and the ethical responsibilities of boards of education.

[39] See, for example, R. Freeman Butts, "Freedom and Responsibility in American Education," *Teachers College Record*, Vol. 54 (1952), pp. 117–124.

It is not suggested that as public servants teachers can with propriety employ some of the extreme technics and tactics often utilized in the rough and tumble of political campaigns. It may well be that there are limits beyond which it would be professionally improper to go.

However, that teachers have the right to keep the needs and problems of schools before the voters cannot be seriously challenged. Also, boards of education have a responsibility and a duty not only to permit, but to encourage such activity by the profession.[40]

Educators and teachers could feel hopeful that despite the pressures that swirled about them they could find strong and loyal friends in their communities if they had the courage and the wit to claim their respect and cooperation, but they found it would take active participation in their professional organizations and genuine exercise of their obligations and responsibilities as citizens.

ISSUES FOR STUDY AND DISCUSSION

1. Do you think it is justifiable to use law and court action to promote equality of educational opportunity or should some other approach be taken? Would you answer differently when discussing racial segregation, religious discrimination, or economic disability? Or do you think that equality of educational opportunity itself is not a justifiable educational goal for America?

2. What is your critical reaction to the following propositions?
"America should maintain public schools and private schools side by side with about the same relative emphasis they now have."
"America should emphasize public schools still further and reduce the status of private schools."
"America should encourage private schools to become the major factor in American education."

3. After your study of the long history of the relations between church and state in America, do you think public funds should be used for the support of religious schools? If so, for what purposes? Do you think religious instruction should be given in the public schools? If so, how would you do it?

4. Looking at the long history of centralization of authority for education, do you find yourself more or less favorable to federal aid for education?

5. As you study the various outlooks toward the educational program, which of the following appeal to you most: the claims of religion, discipline, scholarship, vocational preparation, individual needs, society?

6. How would you answer the person who says modern education is "too soft," lacks discipline, and does not teach children the fundamentals of knowledge and morality? Would you agree with him or disagree?

7. What do you think is the most defensible position to take with respect to the social role of education and the teaching of controversial issues?

[40] NEA, *Journal* (November 1949), p. 622.

8. Are you in favor of laws requiring loyalty oaths for teachers? Do you think members of the Communist Party or fascist parties should be teachers? If not, how would you get rid of them? What do you think is the proper scope and limitation upon academic freedom?

SUGGESTIONS FOR FURTHER READING

Alberty, Harold B., and Bode, Boyd H., *Educational Freedom and Democracy,* Second Yearbook of the John Dewey Society, New York, Appleton-Century, 1938.

American Council on Education, Commitee on Religion and Education, *The Relation of Religion to Public Education,* Washington, D. C., the Council, 1947.

American Historical Association, Commission on Social Studies in the Schools, *Conclusions and Recommendations,* New York, Scribner, 1934.

Axtelle, George E., and Wattenberg, William W., *Teachers for Democracy,* Fourth Yearbook of the John Dewey Society, New York, Appleton-Century, 1940.

Barzun, Jacques, *Teacher in America,* Boston, Little, Brown, 1945.

Beale, Howard K., *Are American Teachers Free?* New York, Scribner, 1936.

Bode, Boyd H., *Progressive Education at the Crossroads,* New York, Newson, 1938.

Brameld, Theodore, *Patterns of Educational Philosophy,* Yonkers-on-Hudson, World Book, 1950.

Breed, F. S., *Education and the New Realism,* New York, Macmillan, 1939.

Brubacher, John S., *Modern Philosophies of Education,* New York, McGraw-Hill, 1950.

————, *The Public Schools and Spiritual Values,* Seventh Yearbook of the John Dewey Society, New York, Harper, 1944.

Butts, R. Freeman, *The American Tradition in Religion and Education,* Boston, Beacon, 1950.

————, *The College Charts Its Course,* New York, McGraw-Hill, 1939.

Childs, John L., *Education and Morals,* New York, Appleton-Century-Crofts, 1950.

Curti, Merle, *The Social Ideas of American Educators,* New York, Scribner, 1935.

Counts, George S., *Dare the School Build a New Social Order?* New York, Day, 1932.

————, *Education and American Civilization,* New York, Teachers College, Columbia University, 1952.

Cunningham, William F., *The Pivotal Problems of Education,* New York, Macmillan, 1940.

Deferrari, Roy Joseph, *Vital Problems of Catholic Education in the United States,* Washington, D. C., Catholic University of America, 1939.

Dewey, John, *Experience and Education,* New York, Macmillan, 1938.

Flexner, Abraham, *Universities, English, German, American,* New York, Oxford, 1930.

Foerster, Norman, *The American State University,* Chapel Hill, University of North Carolina Press, 1937.

Gallagher, Buell G., *American Caste and the Negro College,* New York, Columbia University Press, 1938.

Hook, Sidney, *Education for Modern Man,* New York, Dial, 1946.

Harvard University, Report of the Harvard Committee, *General Education in a Free Society,* Cambridge, the University, 1945.
Hutchins, Robert M., *The Higher Learning in America,* New Haven, Yale University Press, 1936.
Johnson, F. Ernest, ed., *American Education and Religion,* New York, Harper, 1952.
Kilpatrick, William Heard, *Philosophy of Education,* New York, Macmillan, 1951.
———, *The Educational Frontier,* New York, Century, 1933.
———, *The Teacher and Society,* First Yearbook of the John Dewey Society, New York, Appleton-Century, 1937.
Meiklejohn, Alexander, *Education Between Two Worlds,* New York, Harper, 1942.
Monroe, Walter S., *Teaching-Learning Theory and Teacher Education, 1890–1950,* Urbana, University of Illinois Press, 1952.
National Education Association, Educational Policies Commission, *Education for All American Children,* Washington, D. C., the Association, 1944.
———, *Education for All American Youth,* Washington, D. C., the Association, 1944.
———, *Moral and Spiritual Values in the Public Schools,* Washington, D. C., the Association, 1951.
———, *The Purposes of Education in American Democracy,* Washington, D. C., the Association, 1938.
Newlon, Jesse H., *Education for Democracy in Our Time,* New York, McGraw-Hill, 1939.
Pfeffer, Leo, *Church, State, and Freedom,* Boston, Beacon, 1953.
Pierce, Bessie L., *Civic Attitudes in American School Textbooks,* Chicago, University of Chicago Press, 1930.
President's Commission on Higher Education, *Higher Education for American Democracy,* New York, Harper, 1948.
President's Committee on Civil Rights, *To Secure These Rights,* New York, Simon & Schuster, 1947.
Raup, R. Bruce and others, *The Improvement of Practical Intelligence,* New York, Harper, 1950.
Redden, John and Ryan, Francis, *A Catholic Philosophy of Education,* Milwaukee, Bruce, 1942.
Rugg, Harold, *Foundations for American Education,* Yonkers-on-Hudson, World Book, 1947.
Smith, B. Othanel and others, *Readings in the Social Aspects of Education,* Danville, Ill., Interstate, 1951.
Thayer, Vivian T., *The Attack upon the American Secular School,* Boston, Beacon, 1951.
VanDoren, Mark, *Liberal Education,* New York, Holt, 1943.
Van Dusen, Henry P., *God in Education,* New York, Scribner, 1951.
Woelfel, Norman, *Molders of the American Mind,* New York, Columbia University Press, 1933.

16

THE BALANCE SHEET
OF AMERICAN EDUCATION

AS THIS survey of the history of education in American culture draws to a close, it may be valuable to take stock of the present situation in the light of the historical perspective. This final chapter will attempt to formulate some generalizations with respect to the present balance sheet of American education in the light of the past as we face the problems of the future. It can be done only in very brief terms and is presented merely as a basis for continuing study and discussion by the educational profession and by all who are interested in the future of American education. The prior three chapters have emphasized the controversies in American society, in currents of thought, and in educational points of view and thus may have given an exaggerated impression of instability and conflict. As a prelude to this concluding chapter it may be well, therefore, to begin with a short summary of some of the basic characteristics of American education that have been hammered out in more than 300 years of our history. The over-all picture is one to be proud of despite the difficult problems that lie ahead.

SOME BASIC CHARACTERISTICS OF AMERICAN EDUCATION

Viewed historically, the organized educational enterprise in the United States has come to have the following general characteristics:

Centralized authority and decentralized administration. Over-all authority for the sponsorship and control of public education has been increasingly vested in the state, but direct administration of schools has been largely delegated to local units. A long series of developments dating back to colonial times and expressed in state constitutions, state legislation, and court decisions has given the general authority for education to the several states in order to achieve the common advantages that arise from centralization of authority. The day-to-day management and administration of public schools, however, has been largely decentralized and delegated to local units in which the public through boards of education and the profession through its administrators and teachers have been given important roles to play in the policy making and conduct of the schools. This is a genuinely creative social invention designed to achieve a balance between the values to be achieved for the common welfare through centralized authority and the values of flexibility, variety, and originality to be achieved by decentralized management. It contrasts sharply with those systems of education in other lands where centralization applies to control of curriculum and methods as well as to organization and support of education by central governments. It also contrasts sharply with those private systems of schools in other lands where the professional administrators, teachers, and sponsoring agencies do not feel so responsible to the public, the parents, or the children.

Public support from larger and larger units. Financial support for education has come increasingly from public funds and taxation rather than from private sources of endowment, gift, or tuition. Such public funds have been raised from larger and larger units organized for taxing purposes. The proportion of funds raised by local districts, towns, and counties has declined, and the proportion raised by the states and the federal government has increased. Again, the common values of the general welfare have led to the necessity for providing equal educational opportunity for all children despite the inequalities of wealth represented in the several districts, counties, or states. It has been increasingly recognized that poorly educated citizens anywhere are a threat to the common welfare everywhere. Inequality among local units in ability to support education should not be allowed to stand in the way of the need for good education for all.

A single-track system of public education open freely to all. The ideal of equal opportunity for education open to all has led to the development of a single and common public system of education, extending downward to the earliest age levels and upward to include secondary and higher education. This ideal of a single-track system of public education, open free to everyone to climb as far as his talents will take him, has been in sharp contrast to the dual systems of Europe in which elementary education has traditionally been designed for the lower classes and secondary and higher education has been limited to the upper classes. Again the common needs of good citizenship have led to compulsory attendance requirements on the grounds that the general welfare of society and of the individual himself cannot be left to the whims of the illiterate and the uneducated. Free schooling is not distinctively American, but the ideal of equal opportunity from the lowest to the highest levels of education has nowhere else been so explicitly stated or so effectively achieved. The most obvious remnants of a dual system within public education remain in the segregated school systems for Negroes in some of the states.

Democratic methods of control in public education. American education reflects the democratic desire that those most concerned with public education should have some voice in the control of public education. Thus the ideal has come to be stated that the common public interest should be represented through federal, state, and local governments; the professional interest should be represented through administrators and teachers; and the wide ranging interests of parents and the different groupings of the American people at large should be represented through their voluntary associations and community agencies. Each is recognized in the best theory as having a legitimate role to play. If any one of the three elements should exert undue control and thus deprive the others of a legitimate voice, the balance would be broken and the democratic ideal endangered. If state agencies become exclusively domineering, the dangers of totalitarian control become possible. If the profession is given too much power, the educative process may become deadened and disdainful of legitimate social and public interests. If the voluntary groups are permitted full sway, the schools are in danger of becoming the subservient tool of the most powerfully organized minority. Somewhere in a dynamic balance of these forces is to be found the legitimate realm of autonomy and leadership for the profession and the values of freedom for education and for a democratic society in general.

Large freedom for private and religious education. Private and religious agencies have been given considerable freedom to establish, control, and support schools of their own alongside the public schools from the earliest age levels through the universities. In contrast to other nations, private education in the United States has been given wide latitude to experiment and to develop distinctive programs of education so long as the minimum requirements of the states are met with regard to the common values of citizenship and social unity. Diversity has been considered to be a value to be prized in a free and open society. This decision to permit and encourage experimentation for the improvement of education has, however, carried with it the general requirement that public funds shall not be used for the direct support or aid of private or religious institutions. Two major principles were involved in this decision. One was that public control would and should follow the use of public funds by private institutions. The other was that religious freedom and the separation of church and state would be endangered if public funds were used to promote sectarian religious teachings in private schools. Here again was a creative social invention seldom followed in other countries; some nations have set out to repress or destroy the private and religious schools as a threat to the state, whereas others have given public funds generously to the private and religious schools and have therefore seriously weakened the development of public school systems.

A widening task for the educational program. The conception of the tasks to be performed by the public schools has widened enormously since the narrowly conceived schools of 300 years ago. In the relatively simple and agrarian society of the early colonial period it seldom occurred to anyone that a small child would need to know much more than the rudiments of the three R's, and indeed many felt that most children did not even need that. At the higher levels of education the conception of education was much broader, but it was universally assumed that only a small minority of boys either could or should go on to secondary or higher education. Now the vision of the needs of the child and of youth have become vastly expanded in the light of a highly complex form of society. Not only are the fundamental subjects of the three R's required, but the complexities of life require attention to health, vocational preparation for an industrial society, personal adjustment in an age of tensions, and education for citizenship in an interdependent nation and a world full of dangers.

Expansion and complexity of knowledge. The scope and program of the schools, colleges, and universities has also been widened as a result of the sheer accumulations of organized knowledge in a vast array of fields. The developments of research and scholarship and writing have produced information and authenticated knowledge in fields that could scarcely be imagined by the early colonists. This has taken place in every field of knowledge with which the colonists were familiar as well as in dozens of fields that were unthought of in their time. Particularly is this true in the natural and physical sciences, in the social sciences, and in all of their related fields. Not only is there more in quantity to be known, but also the complexities of thought and the research methods ingeniously devised by thousands of scholars have made the processes of education much more complex. This has worked in at least two ways. It has meant that many high school youths are now able to achieve facility in and knowledge of the physical and social world that would have been beyond the ken of many eminent scholars 300 years ago, and it has meant that high level proficiency in sheer understanding, to say nothing of creative and original pursuit on the frontiers of knowledge, now requires a much longer period of college, professional, and graduate study than was ever contemplated in earlier times.

Humane conceptions of human development and educational method. The attitudes toward children and youth have undergone a no less marked change in the course of 300 years. The earlier attitude that the child was born in sin and destined to perform in sin if not rigidly controlled by external discipline has gradually given way to a more sympathetic and humane attitude toward the child as one to be loved, cared for, and appreciated for his own sake.

Similarly, conceptions of learning and discipline that had formerly been based upon authoritarian control and methods of brutal punishment have given way to concern for guidance and help to the child in developing habits of self-control and a sense of responsibility appropriate to his age. The realization that children and youth go through recognized stages of growth and development in their emotional and mental capacities as well as in their physical development has broadened and deepened the teachers' concern to watch and to wait, to help and to guide. Whereas all children were formerly assumed to be alike in their natures, the modern approach realizes that varying interests, capacities, and needs must be taken into account if children are to learn satisfactorily and are to develop into well-rounded, well-adjusted human beings.

A strengthened conception of the teaching profession. In the light of the greatly expanded conception of a desirable education as mentioned in the items above, a new conception of the teaching profession has also appeared. In the early days it was assumed that almost anyone could "keep school" if he had the stamina and strength to keep the unruly children under control and hammer into their heads the rudiments of knowledge. Now it has come to be realized that good teaching requires persons of high ability, insight, and preparation worthy of the other learned professions. To become members of a full fledged profession it was increasingly recognized that teachers would need to strengthen their professional organizations in order to render their service to society and to maintain high standards of admission and performance in the profession. Furthermore, the profession not only needed to achieve an economic and social status high enough to attract and hold able people, it also needed to be authorized by the government to carry out its functions as a public service in accord with a well recognized code of ethics.

Improved professional preparation. Inherent in the development of teaching as a profession was the necessity to broaden and extend the period of preparation required for becoming a practicing member of the profession. In this respect teaching began to lengthen the period of preservice preparation as was done by law, medicine, engineering, and other professions. Since its services must rest upon the mastery of a common body of knowledge and skill and since this body of knowledge and skill had become so much more complex, it was clear that college and university study must now be required for the profession of teaching. No longer was it possible for a teacher to know just enough to keep a page ahead of the students in memorizing a textbook. Thus, the expectations for professional preparation have lengthened in number of years and in complexity of competences required. A distinctively American aspect of this development is the growing practice to prepare elementary school teachers in colleges and universities along with secondary and college teachers. We have not fully achieved this ideal, but it is a significant departure from the European tradition whereby elementary school teachers were trained in normal schools separate from the university-level preparation expected of high school and college teachers. One more step toward breaking down the dual systems of education was being taken.

Enormous gains had been made by mid-twentieth century in realizing the ideals and principles just stated, but many problems and deficiencies remained—enough to challenge the ingenuity and skill of educators for many years to come as they kept at the task of preserving the assets and overcoming the liabilities. The remainder of this chapter will attempt to provide a basis for balancing the books and assessing the credits and debits of a few of the present day problems of American education, especially with respect to the ledgers on educational support and control, the educational program, and the educational profession.

CONTROL, SUPPORT, AND ADMINISTRATION OF EDUCATION

General Availability of Education

As one estimates the over-all success of the American educational system, one needs to keep in mind the great extent to which education has been made available to Americans of all ages. The most startling fact is the tremendous increase in the number of children and youth attending school and college in recent years. In a period of less than forty years the total population of the United States has increased by half, from about 100 million people at World War I to about 150 million in 1950. Similarly the attendance at all schools and colleges, public and nonpublic, increased in the same period from something over 20 million to more than 30 million in 1950 and approximately 35 million in 1953.[1] Within forty years, then, the rapid expansion in sheer numbers of people who need to be taken care of in schools and colleges has presented the nation with many very difficult problems. Recognition of this fact should elicit patience among some for the growing pains attendant upon such a great social experiment, but should prompt others to realize the urgency of making changes to meet the new conditions. More than one fifth of all Americans were attending educational institutions.

Within this general setting of expansion the most striking expansion in the last forty years has been in secondary and higher education. The increase in attendance at elementary schools paralleled in general the increase in total population in the country, but high school and college enrollments were at a much more rapid rate. Secondary schools which enrolled about 1 million students in 1910 and 2 million students in 1920 had increased to more than 7 million in 1940, and then dropped to around 6 million in 1950–1952. To put

---

[1] The figures in this section are based largely upon U. S. Bureau of Census and Office of Education statistics. For a handy summary of these, see NEA research bulletin, *Schools and the 1950 Census* (December 1951).

it another way, high school enrollment was only about 5 percent of the total enrollment in all public and nonpublic schools in 1910; it was over 22 percent in 1950. Similarly, college enrollments which were about 250,000 in 1900 and about 400,000 at World War I had risen to more than 1 million in 1940 and to 2 million by 1950, some tenfold in fifty years. This represented a rise from about 2 percent of total school and college enrollments to about 7 or 8 percent of the total number attending all educational institutions.

The more rapid rate of growth in high schools and colleges, however, did not lessen the problems facing elementary education. Elementary school enrollments had risen steadily and rapidly from 16 million in 1900 to reach a peak of nearly 24 million students in 1930. The numbers declined markedly after 1930, the result of lower birth rates, until they dropped to around 20 million by 1938 and stayed there through most of the 1940's. It looked for a while as though the attendance at elementary schools would become stabilized as the total population did, but beginning in 1947–1948 elementary school enrollments went up sharply again as the increased birth rate of World War II began to have its effect. By 1952 elementary school enrollments reached an all-time high of more than 26 million and estimates were that elementary enrollments would reach as high as 29 million by 1956 or 1957. This caused a dangerous shortage of elementary school teachers and school buildings by mid-century with all of their attendant difficulties. Thereafter, of course, it was predicted that high school enrollments would also sharply rise as the elementary school "bulge" reached high schools whose enrollments were expected to reach 8 million or 9 million by 1960 or 1961.

Thus, elementary school enrollments were due to rise as a result of increased birth rates if the same high proportion of children were kept in school. In 1952 nearly 99 percent of children aged seven to thirteen were actually in school. Progress in getting older children into school was also made, for, whereas only 51 percent of children aged fourteen to seventeen were actually in high school in 1930, some 85 percent were in high school in 1952. Universal high school education was thus considerably short of universal elementary school education. The greatest proportionate gains in this respect had been made in colleges; whereas about 5 percent of the youth aged eighteen to twenty-one had been in college in 1910, some 30 percent of the age group were in college in 1950. Considerable expansion in college attendance, therefore, was also possible if adequate financial provision was forthcoming.

As a result of all this educational activity in recent years, the educational status of the nation was basically sound and improving. By 1947 illiteracy had dropped to 2.7 percent for persons aged fourteen or over. This was an excellent achievement compared with most other nations of the world, but the fact still remained that almost 3 million Americans aged fourteen and over could not read or write any language, and more than 1,000,000 men could not be accepted for military service in World War II because of educational deficiencies. The weak spots were also revealed by the fact that the percentages of illiteracy were considerably higher for nonwhites (11 percent) and for rural farm areas (5.3 percent). By 1947 the median number of years of schooling attained by all Americans was 9.6 years. This meant that half of the population aged fourteen years and over had gone beyond the ninth grade in school and half had less than ninth-grade schooling. Women had slightly more schooling on the average than men, and nonwhites had received on the average about two and a half years less schooling than had whites. Here was another measure of the inequality of educational opportunity for America's largest minority.

These figures point to the enormous assets and gains that America's educational system has made despite great difficulties. They are cause for satisfaction and pride. They undoubtedly have had an untold share in contributing to the essential health and stability of the American people. Nevertheless, they reveal the necessity of continued and even expanded effort in order to maintain the record without falling behind. To render equivalent service to the increased millions that will be flooding America's schools in the coming years, an expansion of 20 to 30 percent in elementary school facilities will be needed just to keep from falling behind, and a similar expansion of 25 to 40 percent is required in secondary school facilities. This means more financial outlay for school buildings, larger staffs, and more adequate equipment. Moreover, special attention needs to be given to improving the present facilities for large groups of Americans, especially nonwhite groups and rural farm groups. These weak spots, together with the need for vastly expanded programs of adult education for a population in which the aged are an increasingly large proportion, should be more than sufficient to overcome any sense of inertia which Americans might have about their school system. Justifiable pride about the achievements of the past—yes; smug self-complacency about the future—no!

While public school educators were having their troubles with these rises in school attendance, they noted with growing concern that enrollments in nonpublic schools were increasing at a much more rapid rate than in the public schools. In 1952 approximately 4 million children attended nonpublic schools and the proportion was increasing. In 1937–1938 enrollments in nonpublic schools amounted to 9.5 percent of all elementary and secondary school enrollments; by 1949–1950 they had grown to 11.8 percent; and, if the present trend continues, they will amount to 13.6 percent, or more than 5 million, by 1960. At the secondary school level enrollments in public schools dropped 16 percent between 1940 and 1950, whereas enrollments in nonpublic schools increased 34 percent, reaching nearly 700,000 in 1952.

By all odds the greatest proportion of nonpublic schools consisted of religious schools, and of these, well over 90 percent were Roman Catholic. The International Council of Religious Education reported in 1949 that Protestant parochial schools had increased nearly 40 percent between 1937 and 1947. Although relatively few in absolute numbers, claims were made that even greater rises in Protestant schools would follow the McCollum decision of the Supreme Court in 1948. But of much greater concern was the rise in Roman Catholic parochial schools which increased their enrollments on the elementary level by 35 percent and on the secondary level by 42 percent from 1942 to 1952. It was reported in a *New York Times* survey that Catholic elementary schools enrolled in 1952 more than 3 million pupils; secondary schools enrolled more than 600,000 pupils; and colleges enrolled 350,000 students for a total of nearly 4 million students.[2] This meant that more than 12 percent of all elementary school children and more than 10 percent of all secondary school children were in Catholic schools, a proportion that was increasing.

A vigorous campaign was being conducted by Catholic leaders to expand buildings and facilities to accommodate the predicted rise of another 23 percent in Catholic elementary schools and another 35 percent in Catholic secondary schools in the next ten years, at which time the total enrollments at all levels would be near 5,000,000. In 1952 it was estimated that more than half of all Catholic children of school age were already in parochial schools, and the avowed objective of Catholic educators was stated by Monsignor Frederick G. Hochwalt, director of the education department of the National Catholic Welfare Conference, as follows: "Every effort will be made to achieve the ideal of a place in a Catholic school for every Catholic child." [3]

RELATIONS BETWEEN LOCAL, STATE, AND FEDERAL AUTHORITY

As indicated earlier, one of the distinctive features of the American school system is the unique relationship between local, state, and federal units of control. Primary legal responsibility and authority for public education is vested in the states with specified powers delegated to the local units and an increasing amount of financial support coming from the federal government. Some of the current practices and problems of each level will be mentioned here.

Local Control and Support

The general theory of educational control at the local level divides responsibility between a lay board of education and a professional staff headed by a superintendent of schools. The theory is that the board of education, operating under powers delegated to it by the state, determines matters of policy which are carried out in practice by the professional staff under the leadership of the superintendent. By 1950 more than 85 percent of all city school systems had boards of education that were elected by the people; in the remaining

[2] *New York Times* (Mar. 30, 1952).
[3] In a speech at the convention of the National Catholic Educational Association in Kansas City as reported in the *New York Times* (Apr. 20, 1952).

cities the boards are appointed, usually by the city council, mayor, city manager, judges, or some other city, county, or state agency. The smaller the city the more commonly are boards of education elected, ranging from 75 percent for cities of from 100,000 to 500,000 to 92 percent for cities under 5,000. In cities of over 500,000 46 percent of the boards were elected and 54 percent were appointed.[4] Most boards of education consist of from five to seven members. Great efforts have been made to preserve the nonpartisan character of school board elections; on the average less than 20 percent of the school districts of the country permit party affiliations of school board candidates to be indicated on the ballots. Very often special elections are held for school boards in order to keep them separate from the political contests in city, state, or national elections.

Another practice designed to keep the schools out of partisan political control is to give school boards a financial status somewhat independent of other local units of government. This is commonly known as fiscal independence. In almost all instances the board of education has the power to prepare its own budget. In 54 percent of American cities the school board budgets are not subject to review by any other city agency, and in another 18 percent the school board budget is reviewed but cannot be changed by certain city agencies. In 22 percent of the cases a city agency can disapprove the school budget and require the school board to change it, but in only 6 percent of all cities can a city agency itself change a specific budget item. The local agencies most commonly given the power to review school board budgets are city or county councils, budget or finance officers, tax agencies, mayor or city manager, and a few other local officers. In about two thirds of American cities the school board has the authority to fix or recommend the tax rate which must be approved by the tax collecting agency. The trend has been toward greater fiscal independence in recent years. For example, in New York State a forty-year campaign by school officials was culminated in April 1950 when the legislature gave to all the school boards in cities of less than 125,000 full responsibility for their budgets so long as they kept within the approved tax rates set by the state. In the six largest cities of the state the school boards were still required to submit their budgets to city administrations for approval.

A running battle has been waged for some years between political scientists and school officials over this question of independence of school districts. Political scientists have argued that schools are merely one phase of local government along with police, fire, and health protection and all the other services rendered by local governments. As such the needs of schools should be reckoned in relation to these other local services, and the amount of financial support for schools should be balanced against the other needs. Thus,

[4] For these and related figures, see NEA research bulletin, *Fiscal Authority of City School-boards* (April 1950).

school requests should be determined by a single over-all local government agency, and school officials should be required to compete for funds and show cause for the necessity of their requests along with the others. They argue that fiscally independent school boards often do not consider the needs of other services and often undertake unnecessary or overlapping functions that cause needless expense and wasted effort. Extravagant demands of school boards may often handicap and set back other worth-while concerns of local government.

On the other hand, school officials have argued that education is primarily a function of the state, and local boards of education operate under the authority of the state in order to serve the goals of citizenship that transcend in importance and in scope the functions of local government. Only in this way can the nonpartisan character of education be preserved from the political contests of local politics. Thus, the financial support of schools should not be put at the mercy of local politicians who may not be as aware or appreciate so fully the needs of education as does a school board elected or appointed especially for that purpose. These values are likely to be lost if schools are made subservient to other interests and if school funds may be diverted to other purposes at the insistence of highway or other lobbies. It was for such reasons as these that education was made a centralized state function in the nineteenth century and not left to the vagaries of local government. Indeed, many school districts antedated in time the modern political organization of the cities and towns in which they now exist.

In most states the school district is legally a separate corporation from that of the city or town whose boundary lines may or may not be coterminous. There are some 90,000 school districts in the United States. The number of school districts was decreasing and the average size was increasing as the movement to consolidate local school districts gained momentum in the twentieth century. This was spectacular evidence of the new potentialities for better education that could be achieved in a day when modern roads and bus transportation could make possible fewer and better schools serving larger numbers of pupils. Two or more poor school districts, each scarcely able to support its own weak school, could now pool their resources to obtain more competent teachers and better facilities. This was a kind of centralization that met, to be sure, opposition from those who would or could not see the advantages but one which received widespread support from educational leaders and was gaining headway in the middle of the twentieth century.

The total amounts of money raised by local taxation in local school districts, in towns, and in counties increased by leaps and bounds to meet the expanded enrollments. The expenditure of funds for public schools throughout the country jumped from something over $2.5 billion in 1930 to nearly $4.5 billion in 1948, but the striking fact was that the *proportion* of money coming from local sources was decreasing. Local sources supplied about

83 percent of all funds for public schools in 1930, but they supplied only about 58 percent by 1948. The difference was made up by the great increase in funds that came from state sources, which jumped from about 17 percent of the total to nearly 39 percent of the total in 1948. This was another evidence of the increasing centralization of school authority, this time in financial terms.

The local administration of schools was, of course, not without its problems. One problem was indicated by the well-known fact that school boards were likely to be composed in large part of persons who were in the upper income brackets or in positions of a more privileged social status. More than half of all school board members in cities were likely to come from the business and professional classes and thus were to this extent unrepresentative of the great majority of people who were in the lower white collar, service, or labor groups. The vast majority of school board members in rural districts were, however, farmers. As organized labor and other groups became more important in the affairs of the nation after 1930, the composition of school boards began to become somewhat more representative of the people as a whole.

Another problem relates to the democratic administration of schools. The prevailing theory came to be that more attention should be paid in policy making to the teaching staff and to community agencies along with the long-established role of school boards and administrators. Many school systems were run as though they were the private domain of the school board members or the hierarchy of chief school administrators. They acted as though any suggestion from parents, teachers, or voluntary groups was an infringement upon their prerogatives or an interference with their business. Such attitudes came down from the days when teachers were ill-prepared and citizens were not expected to know much about education.

In the late 1930's the attitudes began to change, and the theory that parents, teachers, and community groups ought to be more widely consulted about school affairs began to gain some headway in practice as well as in theory. In some communities more or less formally recognized staff councils were organized in order that the base of discussion and consultation could be widened to include teachers as well as administrators. In other communities still wider advisory councils were established in order to give a continuous hearing to the judgments of the public at large. Parent-teachers associations grew by leaps and bounds, and in a few communities even the students began to be listened to with more appreciation and respect as the notion of a "community school" began to capture the imagination and loyalty of those members of the profession and the public who were genuinely devoted to improving their schools.

The improved preservice preparation of school administrators aided these movements greatly. This movement was signalized by the establishment of a large-scale study called the Cooperative Project in Educational Administration supported for several years by funds from the Kellogg Foundation with headquarters at Teachers College, Columbia University. Furthermore, the first steps were taken to establish school board institutes where members of school boards could meet together and discuss their common problems under professional leadership. Perhaps the most extensive and creative program of in-service self-improvement for administrators and school board members was the Metropolitan School Study Council consisting of seventy-two school systems in and around New York City which banded together voluntarily to conduct continuing and systematic study of ways to improve their educational programs and their relationship to their communities. Similar work was carried on with some 190 other systems in thirty-nine different states under the auspices of the Associated Public School Systems.

On the debit side of the ledger, however, were the instances where arbitrary school boards, or autocratic administrators, or selfish groups in the community tried to use the schools for undemocratic purposes. Most such instances gained little notoriety, but a few became so critical that the effectiveness of the school systems was impaired and the profession at large was aroused. Only two instances can be mentioned very briefly. They are both described at length in publications of the National Education Association as examples of the effects of undemocratic school administration.[5]

In McCook, Nebraska, the school superintendent and the board of education acted so arbitrarily in firing several teachers without hearing and without cause that the entire community was aroused in 1946 and 1947. Several teachers resigned in protest, students went on strike, mass meetings were held, and petitions of protest were signed by large numbers of citizens. The morale of the school staff became so low that the NEA investigated the situation and charged the superintendent and school board with neglect of duty, unprofessional and unethical conduct, arbitrary procedures, and contempt for public opinion. Here was a case where the board of education and the superintendent attempted to ignore the legitimate demands of the teachers and the public. The result was a community-wide crisis of serious proportions.

The other case represented a different unbalance of forces. In North College Hill, Ohio, the board of education acted with political and religious sectarian motives to fire the superintendent for unjustified causes. In this case the vast majority of teachers resigned in protest and in support of their superintendent, students went out on strike with the approval of their parents, and large numbers of aroused citizens could get no satisfaction from the majority of the board in response to their petitions and their personal requests at school board meetings. Again the NEA investigated and, this time with the concurrence of the Ohio Education Association, condemned the

[5] Commission for the Defense of Democracy through Education, *McCook, Nebraska* (Washington, D. C., National Education Association, March 1947), and *North College Hill, Ohio* (Washington, D. C., National Education Association, November 1947).

majority of school board members for these actions: their unwarranted dismissal of a competent superintendent, interference with the legal right of the superintendent to recommend appointments and promotions of the staff, conducting board meetings in a secretive and tyrannical manner, ignoring the protests of teachers, students, and citizens, and promoting sectarian religious strife in the whole community. Here again was an example of a community torn asunder by the improper assertion of authority by a local school board. It illustrates what happens when the legitimate role of the professional staff (superintendent and teachers alike), the students, and the community are ignored.

Finally, even more well known were the cases in Pasadena, California, Denver, Colorado, Englewood, New Jersey, and elsewhere where community pressure groups tried to have their way in the schools by attacking the board of education, the administrators, and the teachers alike. With motives of patriotic fervor, or religious animosity, or economy-mindedness, the special interest groups sought to put their will above that of the regularly constituted school authorities and staff. This problem has already been discussed in Chapter 15 (see pp. 538–546) and will thus not be discussed further here. It simply serves to illustrate the dangers whenever any one of the three major elements in local school control oversteps its bounds and tries to dominate the schools for its own purposes. It meant that at times the culprit could be the board of education, or the professional staff, or community groups. At other times each one could be the defender of democratic principles. The hope for the future was that all three could cooperate to promote a better education to meet the needs of children and a democratic society.

State Control and Support

By mid-twentieth century Americans had experienced more than 300 years of state control of education. The beginnings had been laid in the seventeenth century with the Massachusetts school laws of 1642 and 1647. Considerable autonomy was granted to local towns and districts in the eighteenth century, but the state gradually regained more direct control in the nineteenth and twentieth centuries. The states had never given up their authority; they had simply delegated more power to local units. By the middle of the twentieth century the range and scope of activities of local units was determined in large part by state authorities. In their various ways the state constitutions, state laws and school codes passed by the legislatures, state court decisions, and the policies and regulations formulated by state boards of education, state superintendents of schools, and state departments of education all combined to spell out in great detail how the school systems of the states should be run.

It was generally accepted that the state had the authority to do the following things and much more: define the kind, size, and powers of local school units; define the powers of local school boards and school superintendents;

define the kind and amount of financial support through taxation and school funds to be provided for state schools; set requirements for the length of school year and for compulsory attendance; determine minimum standards for school buildings and facilities; establish qualifications and regulate the certification of administrators and teachers; set minimum essentials of the curriculum; and provide the machinery for enforcing its laws and regulations.

There was considerable variation among the states in the way they organized to carry out these measures of control and support, but there were also several general patterns. More than half of the states provided for some form of the district system of local control; most of the twenty-six states with a district system were in the Middle West and the West. Nine states provided for a township or town form of organization; most of these were in the Northeast. Twelve states, mostly in the South, provided for still larger units in the county system; and one state, Delaware, organized the whole state as virtually one school district.

All states have established some form of machinery for regulating and administering their school systems. All but nine states have state boards of education whose duties are somewhat similar to those of local boards in that they are empowered to formulate general policies and have general oversight of the elementary and secondary schools or the whole state system of education. Members of such boards are elected, or appointed, or serve ex officio by virtue of some other state office.

Many states may have special state boards of several kinds in addition to or in place of a general state board of education. These include state boards of regents or trustees for the state universities, state colleges, state teachers colleges, and special schools of various kinds; boards of vocational education and of vocational rehabilitation; and boards to select textbooks, certify teachers, and manage pension and retirement funds.

All states have a chief school officer, commonly known as the state superintendent of public instruction or state commissioner of education, who may be elected in state-wide elections by the people, be appointed by the governor, or be appointed by the state board of education. The best recent theory of school administrators much prefers the latter method as most likely to obtain a person with high educational qualifications rather than with partisan political affiliations.

All states also have established state departments of education that act as agencies of the executive branches of state government under the supervision of the chief state school officer. The range and scope of the work of state departments of education have been greatly expanded in recent years as the school systems have become much more complex and as government in general has expanded its services. There is no one pattern of organization, but the larger state departments are likely to have divisions or departments to give aid and supervision to the general fields of elementary education, secondary education, teacher education, certification, and guidance services, as well as instructional services in such special fields as art, music, physical and health education, education for the handicapped, and the vocational fields (agriculture, home economics, trade and industrial education, commercial and distributive education). There are also likely to be special departments concerned with textbooks, libraries, audio-visual materials, evaluation and research, school buildings, transportation, school lunches, budgets, accounts, finances, attendance, accrediting of schools and colleges, school law, pension systems, veterans' rehabilitation and education, and the like.

Undoubtedly great educational gains have been made by the vast development of such state machinery for the control and support of public schools. The great unifying tasks of raising standards and equalizing educational opportunity have often been promoted far beyond what could have been achieved for the state as a whole under the varying conditions of local autonomy represented by hundreds of small school districts. Equalization funds for providing state aid to poor districts and requiring richer but reluctant districts to put forth greater effort to raise their school taxes have generally been to the good. The great increase in the last twenty years in the proportion of school support that has come from state funds is a symptom of this movement (see pp. 573–574).

On the other hand, educational leaders see dangers in a possible deadening uniformity that may stifle local initiative and originality when state regulations become so detailed and so confining that local units have no scope to experiment with new ventures in curriculum, methods, and community enterprises. Again, a judicious balance seems desirable between state and local agencies. At times an unenlightened local community needs the stimulus and even compulsion of forward-looking state authorities; at other times local agencies need to be freed of the restrictive requirements of backward-looking or political-minded state authorities. No one panacea could fit all cases. The American genius for working out cooperative relationships seemed to be the best hope for the future.

There was one other area of debit concerning state support of education about which most educators were agreed. That is the unequal ability of the states to provide a satisfactory minimum of education for all of their children. This inequality was caused by great differences in wealth and in effort.[6] At mid-century several states had more than an annual income of $12,000 for each child of school age; other states had less than $5,000 income for each school age child. In general the poorer states put forth even more effort than

[6] For details of educational inequality in states, see Council of State Governments, *The Forty-Eight State School Systems* (Chicago, the Council, 1948); and Legislative Reference Service, Library of Congress, *Federal Educational Activities and Educational Issues Before Congress* (Washington, D. C., Government Printing Office, 1951).

the wealthy states; that is, they spent a higher proportion of their incomes on education. But with all their effort some states spent only one fourth as much for each pupil each year as did other states. It was clear that in general the southern states had less resources with which to provide education for their children. Their problems were complicated further by the larger proportion of children in those states to be educated and the added cost of attempting to maintain two separate school systems for Negroes and whites. This meant that teachers' salaries were on the average lower in many southern states than elsewhere, that the salaries of Negro teachers were lower than those of white teachers, and that twice as much was spent on the average for each white pupil as for each Negro pupil. All of these factors showed wide inequality among the states and within some states.

The inequality of ability to support schools among states was further brought home by the realization that migration and mobility of movement of people from one state to another had rapidly increased in recent years.[7] In the decade of the 1930's there was more migration than in any previous decade, stimulated no doubt by the economic depression. In the 1940's the migration was even greater, largely as a result of the movements of people to engage in war work. From 1940 to 1947 some 13 million people moved from one county to another within the same state and some 12 million moved from one state to another. The states with the largest net gains were those of the West, and the states with the largest net losses were those of the South. By 1950 it was estimated that nearly one third of the total population of the United States lived in states other than the one in which they were born. Significantly enough, the states with the highest number of children sent the largest numbers of people to other states. The trend from rural regions to cities was also marked. A study of population movement over a twenty-five-year period in Poughkeepsie, New York, showed that only 47 percent of those who graduated from the high school in 1924 still lived in the city by 1949; 32 percent lived elsewhere in New York State; and 21 percent lived in other states or nations.[8]

All this added up to the fact that the kind of education provided by one state was of concern to other states because of the great migration of people. People who had received a poor education as children were likely to migrate to states where they would have received a good education if they had been born and lived there from the beginning. The facts of inequality and of mobility pointed to debits of the system of state support of education and pointed to the need for general federal aid to education. Federal aid could help the states to equalize their educational facilities, and it could protect the wealthier states and the whole nation from the dangers of inadequate education. Poor education for some anywhere was a threat to all everywhere.

[7] See *Schools and the 1950 Census, op. cit.*
[8] See report in NEA, *Journal* (January 1950), p. 23.

The Federal Government in Education

Much has already been said in Chapter 15 about the struggle for federal aid to education and the arguments pro and con. This section will simply attempt to describe very briefly some of the actual ways in which the federal government has played a role in American education in recent years. All three branches of the federal government began to play larger and larger roles in the conduct of American education despite the fact that the school systems themselves were largely under state control. This happened in several ways.

Federal courts, for example, began to play a larger part in saying what states could and could not do about their own educational systems. As already pointed out in Chapter 15, the United States Supreme Court told the states that they could not destroy private schools (Oregon case), that free textbooks could be provided with state funds for parochial school children (Cochran case), that public funds could be used to provide free transportation for parochial school children (Everson case), that released-time programs of religious education could not be conducted in public school buildings (McCollum case), that such programs could be conducted outside public school buildings (Zorach and Gluck case), and that states must provide equal educational facilities for Negroes (Gaines, Sweatt, and McLaurin cases). Jurisdiction of these cases was assumed by the Supreme Court under the religious freedom and equal rights clauses of the First and Fourteenth amendments of the United States Constitution by which the activities of states are brought under federal review and determination in these respects.

Other principal ways in which the federal government took part in American education were in the form of (1) aid granted by Congress to the states for the support of specific tasks in state schools and colleges and (2) a wide variety of educational activities in the several executive branches of the federal government under authorization by Congress.[9] Some measure of the extent of financial outlay represented in these two activities is indicated by the fact that in 1940 the federal government spent about $100 million for educational purposes, but by 1950 the federal government was spending more than $3.5 billion annually for educational purposes. This is a remarkable increase in itself but appears even more significant when it is realized that the total educational outlay for public schools in the states from all sources was only about $4.5 billion. To be sure, by far the greatest share of the federal expenditures was represented in 1950 by nearly $3 billion spent for veterans' educational and rehabilitation benefits, but nevertheless the facts are rather startling and indicate that proposals to spend $300 million a year for general

[9] Much of the information in this section is based upon Hollis P. Allen, *The Federal Government and Education* (New York, McGraw-Hill, 1950), a summary of a task force study on education for the Hoover Commission on Organization of the Executive Branch of the Government, and also the Legislative Reference Service, Library of Congress, *Federal Educational Activities and Educational Issues Before Congress* (Washington, D. C., Government Printing Office, 1951).

federal aid to education as proposed by the Taft-Thomas bills in 1949 would not be the drastic step that it is sometimes represented to be. Nevertheless, in 1952 the federal government still confined itself to promoting special educational tasks and had not begun to give federal aid to the states for general purposes.

Interestingly enough, danger to the national security and threats to its welfare have been the prime motivations in stimulating the federal government to take action when it did. The early federal programs for vocational education began in the World War I period; a second spurt of federal activity took place in the depression years of the early 1930's; and the great boom of federal activity surrounded the World War II period of the 1940's and the cold war period of the 1950's.

Some of the major special projects promoted by the federal government are as follows:

1. Cooperative extension work in agriculture and home economics was begun by the Smith-Lever Act of 1914 and agricultural research in land-grant colleges began as early as the Hatch Act of 1887. The land-grant colleges themselves had been founded with the aid of the Morrill Act in 1862 in the Civil War period. As a result of several subsequent acts in the twentieth century some $41 million were being expended through the Department of Agriculture for these purposes by 1949. The aim was to improve understanding among rural families concerning agricultural methods for farmers and home economics for housewives. County agricultural agents were authorized to take the lead in conferences, lectures, demonstrations, and publications aimed at raising the level of rural life.

2. School lunches for nonpublic as well as public schools were provided first as an emergency measure in the depression of the early 1930's and later made permanent in 1946 and 1948. The school lunch program grew from $12 million in 1940 to $92 million in 1949. These funds are now disbursed through the Production and Marketing Administration of the Department of Agriculture, and the School Lunch Act of 1948 provides that funds shall be disbursed directly to parochial schools in those states that do not permit state funds to go to parochial schools.

3. Vocational education on a large scale was begun under the Smith-Hughes Act of 1917 in which federal funds were distributed to promote the teaching of agriculture, home economics, and the trades in secondary schools and to aid in the training of teachers of these subjects. Several other acts (George-Reed in 1929, George-Ellzey in 1934, and George-Deen in 1936) expanded the services and funds for vocational education. Aid for education in the distributive trades of marketing and selling was added by the George-Deen Act. Every state has set up a state board for vocational education to supervise the use of federal funds. Some $27 million were expended in 1949 through the Office of Education for these purposes.

4. Vocational rehabilitation for handicapped persons was begun with an act in 1920 and expanded by the Social Security Act of 1936. More than $2 million was distributed in 1949 for these purposes by the Office of Vocational Rehabilitation in the Federal Security Agency. Added to this was nearly $300 million in vocational rehabilitation benefits for disabled veterans distributed in 1949 by the Veterans Administration.

5. In the depression years the federal government gave emergency aid to education of various kinds. The Civilian Conservation Corps (1933) and the National Youth Administration (1935) were designed to give relief and vocational training to unemployed youth. The NYA also helped students to continue in school and college. These agencies were closed down in the early 1940's. The Public Works Administration gave funds to help build school and college buildings, and the Works Project Administration promoted educational activities in nursery schools, adult education, workers education, vocational education, and citizenship education for immigrants.

6. War and defense training was greatly stimulated both in and out of schools in the 1940's. Beginning with the civil aeronautics training program in 1938, the federal government moved into the training of defense workers through a war training program in schools and colleges in such fields as automotive and aviation mechanics, machine and shipbuilding mechanics, radio and electricity, and a host of others. Approximately $500 million were spent between 1940 and 1945 to train some 12 million people for war work. The Immigration and Naturalization Service of the Department of Justice sponsored a program of citizenship education for the 4 million foreign-born who had not become citizens but who were residing in the United States in 1940. The Treasury Department sponsored a savings program in the schools. The Lanham Act gave federal funds to aid the financing of public school buildings and services in regions that experienced special hardships during the war boom days. Some sixteen federal agencies promoted educational programs in the elementary and secondary schools. The war training programs of the Army, Navy, and Air Force were greatly expanded not only in the regular service academies but also in reserve officer training programs in colleges and universities throughout the country.

7. The greatest financial outlay of the federal government was, of course, the Servicemen's Readjustment Act of 1944 (the "G. I. Bill of Rights"). This act provided tuition, subsistence, books and supplies, equipment, and counseling services for veterans to continue their education in school or college. By 1951 when the deadline for beginning training was reached, some 8 million veterans had received benefits under the act at a total cost of approximately $14 billion. College training was received by 2,350,000 veterans; school training by 3,430,000; on-the-job training by 2,390,000. The general consensus was that this was a tremendous educational undertaking at federal expense of untold benefit to the veterans, to the educational institutions con-

cerned, and to the country as a whole. In 1952 a new act was passed to continue the educational benefits for veterans who began their military service with the war in Korea. Whereas the first G. I. Bill had provided that federal funds be paid directly to the college or school concerned, the Veterans Readjustment Assistance Act of 1952 provided for direct payments to the veteran to be used as he sees fit while attending school or college.

8. Another striking innovation originating in the war and postwar years was the extensive program of grants by the federal government to as many as 175 colleges and universities to promote fundamental research and the training of personnel of vital importance to the national security and welfare. These were largely in the nature of grants for research in the sciences, technology, engineering, agriculture, medicine, public health, mental hygiene, and research for the several branches of the armed forces. The Atomic Energy Commission alone spent nearly $80 million for these purposes in 1949. At least nineteen federal departments and independent agencies were promoting research and programs of one kind or another in American colleges and universities, both public and private, amounting to nearly $160 million in 1949; training programs that came to more than $33 million brought the total to nearly $200 million. By 1952 the amount allocated by the federal government to nonprofit colleges and universities had jumped to $300 million.

Thus the role of the federal government in the support of higher institutions had expanded enormously. Including veterans' benefits, the federal government spent nearly $470 million for higher education in 1950, whereas private benefactions amounted to some $105 million. Of the private benefactions, some $40 million came from business corporations, $25 million from church bodies, $15 million from alumni and friends, and $25 million from scores of philanthropic foundations of which the best known were the Carnegie Corporation, the Rockefeller Foundation, and the Ford Foundation.

9. Federal promotion of international training, research, and exchange of persons is on the increase but as yet relatively small. Several federal departments and agencies began to conduct such programs as the following: training Latin-American agriculturalists, internes, and public administrators; cooperative programs with other countries for exchange of scholars and students, under the Smith-Mundt and Fulbright acts; re-education in liberated and occupied areas; and technical assistance programs in education, science, agriculture, industry, engineering, public health, and other fields for underdeveloped regions of the world under the Mutual Security Program (Point 4). Federal support for the United Nations Educational, Scientific and Cultural Organization (UNESCO), which the United States joined with forty-three other nations in 1946, amounted to well over $3 million in 1949.

There was no doubt that tremendous value was received and enormous good done by federal activities in education which were undertaken for purposes that could not or would not be undertaken by state or private agencies. The trend to expand federal educational activities was on the whole a gain for education and a sign of the times that more and more educational problems of national and international scope required the centralizing efforts of federal support. On the other hand, serious debits were evident. Some were afraid that the federal government would establish a unified system of national schools, but most educators agreed that there was little chance of that happening. Considerable concern existed, however, about the haphazard and piecemeal methods by which the several federal agencies were launching educational programs with little coordination of effort. Inasmuch as only about 1 percent of federal funds was being channeled through the Office of Education, it was obviously being by-passed in many significant ways, and much overlapping and duplication of effort was undoubtedly occurring. Many proposals were being made to remedy the situation by strengthening the federal government's role in American education without undue control.

As early as the 1920's a proposal was made that a federal department of education should be created with its chief officer in the president's cabinet, but instead the United States Office of Education was transferred in 1939 from the Department of Interior to the Federal Security Agency together with the Social Security, Public Health, and other agencies. With the vast expansion of federal activities in education noted above, two other major proposals for coordinating federal educational services were being made. One was to elevate the Federal Security Agency to a department of welfare of cabinet rank to include health, education, and social security. This had been proposed by the American Council on Education in 1947 and was sponsored as a reorganization plan by President Truman in 1949, but it was defeated.

A second proposal which gained more support from school officials was to elevate the Office of Education to an independent agency with the Commissioner of Education chosen by a national board of education to be appointed by the President and approved by the Senate. The National Education Association, the American Association of School Administrators, and the National Council of Chief State School Officers held that only thus could a national policy for education be adequately formulated and education be given the status and financial support it deserved. A similar view was taken by the task force on education of the Hoover Commission, and a bill was introduced by Senator Wayne Morse of Oregon to achieve coordination through such an independent agency. Despite the continuing debate no further action had been taken by 1952, but if the activities of the federal government continued to expand, as seemed likely, some reorganization would doubtless come when it was realized that the temporary and emergency measures of the past decades were becoming permanent functions of the federal government. This was particularly likely if Congress should pass a federal aid bill providing for annual appropriations to be used by the states to improve and equalize their school systems.

THE EDUCATIONAL PROGRAM

General Patterns of Organization

As expansion was characteristic of the attendance, size, and financial support of schools after World War I, so was expansion the keynote in the organization and conduct of the educational program. The earlier conception that children would normally start in an eight-year elementary school at age six and continue to age fourteen and that a few would then go on to secondary education in a four-year high school from ages fourteen to eighteen began to be modified as the twentieth century wore on. This arrangement, commonly known as the 8-4 plan, still was a common feature of the educational landscape, but it became increasingly evident that a wide variety of reorganization plans was being tried in order to take account of the particular needs of different age groups of children and youth. The most common rearrangements gave attention to the needs of children younger than six years of age in nursery schools and kindergartens, to early adolescent youth in the junior high school, and to older youth in the junior college or community college.

By 1948 the general picture of plans of organization in city school systems was apparent from a study of approximately 1,600 city school systems amounting to about half of all cities over 2,500 population.[10] The results represented school systems that enrolled about two thirds of the total enrollment in all city school systems in 1946 and therefore are fairly representative. The picture was something like this:

In cities conducting a comprehensive system of elementary and secondary schools, the most popular plan (35 percent) was a six-year elementary school, a three-year junior high school, and a three-year senior high school (6-3-3 plan). Next in order was the more traditional 8-4 plan, retained by 23 percent of the school systems; then a 6-6 plan of a six-year elementary school and a six-year secondary school (16 percent); a 6-2-4 plan (12 percent); and a 6-3-3-2 plan (4 percent) in which a junior college had been added. Together these five plans represented 90 percent of all comprehensive school systems. It is noteworthy that by far the most of these have adopted a six-year elementary school no matter what arrangement may follow, and most of them had some form of junior high school. The remaining 10 percent of the city school systems divided up the usual twelve years of elementary and secondary schooling in a wide variety of ways (7-5; 5-3-4; 7-2-3) or expanded their systems to include fourteen years of schooling (8-6, 6-4-4).

In those relatively few cities (14 percent) where elementary schools were organized and controlled separately from high schools, the prevailing plans reflected a much more conservative pattern; more than half of such elementary

---

[10] The data for this section are taken largely from NEA research bulletin, *Trends in City-School Organization, 1938 to 1948* (February 1949).

school districts retained the eight-year elementary school; and more than three fourths of the high school districts retained the four-year high school.

The junior high school movement made rapid strides from 1910 for some three decades, especially in the largest cities and in the regions of the West. It still seems to be gaining gradually, but the movement is largely stabilized, for in the period from 1938 to 1948 there was relatively little change from the 8-4 plan to a junior high school plan. In this period 89 percent of the city systems that had junior high schools in 1938 had made no change by 1948; 9 percent showed a net increase; and 2 percent showed a net decrease in junior high schools. Again the largest increases were in the largest cities.

At the lower end of the school system considerable provision has been made for younger children to attend pre-elementary schools as a part of the public school system. These take two general forms, the kindergarten for five-year olds and sometimes four-year olds, and nursery schools for two-, three-, or four-year olds. The kindergarten has made much more rapid and widespread gain than has the nursery school. In 1950 there were about 750,000 children four and five years old in public kindergartens and another 145,000 in private ones. By 1947–1948 nearly 60 percent of all city school systems were operating kindergartens as part of the public school systems. Again the highest proportion of these was in the largest cities. The kindergarten was most popular in the West, in New England, in the Middle Atlantic, Middle Western states, and least popular in the South. Between 1938 and 1948 the gains were rapid and substantial: 30 percent of the cities that had one or more kindergartens in 1938 had shown a net increase by 1948, and only 2 percent had shown a net decrease in the number of kindergartens.

The story was somewhat different, however, with respect to nursery schools and child-care centers. In 1948 only 10 percent or 11 percent of all cities were operating nursery schools or child-care centers, but the average was considerably higher in the larger cities. In contrast to the continued growth in kindergartens, the programs for nursery schools and child-care centers, stimulated as they had been by depression measures and the war years, were being curtailed. More than half of the cities that had such nursery schools or centers were curtailing them in 1948, and only about 30 percent were expanding them. Interestingly enough, it was the larger cities that were tending to curtail and the smaller cities that were tending to expand these programs.

At the upper end of the scale the development of the junior college has been one of the most significant aspects of the recent period in American education. After the initial beginnings prior to World War I, the movement spread rapidly, especially in the West. From a total enrollment of some 2,300 students in seventy-four institutions in 1915 the number of junior college students had jumped to more than 575,000 students in 586 institutions in 1952. The number of junior colleges had been even higher in 1948 but began to drop off after the peak of the war years; the enrollments, however, continued to increase steadily. Whereas only 26 percent of the junior colleges were publicly controlled in 1915, 55 percent were public by 1952, but the publicly controlled junior colleges enrolled about 86 percent of the students.[11] Well over half of the publicly controlled junior colleges were controlled by city school systems, and the rest were about evenly divided between state control and a special district organized for the purpose. Almost two thirds of the privately controlled junior colleges were run by religious denominations. The prospects were that the movement had become firmly established and might move in the direction of the community college as defined by the President's Commission on Higher Education.

At the top of the educational ladder was a vast array of institutions that granted bachelors' and higher degrees, collectively known as institutions of higher education. They consisted of (1) universities and large institutions of complex organization that included undergraduate, graduate, and professional schools; (2) the four-year liberal colleges of arts and sciences; (3) the independent technical and professional schools; and (4) separate teachers colleges and normal schools. In 1952, according to Office of Education figures, the total of all institutions of higher education (including junior colleges) was 1,859, about two thirds of which were under private control but with about half of the students enrolled in institutions under public control, a trend that has been increasing in the past twenty-five years. The large universities (some 130 of them) were growing larger and attracting an increasing proportion of students; the independent liberal arts colleges were almost entirely under private and religious control (693 of them); the independent technical and professional schools totaled more than 300; and the teachers colleges totaled about 200, with four fifths of them under public control. Financial support began to come in substantially higher proportions from state and federal funds in comparison with student fees and endowments. The total enrollment in all higher institutions in 1952 (including junior colleges) stood at something over 2 million, a noticeable decline from the postwar peak of 2.5 million in 1949, a decline caused principally by sharp drops in enrollment of World War II veterans in the intervening years. But in the fall of 1952 college enrollments began to increase again for the first time since 1949, and the predictions were that the increase would continue.

As a result of these widespread changes in organizational patterns and rapid growth at all levels of the educational system, it became more and more difficult to refer in the traditional terms to elementary, secondary, and higher education. Were kindergartens and nursery schools a part of elementary or

11 These data are taken from Jessie P. Bogue (ed.), *American Junior Colleges, 1952* (Washington, D. C., American Council on Education, 1952), from figures compiled by the American Association of Junior Colleges. They include junior college divisions of universities and colleges that belong to the association and nonaccredited as well as accredited institutions. By contrast the Office of Education for 1952 lists only 514 junior colleges with an enrollment of only 200,087, apparently including only those junior colleges that are separately maintained and classified.

"pre-elementary" education? Was a junior high school a part of elementary or secondary education? Was a junior college a part of secondary education or higher education? Although each school system and each theorist might have slightly different answers to such questions as these, an emerging and somewhat different fourfold pattern began to appear by the middle of the twentieth century.

Many educators began to prefer a change of names to indicate somewhat the new conception of the developmental patterns in the educational system. "Childhood education" referred to the period from the earliest care and education of children outside the homes up to around the age of twelve or so; "youth education" referred to the educational experiences from early adolescence through later adolescence in the late teens; "higher education" referred to regularized study leading to bachelor and higher degrees; and "out-of-school" education referred to the vast network of formal and informal opportunities for continuing educational experience for young adults through maturity and old age. The older terms of elementary and secondary education would doubtless remain for a long time, but there was no doubt that their meanings were changing.

Childhood Education

As one looks back over the last thirty-five to forty years of educational development, it seems clear that the most radical changes in program and outlook have taken place at the earlier school levels, whereas changes have been somewhat less rapid and less thoroughgoing at the upper school and college levels. Some of the changes in theory have already been indicated in foregoing chapters. Here it can merely be stated that the whole conception of child development has had an important and formative influence. The most common practice in elementary schools of forty years ago had been to stress the intellectual learning of the skills of knowledge in reading, writing, spelling, arithmetic, and the other school subjects by methods of drill and memorizing through books and by ordered arrangements in classrooms. In more recent years the emphasis has been to give greater attention to the well-rounded development of the child, emotional, social, and physical as well as intellectual, through an enriched program of activity and study with greater freedom of discussion and movement.

The tendency among the best modern schools was to try to look upon early childhood education as something of a unitary experience beginning as early as age two or three and continuing to age seven or eight. It was hoped that children of these ages could thus continue from the nursery school through the kindergarten and into the first two or three primary grades without a too drastic interruption. Emphasis was therefore likely to be put upon a wide variety of activities, including development of desirable habits of health, dressing, and eating; direct learning through vicarious experiences and acquaintance with story books and story telling; creative expressions through the arts of dramatic representations, rhythms and dance, music, drawing, painting, and crafts; and the learning of desirable social habits and skills through group planning for work, play, rest, and refreshment. A gradual development of reading and number and writing skills is coordinated with these other individual and social learnings rather than assuming that learning to read and to write was the automatic and exclusive business of children in the first grade. It was found that some children were ready to read before the first grade and some not until afterwards.

Childhood education for older children from about ages eight through twelve or fourteen is designed to carry forward the development of a well-rounded personal and social life and to expand intellectual horizons through the social studies, geography, the sciences, the arts, literature, and the language arts as well as to improve competence in the fundamental skills of reading, arithmetic, writing, and spelling. Acquaintance with the natural world through science and with activities of the wider society through citizenship education became ever more important along with more highly organized play and team games for physical education and recreation.

The background of such a broadened conception of the proper educational program for children had been built up in the modern philosophical, psychological, and social points of view already described in Chapters 14 and 15. Taking their cues from such orientations, many theorists and practitioners began to apply the theoretical principles to education for children. From the 1920's onward many new "plans" were devised and many new names were coined, including the "project method," "unit method," "Dalton plan," "Winnetka plan," "contract plan," "child-centered school," "ability grouping," "homogeneous grouping," "activity program," and the like. The distinctions and merits of such plans are for the students of curriculum development to work out, but the over-all effect seemed to be to break the lock step of routinized and formal learning from books, to give greater attention to the individual child, to stress learning by purposeful activity that improves actual behavior, and to develop healthy, emotionally well-adjusted personality and character.

Some of the earlier plans were, of course, not so much concerned with such over-all aims as these. Some were devoted simply to improved methods of learning subject matter by individualized projects adapted to each child or to separating the more intellectually able from the less gifted so that each group could proceed at its own rate, but by the 1930's the "activity movement" was beginning to embrace the larger objectives, as most notably expressed in the writings of John Dewey and William H. Kilpatrick at Teachers College, Columbia University. From these beginnings the movement spread in the 1940's and included emphasis upon "areas of living," "persistent life situations," "experience curriculum," or "common learnings" which in various ways became the framework for modern curriculum development and methods of teaching.

Wherever serious evaluation of the results of such programs was undertaken, improved learnings and attitudes were found to result. For example, a careful evaluative study of the activity program in several New York City schools was reported in 1939 in which eight activity schools were matched with eight regular schools as controls, and a program of observation and testing was conducted in each.[12] The observational data were highly favorable to the activity classes and showed more self-direction, initiative, participation, planning, experimentation, cooperation, leadership, and critical thinking without loss of discipline or abuse of the freedom involved and with little or no significant difference in achievement on tests of reading, arithmetic, spelling, and language usage. The activity program was later widely extended through the city's public school system.

In city school systems around the country it was found in 1948 that 40 percent of the cities had adopted some form of individualized instruction. More than half of the cities over 30,000 population had adopted such programs, and the trend toward still more individualized instruction for those cities that already used it was strong.[13] Similarly, some form of ability grouping was in use in more than half the cities, especially so in the larger cities, but in this case about as many cities were retreating from this policy as were extending it. Remedial classes, especially in reading and arithmetic, were in use in well over half the cities, and again much more extensively used in the larger cities. As yet, however, the practice of adopting a "no-failure" policy of promoting children each year rather than having them repeat grades has not been widely adopted; only 17 percent of cities have made use of the plan, but where it is in use, it is being extended. Annual promotions, rather than at half year or quarter year, have been widely adopted, namely, in 93 percent of elementary schools, 82 percent of junior high schools, and 72 percent of senior high schools. The trend has been strong in this direction since 1938.

Especially significant, too, in illustrating the broadened conception of a desirable educational program and the movement away from a narrow curriculum consisting of simply a few traditional subjects has been the remarkable increase in adopting special services for the schools in recent years. Outstanding in this respect are the number of school systems that have provided special services in audio-visual education (89 percent of city systems), library service (84 percent), guidance departments (74 percent), school lunch programs (73 percent), school health departments (72 percent), recreation departments (65 percent), school transportation (59 percent), departments of

[12] Arthur T. Jersild, Robert L. Thorndike, Bernard Goldman, and John J. Loftus, "An Evaluation of Aspects of the Activity Program in New York City Public Elementary Schools," *Journal of Experimental Education* (December 1939), pp. 166–207.

[13] NEA research bulletin, *Trends in City-School Organization, 1938–1948* (February 1949), pp. 20–21.

adult education (44 percent), work experience programs (37 percent), and summer sessions (29 percent). The trend toward these services has been especially strong since 1938 with respect to audio-visual instruction, guidance services, school lunches, work experience, and recreation. The percent of cities adopting these services as a whole has been greatest in the larger cities and smallest in the cities of the southeastern states. Despite the criticisms of modern and progressive education noted in Chapter 15 (pp. 540–546), the overwhelming evidence points to the superiority of the newer conceptions and practices of childhood education.

Youth Education

In the long perspective of history the change in attitude toward secondary education was one of the most remarkable and one of the most distinctive features of American education. Whenever critics become too sharp or when educators become discouraged about the high schools, it is well to remember that modern American secondary education is a great experiment and a fairly recent one. Until the twentieth century the dominant conception of secondary education, despite all attempts to change it, was still largely following the European pattern, namely, a school designed for relatively few students, most of whom were destined to go on to college. Thus, the college preparatory function was by all odds the dominant one up to the time of World War I.

To be sure, the curriculum had been broadened extensively in the later nineteenth century to include a wide range of subjects, but this still meant principally that the range of subjects acceptable for college preparation had been enlarged rather than that the basic conception of secondary education had been changed. It was thus possible by 1900 to gain admittance to college by taking many kinds of courses in the social sciences, the sciences, and the languages and literature as well as by taking the more traditional courses in the classics and mathematics.

A second thing that had happened in the nineteenth century was the effort to adapt the high school curriculum to those who were not planning to go to college. This was a notable change and a most significant part of the great American experiment of extending the common school ideal to the secondary school level. But, again, by and large the actual steps taken in this direction were largely to expand the high school curriculum by adding the more *modern academic* subjects to the more traditional academic subjects. Preparation for life rather than for college was thought to consist of the study of nonclassical subject matters in science, social science, and to a lesser degree the arts. By 1900 only about 10 percent of all high school age youth were going to secondary schools, and 75 percent of the high school graduates were going on to college. This highlights the dominantly college preparatory function of the high school at the beginning of the twentieth century despite the growing emphasis in theory upon the high school as a direct preparation for life.

Since 1900, however, a radical change has occurred. The theory and then the practice gradually came to look upon the high school as a place for educating virtually all of American youth, no matter what their immediate destination after high school was to be, whether to go directly into jobs or on to college. This change was signalized in the aims of secondary education as expressed by the Commission on Reorganization of Secondary Education in its famous *Seven Cardinal Principles of Secondary Education* in 1918: health, command of fundamental processes, worthy home membership, vocational efficiency, civic participation, worthy use of leisure time, and ethical character. The only one of the seven that could be considered a direct preparation for college was the command of fundamental processes; the other six were much more concerned with the personal and social competences of life in general. Here was notice that American high schools would increasingly become concerned with education for all American youth rather than simply with the few who could profit from a traditional form of secondary education in the European sense of preparation for higher education. As a matter of fact, this shift was actually reflected in the changes of the next thirty years: by 1950 some 85 percent of high school age youth were actually attending high school, and only about 25 percent of the high school graduates were going on to college. Obviously, the problems connected with such a change of clientele and of purpose were enormous.

This effort to adapt high school education to virtually all youth was reflected in many ways. Nearly all of the important statements on secondary education from the *Seven Cardinal Principles* to the present time have emphasized some variation of the same theme, notably the NEA's Department of Secondary School Principals in its *Issues and Functions of Secondary Education* in 1933, the Educational Policies Commission's *The Purposes of Education in American Democracy* in 1938, and *Education for All American Youth* in 1944, and the statements of the Commission on Life Adjustment Education for Youth from its creation in 1947.

Another evidence of the change has been the very great expansion of the curriculum and activities of the American high schools in the last thirty to forty years. Not only was there expansion in the number, range, and type of the "academic" subjects such as English, speech, the foreign languages, mathematics, the social sciences, and the physical and natural sciences, but also in what many called the nonacademic studies, such as the various branches of physical and health education and recreation, the fine and industrial arts, music, home economics, commercial and business subjects, and other technical, shop, and laboratory studies looking directly toward vocational or occupational employment. Many new services in guidance, psychological testing, vocational adjustment, remedial instruction for the physically handicapped, mentally retarded, intellectually gifted, emotionally maladjusted, and new programs of work experience and extracurricular activities were also vastly expanded.

All of these developments were a recognition in some form that the aims and program of the American high school had drastically altered since the days of the Latin grammar school, the academy, and the early public high schools. Especially unique in the experiment was the dominant view that all of the children of all of the people should attend a comprehensive high school together, no matter what phase of its work they were to take part in. The specialized high school devoted to specific purposes appeared in some cities, but principally in the larger cities. Even in cities over 30,000 population the number of specialized high schools is less than 10 percent of the total; they are usually in the form of vocational, technical, continuation, or commercial high schools. The comprehensive high school has become the most typical kind of institution for youth throughout the country and is largely a distinctively American creation.

This is not to say, of course, that all educators were satisfied with the direction things have taken in American high schools. Many who held to the European ideal of secondary education believed that too many students who were attending high school should not be there and that consequently standards of scholarship and knowledge were being drastically lowered. Others who felt that the primary purpose of high school education should continue to be preparation for higher education were disturbed and annoyed by the presence of the majority of high school students who were not going on to college. At the other extreme were those who were concerned that the high schools were still too much exclusively concerned with college preparation and were not fully aware of or were not accepting their responsibilities to the majority who needed a different kind of education from that recognized for college preparation. Still others felt that the scattering of attention and specialization of students in narrow subject matter fields was leaving a disastrous gap in the general education for citizenship and social responsibility. College educators were especially disturbed that students who came to them were not well enough prepared to do college work.

As a result, much discussion and experimentation have been undertaken with respect to the high school curriculum and program. The college preparatory emphasis has largely thrown its weight behind the traditional subject matter curriculum of the separate academic fields whose main goal was the acquisition of knowledge by the learner. College entrance requirements of a specified number of units in English, foreign language, history, mathematics, and science have helped the "subject" curriculum to maintain its hold. Many schools, however, have been trying in various ways to bridge the gaps between isolated subjects and enable the student to see relationships among the several fields of knowledge. "Correlated" courses, "broad fields" courses, "survey" courses, and other adaptations were made in the effort to enable the student to gain a general grasp of the whole field of social studies or general science or the language arts or the creative arts. These four "broad fields" were the most common. Requirements were often instituted that required the student to do some study in all four fields in the interests of his "general education."

More radical innovations took the form of "problems" courses devoted to certain major themes or basic social issues which became the center of concern and upon which were focused materials drawn from whatever field of knowledge was appropriate; such themes might be citizenship, housing, employment, world peace and war, and the like. Sometimes a "core" curriculum was required of all students for a certain part of their high school program throughout the three, four, or six years; the rest of the time was left free for electives. Sometimes such a core curriculum would be fairly systematically planned to cover study and activities represented by the major fields of knowledge, such as the sciences, social sciences, and the arts; sometimes it was devoted to "persistent life situations" commonly faced by all students, such as obligations of citizenship, family, health, vocation, creative expression, and the like. Still more radical were the free arrangements where part or much of the educational program would be planned by the students and teachers on the basis of the interests and needs of the students and leading toward wider personal and social understanding and participation. This latter was often called the "experience" curriculum.

Considerable emphasis was often placed upon the "community school" in the effort to bring the school much closer to the activities of the community, to use community resources, and to adapt the school to the needs of the local community. Perhaps best typifying the whole movement toward a new type of youth education was the development of the "community college" idea whose principal concerns were to provide an extension of educational facilities for youth in the community beyond the twelfth grade by full-time or part-time study. In this way youth could obtain the added skills, knowledge, or experience that would enable them to improve their competence in citizenship, in skilled work, in semiprofessional and technical fields, or in the general enjoyment of life as their needs and interests dictated. Opportunity to prepare for further college work leading to a degree elsewhere was also usually a part of the community college program.

Only one other significant movement can be mentioned here, and that was the increased attention to large-scale projects to improve educational programs by cooperative effort under the stimulation of organized professional leadership. This took many forms. Instead of being satisfied with separate and isolated effort in individual local schools or with written pronouncements by national committees that were seldom put into practice, leaders in curriculum development tried to promote self-improvement on a state, regional, or national scale. Some state departments of education, teachers colleges, and universities were very active in this effort, especially in the 1940's and 1950's. The Progressive Education Association instituted its "Eight-Year Study" in 1933 in which thirty progressive schools took part. It was found that the graduates of these thirty schools did as well as or better than the graduates of traditional high schools when they got to college. The Horace Mann–Lincoln Institute of School Experimentation under the direction of Dean Hollis L. Caswell of Teachers College, Columbia University, began to work in 1943 with several public school systems across the country on a program of cooperative research and stimulation to curriculum improvement. The Citizenship Education Project under the leadership of President William F. Russell of Teachers College began a large-scale effort to improve the quality and quantity of education for citizenship through increased attention to the knowledge, the attitudes, and the active skills required for effective citizenship in and out of schools.

Whatever the inadequacies and difficulties that still remained in the newer conception of secondary education for all youth, most educators were convinced that the gains outweighed the losses and that no retreat was possible or desirable.

Higher Education

The educational programs at the college and university level leading to the bachelors' and higher degrees reflected many of the same orientations that applied to childhood and youth education but, of course, with differences in emphasis (see pp. 538–540 in Chapter 15). The emphasis upon scholarship and research and the emphasis upon vocational and professional preparation quite naturally continued to determine the curriculum and outlook of colleges and universities to a larger extent than at the lower levels. The greater maturity of the college students, their closer proximity to the necessity of earning a living, and the concern of the faculties for advancing the boundaries of knowledge through research and writing helped to account for this difference. Similarly, the greater hold of traditional values to be found in religion and in intellectual discipline also enabled the higher educational program to remain more conservative than those designed for children and early adolescents. Although some colleges made notable efforts to experiment with newer programs and methods, the emphasis upon the individual needs of students and a forthright attention to social problems seemed to lag behind in the higher educational program. It seemed to be more difficult to make changes at the upper levels than at the lower levels of the educational system.

At World War I the dominant curriculum pattern in most liberal arts colleges was a subject matter curriculum organized by departments and following somewhat the accepted bodies of organized knowledge. Departments of history, economics, political science, sociology, physics, chemistry, botany,

English, Greek, Latin, French, German, and dozens of others ranged from astronomy to zoology. Each department offered a set of courses from which students could choose as the requirements for the degree permitted. The free elective system was much in the saddle, and requirements were often at a minimum. The scholarly interests of the faculty largely dictated the organization of subjects by departments. Students were often permitted or even required to specialize rather narrowly along subject matter lines according to vocational or professional interest. The smattering of knowledge and the lack of relationship among the specialized fields began to cause great concern to many educators. Consequently, several types of changes were instituted, a few of which may be mentioned here.

One of the most common efforts to see that students overcame excessive specialization was the expedient of requiring students to take a certain number of courses in one department for his "major" and then take a certain number of other courses that were distributed among several departments or fields of knowledge in order to be sure that he become acquainted with some other fields of knowledge. The student would typically be obliged to take some courses in English, in history, in one or more of the sciences, and perhaps in one or more foreign languages in addition to those in his major field. This system of "concentration and distribution" or the "major-minor" system were the easiest devices to overcome excessive specialization and excessive smattering, but they did not attempt to change the character of the highly specialized subject matter courses.

Another and more fundamental effort to overcome the ill effects of the free elective system was directed at the narrow conception of the subject matter fields themselves. This took the form of attempting to broaden the conception of what was an appropriate "field of knowledge" for study by students. It was claimed that the old subject matter courses followed the narrow scholarly and research interests of the faculty member who taught his courses as though every student was to become a research scholar in his field. It was thus proposed that "broad field" courses be organized in order to give the student a general introduction to the findings, theories, and methods of inquiry appropriate to broad fields of knowledge rather than narrow ones. Typical of such broad fields were the social sciences, the natural and physical sciences, the humanities, and the arts.

Sometimes the several related departments were brought together administratively into larger divisions; more typically, representatives of several related departments would cooperate in offering survey courses, orientation courses, or integrated courses to give the student a broad overview of the field. Courses in contemporary civilization, the humanities, and general science began to become more popular from the 1930's onward. Somewhat less widely adopted but widely publicized were efforts to focus the curriculum upon selected great books of the Western tradition or upon the study of the whole culture or civilization of a people at a selected time in history. The latter was given impetus by World War II when it was suddenly realized that Americans needed much greater understanding of other peoples in many areas of the world where American armies were going for the first time. Thus, "area courses" devoted to a study of the life and institutions of peoples in Southeast Asia, or Japan, or the islands of the Pacific, or the Middle East, or Soviet Russia, began to be more popular.

Still less popular but more radical were efforts to try to individualize instruction in order to give more attention to the needs of individual students. In the more conservative colleges this effort took the form of small tutorials under the guidance of a faculty tutor, or honors courses, or independent study plans for the better students. More progressive colleges tried to apply the individual methods to all students and even to build a whole curriculum around the needs and interests of individual students through alternate periods of study and of work, study plans that included travel abroad or community activities, independent reading plans, and the like. The great upswing in enrollments in higher education after World War II made such individualized plans very difficult except in those institutions that could remain relatively small.

In general, most colleges were trying to make some adjustment to the claims of a general education as well as to vocational and professional preparation. General education was seen as somehow much more important than ever before in the light of the growing complexity of society and the expansion of knowledge. Social demands of citizenship and world interdependence required everyone to be more aware of his duties and responsibilities in the world, and the vast and rapid widening and deepening in all fields of knowledge required more attention from the educated laymen as well as greater time and effort for those who would become scholars or specialists in any one field. At the same time the new realization of the importance of technical and scientific knowledge in times of war as well as peace gave a great boom to interest in those vocations and professions that rested upon the sciences. Professional schools raised their requirements and lengthened their periods of preparation. The program of higher education had to take account of the social, vocational, and professional demands of the times and the common requirements of citizenship and loyalty to democracy without losing sight of the individual and his own personal development.

Conscientious college educators tried to reconcile these differing orientations and conflicting demands upon the colleges, but often ran into difficulties. When they tried to institute programs of guidance and counseling to take account of the needs of students or build student union centers to aid in the social, recreational, and personal development of students, they were often met with the icy opposition of academically minded professors who deplored this "coddling" of students. When the intellectuals in turn extolled the values of scholarship, research, and high intellectual standards, they were often met with the derision of the practical minded, down-to-earth protagonists of vocational and practical training for a job. When the practicalists were successful in obtaining new buildings and attracting a great many students, the advocates of a traditional liberal education or of a traditional religious education would advocate a return to the tried and true values of the past. Meanwhile the students often seemed to respond most actively to programs of intercollegiate and intramural athletics and extracurricular activities of all kinds. As a result of the interplay of such forces as these, American higher education sometimes made short-sighted adaptations and compromises, sometimes went to extremes of indifference or overenthusiasm for some phase of college life, but on the whole it presented a more healthy and balanced program for thousands of students than was available anywhere else in the world.

Out-of-School Education

The range and vitality of educational programs conducted for youth and adults outside of schools and colleges rivaled those that were conducted within formal educational institutions. The improvement of means of communication made such education more possible and the growing complexity of life in the twentieth century made it more necessary than ever. Only a very few examples of the out-of-school educational movement can be mentioned.

For children a network of publicly and privately sponsored child guidance clinics, family relations centers, health services, camps, day nurseries, playgrounds, parks, and recreation centers has grown in recent years under the impetus of deliberate programs planned by trained personnel in place of the unplanned and haphazard provisions of former years. Churches have redoubled their efforts for religious education on Sundays, week days, and in vacation periods. Enrollments in Sunday schools increased steadily from World War I until the 1930's when it began to drop off, but it picked up again in the years following World War II until it reached well over 26 million children by 1949. This was a large and significant educational enterprise conducted outside the regular private and public school systems of the country.

For older children and youth dozens of organizations began to refine and professionalize their educational programs. Some were religious and non-denominational in motivation, as for example the Young Men's Christian Association and Young Women's Christian Association; some were more specifically sectarian in their Protestant, Jewish, or Roman Catholic affiliations. Others were more general in appeal, such as the Boy Scouts, Girl Scouts, Junior Red Cross, Girl Reserves, Camp Fire Girls; still others appealed to the special interests of city children through neighborhood centers and settlement houses or rural children through 4-H clubs and the Future Farmers of America.

The depression years of the 1930's prompted increased governmental and professional attention to the problems of out-of-school youth. The federal government reached well over 2.5 million unemployed youth in the camps and vocational courses of the Civilian Conservation Corps (CCC) and the work experience and training courses of the National Youth Administration (NYA). The exigencies of World War II directed attention to the educational needs of the millions of youths inducted into the armed services, and vast educational programs became a part of the training for general military service as well as for specialized and technical tasks. Several kinds of proposals were made for universal military training or for extended periods of universal national service for all youth. Whichever way America was destined to go, the chances were that in the future all able-bodied youth could expect to spend extended periods in military or national training programs of some kind which would require increased attention not only to the technical but the educational aspects of such service. Widespread supplements to formal education in school and colleges were provided by the hundreds of courses offered and the thousands of persons reached by the correspondence courses of the United States Armed Forces Institute (USAFI) established during World War II and made permanent in 1946. The attention of educators was forcibly called to the problems of out-of-school youth by the studies and research of the American Youth Commission established in 1935 by the American Council on Education.

The range of educational programs designed for adults would take many pages simply to catalog and define. On the professional side the increased interest in improving adult education programs led to the establishment of the Department of Adult Education of the National Education Association in 1924 and the American Association of Adult Education in 1926; they joined forces in the creation of the Adult Education Association of the United States of America in 1951 in order to coordinate efforts in the professional training for leadership in adult education. Hundreds of voluntary organizations promoted adult education programs of all kinds. They included organizations designed to promote causes that ranged from the religious, humanitarian, and patriotic to programs for social service, public health, social work, recreation, guidance, vocational preparation, and the like. Dozens of such organizations affiliated themselves with one or more national coordinating agencies, such as the National Conference of Social Work, National Health Council, National Social Welfare Assembly, and the American Council on Education. Scores of others did their own work in their own way.

The largest adult education program in the country, if not the world, was the rural, agricultural, and home economics program promoted through the Cooperative Extension Service of the United States Department of Agriculture. An increasing number of urban communities began to coordinate their adult education efforts by launching community-wide programs as early as the 1920's. Public and private agencies in Cleveland, Springfield, Massachusetts, Des Moines, Iowa, San Francisco, Chicago, and New York won recognition in this field. Labor unions began to expand their educational programs designed to promote understanding and skill in labor organization activities as well as general education for their workers. Outstanding were the International Ladies Garment Workers Union, the Workers Education Bureau, the American Federation of Labor, and the Congress of Industrial Organizations. Summer schools, conferences, institutes, and organized classes were conducted by an increasing number of labor unions. Business and industry stepped up the tempo of their training programs, their research activities, and their facilities for adult education among their employees in management and in the labor force. Some spectacular achievements were made by some of the educationally minded industrial concerns.

Almost all national organizations interested in influencing public opinion began to establish educational departments or divisions for research, promotion, public relations, and social action. Some were broadly and generously conceived to promote better civic understanding and citizenship; others were more narrowly conceived to promote special interests or increase sales of products. Libraries and museums broadened the range of their activities and programs. Women's organizations were especially active through such groups as the League of Women Voters, General Federation of Women's Clubs, and American Association of University Women. The American National Red Cross and the agencies of civilian defense greatly expanded their programs during World War II and in the postwar years. The deleterious effect of low-grade entertainment, crime thrillers, and "soap operas" offered by movies, radio, and television caused great concern among educators. Some of the outstanding companies began to look more carefully at the educational influence of their programs and to seek ways of improving their educational and public service features. The Federal Communications Commission in 1952 was persuaded to set aside several high frequency television channels for educational purposes. The media of mass communication presented one of the greatest educational possibilities of all time. It remained to be seen whether the profession, the producing agencies, the government, and the public together could meet the challenge of these media which rivalled in significance the creation of the school itself. Would they become instruments of mind control or of human enlightenment and freedom?

THE PROFESSION FACES THE FUTURE

One of the great paradoxes of American culture is the range of public attitudes toward the teaching profession. In one sense the American people have almost unlimited faith and respect for education, but in another sense they often have low regard for teachers. They entrust their most precious assets, their children, to teachers, but they often pay teachers niggardly salaries and hedge them in with all kinds of social limitations. Teachers have something of the same paradoxical view of themselves; they like to think of themselves as a profession, yet they are often indifferent and reluctant to overcome the conditions and the low standards that stand in the way of genuine professional advancement. This concluding section will point to a few of the gains made in recent years and some of the inadequacies that still remain to be overcome.

Financial and Social Status of Teachers

One measure of the social status of a professional group, though not the only one, is the financial return for its members. Teachers' salaries rose during the 1920's until they stood at a high point around 1930 after which they dropped to their lowest levels by 1935. By 1940 they had regained the losses and were almost back up to the 1930 levels. At the close of World War II they jumped upward sharply until they had reached their all-time high levels in 1951–1952, when average annual salaries for teachers amounted to something like $3,300 for the whole country. Even this figure was low enough, but when these gains in actual dollars are compared with the gains in other occupations and with the increased cost of living, the teachers' plight was even more clear. While teachers' salaries rose on the average some 84 percent between 1925 and 1949, the earnings of production workers in industry were rising 125 percent. Up to 1940 teachers remained ahead of the average wage and salary workers in the country, but they dropped significantly behind during the 1940's. War work brought rapid gains to employed persons between 1940 and 1945, and the teachers never caught up. From 1940 to 1949 teachers' salaries increased about 100 percent, but average wages of other employed persons increased 120 percent. In 1951 the average salary for physicians was $12,518, for lawyers $9,375, and for dentists $7,743.

The comparison of teachers' salaries with the rise in cost of living, however, made teachers' salaries seem still worse. If the average price level between 1935 and 1939 is figured as a base of 100, the price index in 1951 came to about 180. This meant that the purchasing power of the average teachers' salaries of $3,300 in 1951 was equivalent to only about $1,833 in prewar dollars. Thus, the increases in actual dollar salaries for teachers in the last twenty years have virtually been wiped out by the rise in cost of living and the increase in taxes.

Up to this point all the figures have been given in averages which do not indicate the range of salaries or the extremely low salaries paid in some sections of the country. In the fall of 1951 New York State paid its teachers an average annual salary of about $4,500, the highest of any state. At the other extreme, Arkansas paid an average annual salary of $1,700 and Mississippi paid only $1,475. Sixteen states paid some of their teachers as little as $25 a week or less. In general, the lowest salaries went to Negro teachers in the South and to rural teachers everywhere. The larger the community the more likely were teachers' salaries to be higher. In view of the fact that almost any occupation above unskilled labor paid more than teaching, it is not surprising that teachers deserted the schools by the thousands during World War II and that the growing shortage of teachers in the postwar years gave evidence of the difficulty in luring them back to the schools. When members of the other professions, such as physicians, dentists, lawyers, engineers, and architects, averaged from two to four times as much as teachers, it is no wonder that teaching had difficulty in making good its claim to the status of a profession.

Within the teaching profession itself, however, considerable gains were made in overcoming some of the discrepancies among the various kinds of jobs. In the last twenty years the wide gap in salaries between elementary school teachers and secondary school teachers has been narrowed, as has the gap between classroom teachers and administrators. The improvement in elementary school teachers' salaries has resulted from the need to keep teachers in the schools in competition with other occupations and in competition with the rising cost of living. Also, the salaries of beginning and inexperienced teachers have had to be raised in order to attract enough new teachers into the schools to keep them going. Even so, the estimate was made in 1951 that anywhere from one sixth to one half of the elementary school teachers of the nation fell below minimum standards of acceptability.

Great gains have been made in establishing standard salary schedules in most of the cities and states of the country. Virtually 90 percent of the cities have established some kind of definite salary schedule, and since 1940 there has been a rapid gain in the number of salary schedules based upon qualifications of training, experience, and preparation of teachers rather than simply upon the position, the grade level, or subject taught. Tenure, sick leave, and retirement provisions have all been strengthened for most teachers. Improvement has also come in many sections where married women have been permitted to continue teaching and where the proportion of men teachers has increased. In 1947–1948 some states had as few as 10 percent of men teachers in the classrooms; other states ranged as high as 30 percent, for an average of about 19 percent in the country as a whole. If elementary school salaries could be raised significantly close to high school salaries, more men might be attracted to the elementary schools of the nation. Despite the gains made, one great problem that remained before teaching could achieve full status as a profession was the perennial problem of raising salaries sufficiently to attract the most able persons and hold them.

Another measure of the social status of teachers was the pressure put upon teachers to conform to the mores of the community which supported them. Something of the conflict in attitudes toward the social role of teachers has been mentioned in Chapter 15 (see p. 542), and much of this concern by the public is legitimate. But many communities go much beyond these professional matters in insisting upon conformity in the private affairs as well as the public life of teachers. This has been a long tradition in American education going back to colonial times as this book has tried to show. Taboos against smoking, dancing, dating, drinking, card playing, and many forms of amusement and recreation are levied upon teachers long after they have been relaxed for adults in general or for parents themselves. Similarly, pressures are exerted upon teachers to teach Sunday school, remain in the community over weekends, and to shape their personal behavior in other ways in communities where no one would think of requiring similar conduct of its lawyers, physicians, engineers, or other professional personnel. Clergymen and librarians, however, were likely to be subjected to somewhat the same pressures that were felt by teachers.

Teachers as a whole have been subjected to these kinds of pressures for a number of reasons. Most teachers have been women; and until recent years they were either too timid or not accustomed to asserting equal rights of personal freedom and of full citizenship. Teachers are public employees and dependent for their salaries and appointment upon representatives of the community. They have therefore felt that they could not afford to risk offense by expecting the freedoms that others enjoyed. Teachers have come from the middle or lower middle classes in the population where there has been little tradition of organized effort to improve salaries or status by group action. And many teachers have had such meager preparation for their jobs that they were not able to command the respect or exert the leadership expected of competent professional personnel. These were some of the problems that required attention from the profession and the public at mid-century.

Preservice Preparation of Teachers

Since World War I enormous gains have been made in the upgrading of the professional preparation of teachers and the improvement in standards of admission to the profession. Yeoman work has been done to raise the level of expectation in institutions of teacher education. Of great significance here is a gradual rejection of the idea that teachers merely need a minimum of training in the school subjects they were expected to teach. In its extreme form it was sometimes assumed by the public and by educators alike that teachers needed to know but little more than the children they were to teach. Thus, an elementary school teacher simply needed a year or two in a high school or in a normal school to obtain adequate preparation, and a high school teacher simply needed a year or two of college. No wonder it was proper to speak of "teacher training" as a fairly routine affair. But now, the general expectation is that at least four years of college are needed for all teachers of elementary and secondary school subjects. Many states have not yet reached this level of expectation, but a few are even beginning to go beyond this and require a master's degree for beginning teachers in high school.

Not only has the length of preservice preparation been increased, but the quality and content has been upgraded. In earlier days it was often assumed that the essential element in teacher training was simply a mastery of the "methods of teaching" with little attention to general education or the content of the subject matter to be taught. This view outraged many college educators who looked upon "methods" as simply "tricks of the trades," lacking in intellectual content or requiring very little ability. The academic outlook of liberal arts educators was likely to go to the opposite extreme and insist that knowledge of the subject matter to be taught was the only real qualification for teaching and that methods of teaching and everything else would take care of themselves so long as the prospective teacher knew his subject well and was a good scholar. This view dominated the liberal arts colleges and graduate schools and still holds sway in the preparation of high school teachers and college teachers in many of those institutions. It accounts for much of the indifference, disparagement, and even scorn heaped upon "education" in many colleges and universities. These antagonisms have been responsible for many of the difficulties in raising the standards of preparation and in attracting competent people into the teaching profession.

Nevertheless, the level of preparation has consistently improved. One of these improvements has been the replacement of "normal schools" by "teachers colleges." The normal schools served a useful purpose for many years when no other institution was paying much attention to the needs of elementary school teachers. At least they gave one or two years of "training" that would not otherwise have been available, and some of it was of high quality. But they began to give way to the idea that teachers ought to have a longer, broader, and deeper preparation than the normal schools could provide. This could be achieved in a teachers college that offered a four-year course of study leading to the bachelor's degree. In 1920 there were 137 state normal schools and only forty-six teachers colleges in the United States; by 1952 there were only a few normal schools left and more than 200 teachers colleges, most of them state teachers colleges.

Another improvement was the breaking down of the tradition that elementary school teachers needed less preparation than high school teachers and thus could be trained separately in normal schools, whereas secondary school teachers needed a college or university education of longer duration. In recent years, however, the trend has been to raise the level of preparation for both elementary and secondary school teachers and to insist that they equally require a college or university type of education. Leadership in this movement was exerted by Teachers College, Columbia University, in the early decades of the century, a leadership now shared by many of the state and private universities as well as other teachers colleges.

The best theory came to insist that the preservice education of teachers required a good general education as well as professional education for all personnel who were to work in the schools and colleges of the country. General education should consist of a broad background of knowledge and outlook that all citizens should have no matter what their occupational intent. This usually meant an understanding of the basic problems and methods of inquiry in the social sciences, the natural and physical sciences, the languages, literature, and philosophy of the humanities, and the arts.

Professional education came to include at least three major aspects: the foundations of education, a major field of competence, and a period of induction to teaching experiences. The foundations of education, although defined differently, have come to refer to a thoroughgoing study of the culture and of human behavior as these relate to the whole educational enterprise. Just as educators need a general education in common with other citizens, so should all professional workers in education have in common an understanding of the role of education in society no matter what their specific professional task may be. Members of the profession need to understand the basic social trends in our culture, the dominant intellectual outlooks, the deepest values and commitments of democracy, and the conflicts and controversies that affect and shape the educational task. They need also to understand the processes of human growth and development and the mental, emotional, and physical behavior of the learners as well as the psychology of learning, adjustment, motivation, and personality development. This foundational approach is usually identified with courses in the history and philosophy of education, educational psychology and measurement, comparative education, and courses devoted to the social foundations of education (sociology, anthropology, economics, government, and social psychology).

Preparation in the major field of competence includes the subject matter specialization and the methods of teaching, administration, or guidance appropriate to the special position for which the student is preparing. It includes attention to subject matter, curriculum development, materials and methods of teaching, and the whole range of activities whereby teaching may be enriched and improved at the particular level or in the grade or subject concerned. Great gains have been made in these respects not only in the usual subjects of the curriculum, but also in the preparation for special functions in guidance and counseling, psychological services, audio-visual materials, and administrative positions.

The induction to service includes an extended period in which the prospective teacher or administrator may have a wide variety of experiences in actual professional situations. Through observation, participation, student teaching, laboratory experience, and internships the prospective teacher or administrator should gain the best possible insight into the conditions of dealing with students, parents, other teachers, and the community as a culminating experience leading to the first job.

Despite the best theory and the actual gains made, much remained to be done. Many states lagged behind the best theory in their certification requirements which often were stated in terms reminiscent of the older "normal school training" and neglected the well-rounded preparation described above. The length of preparation required was variable among the states. In 1952 only seventeen states required a college degree for elementary school teachers; five required two and one half or three years of college work; eighteen required one and one half or two years of college work; seven required only one year of college work; and one state required no college work for elementary school teachers. The situation was much better with respect to secondary school teachers; in 1950 thirty-seven states required four years of college; four states required more than four years of college; and only six states required less. But even these requirements had often been disregarded in the extremities of the teacher shortage following World War II.

The issuing of emergency certificates to thousands of teachers during the war and the relaxation of certification requirements led the National Education Association to estimate in 1952 that 100,000 elementary school teachers were so inadequately prepared that they were a threat to the children of America. Half of the 600,000 public elementary school teachers did not hold college degrees, and thus they fell below the professional minimum now considered desirable. In many states the private and parochial school teachers were not required to meet the requirements of public school teachers. With the enrollments increasing and the shortage of teachers growing more acute as teachers again left the schools to seek more remunerative employment as they did in the war period, the outlook was such that the profession and the public would need to redouble their efforts simply to maintain the gains that had been made in preparation for the profession.

The Roads to Professional Improvement

Two of the main roads to professional improvement have been mentioned, the raising of the financial and social status of teachers and the raising of standards and quality of professional preparation. A third road remains to be discussed, namely, the continuing in-service education of professional workers on the job. Among the many opportunities for in-service improvement, three are outstanding:

The first is the deliberate and conscious effort to improve teaching by day-to-day supervision and by special periods of study. Radical changes have taken place in supervision from the days when supervisors simply observed teachers at work, rated their performance, and turned in reports of merit or demerit. Rating by check lists, authoritarian inspection, and testing of students has tended to give way to cooperative conference, discussion, and mutual planning by teachers and supervisors as they faced the learning problems of students and sought better materials, methods, and goals for the teaching process.

The key to curriculum development and supervision is now less a matter of handing down printed courses of study worked out by the central office in local or state headquarters and more and more a cooperative process of continuing study and improvement. This change was signalized when the NEA Department of Supervisors and Directors of Instruction changed its name to the Association for Supervision and Curriculum Development. Study at summer sessions and part-time study during late afternoon or evening hours at colleges and universities have become an increasingly important method of improving professional achievement for thousands of teachers and administrators. Opportunity for shorter periods of work and study at institutes, workshops, and regional, state, and national meetings has been utilized by thousands more than ever before. The hope was that few if any teachers would let a year go by without engaging in some such form of professional improvement.

A second approach to professional improvement has been the vast stimulus coming from research, surveys, and the cooperative efforts of local and state school systems, teacher education institutions, and national organizations. Landmarks in the surveys of teacher education were the studies made for the Carnegie Foundation for the Advancement of Teaching in 1920, the Commonwealth Teacher Training Study in 1928, and the National Survey of Teacher Education published by the United States Office of Education in 1933. From 1938 to 1943 the Commission on Teacher Education, established by the American Council on Education, stimulated cooperative effort among some thirty-five institutions to study, improve, and evaluate their programs, always with an eye to the improvement of professional standards of pre-service preparation and in-service education of teachers. Special attention was also given to the improvement of college teachers whose assumptions about education and methods of teaching were so influential upon their students who were to become the teachers in the schools. The range and scope of research by faculties in schools of education and teachers colleges and the doctoral studies of graduate students in education continued to focus major attention upon ways to improve the status and performance of the profession. Much more was known, and proposed, and written about than was or could be put into practice.

A third promising road to professional improvement was the professional organizations themselves. Educators were finally learning that no occupational group ever became a profession worthy of the name without strong and vigorous professional organization. This had been true ever since the organization of the teaching guilds produced the universities themselves in the medieval period. The physicians, lawyers, and engineers of the United States learned the lesson in the later nineteenth and early twentieth centuries. Educators were beginning to learn the lesson in the middle of the twentieth century. In fact they were so eager to form organizations that it was possible they would divide themselves into so many specialized professional groups that they would dissipate their efforts and be unable to act in concert on the serious problems that faced them. The *Education Directory* of the Office of Education takes some thirty-five pages just to list the names of the state, regional, and national associations concerned with education in the United States.

The largest national professional organization is the National Education Association, operating through twenty-nine departments devoted to virtually the whole range of specialized professional interests. Well over 400,000 persons belong to the National Education Association, nearly 900,000 belong to fifty-one state education associations affiliated with the NEA and some 500,000 belong to 2,900 local education associations also affiliated with the NEA. In addition, there are many other organizations devoted to the recognized subject matter fields and major activities of the educational enterprise.

Cutting across subject matter lines to promote some identifiable interest, a large number of other organizations appealed to teachers. The American Federation of Teachers found special advantages in affiliation with organized labor through the American Federation of Labor. The American Education Fellowship (formerly the Progressive Education Association) devoted its attention to experimental programs of education and the social role of education in a time of crisis.

The National Society of College Teachers of Education directed special attention to improving the programs of instruction in the institutions of teacher education, including the foundations of education, curriculum, administration, general education, and methods of teaching. The John Dewey Society concentrated upon scholarly studies of the critical issues facing American education, and the National Society for the Study of Education conducted research in many areas of the curriculum and of teaching. The Association of American Universities, the American Association of Colleges, and the American Association of Junior Colleges devoted attention to their specific levels of education. The American Association of University Professors devoted itself to scholarly study and the improvement of the conditions of college teaching with special attention to problems of academic freedom and tenure. Five national organizations joined together in 1952 to form the National Council for Accreditation of Teacher Education in the effort to replace the several accrediting agencies that have been trying to improve the preparation of teachers. The twenty-one members of the council are to be appointed by the American Association of Colleges for Teacher Education, the National Council of Chief State School Officers, the National School Boards Association, the National Association of State Directors of Teacher Education and Certification, and the National Commission on Teacher Education and Professional Standards of the NEA.

On the international level American educators sought to cooperate with educational agencies of other lands through an increasing number of exchange arrangements and international conferences, especially through the expanding activities of UNESCO and through the World Organization of the Teaching Profession under the leadership of President William F. Russell of Teachers College, Columbia University. In August 1952 WOTP joined with two other international teachers organizations to form the World Confederation of Organizations of the Teaching Profession.

Harassed though they may be by the myriad problems of education in thousands of classrooms in hundreds of local communities, the educators of America could no longer be concerned simply with their own local problems. Many had come to realize that the welfare of individual teachers was bound up with the profession at large in state and nation and that the welfare of education itself depended in large measure upon stronger organization. A few, but a growing number, were now realizing that there were common professional problems facing the world and that organized effort must cross the boundaries of all nations that could be brought to believe in a free world. The prospect was staggering, but the educational achievements of the profession and of the American people over more than 300 years as recorded in these pages gave hope that even so gigantic a task was not too much for the organized efforts of a million teachers dedicated to the methods of intelligence and to the goals of freedom through education.

ISSUES FOR STUDY AND DISCUSSION

1. On the basis of your study and experience criticize the ten basic characteristics of the American educational system as described at the beginning of this chapter. How would you change the statement of these characteristics? What would you delete or add?

2. What do you think of the proposition that control of education should reflect a balance of responsibility exercised by government, the profession, and voluntary associations?

3. What do you think of the proposition that public support for education should be divided among local, state, and federal governments? What do you think would be a proper division of responsibility?

4. Do you think the United States has been wise to launch upon the experiment of a vast extension of educational opportunity downward to nursery schools and upward to the university? Do you think it is wise to expand the opportunities for youth education and for higher education even more than they have been?

5. Which of the roads to improvement of the educational profession do you think holds the most promise?

6. As you tally up your own estimate of the balance sheet of American education, where do you find the most credits and the most debits. Does your over-all balance come out in the black or in the red?

SUGGESTIONS FOR FURTHER READING

Aikin Wilford M., *The Story of the Eight-Year Study*, New York, Harper, 1942.
American Council on Education, Commission on Teacher Education, *The Improvement of Teacher Education*, Washington, D. C., the Council, 1946.
Armstrong, W. Earl, Hollis, E. V., and Davis, Helen, *The College and Teacher Education*, Washington, D. C., American Council on Education, 1944.
Bogue, Jesse P., *The Community College*, New York, McGraw-Hill, 1950.
Brameld, Theodore, *Workers' Education in the United States*, Fifth Yearbook of the John Dewey Society, New York, Appleton-Century, 1941.
Bunker, Frank Forest, *The Junior High School Movement—Its Beginnings*, Washington, D. C., W. F. Roberts, 1935.
Cartwright, Morse A., *Ten Years of Adult Education*, New York, Macmillan, 1935.
Caswell, Hollis L., ed., *The American High School*, New York, Harper, 1946.
———, and Foshay, A. Wellesley, *Education in the Elementary School*, 2d ed., New York, American Book, 1950.
Commission on Financing Higher Education, *Nature and Needs of Higher Education*, New York, Columbia University Press, 1952.
Counts, George S., *Social Composition of Boards of Education*, Chicago, University of Chicago Press, 1927.
Duffus, R. L., *Democracy Enters College*, New York, Scribner, 1936.
Elsbree, Willard S., *The American Teacher*, New York, American Book, 1939.
Fine, Benjamin, *Our Children Are Cheated*, New York, Holt, 1947.
Forest, Isle, *Pre-School Education*, New York, Macmillan, 1927.
Hofstadter, Richard and Hardy, C. DeWitt, *The Development and Scope of Higher Education in the United States*, New York, Columbia University Press, 1952.
Hollinshead, Byron S., *Who Should Go to College*, New York, Columbia University Press, 1952.
Hollis, Ernest V., *Philanthropic Foundations and Higher Education*, New York, Columbia University Press, 1938.
Kandel, Isaac L., *The Impact of the War upon American Education*, Chapel Hill, University of North Carolina, 1948.
Knight, Edgar W., *Fifty Years of American Education*, New York, Ronald, 1952.
Koopman, G. Robert, Miel, Alice, and Misner, Paul J., *Democracy in School Administration*, New York, Appleton-Century-Crofts, 1943.
Koos, Leonard V., *The Junior College*, Minneapolis, University of Minnesota Press, 1924.
Meyer, Adolph E., *The Development of Education in the Twentieth Century*, 2d ed., New York, Prentice-Hall, 1949.
Millett, John D., *Financing Higher Education in the United States*, New York, Columbia University Press, 1952.

National Education Association, Educational Policies Commission, *American Education and International Tensions,* Washington, D. C., the Association, 1949.

———, *Federal-state Relations in Education,* Washington, D. C., the Association, 1945.

———, *The Unique Function of Education in American Democracy,* Washington, D. C., the Association, 1937.

National Society for the Study of Education, *General Education,* 51st Yearbook, Part I, Chicago, Distributed by the University of Chicago Press, 1952.

Olsen, Edward G., *School and Community,* New York, Prentice-Hall, 1945.

Prall, Charles E., *State Programs for the Improvement of Teacher Education,* Washington, D. C., American Council on Education, 1946.

———, and Cushman, Leslie C., *Teacher Education in Service,* Washington, D. C., American Council on Education, 1944.

Raup, R. Bruce, *Education and Organized Interests in America,* New York, Putnam, 1936.

Reutter, E. Edmund, Jr., *The School Administrator and Subversive Activities,* New York, Teachers College, Columbia University, 1951.

Rose, Arnold M., *Race Prejudice and Discrimination: Readings in Intergroup Relations in the United States,* New York, Knopf, 1951.

Russell, James E., *Federal Activities in Higher Education after the Second World War,* New York, Kings Crown Press, Columbia University, 1951.

Smith, B. Othanel and others, *Fundamentals of Curriculum Development,* Yonkers-on-Hudson, World Book, 1950.

Stratemeyer, Florence B. and others, *Developing a Curriculum for Modern Living,* New York, Teachers College, Columbia University, 1947.

Taba, Hilda, and Van Til, William (eds.), *Democratic Human Relations; Promising Practices in Intergroup and Intercultural Education in the Social Studies,* Washington, D. C., National Council for the Social Studies, 1945.

Thayer, V. T., and others, *Reorganizing Secondary Education,* New York, Appleton-Century, 1939.

Warner, W. Lloyd, Havighurst, Robert, and Loeb, Martin B., *Who Shall Be Educated?,* New York, Harper, 1944.

INDEX